A Guide to

STAFFORDSHIRE

and the Black Country

the Potteries and the Peak

Michael Raven

*Dedicated to
my good companions
Pirate, Bruno
and Tess*

A Guide to

STAFFORDSHIRE

and the Black Country

the Potteries and the Peak

Michael Raven

MICHAEL RAVEN
Ashley, Market Drayton
2005

CREDITS

Published by
Michael Raven.
First Edition November 2004
All rights reserved.
Layout and Microsoft Publisher formatting M. Raven
Printed and bound in Great Britain by
The Bath Press, Bath, UK
Publisher's address: Michael Raven,
Yew Tree Cottage, Jug Bank, Ashley,
Market Drayton, Shropshire,
TF9 4NJ
Telephone: 01630 672304

Front cover photograph:
a stained glass window
at Biddulph Grange

ISBN: 0 906114 33 0

BIOGRAPHICAL NOTE

Michael Raven was born in Cardiff of Lancastrian parents in 1938 and was
educated at Towyn Grammar School and Keele University where he studied
geology and political philosophy. He completed his National Service with the
Cheshire Regiment in Malaya and then did a variety of jobs before going to
Spain to learn flamenco. He has always had a keen interest in sport:
in 1956 he was the Midlands' Decathlon Champion and in the army
was a Marksman First Class. For the last 30 years he has earned
his living as a classical guitarist, composer and researcher of folk studies.
Michael Raven has over 60 albums of recorded music and more than
80 books to his credit. This volume is his fifth
topographical work. The others are:
Staffordshire and the Black Country,
Black Country Towns and Villages,
A Guide to Herefordshire
and *A Shropshire Gazetteer.*
Of the latter the *Shropshire Alternative* said:
"It must be the definitive book on Shropshire",
and the *Photographers' Britain* proclaimed it
"uniquely detailed and splendidly opinionated".
Other related books include
Shropshire in Pictures,
Cheshire in Pictures and
Midlands Digest in six books.

FOREWORD

This book contains most of the information previously published in my *Staffordshire and the Black Country, Black Country Towns and Villages* and the Staffordshire articles in *Midlands Digest* Vols 1-6. Also included are updates of this information and a great deal of new material. It has been my intention to produce something that is usefully detailed but of a convenient size and reasonably priced.

For those seeking more information I can recommend the Staffordshire volumes of the *Victoria County History* and Tim Cockin's *Staffordshire Encyclopaedia* which are available for reference in most public libraries.

The photographs were all taken on Nikon cameras, both film (35mm transparency) and digital, and were processed using the Photoshop computer programme. My digital camera is a Nikon D100 with a Nikkor 28-70mm, 1:2.8D zoom lens. This is a rather physically long, heavy lens but by using my left forearm as a rest it can be held remarkably still and free from quiver without having to resort to a tripod. I confess to being a convert to the digital format especially as computer processing is now the norm. As most of my archive was made 10 years ago it is on 35mm slides and the thought of scanning and processing 10,000 of these and a similar number of negatives and prints is daunting to say the least.

This book has taken me nearly two years to complete; that is full time, not just evenings and weekends, but includes the work I put in on the books mentioned in the first paragraph. I rarely write about somewhere that I have not personally visited, and for all those hours of travel I always had a dog for company. So, thank you Lady, Pirate, Bruno and Ricky and their occasional friend, Tess, who lately left us.

Michael Raven
Ashley, 2004

List of Colour Plates

*All the photographs were taken
and processed by Michael Raven*

List of Poems

CONTENTS

A

ABBEY HULTON *1.5m NNE of Hanley and 0.5m S of Milton*

In Domesday Book the manor is Heltone, meaning 'hill town'. The 'abbey' is from the Cistercian abbey founded by the Audley family of Heighley Castle (near Madeley) in the early 13th Century.

After the Dissolution of the Monasteries the abbey was quarried for its stone and today nothing is left above ground. The site has been extensively investigated and the foundations exposed. The abbey lies in Woodhead Road, next to Carmountside County Primary School. There is a prehistoric burial mound 0.5m NW of the abbey, and to the south is a large 20th Century housing estate with an unenviable reputation.

ABBOTS BROMLEY *6m NE of Rugeley*

Abbots Bromley is a small town on the western edge of Needwood Forest, famous for its ancient Horn Dance held annually on the Monday after the first Sunday after the 4th of September.

Six men wearing reindeer horns dance at several venues throughout the day accompanied by a hobby horse, a boy with a crossbow, a jester and a musician. The horns are stored in the church on public display. In origin the dance is probably a relic of a pagan fertility rite, though there are other theories. It is unique within Britain.

The author well remembers the day he was talking to one of the dancers, who had laid down his horns a few feet away. After a few minutes of conversation I casually looked away to see Lady, my Border-Collie-cross, chomping away merrily on 1,000-year-old reindeer horns. I was horrified and the dancer, to say the least, was not best pleased.

The unspoilt village has a 17th Century, hexagonal, timber market cross, pleasantly mellowed brick houses, a stone church with 14th Century arcades and a smattering of black-and-white buildings. The school of St Mary and St Anne is one of the oldest girls' public schools in the country.

The manor house of Abbots Bromley is Hall Hill Manor Farm. It was held by Burton Abbey but after the Dissolution passed to the Pagets, and in 1939 was owned by the County Council. Mary, Queen of Scots, is thought to have spent a night here when traveling from Chartley to Tutbury on 21st September 1586.

A mile-and-a-half north-west of the village lie the forests and farms of **Bagot's Bromley**. On the west side of the road to Uttoxeter, at the junction with the lane to Dapple Heath, is Monument Field. This has a clump of trees and the remains of a moat, now filled with cow dung, in which stands a brick monument marking the site of the manor house of the Anglo-Saxon Lord Bagot. His descendant, Ralph, was to desert this place in 1360 on his marriage to the heiress of nearby Blithfield, to whose Hall he moved. Amongst his descendants were the Earls of Stafford and the Dukes of Buckingham.

Bagot's Park, even in the last century, had a magnificent broad-leaved forest of beech, ash, oak and chestnut. Now it is gone. Lord Bagot sold the timber to pay his taxes and the land was bought by the Forestry Commission who arrayed it with seemingly never-ending lines of coniferous trees. However, they have relented in recent times and are introducing hardwoods with the intention of creating a genuine mixed forest. There are deer, rabbits and badgers in the woods. These woods were a source of fuel for the medieval glass makers known to have operated in the Abbots Bromley area.

On the south-eastern boundary of Bagot's Wood the recently deceased naturalist, author and TV presenter, Phil Drabble, had his home in the most attractive Goat Lodge, situated at the entrance to the Bagot Estate Farm which is located on the north-eastern side of the Abbots Bromley-Uttoxeter road (B5015), signposted Dunstall. Within yards of the concrete estate road stood the last solitary survivor of the ancient forest, the Walking Stick Oak. This lingered as a forlorn sentinel, dead and stark and white, before recently finally falling.

The unique Bagot Goats no longer graze the pastures here, but at least these friendly black-and-white bearded creatures have been saved, and are now at the Shugborough Hall Farm near Stafford.

Blithfield Hall has been divided into three separate houses internally, but the freehold of all three remains with Lady Nancy Bagot. It stands in its park overlooking the 790 watery acres of Blithfield Reservoir, opened in 1953 by the Queen Mother. The River Blythe, whose waters were dammed to create the lake, is the 'Withy' of W M Canaway's 'A Creel of Willow'. The road crosses the reservoir on a spectacular causeway. The Police Underwater Search Unit is no stranger here, it being a handy place to deposit the tools and unwanted proceeds of criminal activities. At Rugeley Turn, 0.75m NW of Abbots Bromley, there used to be an airfield.

ACTON TRUSSELL *3.5m S of Stafford*
In Domesday Book the village is referred to simply as Actone. At that time it belonged to the Bishop of Chester. The local lord was Robert and there were 10 villagers and 8 smallholders. Between them they had a mill, 8 acres of meadow and a small wood. Acton means 'the settlement by the oak trees' and Trussell was the name of a later Norman lord of the manor (from at least 1342). The old Anglo-Saxon village stands on a rise above the flood plain of the River Penk.

The Staffordshire and Worcestershire canal (constructed by James Brindley in 1772) follows the course of the river; so does the M6 Motorway, with a roar that makes double glazing a necessity hereabouts. What little is left of the old village has been swamped by modern middle-class houses, though from a distance the overall impression is of a pleasant little hill town - almost Italian looking.

The church of St James is found in splendid isolation 0.25m south of the village. It has long been suspected that the reason for this is that the original village stood by the church and moved away, either because of the Black Death or possibly because of flooding. Recent excavations have exposed the sandstone foundations and post holes of several buildings to the south and east of the church. Vitreous slag can also be found in the adjacent field to the south. This could indicate either glass or iron-working in the area. To the east the ground is disturbed and there is what appears to be a small quarry. All this confirms that the original village probably stood around the church. What is more, there is evidence of Roman occupation in the vicinity: shards of pottery, numbers of coins and a villa (located to the east of the church) which was excavated in about 1984.

As to the church of St James itself, the nave and chancel are Decorated; the tower is of 1566 in the upper parts and 13th Century in the lower. There was restoration by Street in 1869. Inside, is a monument to Richard Neville, died 1728, and some Clayton and Bell stained glass.

North of the church, on the fringe of the village, is the Moat House, part timber-framed and part 18th Century brick. It stands on the site of an earlier manor house, home of the Trussell family until the end of the 16th Century. In recent years it has been hugely extended as a hotel-conference centre and a venue for weddings. Here, also, is the Old School House of similar construction. On the other side of the road from the church, to the west, is a fragmentary, circular segment of a moat, 615 feet by 110 feet. In the late 1850s fire bricks were manufactured at Acton Trussell.

The name Acton Trussell is the original of Stackton Tressel, coined by the comedy duo, Hinge and Brackett. Dame Hilda Brackett, alias Patrick Fyffe, used to live in the village.

One mile NE of Acton Trussell, on the lane to the A34, is the splendidly-situated haunted house of Acton Hill Farm (SJ 946195). In March 1835 the shepherd, Richard Burton, lost five children aged between two and 17 in a period of 11 days. Another son died in 1838 and two more in 1840. All eight are commemorated on a stone in Baswich churchyard. The cries of ghostly children have been heard by the later occupants of the house.

ADBASTON *6.5m NNE of Newport*
Adbaston is lost in the lanes north of Newport in flat farming country which, with the increasingly large fields of today, can be somewhat bleak. The old village consists of little more than the Hall, the Rectory and the Church. One tries to forget the modern concrete houses and the row of brick bungalows. The Hall is now a colour-washed farm and is older than it looks. In front of the house is a pool much frequented by ducks.

The Rectory is 19th century brick, and the Church of St Michael is essentially Norman - see the chancel windows - with later Perpendicular (1350-1550) rebuilding. The silver chalice and plate are Elizabethan and there is an incised monument to Reginald de Adbaston, died 1441.

Knighton Reservoir, 1.25m NE of Adbaston, is a delightful little lake, constructed as a feeder reservoir for the Shropshire Union Canal, a little to the south. It is almost hidden from the road and looks as though it is a stream temporarily in flood, with grassy meadows reaching to the water's edge. Near the dam end is a derelict farmhouse in a wooded clearing.

Batchacre Hall, 1.25m S of Adbaston, was built for Admiral Richard Whitworth III, died 1811. It sits in isolation amongst windswept fields. The Georgian red brick facade hides a much older building which shows itself in the strange chimneys and mullioned windows in the basement. These probably belonged to the 16th Century Grange held by Ranton Abbey, which preceded it. Over the porch is a tripartite window with a pointed window above. The house and grounds have known better days. There used to be a lake with an ornamental fort on an ornamental island. Only a rectangular fragment of this lake remains. Still there, standing forlorn amongst undergrowth to the south of the Hall, is the porch of Gerard's Bromley Hall which was demolished in 1584. (See Gerard's Bromley.)

The lake had been formed by damming the Lonco Brook and was intended to act as a feeder reservoir for the projected Bristol and Hull Canal which never materialized. Admiral Whitworth used to have mock naval battles on it. Amongst the outbuildings is a 16th Century block called The Barracks because the Market Drayton troop of the Volunteer Cavalry was once stationed here.

At Wood Farm the Sharrod family made a beautiful garden and grotto in, and about, an old gravel pit. Two huge blocks of sandstone were used as gates, which were so well balanced that they could be moved with one finger. The garden has decayed. Only the well-known Tree House remains.

Knighton, 1m SW of Adbaston, is a hamlet that bestrides the Shropshire Union canal and is dominated by the Premier Brands' factory which, until 1986, belonged to Cadbury. Dairy-based confectionary is manufactured here and has been since 1911. There are a few farms, the old Hall, a roadside development of 20th Century houses with hipped roofs arranged in blocks of two or four, a social club with a bowling green, tennis courts and a football pitch. It is about as ordinary as could be, yet it was unique in the whole of Britain. All but three of the houses here lie on land which was formerly part of the estate of Knighton Manor, and by an act of Parliament of 1660 were granted immunity from the payment of local rates and taxes of any kind. The exact wording was very sweeping. The manor was "freed, discharged and acquitted of and from payment of all, every or any manner of Taxes, Assessments or charges Civil or Military".

Why should King Charles II have granted such an unusual boon? The gift was not actually meant to favour Knighton itself. The purpose of the Act was to authorize the setting up of a free school and almshouses in Newport (Shropshire) by William Adams, a citizen and haberdasher of London. To make his new establishment financially independent he endowed it with the manor and Grange of Knighton. The exemption from taxation already detailed made the income from the manor more valuable. But why was this special concession made? It is said that the king was returning a favour to Adams, who had loaned the king £1,000 at a time of great need. In 1990 this taxation privilege was withdrawn.

Flashbrook, 1.75m SSW of Adbaston, is a small, scattered settlement by a Roman road. The Grange formerly belonged to Ranton Abbey. The Manor House of 1556, built by the Barbour family of Stafford, was demolished in 1954 and replaced by a modern house. The Heath stretches into Shropshire and was used as Chetwynd Airfield. The Flash Brook is a tributary of the Lonco Brook.

Shebdon, 1.25m S of Adbaston, is a small hamlet which was Sahebbedon in 1267. The name means 'Sceoba's hill'. Shebdon Heath lies on the north side of the Shropshire Union Canal. Shebdon Pool was drained by 1922.

ALDRIDGE *2.5m NE of Walsall*

The Domesday Book name was Alrewic, which means 'farm amongst the alder trees'. In Anglo-Saxon times it was a Royal Manor. After 1066 it passed to William, son of Ansculf, and under the Normans the area fell just within the southern boundary of Cannock Forest. In the 19th Century the most important industries were coal mining (the last pits closed in the 1930s), brick making and tile manufacture. Limestone was quarried from Roman times until the late 19th Century. Today, there is a variety of light engineering and manufacturing works, and bricks are still made in abundance.

There is very little that is old here. The town centre is full of flat-roofed shops that have the appearance of temporary buildings, the schools are modern square boxes with much glass and there is acre upon acre of post-war housing. The reason for this development is that Aldridge was made one of the overspill areas for the Birmingham conurbation.

That Aldridge was once a great deal more attractive than it is today can be seen by what remains of the old village. It stands around the northern edge of the extremely large and lush village green. Here are three buildings of note: the church, the Moot House and Manor House. The church of St Mary has a 19th Century tower and an aisle of 1841; most of the rest was rebuilt by Anthony Salvin in 1853. Inside there is a Jacobean pulpit, a stained glass window by Powell and a cross-legged knight of the early 14th Century. South-west of the church is the Moot House. This is a handsome stuccoed house of three bays and 2.5 storeys with a curved porch supported by columns. Each of the slightly projecting end bays has a Venetian window surmounted by a tripartite window, and at the top a lunette (moon-shaped) window. The Manor House lies to the other side of the church. It is a large brick-built building of three bays and 2.5 storeys with a hipped roof. The porch does not look as though it belongs. It is of stone, supported by stone Ionic columns, and above it is a pedimented window with stone surrounds. The house is currently used as a Youth Centre.

Just to the east of Aldridge, where the Chester road crosses Little Aston Road, is the Old Irish Harp. The highwayman, Tom King, who had a national reputation, is said to have been born at this old coaching inn and in later life to have frequented it.

Leighswood, due north of the town centre, is split by Northgate, the road to Brownhills. To the east are suburban houses; to the west industrial estates. More interesting is the road to High Heath. This crosses the Daw End branch of the Rushall Canal, passes the giant brickworks of Ibstock and Salvesan and brings the traveller to **Stubers Green**.

Green it still is, complete with its compliment of browsing nags. It is also a watery place with drainage ditches and several pools. Some pools were formed by settlement of the land because of mining; others are old clay and gravel pits. The largest is called The Swag and is now home to the Aldridge Sailing Club. Swag is a local term for land that has sunk due to the collapse of underground mine workings. The lane that leads past the entrance to the Sailing Club brings one to Westgate. Turn left and down the road one comes to the delightfully named Dumble Derry Lane. Dumble is probably of Celtic origin but can mean many things, most commonly 'dark hill'. Certainly there are long views northwards from here. The ancient name does not sit too happily alongside the gleaming silver silos of the BP oil and lubricant plant, which stands beside the canal, guarding the entrance to an industrial estate.

Druids' Heath lies 1m NE of Aldridge town centre. On the upper slopes there is now a pleasant modern residential area. Much of the rest of the heath is now occupied by the links of the Druids' Heath Golf Club. Their yellow brick club house looks down a long slope to the whitewashed Druids' Heath Farm. The Druids were Celtic Iron Age priests. Other than the name, there is no evidence to suggest they had a connection with the Heath. But then there is no evidence to suggest the opposite. Certainly, early man left his mark hereabouts: the Iron Age fort at Holy Bank, a Stone Age axe at Shenstone, and the Roman Ryknild Way. Generally speaking, Celtic names have only survived as the names of rivers and prominent hills - but only generally speaking. The most plausible origin of the name we have come across is that Druid is a corruption of 'Dreux', a Norman family who were medieval lords of Aldridge.

Druids' Heath House is perhaps the same as Druids' Heath Farm, said to be the most 'supernaturally disturbed' house in Staffordshire. It started life as a school but by the 1940s was being used as an annexe to a Dr Barnardo's Home.

By 1984 it had become an old people's home known as Richard House.

Bourne Vale, 1m E of Aldridge, is a modern housing estate. However, just to the north is the former small lake, now reduced in size, called Bourne Pool which is the source of the Bourne Brook, a tributary of the River Tame. In 1955 over 2,000 flint implements of Late Mesolithic age were found to the west of the pool at SP 069997. The site was excavated in 1958 and numerous heat-shattered pebbles of possible Middle Bronze Age were found amongst a surface scatter of Mesolithic flint artefacts, at about SP 069998. (Pebbles were heated in a fire and then dropped into cold water to heat it. If water is heated in porous pots the pots explode.) To the south-west of Bourne Pool, at SP 073997, are the remains of an unexplained rectangular, very-worn earthwork, 80 yards by 25 yards, protected by a treble ditch called Loaches Banks.

Linley, 1m W of Aldridge, was a place of extensive limestone mining, quite probably from Roman times. Letocetum may have been constructed with Linley limestone. There have been several Roman finds in the area – coins in large numbers and a clasp (fibula). In 1856 the Linley Caverns were described as "of immense extant which lead to a large subterranean lake". These were well lit and visited by tourists. The entrances to the caverns have since been sealed. The Linley Lodge Industrial Estate is named after Linley Lodge, which stood SE of Barnes Road. The name Linley means 'the glade where flax grows'.

ALREWAS *5m NE of Lichfield*

Three Iron Age gold torcs were found here by a metal detectorist in 1996 and are now at the Potteries Museum in Hanley. Alrewas is a communications' centre of some importance. Here the A38 (Ryknild Street) crosses the A513, King's Bromley to Tamworth road, and the Trent and Mersey Canal crosses the River Trent. The country around is flat, and sand and gravel are quarried nearby. The village is most attractive with many timber-framed and black-and-white thatched cottages. There is a Victorian cotton mill just north of the church. The name Alrewas means 'alder-wash' or 'alder marsh' and was first mentioned in a land grant by King Edmund in 941.

The village lies on the edge of Needwood Forest which was once heavily wooded. The boundaries of **Needwood Forest** were, generally speaking, the Rivers Trent, Dove and Blithe. It was a natural woodland which, for the most part, lay on a raised plateau. After the Norman Conquest it became a hunting ground of the Ferrers family. A mile-and-a-half west is Alrewas Haye, an isolated farm. This is quite possibly the site of an Anglo-Saxon 'haye', a small, often unenclosed, hunting park. Two ancient trades practised in Alrewas were eel fishing, in the River Trent, and basket making. The area is also noted for the survival of the Borough English custom of passing property to the youngest child, be it male or female.

The church of All Saints is Norman, with two original doorways, but was largely rebuilt in Early English and Perpendicular. In the chancel is a 15th Century wall painting. There are 18th Century memorials to the Turton family who lived at Orgreave Hall, which lies 1.5m NW of Alrewas.

Over the door of a house near the church is this verse:

Traveller, as you pass this way,
A blessing on this house I pray,
And if you've time (I ask your pardon)
Spare another for the garden.

Chetwynd Bridge (1824) lies 1.5m SE of Alrewas. This is in cast-iron and was made at Coalbrookdale. It has three arches and was designed by the County Surveyor, Joseph Potter. It is sometimes called Salter's Bridge and carries the A513 over the River Tame. Half-a-mile downstream the Tame joins the Trent.

ALSAGERS BANK *2.5m NW of Newcastle-under-Lyme*

Alsagers Bank is a large, former mining village which straggles along the B5367, from which there are far-reaching views stretching from Liverpool to the Long Mynde. The name was formerly Auger's Bank after George Auger, who hired out horses to assist in climbing the steep bank on the Newcastle road. Later, this business was taken over by George Alsager of Halmer End Farm (now Minnie Farm). The Farmer's Boy pub probably stands on the site of a cottage in which Adolphus Fielding, a potter, was beheaded with an axe by his lodger in 1845.

Alsagers Bank is adjoined to the north-west by Halmer End, and to the south-west by the recent open-cast coal pits of High Lane. Note, however, that open-cast mines eat their way through the country at a rate of knots and are very much here today and gone tomorrow.

Scot Hay, 0.5m SSW of Alsagers Bank, is a hilltop village in a mining area. The older cottages and terraced houses are on the hill top and the newer bungalows and houses are mostly on the lower slopes. The Hill Top Primitive Methodist church of 1876 is built of blue brick with yellow brick dressings and has lancet windows. On the north-eastern fringe of the settlement is a large cricket ground with pavilions and a car park. Scot Hay is an unexpectedly pleasant little residential place, though it appears to have neither shop nor pub.

The village was the birthplace of Wilf A Bloor, who wrote the Jabez stories in Potteries' dialect, which were published in the Evening Sentinel newspaper between 1968 and 1993. He wrote under the pen name of A Scott.

ALSTONEFIELD *14m NNW of Ashbourne*

The parish of Alstonefield is very large, being 23,000 acres compared to, say, Barlaston at 2,000 acres. The reason is that this is moorland hill country, with a widely-scattered population living in isolated farms and small hamlets. It has been this way since medieval times. The underlying rocks are limestone and the stones cleared to make the pastures were used to build the characteristic white stone walls and cottages of the area.

The village of Alstonefield is at least Anglo-Saxon in origin, if not earlier. It is a pleasant, stone-built place with a perfect village green shaded by large trees and overlooked by the village pub. It is famous for the fact that Charles Cotton, the fishing friend of Isaac Walton, lived nearby at **Beresford Hall**. The Hall was pulled down about 1860 and now lies in ruins, but Cotton's delightful Fishing Lodge of 1674 still stands in its charming setting by the River Dove at the northern entrance to Beresford Dale (nearer to Hartington than Alstonefield).

The church of St Peter at Alstonefield has fragments of Anglo-Saxon interlace sculpture: in the west side of the porch; inside the tower; in the west of the north aisle; and in the north of the north aisle. The chancel is Norman but most of the rest of the church is Decorated (1290-1350) and Perpendicular (1350-1550). Inside there are 17th Century box pews, a fine two-decker pulpit of 1637, and the Charles Cotton pew with its pale green livery. (Note: at Bowman's Farm, SK 137558, Alstonefield there is an 18th Century Quaker burial ground.)

Alstonefield Hall is a small manor house of 1587 which lies to the north of the church. It is of irregular shape and has mullioned windows. One mile south-west is the 17th Century Stanshope Hall. It has gabled wings and a side-facing, five-bay brick front with a projecting surround to the doorway.

In the hills around Alstonefield are several prehistoric burial mounds, or tumuli. These include sites at Narrowdale Hill, Gratton Hill, Stanhope pasture at Hall Dale, Steep Low and Pea Low. Pea Low was broken into twice, once by Bateman and once by Carrington. It lies 0.75m N of Alstonefield, at SK 130564, and is 38 yards in diameter and 10 feet high. There have been numerous finds in the area: 50 Roman coins, fragments of a cup, a round cremation urn, two iron spear heads, a lance head, a knife and an iron arrowhead.

The barrow at Steep Low (or Steepe Lowe), 0.5m NW of Alstonefield, was opened in 1845. Amongst the finds were a skeleton, some smelted iron-ore, a drinking cup, animal bones and three Roman coins: one of the Emperor Tetricus (768-773 AD), one of the Emperor Constantine (307-337 AD), and one which could not be deciphered. Narrowdale, 1m NNW of Alstonefield, is a short, ravine-like narrow dale.

Gateham, 1m NW of Alstonefield, consists of two houses and two burial mounds. The mounds were excavated by Carrington in 1849. One revealed nothing; the other a cremation and a cinary urn. Gateham Grange has medieval cellars and was a grange of Combermere Abbey by 1134. The settlement may have been larger in the 19th Century but declined after the closing of the Ecton copper mines. **Stanshope**, 1m SSW of Alstonefield, has at least four excavated burial mounds and there are three more to the south at **Damgate**, 1m N of Ilam.

(See the Malbonck Forest article for the extent of the old Alstonefield Forest.)

ALTON *3.5m ESE of Cheadle*

We were in the grounds of Wootton Lodge, the most handsome house in the county. Across the lovely deer park and the lakes came the raucous sounds of a rock group. Perhaps the Hall had been bought by a pop millionaire, we thought. But no - the music came from the funfair of Alton Towers nearly two miles away. The owner of Wootton Lodge is Mr Bamford of the earth-moving equipment manufacturers, JCB. He must be furious at this untoward intrusion.

The quiet little village of Alton lies high on the southern bank of the delightful Churnet Valley. There has probably been a settlement at Alton since prehistoric times. Early artefacts found here include a polished stone axe, a flint arrowhead, a Late Bronze Age or Anglo-Saxon, leaf-shaped sword and three roman coins (found 900 yards below Alton Castle).

The village commands the north-south river crossing and the east-west road from Cheadle to Rocester. There is good reason to believe that the settlement lay on an old salt road from Nantwich to Derby, because east of Alton is Saltersford Lane which may have formed part of the route.

Bertram de Verdun built a large castle at Alton about 1175. (He also built Croxden Abbey). All that remains of the castle is part of one tower. This is in the forecourt of the new castle built by Pugin in 1847. Seen from the valley below this is everyone's idea of a fairy-tale castle, a Rhineland fantasy. It has four storeys and three towers, and sits on a precipice with a ravine between it and the adjacent Hospital of St. John. The castle is 'L'-shaped with a chapel wing which converts the 'L' to a 'T' shape.

The chapel has a roof of coloured tiles, the window tracery is geometric and the apse is polygonal. There is an ante-chapel and a chapel proper which is, unusually, rib vaulted in stone. The whole provides an atmospheric place of worship. Today the castle is used as a Roman Catholic boys' school.

Across the moat-ravine, traversed by a bridge, is the Hospital of St John, built between 1842 and 1846 for the 16th Earl of Shrewsbury by Pugin. The castle and the hospital are of one integrated design. It is built in a 'U' shape, the open end facing the castle. The right wing was built last and differs in design from the others. The Hospital, in Pugin's words, was to 'consist of a chapel, school, lodging for the warden, common hall, kitchen, chambers and library, lodgings for the poor brethren and a residence for the schoolmaster'. The schoolmaster's house was actually a conversion of two existing cottages and stands detached. The chapel has a good chancel roof and an ornate plaster reredos. There are brass memorials to the last Roman Catholic Earls of Shrewsbury; the 16th died in 1852 and the 17th died in 1856. Pugin himself died in 1852.

The sizeable village is a quiet place. There is a small, pretty hamlet down in the valley at the bridge head, and from here a delightful lane runs parallel with the river to Oakamoor, some two miles to the north-west. The village church of St Peter at Alton has a Norman north arcade and a 14th Century tower, but was mostly rebuilt in 1830. Probably the best house in the village is the painted Old Coffee Tavern with a pedimented doorway in the centre of three bays. Nearby, is the old, stone-domed Lockup of 1819.

Alton Station lies on the north bank of the river. It was built in the 1840s by H A Hunt and has the appearance of an Italian house. The railway is now dismantled and is used as a footpath. Both sides of the valley are wooded.

The **Churnet Valley** has had a long industrial history and, strange as it seems today, there were many mills here making iron and copper. At Alton there are today two buildings which were formerly working mills. The Old Mill Cafe (SK 072426), formerly Alton Mill, is probably 18th Century. It is built of stone with a tiled roof and brick chimney stacks, and a gabled wing at each end. The actual mill has been pulled down. From about 1734 it drew brass for wire pin manufacture, but later became a paper mill. In 1830 it had three waterwheels. One mile NW of Alton in the Churnet Valley is a watermill (SK 060432), built in 1741 as a lead smelting mill and converted to grind corn by 1784. It has a single, high-breast waterwheel and three pairs of grinding stones.

North of the river is **Alton Towers** which is today best known as a pleasure park. The old house and gardens are very much of secondary importance to the gaudy amusements first introduced by John Broome, a businessman and property developer, in the second half of the 20th Century. There are 78 listed attractions which include rides that are major works of engineering, such as the gigantic corkscrew roller coaster. It is, to all intents and purposes, a small town in its own right. In the summer months hundreds of coaches pour down the surrounding country lanes. On arrival they stand in endless lines in the enormous vehicle park. There can be no doubt that the greatest achievement of the organizers of the pleasure park was the obtaining of planning permission for this development.

So what were the origins of Britain's biggest and most brash funfair? The hill on which Alton Towers stands is called Bunbury, or sometimes Bonebury. There was an Iron Age (BC 600-650) settlement here which was taken over by Anglo-Saxons. It consisted of a double or treble ditch to the north, north-east and north-west sides, with the hill forming sufficient defences to the south. It was very large, covering about 100 acres. In AD 716 Ceolred, King of Mercia, was in occupation of the fortress. King Ina (or Ine) of the West Saxons was advancing to attack him. He camped in a valley, where the Alton Towers' gardens are now situated, and King Ina himself slept in the shelter of a huge rock now called King Ina's Rock, which can be seen on Rock Walk. The next day King Ceolred left his fortress and descended on the West Saxon army. The battle took place in what is now called Slain Hollow. However, the battle was indecisive and both armies withdrew.

The lands of Alton passed to Bertram de Verdun. They were gifted to him by Richard I as a reward for his services in the Holy Land. They later passed to the Talbots in 1412. The Talbots, who were Earls of Shrewsbury, lived at Wingfield in Derbyshire, Worksop in Nottinghamshire and Heythrop in Oxfordshire. All they had at Alton was a small lodge built for their agent. Then, in the early 19th Century, the 15th Earl and his wife visited their Alton estate and were very taken by the grandeur of the scenery. In 1814 the Earl started to lay out the gardens and made Gothic additions to the existing lodge. In 1827, with the work still incomplete, he died but the 16th Earl continued where the 15th Earl had left off, and when the Heythrop mansion burned down in 1831 the Earl moved to Alton.

Many architects were employed at Alton, including James Wyatt and Pugin, but who did what is not known. The house measures 460 feet by 250 feet. It is most ornate and irregular, a fantasy of towers, pinnacles, battlements and turrets. It was originally called Alton Abbey. Today, much of the hall is empty and even ruinous. The Banqueting Hall has a fine timber ceiling and stained glass windows. The Flag Tower is rock-faced with four turrets and stands in good order. The Chapel was remodelled by Pugin. It is high with two west galleries and has a low polygonal apse between two turrets. The Conservatory and the Stables are restored and very good.

The gardens are Alton's glory. More than one observer has declared them the finest in the country. They are heavily planted in a rocky valley that leads down to the River Churnet. There are pools, fountains, terraces, walls, paths and staircases. The two principal gardeners were Thomas Allason (1790-1852) and Robert Abrahams (1774-1850). There are many garden buildings: The Pagoda Fountain (a copy of the To Ho Pagoda in Canton); the Swiss Cottage, now a restaurant but once home to a Welsh harper; a construction called Stonehenge, which is not a copy of the original; and the Choragic Monument, a copy of Lysicrates' work erected in Athens in 344 BC. The gardens include the great Rock Garden, the Star Garden, the Terraced Garden and the Dutch Garden. The 16th Earl gave orders that any Roman Catholic who applied for a job should be employed without question, hence the vast network of paths through the woods - work that could be tackled by the unskilled.

In 1856 the last of the Catholic Earls of Shrewsbury died. There was an unpleasant squabble over the inheritance which finally passed to a remote cousin, the Anglican Earl Talbot of Ingestre, near Stafford. The court case had been expensive and to pay for it the contents of Alton Towers were sold by auction. The sale lasted for 29 days, so much was there to sell. There was a collection of paintings, originally owned by the mother of the Emperor Napoleon - which included works by Velasquez, Van Dyck and Bellini - furniture, arms and armour and, all in all, a countless treasure that attracted buyers from all over Europe. Ingestre Hall became the main residence of the Earls, and in 1860 the gardens at Alton were opened to the public. The family became involved, firstly, with a hansom cab company and then with the Talbot car company. In 1896 the Earl and his Countess separated. She had Alton and he lived at Ingestre. The Earl, however, held the purse strings and at Alton both the house and the gardens were allowed to decay. In 1918 most of the Alton estate was sold. In 1921 the Earl died, in 1923 the Countess left Alton and in 1924 the house, gardens, woods and parks were sold. They had been in the hands of the Earls of Shrewsbury for 700 years.

The property was bought by a group of local businessmen who formed Alton Towers Ltd. The gardens were restored and the public once again admitted. There were boats on the lake and bands on the bandstand, and the gardens were a commercial success. During the Second World War the house was used as an Officer Cadet Training Unit. By the end of the war the Army had done its worst and Alton Towers was in a dilapidated condition. The Army kept it locked up and unused until 1951, when it was finally handed over to its rightful owners. Leaking roofs, dry rot and wet rot made much of the building unsafe so the interior was largely demolished. In 1952 the gardens were once again restored and opened to the public. Then came the modern developments that were to make Alton an international name. One wonders if the 15th and 16th Earls would have quite approved.

AMBLECOTE *0.5m N of Stourbridge centre*

It has its own entry in Domesday Book but is now a part of the Stourbridge conurbation. The name is Anglo-Saxon and means 'the cottage by the river (or the sandbank)'. The river is the Stour which is shadowed here by the Stourbridge Canal. The settlement developed rapidly in the 19th century. Glass making (craftsmen from Lorraine were here from at least 1620), fireclay mining and coal mining were its most important industries. The area was also known for its clay tobacco pipes.

The single-cylinder, steam winding engine presently installed in the Racecourse Colliery engine house at the Black Country Museum in Dudley, came from a small disused coal pit at Amblecote.

At Dennis Hall glass making continues at the works of Thomas Webb & Sons, a world renowned company which came here in 1850. The Georgian Hall is now a part of the factory. The yellow brick church of Holy Trinity was built in 1844 to a design by Samuel Heming. The centre of the Corbett Hospital is a late Georgian house of nine bays, with a Venetian window at the back and a handsome staircase.

ANSLOW *2m NW of Burton upon Trent*

Anslow is an Anglo-Saxon village on the Needwood Forest plateau. In the 10th Century it was called Eansythlege, 'Eanswyth's woodland clearing'. In the late-12th Century it was a manor held by Burton Abbey. In the mid-16th Century it passed to the Paget family of Beaudesert. A field called the Bell Grove records the site of the Curfew Bell Tree. Curfews were held on six days scattered throughout the year to defer evil spirits, witches, goblins and friends.

Anslow Common, 0.75m SSW of Anslow, had a squatter settlement by 1700, before it was enclosed in 1802. **Anslow Gate**, 1m W of Anslow, developed around an entry point into Needwood Forest. Anslow church, Holy Trinity of 1850, is at Anslow Gate.

ARMITAGE *2.25m SE of Rugeley*

It lies on a rise 0.25m south of the River Trent and alongside the Trent and Mersey Canal (1766-1777), which runs parallel with the road from Rugeley for some two miles. This stretch of the canal has recently been improved. The main-line railway passes to the east of the village on its way from Rugeley to Lichfield. Armitage is not an attractive place but it does have several black-and-white cottages, two of which are on the main road. One of these is the once-well-known former restaurant called 'The Farmhouse', now called Spode Cottage. (See below.) The rest of the buildings are mostly red brick. The village is famous for the sanitary products made here, called Armitage Ware.

The church stands alone, to the west, close by the river. The old Church of St John was Norman with a later tower of 1632. All but the tower was rebuilt in 1844, in Norman style, and was very well done. The font is original Norman and is also very good.

About 1m W, along the A513 to Rugeley but on the other side of the canal, is Hawkesyard Priory, latterly called the Spode Conference Centre and now (2004) with an 'Offices to Let' sign prominently displayed. This started as Armitage Park, a stuccoed Gothic house built in 1760 by Nathaniel Lister. In 1839 it was bought by the widow of Josiah Spode III and the alteration in stone, to the left part of the house, dates from that year. The house has battlements and pinnacles but the chimneys were removed in 1963. The rear of the building backs on to the canal. It has three storeys and looks like a warehouse. There was a short tunnel connecting it to the canal. Mrs Spode and her son, Josiah Spode IV, lived in the house, the pottery business having passed to the Copeland family. Josiah IV renamed the house 'Hawkesyard' after the original medieval house that occupied the site. He became a convert to the Roman Catholic religion in 1885 and when he died in 1893 he left the house to the Dominican Order. It was the Dominicans who commissioned the Priory and chapel that lie just above the house. They were built in red brick by Edward Goldie. The chapel has eight bays of large Perpendicular windows and the facade is college-like. The stone reredos has statues of saints. On the north side is the Founder's Chantry where lies buried Josiah IV and his niece, Helen Gulson. The organ (c1700) is outstanding. It came from the chapel at Eton College and bears the coat of arms of King William III, of Eton college and of King's College. These were carved by William Bird who carried out work for Christopher Wren. The Dominicans first used the house as a school but then renamed it Spode House and now hold conferences and retreats there. It still retains a small park.

Close by Spode House, where the canal and the road cross, is Spode Cottage, a black-and-white house that became a restaurant and is now a pub. Behind it is a residential mobile home park. Opposite, is the Plum Pudding Brasserie. In total, a busy little canal-side settlement.

Adjoining Armitage to the east is **Handsacre**. Here was the old moated Hall, of brick with timber-framed gables, probably of the 17th Century. Inside was an older part - aisled, of two-and-a-half bays - of about 1320. This was the home of Sir William Handsacre who, in 1403, rode out at the head of his men intending to join up with Harry Hotspur and Owen Glendower to do battle with Henry IV. The battle took place near Shrewsbury at Battlefield, but Sir William was not there. His neighbour, Sir Robert Mavesyn, whose manor was less than a mile to the north at Mavesyn Ridware, was also riding out that day, but to join King Henry. The two local lords met by the Trent and in the bloody battle that ensued Sir William Handsacre was killed. Sir Robert Mavesyn went on to the great Battle of Shrewsbury where, though he fought on the victorious side, he was slain. Handsacre Hall was demolished in about 1970 but some of the older parts of the building have been reconstructed at the Avoncroft Museum of Buildings near Bromsgrove in Worcestershire.

ARMSDALE AND THE LANGOT VALLEY *5m NE of Eccleshall*
This lovely dale runs from Fairoak to Blore Pipe and is part of the valley of the River Sow. On the western flank is Bishop's Wood, the modern coniferous re-planting of the medieval hunting grounds of the Bishops of Lichfield. In 1298 it was called Blore Park and was an enclosed part of **Blore Forest**. Local people had to provide 84 beaters for three three-day hunts every year. Sir Gerard Bromley, Master of the Rolls from 1581 to 1592, and his son - who became Baron Gerard, Lord President of the Council of Wales and the Marches, and who lived at the nearby 'palace' of Gerard's Bromley Hall - would have known these woods. (See Ashley.) They were certainly well known to the Elizabethan glass-makers from Lorraine, one of whose kilns has been found and renovated - the only one of its kind in the whole country. (See Broughton.) The wood is criss-crossed by many tracks and is a popular place in which to go riding.

At the northern end of the Langot Valley is **Fairoak**. This is a long, straggling hamlet somewhat spoiled by an incongruous row of mundane Council houses. The Freemasons' Arms, the name of which is a reminder that the area was noted for its stonemasons, was de-licensed recently and is now a domestic dwelling. There were several stone quarries in the district and the industry flourished here from at least the 14th to the 18th Centuries. Behind the Council houses is a wooded knoll, the top of which has been quarried. From several sides the hill has the shape of a cone and it is reputed to be a prehistoric religious site. The druids are said to have made human sacrifices on a rock on its summit. The name Langot is probably derived from the Celtic for 'Holy Stone' and the road that runs down the valley is called Langot Lane. An early Bronze Age axe head was found in the village and is now at Hanley Museum. There is also, it is said, an Iron Age fort in Bishop's Wood. **Fairoak Green** is half an acre of common land at the north end of the village.

If ever you are near Moss Farm, 0.5m SW of Fairoak, keep your eyes on the sky. During the Second World War a bomb fell into the moss and is still there, unexploded, and in 1999 an aircraft refuelling hose dropped on the farm. In 1975 the teeth of a wild Pleistocene horse were found on or near Moss Farm.

The valley of the River Sow is quite marshy in places and the name Pipe in local names, such as Blore Pipe, probably refers to drainage channels and conduits. Many of the physical features of the area are the result of glaciation.

Down a lane, about 400 yards south of Fairoak, is Armsdale and Sutton House. It was here that the 2nd Duke of Buckingham hid in a bread oven to escape Cromwell's soldiers during his flight after the defeat of Charles II at the Battle of Worcester. In fact, he is believed to have hidden in the valley for some time before making his way to France. There is a small cave at The Outlands, near **Blore Pipe,** in which he is said to have lived and which is still called Buckingham's Cave. This is in the cliff face behind the red brick Cave Cottage (which has been recently renamed April Cottage). The cottage is the first house on the right on the lane to Walkmill and Offley Hay. One of Buckingham's brothers in arms was Colonel Blague. Charles II had given the Colonel his diamond brooch of the Order of the Garter for safe keeping. Blague was heading for Scotland and, like Buckingham, found himself in the Langot Valley. He was resting at Blore Pipe Farm (which is opposite the entrance to White Farm) when Cromwell's soldiers arrested him, but not before he had hidden the King's diamond brooch. This was retrieved by Royalist sympathizers and taken from the farm to Stafford. From there Isaac Walton took it to London and returned it to Colonel Blague who was imprisoned in the Tower. Shortly after, the Colonel escaped, made his way to France and was able to restore the brooch to the King.

A more macabre incident occurred on 2nd April, 1843 when a farm labourer called Charles Higginson murdered his young son by burying him alive in Bishop's Wood. The inquest on the death was held at the Freemason's Arms and Higginson was later arrested, tried and hanged at Stafford on 26th August 1843.

On the high ground to the east of the valley is a ridge on which there is a remarkable series of sandstone outcrops. The bedding planes dip sharply to the east and the rocks themselves vary from massive to fine, shale-like deposits with many small unconformities. There are many caves in these rocks. Part of the roof over one of the largest and longest of the cave systems collapsed some 30 years ago. The surface crater is about 20 feet deep and 16 feet in diameter. The caves can still be entered but are very dangerous. In this century a man called Joe Wilson used to live in the caves here. He was a real cave dweller. His home was not a rock-house like those at Kinver, which had brick front extensions. He was a troglodyte. For a time a chimney sweep also lived in another cave 'next door'. A few yards to the south is an overgrown ravine, about 40 feet deep and 20 feet wide. This runs southwards and is one of the old stone quarries which has been partly infilled to make it less dangerous. Brambles and briars are rife here. These caves and the ravine can be approached along a dirt track just north of Greatwood Farm (SJ 778312). They are about 400 yards north-west of the farm. The track passes through a rock cutting. To the left (south) are the caves just mentioned and to the right (north) are yet more caves (SJ 776317). Two of these have fresh-water pools in them and this is where the farmer from Greatwood Farm used to obtain his water. He filled milk churns and transported them by horse and cart. The entrances to many of the caves have collapsed. The views from this rocky ridge are far-reaching and the undulating country all around is both beautiful and mysterious. With the shelter offered by the caves and the regular supply of fresh water it seems highly likely that prehistoric man lived here, though we know of no excavations or investigations having been carried out in them. Any remains of early occupants could have been well preserved by being covered with the material from the collapsed roofs. The water holes have deep layers of fine silt in which artefacts may well lie hidden. It must surely be a site worth exploring.

To the south of the ravine is another outcrop in which there are four caves, one of which is quite large, measuring approximately 12 feet high by 10 feet wide and 30 feet deep. They face on to a grassy dale where sheep graze and which leads to Langot Lane, from where the caves can be seen over a five-bar gate just north of Blore Pipe. Bishop's Wood and a great deal of the land in Armsdale and the Langot valley, including the cave-ridge, still belongs to the church and is in the care of the Church Commissioners.

ASHLEY *4m WNW of Market Drayton*
The name means 'the forest clearing by the ash tree'. Today, the village is a modern-looking place. The old centre has been inundated with middle-class villas, not unattractive but with very little character. It is on the outskirts that the old village lingers, in the lanes of Hookgate, Jug Bank and Ashley Dale. Small sandstone cottages are scattered haphazardly in a maze of narrow tracks. This is a typical, early-medieval forest clearance pattern. Men acting individually, and not as part of a planned scheme, hacked out clearings in the forest.

Tracks ran from one clearing to another, ignoring topography or the convenience of straight lines. Even today the hedges reflect this frontier existence. They are planted with a wide variety of trees and bushes, many of which provided a crop such as holly - which was widely used as a winter feed for cattle in medieval times - and a whole range of small fruit trees and bushes such as damson, for the dyeing trade, and blackberry. The fields are still small and irregular and there are very few modern houses. There are least five small sandstone quarries: some are now water-filled, some have been back-filled, and one is used by the council to store crushed road-stone.

There has been a church at Ashley since at least 1205, when King John granted it to the Canons of Montesfunt in Normandy. There are two legendary tales that tell of its foundation: one, that a knight was lost in the forest and, emerging to safety at Ashley, founded the church in gratitude; and the other, that a knight fulfilled a vow he had made prior to undertaking a dangerous journey, from which he returned safely. The church of St John the Baptist that we see today has a 17th Century tower but the rest was built by J Ashdown of London in 1860-2 in 13th-14th Century style. It sits on a raised circular mound, the sign of an Anglo-Saxon or even pre-Christian site. Inside are several monuments, for which the church is well known. The Kinnersley family are more than well represented but the splendid tomb of Sir Gilbert Gerard (d 1592) and his wife (d 1608) is the most impressive sculpture. The interior was richly furnished by Bodley's successor, Cecil Hare, in 1910 and paid for by F G Lindley Meynell of Hoar Cross.

A few yards to the north-west of the church is a substantial man-made mound. Apparently, this has not yet been excavated and there are several local legends which explain its origin. Informed opinion is that it was probably a mass burial ground for victims of the Black Death. There is another mound, a burial site about 15 feet high, in Ashley Dale at SJ 754364.

A one-time rector of Ashley church was John Lightfoot. He was a Hebrew scholar, the foremost of his day, and to remove himself from domestic distractions he bought the field adjacent to the church and built himself a little cabin. Here he worked and often slept. In 1642 he became vice-chancellor of Cambridge University.

Up the hill from the church is the strange little Roman Catholic chapel of Our Lady and St John. The church and rectory are built as one, with primitive, Gothic-inspired ornaments in colour-washed stucco. As for the rest, the village has three pubs, a doctor's surgery and an unmanned fire station.

To the west is an area called **Ashley Heath**. Here are unmade tracks in a dense wood, in which are smart new houses with patios and swimming pools. There is also is a school, a water tower and a controversial radio-'phone mast.

Adjoining Ashley Heath is **Loggerheads**, situated at the crossing of the road from Market Drayton to Newcastle (A53) and the road from Eccleshall to Woore (B5026). The settlement takes its name from the pub, The Three Loggerheads. A loggerhead is a fool. The old inn sign showed two fools' heads; the third fool was the onlooker. Part of the Three Loggerheads is 17th Century and is listed. In the last century the inn was the destination of coach trips from the Potteries. People came for the day and even the weekend.

Loggerheads is really quite interesting because it is a village in the making. Only a few years ago all that was here was the public house. Now there is a garage, a restaurant, a Post Office and half-a-dozen assorted, purpose-built shops. It has effectively taken over as the centre of Ashley.

There are several new housing estates to the north-west of the crossroads, whilst to the south is another area of very upmarket detached villas, again in a wooded setting. This occupies the site of the old tuberculosis hospital, the Cheshire Joint Sanatorium. It was situated here because Loggerheads is on a hill, above the damp air of the lowlands and the soot and smoke that used to drift over from the Potteries. It is noticeable today that the weather on the hill is often quite different from that on the plains around it.

The Sanatorium opened in 1923, on a 230-acre site in Burntwood, and closed in 1969. In 1977 Newcastle-under-Lyme Borough Council bought the estate, and some superior private houses were built on a very small area. There is a football pitch, a children's play area with an imitation steam train, and tracks through some very attractive woodland, including an area of ancient scrub oak wood at SJ 738354, which is now an SSSI in the care of the Staffordshire Wildlife Trust. There is a tradition that the last wolf in England was killed in Burntwood.

Today, this large forest is coniferous, courtesy of the Forestry Commission, but it used to be an oak wood, part of the ancient Blore Forest. The stumps of the great oaks can still be seen. They were mercilessly cut down to make way for the quick-growing crop of softwoods. The whole area around Ashley is quite heavily wooded, with the Maer Hills' Forest to the north, Bishop's Wood to the south and numerous small copses in-between.

The old name for Burnt Wood was Rowney Wood (from Roundhay), and it was more extensive than it is today. Rowney Gate was the area between the Newcastle road and the road to Mucklestone at the Loggerheads' crossroads. The name lingers on in Rowney Farm, 2m WSW of Ashley.

A curiosity is an old railway carriage at Ivy House Farm, now a vehicle repair garage, on the Newcastle road. It is said to have belonged to Buffalo Bill - William Cody. He brought his Wild West Show to The Potteries in 1904. They appeared at the old racecourse, Boothen Farm, Stoke and at the Agricultural Show Field at Birches Head, Hanley. His entourage over-wintered their horses at farms along the A53, between Loggerheads and Market Drayton, for several months. (See Blore in Hales.) There is a collection of documents relating to this in an alcove in the Three Loggerheads pub.

At The Wellings, a house 1m NNE of Ashley, down a long, dead-end track off the A53, is Wellings Cave. It has three rooms carved out of the rock and there is a long tunnel of at least 200 yards, which is said to lead to Maer Hall, a good mile to the east. It was blocked in 1935. Apparently, hounds from the North Staffordshire Hunt often became lost in this cave.

Red Bull, 3m W of Ashley, at the junction of the A53 and the B5415 near Market Drayton, is a hamlet of half-a-dozen cottages and two mounds that might be the grassed-over remains of former buildings. One of these buildings, or former buildings, was probably an inn called the Red Bull. It is not uncommon for pubs to give their names to small country places.

A short distance north-east of Red Bull is Daisy Lake, a most attractive modern house which stands in wooded grounds with a small lake.

Hookgate, 1.25m WSW of Ashley, is a haphazard residential development along the Loggerheads to Eccleshall road. This road forms the boundary of Burntwood, a remnant of the medieval Blore Forest. There was probably a gate to the forest here.

Gerard's Bromley, 1m SE of Ashley, is now a single dairy farm. The medieval settlement is long gone, as indeed is the Hall which was described by Dr Plot in 1686 as being 'the most magnificent structure of all this county'. It was built about 1575 by Sir Gilbert Gerard, who was Attorney-General to Elizabeth I in 1581, and it is said that he built the Hall in the expectation that his queen would be visiting him there. She did not. It was a handsome stone mansion with ogee capped turrets, shaped gables and high windows. The 7th and last Lord Gerard became a Jesuit priest. The hall passed to the Meynell family and it was they who pulled it down in the 18th Century.

All that remains on the site today are the later 17th Century gate piers and a 17th Century barn. Inside the barn is an elaborate plaster frieze depicting a hunting scene. The sole remnant of the Hall itself is the Porch, which was dismantled and re-erected at nearby Batchacre Hall. (See Adbaston.) Here it languishes in a patch of scrub where it serves as a piece of garden furniture. The present farmhouse at Gerard's Bromley stands at the back of the large enclosed yard. It is, in fact, quite probably the original Hall, the home of the Gerards before they built their 'ephemeral palace'. The illustration in Dr Plot's 'Natural History of Staffordshire' (1686) shows the Old Hall, then used as servants' quarters, standing beside and behind the New. In recent times there has been talk of excavating and restoring the formal Tudor Gardens.

Below the farm the land falls away to the substantial mill pool and the now disused stone and brick mill. The stone was probably from the dismantled Hall. The road runs along the dam. The pastures on the northern bank of the pond have medieval ridge and furrow with distances of between 12 feet and 15 feet between the ridge crests. On the other side of this hill is **Podmore Pool**, another man-made lake and the probable site of the medieval ironworks at Bromley.

The Rudge, 1m ESE of Ashley, is now only a farm in attractive rolling country. In the 12th Century the manor was held by the de Muttons. Later, it passed to the Chetwynds, then to the Talbots, and in the 19th Century to the Meynell-Ingrams - illustrious country names all. It was then reduced in size and became a farm. Earlier forms of the name Rudge are Rigge and Ridge. In the 17th Century Jesuits are recorded at Rudge and later at nearby Gerard's Bromley. (The Talbots were Roman Catholic.)

ASTON (near Woore) 1.5m SE of Woore
It lies at the end of a bluff, a delightful village of working farms and upmarket residences. Aston Manor is a three-storey brick house now run as an Equestrian Centre. It is their big, neglected barn with broken cladding that is the traveller's introduction to Aston. It does not so much offer a greeting as growl at you. The only social facility in the settlement is the Village Hall.

The lane that leads to the dairy farm of Aston Cliff comes to an unexpected end at electric security gates. The thoroughbred horses in the adjacent fields belong to the Bearstone Stud and notices warn you that a security company is continuously video recording the area.

On the little green at Cross Lanes there is a water hydrant, and if you take the lane heading for Lunts Farm you will have for company a little stream that runs beside the road. Against the bank are some houses, old and new, in charming disarray. Several owners have hacked into the bank to create space for garages or extensions. At the end of this row is a good cottage, which is half black-and-white and half sandstone. In the paddock is a donkey, a jolly little animal, the sight of which should brighten anyone's day.

Lea Head Manor, 2m SW of Madeley, is a handsome, timber-framed house which was built in 1672 for William Bucknall. The gate post finials are pineapples, a fruit which had only just been introduced to England and which is a token of welcome and friendship. Nearby, is the moat of the previous medieval manor, which was burned down during the Civil War. The River Lea rises close to the house from a reed-fringed lake. It runs through Madeley to Wrinehill Hall where it joins the Checkley Brook. The whole small park is beautifully kept. In the Spring a feature of the pasture fields hereabouts is the profusion of dandelions. You could almost believe they were being grown as a crop.

Sidway Hall and Sidway House, 0.75m SSE of Aston, lie on the A51. The Hall was the seat of the Bowyer family from the 14th Century. In the 1990s there was a bottled water business here.

ASTON *(near Stone) 6m N of Stafford*

A little Catholic enclave hidden amongst the trees and seemingly surrounded by streams, near the junction of the A34 and the A51, just south of Stone. The moated Hall has been a Catholic house since Elizabethan times and today is a home for retired priests. In 1842 Father Dominic Barberi (1792-1849), founder of the Passionists, came here. He was beatified in 1963. A wooden cross attached to a garden wall is said to mark the spot where Barberi is buried.

The timber-framed house is now clad in Victorian brick. Alongside the entrance drive is a small chapel of 1844 with a low tower and spire. The Hall used to belong to the Simeon family who were Baronets of Britwell Salome, Oxfordshire.

The River Trent touches the northern edge of the village and on it was a mill, now a house. In the outbuildings opposite was a small craft pottery. The Trent and Mersey Canal runs within a few yards of the river and parallel to it for many miles hereabouts. The church of St Saviour was built by James Trubshaw in 1846; the spire was added by J R Botham in 1820 and the stained glass windows were designed by C A Gibbs in 1863.

One mile south of Aston, on the A34, is Yarlet Hall School. This is all that remains of the village of **Yarlet**. In 1086 it had 8 households, a large population for its day, but in the 12th Century the monks of Combermere (Cheshire) evicted the tenants, destroyed the village and made a farm - a grange - in its place. Today, there is a pub and a garage on the main road nearby, but these are comparatively recent main-road developments, as are the houses to the south. The old deserted village probably lay around the Hall. The present Hall is a Victorian building in Jacobean style, though it almost certainly stands on the site of the old medieval manor house. It was started in the 1870s by Henry Tunnicliffe and finished by the Reverend Walter Earle, who established the preparatory school here in 1873. At the top of Yarlet Bank, above the school, is a cone-shaped hill, which possibly has prehistoric associations. A Bronze Age flint scraper was found by the Hall tennis courts in 1977, and a socketed spearhead of probable Roman origin was found between Yarlet and the foot of nearby Pirehill.

Pire Hill, 1m SW of Aston, is the hill that gave its name to the Hundred of Pirehill, one of the five Hundreds of Staffordshire. (The others were Totmonslow, Cuttlestone, Offlow and Seisdon.) The headquarters of the Staffordshire Fire and Rescue Service has been established at Pire Hill Hall (or House) since 1941. The Hall is 0.5m ESE of the summit of Pire Hill, which is 463 feet above sea level.

AUDLEY *4.5m NW of Newcastle-under-Lyme*

Audley, called Aldidelege in Domesday Book, is a pleasant small town built on a ridge. There is much suburban housing and a surprise - a small theatre. To the north-west of the church is a good group of three shops, an archway and a house, all in Gothic brick with arches. They were built by William White and were illustrated in 'The Builder' magazine in 1855.

Audley has a 'forgotten castle' which is rarely mentioned in reference books, even today. It seems that historians had assumed that references to Audley Castle were errors and that the ancient writers were actually referring to Heighley Castle, 2.5m SW, both of which were owned by the Audley family. It was almost certainly the Normans who built the castle on what is now called Castle Hill. It lies adjacent to the A52, Newcastle to Nantwich road, and consists of a circular mound with a flat top which covers about a third of an acre. A moat protects the northern edge where the mound is at its lowest. There would have been a wooden palisade and a wooden fortress tower, as only minimal stonework was found when the site was excavated.

The church lies south of the castle, on the other side of the road. This is a typical Norman alignment. There was probably a natural gully between them but this was deepened when the road was improved in modern times. The Audley family (who took their name from the Anglo-Saxon settlement) came into possession of the manor some time after 1086, and it was possibly they who built the castle. In 1226 the fortress was mentioned in a document and again in 1272 at the inquest into the death of James de Audley. By this time the family had built Heighley Castle (see Madeley) and this had become their main dwelling. Audley Castle fell into disuse, references to it ceased and it became forgotten. It was rediscovered by local amateur historians at the beginning of the last century. It had long been used as an orchard but has now been cleared and fenced around.

The most famous squire of Audley was Sir James Audley (ancestor of James de Audley) who led the forces of the Black Prince at the Battle of Poitiers (1356). The battle was won but Audley was badly wounded. The Black Prince is reputed to have embraced him and said: "Sir James, I and all the rest of us deem you the bravest knight in this battle, and to increase your renown I retain you forever as my Knight."

In the church at Audley is the tomb of one of Sir James's squires, Richard Delves, who had helped carry his injured lord from the field of battle. On the chancel floor is a tombstone to Edward Vernon, vicar of Audley, who founded the Grammar School in 1612. The church of St James has a 14th Century tower, a 16th Century aisle and a Jacobean font. It is an impressive building in sandstone, with a large east window by William Wailes, and was restored by Gilbert Scott in 1846.

Shraley Brook, 1m WSW of Audley, lies adjacent to the M6. Most of the male population of this scattered hamlet worked at the Minnie Pit, Halmer End and many were killed in the dreadful explosion of 12th January 1918. (See Halmer End.)

Bignall End and **Bignall Hill** are hamlets to the east of Audley. Bignall Hill itself has an obelisk commemorating John Wedgwood, a colliery owner, who died in 1839. It was originally much taller but was damaged during a storm in 1976, reduced to about a quarter of its original height, and was not restored but merely capped. By 1962 there was a two-million-gallon water reservoir under the hill.

B

BAGNALL 1.75m S of Endon, which is 5m NW of Hanley
The medieval name was Baginholt and possibly means 'Badeca's wood'. It is a hilltop settlement with more than its fair share of charm, despite the 20th Century invasion of detached brick houses. Still, Hanley is only three miles to the south-west, so Bagnall can think itself lucky to still be surrounded by open country. Today, it is a residential village, but in earlier times there was some industry. Iron was smelted here as early at 1560, perhaps at Pool Meadows (SJ 933511), where the stream was anciently dammed and the pond bay still exists. In 1686 Palmer of Bagnall was one of the first potters to use common salt as a glaze. Later, in the early 1700s, Dutchmen introduced the enamelling process to decorate pottery: "to keep their operations secret they fired their ware in a muffle kiln in a garden at Bagnall." However, it should always be remembered that early references to places can be misleading; often, it is the parish that is referred to, and not necessarily the village or town that gave its name to the parish.

Bank Farm, a 16th Century house, was occupied by William Adams, a potter, who is believed to have used the adjacent property, Bank House, as a pottery. He was here between 1794 and 1810 and was a friend of Josiah Spode. Adams also had a flint mill called Stanley Mill on Stanley Pool.

The old village centre of Bagnall encircles a walled green, part of which is now used as a car park for customers of the Stafford Arms. The pub is long and low, and to its right is attached to a most handsome house which has mullioned windows and an ogee-roofed bay. Both buildings are of local stone and both are 17th Century at least. On the other side of the road is the church. St Chad's was rebuilt in 1834 with a battlemented tower, and the chancel was added in 1881. It sits well in the landscape and is embowered in mature trees and attractive gardens.

Opposite the Post Office-cum-general store is Bagnall Hall, a dignified building with hipped roof, five bays, ashlar stone, irregular quoins and dated on a plaque "1603, rebuilt 1777, I.M." For most of the day it lies in its own shadow with the sun on its back. It faces a second small, triangular green on which is a weather-beaten stone cross with a wheel top.

Standing at the village centre one has a choice of three roads by which to leave. One road heads south-west and leads to Highlands' Hospital, a modest red brick building in which the mentally disabled are cared for; one leads north to Stanley, about which more later; and the third leads south-east, steeply downhill, past stone barns in the process of being converted to houses, a disused quarry and St Chad's Lodge. The area at the bottom of the hill is a watery place with a gushing well, the stonework of which was 're-fixed in 1816', and a ford across a stream. It is this stream which was dammed in late medieval times and which now feeds Stanley Pool.

A wooded hill crowded with rhododendrons now dominates the scene. Ranks of rhododendrons usually speak of a country mansion and invariably survive the demise of the building. But here the explanation is more unusual. This hillside, which stretches for 0.33m southwards, was once a part of the Martin's Hill

Nurseries. These are not marked on the map but the entrance to them is at the road junction, just north of Lark Hall, at SJ 934878. Isaac Matthews started the present venture, which is now known as A P Matthews Nurseries Ltd, in the early years of this century. The black peaty soil is ideal for rhododendrons and azaleas, the land being old woodland that has never been limed and is well drained. It is exposed, high on this hill, but banks of mature bushes act as wind breaks. On the 18 acres under cultivation there are between 50,000 and 100,000 plants, at various stages of growth, in up to 60 varieties. Today, most of the stock comes from Holland and is grown on here. In 1992 the wholesale price of an 18-month-old, two-foot-high plant was £5 for a common variety, and £7.50 for a grafted, named variety. They retail at three times this price in some Garden Centres. The plants grown on Martin's Hill have a national reputation for quality, 'second to none' as they say. What is more, the nursery grounds have real character, more like a parkland; such a contrast to the 150 acres of flat, machine-friendly land that the company owns at Rodeheath, near Sandbach, Cheshire.

Furthering this horticultural connection with Cheshire, is the fact that John Ravenscroft was born at Bagnall. Mr Ravenscroft started, and still owns, the internationally-known Bridgemere Garden World, just over the border in Cheshire. It is no secret that he buys rhododendrons from the Martin's Hill Nursery to retail at his garden centre.

Now that you know where to buy the best possible rhododendrons in England at the best possible price, return to Bagnall village and leave on the road that leads down Clewlows Hill. Facing you, at the 'T' junction, is the mellow brick Rose and Crown. Turn right, and after a few yards turn right again into Puddy Lane, past Addlestone Manor (a modest, rendered house) and a great white wall confronts you. This is the overflow chute of **Stanley Pool** dam, built in 1840 as a feeder reservoir for the Caldon Canal. There are a few cottages, a disused quarry, some quaint stone bridges and an abundance of vegetation. On the waters above, men fish and sail boats. Continue left, up the hill, and one enters the attractive hillside village of Stanley, a place of solid detached stone houses. Back on the main road at Endon, and heading home to the Potteries, one reflects that Hanley, Burslem and Tunstall were once hilltop villages like Bagnall. Oh happy days.

Bagnall Grange, 0.75m E of Bagnall, is an 18th Century farmhouse built on or near a grain mill owned by Hulton Abbey. Moor Hall, 1m E of Bagnall, is a stone house of the 16th Century. The name is a corruption of Murhull, from a local family. The moat is a Listed Monument; a stone axe-hammer was found in the grounds of the house.

Tompkin, 1m ENE of Bagnall, is a tiny hamlet on high ground. The name is unexplained but there are folk stories to the effect that it is a contraction of Tom's skin: Tom was a little drummer boy captured and skinned alive at Tompkin Farm by Roundheads during the Civil War. Another tale has Squire Mulhall skinning a Jacobite drummer boy with the intention of using his skin to form a drum. It is said that the skin was unable to be tanned and was hung for a while at Endon church, but was thought to bring bad luck and was burned. Hmm.

BALTERLEY *5m SE of Crewe (Cheshire)*

A scatter of houses along the A52; a charming red brick church of 1901 by Austin and Paley; a Victorian blacksmith's shop with green sliding doors and the old hearth still in place; and the beautiful Hall o' th' Wood. The latter is a late 16th Century, black-and-white house which is one of the best in the county, though it has recently been a little over-restored. It stands at the end of a long drive with a backdrop of trees. The Hall is highly decorated with a motif of five overlapping circles. To the front are two large gables in-between which are two Porch-like projections with overhanging gables, and in-between them is a recessed centre bay with entrance door. The approach drive leads to the back of the house where are to be found some new houses by the pool. The church of All Saints was built in 1901. It is said that the vestry was not consecrated so that the vicar could smoke his pipe there. Half-a-mile to the west of Balterley is the county border of Cheshire.

BARLASTON *3m NNW of Stone*

In Domesday Book the village is called Bernulvestone which means 'Beorrtwulf's estate'. At that time seven families lived here. During the whole of the Middle Ages the village operated the classic Midland Open Field system. There was a single settlement and the boundaries of the small parish of 2,000 acres coincided with those of the manor. At one end of the village lay the manor house and the church, and at the other the village green. The farmers lived together in the village and their three open arable fields lay around the settlement. Each farmer had a number of strips in each field. These were deliberately scattered so that any variation in soil quality was equally shared. This arrangement lasted until the 16th Century. Within the whole parish there were only two exceptions to this scheme. Great Hartwell farm lay two miles east of the village, and was self-contained with its own fields. It also had its own chapel and watch tower, and in the 1480s another isolated farm appeared, 0.75m to the north-east, called Woodseaves, probably in a new forest clearing.

Today there is a considerable suburban sprawl along the Trent and Mersey Canal and the railway. There is a small shopping centre and a well-known and much cursed railway crossing. However, this is nicely kept apart from the old village which lies above it on a well-wooded ridge.

The church of St John has a medieval tower but the rest is the work of Charles Lynham, 1886-8, with a new vestry of 1969 by A G Capey. There are some monuments to the Wedgwood family.

The present **Barlaston Hall** was built about 1756. The architect is not known but was probably Sir Robert Taylor. It is tall, of brick and of a strong design. It has five bays of 2.5 storeys. The doorway has Tuscan columns and a pediment, and at the rear is a large, full-length, central bow with steps leading to the patio. To the sides are canted bays. The interior had good plasterwork and a fine staircase. A few years ago the house stood in great disrepair. It had been bought by the Wedgwood company who wanted to demolish it and redevelop the site. The building was suffering from settlement cracks, caused by coal mining, and they hoped that it would become too bad to repair. They were thwarted by the Secretary of State for the Environment, who rejected Wedgwood's application to demolish the Hall. The company chairman reacted by saying it was a pity that the government hadn't got better things to do than 'save decrepit buildings'. There was a public outcry and Wedgwoods were taken to task in The Times, which spoke of their 'astonishing blindness' to the virtue of what they possessed. The outcome was that Wedgwoods sold the property to a trust for £1. The trust renovated the Hall and converted it into flats, and it now stands restored to its former glory.

Upper House, 0.75m S of Barlaston, was built in 1849 on the Lea estate by Francis Wedgwood, grandson of Josiah Wedgwood. In about 1984 it became a hotel. In 1850 the remains of an Anglian warrior of the 7th Century were found in a rock-cut grave, on top of a 500-foot hill near Upper House, beside an ancient track at SJ 896379. Artefacts found there included a 33-inch-long iron sword, a small iron knife, pieces of a bronze bowl, pottery and two hooked disc brass escutcheons decorated with Celtic designs in chemplene enamel. These finds are now in the British Museum.

In 1938-40, the Wedgwoods built a new factory at Barlaston, 0.5m north of the village, and deserted the old Etruria complex. The new factory is mundane in the extreme and of no architectural interest whatsoever. Apparently, the architect, Keith Murray, was chosen on the strength of some vase designs he had made! **Barlaston Park**, 1m W of Barlaston, is a housing estate of some 200 houses, constructed as a model village by the Wedgwood Company for its workers. The architect was Louis de Soissons. The factory is still a going concern and now has a small museum, a factory shop and a snack bar. Between Barlaston Hall and the Wedgwood Factory is the Park and the Lake.

Hartwell, 1m ENE of Barlaston, is a small, spread-about settlement. The name means 'the hart's spring'. Great Hartwell Farm is built on part of a moated site. In 1282 permission was granted to Adam de Chetwynd for a chapel at the farm. Hartwell Hall was built in the 1860s by the Paddock family, solicitors of Hanley.

BARTON-UNDER-NEEDWOOD 7.5m NE of Lichfield

It lies between Lichfield and Burton on Trent, just off the dead-straight Ryknild Street, the Roman road now called the A34. The name Barton means 'fort-settlement' and Needwood means 'forest refuge'. Barton-under-Needwood was originally a dependent settlement of Tatenhill. Both villages lie in the Trent valley on the fringe of the Needwood Forest plateau. The Forest originally filled the area between the Rivers Trent, Dove and Blithe, and was well-wooded until the 17th Century. Today there is very little of the Forest left, although a few miles north of Barton there are many copses and small woods which can give the impression of a forest.

The village of Barton is quite attractive and is blessed by being a good 0.5m from the roar of the A34. On the road to Dunstall is the charming 18th Century, brick-built Old Hall. In the grounds a deer shelter is preserved, dated 1724. On the opposite side of the road is disturbed ground, possibly the site of old cottages. The Dower House is early 19th Century, rendered with two trellis verandahs and a porch of wooden Doric columns. However, the main attraction at Barton is the church and the man who built it.

The church of St James is rare, in that it was built all at one time by one man and therefore has architectural unity. It is the work of Dr John Taylor and was completed in 1517. The tower is short with eight pinnacles and there is a nave, aisles, clerestory and polygonal apse. In the north wall of the chancel is a blank arch, presumed to have been intended as the founder's tomb. The only alteration made to the structure was the widening of the church to north and south in 1862. The walls were rebuilt to match the originals. The overall style is Gothic Perpendicular. Dr Taylor was one of a set of triplets. This was an unusual event in those days and they were shown, as a curiosity, to King Henry VII. The King made the remarkable gesture of paying for their education. John, the eldest of the triplets, went on to become one of the King's Chaplains, Archdeacon of Derby and Buckingham, Master of the Rolls (1527) and an international diplomat. He attended Henry on the Field of the Cloth of Gold. The church was built on the site of the cottage in which he was born. He died in 1534. Close to the church is the Old Vicarage, a striking stuccoed house with two large, almost semicircular, gables to the front.

Barton Turn, 1m E of Burton, is a hamlet that takes its name from either a basin-like section of the Trent and Mersey Canal, where narrow boats are turned, or from the turnpike on Icknield street. There was a railway station here but it closed in 1957 and was demolished shortly after.

BASFORD *See Newcastle-under-Lyme*

BASFORD GREEN *Im SE of Cheddleton*
From the road, the lakes in the valley and the mock castle can be seen. These are part of the estate of Basford Hall, an ashlar house of 1858, which is superbly positioned with long views over the beautiful countryside to the south-east. It was the home of a junior branch of the Sneyd family, which descended from William Sneyd of Keele, MP for Newcastle-under-Lyme in 1685. A little further along the road is Cheddleton Station, now a Railway Museum with a special emphasis on the 'Knotty', the North Staffordshire Railway. The River Churnet and the Caldon Canal flow by here within yards of each other.

BEDNALL *2m S of Stafford*
In Domesday Book it is Bedehala and was described as waste. Bednall lies hidden away, down anonymous lanes in flat pastoral country, to the west of the Stafford to Cannock road. Bednall is a handsome place of pleasant detached houses and abundant greenery. The early 19th Century Hall is modest but attractive, with its grey render and white porch pillars. It stands near the handsome church of All Saints, a grey stone building with a tall, thin spire, built in 1846 on, or near, the site of a 12th Century chapel. Next to the church, on one side, are the Victorian red brick Junior School and schoolhouse, and on the other is Church Farm. The village also has the convenience of a small general store. The village well is near the junction of Bowling Alley and Common Road.

In 1720 William Alport founded a charity in his will to benefit the vicars of eight Staffordshire parishes, one of which was the incumbent of Acton Trussell and Bednall. There were two simple conditions, but for 34 years two vicars of Acton and Bednall took the Alport money without honouring them.

Bednall Head, 0.5m E of Bednall, is a main-road straggle of mixed houses, a couple of second-hand car lots and a pub.

Gipsy Green, 0.5m S of Bednall, is a hamlet of mostly Teddesley-estate cottages.

At **Springslade Pool** (Stale Pool), 0.5m SSE of Bednall, in Teddsley Hay, there was iron working from at least 1585.

BEECH *1.5m W of Tittensor*
The main access lane passes over the roaring M6 and enters a narrow, wooded dale that cuts into the long escarpment which parallels the motorway. At the foot of the bluff are a series of large, dramatic caves. These are actually sandstone quarries. The mounds are overburden spoil heaps. The stone was used for local building, including Trentham Hall and the Madam's Bridge (1.5m E at SJ 877384) over the River Trent. This bridge was built in 1597 but was later

destroyed and replaced with a modern concoction of steel and concrete. The caves are impressive and atmospheric despite being covered in graffiti. During the Second World War they were used for storing munitions. In 1992 at least five 'rave' parties were held in the caves, which are now part of Lord Stafford's estate. In spring the steep escarpment slopes are covered in bluebells, which flourish in the dappled shade of this ancient woodland. The settlement lies higher up the valley, or coomb, but consists of little more than a few cottages and houses. The name Beech is simply from the beech tree. In 1285 it appeared as Le Bech.

Beechcliff, 0.5m NE of Beech, lies hard by the M6. It is a tiny hamlet consisting of little more than a few cottages, a farm and a bungalow. In the woods on the steep bank west of the motorway, and next to the lane underpass, is Beechcliff Sawmills Ltd. This is a small, characterful, timber-built shed wherein are produced oak beams and oak fencing materials. This is a timeless trade, living in the woods and making real things with time to drink tea and watch the sun go down. Only 30 yards away cars and lorries whiz by in frantic haste. There is a timeline here. The trees at Beechcliff are tall, mixed deciduous and most handsome. As at Beech, wherever they allow dappled sunlight to reach the ground, bluebells emerge in early spring. These woods parallel the motorway for a mile from Knowle Wall in the north, to Beech House Farm in the south.

BENTLEY *0.25m E of Willenhall*

The name is Anglo-Saxon, probably from 'beonet-leah', meaning 'the clearing with bent grass': The settlement stands on an exposed hill and vegetation would catch the wind. Bentley Hay was an administrative division of the Royal Hunting Forest of Cannock Chase. There does not seem to have been much here, except the Hall, until recent times.

Bentley Hall has its footnote in history, because on the 9th September 1651 the fugitive King Charles II stayed here overnight as the guest of Colonel Lane. The following day the monarch was dressed as a groom and left in the company of the Colonel's sister, Mistress Jane Lane. They made their way to Long Marston via Bromsgrove and thence to Bristol. After several adventures the king finally managed to flee England and reached safety on the Continent. However, the word was out that a woman had aided Charles in his escape and Jane and her brother also thought it prudent to depart these shores. They trekked across England dressed as peasants and at Yarmouth took a ship to the Continent. They were met by Charles, who arranged for Jane to stay with the Princess of Orange. On his restoration he gave Jane a pension of £11,000 a year and allowed the three royal lions to be incorporated into the Lane coat of arms above the motto 'Garde le Roy'. These arms are depicted on the sign of the Lane Arms pub, on the main Walsall to Bilston road.

Almost 100 years later, in 1743, another illustrious person came to Bentley, namely John Wesley. His preaching had caused riots in Wednesbury. Furious Anglican colliers brought him to appear before the magistrate, Mr J P Lane. Mr Lane sent word that he was in bed and would they go elsewhere.

Five years later, in 1748, the Lanes left Bentley and moved to King's Bromley. The Hall, too, is gone. It collapsed in 1929, undermined by colliery workings. Some stones from the ruins have been erected as a cairn, topped by a 'megalith' from the nearby hard-rock Quarry of Powk. The notice says it stands on the spot where the Hall once stood, but local people say that the big house was some yards away, below the mound, in the position now occupied by the modern yellow brick library.

The cairn shares the high mound with the modern, yellow brick parish Church of Emmanuel. This was built by Lavender, Twentyman and Percy in 1951. It is dedicated to Alfred Ernest Owen of Rubery Owen and Co, Darlaston, and replaces a church of 1872, by Street, which was destroyed by a landmine in the Second World War. The roof is a startling green, as though to distinguish it from the nearby Roman Catholic church of Mary Immaculate, also in modern yellow brick but with a silver roof. There is more yellow brick in the main shopping block. All they need now is a 'yellow brick road'. Instead, they have one of the ubiquitous black shacks erected by Walsall Metropolitan Council to harbour the Local Neighbourhood Office. In Churchill Road is the Jane Lane school, a rather peculiar modern thing. Within a stone's throw, just over the M6, is the hard-rock Quarry of Powk. The precipitous rock faces have now been made safe by infill but it is still a big hole, now tree clad and romantic.

Most of Bentley now consists of affordable modern housing. There are still some areas of derelict land yet to be reclaimed, but the muddy grey mounds flecked with black betray the area's old mining history. Indeed, to the north, on the Wyrley and Essington Canal, are the remains of the Bentley Coal Canal Wharf and Bridge. Mumper's Dingle is thought to be situated hereabouts. This was where Isobel Berners camped and where he fought the Flaming Tinman in George Borrow's 'Lavengro' (1851).

Today, the industrial activity lies to the south, on the other side of the Walsall to Bilston road. The ground slopes down to the stream where once stood Bentley Mill. On this slope, in Bentley Mill Way, is an industrial-engineering estate, a large Habitat store, a massive Showcase Cinemas complex (12 screens), a traditionally grubby car-wreckers yard, derelict land and allotments. A parallel road, Bentley Mill Lane, has some shops, some semi-detached houses, a New Life Centre Apostolic Church (in King Charles Crescent), and an awful lot of humpy derelict land - a place of electric pylons and gipsies.

On the east side of the M6 is **Bentley Moor**. Here are a variety of modern industrial units and warehouses, Reedswood Park (landscaped spoil mounds opened in 1877), an electricity power station, some older residential developments, and the Quarry of Powk, already mentioned. In Bentley Lane there have been several occurrences of a phenomenon in which an invisible force bangs on the windscreen of moving motor cars. The Bentley Canal (1840-4) is only four miles long. It connects to the Wyrley and Essington Canal but was closed in 1961 and is now derelict. The author has written a poem-song about the sad plight of the Bentley Canal.

BETLEY *6m NW of Newcastle-under-Lyme*
Betley is a most attractive village. It stands along the A531, in the north-west of the county, close to the Cheshire border. The buildings are a pleasant mixture of red brick and black-and-white. The Old Hall of 1621 has a fine panelled Court Room, and amongst the farm buildings are some excellent two-tier vaulted cow shippons built by George Tollet IV.

South of the Hall, at the other end of the village, is Betley Court. This is a large, handsome, 18th Century, chequered-brick house with a 20th Century porch, which was for long a home of the Fletcher-Twemlow family. In recent years it has been renovated by the present owner, Godfrey Brown, Emeritus Professor of Education at Keele University. He has written a book called 'This Old House' which is an account of the trials and tribulations of restoring an old building. He also commissioned a handcrafted reproduction of the internationally famous Betley Window, which was at the original Betley Hall (now demolished) and is now in the Victoria and Albert Museum in London. This small medieval stained glass window has diamond-shaped panes on which are depicted six Morris Dancers together with a Fool, a Fife and Tabor Player, the Queen of the May and a Hobby Horse 'ridden' by a King. Its exact age is unknown, but it is probably the earliest pictorial representation of traditional Morris Dancers in Britain and is of considerable historical interest. The reproduction is installed in the wing of Betley Court, which is currently used as a commercial gallery of art, ceramics and antique furniture. The gallery is open to the public and has an excellent selection of beautiful objects. The Court has some splendid iron gates, which have been renovated with the assistance of English Heritage. The stable block has been converted into dwellings.

The village is larger than it may at first appear and there are some small estates of modern houses, though these are tastefully tucked away out of sight. The village cricket ground is nicely sited on a hill adjacent to the church but is spoiled by the advertising boards that surround the playing area.

The church of St Margaret is unusual in that it is basically a timber structure with a stone tower and stone aisle walls. Wooden piers carry a wooden clerestory and a heavy wooden roof, which is highly ornamented in the chancel. The chancel was rebuilt in 1610. There are monuments to the Fletcher and the Fletcher-Twemlow families and a 17th Century monument to Ralph Egerton, died 1610. The exterior was restored in 1842.

To the south-west of the village, approached through a farm, is Betley Mere, a beautiful lake with tall rushes and grasses and wild birds. Adjacent to the Mere is Cracow Moss. In Domesday Book Betley was called Betelege. It was held from the king by Wulfin. Prior to the conquest it was owned by Godric and Wulfgeat. There was once a market at Betley.

At **Buddileigh**, 1m NW of Betley, on the main road, is The Beehive, an engaging half-timbered house of cruck construction with a date of 1662 on the porch, but which is probably much older. Here also is **Doddlespool Hall**. The original Hall was built in 1605 but what we see today is Victorian mock-Tudor. The name is derived from 'toad's pool'. The Hall is now an old people's home.

South of Betley is **Wrinehill** and here is the Summer House, an old home of the Egerton family which has also been a barracks and a shop. It is built of brick on a stone base and inside is a handsome oak staircase. It is a timber-framed house of about 1580, encased in brick shortly after. The flat roof, it is said, was for the Earl of Wilton to use as a view-point to watch the fox hunt.

Craddock's Moss, 1.5m E of Betley, is a large raised moss some 600 yards wide. It lies in a flat-bottomed valley. Immediately to the west of Craddock's Moss Farm are a number of crop marks, which include two small ring ditches, two linear features and an enclosure.

BIDDULPH *7m NNE of Hanley on the A527*
At the time of the Norman Conquest Biddulph was held by a man called Grufydd (Gritin), presumably descended from either an original Celtic pre-Roman settler or a later immigrant Welshman.

Today it is a large, sprawling, somewhat-characterless place on the edge of the Moorlands. The name is from the Anglo-Saxon and means 'the place by the mine (diggings)'. There are records of iron-ore mining in Biddulph from the 14th Century, and In 1880 Robert Heath had iron furnaces at Biddulph, Ford

Green and Ravensdale (part of the Fowlea Brook valley – Ravenscliffe?).

At Bailey's Wood, to the west of Biddulph Grange, is a 'D' shaped earthwork overlooking the Biddulph Brook that could be either Iron Age or Norman. Later, a residence was built here which was the forerunner of Biddulph Old Hall. The earthwork is a listed monument.

The Old Hall was built by Francis Biddulph in 1588 and extended in the late 17th Century. It is situated 0.5m NNE of Biddulph Grange at Ordnance Survey reference SK 894003. It was destroyed during the Civil War by the Parliamentarians and today stands in ruins, hidden from sight by a large farm. Parts of the front facade remain and a porch leads to the central courtyard. One ogee-capped turret also survives. An area at the back of the house is still lived in. The 17th Century burial pit, in which members of the Biddulph family were interred, lies behind Biddulph Old Hall. It is called Kate's Pit after the family's governess, an Italian lady who had a very beautiful singing voice and who joined them in 1647. She died of bubonic plague.

The new hall, Biddulph Grange, was built for James Bateman (1811-97), but it is for the gardens that it is famous. James was the son of John Bateman of nearby Knypersley, who had made a fortune manufacturing steam engines in Manchester. He was a keen gardener, even in his student days at Magdalen College, Oxford, and was later, in 1864, to lay out the University parks. In 1842 James bought an old farmhouse at Biddulph. It was surrounded by marshy ground on a desolate hillside. Over the next 25 years he laid out the gardens, which were to achieve national fame. In 1869 the Batemans moved to Worthing for health reasons and the house was bought by Robert Heath. After a fire in 1896 much of the Hall was rebuilt but the porte-cochere, the outer hall and the low parts of the garden side are original. The main garden facade is of the rebuilding. In recent years the Hall has been used as an orthopaedic hospital and there are some quite awful extensions. Today, it has been divided into apartments.

Amongst the set pieces of the gardens are a Chinese Garden, which is approached through a tunnel; the Egyptian garden, which consists of clipped hedges in imitation of pyramids and temples; and the Obelisk Walk, which attempts to give the impression that the path is really an obelisk in the distance that melts away as you approach it. On the high ground is the water-lilied lake. The National Trust took over the care of the gardens in 1987, and raised a million pounds to fully restore and maintain them. They are, of course, open to the public.

The church of St Lawrence has a Perpendicular tower and an Early English arcade of four bays. Most of the outside of the chancel is of 1833 by T Trubshaw, and the south chapel is by Ernest Bates, of 1873. There are some good monuments including one to Sir William Bowyer, died 1640, and the large tomb of William and Mary Heath by Matthew Noble (1872) in the south chapel. There is a 16th Century Flemish, stained-glass west window and a Norman font. Around the churchyard walls are tombstones incised with crosses and swords, perhaps from the graves of knights returned from crusades to the Holy Land.

Moor House, in Overton Road, was the seat of the Stanier family of industrialists. The present house is of about 1843 and was later lived in by Thomas Twyford, the inventor of the one-piece ceramic water closet. A conical mound at **Lea Forge**, 0.25m N of Biddulph church, was an early Norman castle motte. The dwelling later built on it was probably the manor house before Biddulph Hall was constructed. Iron-forge slag found here is probably late medieval.

Brindley Ford, 1.75m S, on the Biddulph to Tunstall road, is a small main-road settlement. The name is from James Brindley, the canal engineer, who is buried at Newchapel, 1m W of Brindley Ford. There used to be a ford near the Board School but the stream has now been culverted.

Whitemoor, 1.25m NNW of Biddulph parish church, is a hamlet which was occupied by at least 1500. During the siege of Biddulph Old Hall in the Civil War the Parliamentary troops were based at Whitemoor.

The spectacular **Bridestones**, 3.5m NNE of Biddulph at SK 906622, lie just off the minor road that joins the A527 at Dane in Shaw (south of Congleton), and the A523 at Ryecroft Gate. These are the remains of a huge prehistoric burial mound/long barrow. The stones of the central chamber are still standing, and nearby are great mounds of rocks that have been removed from the grave. Local legend has it that a Viking invader married a Saxon maiden and settled down here, but there was still hostility to the northern newcomers and the couple were killed soon after the marriage and buried under the Bridestones.

In fact, the grave was more likely to have been from a much earlier period, at least Iron Age. The site is on the edge of the moors overlooking the plain below. The Bridestones can he seen from the road and there is a right of way to them down the entrance drive of the adjacent house. The border with Cheshire passes through the site. (Note: some of the Bridestones were removed to Tunstall Park.)

Half a mile to the east is **Earlsway House**, a reminder that this minor road was once part of the ancient route from Chester to Coventry, which was used by the Earls of Chester when visiting their Midland estates. This is also probably the route followed by Sir Gawain in the medieval romance poem 'Sir Gawain and the Green Knight'. It is now believed that this was set in the area of Swythamley Hall, which lies 4.5m NE of the Bridestones. (See Swythamley.)

BIDDULPH MOOR *Im E of Biddulph*

There is a small centre to this substantial village but most of the older cottages and houses are scattered over the bleak moorland slopes. Telephone wires and electricity power cables, with their supporting poles, constitute a major land-scape feature. There is, without doubt, an atmosphere to the place - a feeling of the frontier, of a certain wildness.

Perhaps this has contributed to the widespread belief that a part of the population is descended from Saracen slaves brought here from the Holy Land by the medieval knights of Biddulph. The story goes that a local lord brought back captured Turks and set them to work carving the stones of the church of St Chad in Stafford.

When the church was complete they were then employed on the Biddulph estates and made bailiffs of the wild moors above the village. They married within their community and, as late as the beginning of this century, local people knew them as a separate people. They were called gypsies and the family name was Bailey. The local scout troop is called 'The Saracens' to this day though older people in Biddulph are loath to talk of the matter. The Moors rise to 1,100 feet.

The Wicken Stones is a thin, grit-stone ridge below Rock End, at the top of Park Lane. Many of the rocks have names given to them by climbers.

The source of the River Trent is at Knypersley Reservoir, 2m S of the village of Biddulph Moor. The reservoir now forms a central feature of Greenwaybank Country Park. (See Knypersley.)

BILLINGTON *2m SW of Stafford*

Billington is a hamlet on the south side of the Stafford to Newport road. Billington Hall is a brick farmhouse of about 1800. Nearby, is Billington Hall Farm, which has the remains of a medieval wayside cross. This might have been associated with the now-vanished St Margaret's Chapel, which stood on Billington Bank (A158), but its stones have been removed. The name Billington is Anglo-Saxon and means 'Billa's (or a similar personal name) farmstead'.

Berry Ring (SJ 887211) is an Iron-Age fort of the 2nd to 1st Centuries BC and lies on the north side of the main road. It covers seven acres enclosed by a single bank and ditch with remnants of a second ditch on the north side. There are entrances on the north and east sides. The site has not been excavated but some finds of Roman origin and a flint knife have been discovered here. East of Berry Ring, near the motorway, is a moated site thought to be where Edward de Stafford had an early castle, a predecessor to Stafford Castle. Stafford Castle was begun about 1348.

BILSTON *2.5m SE of Wolverhampton*

Bilston is a flourishing Black Country market town which has survived the closure of its major employer, the huge Bilston Steelworks. It has as many dour suburban streets as any other town in the conurbation, but the centre of the town is cheerful and busy. The large Thursday Market attracts customers from far and wide, and at times has the air of a country place; but that it has not been for several centuries.

In Domesday Book we are told that the settlement still belonged to the King, that there were 8 villagers and 3 smallholders with 3 ploughs, and that there was an acre of meadow and a wood 2 miles long by 2 miles wide. The name Bilston is derived from the name of a tribe of Angles who came up the Trent valley and settled here in the late 6th Century - the Bilsaeton or Bilsonii.

Coal was probably being mined in Bilston during the late Middle Ages but it was not until the middle of the 18th Century, when John Wilkinson (1728-1808) set up his ironworks at nearby Bradley in 1757-8, that the town began to expand. Wilkinson used the new process, developed by Darby in Coalbrookdale, which allowed coal, as coke, to be used for smelting iron ore. Previously, charcoal had been used because coal would not burn with sufficient heat. Bilston was on the rich '30-foot' coal seams and so had an ample supply of fuel. It has been fairly stated that Wilkinson's arrival at Bradley marks the beginning of iron-making as a major industry in South Staffordshire. 'Iron-mad' they called him and his innovations in iron making, casting, machining and engineering were legion. However, he was not a scrupulous man. As well as legitimate steam engines made to the order of Boulton and Watt, he manufactured many 'pirate' versions at his Bersham, Denbighshire works, on which royalties were not paid; and during our wars with the French he had no hesitation in supplying the enemy with gun barrels expertly bored at his Willey, Shropshire, works. Mark you, in this he was only ahead of the modern fashion; today, it is a practice actively encouraged by governments.

By 1836 Wilkinson's ironworks had passed into other hands and had been crenellated to give them the appearance of a castle. The Wilkinson works were only the beginning of a large-scale iron-making, steel-making and heavy engineering industry, which 'caused the ground to shake and the night sky to burn like the fires of hell'. Other ironmasters followed: Baldwin, Ward, Sparrows, Thorneycroft and Hickman. Hickman owned the mighty Bilston

Steelworks that sprawled over many acres next to the old Bilston Quarries, south east of the town centre, adjoining Ettingshall. The last furnace, Elizabeth, was closed in 1979 and the works demolished in 1980 - a sad day for the Black Country for this was the end of steel-working in the area.. (See Ettingshall.)

Bilston was also famous internationally for its more delicate, decorated products such as enamelled ware, which flourished between 1730 and 1830, and Japan ware (goods made of either papier mache or tin-plate and varnished to give a high gloss finish). Japanning was a dead art by 1900 but a firm called Bilston Enamels has recently revived the enamelling crafts and is doing very well, especially in the limited edition collectors' market.

Note: Papier Mache is a misnomer although the term was used by the trade at the time. The articles were actually made from sheets of a special paper pasted together and then stamped into shape. They were originally called 'paper ware' but the public preferred the French name. Examples of both japanning and enamelling can be seen at Bilston Museum (which is above the town library), and in Bantock Park House, Wolverhampton.

The early industrial towns were squalid places and in 1832 there was a severe outbreak of cholera in Bilston. The local vicar demanded the rebuilding of 'brick graves called courts, alleys and back squares where the poor are buried alive, amid gloom, damp and corruption . . .' The old courts were pulled down and replaced by streets of terraced houses which, though not by any means opulent, were at least more sanitary and even had small back gardens. However, many of these gardens were later built on. Small workshops and sometimes more houses were crammed in by the owners and landlords.

Bilston has been fortunate in having good communications. The Holyhead Road used to pass through the town until the 1820s when Telford built a bypass. Between 1772 and 1786 Brindley constructed the Birmingham canal which linked Bilston with other Black Country towns and Birmingham, as well as the rest of Staffordshire and Worcestershire. The Metro railway came in the 1990s.

The parish church of St Leonard is something of a surprise - a great white piece of stucco that commands the attention. It lies in the centre of the town and was built in 1825 by Francis Goodwin. It replaced the old medieval church but is of a classical design. It was rendered in 1882-3. The windows of the sides are long and arched and the front has five bays and a chamfered turret. The interior is quite elegant with galleries and Ionic columns, and a sense of space. It is nice to see monuments to other than landed gentry. Here they are to Mrs Williams, died 1834, Mrs Riley, died 1835, and Mrs Pearce 'descended from three children of Edward I'.

There are two Commissioners' Churches in the town - St Luke of 1851 in Market Street, and St Mary of 1857 in Oxford Street, by Francis Goodwin. Commissioners' Churches were built with financial assistance from the government under the Act of Parliament of 1818, which established a fund of one million pounds to provide churches in districts of greatest need. The Roman Catholic church of Holy Trinity is also in Oxford Street. It is of 1883 with a chancel by Pugin. The Town Hall of 1872 has a tower and Gothic capitals but has a style that leaves all the experts baffled. The most notable secular building is the Greyhound Inn in the High Street. It is of about 1450. The handsome black-and-white timber framing has closely-set uprights and two gables. Inside, is a good Jacobean plaster ceiling with leaf scrolls.

Sir Henry Newbolt (1862-1938), poet, naval historian, man of letters and the author of the song 'Drake's Drum', was born at St Mary's Vicarage, Bath Street,

Bilston. The house was demolished in 1969 to make way for a sports' centre. Well done, everyone: I mean, Bilston is simply heaving with historically interesting buildings.

The Lunt lies 0.75m ENE of the town centre. It is a large area of derelict land now grassed over but by no means reclaimed. It is cut through by a stream, there are pools, and a canal skirts it to the east where it adjoins the George Rose Park. It is now cut through by something more substantial than a stream, namely the Black Country Way. The name Lunt is ancient and is interpreted as 'an open space into which game is driven prior to slaughter'. At the moment parts of the Lunt are grazed by a herd of ponies and horses. These gentle creatures are used for the harmless sport of recreational riding, but in the 19th century Bilston was a centre of blood sports, especially cockfighting.

The leading trainer of fighting cocks in the whole of Britain was 'Cockie' Potter. He was born in Bilston. At the age of 11 he began work in a coal pit but then found a job as a pot-boy at the Britannia Inn, Moxley. The landlord kept fighting cocks and here Potter learned the art of feeding and training the birds. He had great success at local 'mains' and his prowess came to the attention of Lord Stanley, 12th Earl of Derby. Lord Derby employed Potter as his Cock-Master General in charge of the 2,000-3,000 prize-fighting cocks he kept on his estate. This was a position of high prestige. Even after his retirement Potter was treated like royalty whenever he returned to visit Bilston. It is hard to believe now but some of the mains were major social and sporting occasions attended by thousands of spectators. Duddeston Hall, Birmingham was a major venue. In 1824 'Cockie' Potter officiated there for Staffordshire in: "A main of Cocks fought between Lord Anson (Shugborough) and Molyneaux (Wolverhampton) for Staffordshire and Colonel Yates and Edmund Peel Esquire for Worcestershire for 25 guineas a battle and £500 the main". These were large sums in their day, but as nothing to the amounts wagered. Cockfights were frequently held as secondary attractions at racehorse meetings, though in fact they often drew the larger crowd. Body-snatching and coin forging were rife in Bilston. In the 19th Century a watchman was employed to guard new graves for several weeks after the burial, and coiners in the area were investigated by officials sent here by the Home Office.

Bradley lies 0.75m S of Bilston town centre.

The Devil stood on Bradley Moor
And heard the forges roar.
Quoth he: "I've heard a row in Hell,
But none like this before."

The name is pronounced Braidlee and means 'the broad clearing in the forest'. It had its own entry in Domesday Book and was for long a separate settlement. Then came John Wilkinson and coal-field iron-making, but that has already been discussed. Today it is but a shadow of its former self. Bradley stands on high ground and is most easily approached down Loxdale Street, off Oxford Street. Here we start a journey to get a flavour of the place.

At the crossroads are ELS and B&Q, then the old GKN Sankey works and Loxdale Sidings by Pothouse Bridge, where the canal has river-like, grassy banks; then semi-detached houses, Steel Stockholders, the White Hart, Buxton Sheet Metal Ltd., Fesswick Steelholders (Carbon and Alloy Steel Bar, Bright and Black), two rows of shops, and a snooker club; into Ash Street, Tipton Non

Ferrous Foundry, the Daisy Bank Social Centre (in the old Sedgley Board Schools building); down Brierley Lane, into Hall Green, over the hump-backed railway bridge, past the Dudley Tubes Works, complete with attendant gypsy camp and almost surrounded by a large area of greened-over mine spoil heaps; past Batman Hill, then an industrial estate - nuts and bolts and plastics - and the Ironmaster pub; up the hill, past the recreation ground where at Easter three large wooden crosses are displayed beside the War Memorial, on an old coal spoil mound beside the road; now out of Hall Green and into Wilkinson Avenue and estates of modern houses.

Stop at the Wilkinson Primary School (where Walter Street meets Wilkinson Avenue). The school stands on the site of John Wilkinson's famous ironworks. We now continue, past the forbidding brick school of St Martin in Slater Street, which is now a Church Centre with loud, large, blue-painted windows; past the impressive church of St Martin in King Street, of 1868, to a design by G Bidlake, and back to Loxdale and the Pothouse Bridge, the name of which reminds us that there were potteries in most of the industrial towns. There was as much clay in the ground as coal and ironstone. What struck us most about Bradley is that almost all the houses are of this century, and most are very recent; Victorian terraces are few and far between.

Lower Bradley adjoins Bradley to the south east and abuts Great Bridge Road. It is very much a place of 20th Century housing estates, mostly belonging to the council. The surprise is the Rocket Pool (there were two pools but they have been made into one). This circular lake has two small islands and is surrounded by houses, bungalows, blocks of flats, a youth club and a pub. A long, gentle incline (called the Black Path by local people) leads up to a large area of recently reclaimed industrial wasteland. The only accesses to the Rocket Pools estates are from the north, off Bradley Lane. This is to isolate them from the privately-owned and more up-market estates of Wednesbury Oak, which they adjoin to the south. The Black Path Incline seems at one time to have connected with the canal that now ends at the romantically derelict Bradley Locks. These can be seen from Bradley Bridge on Great Bridge Road. Like the canal the Wolverhampton-Bilston-Walsall railway line is now disused and the track has been dismantled, but the viaducts that carried it over the road and the canal are mostly intact. With plans for the new Metro railway still proceeding, these may well be put back into service.

Lanesfield, 1.25m WSW of Bilston, took its name from the Lane family. The area developed in the early 19th Century. The Coseley Engineering Company was one of the world leaders in the supply of prefabricated, steel-framed buildings from the 1950s. The Birmingham Canal (Old Cut Old Main Line) passes close by Lanesfield.

Wildfire, Firing of the Damp and Pseudo Volcano are alternative names for the spontaneous combustion of coal seams that can sometimes explode. In 1851 Bradley Moor was reported to have been burning (or smouldering) for nearly 70 years. Several miners were killed by exploding coal in Bilston coal pits. Clay that came into contact with the burning seams was 'fired' and used as roadstone and for the foundations of buildings.

BISHOP'S OFFLEY *See Offley*

BISHOP'S WOOD *6.5m E of Oakengates (Telford)*
The village lies 0.75m S of the A5 in pleasant rolling country and has a church

spire which is a well-known landmark. The scattered settlement expanded by squatters building cottages on common land belonging to Brewood Manor. It takes its name from the now-lost forest which only remains as isolated copses. In 1135 the bishops of Lichfield were given hunting rights in the forest.

The church of St John lies just outside the village to the south-east. It was built in 1851 by G T Robinson, much in the style that had developed in the second quarter of the century by the constructors of Commissioners' churches, i.e. those wholly or partly financed by the government under the Act of 1818, which allotted one million pounds to provide places of worship in districts of greatest need. They were often very utilitarian and there are many examples in the Black Country.

The Bishop of the name Bishop's Wood would have been the Bishop of Chester, whose diocese used to include all the land between Chester and Lichfield, including the cathedral town itself. Two miles to the west of Bishop's Wood is Weston Park, home of the Earl of Bradford, and two miles south-west is Chillington Hall, home of the Giffard family. The famous Boscobel House and the Royal Oak Tree lie 0.75m south. (See Chillington.)

Ivetsey Bank, 0.5m N of Bishop's Wood, is a small settlement on the north side of Watling Street, along the lane to Wheaton Aston. Indeed, both the New and Old Wheaton Aston Halls are at Ivetsey. The main road marker is a large white inn. It is dangerous to quote pub names these days because owners have developed an annoying habit of changing them, often many times. In the 13th Century Ivetsey was Uvetshay, which means 'Ufegeat's enclosure in the forest'. Bank is a later addition and refers to the hill on Watling Street.

BLACKHEATH *4m SSE of Dudley*

It lies on a low hill surrounded by residential areas and industrial estates. The meaning of the name is self-evident, but what exactly made it black is not clear. The settlement developed as both a mining village and a cross-roads' community. Most of the High Street remains intact and unspoilt by 'development'. There are a number of small shops and service offices (banks, solicitors, estate agents etc.) and there is a friendly atmosphere. On the highest point stands not the parish church, as is usual, but the High Street Methodist Church, in hard red brick with a castellated tower and arrow slits. Nearby, at the junction of Powke Lane and Holly Road, is a nice example of street art: three flying birds in yellow and black brick on the gable end of a small shop. Blackheath Station lies on low ground half-a-mile east of the town centre. Somewhat confusingly, it is called Rowley Regis Station because that is now the collective regional name for this area.

To the north-east is **Whiteheath Gate**, a largely residential district that adjoins the lethal Wolverhampton-Birmingham New Road. To the west is Old Hill which lies in the deep valley that carries the Dudley Canal. From The Bush pub there are long views over the broad flanks of Netherton Hill and Regis Hill. Amongst the factories and houses are patches of rough, scrubby wasteland (or moorland, to be kind). As proof that things were once very different, just look at the settlement names: Brickhouse Farm, Tippity Green, Springfield, Primrose Hill and the delightful Mouse Sweet.

From The Bush the road descends steeply towards the gleaming white granites of the crematorium/cemetery, past factories and old slag heaps to Darby End. (See Netherton.) From Darby End the scrubby slopes of the hill on which Blackheath stands look dark. The low bushes crouch in their own shadows.

Perhaps this was why it was called Blackheath.

Hurst Green is a largely residential area 4m SE of the town centre. Hurst is from the Anglo-Saxon 'hurst', which can mean 'a hill, or a wood, or a wooded hill'. The Recreation Ground and the Shopping Centre both adjoin the M5. John Rose, the noted traditional fiddle player, lived in Oak Barn Road.

South of Hurst Green is **Quinton**. The name means 'the manor belonging to the Queen'. It is a place that has acres of affordable housing for the living and a large cemetery to cater for the dead. Both Hurst Green and Quinton now have Halesowen postal addresses and are administered from Dudley.

BLAKE MERE *5m NE of Leek*

Blake Mere, or Blackmere (SK 030613), is a small pool in the moorlands between Leek and Buxton. It lies alongside the spectacular road which follows the Morridge - literally 'the moorland ridge' - an ancient track that must have been well used by prehistoric man. It is most easily approached off the A53 at Stake Gutter, which is 2m NE of Upper Hulme, but can also be reached via Thorncliffe.

All manner of tales and superstitions are connected with this 40-foot, heart-shaped pool: animals will not drink there; birds will not fly over it; the pool is bottomless; it can never be drained; there is a mermaid who protects it from harm, etc. It is said that in recent years there was a moorland fire and the fire brigade pumped water out of the pool non-stop for many hours without the level lowering. It is very likely that Blake Mere had religious significance for early man and that these legends are a folk memory of ancient beliefs.

Some say the mermaid story originated in medieval times when Joshua Linnet had a young girl branded as a witch and drowned in the pool. As she floundered in the water she cursed her accuser and said he would suffer the same fate. Three days later Joshua Linnet was found drowned in the lake with his face torn to pieces. The mermaid has been known to walk alongside travellers and try to entice them with her deep green eyes to follow her to her watery home.

In 1679 there was a murder here. Andrew Simpson, who worked at the Red Lion in Leek, overheard a young woman speaking of how well she had done selling her lace, wool and thread. He followed her home across the moors and murdered her for her money. He threw the body into Blake Mere but the corpse was found and he was hanged on Gun Hill.

Just south of Blake Mere is a prehistoric burial mound called Merryton Low, and south of that is the stone-built and gabled Mermaid Inn. This is all that remains of the village of Blake Mere. In the 16th and 17th Centuries there were several houses, a chapel and a pub, the original Mermaid Inn. At that time the present pub was a house, called Blake Mere House. The remains of the old hostelry are at the end of the car park. The field opposite the inn is used by a Gliding Club. All around are wild moors, parts of which are used by the army for exercises.

BLITHFIELD *8m E of Stafford and 3m N of Rugeley*

In 1066 Edmund held Blithfield. By 1086 it had passed to Roger de Montgomery, the right-hand man of William the Conquerer. It was held from him by another Roger who had four slaves. There were also seven villagers, a priest and a smallholder. For its time this was quite a substantial settlement. In 1367 the manor passed by marriage to the Bagot family of nearby Bagots Bromley. It remained in their hands until this century. The present Hall has an

Heath, the second battle of the Wars of the Roses (23rd September 1459), which is re-enacted each year on fields belonging to the farm. There are knights in armour and a host of side-shows, which include period musicians and a hog roast. The farmer and his associates are very knowledgeable and give talks on military weapons and tactics of the time. The actual battle is well documented in national histories. Suffice to say here, that the Yorkists defeated the Lancastrian force under Lord Audley by feigning a retreat and then trapping the Lancastrians in a ravine-like gully of the Hemp Mill Brook (Wemberton Brook in the 15th Century), where they were slaughtered. The Hemp Mill (SJ 713353), which now occupies the gully, would appear to be of a later date than the battle. Today, it is a private cottage with a small pond. Lord Audley was killed and a stone cross (SJ 706353) marks the spot where he is reputed to have fallen. This is in a field on the opposite side of the road from Audley's Cross Farm. Sir Richard Neville, Earl of Salisbury and commander of the victorious Yorkist army, camped on Salisbury Hill, Market Drayton, after the Battle of Blore Heath.

For Blore Pipe, 3m SE of Blore, see the article on Armsdale and the Langot Valley

BLOXWICH *1.5m N of Walsall*

The name Bloxwich probably means 'the dwelling place of Blocca'. It adjoins Walsall but is by no means a suburb of the larger town. Bloxwich grew rapidly in the 18th and 19th Centuries on coal mining, brick making and manufacturing, especially of saddlery and its associated ironmongery. In Bloxwich Park there is a monument - a pile of stones formerly used as anvils. In the harsh, rough days when the Black Country earned its name, Bloxwich people participated in cruel blood sports such as cock fighting, bear baiting and bull baiting. There is a well-known 19th Century broadsheet song, called 'Ye Three Tall Men', about a bull bait in Bloxwich. There has been a settlement here since at least 1086 when it belonged to the manor of Wednesbury, which in turn belonged to the King himself.

Today, unlike many Black Country towns, Bloxwich has a centre with a real sense of character. In fact, it has two centres: at one is the church and the Hall, and at the other a pleasant 'village green' with a colourful fountain. They are connected by the main shopping street. The church of All Saints is of 1791-4 but was much altered and a new chancel and tower built in 1875-7 when it was Gothicized. On the roll of honour for the First World War is the name of Harold Parry, a local poet cut down at 21 years of age in Flanders. At school he had been Head Boy, Captain of Cricket and Captain of Football. He had won a history Scholarship to Oxford but joined the army out of a sense of duty. What he said of a comrade may well be said of him: 'England has lost another who would have been an even greater credit in life than in this most glorious death'.

Opposite the church is the old Hall. For many years it lay derelict and looked very sad indeed, but now it is fully renovated and used as office accommodation. Almost adjacent is the police station and nearby is the colourful nightclub called 'Starlight' (was 'Flix'). At the other end of the High Street is the real community centre of the town. Here are some old houses, a country-like pub, the bus station, shops and a school - a friendly place around the green. As befits the village it once was, there is a spacious cricket ground and, as becomes the town it now is, it has a golf course.

Perhaps Bloxwich's best known son was Pat Collins (died 1943), the 'King of Showmen', whose funfair still tours nationally. He was Mayor of Walsall in

1938, and for two years was the town's Member of Parliament.

Leamore stretches southwards from Bloxwich to Walsall, a busy area with much industry. Here are the new South Staffordshire Water offices (in red brick and dark glass to a 'Hanging Gardens of Babylon' design) and the big white MEB block. Manufacturers include Sterling Tubes, Alpha Zinc and Press Components. Amongst all this it is nice to see a small traditional pub, the White Horse, in cream and green with typical canted bays. There are also large residential areas in Leamore, mostly to the east of the A34. The name is from the Anglo-Saxon and probably means 'the glade in the wood on the moor.'

Wallington Heath lies east of the north end of Bloxwich High Street. Tall tower blocks face the King George V playing fields across Bell Lane. The name is Anglo-Saxon and probably means 'the heath of Wealh's people'.

Blakenall Heath, 'the hall (or the remote place) on the black heath', is an eastern residential suburb of Bloxwich. The Victorian terraces near the town centre give way to a sea of modern estates of high-rise blocks of flats, which climb the hill to the striking white Christ Church with its battlemented tower. This was built of limestone 'bricks' in 1872 to an Early English design by Henry Naden. If many of the estates on the Heath are dismal, at adjoining **Harden** there is disgrace. Some of the council houses in Shakespeare Crescent are in a deplorable state - not just those that stand vandalised and empty, but those in which people live. Do not blame the council. It is not they who destroy roofs, burn down doors, spray graffiti, break windows, turn front gardens into cesspits and scrap yards, chop down hedges and litter the roads with derelict cars. It is some of the people who live there. The centre of Harden is at the top of the hill on Harden Road where there is a service station, a Bahia super food store, a row of iron-shuttered shops and a boarded-up pub. No one takes their holidays at Harden.

Half-a-mile east of Bloxwich is the new **Mossley** housing estate and the big new Sneyd Secondary School. The school stands beside the Sneyd Reservoir, constructed as a feeder pool for the Wyrley and Essington canal (1797). The canal is now disused, but considerable stretches of it still exist. Sneyd Farm, from which the reservoir and the school take their name, stands near the pool. It is of red brick, 2.5 storeys high, and is embowered amongst conifers and hardwood trees. When we visited Mossley the pool was alive with young people cavorting on noisy water motor-scooters. Not that noise can be complained of here, not with the M6 roaring by on a raised embankment only yards away. Both to the north and the south of the reservoir are more pools, set amongst a bumpy landscape of rough grass and scrub woodland. This now forms part of the Mossley-Short Heath Nature Reserve. Just south of the Sneyd Reservoir, across the A4124, is a delightful wilderness of pools, marshes, bridges, dry docks and canal basins that was once a British Waterways Maintenance Yard. The approach track is incredibly bumpy - be warned. If the walker continues southwards he will come to the unexpected woods of Short Heath. (See Short Heath.)

Little Bloxwich is a north-eastern residential suburb of Bloxwich: the Bridgewater pub, high-rise and low-rise blocks of flats, affordable modern houses, and a bridge over the Essington and Wyrley Canal (1797).

One has to pass through Little Bloxwich to get to **Fishley,** 1.25m NNE of Bloxwich. The name is Anglo-Saxon and means 'the fisherman's clearing in the wood'. The fishing lake has been replaced by Bloxwich Golf Course but the land is still easily waterlogged, as is evidenced by ditches brimming over and field pools. Fishley is a scattered hamlet with a derelict mill (guarded by a Rottweiler) and an old man, who lives in a derelict caravan amongst heaps of cut wood and the skeleton of a gipsy "varda" (traditional caravan). Poplar Farm is the oldest farmhouse in the Bloxwich area. Just south of the golf driving range is the now-abandoned Lord Hay's Branch of the Essington and Wyrley Canal. Fishley Church (SK 012048) is a large boulder on Pelsall North Common, said to be the place where five parishes meet. The Fishley Charity Farm, 0.75m NNE of Fishley, was purchased and endowed in 1657 with charity funds supplied by William Parker, a London merchant, who was born in Bloxwich. The Charity helps in the education of needy children.

Newtown, 1m N of Bloxwich on the A34, is a main-road settlement and has developed around two old pubs, the Ivy House and The Freemasons. In recent times they have been joined by Hardy's (of Laurel and Hardy) Cabaret Club, a service station, a cafe and a handful of modern houses. Tom Hodson, once the landlord of the Ivy House, was the owner of White Eye, the world champion whippet. In 1888, at Lea Brook, Wednesbury, White Eye ran 200 yards in 12 seconds, a record than still stands.

In the open country to the north of Newton is **Hobble End**, a township of one grandly-modernised and extended cottage and a red brick dairy farm.

Springhill is a small mining village in open country, 1.5m NW of Bloxwich town centre. The land is very flat and there is nothing now that could be called a natural hill from which a spring could emerge. But then the ground here has been so dug up for coal and clay, and then covered with spoil heaps, that this is not altogether surprising. The settlement lies along Broad Lane, the B4210. The road is lined with houses - semis, a few detached and some old Victorian terraced villas. Springhill Farm is probably the oldest building. Services consist of little more than a Progressive Working Men's Club and the Why Not Inn, quite striking with its green and white livery and glazed verandah. Coal was still important at Springhill into the mid-1990s. Near the huge spoil mound was the Yew Tree Coal Company, and further south the Powell Duffryn Coal Preparation Springhill Disposal Point. In the company's modern, grey-green towers and sheds, coal from the Horsefields Colliery was crushed, graded and blended before being taken to Rugeley 'B' electricity power station. To the east the old LMR Walsall-Cannock railway runs along a raised embankment, but the Essington and Wyrley Canal has been abandoned and partly filled in. Note: the large brickworks, 0.25m W of Springhill, still shown on most maps, has been demolished and the ground levelled.

BLYMHILL *6.5m E of Oakengates (Telford)*

The name Blymhill is thought to be derived from 'plym hyll' which means 'the wild plum tree hill'. It lies on the estate of the Earl of Bradford, directly north of Weston Park and 1m N of the A5. In 1086 it was held by Warin and there were 7 villagers, 4 smallholders and 1 slave working the land, which was then owned by the Norman lord, Robert of Stafford. Today, the red brick village is small and trim, though in recent years it has been somewhat spoilt by the erection of black, corrugated-iron barns and the construction of new houses and bungalows.

The church is situated at the end of a cul-de-sac in a group which includes the Old Rectory and the Old School. There was a church here in the late 12th Century. The present building has an Early English south arcade, a Decorated chancel and a Perpendicular tower. The rest belongs to G E Street, who did the restoration of 1856-9 in Early English style. The botanist parson, Samuel

Dickenson, was a vicar here for 46 years. He retired in 1823.

Next to the church, but hidden behind a screen of trees, is the Old Rectory. The original house was partly demolished and partly rebuilt by Street. What we see today is a gracious four-bay, grey-rendered, Georgian-style house with a hipped roof. It is most pleasantly situated with views over sheep meadows to the side. In the village are some black and white cottages and a post office.

South-west of the village is High Hall. This is a 17th Century brick farm-house on a stone plinth. It is built on the site formerly occupied by the old Blymhill Manor House. The house stands on a bluff with good views all around. At the bottom of the hill is another farm, at the back of which is a moat. This might well have been the site of the very first Norman manor house, before the lord moved up on to the hill.

Wrestlers' Farm, 1m NE of Blymhill, is a house which was formerly known as Wrestlers' Inn. It was a famous sporting house – a venue for cock fighting, wrestling matches and gambling. Being close to the Shropshire border, partici-pants could quickly escape the Staffordshire authorities if needs be.

Brockhurst Farm, 1m SW of Blymhill, is a tall red brick house of the 18th Century. The main doorway faces away from the road and is surmounted by three central windows and a wide, semi-circular, recessed arch. To the south-eastern side of the house, and adjacent to the road, is a square moat with a raised mound within. The side furthest from the road is water-filled and is used as a duck pond. Seventy-five yards south-west is the line of the second moat, now a deep ditch. These moats were probably the defences of an isolated medieval farmhouse. 'Broc' in a place name usually means either stream or badger. 'Hurst' can mean either a wood or a hill, or a wooded hill or even a sandbank in a river. As there are no streams, hills or sandbanks here it might be fair to interpret the name 'Brockhurst' as meaning 'the wood (or clearing in the wood) which has a badger set'. Close to the farm are two blocks of semi-detached estate houses, built in 1954 on the site of two timber-framed cottages which were demolished. The present houses here have wood shingles to the upper storeys and ugly shack-like garages in the front gardens. The road has deep ditches to either side, a sign of wet land.

White Sytch, 1.5m W of Blymhill, is a lake. This is the centre of a sporting estate owned by the Earl of Bradford. In the woods that surround it pheasant are bred. The lake is fished and there is a large population of wild geese and ducks. A forestry road encircles it. The woods are mixed deciduous and coniferous but it is noticeable that most recent plantings are evergreen softwoods. It is sad to see the stumps of ancient oaks, which have been felled to make way for a more profitable, quick-growing crop. The entrance to White Sytch is just east of Blymhill Common at Ordnance Survey reference SJ 794127. One-and-half miles south-west of Blymhill is the Bradford Estate sawmill and tree nursery. It lies adjacent to the A5, almost opposite the entrance to Weston Park. Only small timber appears to be processed here, the kind used to make fences and garden furniture. We have noticed on many occasions the almost instinctive respect and loyalty of country estate workers to their lordly masters. The atmosphere is almost medieval. Men doing humble jobs and living in humble houses feel no jealousy towards those of a higher social station and greater wealth.

Brineton is a hamlet 0.75m N of Blymhill. The name is from the Anglo-Saxon and means 'Bryni's settlement'. Brineton House is of the 17th Century. Laurels Farm is a brick house of 1678.

BLYTHE BRIDGE *3m SE of Longton*

As you approach Blythe Bridge you pass superior houses, and as you leave you pass good detached homes. The small centre of the village is less decorous with a few small work-a-day shops and a handful of businesses.

The settlement is actually something of a communications' funnel: The River Blithe is paralleled by the Stoke to Uttoxeter railway (1848) and Ryknielde Street. Ryknielde Street is the medieval name for the Roman road from Little-chester, near Derby, to Rocester to Chesterton, now called the A521. (Confusingly, there is another road called Ryknild Street which ran from Littlechester to Metchley, near Birmingham, which in Staffordshire is followed and paralleled by the A38).

Most travellers do not give Blythe Bridge a second glance, unless they are held up by the level crossing. The Foxfield Railway Museum Station is at Blythe Bridge.

Sergeant Albert Edward Egerton (1897-1966) was born in Longton but lived at Blythe Bridge and is buried in Forsbrook churchyard. He was awarded the VC for making a solo attack on an enemy dugout in 1917 during the battle of Ypres.

Blythe Marsh is a residential area adjoining Blythe Bridge to the east. A prehistoric perforated stone axe-hammer head was found here by Mr Day, the headmaster of Blythe Marsh School.

Forsbrook, to the NE of Blythe Bridge, and Blythe Bridge are to all intents and purposes one settlement these days. (See Forsbrook.)

Paynsley Hall, 2m NE of Blythe Bridge, lies on the west side of the River Blithe. In Doomsday Book it is Lufamesles. There are numerous earthworks and entrenchments in the surrounding fields, the remnants of moats or defences. The Hall was the seat of the Draycott family from the Norman Conquest until the early 18th Century when it passed by marriage to the Lords Stourton. It then became a farm and most of the old buildings have disappeared. All that remains is a very large stone chimney.

BLYTHBURY *2m NE of Rugeley*

The name means 'the fort on the River Blithe', although today the village is 0.75m W of the river. Blithbury Priory stood 0.75m NE of Blythbury on the west side of the river at SK 091208. It was founded by Hugo Mavesyn in about 1140 for Benedictine nuns.

By 1789 there was a farmhouse on the site, and the last remains of the priory were demolished by 1795. Some bits of stonework and stained glass were incorporated into a later fishing lodge attached to the farmhouse. The lodge still stands. The local inn is The Bull's Head, but at some time the animal representing the name on the pub sign acquired a pair of spectacles and the hostelry is now known as the Bull and Spectacles.

BLYTHEBRIDGE *1m SW of Kingstone*

Blythebridge (all one word) is a minute hamlet. Blythe Bridge Mill (sic) is the nucleus of the settlement and is not unhandsome. It has a quatrefoil panel above the first-floor door, which matches the openings on each side. It contains the coat of arms of Robert Shirley, 7th Earl Ferrers of Chartley Castle, and the date 1825.

Blythe Bridge Hall, 1.25m SW of Kingstone, was the home of the historian, Sir Simon Degge (1612-1705), the son of William Degge of Stramshall. Amongst other works, he was the author of 'The Parson's Counseller'.

BOBBINGTON *6m ESE of Bridgnorth*

Bobbington is small hamlet in flat country close to Halfpenny Green aerodrome. (Halfpenny Green itself lies lm NE). This is the kind of place into which adventurers smuggle diamonds from Africa: fairly remote, run down and scruffy, yet with a romantic aura. Here you can learn to fly or risk your neck parachuting. In 1972 Prince William of Gloucester flew out of Halfpenny Green and was killed when his aircraft crashed.

The airfield was opened in 1939 by the Air Ministry and in 2000 was officially named the Birmingham Business Airport, but it is now the Wolverhampton Airport. In 2004 planning permission is being applied for to move and extend the runway to enable passenger aircraft to land and take off from here. If permission is granted a most handsome and healthy roadside sweet chestnut tree, 900 years of age, will have to be cut down. Local people are protesting volubly.

The church at Bobbington has a Norman north arcade of four bays and a smallish Victorian tower. There is a large yew in the churchyard, with a girth in excess of 21 feet, and a Victorian vicarage. Bobbington Hall, 0.75m SW, is 17th Century brick with stepped gables and mullioned windows.

Leaton Hall, 0.5m SE of Bobbington, is dated at 1817 but was modified in the early 19th Century when stucco was applied to the front and the rear was extended. It has eight bays of three storeys and a porch with Tuscan columns. The Air Ministry occupied the Hall during the Second World War.

At **Upper Whittimore Farm**, 2m NE of Bobbington, a white wine vineyard was established in 1983. It is the only vineyard in Staffordshire and gets regular mentions on local television news programmes.

Bobbington is an ancient place. Domesday Book records that in 1066 the Saxon, Wivar, held it. By 1086 it had passed to Helgot who held it from his Norman overlord, Robert of Stafford. The lord of the manor had 4 slaves and there were 5 villagers and 3 smallholders. There was land for 6 ploughs and some woodland pasture.

Lutley, 1m SSE of Bobbington, is a small hamlet with a moated site in which coins and a stone font have been found. South of Lutley Farm there might have been a medieval village deserted between 1377 and 1524.

BRADLEY *4.5m SW of Stafford*

The name means 'broad glade in the wood'. In 1066 the lord of the manor was the Saxon Earl Edwin. It was an extensive manor in 1086 and had several dependent outlying villages which included Silkmore and Littywood. It had a mill, 12 acres of meadow, woodland 1.5m long by 0.75m wide, and belonged to Robert of Stafford. The country around the village is flat and attractive in a subdued way. The settlement lies on a slight rise and is considered locally to be a pleasant place in which to live. There is a well-known pub and the even better known Fosters Garden Centre.

In 1987 the church of St Mary and All Saints featured on national television as the setting for the 'Wedding of the Year'. The north chapel and chancel are late 13th Century; the chancel east window, with its flowing tracery, and the three-bay north arcade are early 14th Century. The top of the tower is Perpendicular and the arch to the nave probably Decorated. There are Norman stones in the west wall of the tower, and the font is also Norman. Walter Collins was rector here for 54 years in the 18th Century. The little church at nearby Coppenhall was originally built as a chapel to Bradley.

At White House Farm, Bradley, there was a stone, the Webb Stone. A farmer moved it and all his cattle died. It now stands near a bungalow on the lane to the farm and is said to turn completely around at one minute to midnight. Spinsters should bow to the stone as they pass, for if they do not they will never marry. The Webb Stone is the largest of three boulders in Bradley. The name is from the Webb family, who are local farmers.

Three-quarters-of-a-mile NE of Bradley is one of the country's historical gems. At Littywood is a medieval manor house surrounded by a large double moat. The outer ditch has a diameter of 650 feet. The house is timber-framed with a later facing of brick. The inner core is dated at 1400. The old 'great hall' has been sub-divided but much of the structure is still intact. It is 20 feet long by 21 feet wide and 30 feet from floor to ridge. The house has two bays and a screen passage. The west truss of the hall has crucks. To the west of the hall was the solar (living room). The mid-truss of the hall has arched braces to a collar beam. Until 1954 the house was thatched. Littywood has long puzzled historians because the fortifications seem far too substantial for a mere farmhouse, yet there are no records of it being the home of a lord of any importance. The most recent supposition is that it could have been the site of the original home of the de Stafford family, who were major landowners in the county, and whose base, prior to their occupation of Stafford Castle in the 13th Century, is unknown. The present house was built by the Caverswall family. It is very likely that there was an Anglo-Saxon settlement here and it is possible that the moat defences were pre-Norman. The site has yet to he properly investigated.

Mitton, 1.5m S of Bradley, is a tiny hamlet on the Church Eaton Brook. Mitton Manor is now a mid-19th Century brick house with stone dressings. It stands near the confluence of Church Eaton Brook and the Whiston Brook. The name Mitton (or Mytton) means 'the settlement by the meeting of two streams'.

Shredicote, 1m SW of Bradley, is a tiny hamlet, the name of which means 'cottage on a piece of detached land'.

BRADELEY IN THE MOORS *3m ESE of Cheadle and Im SW of Alton*
A pleasant place, high above the River Churnet on the opposite side of the valley to Alton Towers. It belonged to the Englishman, Leofric, but was taken by William the Conqueror for himself. Today, it consists of a few cottages, farms and the church of St Leonard which was built in 1750 and, unusually, has not been altered or added to since then. One mile south are the substantial remains of the great Croxden Abbey which lies secluded, though well signposted, down a tunnel-like lane.

BRAMSHALL *1.25m W of Uttoxeter*
The village stands on a hill in rolling countryside. Domesday Book tells us that half the land belonged to the king and half to the local landlord, Robert, but that Robert had annexed the king's part 'and for this must answer'. There is a lot of modern housing. In the valley below is a railway crossing. The church of St Lawrence was rebuilt by the 16th Century Lord Willoughby de Broke in 1835. In one window there are fragments of medieval glass. These include a kneeling figure in a white flowered dress inscribed 'Alice Tame, Lady Verney'; she was an ancestor of Lord Willoughby. The church has a substantial tower but no aisles or chancel and is ashlar faced. Half-a-mile south, on the A518, Stafford to Uttoxeter road, is Loxley Hall, now a school but reputed to be the Loxley mentioned in ancient ballads as being the place where Robin Hood was born.

The rendered facade hides a much older inner core. *(See Uttoxeter.)*

BRANSTON *2m SW of Burton on Trent*
Once owned by the Countess Godiva, but confiscated by the Normans and given to the Abbey of Burton, Branston is today a red brick suburb close to the busy bypass of Burton on Trent. The church of St Saviour was built by Street in 1864.

The well-known Branston Pickle was first manufactured commercially in a factory originally constructed by the Enfield Armament Company, in which machine guns were manufactured. Crosse and Blackwell took over the works in 1921 and began producing their famous pickle. However, they only stayed here until 1926 when the premises were taken over by an artificial silk manufacturer, and then by the War Department as an Ordinance Depot until it closed in 1964.

Sinai Park, 1.75m WNW of Burton, was a medieval deer-park enclosed from woodland by Burton Abbey. The name might be from 'seyne', Old French for 'holiday'; perhaps the monks considered it to be a retreat. The present 'E'-shaped, timber-framed, brick and stone house is surrounded by a moat dated to 1334. The two wings are dated to the 15th Century and the central block to the 17th Century. In the 18th Century it was 'Georgianised' and stuccoed. William Wyatt lived here at that time. He was steward to the Paget family (Earls of Uxbridge), and related to James Wyatt, the noted architect. It then became derelict and housed pigs until about 1993, when private restoration was begun. Lord's Well, a chalybeate spring near the house, has a stone wall and stone steps leading to the water. It was rebuilt by William, Lord Paget in 1701.

Prehistoric remains found at Branston include a near-complete Mesolithic female skeleton and the remains of settlement huts dated at circa BC 7000. These were found in lagoons 800 yards south-west of Gallows Bridge. At various other locations the following Roman artefacts have been discovered: an iron key, building mortar, a spear-head, a lead weight, and pottery fragments.

BRERETON *1m SE of Rugeley*
The name is from the Anglo-Saxon and means 'the briar covered hill'. From at least the early 19th Century there was coal mining in the area.

To all intents and purposes Brereton is now a part of Rugeley, with extensive new building along the busy Lichfield road. There are two notable 18th Century houses: Brereton House, brick with five bays and a doorway with Tuscan columns; and the Cedars Hotel, which has a fine tree to the front and an unremarkable modern extension to the rear.

The church of St Michael was built by Thomas Trubshaw in 1837 but was enlarged by Sir Gilbert Scott, who added the transepts and chancel in 1877. Inside, is a very good painted frieze by Heywood Sumner of 1897. Also on display in the church is the map left by Dr Livingstone, the explorer of Africa, when he lectured at Redbook Lane School in 1857. To the west and south-west, between Brereton and Hednesford, is Beaudesert Old Park, a part of the wooded acres of Cannock Chase.

Ravenhill House, Raven Hill, Brereton, is a late 18th Century house with 19th Century additions, built by the Reverend George Talbot who died in a hunting accident and may be responsible for the many hauntings experienced here. It was a military hospital during the Second World War and from 1948 was occupied by an electronics' company. Incidentally, the name 'raven' is from the Norse 'hrafn', which means 'raven'. The Vikings used the raven on their war flags and were known as 'the men of the raven'. Raven became a personal name amongst both Norsemen and Anglo-Saxons, presumably to describe very dark-haired people or those who showed aggression. Therefore, in place names 'raven' may refer to a person, not necessarily a big black bird that croaks.

BREWOOD *8m NNW of Wolverhampton and 2m SW of Gailey Island*
The name means 'the wood on the hill', and has a Celtic origin. The village lay in the Forest of Brewood, which was disafforested (that is, was released from the restrictions of Forest Law) very early - in 1204. Nevertheless, it remained heavily wooded until quite late and today the country between Brewood and Ashley shows all the signs of protracted and haphazard woodland clearance: winding lanes, irregular-shaped fields and small scattered hamlets. This is the slow, piecemeal work of unorganized individuals hacking out homesteads - not planned and controlled by large landowners. The woodland was not totally cleared until the end of the Middle Ages, though the numerous coppices, parks and wooded hedgerows can still give the impression of forest.

The village is most pleasing and has survived, becoming a dormitory town for Wolverhampton. The new estates lie around the old centre. The houses and shops are largely of local red brick. The most eye-catching building is Speedwell Castle, which is not a castle at all but a house elaborately decorated in Gothic style and built about 1750. The facade is dominated by two large bays, on which are clustered ogee-shaped traceried windows. It is best considered as a piece of whimsy and, indeed, it was born in jest, the owner having promised to build a castle if the horse he backed had won. The horse, called 'Speedwell', duly obliged. Inside, is an elaborate plaster ceiling and a Chinese-Chippendale staircase. Of the many modest but attractive houses in the village, three deserve specific mention: West Gate, The Chantry and Dean Street House, all of which are in Dean Street.

The church of St Mary and St Chad has a 13th Century chancel, a 14th Century nave and a south aisle by Street, of 1878-80. Inside are four monuments to members of the Giffard family: Sir John Giffard, died 1556, who was Henry VIII's standard bearer; his son, Sir Thomas Giffard, died 1560; Sir John Giffard, died 1613; and Walter Giffard, died 1652. All were Roman Catholics and the last two were persecuted for it. The Roman Catholic church is by Pugin, of 1843. Pugin also designed the school and the Priest's House. Brewood Hall lies on the edge of the village engulfed by new houses. The Shropshire Union Canal runs through a cutting along the western edge of the village.

In 1736 Samuel Johnson applied for the post of usher at Brewood Grammar School (founded by Edward VI), but was turned down on account of his gaunt, pock-marked face and the uncontrollable twitches of his arms and legs. Probably the best known old boy of the school is William Huskisson, the Colonial Secretary who was knocked down and killed by a train at the opening of the Liverpool to Manchester Railway in 1830. Gilbert Giffard (born about 1561) was the black sheep of the Giffard family. He was involved in the Babbington Plot, and it was he who devised the false-bottomed beer barrel scheme by which letters were smuggled to and from Mary Queen of Scots whilst she was imprisoned at Chartley Castle - not the castle on the hill that can be seen from the road, but the castle on the site of the present moated house in the wood below.

Ackbury Heath, 1m SW of Brewood, is a tiny hamlet near Giffard's Cross. In the 12th Century it was Herkebarowe, 'the burial mound of Herke'. The moat at the junction of Port Street and Chillington Street is probably the site of the now-lost manor house.

Chillington Hall, 1.75m SW of Brewood, was formerly called Chillington Castle. This has been the home of the Roman Catholic Giffard family, who came over with William I, since 1178. The Hall is approached from the direction of the village by a lane that parallels the old Upper Avenue. This links the house to the lodge at Giffard's Cross, which is so called because a cross marks the spot where a panther died in the 16th Century. The story is that Sir John Giffard had a private zoo from which, in 1513, the panther escaped. The animal was spotted at the end of the avenue and was about to pounce upon a young mother with her child. Sir John, from a position in the Hall, took his crossbow and shot it dead at a range of about one mile. The old oak cross was recently replaced by a new one and lies in the front garden of the lodge. A leopard's head is contained in the family coat of arms. The Upper Avenue connects with the now-disused Lower Avenue.

The Hall stands in a large park divided into four parts. To the east, in front of the house, is a deer park which adjoins in succession an area of meadow, The Pool and the Big Wood. Local gossip has it that the island in The Pool was used in Victorian times for society parties of a salacious nature. The laughter that drifted across the woods and waters on summer evenings spoke of more than mere jollity, so an old game-keeper told us. The M54 now runs through the southern tip of the wood. The park was landscaped by Capability Brown, and in it are to be found: the Bowling Green Arch, of about 1730; the Dovecote by the stables; the Bridge designed by Paine; the Gothic Temple by the lake; the Ionic Temple of 1771, also by the lake and probably by Robert Adam; a Sham Bridge; and a Grecian Temple. A decorative canal leads from the lake towards the house.

The Hall itself dates from 1556, when Sir John Giffard replaced the original dwelling with a courtyard house, the courtyard of which was incorporated into the rebuilding by the architect, Francis Smith of Warwick, for Peter Giffard. The east facade, which faces the entrance gates, is of 1786-9 by Sir John Sloane. It has a giant portico, with unfluted Ionic columns carrying a pediment. The south-west side is of brick with stone quoins. Inside, is a fine staircase hall of about 1724, spacious and of great style with heraldic glass of about 1830 by John Freeth of Birmingham. The saloon occupies the old Tudor courtyard and contains a chimney piece which depicts the panther story. To the south, just outside the park but belonging to the estate, is the White House. This has a north facade of about 1770, which faces the Hall and behind which lies a large farmhouse of an earlier date. The facade is an 'eye-catcher', with Tuscan columns and pediments, and blocked arches to give the impression of a Triumphal Arch.

Boscobel, 1.5m NW of Chillington Hall, lies just over the border in Shropshire. The name is derived from the Italian Bosco Bello, 'the house situated in the beautiful woods'. Here stood the now legendary Royal Oak tree in which King Charles II hid whilst on the run after the Battle of Worcester. Captain Careless, or Carlos, who accompanied him during this famous incident, is buried in Brewood church; Boscobel belonged to the Giffard estate at the time.

Two miles to the west of Brewood is the very fine house called **Blackladies**. It stands on the site of a Norman Benedictine Nunnery ('Black Nuns') of about 1140. Parts of the old nunnery are incorporated into the fabric of the house, which is brick-built with gables and mullioned and transomed windows. In 1276 King Edward I hunted a stag out of Cannock Chase and into the Forest of

Brewood where John Giffard shot the animal. It died in the fish pool at Blackladies, which then lay in the Forest of Brewood. Sir John was charged with killing the king's deer and was tried before the Forest Court. However, because Brewood had been disafforested he escaped the death penalty and was merely fined. The fish pool is probably the same pool that lies to the right-hand side of the present house.

Kiddemore Green straggles along the road between Brewood and Bishop's Wood to the west. The name is from Kerri-moor, meaning 'marshland where brush grows'. The Oakley Country House is at Kiddemore Green, a venue for weddings with a lake and attractive gardens.

Somerford Hall, 1m SE of Brewood over the River Penk, is set in a pleasant park. The present house is of the mid-18th Century: stuccoed with three storeys, seven bays and low one-bay wings with arched windows and broken pediments. It was the home of the Monckton family though it is now divided into flats. The family now lives at Stretton. Facing the Hall across the park is Somerford Grange in the hamlet of Somerford. The Grange has three storeys and is built of brick with Gothic ornamentation and battlements. This is all a sham facade to an ordinary house designed as a park ornament. It is reminiscent of Speedwell Castle in the village of Brewood. Near the bridge, by Mill Farm, is the Somerford Water Pumping Station, built of red brick by the South Staffordshire Water Works Company in 1922 and still functioning.

There are two ancient metal working sites in the area of Brewood. One is near the end of the Chillington Hall Lower Avenue, where it joins the road to Coven (SJ 899075). There are some substantial remains: mill pond, pond bay, the foundations of a rectangular building, a waterwheel pit and cinder in black earth. This might well be the site of the fulling mill at Brewood mentioned in Domesday Book and again in 1717 in Taxatio Ecclesiastica. It may also have been the site of the forges mentioned by King about 1680 and again in 1717. The other site has less to show. It is in the gardens at Cinder End House (SJ 905073), near the Sewerage Works at Lower Green, Coven, where there is black soil, cinder and slag, probably the spoil from a bloomery forge.

Belvide Reservoir, 1m NW of Brewood, was built in 1843 as a feeder reservoir for the Shropshire Union Canal, but is now also a recognized nature reserve. A small stretch touches Watling Street, just to the west of Telford's aqueduct which carries the canal over the road.

BRIERLEY HILL *2m SW of Dudley*

*When Satan stood on Brierley Hill
And far around him gazed,
He said,. "I never more shall feel
At Hell's fierce flames amazed".*

Today, there is a friendly high street with a good range of traditional small shops, the Moor Shopping Centre and service offices, but until the middle of the 17th Century Brierley Hill was a waste common land, an area of rough scrub. Then came the glass makers. Craftsmen from Lorraine had been active at several small and often isolated sites in Staffordshire since about 1580. After 1620 the industry became centred on the area around Brierley Hill and has stayed there ever since. Here the glass makers found raw materials in abundance. There were ferns (burnt to make potash) and sand, but in particular the area had ample supplies of very good fireclay. What is more, in 1615 an Act of Parliament forbade the use of timber for firing the glass furnaces, and so an alternative source of fuel had to be found. In the Kingswinford area (Brierley Hill was in Kingswinford parish) there had been early successful experiments using coal. The Tyzack and Hanzey families were the most notable of the Lorraine glass makers who settled here. Paul Tyzack had first operated in Bishop's Wood, 4m W of Eccleshall.

The Hill was also settled by squatters who mined the shallow coal seams, dug the clay for bricks and built small forges to work iron. Irregular hamlets and individual cottages developed, and from all accounts the area was industrialized but still relatively pleasant; relative that is, to the burgeoning Black Country towns below the hill with their dark, smoky and overcrowded squalor. Trade was given a boost in 1776 with the opening of the Stourbridge Canal, and in 1813 Nightingale was writing of the 'elegant villas of the capitalists of the glass trade'. Many of these good Georgian houses still exist in the area; not so the distinctive, cone-shaped kilns that were such a feature of the townscape. Only one now remains, at Wordsley, and this is kept as a museum piece by the firm Stuart Crystal. Today the kilns are fired by gas or electricity. The area is known internationally for its glass products, especially cut-glass decorative ware. Most of the large manufacturers have factory shops which are not only open to the public, but open on Sundays as well. One such is Royal Brierley Crystal. Their works date from 1776 and are believed to be the oldest in the area.

Other industries that became established in Brierley Hill include tin plating and galvanizing, holloware production and heavy steam engineering.

From the parish church of St Michael, at the top of the hill, there are fine panoramas which encompass much of the Black Country and Birmingham and the countryside beyond. The church of St Michael was built in 1765. It is very plain, of red brick in a Georgian style and in a way quite charming, probably because it fits in with the landscape around as so many rock-faced Gothic churches do not. St Michael's was restored in 1873-88 and the tower was largely rebuilt in 1900. One of the 18th Century vicars was Thomas Moss, a minor poet. There are four other churches, including the brick Roman Catholic St Mary's, of 1872, by E W Pugin. Near the top of the hill, opposite the parish church, are 10 very high blocks of flats which interrupt the view and do little for the landscape.

However, they are paragons of good taste compared to the new **Merry Hill** Shopping Centre erected by the Richardson brothers - millionaire scrap metal merchants turned property developers. This extravaganza of parking places and bright plastic has been built by the site of the old steelworks and is having a dire effect on small town shopping centres for miles around. The Merry Hill centre is garish and not very nice at all. It is also very spread out and soulless. Even the waterfront developments of brick-clad offices and the sleek airborn monorail do little to redeem the place.

A remarkable survivor from happier times is 142 Hurst Hill. This grey rendered cottage faces 'moon city' but hides behind a high hedge. Peek over the garden gate and there you will see a little piece of traditional rural England.

The Merry Hill centre lies adjacent to the vast acreage of derelict land created by the demolition of the huge **Round Oak Steelworks** in the early 1980s. There had been large scale iron-working on the site since 1784. The Round Oak Works themselves were built by William, 11th Baron of Dudley, in 1857, and were turned to steel manufacturer in 1894 when the Bessemer process was developed. At one time 3,500 men were employed at 'The Earl's Works', as it was known locally. The area is now an Enterprise Zone and is being cleared in preparation for redevelopment. Incidentally, the church on the gorse-covered hill, which can be seen from the Merry Hill centre, is St Andrews at Netherton.

Another large industrial enterprise, for which Brierley Hill was well known, was the Marsh and Baxter sausage and pie factory, reputed to have been the largest in the country. This is gone and the site is now partly occupied by the Moor Centre. Redevelopment is no stranger to Brierley Hill. Stretching south-west of the town, between **The Delph** and Stourbridge, were numerous coal mines and clay pits. These have now been cleared and in their place is a mammoth housing estate. The Delph is synonymous with the Nine Locks that carry the Dudley Canal No 1 up the hill of the ridge on which the town stands. There are actually only eight locks now, one having been lost during rebuilding in 1957. They are in very good repair and the area is most attractive. Half-way up is the restored stable-block, once used by the canal horses. The canal lies to the south-west of St Michael's church, below the nine looming tower blocks built in 1965. These flats stand in the area of the original squatter settlement.

Archie Hill, novelist, radio playwright and broadcaster, was born in Brierley Hill. His autobiography, 'A Cage of Shadows', describes his childhood in the slums of the Black Country.

At **Withy Moor** ('the willow-moor'), a residential area adjoining the Delph, is The Vine pub which is famous for its home-brewed ale. Locals know it as the Bull and Bladder. Another inn, the Robin Hood on Pedmore Road, Merry Hill, is home to the Citizens' Theatre where, amongst other attractions, there were regular performances by the popular 'Black Country Night Out' group of local singers and comedians, which was first devised and organized by Jon Raven of Wolverhampton. **Harts Hill** is 1m N of Brierley town centre. Canal street and Brick Kiln street hint at heavy industry and the old Brierley Hill Iron Works confirm that it has been many a year since wild deer frequented the hill. The Stourbridge Canal is now disused. **Woodside** adjoins Hart's Hill to the north. It is a small residential area with a park, a school and a library at the junction of Stourbridge Road (A461) and Highgate Road (A4036).

Brockmoor lies 4m NW of Brierley Hill town centre. The name can mean either 'the moor by the stream' or, more likely, 'the moor where badgers live'. Today, it is a mixed residential-industrial area. A few terraced houses mingle with modern semis, schools and some surprisingly large open spaces - The Leys, The Dell, the Wide Waters and the Three Pools (Grove, Middle and Fens). Adjacent to part of this green belt lie the heavy industries. In Leys Road there are engineering firms, the Cookley Wharf Industrial Estate, and the mighty British Steel Strip Mill contained in its big, bright, modern sheds. Adjacent to the mill is the Norman-style church of purple brick with yellow brick dressings and a bellcote. Local people know it simply as Brockmoor church but officially it is called St John's. It was built in 1845 as a Commissioners' church to a design by Thomas Smith. There are a few shops, The Woodman, The Fish, a running track and one of the drab black huts called Neighbourhood Offices that Walsall Metropolitan Council inflicts on everyone but itself.

Brockmoor's most famous son is Frederick Carder, who was born here in 1863. He was the leading craftsman in glass in the Stourbridge-Brierley Hill area but early in his career he emigrated to America. He built the famous Steuben glass works, later taken over by Corning.

One mile east of Brierley Hill town centre is the Nature Reserve of Saltwells. (See Netherton.)

BRINDLEY HEATH AND VILLAGE *2m NNE of Cannock*

Brindley Heath, an area of Cannock Chase, north-east of Pye Green, takes its name from a forest keeper named Brindley who was alive in 1595. Brindley Valley, on the east side of Brindley Heath, had a forge and furnace in the early 18th Century. The upper and lower Brindley Pools, the Furnace Pool and Brindley Pool were made to control the water flow to the mill(s).

Brindley Village (SJ 993150) was actually a military hospital of the First World War which was taken over as a hostel by West Cannock Colliery. By the late 1950s it had been demolished and the inhabitants re-housed in the new Brindley Heath Estate.

RAF Hednesford lay on the south side of Marquis Drive in the Second World War but had no airfield. In 1956 it housed Hungarian refugees and in 1984 part of it was used to house the Cannock Chase Visitors' Centre.

BROCTON *3.5m S of Stafford*

Brocton lies between the A34, Stafford to Cannock road, and the A513 to Rugeley, on the eastern fringe of Cannock Chase. The village is of Anglo-Saxon origin and the name means either 'the settlement by the brook' or 'the settlement by the badger's den'.

There are several black-and-white, half-timbered houses, probably the finest being 'The Cottage' in Pool Lane. However, in the 20th century the area became an up-market dormitory for the county town of Stafford. There are many attractive modern houses in the leafy lanes but this is not a real village - there is no church, no pub and no feeling of community.

However, there is a golf club. The clubhouse occupies the old Brocton Hall. This is an early 19th Century rendered house of five bays. After a fire in 1939 the top storey was removed. The entrance is in the central bow with giant Tuscan columns. Inside, there is an impressive entrance hall and a fine staircase with an iron trellis handrail.

Near the house is an octagonal Dovecote with Gothic ornamentation, and between the kitchen garden and the pond are two genuine Gothic arches, one for a window and one for a door, said to have been taken from St Thomas's Priory (now a farm) at Baswich. A junior branch of the Chetwynd family lived here: Sir George Chetwynd was created a baronet in 1795 and was Clerk of the Privy Council.

In Domesday Book Brocton was said to be a 'waste', that is, there were lands here that had been cultivated but had then been abandoned. Indeed, the soils are poor, consisting largely of sands and gravels, though in this age of concrete these are valuable materials, and 0.25m E of the village is a large disused quarry.

North-east of the quarry is one of the county's treasures, a remnant of medieval oak forest called **Brocton Coppice**. Most of the trees are no more than 200 years old but we know from the insect life and other vegetation in the area that this has been a deciduous forest for many, many centuries. Robin Hood would have been at home here. It is approached along a lane leading off the village green. Near the top of the hill, just past the quarry, is an unmade track on the left. This leads to a parking area from which a well-trodden footpath leads to the wood.

In the early 19th Century flax was grown at Brocton.

On Coppice Hill, 0.75m ESE of Brocton, at SJ 978188, is a gravestone commemorating Freda, a Dalmatian dog who was the mascot of the New Zealand Rifle Brigade. She died in 1918.

BROUGHTON *5m W of Market Drayton*

Broughton lies in what is often called the woodland quarter of the county, that is, the north-west corner which has few villages or towns of any size, virtually no industry and a most pleasant rural aspect, almost medieval in places. The gently rolling country provides views not obtained in flat areas where hedges, important as they are as wild life habitats, often obscure the land they lie in. Broughton is in the parish of Eccleshall which, at around 20,000 acres, is the second largest parish (after Worfield) in the county. To the south of Broughton was marsh - the name of nearby Wetwood perpetuates the memory - and around and beyond the marsh was, and still is, the forest of Bishop's Wood. Today, this is largely stocked with coniferous trees by the Forestry Commission, but amongst their endless ranks can be found the stumps of the oak trees which once flourished here when Bishop's Wood was a part of the larger Blore Forest. It is likely that the villagers of Broughton depended quite heavily on the forest because at the time of the Domesday the arable land was described as waste.

The name Broughton means 'the settlement by the fort' and the settlement was almost certainly of Anglo-Saxon origin. It was never more than a hamlet but today only the Hall and the chapel to the Hall remain. However, they are both splendid buildings. The Hall lies north of the road, from which it can be glimpsed through the woods of its park. It was the home of the Delves-Broughtons from the 13th Century, although the present house is dated at 1637. It is without any doubt the finest black and white house in the county.

The Delves-Broughtons moved to Cheshire in the 18th Century and only used Broughton as a second home. Members of the Delves-Broughton family were main players in the 'White Mischief' scandals in Africa in recent times. They sold the house in 1914, and between 1926 and 1939 it was renovated and greatly extended. Most of the stonework is of this date, including the great hall, now a chapel. Inside, there is a good staircase of the 1630s, and in the long gallery is a frieze depicting monsters and other beasts. The house has three storeys with gables over the right and left wings. Attached to the Hall is a park with meadows, a lake and a large walled garden.

During the Second World War the Hall housed two evacuated schools. Pupils at these included Michael Heseltine MP and the late Sir Julian Critchley MP. When the owner died the house was given to the Fransiscan Order (in 1952) and became a home for retired lady missionaries. Once a year the nuns held a summer fair. They also sold fresh eggs. In 1993 it was put up for sale and subsequently bought by the multi-millionaire, John Caudwell, a second-hand car dealer who went into mobile phones and has acquired a personal fortune of some £850 million. His marketing company is called Phones 4 U.

Broughton Hall is not only a splendid house it also has a splendid ghost, a Royalist cavalier of the Civil War who wears period dress and Red Stockings. He was fatally shot by Roundhead soldiers whilst taunting them from a window in the Long Gallery and died in a room adjoining it. A bloodstain was found there in 1926 during restorative work and the ghost of Red Stockings has been seen on several occasions.

On the opposite side of the road from the hall is the delightful church. This was built in 1630-4 as a private chapel to the Hall, though it is now the public church of St Peter. It is of a Gothic design and has an east window over the chancel arch, which contains some sparkling 15th Century glass with figures of the Broughton family. There is also a beautiful Pre-Raphaelite-style window. The monuments are, as one would expect, mainly of members of the Broughton family. It is very likely that the church occupies the site of the old Anglo-Saxon fort. The vicarage is in Wetwood, 0.5m to the west.

Reynold's Orchard lies 0.25m SE of Broughton church at SJ 768335. The story goes that a Yonge of Charnes Hall had a wager with a Broughton of Broughton and lost Reynold's Orchard, but only for three harvests. Lady Broughton sowed the land with oaks, some of which were cut down during the Second World War, but some of which are still there 150 years or more later. There is a listed, moated site within the orchard, at SJ 768339.

Iron was probably being worked at Broughton in the 14th Century; one of the tax payers was called Roger Iremongere (Ironmonger). There is believed to have been a supply of iron ore in Bishop's Wood and, of course, the forest provided an ample supply of fuel. What is more certain is that glass was manufactured hereabouts. In 1580 Bishop Overton, Bishop of Lichfield and the owner of Bishop's Wood, brought Lorraine glass-makers from Hampshire and established them in the forest.

Glass was a very profitable business at that time because the owners of large houses and stately mansions were building much larger windows and enlarging those that already existed. Glass was also beginning to be used in the homes of the developing middle classes - farmers, craftsmen and merchants. In the Wood the glassmakers had all the necessary raw materials - sand, clay, ferns (which were burnt to make potash) and, of course, timber for fuel. Two of the glass families were the Tyzacks and the Henzeys (or Hennezels). In 1615 there was great concern nationally about the depletion of the country's timber supplies, and a law was passed prohibiting the use of wood as fuel in glass furnaces. Much to the Bishop's regret the glass makers were forced to leave. Some went to Newcastle on Tyne and some to Brierley Hill, in south Staffordshire, where coal was available to fire their furnaces legally.

However, they left a memorial. In the 1930s the remains of one of their furnaces was found and renovated. It is the only surviving 17th Century glass furnace in the whole of the Britain. It lies just off a track in Bishop's Wood at SK 760312, half-a-mile NW of White's Farm. The forest here is most attractive. The furnace is covered by a substantial, but somewhat wonky, open-sided timber shed. The furnace is about seven feet square and three feet high. It is constructed of sandstone lined with vitreous shards. There are four crucibles on two platforms which lie on both sides of a sunken, two-foot-wide fire tunnel.

At Fairoak Grange Farm, just north of Bishop's Wood, near Hookgate, Ashley, are some fields called 'the Songles'. In the parish registers of Eccleshall church the Songles are shown as the residence of James Leggeye, a French glassmaker, and Judith Tyzake, presumably of the Lorraine glass-maker family.

The road from Wetwood, south to Fairoak and on to The Outlands and Bishop's Offley, follows the lovely valley of the River Sow. The source of the river is at two attractive pools, some 250 yards south-west of the farm called Broughton Folly, which is on the main Loggerheads-Eccleshall road, 0.5m NW of the church. The Ordnance survey map still shows the wood called Broughton Birches, a little further north-west from the farm, but this was ripped out over 20 years ago to make pasture. A few token trees were left along the roadside.

Wetwood is a crossroads' hamlet on the B5026. Wetwood Manor is of 1642, with additions of 1920, and is presently occupied by John Caudwell's former wife. In the 13th Century Dieulacres Abbey had a grange at Wetwood, probably at Lower Wetwood.

BROWN EDGE *3.5m NE of Hanley*

The old stone-built village lies to the north of the considerable suburban development along the main road from Burslem to Endon. It adjoins the southern slopes of Cowall Moor with untamed areas still under gorse and heather. The settlement originated as a squatter community. Miners seeking work in the area built small cottages on the Common belonging to Norton Manor.

The present church of St Anne at Brown Edge was built in 1844 by James Trubshaw (junior) in Norman style. The spire was added by Ward and Son of Hanley in 1854. The west doorway and the arch between the tower and the nave are very ornate and there is a beautiful William Morris-Burne Jones window of 1874. The parsonage looks to be contemporary with the church. Also of the same date, is the unusual stable and coach house placed in front of the church. This was built for his own use by Mr Williamson, a wealthy local worthy, who paid for the steeple. Perched high on a ridge, and facing the prevailing winds from the north-west, Brown Edge is a notoriously chilly place.

In 2000 the custom of well dressing was revived at Brown Edge. There are two wells: Spout Well in Sandy Lane, and Sytch Trough in Sytch Road.

To the north-west of Brown edge by half-a-mile is Greenway Bank Country Park, with its attractive lakes and woods. The River Trent has its source there. (See Knypersley.)

BROWNHILLS *5.5m NE of Walsall*

The main shopping street of Brownhills is the Chester Road. It runs in a dead straight line, north-west to south-east. To the north-west the town is approached via **Holland Park**, an old mining area. Most of the spoil mounds have been levelled and it is now a surprisingly wild place with rough grass, gorse, scrub woodland and a few coniferous plantations. In the High Street the shops are very largely of the 20th Century and have little character, but are nevertheless well patronized. To the south-west the shops give way to blocks of skyscraper flats at **Catshill** ('the hill of the wild cats') and then to semi-detached suburbia. No one goes out of their way to visit Brownhills.

However, the A5 skirts its northern fringes making the name known to many. In fact, the town is situated on one of the two main routes from London to Chester. The Royal Mail coaches came along the A5 (Watling Street) from London and then turned north-west, via Lichfield, Rugeley and Stone, and on to Chester. A much used alternative route came up from Coventry via Castle Bromwich and joined the A5 at Brownhills. It followed the A5 for 14 miles before leaving it at Weston-under-Lizard to go to Whitchurch and on to Chester. This road was much favoured by cattle drovers, because the country was more open, and by passenger stage coaches which found it was a faster route.

Brownhills lies on the Cannock Coalfield, and shallow pits had been worked here long before the boom years of the mid-19th Century. Cannock coal lies deep, and it was not until the mines of the Black Country failed to keep pace with demand that deep mines became economically viable. Iron had been smelted and worked at Cannock up to the mid-18th Century using charcoal as fuel. When coal, as coke, began to be used, Cannock could not compete in the iron trade because of the costs of obtaining the deep coal and the lack of transport. By the time the Wyrley and Essington Canal arrived in 1797, and the spur to Brownhills was built a year or so later, it was too late and the iron trade was dead. However, the canal and the new financing methods (the formation of

Joint Stock Companies) did save the coal trade, and today the area is littered with spoil heaps as a memorial to the success of the industry.

In the summer of 1992 there was a meeting of the Ku-Klux-Klan on waste land at Brownhills called The Mound. A five-foot-high wooden cross was burned and the incident was attended by the police and the fire brigade.

On the northern fringes is a suburb called **Newtown**. This consists very largely of a new industrial area centred on an iron foundry called Castings Ltd, established here about 1960. This is surrounded by similar and connected businesses such as steel stockholders, toolmakers and pressing manufacturers. Brownhills is still very much an industrial area, but unlike the Potteries or the Black Country has little character.

Just over a mile to the north-west is the vast expanse of **Chasewater**, a reservoir used for various water sports such as sailing, canoeing, sail-boarding and power boat racing. There is a permanent boat club and on the opposite shore to this is a pleasure area which, in the summer months, is akin to a seaside holiday resort. An added attraction is the Light Railway and Museum which has a collection of industrial locomotives and rolling stock, from the period 1875-57, and half-a-mile of single gauge track. Chasewater, formally called Norton Pool, was constructed in 1799 as a reservoir for the Essington and Wyrley Canal and the Birmingham Canal. In character with the area in general, however, even Chasewater is somewhat scruffy and the nearby Raceway buildings are an absolute disgrace.

Hammerwich is a hamlet on high ground, 0.5m N of the A5. The church of St John the Baptist was rebuilt in 1872. In the 14th Century Hammerwich had three village centres: Middleton, Netherton and Overton. In 1262 action was taken against the villeins of Hammerwich in the Cannock Forest court for setting fire to the woods to clear land - possibly where Burntwood now stands. There is a wild Morris dance, performed by the Lichfield Morris, called The Vandals of Hammerwich.

Hammerwich Hall is more properly called Hammerwich House. It started life as a 19th Century farmhouse and has since been a girls' remand home, a children's home, a hospital annexe and an old people's home.

Hammerwich Square, a hamlet to the west of Hammerwich, was settled by 1871 when several coal mines were in operation here.

Clayhangar, 0.75m SW of Brownhills, is a small village which had developed on the west side of Clayhangar Common by the early 19th Century. The name means 'the clayey hanging wood', referring to the red marls on a wooded slope still evident. The new multi-purpose church building of about 2000 is dedicated to the Holy Trinity.

Triangle, 1m N of Brownhills, originated as a settlement of miners in the 1860s and greatly developed in the 20th Century. It takes its name from a triangle of roads 0.75m N of the A5 (Watling Street).

Muckley Corner, 1.75m ENE of Brownhills, is a small crossroads' settlement where the Lichfield to Walsall road (A461) intersects Watling Street . The prominent inn (Ye Olde Corner House) was here by at least the 1790s. By the mid-19th Century, until 1883, petty court sessions were held at the inn. The lime-kilns, known to be in existence by 1845, probably ceased working in the mid-1890s.

Shire Oak is a suburban area south of Brownhills. The tree that gave its name to the settlement was believed to be some 2,000 years old when its stump was removed in the 1890s. It stood near the top of Shire Oak Hill and marked the boundaries of Walsall and Shenstone ancient parishes. The wood in which it stood was described as a den of thieves and was used as a hideaway by highwaymen. There is a tradition that when travelling to Ireland Dean Swift met a tramp and his female companion beneath this tree whilst sheltering from a storm. The couple had just indulged their passion for each other, which so inflamed Dean Swift that he married them on the spot and by way of a marriage certificate wrote this verse:

Beneath this oak in stormy weather
I joined this whore and rogue together.
And none but He who made the thunder
Can put this whore and rogue asunder.

BUCKNALL *1m E of Hanley*

Bucknall was once a separate settlement but is now a suburb of Hanley. In Domesday Book it is Buccenhall and means either 'Bucca's nook' or 'Bucca's hill'. There were two early churches at Bucknall but the present building is of 1854-56 and is dedicated to St Mary. The Bucknall Bull Ring was attached to a large stone and was lost until discovered beneath a wayside cross at Bagnall. The River Trent flows to the side of the village and there was once a mill close by the railway station. In Bucknall New Road there is a water trough with two levels, one for horses and a lower one for dogs.

Today, Bucknall is a residential area with a large green space complete with pool, the Hanley Town Football Club ground, and the Newhouse Special School. It also has the doubtful privilege of adjoining Abbey Hulton to the north-east.

In 1974 Brook House, a half-timbered house that stood at the bottom of Brookhouse Lane to the east of Bucknall, was sold to Ian Bailey for £2. Mr Bailey rebuilt the house in Smithy Lane, Knighton near Mucklestone, and it still stands.

Peter Whelan, the playwright, was born at Bucknall in 1932. After attending Hanley High School he went to Keele University. Another native is Angela Smith, the World Champion squash player.

Ford Hayes (House) Farm, 1.5m SE of Bucknall, was the birthplace of Hugh Bourne (1772-1852), the founder of Primitive Methodism. At the age of 16 he moved to Bermesley Green.

BURNTWOOD *3m W of Lichfield*

A colliery town on the Cannock Coalfield that offers a dismal prospect. Burntwood lies in an area of Cannock Chase which was cleared of woodland as late as the Middle Ages. (Much of the forest of England had been cut down and most of the settlements established by the time of the Norman Conquest.) The name Green, which occurs in the names of nearby villages such as Goosemoor Green, Cresswell Green and Spade Green, refers to a clearing in forest - a green field amongst the dark woods. The name Burntwood itself implies that the land here was cleared by burning. Between Burntwood and Cannock Wood, and Longdon to the north, are a characteristic tangle of little lanes linking small hamlets and isolated farms.

From the early 17th Century there was iron-working in the Burntwood area, and from the 18th Century there was brick making and stone quarrying. By the mid-19th Century nail-making and coal mining were important here.

The parish church of Christ Church was built in 1819-20. Between 1961 and

1971 the population of Burntwood nearly doubled when it became an overspill area for people from Birmingham and the Black Country.

On the eastern fringes of the suburban growth is **Burntwood Green** and here, on the main road to Lichfield, is Edial House (pronounced Ed-yal). This is where Samuel Johnson opened his school in 1736. His famous advert read: 'Young gentlemen are boarded and taught the Latin and Greek languages by Samuel Johnson'. It was a disaster. The school had only three pupils and closed the following year. Johnson left Burntwood and went to London accompanied by one of these three pupils, a young man by the name of David Garrick, who was to become the country's leading actor.

Hobstone Hill lies 1m E of Burntwood near Woodhouses. A lunatic asylum was built here in 1864 to a design by W L Moffatt. As always with such institutions, there have been later extensions. In 1947 it became St Matthews Hospital. Near the hospital, on the road from Burntwood to Woodhouses, a tall spectral man has been seen walking a dog.

To the east of Burntwood, and almost in Lichfield, is Maple Hayes, a good late Georgian house where Erasmus Darwin laid out his Botanic Gardens. The house later became the property of the Worthington brewing family. Today, it is a boarding house for Lichfield School. In 1840 a racehorse meeting was held at Burntwood. It was held annually for 10 years and at one time nearly ousted the long-established Lichfield Races.

BURSLEM *3m NE of Newcastle-under-Lyme*
Burslem is a hill town, a nice town and is quite rightly called the Mother of the Potteries. There was a flourishing pottery industry here by the mid-17th Century. Local farmers had kilns (about eight feet high) in which they produced rough ware such as butter-pots for Uttoxeter market. There were some 20 small potteries using clay and coal dug locally from open-cast pits.

The town developed around the old Anglo-Saxon village. The name Burslem is a corruption of Burgheard's Lyme, meaning either 'Burgheard's woods' or 'Burgheard's clearing in the Forest of Lyme'. By 1710 there were 43 pot-banks in Burslem out of 52 recorded in the whole area. It is believed that the quad-rangle format of many of the later factories was a perpetuation of their origin as farmyard buildings. By the 1750s the trade was growing rapidly and the quality and variety of wares was increasing greatly, though Burslem was especially known for its white crockery ware.

About this date Thomas John Wedgwood had a windmill at The Jenkins, constructed by James Brindley (the canal builder) who had recently set up as a millwright in Burslem. It stood to the north-east of the present Market Place, and wet ground flint until 1832. The first large and important, and traceable, pot works was the Brickhouse Works. It became well known when in the ownership of John Adams (died 1687). It covered most of the land south of the Town Hall to Queen Street, which includes the site of the present Wedgwood Memorial Institute. The Adams family were there until 1762 when the tenancy passed to Josiah Wedgwood I. This is where Wedgwood developed his Egyptian Black and Cream Ware, called Queen's Ware, after Queen Charlotte.

The town, and the Potteries in general, were still comparatively isolated, but in the late 18th Century the roads were turnpiked and improved, and in 1777 the Trent and Mersey Canal arrived. In 1829, despite being thoroughly industrialized, Burslem was described by a visiting clergyman as 'spacious, airy and clean'. Today, although it has its share of grim Victorian terraces, the town could still be so described. The overall impression is of a Georgian market town, though the impressive Old Town Hall of 1852-7 by G T Robinson, with its giant columns and baroque decoration, speaks of civic pride rather than rural charm.

Ceramica is a museum and shop devoted to the pottery industry of Burslem and North Staffordshire. The Old Town Hall houses the museum displays; the shop is in the adjacent new, wing-shaped piece of modern architecture which is not without its critics.

Behind Ceramica is an area of cleared land once occupied by several large pottery firms, including Wade's. Some 900 houses are scheduled for this site at the time of writing (2004). Also at the time of writing, the Royal Doulton Factory in Nile Street is to close. Royal Doulton have been making pottery in Burslem since 1877, but the factory has been sold for two million pounds and production will now go to Indonesia.

South of the old Town Hall is the Leopard Inn with three storeys and columns between the parts of the bows. Still in the centre of the town, on the corner of Wedgwood Street and Chapel Bank, is Wedgwood House, the finest house in Burslem. It was formerly a home of the Wedgwoods. Inside are the initials of Thomas (father of Josiah) and John Wedgwood, and it is dated at 1751. It later became the Midland Bank and is now owned by a firm of architects who have restored it to its former glory. The house has five bays, 2.5 storeys, a one-bay pediment and a Tuscan-columned porch.

Opposite the Wedgwood House (the Big House as it used to be called) is the site of the Ivy Works, which was rented by Josiah Wedgwood in 1759. It is now a lawned area with public toilets and a bandstand.

The new Town Hall in Wedgwood Street is in Classical style with pairs of columns and was built in 1911 to a design by Russell and Cooper. One of the best known buildings in the Potteries is the Wedgwood Memorial Institute in Queen Street. It is built of red brick and terracotta, in what has been described as Venetian Gothic; with some large and very fine sculptured figures and a statue of Josiah Wedgwood, by Rowland Morris, above the lavish porch. It was purpose-built to house the museum, library and art gallery.

The impressive Burslem Sunday School in Westport Road is of 1836, by Samuel Sant. It has five bays, eight columns and a pediment. Adjacent to the Sunday School stood the Wade Heath Pottery, of 1814, one of the better pottery works with a typical Georgian façade, consisting of a canted arched doorway, a Venetian window and a pediment.

Close by, in Hall Street, is the Roman Catholic church of St Joseph, by Sydney Brocklesby, of 1935-7, a pleasant enough building but one which would look more at home in the sunshine of Tuscany.

The parish church of St John the Baptist stands with a quiet dignity in most undignified surroundings. It lies a little way from the present town centre, down the hill towards the canal. The medieval stone tower is of about 1536, the brick chancel is of 1788 and the rest is brick, of 1717. Inside, are two terracotta figures by a teenage Enoch Wood, later to be a potter of some stature in the town. In the large churchyard, close to the church, is the grave of the witch Peggy-Lee. Margaret Leigh, to give her her proper name, was reputed to have caused herds of cattle to die, chimneys not to draw and other such evils. When she died in 1748 she was buried in the churchyard, just south of the church. However, when the funeral party returned to her home they found her there knitting by the fire. To lay the spirit her body was dug up and re-interred in a new grave, which had been cut north-south. Close by Peggy Lee's grave is a stone coffin believed to have come from Hulton Abbey. Lanes lead from the church down to the wharves of Longport, Middleport and Newport on the Trent and Mersey Canal.

From the town centre the A50 heads southwards along the Waterloo Road. This road was begun in 1815 and named after the famous battle of the previous year. The George Hotel stands at the Burslem end. This was The Dragon of Arnold Bennett's novels, a Georgian-style building of the 1920s. Arnold Bennett lived at number 198 and also at number 205, which was once a museum dedicated to him but is now an old people's home. On this road is the America Inn of 1830 with one large bow window.

Westport Lake, 0.75m WNW of Burslem, was formed by mining subsidence in about 1880. It was developed and landscaped, and in 1971 was opened as a public amenity area. (For the Wildlife Rescue Centre see below.)

Longport, 1m W of Burslem, was called Longbridge before the canal came. This was a 16th Century bridge which, by the mid-18th Century, was a one-hundred-yard-long, wooden plank construction which crossed the marshes of the Fowlea Brook. It carried the packhorse route from Burslem to Newcastle-under-Lyme and was turnpiked in 1760. The settlement developed from 1775 to serve the new Trent and Mersey Canal. Today, the area around the bridge over the canal is one of the most picturesque in the Potteries, with the busy boatyard, old beehive pottery furnace and the world-famous Woods' teapot works - now taken over by Lorna Bailey as a ceramic crafts' centre. Here, too, is the Westport Wildlife Rescue Centre, an animal sanctuary in a small piece of woodland off the beaten track, near southern end of Westport Lake. Visitors are welcomed.

Port Vale Football Club is presently housed at a ground in Hamil Road, 0.5m NE of Burslem. However, it started life as Longport Football Club in 1876 and its headquarters were in Port Vale house in Scott Lidgett Road, Longport. 'Port' is from the wharf on the Trent and Mersey Canal, and 'Vale' is from Fowlea Brook Vale. The club had six different grounds between 1919 and 1968.

Gertie Gitana (1887-1957), the music hall artiste, was born in Shaley Street, Longport. Gitana Street in Hanley is a named after her.

Bradeley, 1m NE of Burslem, has a purpose-built Retirement Village, opened by the Council in 1994. It was intended as a self-sufficient community with its own social services such as a shop, library and health centre. This inspired a similar scheme in Berry Hill, west of Hanley.

Hamil, a former hamlet, 0.75m NE of Burslem, is remembered today by Hamil Road. Opposite the Port Vale football ground is the site of Hamil Grange, a cottage which was the home of the Leigh family from the early 17th Century. Molly Leigh was born here. She was ridiculed for being very ugly and, because of this, shunned society and did not attend church. Consequently, she was labelled a witch. A very early pottery kiln and two coarse saggars were found in a field at Hamil in the early 18th Century.

Sneyd, the ancestral homeland of the Sneyd family, no longer carries its traditional name. It is the Hamil Road area of Burslem, near Port Vale football ground. In 1256 it was Sned, from the Anglo-Saxon Snede meaning 'an outlying, detached piece of land'. The parish church of holy Trinity became unsafe and was demolished in 1959. St Werburgh's church then became the parish church and was re-consecrated Holy Trinity. To the south of Sneyd is **Sneyd Green**, where the Sneyd Cricket Ground is to be found on Sandbach Road, and Sneyd Green CP School is in Sneyd Street, which faces Hanley Central Forest Park. The parish church of St Andrew was built in about 1962. Noah Heath, potter and poet, was born at Sneyd Green in about 1780.

BURSTON *4m NE of Stafford*
A tiny, pretty village in a quiet cul-de-sac, off the busy A5l, between Weston and Stone. There are a row of terraced houses, several cottages, a large red brick farmhouse facing a pool frequented by ducks, and a church built in 1859 on the site of a ruined chapel. The mission church is dedicated to St Ruffin, second son of King Wulphere, who was murdered by his father for converting to Christianity. Ruffin was reputedly buried at Burston where his mother, Queen Ermenilda, built a chapel which was later much visited by pilgrims. The pool was constructed as a part of a watermill complex. The mill was at Burston Villa Farm, just downstream. It has been demolished but was grinding corn up until about 50 years ago. In 1979 a small hoard of bronze Roman coins was found in Jolpool Brook, below Beck House. Within half-a-mile to the west lie the River Trent, the Trent and Mersey Canal and the main-line railway to Stoke-on-Trent. Despite all this hustle and bustle, the village slumbers peacefully and remains quite rural. To the south-east is Sandon Park, the seat of the Earl of Harrowby. (See Sandon.)

BURTON UPON TRENT *11m NE of Lichfield*
In the early 7th Century the Angles came into the Midlands along the valley of the River Trent. At Burton they built a fort, around which developed a small settlement, hence the name 'burh-tun', (fort settlement). Today, of course, the name Burton is synonymous with beer:

Say for what were hop-yards meant,
Or why was Burton built on Trent?
A E Housman

The trade was first developed by the monks of Burton Abbey. After the Dissolution of the Monasteries local inn-keepers manufactured their own beer, and by the beginning of the 17th Century ales brewed in Burton were being sold in London. At the end of the 17th Century the river was improved and became navigable between Burton and Gainsborough in Lincolnshire, thus allowing rapid and cheap transport to the east coast. In the 18th Century the town thrived on trade with the Baltic and Russia, and the foundations of the modern industry were laid. (Catherine the Great is said to have been 'immoderately fond' of the ale brewed in Burton.) In 1777 the Trent and Mersey Canal opened, and facilitated transport both to the east and the west coasts. During the 19th Century the brewers developed the famous East India Pale Ale and enjoyed great success in the huge Indian sub-continent. In 1839 the railway arrived and trade was given its biggest boost yet, because Burton brewers could now compete more effectively with local breweries in other parts of England, and they greatly expanded their home business.

The secret of Burton's success was, and is, the special qualities of its hard water. This is pumped to the surface from subterranean springs. The rocks here contain gypsum and the water dissolves out and absorbs minerals such as magnesium and calcium sulphates. (In the past, brewers from other parts of the country have actually sunk wells at Burton and transported the water, at great expense, to their breweries.) The breweries at Burton totally dominate the town. Beer is a bulky product. It needs large vats to produce it and huge containers to store it; and the maltings require massive areas of floor space for the grain to be spread over and turned, to dry the malt and encourage germination. Until 1967

Burton was criss-crossed by an elaborate system of private railways, which connected the maltings on the outskirts of the town with the breweries in the centre. In this century the industry has been rationalized and is now controlled by a handful of big amalgamations and alliances. Despite their 'chemical beer' they still dominate the market, but in recent years they have been troubled by the growth in the Real Ale movement The wheel could go full circle for there are now many small breweries, and they are back in the countryside operating the length and the breadth of the land. Things could be returning to how they were in the Middle Ages when every locality had its own special brew and was proud of it. Still, the brewers of Burton won't be short of beer to cry into.

Burton has had a market since the year 1200 when the Abbey created the borough, and the heart of the town is still the Market Place. It is one of the few areas in Burton with any character. Around the square are shops, and facing the main road is the parish church of St Modwena, named after the Irish lady saint who, in the 7th Century, is reputed to have built the first church here on the island of Andressey (St Andrew's Island) in the Trent, which lies at the back of the present church. The church was rebuilt in 1719-26 by William and Richard Smith and completed by Francis Smith. The churchyard has been cleared and is now a Garden of Remembrance for the dead of Second World War.

To the right of the church, at the rear of the covered market, is a re-erected wall with arches and sculptures. These are some of the few remains of the great Abbey of Burton, which was centred on the site of the present day Market place, Market Hall and part of the Remembrance Garden. The abbey was founded by a Saxon Earl, Wulfric Spot, in 1003 for the Benedictine Order. It dominated the life of the town in the Middle Ages and the Abbot was a major landowner. (The Abbey also carried out valuable surveys of its estates showing the existence of a whole class of rent-paying tenants, which is not mentioned in Domesday Book. This class might well have encompassed two-thirds of the population.) The Abbey was the largest and wealthiest in Staffordshire. After the Dissolution in 1537 the town sank to a mere village, until it was revived by the development of the beer trade already discussed. The beer barons may have made fortunes but they spent very little of it on either their factories or the cottages of their workers.

The old centre of Burton is pleasant enough and any town that has a decent coffee shop cannot be all bad. Burton has Café B in the High Street, a road of traditional three-storey shops. However, for the most part Burton turns its back on the attractions of its broad river. It is the car parks and modern buildings which spoil the townscape; and the fact that it is so flat means there are no vistas. In recent years the Almshouses of 1593 were demolished to make way for a large shopping centre, wherein you will find branches of all the major national chain stores such as Boots and W H Smiths. This was a dastardly deed as Burton has so little that is old. There are some public buildings and churches worthy of mention, which were largely paid for by the breweries, but there is little that is charming or beautiful.

Top of the list comes St Chad's Church, designed by Bodley and paid for by Lord Burton, of the Bass family, in 1903-10. The Town Hall was built in 1878, with additions in 1894 and a disastrous right-hand extension of 1938-9. It really is Gothic gone wrong. The proportions are most peculiar and it is probably best thought of as an amusing folly. It lies an inconvenient and considerable distance from the centre. This is because it was originally built as an Institute, attached to the adjacent church of St Paul, and did not achieve its present status until 1894, which does not, of course, explain why it was chosen to be the Town Hall. One of the few old buildings left in Burton is the 17th Century, gabled Manor House. This was used as an estate office by the Paget family, Earls of Uxbridge and Marquesses of Anglesey, who are still Lords of the Manor here. They acquired much of their property from the Abbey when it was dissolved. Behind the Manor House is the Abbey Club, a large Victorian house built in the old grounds of the Abbey and incorporating the original Abbey Infirmary. Some of the best buildings in the town are in Morninglow Street. Here is a series of good 18th Century houses and the baroque, domed Magistrates' Court. There are many churches scattered around the town; likewise, many malthouses and breweries, in one of which Bass has a well-advertised museum.

In 1867 the old medieval bridge was pulled down and a new one built to replace it. The river and the flood plain meadows are very broad here and the bridge is long, multi-arched and most impressive. It is seen to its best advantage from the east bank. There are prettily-painted boat houses and almost romantic views of the large Drakelow Power Station which lies upstream, just over the border in Derbyshire. Today, Burton is bypassed by the busy A38 and most travellers will only see it as a built-up blur as they journey from Lichfield to Derby.

Finally, two curiosities: the first is that Burton had the first recorded cricket club in the county. The game had undoubtedly been played throughout the shire at village level for many years, but by 1831 Burton had a first-class ground and the town team played matches against the Leicestershire County side. In 1837 they beat Leicestershire by an innings and five runs. Among the batsmen were C Allsop and Abram Bass, who was to become known as the Father of Midland's cricket. The second curiosity is that Catherine Mewks, 1802-1822, lost her sight at the age of seven but regained it every Sunday. Her claims were verified by four surgeons and she became something of a celebrity.

On a sadder note, in 1951 Miss Winifred Mulley, aged 51, the headmistress of Burton Girls' High School, was murdered in her house by an army deserter in search of food and shelter. The house stands in the school grounds and is called The Woodlands.

Stapenhill, 0.5m SE of Burton on Trent, was once a village but is now a suburb of Burton. In 1881 an Anglo-Saxon necropolis (a large cemetery) was found by men working in a brick-yard between Rolleston Road and Stanton Road. The prefix of the name Stapenhill is from 'Stapol', a boundary pole or pillar. There were 36 burials and part of the site was later found to be Roman. The church of St Peter was built in 1880-81, probably on the site of earlier Anglo-Saxon and medieval churches. Horse Holme is an island in the River Trent opposite Stapenhill Gardens. The name means 'Horsa's island'.

Shobnall is a substantial hamlet which stands below the slope of the Needwood Forest plateau, 1.5m WNW of Burton on Trent. By 1325 it was a grange of Burton Abbey and by the mid-16th century it was owned by Sir William Paget of Beaudesert Hall. By 1887 Bass, the brewers, had extensive maltings at Shobnall. The parish church of St Aidan was built in 1884. Shobnall Grange, near the church, has some 17th Century brick and mullioned and transomed windows, which were quite probably a part of the Burton Abbey grange.

Horninglow, 1.25m N of Burton, was held by Burton Abbey before the Dissolution of the Monasteries. It then passed to William Paget of Beaudesert Hall. The name Horninglow is not properly understood but could mean

'Horning's Burial Mound'. Today, it is a suburb of Burton - a mixed residential area with several pubs, a Victorian Infants' School and some traditional small shops. Approached from the north-west the land is very flat and one passes a National Forest sign. The railway station opened in 1868 and closed in 1940. A looped, Bronze-Age palstave (bronze chisel) was found on the site of the station (SK 251248). The church of St John the Divine was built in 1864-66.

Stretton, 2m NNE of Burton, lies in flat country near the confluence of the River Dove and the River Trent. Approached from Burton one passes through a large industrial/warehouse/business area to emerge into a pleasant and well-greened residential settlement, most of which lies on the west side of the A38 and the Trent and Mersey Canal. There is a parade of modern shops; the church of St Mary is sandstone; the Bitham Clay Pit Conservation area is close to the Swimming Pool; and hiding down a private drive is the de Ferrers school.

Winshill lies on high ground opposite Burton, on the east bank of the River Trent, and is now a suburb of Burton. In the 11th Century it was held by Burton Abbey and was a manor with its own manor house, mills and gallows. The gallows were probably at **Hanging Hill**, at the Winshill end of the bridge over the River Trent. Approached from Burton, over the A444 bridge, one is struck by the greenness of the wooded lower slopes of the steep hill on which Winshill lies. This east-bank river area is most attractive with mature houses and a very large, four-storey flour mill in the process of being developed into apartments. The road up to the centre of the village passes through a deep, wooded cutting and brings one to the church, with its tall, thin spire and its impressive churchyard gate posts facing the Travellers' Rest Inn. There are shops, a Post Office and some Victorian terraced houses. All around the old centre are estates of 20th Century bungalows and houses.

BUSHBURY *2.5m N of Wolverhampton town centre*
The name Bushbury is derived from Byscopesbyrig (996), the Anglo-Saxon name which means 'the manor belonging to the Bishop'.

Bushbury is now a residential suburb of Wolverhampton, but until the 19th Century it was a village in its own right. Before the Norman Conquest the Anglo-Saxon, Wulfric, held the manor but under King William it passed to William, son of Ansculf. In 1086 there were 3 villagers and 4 smallholders with 2 ploughs, and the lord of the manor was Robert.

The Church of St Mary is medieval and although over-restored in Victorian times much of the original fabric survives: the Perpendicular tower, the Decorated nave and Decorated chancel with its fine sedilia and Easter Sepulchre niche. The font is late Norman and the two small figures in a south chancel window are early 14th Century. Among the monuments are the effigy of a 14th Century priest, a tablet to John Gough, died 1665, and a memorial to Thomas Whitgreave of Moseley Old Hall, who aided Charles II in his escape after the Battle of Worcester. (See Moseley Old Hall.) In the churchyard is part of a circular Anglo-Saxon cross.

In 1645 Charles I is said to have watched a skirmish from Bushbury Hill when a Parliamentary squadron attacked a detachment of Royalist horse, killing 16 men and capturing 26 horses. Charles was staying at Bushbury Hall at the time. Bushbury Hall lies just to the east of the church, and is now a grey-rendered, Georgian-style house of five bays.

Today, Bushbury is no longer a village. It is a place of modern houses and of one estate, in particular, namely **Old Fallings Park**. This is a large 'garden suburb' planned by Thomas Adams and laid out in 1907. It has a symmetrical axis, based on three ellipses, but the outer edges are irregular. Despite its wide streets, its houses of some character, its pink-blossomed trees, its social and shopping centre (Showell Circus), it is not considered to have been a great success. Old Fallings Hall still survives as St Chad's College. It is a large, early 18th Century house of five bays with a hipped roof and giant angle pilasters supporting Corinthian capitals. North of the church is a cemetery and a crematorium.

Showell's Circus, by the way, is a memorial to the medieval moated manor house and estate that once occupied the area. The name Showell is thought to be from the Seofan Wyllan (Seven Springs) of King Ethelred's charter of 985.

There is also a well-known Public Baths at Bushbury, designed by A Chapman and built in 1964-6 of yellow brick and concrete with a large sloping roof. It lies on the lower grassy slopes of **Low Hill,** atop which is an estate of predominantly cream-painted houses.

Northicote Farm is a timber-framed farmhouse, built about 1600 by the Underhill family. The house and 80 acres were bought by Wolverhampton Borough Council in 1978. They restored the farmhouse and it is now a country educational centre. In July each year a free weekend folk festival is held here, a most friendly and well-attended event. In the 1990s a popular contemporary folk group called The Bushbury Mountain Daredevils emerged from the area.

In 1993 Northicote Secondary School was the first school in the country to be failed by OFSTED inspectors. A new headmaster, Geoff Hampton, was appointed and he brought about a dramatic improvement. Geoff Hampton was knighted that same year (1993), the first serving headmaster of a state school to be so honoured.

BUTTERTON *2.5m SSW of Newcastle-under-Lyme*
The village lies in the triangle between the A53, the A5128 and the M6 motorway in wooded, rolling countryside. The Hall was pulled down in 1924 and only the stables remain. Some of the stone was reused in the construction of Newcastle-under-Lyme Golf Club. The Hall had been built for Thomas Swinnerton in 1830. He was a member of a minor branch of the Swynnerton family of Swynnerton. The heiress of Thomas Swinnerton married Sir William Pilkington (the 8th Baronet) and their son was burdened with the name William Milbourne Milbourne-Swinnerton-Pilkington.

Near the stables, in a corner of a field and visible from the lane, are the romantic, ivy-clad ruins of the old sandstone Tudor manor house. A chimney breast and some walls remain. There is a good brick house on the opposite side of the lane. Most of the village houses lie a little further northwards. They are, for the most part, largish and well-heeled.

The church stands apart, at the end of a cul-de-sac, on the edge of the old Park. It was built by Thomas Hopper in 1844, in Norman style with a central tower and low pyramid spire. Inside, there are box pews and monuments to the Milbourne-Swinnerton-Pilkington family.

An exposure of the Butterton Dyke, discovered by Charles Darwin in the Hanchurch Hills, can be seen in a disused quarry, 330 yards SSE of Butterton church. The dyke consists of hard volcanic rock injected between the sandstone beds. The same dyke has been traced at Swynnerton.

Away from the village, and with its own approach road off the A5182 (close to exit 15 on the M6), is Butterton Grange Farm. This was built for Thomas

Swinnerton by Sir John Sloane in 1816. It has overhanging eaves, a tall central chimney-block, giant entrance pilasters and is constructed of red brick - a worthy house but it does not look well from the road: classical lines and the clutter of a farm are not altogether compatible. Opposite the house, on the other side of the road, is a small fishing pool. This was constructed after an oil exploration rig had operated here a few years ago.

BUTTERTON *(in the Peak District) 5m E of Leek*

There is lovely moorland country all around Butterton. It is an archetypal village. Almost all the buildings are of the local grey stone. New houses are few and are constructed in the traditional manner. There is a shop, a butcher, a Post Office and the Black Lion pub. The church of St Bartholomew was built in 1871 by Ewan Christian and the tall spire, which is a landmark for many miles around, was added in 1879 by Sugden. Seen from a distance the village is surprisingly well-wooded. Salt is a very common surname of inhabitants hereabouts. One mile ESE is **Wetton Mill** on the River Manifold. On a hot summer's day local people flock here and there is much splashing and jollity; yet in the hills around are the silent caves and burial mounds of prehistoric man.

CALTON *5m NW of Ashbourne*

Most easily approached off the A523, Leek to Ashbourne road, Calton is a small well-wooded, stone-built village in lovely moorland country. It seems likely that this was a planned settlement of the early 13th Century made by the lords of Blore, Mayfield and Waterfall, and deliberately sited away from neighbouring villages to avoid competition.

The little 18th Century church of St Mary has a bell turret and inside there are High Church furnishings and some very good Continental altar rails. Just over a mile north, on the lane to Ilam, are the splendid ruins of Throwley Hall. In the hills around Throwley and Calton there are many prehistoric burial mounds and caves. (See Throwley.)

One mound, at SK 198512 near Lower Green House, is unusual in that it has a raised central platform surrounded by a bank. Carrington invaded it in 1849 and found the skeleton of a child, a thick-backed knife and signs of an Anglian burial. I hope he felt better having established that, but I don't suppose the child's parents were best pleased.

Musden, 1.5m NE of Calton, is today represented by Musden Grange House. In the 12th Century the Musden estate of about 600 acres was given to Croxden Abbey. The Abbey depopulated the sizeable village and established a grange farm. The grange buildings lay to the west of the present house and the site was surveyed in 1985.

Musden Low is a hill above a bend in the River Manifold and has at least four burial mounds on it. Sorry, but if you want more details of these look elsewhere. The author finds the subject repetitively boring and, what is more, gets very angry at the desecration of graves. These tombs were holy and revered places to those who made them. Would it be too much to let those interred RIP?

CANNOCK *10m SSE of Stafford*

Cannock town and Cannock Chase should not be confused. They share the same name but little else. The town developed as a centre of coal mining in the 19th Century, whereas the Chase is an officially designated Area of Outstanding Natural Beauty (1985). Here we treat only of the town. Cannock is a pleasant enough place with wide roads and a good shopping centre. In the last few years there has been a great deal of rebuilding. Private enterprise is producing a bright, almost trendy town, but though the council developments are not altogether inspired at least their mini skyscrapers are clad in traditional red brick. There are but a handful of old buildings of any consequence.

The parish church of St Luke sits amidst lawns with embattled tower and aisles. In early medieval times it had a grammar school and chantry attached to it. The present church has a tower and west nave of the 14th Century. In 1878-82 it was extended by two bays (to the east) and the chancel was rebuilt. In 1949 a war memorial chapel was added and in 1957 the handsome, old-style porch was replaced by a new one in Perpendicular style.

North-west of the church is the Old Council House, a good 18th Century building clad in colour-washed stucco with wrought iron gates. It was once the home of Henry Cary, friend of Wordsworth. It faces the High Green, which in turn faces the Market Place. There is a modern covered market and market days are Tuesdays, Fridays and Saturdays. Between the High Green and the Old Council House is a red sandstone structure which looks like a dovecote. This housed the water conduit access point and was built in 1736. For over 200 years the people of Cannock obtained their water from the Cannock Conduit Trust (disbanded in 1942). The town is built on gravel which does not hold water and so it had to be pumped from Stringer's Meadow, Rumer Hill, Leacroft.

Longford House, 1.25m SW of Cannock, lies at the junction of the A5 and the A460. This imposing brick and stone house for long lay derelict, but has recently been restored as a social club. Close by is a huge, second-hand car mart which attracts people from a large area.

The name Cannock is Celtic and means 'high place'. In the 11th Century the town was the property of the Anglo-Saxon Earl Algar of Mercia. When he died in 1062 it passed to his son, Edwin, who continued to have some control even after the Norman Conquest. However, Edwin took part in a revolt against King William I. In 1071 all his property was confiscated and the land was laid waste by the King. In 1189, as a part of Cannock Forest, the manor was sold to the Bishop of Coventry and in 1259 Henry III granted a market. The settlement remained little more than a village until the 19th Century when it became a centre of coal mining.

In 1863 the Cannock Extension Canal arrived, one of the last to be built in the whole country. By the end of the 19th Century half the coal produced from South Staffordshire came from the greater Cannock area. The population of Cannock town grew from 3,000 in 1861 to 24,000 in 1901. The last mine to close was Littleton Colliery at Huntington, a northern suburb of Cannock. There is a variety of light industry but the major employers are the service industries - shops, local government, estate agents, banks, solicitors etc. The Cannock Chase District Council administers many nearby towns such as Rugeley and Hednesford, which are described in this book under their own names.

Rumer Hill, 0.75m SE of Cannock Centre, is a residential suburb of Cannock. Rumer means 'rough marshland'. The Cannock conduit was fed from a spring at Rumer. In 1842 there was a celebrated court case over mining rights between Lord Hatherton and the Marquess of Anglesey. Hatherton lost.

Heath Hayes, 1m E of Cannock, lies adjacent to the north side of Watling Street (A5). It takes its name from a farm called Heath Hayes, now confusingly called Farm Grange. The settlement is largely modern. The church of St John the Evangelist was built in 1902. Tom Lunn, of Stafford Street, Heath Hayes, was Wolverhampton Wanderers' goalkeeper when they won the FA cup in 1978.

Pye Green, 2.5m NNE of Cannock, is a modern residential area with a Post Office, on a high point on Cannock Chase. The Post Office tower, is 258 feet high and was constructed in 1970. It broadcasts TV and radio progammes and is a major landmark. 'Pie' is Anglo-Saxon for 'gnat'. A green was a clearing in woodland.

CANNOCK CHASE *between Stafford and Rugeley and S to Cannock Wood*
Cannock Chase covers 25 square miles of varied country, from wild heathland to gentle wooded valleys, marshlands and coniferous forests. It is a remnant of the great Royal Forest of Cannock, which in medieval times extended from Stafford in the north to Wolverhampton in the south, and from the River Penk on the west to the River Tame on the east. There were wolves here as late as 1280 and there are still substantial herds of deer: red deer, roe deer, barking deer and fallow deer. One of the old deer leaps has recently been restored by the Forestry Commission. (See Rugeley.)

The Forest had been a Royal hunting ground in both Anglo-Saxon and Norman times. The term 'Forest' was a legal one. It meant that the land belonged to the King and that forest law applied. It was well-wooded but there were also large areas of moor and meadow. Some of these open areas would almost certainly have been cleared by prehistoric man. The extensive Neolithic flint working 'factory' discovered at Court Bank Covert, and the eight-acre Iron Age hill fort of Castle Ring, both near Cannock Wood, speak of a considerable pre-Roman population.

In 1189 Richard I, desperately seeking funds to finance a Crusade to the Holy Land, sold the Forest to the Bishop of Coventry and Lichfield, and from this date we must refer to Cannock Chase, not Forest. The Bishops built a palace at Beaudesert near Upper Longdon. In 1546 Henry VIII bought back the Chase and gave it to one of his 'new men', Sir William Paget, reputedly the son of a Wednesbury nailer. Beaduesert was held by the Paget family from 1546 to 1918, except for one short period between 1584 and 1597 when the 3rd Baron was in exile for treason. (He was a Roman Catholic and was suspected of being involved in the Throckmorton Plot). In 1815 Henry Paget was made Marquis of Anglesey as a reward for the services he rendered at the Battle of Waterloo. In 1935 the magnificent Beaudesert Hall, the Paget home for many generations, was pulled down and the stone sold by auction. All that remains today is the early 19th Century lodge and a fragment of the Tudor great hall. The lands of the estate are now home to a golf course and a camp site for scouts and guides.

It was the Pagets, and in particular their lessee, Sir Fulke Greville, who were largely responsible for the destruction of the forests of Cannock Chase. During the 16th Century the trees were cut down, converted to charcoal and burned as fuel to smelt iron. By the beginning of the 17th Century Cannock Chase was a heathland - a wild moor covered in grass, heather and gorse. Some of this land was cleared by burning, cultivated for five years and left to return to waste. For 300 years the Chase remained a bleak moorland. Natural regeneration of the woodland was prevented by the grazing of sheep, deer and rabbits who ate the seedlings before they could become established and grow into trees. As early as 1582 there were 6,177 sheep recorded on the moors. Trees were only re-introduced in the 1920s when the Forestry Commission planted hundreds of acres of coniferous forest. The endless ranks of dull, dark green have in recent years been softened by the planting of mixed deciduous species, especially alongside roads.

By 1570 there were two furnaces and two forges on Cannock Chase (that we know of). The furnaces smelted iron out of the ore and the forges beat out the impurities to make the metal less brittle. One of the furnaces was probably the first blast furnace in the Midlands. Giant bellows worked by a waterwheel forced air into the furnace, which created much higher temperatures than before and increased production dramatically. Some small remains of this, in the form of slag heaps, are still visible in the valley of the Rising Brook between Cannock and Rugeley. They can be seen on the right-hand side of the causeway that leads from the road to the new industrial estate, which stands on the site of the old No. 5 colliery. They were once more numerous but many have been removed for re-smelting and for use in road making. (Note: The name Rising Brook is a corruption of Hrisen Brook, meaning 'a stream with scrub wood on its banks'.)

At Fair Oak is a dry hollow, which was the mill pond where the iron was worked. There was a slitting mill, which cut iron bars into widths suitable for nail making, on the Paget estate, and it was probably the one at the village of **Slitting Mill** near Rugeley, built for Thomas Chetwynd in 1623. A large brick waterworks has been built on the mill site but the now dry pond and some brick and stone walls still remain by the stream (SK 029171). The iron ore used in the Cannock Chase furnaces came from Walsall. There was some ore on the Chase but its quality was too low to be worked commercially.

Coal had been mined on Cannock Chase since early medieval times but not until the 19th Century did the industry develop to a noteworthy degree Then it did so with a vengeance. Small picturesque villages and hamlets like Heath Hayes, Norton Canes, Great Wyrley and Cheslyn Hay became grimy colliery towns. (A 'hay' could be either an agricultural enclosure or a division of forest land.) They were virtually new towns, changed out of all recognition. One completely new town was Chasetown, developed about 1850 and given parish status in 1867. From 1850 onwards the railways came, though they were essentially commercial lines.

Today, much of Cannock Chase is owned by local councils and the public has almost total access. (There are some nature reserves which are protected.) It is the natural charms of the Chase which are the attraction: hills, valleys, streams, ponds, trees, bracken-covered moors and the delights of Brocton Coppice, an oak grove which is a remnant of the ancient medieval Royal Forest. (See Brocton.) There are some man-made curiosities: the remains of the army's First World War training camps and railway track; the beautiful German Military Cemetery, designed by Diez Brandi; and the touching memorial erected by the local Polish community for those who were killed in the Katin Forest of their homeland. The much-visited German Cemetery is most easily approached off the A34, Stafford to Cannock road, from which it is well signposted. Many of those buried here died in the Spanish 'Flu epidemic of 1918. The Cannock Chase Forestry Commission Visitors' Centre is in Birches Valley, 1m SW of Rugeley.

There are three separate localities called Severn Springs on Cannock Chase but the best known and most visited is that at the north end of the chase, south of

Weetman's Bridge, at SK 005206. Beware though - a tall dark lady with a pale complexion and dressed in black haunts this beauty spot.

Cannock Chase had a hermit, a young man called Reynold Raddock, who lived in the 18th Century. He fell in love with his cousin, Bertha Wheatwell, but she was enamoured of another. Raddock never spoke of his feelings, and after a serious accident, which crippled him, he repaired to Cannock Chase where he lived as a hermit. At first he had many visitors but in time found himself alone except for the company of a wild hare. Raddock and the hare became close companions. Then, one day, the hare was killed by dogs. Broken hearted the hermit's thoughts turned to Bertha. He made enquiries and found that she had gone to London to marry her betrothed, only to be spurned by him. She was pregnant and destitute and had returned to her parents' house, only to find that they had died of heartbreak on losing their daughter. Bertha was put in the Cannock Workhouse where she died soon after. Stricken with grief for a second time, Raddock lost his mind and was also put in the workhouse where he too died. He was buried next to his beloved Bertha.

CANNOCK WOOD *4m ENE of Cannock*

The settlement lies on the present-day southern boundary of Cannock Chase. It is not so much a village as an area of housing. The land here is all hills and dales. The woods and moors are dotted with modern villas, old-style cottages and some pleasant, up-market estates. They are served by a somewhat down-market garage and village shop, but overall this is a most attractive place. It adjoins the old village of **Gentleshaw**, which has a friendly-looking, red brick church of about 1840 (no one seems to be quite sure of the exact date), with additions to the east in 1903. The school lies close to the church but most of the houses are in small scattered enclaves further down the hill. The Gentleshaw Wildlife Sanctuary has moved to Fletcher's Garden Centre at Eccleshall.

The area around Cannock Wood is rich in sites of historical interest. Foremost, is the prehistoric fort settlement of Castle Ring (SK 045128). This lies just north-west of the village. It is not well signposted but all the local people know where it is. The fort lies on high ground and, were it not surrounded by trees, would have good views in all directions. In Iron-Age times the trees would have been cleared. It has three defensive banks and ditches on its east side and only one larger bank and ditch on its steeper north side. The banks would have been topped with palisades and the entrance protected by a large wooden Gatehouse. In the north-east of the enclosure, which encompasses eight acres, are the sandstone foundations of a Royal Hunting Lodge, dating from the time of King John. This has yet to be properly excavated. There is a car park at the entrance to the site, which lies opposite the Park Gate Inn.

To the south-east of Cannock Wood, by only 0.25m, is a little valley that has had an interesting and intriguing history. This valley is served by two small streams, which join at a small wood called **Courtsbank Covert**. (This is not named on the 1.25 inch Ordnance Survey map but is the wood just to the east of Red Moor – SK 042116.) There are seven sites of interest:

1. The Neolithic flint working site was quite extensive - a veritable factory - but this was totally destroyed during the early years of the Second World War when the eastern banks of the stream were subject to open-cast coal mining. Three train-loads a day were stripped by a huge American drag bucket machine, the farmer told us. Flints from the site are at Birmingham University.

2. The Nun's Well was an ancient well lined with sandstone and capped with

a brick arch. The waters were thought to have healing properties for complaints of the eye. Just after the end of the Second World War the woods around the well were cut down by a local timber merchant, a Mr Barratt. He used teams of eight horses to drag the trees away. A few old oaks were left and stand there today, but most of the area was bulldozed level. The well was capped with corrugated iron sheets and now lies below about 4 feet of earth. Some years after the well was capped a man working a dredger said he saw the ghost of a nun.

3. Just north of the well is the reputed site of Radmore (Redmore) Abbey. That this existed is beyond dispute. It was originally a Hermitage endowed by King Stephen. About 1145 it became a Cistercian Monastery, but later Henry II gave the monks land at Stoneleigh in Warwickshire in exchange for Radmore Abbey. The site was investigated after the Second World War but nothing was found. It has been suggested that the Abbey was only made of timber. Since that investigation the land has been bulldozed, as already mentioned, so any post holes or differences in earth colouring are now long gone.

4. The King had acquired Radmore Abbey because he wished to build a Royal Hunting Lodge there. No trace of this has ever been found but we know that Henry II stayed there in 1155. It has been suggested that the lodge could have been built a little further downstream in the woods where there is a rectangular 'moat' (SK 043117). However, it is now suspected that this 'moat' was actually a pond reservoir for a medieval, water-driven wheel which worked the hammers of an iron-working factory, that is, a 'bloomery'. Slag has been found over quite a wide area and the farmer has found irregular, coarse bricks up to a foot square by three inches deep, both in the stream and in the field in the area marked on the map.

5. Up the hill to the east is a pond (SK 044118), which was quite clearly created by a man-made dam. This is thought to have originally been a fish pond for the Abbey, and was later used as a millpond in connection with medieval iron works.

6. The westerly stream runs red. This is because it cuts through ironstone rocks and earth. The road to the north is called Ironstone Road. (By the pub at New Hayes it becomes Cumberledge Hill). The westerly stream has been channelled along underground pipes from the hillside pond to the Courtsbank Covert. (Note: for a map of these sites see 'Staffordshire and the Black Country' by Michael Raven.)

7. All in all, this is a fascinating site and ought to be properly investigated. Visitors should beware of the nasty little Black Bog. There is a considerable depth of soft peat here. The ground is thoroughly putrid and nothing, not even mosses and lichens, live here. It is an evil place if ever there was one. The entrance to the valley and all the sites listed above is off Hayfield Hill. A five-bar gate gives access to a track between a row of houses at SK 046117.

In 1342 some Lichfield merchants sent two of their servants to Stafford. They were carrying goods to be sold at the market there, but as they passed through Cannock Wood they were set upon by Sir Robert de Ridware and his men who robbed them of their silks and spices. Sir Robert repaired to the priory at Lapley where he shared out the goods with other robber Knights, amongst whom was Sir John de Addyngesles. Sir Robert then rode to Blithbury but the abbess there refused him hospitality, whereupon the knight broke into the barns and took fodder for his horse. Meanwhile, one of the servants who had been robbed escaped and reported to the Sheriff of Lichfield. The Sheriff and his men intercepted Sir Robert and his band and a battle ensued. The Sheriff won the encounter, recaptured the stolen goods and beheaded four of Sir Robert's men on the spot. The robber knight, however, escaped and rode to Hamstal Ridware to seek the assistance of his relative, Sir Walter Ridware. Together they led a band of men, attacked the Sheriff and retrieved Sir Robert's booty. The Lichfield merchants went to Stafford to seek justice but found the town gates locked and manned by men from Ridware. The plaintiffs were forced to flee for their lives. This is a true story. Medieval lords and knights lived very much by the sword, and the sword they wielded was not always that of Justice.

CANWELL *6m SSE of Lichfield*

Canwell lies lm NE of the intersection of the A453 and the A38. There is no village, only a park and a church. The Hall is long gone. It was the home of the Lawley family, Lords of Wenlock, who are buried at Hints church. The attractive church at Canwell was built by Temple Moor in 1911. It has a vaulted roof and Decorated-style windows.

Canwell Priory was founded in about 1140 by Geve, the illegitimate daughter of Hugh d'Avranches, Earl of Chester. It was a Benedictine monastery for monks and was dedicated to St Giles. By the mid-18th Century the priory had all but disappeared and the new stables of Canwell Hall were built utilizing the remaining ruins.

The large park lies to the east of the busy A38, which at this point follows the route of one of the country's most famous coaching roads - the road from London to Chester and Holyhead - described in John Ogilby's road book of 1675 as 'one of the most frequented in the Kingdom'. It entered Staffordshire at Bassett's Pole, lm SW of Canwell Gate in Canwell, and proceeded to Lichfield, Rugeley, Wolseley Bridges, Stone and Darlaston (near Stone), Woore (Shropshire) and Nantwich (Cheshire). In the 13th and 14th Centuries the route was slightly different. From Stone the road went to Newcastle-under-Lyme and then to Nantwich.

Green Wood, 0.75m NNW of Canwell, became a camp in 1997-98, and was manned by demonstrators protesting against the construction of the Birmingham Northern Relief Road through an ecologically sensitive area.

CAULDON (or Caldon) *7m SE of Leek*

The name is thought to be from the Anglo-Saxon 'celfdun', meaning 'calf hill'. Cauldon is a tiny village on the northern Weaver Hills. Godiva owned it in 1066. It then passed to the Norman, Robert of Stafford, the younger son of Roger of Tosny (or Toeni). In 1086 it was described as 'waste' and could well be so described today, for the village lies below the hill of Cauldon Lowe which is being rapidly diminished by quarrying. In 1906 the floors of caves at Caldon Low Hill yielded the bones of many animals including bison, deer and woolly rhinoceros of the period 8000-4000 BC. According to local tradition the hill is inhabited by a race of fairies. To the south-west are several disused quarries and there is a certain grimness to the country hereabouts.

The village consists of the Yew Tree Inn, a few stone cottages and a little 18th Century church with a tall 17th Century house close by. There was a church at Cauldon in the 12th Century but the present church of St Mary and St Lawrence was built in 1781-84 on the site of a medieval church.

A stretch of road from Cauldon to the Crown Inn at Waterhouses is called 'Yarlsway'. This is a corruption of Earlsway, the name of the romantic medieval road used by the Earls of Chester when they visited their estates in Staffordshire, Derby and Nottingham. It was a well-used route from the 11th to the 13th Centuries and is almost certainly that taken by Sir Gawain in his quest for the Green Knight, whose castle was probably sited at Swythamley Hall. Today, it is a series of minor roads running parallel with the main road to Leek.

The 'low' in the name Cauldon Lowe refers to the ancient burial mounds found there, in particular the Big Low. There can be little doubt that more prehistoric remains were here but they have been destroyed by the limestone quarry workings. Near the top of the hill Tarmac produce road metal, and lower down Blue Circle have a cement works. To some people quarries are a blemish on nature's handiwork but to others they have a gaunt attraction. What is beyond doubt, is that the materials produced are essential and have to be obtained from somewhere.

Quarrying on a large scale began here in the late-18th Century when the Trent and Mersey Canal Company bought the mineral rights, and in 1777 brought a spur of the Caldon Canal to Froghall Wharf. The canal was connected to the quarries by a plateway. The stone, as lime, was used in ironworks as a flux, by builders for lime mortar, and by farmers as a fertilizer. The stone itself was used locally for house building. In the 1890s the firm of Brunner Mond, later to become ICI, bought large quantities of limestone from here for their alkali works in Cheshire. Today the canal is only used by pleasure craft and the stone and cement are transported by lorries. The Blue Circle Cement works can be seen quite clearly from the A52, between Leek and Ashbourne, near Waterhouse. In ancient times copper and lead were also mined in the Cauldon area.

The Staffordshire Peak Arts Centre is located in the Old School, Cauldon Lowe, on the A52. All manner of local arts and crafts are exhibited and most of the goods displayed are for sale. There is also a restaurant specializing in whole foods and a snack bar.

Caldon Grange, 0.5m SE of Cauldon, was a grange of Buildwas Abbey in Shropshire.

CAVERSWALL *2.5m E of Longton*
Caverswall lies just beyond the suburban growth of the Potteries and is still very much a place with its own character. It has a superb castle and two churches, and north of these a little village square. There was a castle here in medieval times, (Licence to Crenellate was given in 1275), but in 1614 Matthew Craddock had the present fortified house built within the old castle. (Matthew Craddock came from a wealthy wool merchant family based in Stafford.) A dry moat surrounds the balustraded inner gardens in which the house stands tall, elegant and most handsome. At the corners of the moat wall are polygonal towers. The house is approached via a bridge that leads to a small gatehouse. As late as the last century the moat held water, and old pictures show the castle apparently sitting amidst a lake.

Ownership of the castle passed through several hands until it was purchased by a long-established, local Roman Catholic family, the Coyneys; and in 1811 they gave it as a convent for Benedictine nuns from Ghent, who had fled in fear of the excesses of the French Revolution. In this century it was still in the hands of the nuns who ran it as a kind of guest house. When they left it became somewhat run-down. About 20 years ago it was bought by a businessman and restored as a private house.

There are two churches, one on either side of the entrance drive to the Castle. The parish church of St Peter has a long nave with an arcade rebuilt in the 17th Century, a long chancel and a Perpendicular tower. There are monuments to the Craddocks and the Parkers of Park Hall, Longton. Outstanding amongst these is the monument of 1818, by Chantrey, to Countess St Vincent, who was the wife of Admiral Parker and daughter of Lord Chief Baron Parker.

However, the treasure of St Peter's is the remnant of a tympanum discovered during restoration work in 1962. The sill of the east window in the north aisle was removed and the underside was found to be carved. It was determined that the stone had formed a part of a 12th Century tympanum (the area between the lintel and the arch above a doorway). This had been removed in the 13th Century and left outside for some considerable time. (The marks of grass roots were found.) The back of the stone was then cut into shape to form a windowsill, the carved side being embedded into the mortar. The carving consists of a human figure between two griffins, with wings and feathered bodies and four-clawed feet. The top half of the picture is missing.

Scholars have concluded that the carving represents the celestial journey of Alexander the Great. Alexander wished to ascend to heaven. He sat in a basket attached to two eagles. To encourage the eagles to fly upwards he attached meat to the ends of long rods and held these above their heads. In art this story became modified. The basket became a quadriga and was then confused with the bottom half of Alexander's dress. The rods became sceptres. The philosophical meaning of the story here was man in communion with animals, not 'pride before a fall' as is sometimes represented. The carving is on display inside the church.

On the other side of the entrance to the castle is the Roman Catholic church of St Filomena, of 1864, designed by Gilbert Blount.

CHAPEL CHORLTON 7m NE Stone

Chapel Chorlton is most easily approached by turning off the A51 at the Cock Inn, Stableford. The lane heads south-west, uphill. Near the top of the hill, on the left-hand side, is a rusty five-bar gate near a little wood. This leads to one of the old sandstone quarries for which the village was once famous. The rock face has been earthed over and grass now grows on the steep slope, but the stone can be seen at surface outcrops only feet away from the gate. This stone is fine, white and stain-free, and was used for prestige buildings.

At the top of the hill is the large, triangular village green with an oak tree near the centre. The ground is slightly marshy in places. On the north edge of the green is a large, reed-edged pool. The whole area is pleasantly open, with only a handful of red brick farms and a white stuccoed cottage to take advantage of the views over the forest of Swynnerton Old Park to the north-east.

The small church of St Laurence lies slightly downhill, on the lane to Lower Hatton. It stands on a high mound with two ancient yew trees, one of which is hollow. The stone tower is medieval but was remodelled by James Trubshaw (Junior) in 1826, who also rebuilt the nave and chancel in ashlar. The nave has five windows and the east window has a lunette. The pulpit is Jacobean. Opposite the church is Schoolhouse Farm, a large, red brick complex. All in all, Chapel Chorlton is a charming place.

Along the lane to Maer from Chapel Chorlton are some new houses, perched on the edge of the high ground. Just past these a right-hand turn leads down a delightful deep and wooded hill to the main road. This is the eastern fringe of

Hill Chorlton, where are located the grey grim bastions of the Kennels of the North Staffordshire Hunt. Near a farm called Springfields there is an unusual old stone mill, rebuilt by the Duke of Sutherland and until recently almost forgotten; it was only Listed in 1987. It has now been renovated and converted into a dwelling house. Most of the village lies further west along the main road. The undulating wooded country between Stableford and Woore is really most attractive.

Stableford, 0.5m NE of Chapel Chorlton, is a fair-sized settlement, albeit one of caravan dwellers in a mobile-home park. It comes complete with a club called Madonna's and a large pub, the Cock Inn, which is boarded up at present and awaiting development. The main road here makes a nasty, right-angled turn to cross the Stafford to Crewe railway. The lane to the east takes one to the coniferous forests of the Hanchurch Hills, a place where the author often walks his dogs.

CHARTLEY HOLME *7m NE of Stafford*

The Anglo-Saxon Earl Algar held it before the Norman Conquest when it passed to the king. Today, the hamlet is small and scattered around the Stafford to Uttoxeter road, east of Weston. There are a few cottages, two blocks of modern semi-detached houses, a medieval castle and the Old Hall. Hidden behind a hill is another attraction, far less well known - the large 'quaking bog' of Chartley Moss. The settlement is located on the edge of the Trent Valley, on the hills of the attractive rolling country that stretches from Chartley to Uttoxeter. The view from the mound of the castle keep is well worth the short climb. There are three ancient sites: the castle itself, possibly built within the earthworks of a previous prehistoric fort; the moated Hall to the west; and a rectangular earthwork on the hill to the north.

The original castle was probably of timber, built by Ranulph de Gernon, the Earl of Chester, and was in existence by at least 1153. In 1232, on the death of his grandson, Ranulphe de Blundeville, also Earl of Chester, the castle passed to William de Ferrers, 4th Earl of Derby, who had married Ranulph's sister, Agnes de Blundeville. In the early 13th Century the castle was rebuilt in stone. It has a motte (keep mound), and two baileys (enclosures) protected by walls and towers. The walls are 12 feet thick and the towers have arrow slits. The inner bailey is 83 yards long by 43 yards wide, and the outer bailey is 66 yards long by 60 yards wide. There is an engraved cross, a mark that the builder had been on a crusade to the Holy Land.

In 1461 the castle passed by marriage to Walter Deveraux, who was created Baron Ferrers in the same year. By that time the castle had already been abandoned and a moated timber manor house, Chartley Hall, had been built at the foot of the hill, just to the west. By 1540 the castle was in ruins. In 1575 Queen Elizabeth I visited the Hall and stayed for 10 days. The queen was entertained at Chartley by her cousin, Lettice, who had married the 1st Earl of Essex, the grandson of Walter Deveraux. Robert, the son of the 1st Earl, would almost certainly have been at Chartley then and would have met the queen. The following year his father died and Robert became the 2nd Earl of Essex. He was introduced to Court and became the Queen's favourite. He so arranged things in Staffordshire that he was able to nominate six of the county's 10 Members of Parliament in 1592. Subsequently, he lost his earldom and was executed in 1601 after an attempted rebellion.

On the accession of James I in 1603 the 2nd Earl's son, also Robert, was restored as the 3rd Earl. During the Civil War he was the parliamentary commander-in-chief. In 1646 he died childless and the Chartley estate passed eventually to Sir Robert Shirley, the grandson of the 3rd Earl's sister. In 1677 he was created Baron Ferrers and in 1711 his son became the 4th Earl Ferrers. In 1760 the 4th Earl killed his steward. His punishment was death. Somewhat bizarrely, he dressed himself as a bridegroom and was driven in his state landau to Tyburn Hill in London, where he was hanged before a crowd of 200,000 people.

From December 1585 to September 1586 Mary Queen of Scots was held captive at Chartley Hall before being taken to Fotheringay Castle, in Northampton, where she was duly tried and executed. It was whilst she was staying at Chartley Hall that Gilbert Giffard of Chillington smuggled letters to and from her in beer barrels and laid the trap that was the Babington Plot.

In 1781 Chartley Hall was accidentally burned to the ground. The present house was built in 1847 but an older wing survives at the back. It is approached along a wooded avenue and lies within the old moat. To the front of the house is the lake, which forms part of the moat, and beyond that are the ruins of the castle and the park. There are woods all about and the setting is delightful. The Hall remained in the hands of the Shirley family until 1905 when it was sold. There have been several owners since.

On the hillside north of the castle is an earthwork. It is a perfect rectangle, measuring 57 yards by 31 yards, with a bank and ditch on the longer sides and a ditch only along the shorter sides. It is marked on the Ordnance Survey map as a moat but has yet to be properly investigated.

From time immemorial the Chartley estate was the home of the famous wild Chartley cattle. These were a pale tan in colour, with black ears and long curved horns. They are believed to have been descended from the prehistoric British Aurochs that roamed wild in nearby Needwood Forest. In the early part of this century they were struck down by disease and the survivors cross-bred with Longhorn cattle. Their progeny are now at the Duke of Bedford's Estate at Woburn.

Half-a-mile along the main road towards Uttoxeter is Chartley Manor Farm House, a good early 17th Century, black-and-white, timber-framed building with gables. It stands on higher ground than the castle and the road that climbs the hill has some misleading bends, which have been the cause of several fatal car accidents.

Across the fields, less than 0.5m S of Chartley Manor Farm, is **Chartley Moss**. It lies on the western edge of the wood and adjoins the overgrown track of the disused railway. (The Moss is centred on SK 021279). This is a very special place. It has been virtually untouched by man since its formation in a glacial hollow 20,000 years ago. It looks today much as it did then. In a basin, 70 feet deep, is a pool of muddy water. On the water floats a thick layer of peat and sphagnum moss. As one walks across the surface of the Moss it moves, or trembles, and for this reason is called a 'Quaking Bog' or Schwing-moor. Trees grow in the peat layer but as they grow taller and heavier they slowly begin to sink and small black pools appear around their boles. When they exceed about 24 feet in height they become unstable and collapse. Because of the special conditions here there are many rare plants. The site is not only the best example of its kind in Britain, but is probably the best of its kind in the whole of Europe. The Moss is a Nature Reserve of the Nature Conservancy Council and entry is by permit only. Surrounding the Moss is an Area of Special Scientific Interest.

The whole site covers 104 acres. Anyone venturing on to Chartley Moss should remember that it can be very dangerous. In particular, beware of areas where trees do not grow; it probably means that the peat cannot take their weight. Snakes, especially adders, are here in great numbers and in the summer there are some very nasty biting insects. This is a wild and interesting, but potentially dangerous, place. To the south and west are drainage ditches.

A mile north-east of the Manor Farm, along the road to Uttoxeter, is the hamlet of **Grindley**. The houses lie along the lane to the south-east and there is no sign of a village on the main road. Between the main road and the disused railway line is the site of **Grindley Forge** (SK 043296). It lies on the land of Grindley Forge Farm. Here are the remains of an early 17th Century forge. There is a large mound of black earth and forge cinder, and the leat and forge stream still survive. The leat drew water from the River Blythe. This forge worked 'rough iron' and produced 'merchant bar'. The supplies of iron came mainly from Meir Heath and Vale Royal (in Cheshire).

CHASETOWN *4m S of Cannock on the A5190*
The village did not exist before about 1850 and was built to house the colliers who worked in the nearby pits. The Cannock Chase coalfield was heavily exploited in the second half of the 19th Century. By 1900 there were some 40 mines in the area. It is a dull, drab place of endless rows of modern houses and straight roads, and is noticeably lacking in trees for somewhere so close to Cannock Chase. All around are slag-heaps and waste land, a dismal place like Brownhills which adjoins it to the north.

The church of St Anne at Chasetown is most unusual. It was built in 1865 to the design of Edward Adams, who worked for the South Staffordshire Railway Company and the South Staffordshire Waterworks. It is neo-Norman, of red, purple and black brick. It does not have a tower and the nave and chancel are as one, with a low apse and high windows. Inside, are brick columns with Romanesque capitals inlaid with black, jagged arches and an open timber roof. There is a marble bust of John Robinson McClean, a local coal owner, who founded the church.

Tom Langley, a retired policeman who wrote the ballad, 'The Darlaston Dogfight', and was the author of many books on pugilists, including the Tipton Slasher, was born at Chasetown and educated at Lichfield Grammar School. The author met him at his home whilst researching Black Country folklore and found him to be a most gentle, self-effacing and pleasant man, despite his interest in such gory subjects.

CHATCULL *3m NW of Eccleshall*
Chatcull is a small rural village in lovely rolling country that laughs at weary travellers lost in the lanes trying to find it. In Domesday Book it is Ceterville and is described as 'waste'. The name probably means 'Ceadd's kiln', the suffix 'cull' being from the Middle English 'culne', a 'kiln'. Chatcull Old Hall, an irregular brick and stone house with substantial farm buildings, is said to have a core dating from the mid-12th Century. The Gervoyse, later Jervis, family were here by the mid-14th Century. In the 17th Century Elizabeth Jervis of Chatcull married into the Jervis family of Meaford (near Stone). Elizabeth I is said to have stayed at the Old Hall.

Admiral John Jervis (1734-1823) of Meaford Hall was a frequent visitor to Chatcull (New) Hall, a 'Georgianesque' house with a tower in rather good grounds with a high walled garden. Whilst we were there the sound of sporting gun fire disturbed the peaceful solitude of this place, but was compensated for by the delightful smell of wood smoke.

CHEADLE *8m NW Uttoxeter*

Cheadle is an unassuming little market town that stands on a hill in the Moorlands of North Staffordshire. There are several good houses in the High Street: the Police House with ashlar front, fluted capitals around the doorway and Venetian windows; the Wheatsheaf Inn with a Tuscan porch; and No. 77 with its timber-framing and decorative motifs. The Market Cross is probably of the 17th Century. The Market Place is an open area off the High Street, formed by the setting back of a terrace of late-Georgian, three-storey houses. In Tape Street the large textile mill of J & N Philips once stood, but this was mostly dismantled in 1973. Only the warehouse remains with its central pediment. In Watt's Place is the former Workhouse of 1775.

The dominant building in Cheadle is the lavish, red-stone Roman Catholic **church of St Giles**, built in 1841-6 by Pugin. The Earl of Shrewsbury, of nearby Alton Towers, commissioned and paid for the church. Pugin was told to spare no expense and decoration here runs riot; indeed, the overall style is Decorated. The steeple is a very good piece of Gothic revival with a sharp spire and two sets of pinnacles. Inside, the church is painted throughout and stenciled with crowns, crosses, flowers and trellises - a colourful place. The church has a matching school, the Convent of St Joseph, and a Priest's House (in Chapel Street).

The Anglican parish church is also called St Giles and was built in 1837-9 to a Perpendicular design by J P Pritchett. It stands on higher ground, on the other side of the High Street, and replaced the medieval church. There is a Toll-house of 1833 by George E Hamilton, 0.5m SW of the town centre, on the Cheadle to Blythe Marsh and Calton Moor Road.

Woodhead Old Hall, 1.25m NE of Cheadle, was demolished in 1719. The present house was built for W S Allen in 1873. The architect was William Sugden. From 1937 it was used by the Ministry of Defence as a wireless communications' centre. By 1994 it was the property of the Crown. There were many aerial masts in the vicinity and it was said to be a 'government listening station'. This closed in about 2000 and some new houses are appearing.

The Woodhead Plateway (completed in 1827) was built to carry coal from the Shower Pits at Woodhead Colliery to East Wall, where it joined the Uttoxeter Canal. On the reverse journey lime was taken to the Cheadle road at Woodhead Wharf. In the wall fronting the road can be seen stone sleeper blocks with iron spikes that were taken from the now-dismantled plateway. A double-track inclined plane, 900 feet long, ran through Gibridding Wood. The Woodhead Colliery pits closed in the 1890s because of badly faulted seams.

Hales Hall, 0.75m ENE of Cheadle, lies just off the B471, Cheadle to Oakamoor road. It is dated at 1712 and is very much in Queen Anne style: tall windows, hipped roof, brick with even stone quoins, three dormers and two storeys. It is now used as the nucleus of a caravan and camping site.

The Hales Hall Pool is 'a special wildlife wetland open to the public', and has a good car park off the main road. Opposite the entrance to the car park is a most surprising large building, which is a kind of architectural jigsaw puzzle. It is called Hales View Farm but the strange brick buildings are not old farm buildings but are the work of Les Oakes (died about 2001), who came here in 1960 and set up his architectural reclamation business. His son now runs this and continues to store the approximately 700 horse-drawn vehicles the family has collected. This is an historically important private collection.

The name Hales is from Chief Justice Sir Matthew Hales, one of four lawyers who were each bequeathed a quarter share of the Cheadle Grange estate in 1653. In 1947 the Hall was the property of the Air Ministry, presumably in conjunction with the Wireless Communications' Centre at nearby Woodhead Hall, already mentioned.

There were several long flame coal mines in the Cheadle area; the last was Foxfield. In the 12th Century iron was mined at 'le Brodedelph'. In the 18th Century copper from the Ecton mine was smelted near the town. In medieval times Cheadle lay on the Salt Road used by packhorse trains travelling between Nantwich and Derby.

In 1686 Dr Plot, on his journey through Staffordshire, says he saw conical houses made entirely of turf in the Cheadle area. We tend to forget that up to about the beginning of the 18th Century the houses of poor country people were often little more than mud huts. They were made of 'cob', earth and cow manure, and were white-washed to make them waterproof, and roofed with thatch and turf. Such buildings can, if properly maintained, be quite durable as evidenced by those that exist in Cornwall today. However, they soon disintegrate if left unattended and almost literally melt away, leaving little sign that they ever existed. We recollect a farmer in Churchtown, near Mainstone in Shropshire, telling us that he could remember just such primitive dwellings in a state of collapse on the hillside above the church there.

Freehay, 1.5m SE of Cheadle, is a spread-about village centred on a crossroads. At least it was a crossroads, but rather carelessly it has lost one limb of its cross. The lane northwards from the new roundabout has been swallowed up by one of the five quarries that surround the village. The lane is now a cul-de-sac, at the end of which is a viewing platform with a security barrier and an information board that overlooks the huge gravel quarry with its precipitous banks and lake.

The Hulland and Lawley Quarries were opened in the 1930s; then, in the late 1940s Walter Dinwoodie, a mining engineer, acquired grave-bearing land at Freehay, and in 1951 the Croxden Quarry Company was formed. These quarries were one of the largest, if not the largest, providers of gravel in Europe, with an output of two million tons a year.

Tarmac now operate the quarries, most of which are hidden from sight behind earth walls and small woods, but a glance at the Ordnance Survey map shows how they virtually encircle Freehay.

There is no real centre to the village. It is a scattered community in attractive country, and we spotted a couple of very nice traditional stone cottages on the lane to Winndale. There is a pub, the Queen's, by the roundabout and the parish church of St Chad, 0.75m SW of the pub.

St Chad's (1842-3) is a simple, grey stone, chapel-like building with a bellcote, lancet windows and a steeply-pitched roof. The architects were Scott and Moffatt. Adjacent to the church is the school and schoolhouse, also in grey stone. The ensemble is embowered in tall trees and makes a handsome group.

Mobberley, 1m WSW of Freehay, is a small hamlet on the A521, Cheadle to Uttoxeter road, in the Tean Valley. There are Tarmac sand and gravel quarries to the south and west. At Mobberley the two head-water streams of the River Tean meet and from this confluence the Tean is said to start.

At the road junction is the substantial, cream-painted Queen's pub. This faces a clutter of old rusting cars and vans. A few yards up the hill, in the direction of Uttoxeter, is K & K café and the road passes through a rock cutting.

A little further on again is the right-hand turn to **Huntley**, 1.25m S of Cheadle. The lane dips to the valley bottom, passes a 10-bay building (now a smart house), crosses over the River Tean and then under the railway bridge. The village of Huntley immediately appears, a very nucleated, huddled settlement of farm buildings, cottages and bungalows.

The lane south takes one to **Teanford**, a watery place but the ford is long gone. The River Tean is little more than a stream. The community is scattered. Only a terrace of six humble cottages and a recent house with haughty pretensions, locked behind security gates, stand by the river. On the main road to A521 is the Anchor Inn.

Winnothdale, 1m SE of Freehay, is a scattered hamlet of farmsteads and cottages centred on a country lane crossroads in a most pleasant dale. The red brick Methodist chapel, known as The Chapel in the Valley, was built in 1899, closed in 1969 and is now boarded-up and looking very sorry for itself.

CHEBSEY 5m NW of Stafford

Chebsey lies just north of the A5013, Stafford to Eccleshall road. The country from here, westwards to the border with Shropshire, is most attractive. The village lies close to the River Sow, which is joined by the Meece Brook less than a mile to the south-west. It is a quiet place of old cottages, Victorian houses and some modern villas, not especially pretty but quite pleasant.

The Norman church lies on an ancient site, high-mounded with a watery ditch forming an enclosure to the south-west. In the churchyard are the remains of an Anglo-Saxon cross, a thick round shaft becoming square and decorated mainly with interlace. There was almost certainly an Anglo-Saxon church here, and before that quite probably a timber stockade-fort. The present church has a Norman window in the north chancel, a Norman window in the north nave, a late Norman north doorway, several shallow Norman buttresses and Norman masonry. The four-bay south arcade, the south doorways and the chancel arch are Early English and the tower, with its eight pinnacles, is Perpendicular. There are several William Kempe, and Kempe and Tower windows. Wriothesley Noel, who died at sea in 1941, whilst serving with the Royal Navy, is commemorated by a tablet. He was descended from Robert and Celestia Noel, who founded nearby Ranton Abbey in 1147. (See Ranton.)

In Domesday Book Chebsey, called Cebbisio, is recorded as having 20 villagers, 9 smallholders and a priest with land for 12 ploughs. The village was owned by Henry Ferrers and within the manor was the land on which Stafford Castle was built. This would have been the castle at Broadeye, near the present windmill. It had been built on the orders of the King but was destroyed prior to 1086, also on the orders of the King, because some of the Anglo-Saxon lords in the area had been rebellious.

Walton Hall, 0.5m SW of Chebsey on the Eccleshall to Great Bridgford road, is a substantial Victorian house in Classical style, dated at 1848. It has good ashlar masonry and at the back there is a very large coach-porch with impressive Tuscan columns. It is now a school and there are some unfortunate modern structures scattered about in the grounds. The tiny hamlet of Walton lies 0.5m ESE of the Hall. Waltonhurst, a house, lies in splendid isolation, 0.5m S of the Hall, at the end of a long, dead-end lane.

Norton Bridge, 1m NE of Chebsey, is a small settlement close to the Meece Brook. The railway station opened in 1837. The railway from Stafford branches here, one line going to Stoke and the other to Crewe. The mission church of St Luke was built in 1893 and there is a large white stucco pub, The Railway. The red brick Junction Farm has curious, large-diamond, cast-iron windows. A rusty grey grim footbridge leads over the tracks to the new holt-style station platform; most of the trains hurtle by without stopping. Norton, of course, means 'north-town'. As to the bridges, there are three: the two main-road bridges over the Crewe line and the Meece Brook, and the Stoke line over the Meece Brook. There is a Quaker burial ground, marked by a stand of trees about 0.5m from Norton station, on the north side of the Chebsey to Shallowford road. The last burial was in 1859.

Shallowford, 1m NE of Chebsey, is a tiny hamlet made famous by the presence of Izaac Waltons's cottage. The author of 'The Compleat Angler' spent a lot of time here in his later years. The River Sow passes close by, as does the electrified Inter-City Railway line with its hideous overhead electric supply cables and their supporting gantries. The cottage we see today has been very heavily restored. It had previously been terribly neglected and then burned. The external restoration is not altogether sympathetic, though it is better inside where there is a small museum. The cottage is now owned by Stafford Borough Council. They have installed a resident caretaker who, amongst other things, cultivates the now well-established Herb Garden.

Worston Mill, 1.5m SE of Chebsey, is now a pub-restaurant. Part of the old mill machinery has been renovated and is on public display. It is believed that there might be a lost medieval village in the vicinity of the mill. Wilmot Martin (1875-1963), the 'Staffordshire Harry Lauder', was born at Worston Mill. His father was a corn miller. The mill wheel was driven by the waters of the River Sow.

CHECKLEY *4m* NW *of Uttoxeter*

This really is the most unassuming but charming little village, having a variety of mature properties with flowers in the gardens and evergreen trees in the churchyard. The ancient grey stone church faces the mellow red brick Red Lion and there are meadows down to the River Tean, which is crossed here by a ford. Most of the village lies along a side lane to the West of the Cheadle to Uttoxeter road and is therefore traffic free. Only the Victorian School stands on the main road. There is a friendly feel to the place and even their resident ghost is far from frightening. This is the spirit of a little white dog that walks through the walls of the Rectory.

At the time of Domesday Book there were 3 villagers, land for 3.1/2 ploughs and 2 acres of meadow. There is rather more of everything now but the church of St Mary and All Saints is the subject of greatest interest here. Some 25 feet from the south porch are fragments of two (and perhaps three) Anglo-Saxon or Danish crosses, decorated with interlace and figures believed to be bishops killed by the Danes in a battle at **Deadmans Green**, 0.5m SE on the A522. However, there are other folk tale explanations of that name.

The present church at Checkley is a Norman foundation. The 15th Century tower rises from a massive Norman base; the Jacobean porch encloses the 13th Century doorway; the clerestory and north aisle windows are 17th Century; the chancel and chancel arch are late Norman and very fine; the front gate is also

Norman and has carvings of an ass and palm trees. In the chancel is some lovely 14th Century narrative stained glass. The stalls are of 1535 with carved poppy heads. Amongst the monuments are a cross-Iegged knight of the early 14th Century; the tomb of Godfrey Foljambe (sic), died 1560, and his wife; and memorials to the Philips family, 18th Century mill owners in nearby Tean. Three of the family have been vicars here.

CHEDDLETON *2.25m S of Leek*

The village lies around the A53, on a hillside above the River Churnet, in moorland country south of Leek. Alongside the river are the Caldon Canal and the track of the old Churnet Valley Railway; there is a Railway Museum here. In 1086 the manor was owned by Earl Roger and there were 3 villagers, 1 smallholder and land for 4 ploughs. Historical references to early industry are scanty. In 1413 the Abbot of Dieulacres Abbey, along with others, stole ironstone from William Egerton's Park at Cheddleton. There was a Silk Mill here but all we know is that it had ceased production by 1838. There was a weaving industry, as is evidenced by some three-storey weavers' cottages, and today there is a large agricultural engineering firm called Batemans.

There has also been a tradition of paper making at Cheddleton. In 1797 Mr William Adams built a paper mill that was later taken over by the Fourdrinier brothers. This large works is now operated by Brittain Ltd. They make specialist thin tissues for the pottery industry as well as carbon, insulating, transfer and cigarette papers.

However, it is for the Flint Mills that Cheddleton is famous. They lie alongside, and to the west of, the main road. There was a mill at Cheddleton in the 13th Century and there have been mills there ever since. The south mill (the one adjacent to the Miller's Cottage) was originally used to grind corn, but in the first half of the 18th Century it was converted to crush calcined flint. Flint was used in pottery production, first in stoneware and later cream earthenware, to give the material extra hardness, whiteness and the ability to withstand high temperatures. At first the flints were smashed with iron balls in iron pans, but this created a terrible dust and caused pneumoconiosis - a disease which destroys the lungs. In 1732 Thomas Benson patented a 'wet' method, which was admirably suited to the machinery already installed in the old water mills.

The process at Cheddleton was typical. The flints were calcined (that is heated to make the stones more brittle), broken up in a Marsden Granulator, loaded into a small wagon and trundled to the mill where they were crushed. The wet slip was then dried in a Drying Kiln, cut into slabs called 'cakes' and transported to the Potteries. The North Mill was built by James Brindley, in about 1756-65, specifically to grind flint. Brindley surveyed the route of the Caldon Canal but died in 1772. The Canal was completed in 1777 and greatly facilitated the transport of the flints from Kent and Sussex to the mills at Cheddleton, and the finished 'cake' to the Potteries. The mills were operated until 1963. In 1967 they were sold to a charitable trust who maintain and keep them open for the public. There is no entrance charge. It is a charming site and contains the original equipment and buildings in surprising completeness. It is also a real place, not tarted up for tourists.

The parish church of St Edward stands high on the hill, above the river, overlooking the mills. It is built of stone, as are most of the older buildings in Cheddleton, and is approached up Hollow Lane, off the main road. For company it has a row of traditional cottages and the low-ceilinged Black Lion pub. St

Edward's has a high Perpendicular tower and south arcade, an Early English north arcade and a very good Decorated chancel. The windows are also Decorated, except for the large east window and south aisle windows. These are by the son of George Gilbert Scott, who restored the church in 1863. The interior was largely decorated in Victorian times and of special interest are the stained glass windows by William Morris. Thomas Wardle, a friend of Morris, was a church-warden here. He owned a silk-dying factory at Leek Brook. The church contains work by Morris from 1864 to 1869, during which period his style matured considerably. He also added wings to a 15th Century Flemish relief of the Annunciation, making it into a fine Triptych. There is also a window with three large angels by Burne Jones in the south of the south aisle. The lecturn is a striking Flemish brass eagle and there is a Gothic tablet of the Fynney family. The school and library were also remade by Scott (Junior), prior to 1871.

In the valley there is a small, pretty railway station in neo-Tudor style, built by the North Staffordshire Railway Company in 1849 and now the heart of a Railway Museum. Half-a-mile north of the river is the County Mental Hospital, now called St Edwards Hospital, a large Victorian neo-Elizabethan building with a central block of brick and a tower of 1895-9. The whole complex is now being developed for private residential use.

The Potteries' Folk Club currently meets at the Red Lion in Cheadle Road, Cheddleton. For many years this club has been run by Jason Hill of Burslem, one of the unsung heroes of the Folk Revival and a talented musician and singer.

Cheddleton Heath, 0.5m NE of Cheddleton, was once common land and is now a hamlet. In 1945 a Mosquito KB 206 crashed on Cheddleton Heath killing the two crew members. By 1379 there was a deer park in Cheddleton, now lost.

Ashcombe Park lies 0.75m south of the village. It is set in a small park and the house was built between 1807 and 1811, by James Trubshaw, for a junior branch of the Sneyd family of Keele Park. The house is of ashlar, with two storeys, four projecting bays and a Tuscan coach-porch. (In 1994 we made a brief visit but could not find the house, only a sewage works by the river.)

Shaffalong, 0.5m SW of Cheddleton, is a quaintly-named hamlet and a coalfield area. Mining ceased here in 1912.

The **Deep Hayes** Reservoir, 0.75m WNW of Cheddleton, was built to supply the River Churnet, to compensate for water extracted from tributary streams, but problems occurred in 1979 and it was abandoned. Later, it was redeveloped into three pools and the valley became the Deep Hayes Country Park.

Basford Green, 0.75m SE of Cheddleton, is a small hamlet. Basford Hall was home to the Debanks, Sneyds, Bradshaws and the Scott-Moncrieffs. By 1948 it was a school for maladjusted children. In the grounds is a Bathhouse, designed as a sham castle and built in 1841, and an ice house built into the side of the hill by French prisoners of war in 1824. At SJ 988513 there is a Quaker burial ground. A small stone barn was once a Quaker meeting house.

CHURCH EATON *5m SW of Stafford*
Church Eaton lies in flat and plain but pleasant country to the south-west of the county town. There are several old cottages and one in particular, near the church, has recently been totally restored and re-thatched. Just around the corner is a neo-Tudor Victorian Hall. The village straggles along the main street, and has not been too badly affected by new house building.

The church of St Editha stands on a high, roughly-circular mound, the probable site of a prehistoric or Anglo-Saxon fort. The tower is Norman, late

12th to early 13th Century, as are the west wall and the arch to the nave. The spire is 15th Century, the north wall is Decorated, and the north chapel and the enormous seven-light east chancel window are Perpendicular. (Local people say that this window came from Old St Paul's in London.) The broken font is Norman. Most of the stained glass, including that in the east chancel window, was designed by Kempe between 1893 and 1906. The vicarage is of 1712, a substantial house approached by a long drive.

The advowson (the right to choose the vicar of a parish) of Church Eaton was bitterly and protractedly fought over, over a period of 200 years in the Middle Ages, and involved none other than the Pope and Edward II.

From at least 1620 there was a Grammar School at Church Eaton. It stood in the churchyard until 1857 and was demolished shortly after the First World War. The site of the medieval Manor House of Church Eaton has not been located.

The Shropshire Union Canal traverses the country here in short straight sections, connected by several gentle dog-leg bends. In 1066 Church Eaton (called Eitone) was owned by the Saxon Wilgrip. After the Norman Conquest it was given to Henry Ferrers. In 1086 it was a sizeable settlement with 8 villagers, 8 smallholders and their families and a priest. It is now believed that the Domesday Book omitted up to two-thirds of the people in Staffordshire because they owed no feudal services to the local Lord of the Manor. The Lord of the Manor here was Godric (he held it from Henry Ferrers), and he had three serfs or slaves. By 1340 there was a fulling mill at Church Eaton, though it probably only processed local wool for local markets.

One mile south-west of Church Eaton, over the canal, is **St Editha's Well** (SJ 836164). The well has a sandstone lining and steps, and is covered by a shelter which consisted of a thatched roof supported by four wooden posts. The thatch has now rotted away. The well can be seen from the bridge over the canal, but it is not easily approached from here because of the electric fences, barbed wire and deep ditches of a horse breeding establishment. The best route is from Little Onn and through a dairy farm on whose land it is situated.

Little Onn, 1m S of Church Eaton, is a settlement that stretches for half-a-mile to the west of the Shropshire Union Canal. It lies at the foot of the hill on which stands High Onn. Little Onn Hall, 1.5m SW of Church Eaton, is Victorian Gothic, of about 1870-5, with later additions and alterations. It looks quite impressive when glimpsed through the trees that surround it - large, rock-faced with a turret and gables. The gardens were laid out by T H Mawson and the Summerhouse is also by him.

High Onn, 1.25m SW of Church Eaton, is a small hilltop hamlet. Just to the west of the settlement is the route of the Roman road, which ran from Watling Street at Stretton to the west of Market Drayton. In Welsh 'onn' means 'ashtree'. Windmill Field, at SJ 827162, probably marks the site of a long-gone, medieval windmill. There may have been a deserted medieval village by High Onn Manor, a once-moated house demolished and rebuilt in the 19th Century. By 1230 the early house was held by the Priory of Ware in Hertfordshire.

Wood Eaton Hall, 1.5m SW of Church Eaton, is of 1755 by William Baker, and is built in brick with three bays and a central gable. South-west of Little Onn is a disused wartime aerodrome with a scatter of derelict buildings, romantic in association and looking very forlorn. Its official name was RAF Wheaton Aston. Between 1941 and 1947 it was a training school, and during the Second World War was one of the busiest in the county. The track of a Roman road runs through the site. The airfield was abandoned in the late 1940s and is now a pig farm. On the southern boundary of the aerodrome is the delightfully named Shushions Manor, an early 19th Century house with a moated site to the east.

Joan Eaton was a witch and was reputedly burned at the stake at the junction of lanes (SJ 839171) just to the south-east of Church Eaton, marked by a small triangular patch of grass. There was a cross here, but there is no more. One of the stories told about Joan Eaton is this: she was challenged by the farmer of Red House Farm, Little Onn, that she could not milk his best cow dry. She tried and tried but the cow grew restless, kicked Joan off her stool, broke loose from her tie and ran to Worcester ,some 30 miles away, where she died and was buried by the cathedral. As she broke loose, the cow left an imprint of her hoof on a boulder. The witch, Joan Eaton, cursed this stone and said that should it ever be moved all the cattle on Red House Farm would die. Many years later, the curse almost forgotten, a Colonel Ashton moved the stone and all the cattle on Red House Farm died soon afterwards.

Apeton, 0.5m NE of Church Eaton, is a hamlet clustered around a circle of lanes. On the road to Bradley there is a ford. In Domesday Book the name was Abetone, meaning 'Abba's homestead'.

Allimore Green, 1m NE of Church Eaton, is a small hamlet with a Common of Wetland Meadow, which is an SSSI in the care of the Staffordshire Wildlife Trust. The name Allimore means 'the path through the marsh'.

CHURCH LEIGH *4.5m WNW of Uttoxeter*

Prehistoric finds in the parish include a bronze spearhead, a Neolithic or Bronze Age stone axe and a perforated, naturally-shaped stone. In Domesday Book the settlement is called Lege, Anglo-Saxon meaning 'meadow or pasture'. The village of Church Leigh lies on a hill, south of the A50 trunk road, between Uttoxeter and Cheadle. It is the centre of a scatter of hamlets with similar names - **Upper Leigh**, **Lower Leigh** and **Dods Leigh**.

The country around is attractive, though unspectacular, but the church of All Saints is a surprise. It is a large, commanding ashlar structure built by Thomas Johnson of Lichfield in 1846, and paid for by the Bagot family of Blithfield. It lies on the highest point in the village. The tower is at the crossing and incorporates parts of the previous church. The style is uniformly Decorated with consistently accurate details of ornament. Especially noteworthy is the stone rib-vaulting of the tower and chancel. There is old stained glass in the south-east and north-east chancel windows, including a 14th Century crucifixion and other figures. The Victorians are also well represented with glass by C A Gibbs, Burne Jones and William Morris. The church had a curfew bell which was rung each evening at eventide until 1940.

There is a pub, The Star, and several large brick houses with an ominous development of new villas at the entrance to the church.

Park Hall lies 0.5m N of Church Leigh. It has good wrought iron entrance gates and close to the house is an old moat, presumably the site of the medieval farmstead. At the back of the Hall is a wood called Hell Clough. At Upper Leigh is the modest but attractive Manor House of three bays, 2.5 storeys and a hipped roof, set at the end of a long drive that commences at Lower Leigh and traverses the park in which three donkeys were grazing at the time of our visit. There is a village green at Lower Leigh. To the east of Church Leigh is the curiously-named Nobut Hall and the hamlets of **Upper Nobut** and **Lower Nobut**. The name Nobut could be derived from the Celtic Irish 'noeb', meaning 'holy', hence 'holy wood'.

CLAREGATE *2m NW of Wolverhampton*
The first element of the name could have several meanings depending on its derivation: the Welsh 'claear' meaning 'bright'; the Middle Welsh 'clayar' meaning 'gentle' (as of a slope); the Anglo-Saxon 'clayfren' meaning 'clover'; or a corruption of 'clay'. Today, Claregate is a residential area of mostly semi-detached houses, with more individual, detached dwellings on the road to **Palmers Cross**, which back on to the Golf Course. The centre lies around a crossroads - a few shops, a service station and the Claregate pub.

Down the slope to the east is **Aldersley Stadium**, where there are athletics' and cycling tracks and a shooting gallery. As a young man the author trained here before going on to win the Midlands' Decathlon Championship at Loughborough. The stadium stands beside the Staffordshire and Worcestershire Canal and overlooks the Dunstall Racecourse.

To the north is **Autherley Junction** where the Staffordshire and Worcestershire Canal joins the Shropshire Union. This is a pleasant spot of wide greens, trees and old canal buildings. There are several waterways-based businesses and numerous road and rail bridges, the most elegant of which is the curved canal bridge at the junction of the canals (best seen from Blaydon Road). There is also a very large sewage farm with an extraordinary number of cars parked within the security fencing.

North of Autherley is **Pendeford,** the site of an old wartime aerodrome. This was protected by American anti-aircraft guns at Coven Lawn, where the concrete emplacements still remain. The airfield is in the process of being developed and there is already a brand new Business Park and many acres of 'affordable housing', complete with shopping centre and Pendulum pub. On the Wobaston Road (which runs from Codsall to Fordhouses) are the numerous blue sheds of Dowty. They have taken over here from Boulton and Paul, an illustrious name in engineering and a company that did much in the development of the jump jet Harrier fighter aeroplane.

Pendeford Mill stood at SJ 889035, at the confluence of the Moat Brook and the River Penk. The mill house is now a pair of cottages but the mill was demolished in 1961. It has its footnote in history because Charles II called here on his flight after the Battle of Worcester in 1651. He had travelled from Boscobel on horseback but continued from Pendeford to Moseley Old Hall on foot. Later, the Reverend Henry Higginson, (known as the Roving Ranter'), a Primitive Methodist preacher, was born at Pendeford Mill(s) in 1805.

CLAYTON *See Newcastle-under-Lyme.*

CLIFTON CAMPVILLE *9m S of Burton upon Trent*
The name Clifton is Anglo-Saxon and means 'settlement on a slope', from 'clif', which to Anglians was not just a rocky precipice as it means today. The de Caunvil or Camville family were lords of the manor here from 1200 to 1315. They, in turn, took their name from Canappeville in Normandy.

The village lies in flat country watered by the River Mease. In 1086 the manor was owned by the King himself and it was a sizeable village with 33 villagers, 7 smallholders, 2 slaves and a priest, plus all those who did not owe service to the lord and who were therefore not recorded in Domesday Book.

Today, the village is dominated by the church of St Andrew with its tall elegant steeple (a term meaning the tower and spire together). It is a spacious building, largely of the 14th Century, and has some interior decoration of the same period: the south chapel screens, the seven misericords and the painting in the south aisle. There is a brass plate of a lady of about 1360, with a fragment of a knight on the back, and a fine alabaster monument to Sir John Vernon (died in 1545) and his wife, with some excellent sculptures around the tomb chest. In the chancel are non-figurative monuments by Rysbrack to Sir Charles Pye (died 1721) and Sir Robert Pye, the 4th and last Baronet (died 1734). There is a curiosity in the small north transept. Above the vaulted chapel, partially hidden by a modern oak screen, is a priest's chamber with a fireplace, a garderobe (lavatory) and a gilded crucifix in the medieval altar recess.

As to the rest of the village: the Vicarage stands to the north-east of the church, Manor Farm has a large brick dovecote and a square gazebo, and there has been the usual invasion of modern villas in the main street.

Less than 0.25m E is Clifton Campville's second curiosity, Clifton Hall. At the end of a rough track are two stately 18th Century brick pavilions, each of seven bays and each with two imposing doorways. These are in fact the two wings of the house, the centre part of which was never built. The architect was probably Francis Smith but his design was not completed because the owner, Sir Charles Pye, ran out of funds. However, he and his family and their descendants have lived there quite happily for some 200 years. Latterly, these noble structures have lain derelict and been used as farm store rooms.

Haunton, 1m W of Clifton Campville, is a hamlet with a Georgian Hall, which has a chapel of about 1848 by Charles Hansom. It became the Convent of St John of Bordeaux by the 1970s, a school by 1988 and an old people's home by 1995. The first element of the name Haunton is from an Anglo-Saxon personal name, such as 'Hagona'.

CODSALL *3m NW of Wolverhampton*

Codsall is basically a dormitory town for Wolverhampton, but amongst the acres of suburban housing is a pleasant shopping centre and a little railway station.

The church of St Nicholas is most pleasantly situated on high ground on the northern fringe of the settlement. It has a Norman south doorway, a restored Perpendicular tower and the rest is of 1846-8, in Decorated style, by E Banks of Wolverhampton. There is stained glass by O'Connor, of about 1870, and by H Bryans, of about 1900. Walter Wrottesley, died 1630, lies here in effigy.

A short distance north-east of the church, near the end of Mill Lane, is a red brick tower Windmill, now converted to a house. It was built some time before 1775 and in its heyday had four sails, a boat cap, a weather vane and a long tailpole. It was disused by the mid-1880s.

Sir Charles Wheeler, sculptor and President of the Royal Academy from 1956 to 1966, was born at 12 Church Road, Codsall.

Leper House Farm, 0.5m N, is an 'L'-shaped, timber-framed building of 1716 clad in old red brick. It is connected to the church by an ancient pathway. Tradition has it that lepers were blessed by the priest and then made their way down the hill, and across Moat Brook, to bathe in the sulphurous waters of the Lepers' Well (SJ 870048). The well is still there a hundred yards or so down the lane from the present Leper House, in the direction of Gunstone. It stands beside the road, protected by an oak fence and overhung by bushes. There are stone steps leading down to the waters. The circular well walls are bricked around and measure about five feet across. My dog, Lady, drank long and deep there. Note the hedges. There are many species of plants in them - ivy, holly, hawthorn, oak etc. - a sure sign of considerable age. In the late 17th Century the old Leper

House was replaced by the Brimstone Alehouse, where ale was brewed using water from the Lepers' Well.

Gunstone stands on high ground, a little way down the narrow winding lane to the south-west of the Lepers' House. It is a most attractive hamlet in lovely rolling country, full of horses of all kinds and colours. Their numbers are explained by the fact that Gunstone Hall is now a Riding Centre and that at Barn Farm there is a Riding and Livery Yard. The Hall is irregular and rendered and has hooded mouldings over the windows. However, this rural idyll is somewhat marred by a nasty and persistent drone from the nearby M54. The first element of the name Gunstone is probably from an Anglo-Saxon (or Scandinavian) personal name, such as Gunnar or Gunild.

Wood Hall Farm, 1.25m WNW of Codsall, is a moated site, and at Kingswood Common, 1.5m ESE, is a small church of 1861 and areas of rough scrub woodland and heath that give a good idea of what the country around would look like if left uncultivated.

The Myron, a house at Histon's Hill, Codsall, was the home of Rex Farran. In 1948 he was killed by a parcel bomb intended for his brother, Captain Roy Farran, who was an undercover agent for the British Army in Palestine. The bomb came courtesy of the Stern Gang.

Adjoining Codsall to the east is **Oaken,** a charming tree-lined place of mature detached houses overlooking fields and woods. Of particular note is Oaken House: 18th Century with three bays and three storeys, a pedimented doorway and parapets to the gables. Today, Oaken is a suburb of Codsall, but in 1086 it was the larger of the two villages. A nature trail starts at Oaken Lane, opposite the foot of the railway drive. A leaflet is available from nearby shops.

South-east of Oaken, and on the other side of the A41, Wolverhampton to Shifnal road, is the entrance to **Wrottesley Hall** and Park. Here lived the Wrottesley family who, like many Norman settlers, took the name of the Anglo-Saxon manor they occupied after the Conquest. They were in unbroken succession for 23 generations, from 1164 to 1963. Amongst their forebears were Sir Hugh Wrottesley, who became Governor of Calais, and Major General Wrottesley, the 19th Century historian. The family was awarded a baronetcy in 1642 and a barony in 1838. During the Civil War they were Royalist. In 1963 the 4th Lord Wrottesley died and the entire estate was sold.

Wrottesley Hall stands on rising ground, with good views over the attractive though undramatic Staffordshire countryside. The original mansion was built in 1696 and had a central block of three storeys with a pediment and projecting wings. However, the house was virtually destroyed by fire in 1897 - only the walls were left standing - and was not rebuilt until the 1920s. The central block was lowered to two storeys and the wings to one storey. The original pediment has been reused but is not of the correct proportion for the smaller house. Nevertheless, it is a handsome place and so much better than the alternative of total demolition and rebuilding.

The Wrottesley coat of arms in the pediment maintains a tenuous link with the old family. The Hall has been several things since 1963, including a Country Club, and in the grounds is a small golf course. Most of the extensive Park has been dispersed. Close to the house is a long Georgian stable range surmounted by a cupola. Although there is some commercial activity in the grounds the house itself is now, once again, a private residence.

In 1066 the Saxon Hunta owned the manor of Wrottesley, but after the Norman Conquest it was taken from him and given to Robert of Stafford. In

1086 there was a small village here but by the 17th century this had disappeared, almost certainly destroyed by the Wrottesley family when they extended their Park. This was an unkind but not uncommon practice amongst the landed gentry.

Wrottesley has an intriguing archeological mystery, namely an ancient **Lost British City**. In 1686 the reputable and learned Dr Robert Plot published his 'Natural History of Staffordshire'. In it he tells of having seen the remains of a large stone-built city, or fort, between Wrottesley and Patshull. Since Dr Plot wrote his account squared stones have been found in the area at various times, but little else of interest has come to light. All trace of the settlement seems to have disappeared. Within the locality is Low Hill Field where many human bones have been found. However, it appears that there has never been a thorough, modern investigation of the site, which is quite remarkable when one considers the potential importance. This is Dr Plot's account:

"It being thus made at least probable that the original inhabitants of this county might also be Iceni, as well as those of Norfolk, & c. who though they at first carried themselves fair to the Romans, yet seeing them use their neighbours in that manner as they did, thus stoutly interposed: let us next take a view of what markes there yet remains, of their places of habitation, defence, & c. to one or both of which I think I cannot refer that noble antiquity near Wrottesley in this county, where there yet remains, either the foundation of some ancient British city, or other fortification, of great extent; it including above a moyety of Wrottesley, and part of Pateshull, Pepperhill, and Bonningal parks; also some parcell of the two Commons of Kingswood and West-bach, the whole containing in circuit about 3 or 4 miles, lyeing part of Staffordshire and part in Shropshire, as mark't out by the shaded line in the map. Within the limits whereof there are several partitions yet visible, running divers ways like the sides of streets, tho' hard to be fully traced, because interrupted both by the mattock and plow, the foundations being dayly dugg up by the former, to mend high-ways, make inclosures, and pavements; and then all levell'd by the latter: which together with the large hinges for doores, an antique dagger, that have been found here, and some of the stones square; make me rather think it some ruinated city, than a fortification only: otherwise I could have been content to have thought it some such British vallum, or encampment, as Tacitus acquaints us Caractacus made upon a hill in Shropshire, upon the banks of the River Clun, with great stones rudely heapt upon one another, to defend him from the impressions of the Roman army, the remains whereof, faith Camden, are to be seen this day. Such a Rampire as this I say, I could have easily believed it, there having been just such great stones found hereabout, as we read Caractacus, and other British princes, were used to fortify withal: whereof I was told of one, that contain 100 loads: another so great, that after 10 loads of stone were hewed off it, required 36 yoaks of Oxen to draw it, and made the great Cistern in the Maulthouse at Wrottesley, which though left very thick both at bottom and sides, is yet so capacious, that it will wet 37 strike of barley at a time. Or at least I could have thought it some camp of the Danes, who as Simeon Dunelmensis, John Brompton and Florentius Wigorniensis all testify, were overthrown at Totenhale, Teotenhale, or Tbeotfanbele, now Tettenhall not farr off; the whole, or greatful part of it, being I think in that parish at this very day: but that the parallel partitions within the outer wall, whose foundations are still visible, and represent streets running different ways, put it I think out of doubt, that it must have been a city, and that of the Britains, for that I could hear of no name it ever had, nor have the inhabitants hereabouts any tradition concerning it, of any sort whatsoever, somewhat whereof would have certainly been preserved, had it either been Roman; or so late as either Saxon, or Danish conquests of this nation".

Codsall Wood, 2m NW of Codsall, is a small village which developed on the common before it was enclosed in 1824. There were tea rooms at Codsall Wood in the early 1900s and the village was, and still is, a day-trip destination for Black Country people, especially at the time of its annual flower show.

It is a mature residential area with a wide variety of dwellings, from little 'two-up-and-two-down' cottages to dignified Victorian villas of some substance. There is a dinky little red brick church of St Peter (1885) with a bellcote and a chimney, a Post Office-stores, and two surprisingly large pubs: the Cross Guns and the Crown.

The impressive **Pendrell Hall** hides behind trees on the road to Codsall. It was built in 1865 by Mr Viles, a Bilston businessman and Editor of the Gentlewoman's Journal. It is of red brick with yellow stone dressings and is ornamented with battlements and stepped gables. Other features include a tower and two-storey bow windows. The interior wood panelling and carved pillars were installed by Mr Frank Gaskell who bought the Hall in 1910. In 1954 the Gaskells left and the following year the house and its landscaped grounds were bought by Staffordshire County Council. It is now a College of Residential Adult Education and a public service conference centre. (Note: Pendrell Hall is named after the Pendrell family, who helped king Charles escape after the Battle of Worcester in 1651, but they have no other connection with it.) In recent times some scenes from the TV series 'A Very Peculiar Practice' were shot here.

Whitehouse Farm, 0.25m E of Codsall Wood, is a large, three-storey building, which has a cluster of attached outbuildings with roofs at a surprising variety of levels. The house belongs to the Chillington Park estate, although it lies beyond the park walls. In the 1770s Capability Brown landscaped the park, and Whitehouse Farm was given a sham northern facade (a pediment with Tuscan columns) so that from Chillington Hall it appeared to be a Classical Triumphal Arch. However, it was not meant to be seen too closely and its blandness is now all too evident to the thousands of people who daily pass within a few yards of it on the M54. Almost opposite Whitehouse Farm is the entrance to Moor's Farm and Country Restaurant.

Bilbrook adjoins Codsall to the east. It has its own railway station, schools and shopping parades, but is now effectively at one with Codsall. It is a place of modern housing estates. Most of the local employment is service orientated - clerks in the big new council office block, firemen, teachers, shop workers etc. The name Bilbrook means 'the brook in which watercress (billers) grows'. The Moat Brook, which is crossed by Watery Lane, is probably the waterway referred to. (Streams, unlike rivers, often change name, not just from one historical period to another but along their course.) **Lane Green** is another modern residential area. It lies off Duck Lane and is a part of Bilbrook.

COLTON *2m NE of Rugeley*
It lies between Rugeley and Blithfield Reservoir. Though not large it was a borough by 1364, one of only 23 towns in the County It was small and agricultural, but the people who lived within the boundaries had rights and privileges above those of their neighbours. The church of St Mary has an Early English tower with twin lancet bell openings, and a late 13th Century south chapel with lancet windows. The rest was rebuilt by G E Street in 1850-52. He also supplied most of the furnishings. There are three misericords, brought here

from Tenby, and some stained glass windows by William Wailes.

Colton House is a brick mansion, with nine bays, of about 1730. Like so many large houses close to towns and villages the grounds have been sold off and filled with modern villas, a practice to be deplored. Bellamour Hall is long gone - demolished between the Wars - and all that remains is the wall that enclosed the Park and a two-storey fragment in ashlar, about 10 feet square, with mullioned and transomed windows. The village green is quite remarkable. It is a roughly-circular raised platform, some three to four feet high and about 55 yards in diameter. About it stand the church, the school and a couple of large houses. A stream runs close to the green and is crossed by a brick-built bridge. It is altogether a most attractive ensemble. Up the hill, the Victorian developments have been greatly extended in recent years and the village is now quite substantial.

Today, Colton is probably best known for the Collie Rescue Centre, a most admirable establishment. It is from here that the author obtained his dog, Ricky, in 2002.

Colton Old Park, 1m NE of Colton, was a medieval deer park enclosed out of forest. The earthworks of the park pale can still be seen. Littlehay Manor is of 16th Century origin, but only the two chimney stacks survive from the original house. North of Colton, and almost adjoining it, is **Stockwell Heath**, a charming hamlet set around a quarter-acre green which has a small pool in the middle.

COLWICH *2m NW of Rugeley*

The village has achieved national notoriety as the scene of two terrible railway crashes, both of which involved substantial loss of life. The main lines from Stafford and Stoke meet here before going on to Lichfield. Colwich is little more than a dormitory town for Stafford and has never developed as it might have done, considering its excellent communications. As well as the railway lines there are two main roads, the River Trent and the Trent and Mersey Canal.

Between Colwich and the adjacent village of Little Haywood is the Abbey of St Mary, in which resides a Benedictine order of contemplative nuns. The order was founded in Paris in 1651 and settled here in 1834. The abbey was originally a private house known as Mount Pavilion. It had been built in about 1825 for Viscount Tamworth, the son of the 7th Earl Ferrers, but he died before it was completed. The house is of stone and constructed in a neo-Tudor-Gothic design with battlements to the long main front. There are good views over the water meadows of the River Trent to the hills of Cannock Chase. Not far from the Abbey is the gabled Tudor station, built in 1847 to a design by Livock. The School is of 1860 by Ewan Christian.

The church of St Michael has a Gothic tower, dated at 1640, but most of the rest was rebuilt by H J Stevens of Derby in 1856, though inside there are Early English arcades. The chancel is highly decorated and the stalls are canopied. Overall, the church is large and spacious. There is an alabaster monument to Sir Robert Wolseley, died 1646; a tablet to Charles Trubshaw, the architect and builder, died 1772; and monuments to the Anson family of Shugborough Hall.

The architect, Charles Lynam, who was active in Staffordshire, was born at Colwich in 1829. Later, he lived at The Quarries, Hartshill, Stoke on Trent.

The Wolseley family lived one mile SE of Colwich at **Wolseley**. They took their name from the manor. The family crest includes a wolf's head, a reference to their legendary role as slayers of wolves in medieval times. (Wolves lingered long in the local forests.) The main entrance to Wolseley Park is on the A51 at

Wolseley Bridges, just opposite the big barn with green doors which is used as a craft shop. The iron gates are locked now because the old Hall was demolished some time ago. The Wolseleys were established here by the 10th Century and a Wolseley still lives here, in a new bungalow with an entrance a little further up the road towards Rugeley. In the 1990s they developed the park as a Garden Centre. This failed and the family was bankrupted. It has been taken over by others and is now called the Wyevale Garden Centre. Incidentally, the Wolseley Bridges' road junction is on a notoriously dangerous bend. So what has the council done? Unbelievably, they have inserted two small islands which confuse everyone and encourage dangerous manoeuvres, in an attempt to allow a safe entrance to the Garden Centre. The fact is that the entrance to the Garden centre should never have been allowed to be placed here.

The Irish branch of the family produced Field Marshall Wolseley, a leading soldier of his day who saw service in the Crimean War, the Indian Mutiny, the Chinese War of 1860 and in Canada. It was he who led the force sent to relieve General Gordon at Khartoum, but which arrived too late. The elegant Wolseley Bridge, which carries the A51 over the River Trent, was built by Sir John Rennie in 1800. This replaced the previous bridge, which had carried the famous stage coach road from London and Lichfield to Stone and on to Chester and Holyhead - 'one of the most frequented roads in the kingdom', said Sir John Ogilby in 1675.

Less than 0.25m NE of the bridge is Bishton Hall, an attractive Georgian House of seven bays with a pediment, a four-columned porch and Victorian extensions. It was formerly the home of the Sparrow family, who built the house in about 1770, and later a branch of the Sneyds lived here. Today, it is a Roman Catholic preparatory school called St Bede's, which was founded in 1936 by Cecil Stafforde Northecote. Bishton is a charming little place, with trees and fields, a cricket pitch and a definite atmosphere. There is a circular earthwork, 400 yards east of Bishton Hall, which is a listed monument. The name Bishton might mean 'the settlement belonging to the bishop'.

In ancient times there was some industry in the Wolseley area. Glass making was established here very early, probably in the 13th Century, and by the middle of the 15th Century it was a flourishing business. The Wolseleys were selling fern (used to make potash and essential for glass making) to the local glass house, which was recently discovered at the Wolseley gravel quarries. (See Rugeley.) In the 1470s there were two watermills on the Wolseley estate. These were used in connection with an iron-working forge believed to have had a substantial output. The sites of the mills have yet to be located.

COMPTON *2m W of Wolverhampton town centre*
The name is Anglo-Saxon, from 'cumbton', meaning 'the homestead in the narrow valley'. Indeed, the valley of the Smestow Brook here is narrow and the sides quite steep. Compton is effectively in a pass, a pass used by the Stafford-shire and Worcestershire Canal and the Bridgnorth road. The construction of the canal started at Compton in 1766 and was opened in 1772. James Brindley was the engineer.

In recent times a small shopping centre has developed at the crossroads. This is dominated by the Oddfellows Hall pub, and odd it is with all the decorative wood which has been lashed on to the original brick. The Swan, which stands opposite, is content with its traditional garb. Other facilities include a social club, a boys' club and a canal boatyard.

Compton Hall hides behind hedges, a modest ashlar-rendered building with curved bays and moulded window surrounds and quoins. The present house dates from about 1845. The last wallpaper that William Morris designed was made for this house and he called it 'Compton'. A handful of old cottages survive amongst the 20th century houses in the river valley. On the heights of the south side are some substantial Victorian piles, such as The Cedars and Compton Grange. The even steeper northern flanks have many more well-heeled houses set in wooded grounds. A little way downstream is the old watermill. At the top of the hill, south of Compton, is **Finchfield**, a mature mixed residential area with a shopping centre and a Mitsubishi dealer.

CONSALL *1m SE of Wetley Rocks, which is 5.5m S of Leek*
The hamlet of Consall is situated in the North Staffordshire Moorlands, to the east of the A522, 1m SW of Wetley Rocks. It lies amidst pastures on the edge of the Hidden Valley of the River Churnet and consists largely of stone-built cottages and farms.

There is no church here but there are two Halls, the Old and the New. The biggest house actually in the village is Lower Farm, a black-and-white building constructed on a stone plinth with red brick chimneys and dated at about 1620. Consall Old Hall stands amongst trees, 0.25m NE, on the lane to the delights of Consall Forge. It is a fine 17th Century stone house, originally of three bays and two gables, which has been very well extended by another bay to the right. The windows are mullioned and transomed and the leaded glass lights look to be very old. A little further along, the lane bends to the right. On the bend is the start of the old footpath that leads across the field to Consall Forge.

A little further along again is Consall New Hall, hidden behind a screen of trees and outbuildings. The public never gets to see the New Hall, which is a great pity because it has the most splendid gardens which fall away from the house down a valley. There are several pools with ornamental bridges, trees, shrubs and small statues. The Hall itself is a modest, red brick, Georgian house of five bays and two storeys. It has stone casings around the windows, in which are set unsympathetic, modern double-glazed units. There is a central stone portico of columns and entablature, and above this is a Venetian window. The owner is Mr Podmore, an industrialist with factories in the Potteries. His family used to own most of the land hereabouts, including the adjacent stretch of the Churnet valley. The large collection of architectural stone pieces, visible from the lane that leads down to the newly constructed Consall Nature Park, have been collected from far and wide by Mr Podmore. They are not from the Hall or an older house on the site.

CONSALL FORGE *1.25m ENE of Consall, which is 6.5m S of Leek*
Consall Forge is a delightful hamlet deep in the wooded 'Hidden Valley' of the River Churnet It can be reached along the river-canal or by one of several footpaths. Most people will probably choose to park their cars at the Information Centre of the Consall Nature Park. There is a vehicular track from here that leads down the hill, and divides northwards to Consall Forge and southwards to the old Slitting Mill. However, this is only supposed to be used by residents or the disabled or infirm. By the Centre are two pools, caused by the damming of a stream. It seems likely that these were mill pools connected with iron working.

At Consall Forge there was an iron forge (a bloomery) with waterwheel-powered hammers. All that remains of this is a mound of dark earth opposite the

Black Lion pub, in the small copse between the river and the railway close to the river weir. Pig iron from the furnaces at Meir Heath was refined at Consall Forge, that is, the impurities were hammered out of the reheated iron. The iron bars were then cut into rods, about one inch square, at the Slitting Mill and sold to the South Staffordshire nailing trade. (The Slitting Mill is a little further downstream.) Some sources say that at a later date the iron was taken down the valley by pack mules to the Oakamoor tin works. These were established in 1777 but only had a short life. The iron was rolled into sheets and then dipped into tanks of molten tin to make tin plate.

Iron was worked at Consall Forge between at least 1688 and 1750, and probably later. For much of the time (1688-1710) it was part of the Foley family empire, which had furnaces at Oakamoor, Meir Heath and Heighley (near Madeley); forges at Oakamoor, Keele, Newcastle, Rugeley and Grindley (near Chartley); and a slitting mill at Rugeley. They were also active in Shropshire. Ironstone was also mined in the Churnet Valley, and several men became rich as ironmasters here. One, called Ironstone Smith, lived at Consall New Hall. He is buried in the churchyard at Wetley Rocks.

The huge limestone kilns, which stand against the south bank, were owned by the North Staffordshire Railway Company and are reputed to have been working until 1921. The limestone came from Cauldon Lowe to Froghall by a plateway, and by canal from there. The Cauldon Canal was opened in 1777. (The Railway did not arrive until 1876). To the left of the lime kilns there is a flight of 203 concrete steps, that head up the valley side to the top of the hill, where they connect with the old path that comes out near the Old Hall. A similar set of steps on the other side of the valley is called the Devil's Causeway. In the field near the top of the hill, the path passes by a small pool bordered with rushes, and through mounds of black earth. There are trees here and the total area of disturbed ground is about two acres. This is probably the site of an iron works (SJ 994494).

Back in the valley, a low embankment runs alongside the lime kilns. This marks the beginning of the Consall Plateway, which can be traced northwards up the valley and past a disused sandstone quarry, as it climbs out of the valley and heads south-west for seven miles to Weston Coyney. It was used to transport the processed lime and closed in 1849. In time three more tramways were constructed and were collectively called Cauldon Lowe Tramways. To the left of the lime kilns are two cottages built on the infill of an old quarry. Opposite the quarry is another cottage. There are only three in the whole hamlet. There used to be more against the south bank, by the weir, but these have been demolished.

The Cauldon Canal and the River Churnet are one for 1.5m N of Consall Forge: that is, the river has been canalised but the two parts separate again here. The canal swings east and the river passes over a weir which has floodgates to protect the canal when the waters rise. The river and the canal run parallel but separately from now on. The old North Staffordshire Railway line is still intact and follows the valley to Oakamoor. Until recently it was used by one train a day. This carried sand from the Moneyash quarries of British Industrial Sand at Whiston Eaves to the Pilkington glass works at St Helen's, Lancashire.

A little way downstream from the weir are the ruins of Crowgutters Mill. Messrs Podmores ground flint here until 1947 when the water pipes were damaged in the bad winter of that year and the mill was abandoned. Since then it has been vandalized. Further downstream again there is a block of red brick railway cottages. Beyond them is Podmore Bridge. This bridges the river and was built in 1952 as a replacement for the old London Bridge, which was so called because it had been erected by a London company which mined iron ore in the valley. The lane that crosses this bridge, and leads on through the Wildacres Estate, follows the route of a plateway used to transport the iron-ore. This lane leads southwards past a stone cottage, now a Pottery, to a row of cottages and a large mill.

The mill lies between the canal and the river and was working up until about 1950. Part of it is now inhabited as a house. It was originally driven by one waterwheel but to this were added another two, called Jack and Jill, and finally a turbine was installed. Prior to its use as a flint mill it was a slitting mill. In fact, it was the slitting mill which processed the iron from the forge up-river. There has been a mill here since about 1525 but most of the structure that we see today was built in 1778. There was a Newcomen steam engine here but this was removed to Cheddleton Flint Mill a few years ago. However, much of the old mill machinery was stolen. The pieces that were taken were massive and the thieves brought their own crane. Little wonder that the present owner keeps large Alsatian dogs, as do some of the occupants of the row of cottages at the back of the mill.

The canal at the top of the lock, above the mill, is especially wide because iron ore was loaded at this point. There were several iron mines in the area. Those on the south bank of the river were connected to the canal by a plateway which crossed the river via a spindly wooden bridge, the foundations of which can still be seen. Downstream from the mill is a metal cross-over bridge. By this bridge is the 'petrifying stream' noted by Dr Plot in 1686. By the railway line there was a row of cottages, now demolished, and behind the site of these are the ruins of another flint grinding mill and mill pond with some old wooden machinery still in situ. Further down the valley is Cherry Eye Bridge, named after the Cherry Eye Mine. From here a bright red iron-ore was extracted which made the miners' eyes look red. It was worked until 1921.

COPMERE END *1.75m W of Eccleshall*
Copmere End is a tiny settlement at the end of Copmere and consists of a few cottages, a farm and a pub, The Star.

The attraction though is the lake itself, a large, beautiful sheet of water fringed with rushes and woods and alive with water birds. It is private property, belonging to the Sugnall Hall estate, but casual visitors are not made unwelcome. The mere has many happy memories for the author who has taken all his dogs there over a period of 30 years. Copmere is fed by the River Sow and lies in a natural glacial hollow which was scraped out during the last Ice Age. It covers about 45 acres and its name means either 'Coppa's lake' or 'Great lake', ('Cop' being Celtic for 'big, top, high').

The boathouse was built in 1735 but rebuilt in the early 19th Century. The flat-bottomed punts moored all around it are for the use of fishermen. Originally, the fishing rights were held by the Bishop of Lichfield but the Lord of the Manor of Charnes had the right to fish in the lake 'as far as a man could throw a two-penny hatchet'.

This custom continued into the 19th Century by a large man throwing a hammer. On the north bank of the mere is an old folly building, probably designed as a fishing lodge. The entrance to the grounds around the mere used to be a high stile, where a gamekeeper is said to have hanged himself and which has since been haunted.

COPPENHALL *2.25m SSW of Stafford*

Coppenhall is a hilltop hamlet to the south-west of Stafford and is now almost joined to it by a chain of modern houses, stretching through Hyde Lea to Burton Manor and Rising Brook. Nevertheless, it still feels rural.

In Domesday Book it is Copehale, which is Anglo-Saxon and means 'Coppa's meadow'.

In the 12th Century the manor came into the possession of the monks of Stone Priory and it was probably they who built the church of St Lawrence in the 13th Century. This is how country churches used to be - small and very plain without towers and transepts - like little barns. The timber bell-turret is a Victorian addition. It has lancet windows and the minimum of decoration; a far more Holy place than many a great and grand church.

Coppenhall Hall is a timber-framed and brick house of at least the 16th Century. Depressions around the house may be the remains of a moat.

Hyde Lea, 0.75m N of Coppenhall, is a village that appears to have grown out of squatters encroaching on common land. Hyde Lea Mottes, 0.25m NW of the village, are two adjacent moat-like earthworks. They are thought to lie on the site of a house (or houses) of the Bagot family, who acquired the Stafford barony by marriage in 1194 and assumed the Stafford name. The Bagot name is perpetuated in two field names: Upper Bagot's Oak and Lower Bagot's Oak. (Note: medieval house moats were not serious defensive works; all they could do was deter vagabonds. They were primarily status symbols and used as fishponds.)

. At **Butter Hill,** 0.5m WSW of Coppenhall, there is a large house, now used as an old people's home. Behind the house is a derelict windmill (SJ 898191). It has four storeys, is built of brick and measures 28 feet in diameter at the base. A little of the machinery is still in place.

COSELEY *2.25m N of Dudley*

Coseley lies on a hill deep in the Black Country. It stands astride the Birmingham New Road, which runs for 9.5 miles from the western outskirts of Birmingham to Wolverhampton. This was constructed in 1924-7, as part of a scheme to provide work for the unemployed and to stimulate commerce in the Black Country. The name Coseley is Anglo-Saxon and means 'Cossa's glade in the wood'. The village became a town to service the developing coalmines. In the 1830s there were more than 50 pits within the town boundaries and the availability of fuel attracted manufacturing industries, especially those based on iron. Several of the buildings that housed the old works still exist. The Cannon ironworks (1826) has some parts remaining and the works of Thomas Green and Benjamin Parkes still stand, though substantially modernised. Coseley was one of several centres that specialised in the manufacture of nails, a most important industry in its day.

The people of the area were known for their religious fervour and there are still several Anglican and Nonconformist churches and chapels hereabouts. Christ Church, of 1830 by Thomas Lee, is built of stone with lancet windows and has three galleries. It stands in a large, well wooded cemetery opposite a secondary shopping centre and near to the station. The Ebenezer Baptist Chapel is of 1856 and is situated on the Birmingham New Road. It has stuccoed walls, giant pilasters and a pediment. Nearby is the substantial red brick parish church of St Chad, which stands adjacent to a charming white-washed windmill (of about 1795), now occupied as a dwelling, and faces the Silver Jubilee Park.

On the other side, the east side, of the Birmingham New Road is the new shopping centre. With the exception of the pubs most of the buildings are modern, flat-roofed blocks, though it is a cheerful enough little place. There is also a range of shops on the main road.

Coseley is served by the main-line railway from Birmingham to Wolverhampton, with a station in Havacre Lane, and also by the Birmingham Canal, constructed by James Brindley in 1769. The purpose of this canal was to link the South Staffordshire coalfields to the factories of Birmingham. It succeeded to the mutual advantage of both areas. The price of coal in Birmingham fell from 13 shillings to 7 shillings a ton. This stimulated industry in Birmingham and led to an increased demand for Black Country coal.

Deepfields, 0.5m NW of Coseley, is a former hamlet, now part of the Black Country conurbation. In the 18th Century there were two blast furnaces here and in 1718 the Penn brothers set up a huge coke furnace, one of the largest in the Midlands. Cannon Industries in Deepfields is probably the best known firm established in Coseley. Their electric cookers and 'Gas Miser' fires are leading brand names. The company was founded in 1826 by Edward and Stephen Sheldon who established a foundry to make holloware, i.e. pots and pans, including the 'Kaffir' cooking pots sold in Africa. The old factory was burnt down in 1980 but the firm still has a large presence in the town. **Wallbrook** is an established residential area, east of the railway, which adjoins the Tipton Industrial Estate to the south.

Now, a few words about the fringe areas of Coseley that lie to west. **Hurst Hill** stands on a hill but is locally known as Hurst Green. Indeed, there are still several grassed and wooded areas hereabouts. The largest are the slopes that lead down to Woodsetton. At the top of the hill the main road passes through a cutting in the limestone rock. Adjacent to this is the yellow-stone church of St Mary the Virgin and St Cyprian's Hall, a modern Activity Centre. The Old Gate pub faces a handful of shops and all around are modern houses. Hurst Hill was once famous for its pigeons - homing pigeons that is. An old joke was that if a man was leaving the area he would put his pigeon loft up for sale, with house attached. There is little sign of the old lofts now, though.

Down the hill, to the south-east, are the mainly residential areas of **Roseville** and **Bromford**. Near the junction of the A457 and the B4483 at **Swan Village** is Holden's Black Country Ales Brewery, one of the original Real Ale houses.

The **Woodsetton** toll house stood nearby on the A457. This was dismantled and reerected at in the Black Country Museum in Dudley. Woodsetton is a small residential area to the west of Swan Village. The name means 'the animal fold in the forest'. In early medieval times Woodsetton was one of the nine villages of Sedgley Manor. Its lands were extensive and encompassed most of present-day Dudley.

As the main road rises towards Sedgley there are some elegant Victorian houses with a variety of infill. Old stone walls and the Prince of Wales would seem to indicate the centre of Woodsetton. Adjacent to the south side of the main road is a modern housing estate complete with two substantial schools.

Driving around the Black Country in general, and the western fringes in particular, one is struck by the large number of horses and ponies that graze on the even-more surprising number of green spaces. No lean and mean hunters these, but woolly, lovable little creatures worth more to their humble owners than any thoroughbred could ever be to its lordly master.

COTES *0.75m SW of Swynnerton*

Cotes is a hamlet of red brick farms and cottages on a slope on the edge of the Swynnerton parklands. In Domesday Book 'Cota' is described as waste. The name is Anglo-Saxon and means 'a cottage'. Cotes Heath lies 0.5m W of Cotes and is the larger settlement. On the Eccleshall to Newcastle-under-Lyme road is the small, red-stone church of St James which was built in 1837 and has a bellcote. Behind the church is a collection of what appear to be ex-council houses – worthy but uninspired semi-detached – which have been befriended by a Victorian village school with newly-attached Village Hall.

Cotes Heath proper lies 0.25m W, at a crossroads with trees, some cottages, a block of flats and a side turn that leads to the rear of Cotes Hall, an irregular stuccoed house of 1796. In 1924 the occupant was Bartholomew Snowball. To be called Snowball is an accident of birth; the adding of Bartholomew is an act of rapscallion malevolence.

The embowered lane leads past the Hall to what might have once been an area of heathland. Today there are a number of attractive, mature, detached houses of substance with gardens and paddocks; Westfield House even has a Victorian walled garden.

Cranberry, 0.5m N of Cotes Heath, is reached by a lane which parallels the main-line railway between Stafford and Crewe. With its gantries, overhead power cables and frequent high-speed trains it is neither a thing of beauty nor an affable companion. However, the village along the road has a charming mix of old cottages, mature houses and new villas. There are the yards of a haulage company and a general store; the country around is attractively undulating.

COTTON *4m NE of Cheadle*

It lies in a deep, wooded valley in the Staffordshire Moorlands north-west of Oakamoor. St Wilfred's College, better known as Cotton College, is a Roman Catholic School. In 1846 Lord Shrewsbury of Alton Towers gave the Georgian house to Father Faber and his Brothers of the Will of God. They amalgamated with the Oratorians of Birmingham but left in 1849. In 1850 the Passionists came, and duly departed, and in 1868 the school was established. To the original Georgian house have been added many buildings at various dates. Pugin built the stone range, with three gables and ogee leaded windows, and the brick range to its left. The Chapel is also by Pugin, 1846-8, and was lengthened in 1936 by George Drysdale. The style is of 1300.

Close to the Catholic church is the Anglican St John's, of 1795, a humble but very right-feeling little brick, barn-shaped building with battlements, pinnacles and a circular window. This church was founded by Thomas Gilbert of Cotton Hall.

Gilbert had made his fortune by buying the leases of many small, local copper mines from their lordly owners and subletting them to 'adventurers' (that is, partnerships of miners and merchants) or simply to individual miners. The rent was always in kind - a proportion of the ore obtained, usually 1/13th - and the miners contracted to keep the mines open for a certain number of months in the year. Gilbert also had interests in smelting works at Greenlowfield in Alstonefield parish and on Alton Common.

Half-a-mile to the east of Cotton are two prehistoric burial mounds, one The Cotton Plane was a plateway (railway), one of several that linked the high Cauldon limestone quarries with the low Caldon Canal at Froghall.

At **Threelows**, a fragmented hamlet in the Weaver hills 0.5m E of Winifred's

Cottage, Thomas Bateman excavated five burial mounds in 1849-50. Two cannot be now located. Two lie either side of the on either side of the road from the Threelows to Ramshorn.

Ramshorn, 1m SE of Cotton, is a small settlement on the edge of the Weaver Hills and lies between the woods of Ramshorn Common to the north-west and Wootton Park to the south-east. A cup-marked stone of Neolithic or Early-Bronze-Age was found at Ramshorn Farm in 1993. The name could mean several things but 'ram's bank' is the most favoured. Ramshorn was an early centre of Primitive Methodism in Staffordshire. The large limestone quarries of the Cauldon Low group lie just to the north and the east of Cotton.

COVEN *4m N of Wolverhampton*

Coven is an old village off the A449 between Wolverhampton and Stafford, but much built around in recent years. The cruciform church of St Paul is by E Banks of Wolverhampton (1857). To the west of the church is Grove House Farm, a good timber-framed house of about 1600. It has an unusual decorative motif of small arches on columns. The front facade is now all of brick painted white with 'framing' painted in black. There are two small shopping precincts in the village, a service station-cum-car dealer, and on the main road is Palfinger Cranes who hire out cranes attached to the back of trucks.

In 1066 the Anglo-Saxon Alric held the manor of Coven but it was taken from him and given to the Norman, Robert de Toeni of Stafford, who let it to Burgred. Robert was a major landowner in the county. In 1086 there were two villagers, two smallholders and the lord of the manor had four slaves, or serfs.

At **Coven Lawn**, 1m SSE of Coven at SJ 903053, are the remains of concrete foundations upon which were fixed American Guns and the service buildings associated with them. The site covers some five five acres and has been used in post-war years by the Territorial Army. The guns protected the Boulton and Paul aircraft factory 2m SSW, and Pendeford Aerodrome 2m due S. The aerodrome has been developed for housing. (See Brewood for mention of an old iron working site near Coven Sewerage Works.)

Coven Heath adjoins Coven to the south and is basically a main-road residential straggle with a plant nursery and signs to a Vehicle Testing Station.

Four Ashes, 1m N of Coven, has two pubs at a crossroads on the A449. One of these, the Four Ashes, once had four ash trees within its curtilage and the sign reflects this. On the lane to Calf Heath there is an industrial estate, which has grown up in the shadow of the enormous chemical works that dominates the skyline to the east of the main road. This looks for all the world to be some secret establishment about to be blown up by James Bond.

The Four Ashes crossroads can be very dangerous because traffic on the main road travels very fast. The author once saw a car on the main road overturn here whilst swerving to avoid hitting a slow-moving vehicle emerging from the Calf Heath Lane. Quite dramatic it was. The car ended up upside down but the driver emerged unscathed and chatted as though nothing had happened. Talk about cool. A good man to have with you in the jungle, methinks.

Standeford, 0.75m NNE of Coven, is a tiny hamlet on the Wolverhampton to Stafford road. The name means 'stoney ford' and refers to the crossing place of the Roman road from Pennocrucium to Metchley over the brook here. The Anglo-Saxon Stafford to Warwick road called Portstreet is also thought to have passed through Standeford.

Rodbaston, 1.25m S of Penkridge, is a scattered hamlet which lies in low, wet land just to the east of the A449 Stafford to Wolverhampton road. In Domesday Book it is called Redbaldestone ('Redbalde's town'), and was held by Richard the Forester (Richard Chenven). His fortified manor house, sometimes called a castle, is thought to have been at the moated site 0.5m N of Rodbaston Hall. There are 11th Century references to a castle at Rodbaston, occupied by the Broc and the de Loge families, Head Foresters of Cannock Chase. Rodbaston Hall is a mid-19th Century house which is now the centre of an agricultural college.

In 1919 the War Agriculture Committee, based at Dunston, 2.75m N of Rodbaston, opened an agricultural training centre in their former tractor depot. A little later that year Staffordshire County Council bought Rodbaston Hall and the nearby Hall Farm, and the Grange and agricultural centre moved there. In 1921 it was named Rodbaston Farm Institute; in 1967 it became the Staffordshire College of Agriculture; and in 1994 it became independent of the Council and is now Rodbaston College. The earthworks, about 0.5m S of Rodbaston Hall, might be of the 11th Century village, since deserted.

Rodbaston Old Hall and its private chapel stood on or near the site of the present Rodbaston Stables at SJ 925120. The Eginton family were tenants of Rodbaston from the 1380s to about 1768, first at the Castle and from at least 1690 at the Old Hall, which has now vanished without trace.

CRADLEY and CRADLEY HEATH *1.5m SE of Brierley Hill*
The name is Anglo-Saxon and probably means 'Crada's clearing in the wood'. Industry came early. In the first part of the 17th Century there was a water-driven forge which was operated by Dud Dudley. It is thought likely that it was here that he made his famous experiments using coal to smelt iron. The mill he used stood on the banks of the River Stour. The original settlement of Cradley lies on the steep southern slope of the river valley. As industry developed in the 18th Century squatter settlements sprung up on the heathland of the northern slopes. These merged together to form Cradley Heath.

However, one still has a separate identity, namely **Mushroom Green**, off Quarry Road. It is a delightful hamlet of old brick cottages (the oldest is No. 9), gardens, hedges, lanes and an overgrown piece of heath by a stream, all surrounded by bland modern housing estates. The squatters engaged in a variety of trades but here they specialised in chains. One of the old chain shops has been restored and is in local council care. The forge is in working order and demonstrations are given at regular intervals. Incidentally, most of the visitors to this craft chain shop will pass the modern Griff Chain factory without a sideways glance; but buried amongst the big modern sheds are the original (1835) one-storey, brick-built workshops arranged around a central courtyard.

Well into this century Cradley and Cradley Heath were famous for hand-made chains, especially the large anchor chains used by ocean-going ships. In the old forges men stripped to the waist in open-fronted workshops, even in the depths of winter, so hot were the fires and so strenuous their task. The last of these traditional chain shops was that of Noah Bloomer which only closed about 1990. For many years small chains have been made by machines in modern factories, and now even large chains can be made mechanically.

The other important local trade was nailmaking, the cottage and squatter industry par excellence. At the back of his house the nailer had a little workshop which housed a hearth and the few simple tools needed. Iron bar was supplied by a local nailmaster who took away the finished nails and paid the nailer a pittance. Whole families slogged away day and night to scrape a living. A nail was not just a nail: there were dozens of varieties of all shapes and sizes. Indeed, it was this variety that delayed their production by machine.

Cradley is reputed to be the home of the Staffordshire Bull-terrier, a cross-breed developed specifically for the baiting of bulls but also used for dog fighting. Blood sports were widely practised in the Black Country and illegal cock-fights and dog-fights are still held, one regrets to have to say. One of the most famous dogs was Champion Gentleman Jim who died in 1947. In 1935 the breed was acknowledged by the Kennel Club, largely due to the efforts of Joe Mallen (1891-1975), a giant chainmaker and later the landlord of the Old Cross Guns.

Today Cradley Heath High Street has most of the shops, including a precinct in which many of the national chain stores are represented. It also has the railway station which is located close to the Five Ways crossroads, the accepted town centre of the Cradleys. Cradley itself has the parish church of St Peter and the large High School, both situated on Homer Hill. The church was built in 1789 as a Nonconformist Chapel. The minister then changed sides, became an Anglican, and was later to become the Bishop of Worcester.

From the church's large and romantically unkempt graveyard there are wide views over the Stour valley, towards Cradley Heath and Netherton church (to the left) and the Rowley Hills (to the right). As we surveyed the scene a flight of homing pigeons circled above before descending to their suburban garden loft; a common enough sight perhaps, but not nearly so common in the Black Country as it once was.

As to buildings of any note there are few: Barclay's bank, housed in the striking Victorian Gothic structure erected for the United Counties Bank; the Commissioner's church of 1843 (with chancel of 1874) that stands opposite; and Corngreaves Hall, an 18th Century house with a 19th Century castellated, Gothic facade. This was once the home of the local ironmasters, the Attwood family. Their vast ironworks and colliery complex dominated Cradley between 1810 and 1894, when they closed. The site became derelict and not until the 1970s did new, smaller units of industry move in. Adjacent to the Hall is a golf course.

At **Two Gates,** Cradley, is a Ragged School of 1867. There were many of these schools in the Black Country but only a few have survived. William Caslon (1693-1766), the type-founder who gave his name to a printer's type still used today, was born in Cradley. Halesowen's Caslon Hall is also named after him. Perhaps Cradley's greatest claim to fame is its motor-cycle speedway team, 'The Heathens', whose supporters slogan is 'Ommer 'Em Cradley!'

Codsall Coppice, 0.5m SE of Cradley Heath and on the north side of Barrs Road, is a small area of ancient coppice woodland now surrounded by suburbia. The wood was regularly harvested to make charcoal for iron smelting. There is also an area of disturbed ground on the west side which marks a surface coalmine, once very common in the Black Country. This is a very rare survival.

CRESWELL *5m SE of Longton*

Not a place to linger over long. Here are suburban houses, a large factory, the main line railway, the River Blythe (or Blithe) and some old houses in Creswell Old Lane. Attached to one of the latter is the simple Roman Catholic church of St Mary, built of brick in 1816, with lancet windows and a stained glass window of the Annunciation by Pugin. The name probably means 'the well (or stream) where watercress grew'.

CRESWELL *2m NW of Stafford*

Creswell is no longer a separate community but is now a suburb of Stafford on the road to Eccleshall. Junction 14 of the M6 Motorway has divided the old settlement into two parts. To the south-east is Creswell Manor, hidden from sight in its well-wooded grounds. A new, largely Georgian-style housing estate has been built on land once belonging to the manor. At the back of this estate is the River Darling and the Doxey Marshes, an important wildlife site. North-west of the motorway is an area of inter-war style houses and the site of The Mount, an old mansion now demolished. In the garden of The Mount a prehistoric polished stone axe was found in 1960. The entrance gate and some of the outbuildings of the house remain, and in the grounds are the ruins of Creswell church (SJ 896261), which lies opposite another set of iron gates a little further along the road towards Eccleshall. This was once a substantial church but it has been a ruin for many years. All that remains is a part of the chancel with lancet windows. Occasional open air services are still held at the church.

Around it is some disturbed ground, probably shallow sand and gravel workings, but it is believed that some of these are the remains of a medieval village, which was known to have existed here and to have been was deserted by 1539. Domesday Book also mentions that there was a mill at Cresswell. The manor was then owned by Earl Roger de Montgomery, King William the First's right-hand man and most trusted friend. (The King left his Queen in Normandy under the protection of Roger de Montgomery whilst he made his Conquest of England in 1066.)

CROXALL *5.5m NE of Lichfield*

Croxall is most easily approached off the A38 at Alrewas. The name means 'Croc's secluded place' and is thought to be of Danish origin. Croxall was in Derbyshire until 1894 and much of that county was in the Danelaw, where a high proportion of invading Danes settled and where in Anglo-Saxon times a modified form of Danish law prevailed.

The little hamlet is best known for an incident recorded on the wall monument in the church to Sir Robert Wilmot-Horton and his wife, Anne, of Catton Hall. It was Anne who inspired Lord Byron to write his famous poem which begins:

She walks in beauty, like the night
Of cloudless climes and starry skies:
And all that's best of dark and bright
Meet in her aspect and her eyes.

Byron first saw Lady Anne at a ball. She was wearing a black gown with starry spangles, and the poet was so taken with her that he wrote his immortal lines that same evening.

The wide church, which has no aisles, lies on high ground amongst trees to the east of the hamlet and is approached across a field. It is mostly of the 12th and 13th Centuries and contains a great number of monuments and tablets, mostly to members of the Curzon family of Croxall and the Horton family. First amongst the tablets is that to Eusebius Horton, died 1814, by Sir Francis Chantrey.

Croxall Hall is a large, handsome late 16th Century 'L'-shaped house built of brick with additions and alterations after a fire in 1868. It has wide courtyards and stands amongst meadows close to the River Mease. The windows are mullioned and transomed and the chimneys are tall. Near the road there is a Dovecote with a cupola roof. The Curzons lived at Croxall Hall and in 1557 Joyce Lewis, the daughter of Sir Thomas Curzon, was burned at the stake, in the Market Place, Lichfield, for heresy . After the Curzons the Hall went to the Earls of Dorset by marriage. In 1779 Thomas Prinseps bought the Hall. He was a noted agriculturalist and breeder of longhorn cattle, of which he had a large herd.

Half of the villages in the area around Croxall have been deserted, mostly in the period 1330-1530, probably due to depopulation through plague and famine but also, it is believed, because of flooding. The remains of the deserted ancient village of Croxall are in fields opposite The Grange, which is on the south-east fringe of the hamlet.

South-east of the churchyard, against the River Tame, is a burial mound with a diameter of 117 feet and a height of between 18 feet and 29 feet. There is also a moated site.

Catton Hall lies 1.25m NE of Croxall. It is a modern house set in a small park. In the grounds is a rockery, in which are the fragments of windows and a font believed to be Anglo-Saxon, the last remains of a chapel now long gone. Oakley Farm lies 0.5m SW of Croxall. It once belonged to John Stanley, ancestor of the first Earl of Derby, died 1474. Edward IV was often a visitor here.

CROXDEN *45m NW of Uttoxeter*

Croxden is most easily approached from the minor road between Rocester and Tean. A sunken, tree-lined lane leads northwards from this road to the remote, spectacular ruins of Croxden Abbey, the finest Abbey ruins in Staffordshire. Croxden means 'Croc's Valley', a Danish name.

The Abbey was founded in 1176 by the Crusader, Bertram de Verdun, who also built the first castle at Alton. It was constructed of sandstone taken from the Hollington quarry, a mile to the south-west. (Stone from this site is particularly good, being soft and easy to cut when first quarried and becoming most durable when exposed to the air). The Abbey was a Cistercian house of monks from Aunay in Normandy. Cistercians were sometimes called White Monks because of the light colour of their robes. They sought out remote places and were attracted to the Moorlands of North Staffordshire where they had several monasteries. One of their members, William de Shepesheved, kept a chronicle of the Abbey during the 14th Century, and this valuable document is now in the British Museum. The heart of King John lies either here or in Croxton in Leicestershire. (His body lies in Worcester Cathedral). The Abbey was built between about 1179 and 1280 and the church was consecrated, first in 1181 and again in 1253.

The two largest fragments still standing are of the south wall of the south transept, and the west wall of the nave. Both have tall, elegant lancet windows and the west wall has a superb doorway with clustered pillars. The east wall of the cloister court still stands with three arches of clustered pillars, the middle one being the entrance to the Chapter House. There are many other smaller remains of parts of the kitchen, the common room, the Abbot's House, the sacristy and the 14th Century Guest House. The choir plan is marked out in the grass; it is to the French 'chevet' plan of five radiating apsidal chapels and ambulatory - most unusual in this country. The present road, almost unbelievably, cuts through the site of the abbey church.

The Abbey Chronicle tells of the Great Famine of 1316, of the Murrain of

Cattle in 1319 and of the Black Death of 1349. Little wonder the 14th Century saw a general decline in the population of the country as a whole. The monks cleared woodland in the valley and sold it for charcoal, probably for use in the Churnet Valley ironworks.

Today there is a small hamlet at Croxden comprising a few cottages, the five-bay, Georgian-fronted Abbey Farm and the little village church of St Giles (1884), which replaced the former chapel. The church is rock-faced, of early 14th Century style and was paid for by the Earl of Macclesfield, who no doubt occupied the south chanel pew which has a fireplace. The valley is still secluded and well-wooded, and the streams are pounded in several places, the haunt of fishermen.

At Butterley Bank Farm, 0.5m S of Croxden, and at Brook Farm there are fields in which the ridge and furrow plough marks of the former open field system are clearly defined.

Croxden Common, in the N of the parish, is on high ground and was enclosed by the Earl of Macclesfield in 1814. Today there is a large gravel quarry in the Bunter Pebble Beds.

Greatgate, 0.75m WNW of Croxden, is a crossroads' settlement which comes complete with a whipping post, a lost animal pound, a set of stocks, and a four-foot-high sandstone pillar with clamps on both sides. An early form of the name is Greetyartswood, meaning 'the gate into the wood called Greet'.

CROXTON 9.5m NW of Stafford

In 1086 Croxton was a part of the Bishop of Chester's extensive Eccleshall estate. It is likely that this was previously an old Anglo-Saxon estate which continued intact after the Conquest.

The village lies on the B5206 in the handsome wooded country between Eccleshall and Loggerheads. There are houses, old and new, and several farms. Today the fields are mainly laid to pasture, but 150 years ago this was arable farming country. Croxton is quite a long village. Most of the main road development is somewhat nondescript, but at either end of the village are two little off-road centres that are most charming.

The south-east centre has a handful of old Georgian brick houses set above the steep banked lanes, one of which leads to a disused windmill (1777) at the top of the hill. Opposite the windmill is a tall, modern scaffold-tower from which clay pigeons are fired. The north-west centre is again high-banked and here is found the small church of St Paul by Ewan Christian, of 1853, with its polygonal apse and bellcote. The rectory was built about the same time and lies adjacent to the church. Together they occupy a site which may well have been favoured by the earliest settlers - easily defended and with good views. The road from the top of the edge to the valley below is steep and winding. Here, on the fringe of the village, is the Vernon-Yonge Arms, named after the family who used to live at Charnes Hall, which is 1.25m NW of Croxton.

On Croxton Bank, about half-way up the long, energy-sapping hill north-west of Croxton, is a water trough fed by a spring that has never been known to run dry. It stands on the roadside by Butterbank House and has recently been renovated.

At the top of the hill is the turning to **Charnes**. The Hall is 17th Century, with an 18th Century facade, and has a most attractive park. In fact, all the country around here is quite delightful. There is, however, a gruesome tale told hereabouts. Some 300 years ago the young wife of one of the Yonge family took ill and died. On the night of the funeral, a coachman broke into her tomb. He tried to remove the valuable jewelled ring that she wore but it stuck fast to her finger. In desperation he took out his knife and cut her finger off. As he did so the finger spurted blood and the corpse sat bolt upright. The coachman, still clutching the ring, ran off in terror. The young wife staggered back to the hall and lived for many more years. She had, in fact, been buried alive. The tomb was in Chapel Wood, opposite the entrance to the Hall. The ghost of the girl is said to haunt the house looking for the ring which was so cruelly, yet so fortunately, taken from her. There is not a village at Charnes and it appears that there never has been.

Another gruesome tale relating to Charnes Hall is that a retired colonel was renting the house when he married a young woman. She was travelling to Charnes after the marriage when her horse bolted at Eccleshall. She slipped in the saddle, caught her foot in the stirrups and was dragged along the ground all the way to the Hall, a distance of three miles. She arrived rather dead.

Charnes Old Hall is old no more. It was pulled down in about 1890 and replaced by a new house on the same site. Part of the moat still exists as a pond at the front of the house; to the right are brick farm buildings.

Whittington, 0.5m E of Charnes, is a small hamlet, in pleasant rolling country, which was formerly a small village.

CURBOROUGH 1.75m N of Lichfield

Curborough is a small, scattered settlement without a recognisable centre set in very flat country. Curborough Hall Farm dominates the settlement. It is a red brick ensemble that has been developed in recent times as a Craft Centre, Plant Nursery and fishery. Amongst other attractions there is an assortment of small shops, a furniture restorer, a farm shop, the art gallery of Alan Walford (landscape painter), and a teashop. For the rest there are a few houses and, 0.5m north of Hall Farm, the large Severn-Trent Sewage Works.

Originally there were two, now lost, settlements. **Great Curborough** stood around Curborough Hall Farm. The Hall itself stood just to the north of the farm but was demolished in 1848. **Little Curborough** was centred on Curborough House. The present Curborough House dates from the 17th Century. Little Curborough was also called Culborough Somerville after the Somerville family, Lords of Wychnor, who had land here in the 13th Century. The name Curborough could be from the Anglo-Saxon 'cweorn burna', meaning the 'mill-stream'. A stream, a tributary of the River Trent, runs close by Hall Farm to the east

D

DANEBRIDGE *0.75m NW of Swythamley and 7m N of Leek*

Danebridge is a picturesque hamlet in the steep-sided, wooded valley of the River Dane. The river forms the boundary here between Staffordshire and Cheshire. The settlement developed around the now-ruined, 18th Century cotton mill. The 14th Century bridge was placed at a medieval ford called Sclicher ford, meaning 'slippery ford'. The present sandstone bridge was constructed in 1869.

The handful of cottages, which include a three-storey terrace and the Methodist chapel of 1834, are all built of sandstone. The name Dane is not a reference to Viking marauders: it is a dedication to Dana, the Celtic goddess and wife of Lud, the God of Light.

The ruins of the water-powered, four-storey textile mill lie on the east bank, a short distance downstream of the bridge. It was last used to manufacture shoe polish. The bulk of the stone was reused in the construction of the northenmost cottage on the left bank. On this side of the river the banks are very steep and landslips constantly occur.

On the opposite bank lie the recently constructed Danebridge Fisheries, based on Pingle Cottage. Few welcome this addition to the landscape. Concrete tanks, an artificial lake, wire netting, wooden huts and warning signs do little for this romantic spot. But do not be deterred. There are some splendid river views beyond, especially at Bearda.

Northwards from the bridge are more footpaths and more lovely views between here and Gradbach. Little wonder that even on rainy days in winter you will find a cluster of cars parked along the road whilst their owners commune with nature and ancient river gods.

Bearda is half-a- mile south of Danebridge. It is a delightful valley with a single cottage, Bearda House, at the confluence of two fast-flowing streams, which form a tributary to the River Dane. There was a settlement here in 1340 when it was called Berdeholm. Just south of Bearda House, at SJ 963642, are the ruins of a watermill. The stream flowing from the east has been dammed to form a pool, some 40 yards wide by 60 yards long. It is now reed-fringed and the valley banks are wooded. The waterwheel has long gone but the wheel pit is in good order. This measures 5 feet by 20 feet and is constructed of rough-hewn sandstone blocks. The water emerges from an iron pipe and cascades into the pit before flowing out of a modern concrete pipe culvert under the road. Blocks of stone lie scattered randomly in the undergrowth. The only upstanding building is a small stone shed against the north bank. To the right of the wheel pit is the overflow race, constructed of stone and in good condition. (Note: neither the mill ruins nor the pool are marked on the 2.5 inch to 1 mile Ordnance Survey map.) We know nothing of the mill's history but it is extremely likely that it was one of the textile spinning factories for which the River Dane is so famous. Congleton lies on the Dane and grew rich on spinning first silk, from the 1750s, and then cotton also, from the 1780s, as did Macclesfield a few miles north. An old lady told us that the Bearda mill was last used for sawing timber by the Swythamley estate workers. She also said that there was a gas-making plant on the high ground between the mill and the Dane. As to the name Bearda, it is an Anglo-Saxon personal name, though it could be derived from *brerd*, meaning 'bankside'.

Adjoining Danebridge to the north is the spread-about village of **Wincle**. Indeed, the Ship Inn and Wincle Grange belong more to Danebridge. The Grange is a substantial, irregular stone house with some mullioned windows, which stands esconced in a bower of holly bushes and mature trees. It belonged to Combermere Abbey (near Nantwich) until the Dissolution. Behind The Ship Inn is a more recent big house, the rock-faced Mellor Knowle. At Bartomley Farm (SJ 964657), two fields away, along a public footpath that begins at The Ship Inn, a small treasure of gold rings and chains of early Anglo-Saxon or late Celtic origin has been unearthed.

Wincle proper is further north, up the hill and then down into a shallow valley. It is so refreshing to see a village so unspoiled, but Wincle is in Cheshire.

DARLASTON *4m ESE of Wolverhampton*

The name is Anglo-Saxon and means 'Deorlaf's homestead'. This is not the Darlaston mentioned in Domesday Book; that is the Darlaston near Stone. It owed its early industrial development to its position on the '30 foot coal', a rich seam which actually outcropped here but which is never more than 400 feet below the surface. The most important metal-working industry was gun making, especially the manufacture of the firing mechanism - the lock. These were sent on to Birmingham where the finished guns were assembled. By the mid-18th Century the trade was booming. One of the most important markets was Africa where guns were traded for slaves. In Darlaston at that time there were more than 300 gunlock filers, and more than 50 gunlock forgers. With the abolition of slavery the trade went into recession but recovered, specialising in quality guns, and has survived into the present century.

The other trade especially associated with Darlaston is the manufacture of nuts and bolts. Indeed, the town has a claim to be the home of the modern industry because the first machine to make nuts was invented by a local man, Thomas Oliver. One of his machines is in Bilston museum. By 1860 the trade was firmly established in the town, with eight large manufacturers and many smaller concerns. The largest single company in Darlaston was Rubery Owen, formed in 1893 by John Turner Rubery and Alfred Ernest Owen. This concern manufactured a variety of components for the cycle, motor vehicle and aviation industries. Their Booth Street factory closed in 1980 but the firm continues. There are many other industries in the area and many factories, large and small, making the most diverse products.

During the Industrial Revolution the lot of the labourer was hard. Even skilled men were poorly paid and lived in small, dark, unhygienic houses. This can, perhaps, partly explain the prevalence of blood sports. Cock-fighting, dog-fighting, bull-baiting and bear-baiting were widely practised in the Black Country, and Darlaston is well known for its Bull Stake. This is both an area of the town (now a shopping precinct) near the Library and the actual stake, a large iron ring. This is normally on public display at a site close to the original position. Bulls and, on occasion, bears were tethered to the stake and attacked by bull-terriers. The 'sport' was practised in medieval times but was widespread here through the 17th and 18th Centuries until 1825 when it was made illegal.

There is believed to have been a church at Darlaston from 13th Century but the first parish church of St Lawrence dates from the 17th Century. This was rebuilt in 1721, rebuilt again in 1801 and rebuilt yet again in 1872 by A P Brevitt. In 1907 it received a new tower and spire. Inside there are two galleries supported by cast-iron piers and large cast-iron capitals. In the churchyard is a Mother and Child sculpture by Thomas Wright, 1958. Wright also made the statue of St George, 1959, which stands at the north end of The Green.

In Walsall Street is the modern church of All Saints, of 1952, by Lavender, Twentyman and Percy which replaces, somewhat belatedly, the previous church of 1872 by Street. This was destroyed by a landmine during the Second World War. The church of St George at The Green is of about 1852 by T Johnson.

In the 1960s Darlaston was in danger of dying but the centre was revitalised with the development of the new shopping area and the construction of new housing estates. Today the town looks prosperous enough and has an openness and a feeling of the fresh air that belies its location. This is partly due to the landscaping of the old railway cutting, which now forms a welcome green area close to the town centre. The George Rose Park was opened in 1924 and is named after a local nut and bolt manufacturer. It encompasses Darlaston House, once the home of the Mills family, the first ironmasters in Darlaston. Darlaston's literary claim to fame is that in the 1890s Mrs Henry Wood wrote her novel 'King's Lynne' whilst staying with relatives at The Poplars, a house now demolished, which stood in King Street.

The town itself was immortalized in a song written by Tom Langley, a retired policeman, and called 'The Darlaston Dogfight', which was recorded by 'The Black Country Three' in the 1960s. One of the men who participated in this saga was Rough Moey, also known as Ruff Moey, Moses Whitehouse and Ralph Moody (circa 1779-1840). He kept the recently demolished Mine Borers' Arms at Darlaston and was a character who became a legend in his own lifetime. His face was not only pock-marked but also badly scarred by a pit explosion; he had a wooden leg and had lost one eye; he was stocky and always game for a fist fight; he fought cocks, organized bull baits and was the last man to sell his wife in Wednesbury market.

Fallings Heath is 0.5m E of Darlaston town centre. Falling is probably from the Anglo-Saxon 'fudging', meaning 'newly cultivated land.' At the junction of Darlaston Road and Park Lane stands the brooding hulk of the now-abandoned steelworks of F H Lloyd, which closed in April 1990. We photographed the massive iron vats standing, rusting as they awaited auction. A sad sight, but a sign of the times. Facing the road island is a solitary little house, tall and narrow; the terrace of which it was once a part long gone. The area is mainly residential now but some industry does survive - Servis, Ackers Janet and Standard Tools, and others.

Rough Hay, the north-west area of Darlaston, was barren land in medieval times. In the 18th and 19th Centuries it was much mined for coal and left a wasteland of clay, pit mounds and waterlogged holes. For a time in the 19th Century there was an ironworks here. In the 1920s the council started to develop the area for housing and there is a mission church dedicated to St Christopher.

DENSTONE *5m N of Uttoxeter*

The largely modern village lies in the valley of the River Churnet, some two miles north of its confluence with the River Dove. There are two houses of note: the Stone House of 1712 and Barrow Hill House (latterly the Corbellion Restaurant) of 1780. The village is known for its small damson trade. Fruit grown here is sent to Lancashire dyers.

The church of All Saints was paid for by Sir Thomas Percival Heywood of the Manchester banking family, designed by G E Street and built in 1860-2. The style is English Gothic of about 1300 (Middle Pointed) and is considered to be an example of Street at his best. The chancel is, unusually, higher than the nave, and outside is a round, turret-like tower capped with a tile-clad spire. The stained glass is by Clayton and Bell and the font carving is by Thomas Earp. Street also designed the lych-gate, the School and the Vicarage.

The well-known Denstone College lies 0.75m WSW of the village, in a high position, with good views all round but especially northwards to the Weaver Hills. It is a 'Woodward School', one of the colleges established by the Rev Nathaniel Woodward, who had a mission to achieve 'union of classes by a common system of education'. He built schools at Hurst Pierpoint (1851),

Lancing (1854), Bloxham (1860), Ardingly (1870) and Denstone (1873). Denstone College is in Middle Pointed Gothic style to an 'H' layout. The buildings were designed by Slater and Carpenter (Junior) and constructed in pink sandstone. The chapel was built later (1879), with a polygonal apse and a tall lancet window. Overall, the school and its chapel are impressive but unfriendly structures.

Riverside Doveleys is a farmhouse which lies close to the River Dove. It was rebuilt in 1848 as a country mansion by Sir Percival Heywood. (He it was who gave the land to the Woodward Schools for the construction of Denstone College, 1.5m SW of Riverside Doveleys.) In 1946 Doveleys itself became a school. When we visited in 2004 it appears to have been used as a hotel and there has been a development of superior new houses and a garden centre. The opening-up to the public of such quietly romantic places hidden in woods by a misty river is very democratic, but the magic is lost forever. What was once a little piece of heaven belonging to a rich man is now something rather ordinary which belongs to 'everyman'.

Quixhill, 0.25m NNE of Denstone, is a hamlet which faces Denstone over the River Churnet. The name is from the Anglo-Saxon personal name and means 'Qwic's hill', but the settlement actually lies in the valley bottom. Quixhill Lodge, in Quixhill Lane, consists of a free-standing arch between two lodge houses and was a lodge to Alton Towers.

Stubwood, 0.5m S of Denstone, is a fair-sized hamlet with a telephone box. Local tradition has it that at White Gate Robin Hood shot arrows to a burial mound at Lowfields.

DERRINGTON *2.5m W of Stafford*

At the beginning of this century the population of Derrington was probably little more than at the time of the Domesday Book, when the lord of the manor, William, held it from the great Earl Roger de Montgomery. Earl Roger held most of Shropshire and was a Palatine lord with powers normally held by the king. There were three villagers and one hide of land (about 120 acres).

Today it is a place of modern villas, pleasant enough but with little or no real character. There is a pair of black-and-white cottages and the half-timbered Blue Cross Farm of 1612 to remind one that the settlement is ancient.

The church of St Matthew was designed by a local architect, Henry Ward of Stafford, and was built in 1847. It has a nave and a chancel in one with 13th Century details and a bellcote. A practice occurs here which is to be frowned upon, namely the broadcasting through public address loudspeakers of pre-recorded bells to announce the Sunday morning service.

The principle is distasteful enough but it is compounded by the choice of bells - great cathedral-like swirls of sound apparently emanating from a humble village church. On occasion the tapes get mixed up and more than once worshippers have been summoned to prayer by Bing Crosby and Frank Sinatra singing songs better suited to a nightclub. Floodlit at Christmas, though, the church looks very pretty.

On the approach lane to the village from the Stafford to Newport road, is an untidy factory. This used to produce dog food and the smell was awful. Mr Boon, the owner, was forced to desist by a High Court order. There is also a Village Hall, paid for by Mr Boon, a shop-cum-Post Office and a pub, the Red Lion, in the village.

They also have Mrs Hilda Hodson, who started the Stafford and District

People's Animal Lifeline Society (SADPALS) in 1977. With a small group of helpers she re-homes 250 cats and dogs a year. In a world full of pheasant shooters, badger-baiters and fox hunters these ladies shine like stars in the night. My dog Bruno, the best friend I ever had, came courtesy of Mrs Hodson.

The track of the now-disued Newport to Stafford Railway passes through Derrington. In the year 2000 The Way for the Millenium was opened at the Red Lion. This is a long-distance footpath that uses disused railway tracks and canal towpaths and runs from Newport (Shropshire) to Burton upon Trent.

Stallbrook Hall, 0.25m W of Derrington, stands close to the disused railway track. It is thought to date from the 14th Century and was restored in the 1990s. It was originally moated and the Bowyer family were here in the 16th Century.

DILHORNE *1.75m NE of Blythe Bridge, which is 2m SE of Longton*
The small villge lies in high hill country. The older houses are of red brick and there is a white-painted brick pub, the Red Lion.

Dilhorne Hall was the home of John Holliday who planted many thousands of trees on the moors hereabouts. Here also lived the Bullers and the Manningham-Bullers in the 19th Century, and Lord Dilhorne, a former Lord Chancellor, took his name from the village. Dilhorne Hall was demolished in the 1930s. All that remains of the Hall are the red-brick, Gothic, turreted gatehouse; the gabled lodges; and the ice-house. By the 1980s Dilhorne Recreational Centre had been built on the site.

The church of All Saints is noteworthy for its octagonal tower, one of very few in England. It is 13th Century in the lower part and 13th - 14th Century in the upper part. The four-bay arcades are 13th Century and the chancel late medieval, restored by Ewan Christian. The aisles are of 1819 and the doorways rusticated Gothic. The communion rail is Jacobean.

The Old Parsonage has four storeys, three bays, a semi-circular porch and Venetian windows. Houses of note nearby include Heywood Grange, 1.25m NW of Dilhorne, dated at 1672; and Stansmore Hall, lm WNW of Dilhorne, an early 17th Century house of stone with gables and mullioned windows. Susie Cooper (1903-1995), the ceramics designer, spent part of her retirement at the Old Parsonage, Dilhorne until 1987 when she moved to the Isle of Man.

Godleybrook, 0.75m NNE of Dilhorne, is a hamlet of old red brick houses with modern infill. The road runs downhill from Dilhorne and at the bottom the tree-clad spoil heaps of the Foxfield Colliery loom up on the left. The site of the mine is by a wayside memorial obelisk higher up the bank as one climbs out of the valley. The pit closed in the mid-20th Century and all that now remains are a few out-buildings. These are now occupied by Minelco, a mineral supply company, who have added their own sheds and hoppers. Here they crush, grade and pack a variety of minerals. When we visited they were turning a clay imported from Greece into a fine powder to be used in steel foundries.

The Foxfield colliery was one of the last coalmines in the area and is linked to the Uttoxeter-Stoke line at Blythe Bridge by a mineral railway. In 1967 the Foxfield Steam Railway Society was formed to preserve and run the railway. Some of the locomotives and rolling stock have been renovated and 'steamings' take place on Sundays and Bank holidays during the summer. The station is at the Blythe Bridge end of the track.

If the traveller continues on up the hill he climbs the long steep bank, through attractive hill country, until he reaches the high moorland plateau with wind-battered broken hedges and low stone walls all-a-tumble. The road meets the main road, the A52, at **Overmoor**, a crossroads' settlement consisting of a few scattered farms.

Boundary, 1m SE of Dilhorne, lies just off the A521. Turn off the main road and you are greeted by the rendered Red Lion Inn. This is on Daisy Bank. A little further up is a turn to the left. This is Commonside and here hides a tiny brick Methodist church, as plain as plain can be. Back on Daisy Bank one gets a good view of the Common – scrub woodland and pitted ground – and even better views of Cheadle which lies a million miles below, it seems. The residents of this hamlet live either in old cottages, many of which are being renovated or extended but with a gypsyish air to them, or in smart modern bungalows. Something of a culture clash, methinks, but a place of some character.

As to its name, the meaning is self-evident, but just what boundary we do not know. Boundaries can come and go and be of many things.

DOSTHILL *2.25m S of Tamworth*

To all intents and purposes Dosthill is a southern suburb of Tamworth. The River Tame runs close by to the west and the A5 (Watling Street) passes by to the north. It is mostly a modern place. The church of St Paul has a remarkable, if not comical, small broach spire. The old church stands to the north-east with Norman doorway and windows, and is now used as a parish hall. North of the old church is a barn, probably of the early 15th Century, with very good crucks (inverted curved 'V' shaped frames). Sitting by itself beside the river is Dosthill House, of 1830.

DOVEDALE *The southern entrance near Thorpe is 4m NW of Ashbourne*

It is a place of unsurpassed natural beauty, with scenery that varies from precipitous limestone cliffs to gentle meadows with caves and woods and secret corners. Dovedale lies between St Mary's Bridge (SK 146514), 0.5m W of the village of Thorpe, and Hartington Bridge (SK 121508), 0.5m W of Hartington, a distance of 7.5 miles. The most dramatic and most walked stretch is the Dovedale Gorge. This runs for 2.5 miles northwards from the car park near the Isaac Walton Hotel to Viator's Bridge at the picturesque hamlet of Milldale where there is also a car park. The journey can be made from either direction but we shall start at the south and head upstream.

The word 'Dove' is from the Celtic word meaning 'dark'. It is the 'dark river'. For much of its course and for the whole of this journey it forms the boundary between Staffordshire and Derbyshire. The car park is on the west bank of the river, the Staffordshire side. As one walks northwards, along the main path, the hill to the left is Bunster Hill (1,000 feet). The conical hill on the right is Thorpe Cloud (942 feet). After about 0.75m the river makes a sharp left-hand turn and at this point are the Stepping Stones which we use to cross to the east bank. The flat area of grass here is called Sow Sitch. On the left, on Bunster Hill, is the rock called Dove Dale Castle (or Dove Dale Church), and on the corner of the next bend are the limestone outcrops called The Twelve Apostles.

By now the woods are established and will be our companion for much of the way: this is a natural forest. The trees are predominantly ash and provide a rich sea of green that contributes greatly to the valley landscape. The walls of the gorge stand high now, to about 450 feet above the river. Opposite the Twelve Apostles the path rises to a promontory of rock called Sharplow Point. This is also known as Lover's Leap because a young girl who had been jilted by her lover leapt from the rock in an attempt to commit suicide. Fortunately, however, her fall was broken by the bushes and she survived.

The path descends to the river, passes Tissington Spires on the right and beyond them leads to Reynard's Cave. A short, steep side track leads through the impressive entrance arch to the cave itself, which is some 30 feet high and 15 feet wide. To the left of the main cave and a little above it is another smaller cave called Reynard's Kitchen. In July 1761 Dr Langton, Dean of Clogher in Northern Ireland, had picnicked near Reynard's Cave and was riding up the steep hill towards Tissington, with a young lady in the saddle behind him, when his over-loaded horse lost its footing and threw its riders. The young lady recovered from her fall but the Doctor died from the injuries he sustained.

The riverside path continues to The Straits, where the rocks on either side press hard against the river. Beyond lies the large crag called Lion's Head Rock, again on the right-hand side. High above the Lion's Head is the Watch Tower. Next come the great rock walls of Pickering Tors and opposite them, on the Staffordshire side of the river, is the bulk of Ilam Rock, which is usually in shadow. There is a footbridge across the Dove here which leads to Hurts Wood and Hall Dale, the upper northern slopes of which are bare and are called the Greek Temple. The main path continues on the Derbyshire bank, the right-hand side, and the ground rises again before the descent to the spectacular Dove Holes. These are big shallow caves, the largest one being about 55 feet wide and 30 feet high.

The valley now opens out. On the left-hand bank are the Shepherd's Abbey Rocks and beyond them the cliffs of Raven's Tor, set back from the river above a steep grassy bank. Dry stone walls appear and sheep are seen grazing. A long, narrow meadow leads to the ancient packhorse bridge called Viator's and the charming stone-built hamlet of **Milldale**. Here there is a car park and a tea shop. Several tracks converge at this point. There are footpaths to Wetton, Hope and Alstonefield on the Staffordshire bank and tracks through the hills which join the Buxton to Ashbourne road on the Derbyshire side.

For half-a-mile the metalled road now becomes the route along the left-bank of the river as far as Lode Mill. Here the walker crosses the bridge to the Derbyshire side under the shadow of the hill of Shining Tor. The valley is pastoral with occasional rocky outcrops. At Iron Tors the hill is clad in conifers, and half-a-mile further on Biggin Dale joins the Dove valley from the east (the right-hand side). From now on the valley of the Dove is called Wolfscote Dale, after Wolfscote Hill, which rises to 1,272 feet to the east After a mile of cliffs, pinnacles and screes the hills fall away and a path leads over a meadow and across a footbridge to Beresford Lane, a metalled road which ends at the river in a wood.

The traveller is now in **Beresford Dale**. The river flows through high-banked woods, over weirs and through Pike Pool (named after the rock that sticks out from the pool, not the fish) to the Charles Cotton Fishing Lodge of 1674, which still stands in good repair but which is not accessible from the Derbyshire bank. The Fishing Lodge (SK 126592) is stone-built, about 17 feet square and has a tall pyramid roof. The round-headed doorway has Tuscan pilasters to the sides. It is placed on a little promontory in a well-wooded area. The approach to it is somewhat boggy, and is being deliberately left like this as a small nature reserve. Access to the Fishing Lodge is gained from the big gate pillars on the B5054, which are 300 yards south-west of Hartington Bridge (about 0.75m SW of Hartington village). The gate fronts a long, dead-straight drive which leads to the site of the old Beresford Hall. This is now a mere pile of stones behind a stone wall, 40 yards to the left of the gate at which the drive ends. In the woods between the gate and the river are three abandoned statues. Incidentally, near its end the drive curves around an old stone barn with massively thick walls. This is called Og's Barn and is almost certainly very old indeed. The name is Celtic. Strangely, it is not marked on the 2.5 inch Ordnance Survey map.

To return to the Fishing Lodge, this can be found on the river bank, on the left of the drive, about half-a-mile beyond the gates on the main road. It is difficult to see until you are very close to it. The Tower, which lies in the grounds of the old Hall, also still stands, less than 0.25m S of the Lodge. North of the Fishing Lodge the country is open and the path leaves the Derbyshire bank of the river to terminate near the Charles Cotton Hotel at the village of Hartington.

DRAYCOTT IN THE CLAY *4m SE of Uttoxeter*

It lies in the little valley of the Salt Brook. A saline spring near Draycott Mill, 1m NNE of the village, provided salt for the nuns of nearby Hanbury Priory. In the early 19th Century the Phillips family of Upper Tean had textile machinery at Draycott.

The first element of the name Draycott might be from 'drogg', Anglo-Saxon for 'a porterage', a place where a boat had to be taken out of the water and carried around an obstacle. The church of St Augustine was built in about 1924.

Coton in the Clay, 1m NE of Draycott in the Clay, is a hamlet near the northern escarpment of Needwood Forest plateau. The old Elizabethan, timber-framed manor house was pulled down and the present new Hall built in 1790.

Greaves, a tiny hamlet south-east of Draycott, has a large wood, called Greaves Wood, which is part of Needwood Forest. In 1848 a servant of Queen Victoria discovered a 2nd Century BC, Iron Age gold torc (neck band), which had been dug up by a badger or a fox. It weighs 15.25 ounces and consists of eight twisted wires, each of which is made up of three wires with solid perforated ends. The torc is now at the British Museum.

DRAYCOTT IN THE MOORS *4m ESE of Longton*

It lies on the A521 Longton to Uttoxeter road. Approaching from the north it is disappointing, just 20th Century houses and bungalows along a busy main road. However, the old village centre, though small, has real character. It lies on a bend in a small dale - just a few mature houses and a pub with a timeless feel. The road passes through a rock cutting and descends to the suburbs of Upper Tean.

The main road actually follows the line of the Roman road, Ryknilde Street, and the Romans had a legionary outpost at Draycott. The ledges carved into the rock face at the back of the Post Office were probably carved by the Romans to store the tools used by their blacksmiths and cobblers. An ancient smithy stood here as late as 1956. The cockpit said to be at Draycott is probably that at SJ 984399.

The parish church of St Margaret was consecrated in 1286. The sturdy tower and north chapel are both 13th Century; the nave and chancel are Decorated. One north window is by Kempe and there are monuments to an unknown cross-legged knight, circa 1300; Sir Phillip Draycott (died 1554); and more 16th and 17th Century Draycotts.

At the time of Domesday Book Draycott was held by Henry Ferrers. There was land for 1 plough, 12 acres of meadow, 0.5 square league of woodland, 4 villagers, and 4 smallholders.

DRAYTON BASSETT *3m S of Tamworth*

At the time of Domesday book Drayton Bassett was simply Draitone. The manor belonged to the King who had 2 mills, 9 villagers, 3 smallholders and 8 burgesses of Tamworth who worked here. The Bassett suffix was added later when the Norman knight of that name became the lord of the manor. Today the village is best known for having been the home of Sir Robert Peel (1788-1850), who was Prime Minister in 1834-5 and 1841-6. He was a Conservative but also a reformer. He repealed the Corn Laws and produced the Tamworth Manifesto (1834).

Drayton Manor had been rebuilt by his father, a wealthy Lancastrian textile manufacturer, who came to Staffordshire in 1791 and rented the Castle Mill in Lady Meadow, Tamworth, for a cotton factory and the Castle banqueting hall for a forge. By 1795 he also had two cotton-spinning factories and a calico printing mill at **Bonehil**l (Fazeley), about lm SSW of Tamworth. The Bonehill Mill (SK 199021), used for calico printing, subsequently returned to grinding corn by water power and did so until 1965. The iron breastshot wheel is 12 feet in diameter and 14 feet wide, which is unusually wide. The four-storey, brick-built mill is now used as a builder's workshop. One of the two cotton mills has also survived and stands at the end of Mill Lane, now known as the Old Mill and owned by William Tolson Ltd, smallware manufacturers. The main block is of brick, three storeys high, 164 feet long and 33 feet wide.

Sir Robert Peel was very fond of his home at Drayton Bassett and regularly bought plants and seeds for the gardens there. The Manor was demolished some 60 years ago and today it is the site of the well-advertised and well-signposted Drayton Manor Park and Zoo. Some of the Gothic estate houses remain, as do parts of the gardens which were laid out by Gilpin.

The village of Drayton Bassett lies lm S of the zoo. The church of St Peter has a Perpendicular tower, a nave of 1793 and a chancel of about 1855. There is a monument to Sir Robert Peel, an inscription in black under a Gothic canopy. North-east of Drayton Bassett and close to the main road (A4091) is a foot-bridge over the Birmingham and Fazeley canal with round, Gothic brick towers.

DUDLEY *5m SSE of Wolverhampton*

It is a bright, busy place with an excellent range of shops and social facilities. Dudley has been styled 'Queen of the Black Country', and, indeed, if there was one town that does not conform to the popular, grim conception of the region it is Dudley. The town sits on a limestone ridge which is a watershed. Rivers and streams flow east from here to the North Sea and west to the Atlantic. Paradoxically, although the castle has always been in Staffordshire, the town has for centuries been a part of Worcestershire - an island in an alien sea. In 1974 the whole of the Black Country was removed from Staffordshire and became part of the West Midlands Metropolitan County.

The history of the settlement starts with Dudley Castle which stands on a mound high above the town. The castle site was occupied in Anglo-Saxon times when it was held by Earl Edwin during the reign of Edward the Confessor. In 1066 it passed to William Fitz Ansculf who also owned 25 manors in Staffordshire, 14 in Worcestershire and five in Warwickshire, as well as others elsewhere in the country. Little is left of the 11th Century castle. Most of what we see today - the gatehouse, the barbican and keep - is of the 14th Century. The castle passed to the de Somerys and from them to the de Suttons, who became Lords of Dudley. In the 16th Century John Dudley, the Duke of Northumberland, built a Tudor mansion, or Great Hall, within the old castle. In 1575 Queen Elizabeth stayed here. The Sutton family line ended in 1621 and the castle passed to the Wards who later became, and still are, Earls of Dudley.

During the Civil War the castle was a royalist stronghold, until captured by Cromwell's soldiers in 1646 when the defences were slighted. However, the Tudor mansion was left intact and many splendid balls were held in the great state rooms until 1750, when it was destroyed by a fire which raged for three days. The shell of the mansion, with its mullioned and transomed windows, still stands and forms the inner court. After the fire the castle was abandoned and the Wards moved to Himley Hall. About 1850 the castle became a place of recreation and an annual three-day Whitsuntide Fair was held here. In 1916 as many as 20,000 people attended the festivities.

In 1937 Dudley Zoo was built in the grounds and the earthwork defences of the castle. (There are seals in the moat). The concrete buildings were designed by Messrs Tecton who had also designed London Zoo (1934). Their work was unorthodox for the time but has since been accepted and even applauded. The curved entrance gates are a listed building. The Zoo company (now a charitable Trust of 1978) has invited and encouraged excavation of the castle site and this is now proceeding.

The town of Dudley grew up around the foot of the castle. There are few old buildings and the settlement seems to have developed largely in the 18th and 19th Centuries. It is not noted for its involvement in any particular industry although nails, fine glass, anvils and vices, ironwork for bridges and railway stations, cars (Bean's), beer and GPO post boxes have all been made here. It has a wide market place in the High Street, (the Old Town Hall stood here until demolished in 1860), and a fine fountain of 1867 which was exhibited at the Paris Exhibition of that year.

There are Council Offices of 1935; the Italianate County Court of 1858; the Baroque Central Library of the early 18th Century; a Technical College; a Grammar School; a Girls' High School; and near the entrance to the zoo is an Odeon (now used by Jehova's Witnesses as a meeting place); and the Hippodrome (built as a music hall in 1938 but now reduced to Bingo). In recent times the many streets of shops have been supplemented by the Churchill Precinct, complete with painted glass screen depicting Churchill. On the site of the old station there is now a Freight Liner terminal. As a shopping centre Dudley has been badly affected by the nearby Merry Hill development.

The ruins of Dudley Priory lie on the north-west fringes of the town centre in a grassed park area, at the foot of the castle hill. It was founded by Gervase Pagnell about 1160 for Cluniac Benedictine monks. It was never very large and there were never more than four resident monks, though there would no doubt also have been several guests staying at any one time. In brief, the remains consist of a nave of the early 13th Century, the south transept, the choir, two chancel south chapels, the outline of the cloister, the west wall of the west range and a spiral stair on the east range. After the Dissolution of the Monasteries the buildings were occupied by a tanner, a thread manufacturer, glass grinders, polishers of fire irons and polishers of fire fenders. The neo-Tudor Priory Hall was built in 1825. It is now used as offices.

There are six churches worthy of mention: St Edmund in Castle Street, (1722-4) of brick and stone with monuments to Edward Dixon, died 1806, and Thomas Badger, died 1856; St Augustine (1884) with lancet windows; St James (1840); St John (1840); Our Lady and St Thomas (1842) by Pugin; and St Thomas (1815-18) by William Brooks, attractive and with some unusual features and iron window tracery.

The Priory Housing Estate, built about 1930, stretches from the town almost to the foot of **Wren's Nest** Hill to the north-west. Here are now fenced-off entrances to the old limestone mines. Huge black holes in the rock face lead by way of passages and shafts to a multitude of great caverns. The workings are very extensive and not at all properly mapped. There have been some alarming collapses - craters appearing overnight in playing fields and houses subsiding. The Government has authorized the spending of considerable sums of money in order to attempt to fill in these workings, but the job will take many years. Fossils, especially trilobites, were once commonly found in the outcrops but these are now rarely found such has been the extent of depredation by collectors. At one time there were three fossil shops in the town. One of the 'Dudley Locusts' appears in the town's coat of arms. The Wren's Nest Hill is now a nature reserve with two organized trails.

At 3,172 yards (nearly two miles) the Dudley Canal Tunnel is the longest in Staffordshire. It was built in 1792 and connects the Birmingham Canal to the Stourbridge Canal. An extension of 1,227 yards leads from the main tunnel at Castle Mill basin (which is open to the sky) to an underground basin at Wren's Nest. This was paid for by the Earl of Dudley because its purpose was to serve his limestone mines there. British Rail had plans to seal off the canal to make safe an embankment above its Birmingham New Road entrance, but local enthusiasts formed a Preservation Society in the 1960s and through their efforts the tunnel was saved. They wrote a song called 'Push Boys Push' (recorded by 'The Black Country Three') which describes a journey through the tunnel. The title refers to the means of propulsion which is by 'legging'. There is no towpath so in the days before engines the horses were led over the hill and the boatmen lay on planks and propelled the boat by pushing with their feet against the tunnel walls. Regular trips for the public are run through the tunnel to the limestone caverns, and some 100,000 people a year avail themselves of the service. In recent years a new 65-yard-long tunnel was cut to the Singer Cavern, the first new tunnel of its kind to be constructed in Britain for over 100 years.

The **Black Country Museum** was established in 1975 on waste ground between the Birmingham New Road and the entrance to the Dudley Canal Tunnel. It is a remarkable enterprise. Buildings from all over the Black Country have been dismantled and re-erected here to form a typical street of the region. There is a reconstructed Newcomen engine, a tramway, a traditional fair, a pawnbroker's shop, an ironmonger's shop from Oldbury, a chemist's and a chapel from Netherton, a row of cottages from Old Hill, a pub from Wordsley, a bridge from Wolverhampton, a stable-block (now a restaurant) from Wednesbury, the headgear of a colliery, a boat-building dock, a rolling mill, a bakery, a chainshop and more. All this was initiated by local enthusiasts, ordinary people, not by professionals or local government. This is a reflection of an awakening pride in the region's history and traditions which occurred in the 1960s with performances of local songs by 'The Black Country Three' on Midlands Television in 1964, the publication of several books by M & J Raven in 1964-5 and the formation of the Black Country Society in 1966.

Opposite the Black Country Museum, in Tipton Road, is the Guest Hospital. It began as an asylum of 26 sandstone cottages, to accommodate men who had become blind whilst working in Lord Dudley's coal and limestone mines. However, they proved unpopular and remained empty until Joseph Guest paid for a hospital to be built around them. It is still a going concern with specialist facilities but Russell's Hall Hospital (opened in 1984) has usurped its premier position.

Dudley has produced two great ironmasters and innovators of iron-making techniques. They are Dud Dudley (1599-1684) and Abraham Darby (1678-1717). Dud Dudley was one of the 5th Earl of Dudley's 11 illegitimate children. In 1619, at the age of 20, he took charge of his father's ironworks in the town. At that time iron was smelted using charcoal as a fuel. Coal would not burn with sufficient heat. However, timber supplies in this country were being depleted at an alarming rate, and because of insufficient fuel the production of iron was curtailed. Imported iron was coming in from Spain and Sweden and a crisis was imminent. Dud Dudley experimented with coal as a fuel and it is likely that he did tests using coke. He made unambiguous claims to have succeeded in smelting iron with coal and it is now acknowledged that there is no reason to disbelieve him. In 1665 he published 'Martallum Martis', an account of the contempory iron trade and its problems. Dud Dudley had many trials and tribulations - rioters and floods damaged his works and competitors persectuted him with lawsuits – and finally the Civil War curtailed his experiments. He fought for the King as an engineer, casting iron and fortifying towns. At the end of the war he became an ironmaster again, but after the Restoration was denied the patents he had earlier been granted. He died in 1684, embittered and poverty stricken. With him died his secret coking process.

In 1677 Abraham Darby was born at Old Lodge Farm, Heath Green, Upper Gornal, 0.5m W of Wren's Hill. (See Gornal.) His father, John, was a Quaker farmer and locksmith. Abraham became interested in iron-casting, especially of pots and pans which were being imported from the Continent. He went to Holland, returned with Dutch craftsmen, and established a successful foundry, first at Bristol and then at Coalbrookdale in Shropshire. He initially used charcoal to smelt his iron but after several years of experimenting achieved success with coke as a fuel. The results were dramatic and enabled him and his successors to produce vast quantities of iron, cheaply and quickly, with a fuel supply that was virtually inexhaustible. He died in 1717 and his sons carried on refining the process which, much to their credit, they did not attempt to patent and which was very soon adopted by all their competitors.

Personalities in other fields born at Dudley include Dorothy Round (1909-82), who won the Ladies' Singles Championship at Wimbledon in 1934 and 1937, and was three times mixed doubles champion (twice with the great Fred Perry); and Duncan Edwardes, considered by many to be the greatest and most versatile professional footballer ever. He died in the Munich air crash which virtually wiped out Manchester United F C in 1958. He was born on the Priory Estate and there is a stained glass window to his memory in the church of St Francis. Billy Russell (1893-1971), the comedian, was born in Birmingham but brought up in Dudley; he was the first popular exponent of Black Country humour. Fellow comedians Billy Dainty and Lenny Henry are also natives of Dudley. Many famous rock musicians from groups like Led Zeppelin, Black Sabbath, Killing Joke and Slade have traded equipment and passed the time of day at Modern Music on Castle Hill. 'Devil' Dun of Dudley (died 1851) was a very famous 'wise man' who specialized in charms that enabled stolen property to be recovered. He had a national reputation and clients came from all parts of the country.

Now, a few notes on areas around Dudley that have their own local names. **Mon's Hill** adjoins Wren's Nest to the north. The hill has yellow cliff faces topped with small scrub trees. Below it, along Wren's Nest Road, are dirt stained Council houses, blocks of flats, the Washington Ashes and a few shops. The Mons Hill School is perched on top of the hill, waiting for the day when subterranean limestone workings collapse and take the school with it. Parts of the playings fields have already subsided.

Oakham, 1m ESE of Dudley centre, has long historical roots as its name proclaims 'homestead in the oakwood'. It is now a suburb of Dudley. Undoubtedly the most colourful character to have emerged from Oakham is a somewhat mercurial character called Lillian Lima Valerie Barker (born 1985), who reputedly posed as her husband, a colliery manager at Oakham, on his death. She then became Col Sir Leslie Victor Gauntlet Bligh Barker, DSO, Bart, and obtained several posts as such. She married two women at different times and went to prison for deception and indecency. Her last identity was as Geoffrey Norton and she is thought to have died in Suffolk in 1960.

Russell's Hall, 2m E of Dudley centre, is a recently developed housing estate, complete with a few shops, a small yellow brick church and several schools. The estate is called Russell's Hall because it stands on land that used to belong to the owners of Russell's Hall. Virtually nothing is known of the Russell family who once occupied this house, but they were gone by the late 13th Century when the estate passed to Bishop Robert Burnell, treasurer to the king. He owned a vast amount of property and quite possibly never even saw Russell's Hall. It then passed to the Lovels and later to the de Suttons, who became the Lords of Dudley. They probably rebuilt the house in the early 16th Century. It was altered again in about 1733 by the Lea family and demolished in 1844. The exact site of the house is not known, but it was probably where Occupation Street, on Eve Hill, is now. The valley below was ripped open for coal. There were at least four pits. Their shafts have been capped, their spoil heaps levelled, and on these unsure foundations stand the houses of Russell's Hall today.

Holly Hall is a mixed residential and industrial area that stands around the junction of Stourbridge Road and Kingswinford Road. The Holly Hall School and Dudley Drop Forgings are noted institutions here. At **Springs Mire**, a little to the west of Holly Hall, is the large, 408-bed Russell's Hall Hospital which was opened in 1984. The name Springs Mire reflects the wet scrubland from which several streams emerge. **London Fields** is a recently constructed residential estate of affordable houses on the northern slopes of the Russell's Hall valley. Adjoining it is the Milking Bank estate, still under construction.

At **Eve Hill** 0.5m W of Dudley town centre, the Himley Road crosses the busy Wolverhampton Road. Around the island are: the parish church of St James the Great, neat, attractive, of small limestone 'bricks', with a tower over the entrance, built in 1840; the Wolverhampton Polytechnic Dudley Campus; the towers of 20-storey blocks of flats; and the Grange Inn. These are not really on a hill, but the Dudley-Wolverhampton ridge. Eve could be personal name, but also could be a corruption of 'eave', meaning boundary.

Adjacent to Eve Hill, to the north, is **Shavers End,** an ill defined residential area of semis such as those in Nith Place. Facilities include The Salamander, The British Oak, and the Dudley Christian Fellowship Centre. There was once a windmill here at SO 933908. It had a sandstone tower, two pairs of stones and a dressing machine. Built before 1800, it was demolished in the 1930s. Today there is concrete water reservoir in its place. **Blower's Green** lies 0.5m SW of Dudley centre. A 'blower' was the man who operated the bellows that blow air into the furnace of a nail or chain shop. Downhill from the red brick Sir Gilbert Claughton School and a row of terraced houses is a valley full of large industrial sheds. The biggest of the estates is down Pear Tree Lane where there is an Enterprise Zone. Enterprise Zones bestow certain financial advantages on participating firms. This is a manufacturing area - steel engineering, fastners, power presses - but there are also warehouses and research units. Where the yellow sheds of the Grazebrook Industrial Park meet the multi-coloured sheds of the Blackbrook Estate is a bit of the 19th Century - the Blower's Green Canal Depot. It stands in its original condition, preserved through neglect: a blue-brick warehouse, locks, a reed-fringed canal basin, a couple of canal-side cottages and a railway viaduct – a charming scene despite the clatter and dust from the concrete works next door. Back on the main road, now called Cinder Hill, is the Hillcrest Business Park, arising out of the ashes of a large, abandoned sheet metal works.

Adjoining Blower's Green to the north is **Scott's Green**. This is a mainly residential area which straddles the A461 Stourbridge Road. What catches the eye are the broad blocks of flats - five storeys high and 24 bays wide - that stand opposite the wooded cemetery. Nearby is an Islamic School.

Kate's Hill, 0.33m SE of Dudley centre, is a place of rendered council houses, cleared green spaces, and Victorian terraces. From the upper slopes there are good views across the railway to the castle. In the graveyard of St John's Church (1840) lie the bones of the mighty Tipton Slasher, bare-knuckle champion of Britain. As to the Kate of the place name, could it be a dedication to one of the five Catherines who have married English Kings?

St John's Road runs into **Dixon's Green** where there is a Central Clinic, an orange brick Methodist Church, some larger Victorian houses and roadside trees. Turn into Blackacre Road and you are in **Paradise**. A small park called The Buffery is surrounded by small terraced houses. These huddle below the looming CWS works with its tall, thin chimney. At the town end of this complex is an exposed coal mine spoil heap - within a bowshot of Beatties.

Tansley Hill is a residential area north of Dixon's Green and adjacent to the Oakham Road, along which are attractive semis and detached houses with trees and hedges. There are long views over Warren's Hall Park to the Clent Hills from Elizabeth Grove. But soon we are upon monotonous modern housing estates. They swarm all over these Rowley Hills. **Oakham Centre** is a barricaded brick shed on top of **Darby's Hill**. Above it towers an aerial mast. There are wondrous views to the south, and disused hard-rock quarries to the north. In City Road is a small shopping centre, schools, a quarry spoil heap, an Evangelical church and The Wheatsheaf. We are now in Turner's Hill. (See Rowley Regis.)

DUNSLEY *0.5m E of Kinver*

Dunsley lies south-west of Stourton and to the east of Kinver. The sizeable settlement stands on a high escarpment with splendid views over the River Stour and the Staffordshire and Worcestershire Canal. The name is from 'Dane's lea'. There is a 25-yard tunnel on the canal at Dunsley. In Mill Lane is the site of a windmill. Dunsley Manor, 0.75m NE of Kinver church, has a timber-framed range of the 16th Century which was later encased in brick. Dunsley Hall, 0.75m SW of Stourton, was the manor house of Dunsley and was occupied by Gilbert de Dunsley in 1316. The present house is 16th Century but has many later additions.

In the early 19th Century a tenant of the Hall, Mr Robbins, is said to have been murdered by a highwayman.

Gibralter is an area on the east side of the Staffordshire and Worcestershire Canal, south of Dunsley House (0.5m NE of Kinver church). By 1830 there were 12 cave dwellings carved into the sandstone rock face. By 1851 there were 18 households here, some of whom worked as labourers at the canal wharf. By the 1880s the cave houses were condemned and have degenerated very much since. In 1846 the Wesleyan Methodists are said to have held religious meetings in one of the rock houses.

DUNSTALL *(near Barton) 1m N of Barton-under-Needwood*
Dunstall is a small, pretty village on the edge of Needwood Forest. In the 13th Century the name was Tunstall, 'enclosed farmstead', which here presumably means enclosed out of Needwood Forest. In the 14th Century the land at Dunstall was held from the Lord of Wychnor. By 1553 there was a chapel here.

The approach to the church of St Mary is lined with holly trees. It was built by Henry Clutton in 1852 and paid for by John Hardy of Dunstall Hall. The south-west tower has a round staircase projection and is topped by a tall spire. Inside it is vaulted, as is the porch. The chancel is lined with alabaster. Clutton also designed the School and the Rectory. In the church is a tablet engraved: 'In memory of Charles Arkwright Esq of Dunstall, founder of this church and the schools connected with it. Fifth son of Sir Richard Arkwright of Willersley, Derbyshire.'

There is believed to have been a medieval village in the vicinity of the church, the Old Hall or the Hall which was probably deserted in the 18th Century. Dunstall Hall (not the Old Hall) was called Dunstall Lodge until 1850 and was the principal house of the area. Early occupiers were the Newbolds, Boyntons and Turtons. In 1997 Stan Clarke, the property entrepreneur, bought Dunstall Hall and began a fastidious restoration project with commercial intentions. Dunstall Hall is something of an enigma, but by 1850 it existed much as we see it today. The original house was just the four-bay centre. The 10-bay garden side, the seven-bay orangery, and the entrance side (which has a porte-cochere and a turret-like attic) came later. Inside there is an authentic Roman mosaic floor, thought to have come from Tivoli, which depicts Cerberus in the centre. The staircase and the front door were handsomely and lavishly carved by Edward Griffiths in about 1900. Animals and landscapes predominate. There is also some much-admired stained glass, in particular the leaves, flowers and shields in a corridor by an unknown artist who might have been Rowlands.

DUNSTON *3.5m S of Stafford*
It lies on the A449, close to Junction 13 of the M6 motorway. Dunston is a small, scattered hamlet which was for long in Royal ownership, being first the possession of the Anglo-Saxon King Edward and then of William the Conqueror. The present Italianate stuccoed Hall was built in the 1870s. Lord Thorneycroft was born in this house. There has been a building on the site since the 13th Century when there was a farm here. The present stable-block pre-dates the present Hall, which is today owned by the Staffordshire County Council and

leased to the North Staffordshire Polytechnic who use it as a student hostel (80 places).

The large, rock-faced church of St Leonard dates from 1876, was designed by W D Griffin of Wolverhampton and paid for by F C Perry, who lies outside in an enormous marble tomb. It replaced an earlier church. The brick Rectory lies further south and has been divided into several separate homes. The M6 cuts through the country here on a raised embankment, broadcasting its incessant drumming din.

EARLSWAY

The Earlsway is a route from Chester to North Staffordshire, and is thought to have been used by the Earls of Chester to visit their Staffordshire estates from at least the 12th Century. It is possible that the route was originally created by pre-Norman, Anglo-Saxon earls. Earlsway enters Staffordshire at The Cloud (east of Congleton) and passes through Rushtonhall (near Rushton Spencer), Abbey Green, Leek, Bradnop, Lower Lady Meadows Farm (1.75m SW of Bradnop), and Waterhouses to Ashbourne (Derbyshire). Earlsway House is on the Earlsway, 1m WNW of Rushtonhall. There has been a house on this site since at least 1350.

ECCLESHALL *7m NW of Stafford*

The name is pronounced locally as 'Eccle-shawl'. Eccleshall lies in the midst of well-wooded, undulating country. The name means 'the place of the church' and it is likely that the Bishop of Chester's extensive medieval estate centred on Eccleshall, which was previously an Anglo-Saxon or even a Romano-British estate which was passed on more or less intact. There was certainly an Anglo-Saxon church in Eccleshall, probably founded by St Chad in the 6th Century. There are reused carved Anglo-Saxon stones in the south arcade of the tower of the present church, and also a stone in the vestry with carvings of two men, one thought to be a bishop and the other St Chad mounting a horse. The nave of the church is 12th Century, the chancel and tower 13th Century and the clerestory 15th Century. Internal features include stained glass by Clayton and Bell (1870), the reredos by Champneys (1898) and a finely carved Lady Chapel and organ case by Caroe (1931). In 1866 the church was restored by Street and it was he who rebuilt the east wall with its fine, stepped lancet windows. The tower, the clerestory and the south aisle have battlements and pinnacles. It is a large church but well-proportioned and held in high regard by students of architecture.

Five bishops are buried here. The earliest is Richard Sampson, chaplain to Cardinal Wolseley and friend of Erasmus. He also assisted Henry VIII to obtain his divorce from Catherine of Aragon. The others are Thomas Bentham, William Overton, James Bowestead and John Lonsdale. There is possibly a sixth bishop buried here. This is Robert Wright, who garrisoned the church for King Charles during the Civil War, and whose monument may be the worn stone figure that lay for many years in the churchyard but is now inside the church.

Eccleshall Castle lies just to the north of the church but is hidden from view by a small wood, which was grown for this purpose, and is approached off the Eccleshall to Newcastle road, the A519. It is quite possible that the Anglo-Saxon bishops had a house on the site. Certainly, this has been the main residence of the post-Norman Bishops of Lichfield and before that of Chester. (William the Conqueror gave the Saxon diocese of Lichfield to the Bishop of Chester but it was later reinstated.) A licence to crenellate a castle here was granted as early as 1200, but the first castle of which we have certain knowledge was built by Bishop Walter de Langton in the late 13th Century. All that remains of this castle is a nine-sided corner tower with small, pointed, trefoiled windows. The site is surrounded by a moat, crossed by a 14th Century bridge, and probably had four towers originally.

In 1643, during the Civil War, the Castle was besieged and Bishop Wright was killed participating in its defence. The fortress fell and was partially dismantled. In 1695 Bishop Lloyd built the substantial 13-bay brick house with projecting wings that we see today. The house continued to be used as the Bishop's main residence until after the death of Bishop Lonsdale in 1864. (The new Bishop's palace at Lichfield was built in 1687 but was little used.) The castle was sold and in about 1900 it passed to the Carter family, who are the current owners.

There is a small mere in the castle grounds, a remnant of the old marshes and pools that formed part of the defences. The mere and the wet meadowland that fringe it are a Nature Reserve containing many wetland plants. The bishops had an important corn mill, which stood on the bar north of the town along which Castle Street runs and which was, in fact, the dam wall that held back the waters of one of the branches of the River Sow. This formed the large mill pool that lay north-west of the Castle.

With regard to employment the leather trades such as cordwainers, saddlers and tanners were important in Eccleshall and in the mid-19th Century shoe-makers were only exceeded in numbers by farm workers. Eccleshall is not so much a village as a small town. It is sited at the meeting of many roads. The High Street is wide and until about 2000 it had distinctive cobbled verges. There is a good selection of shops and many Georgian houses. The Royal Oak and the Crown have attractive arcades over the pavement. The town has a typical village cricket pitch adjacent to the church and a rugby club. In medieval times there was another street called Usulwall Street which ran south of, and parallel to, the High Street but this wasted away through depopulation and is now given over to gardens.

On the road to Newport is the new Fire Station with an old cart-type fire engine very nicely displayed. Johnson Hall, 0.5m SW of Eccleshall, with access off the Newport Road, is a large neo-Tudor mansion set in pleasant agricultural grounds. In 1978 it was bought by an arms dealer, Mr Rawlins, who runs his mail order business from the Hall. Nearby is the Foster's (Plant) Nursery.

On the fringe of the village, on the road to Stone, is a brick-built Roman Catholic church and further along is Fletcher's Garden Centre. Attached to this is the Gentleshaw Wildlife Centre. Animals tend to come and go but there is always a large and varied selection. When we filmed there the cast list included: llamas, baby barn owls, a lynx, a dozen different birds of prey - including a golden eagle - monkeys, snakes and numerous small furry creatures. Indeed, it is a veritable zoo. Sadly Rob Smith, the avuncular founder, died in 2004. He was in his prime and will be very much missed, but he left a dedicated band of helpers and his work continues.

The folklorist Charlotte Sophia Burne (1850-1923), whose book 'Shropshire Folk Lore' (1881) is internationally known as an important and early work on British traditions, songs, games and customs, lived at Pyebirch Manor, 1m SE of Eccleshall, towards the end of her life.

The road from Eccleshall to Swynnerton, 4.5m. NNE, takes one past the Raleigh Hall Industrial Estate, Drake Hall open Prison, the now-abandoned Army Weapons' Testing Depot at Coldmeece and the Old Army Camp at Swynnerton, now fenced off and guarded. It is here that radioactive dust was scattered over a vast area during an exercise and here that atomic weapons' convoys stay here overnight on the journey from Scotland to the south. By the time you reach Swynnerton you might be thinking you are lucky to be alive! Drake Hall, 1.25m N of Eccleshall on the road to Newcastle-under-Lyme, is an encampment that was built about 1938 as a hostel for workers at the Royal Ordnance Factory at Swynnerton. It is now a women's prison. The name is from Sir Francis Drake.

Sturbridge was a minute hamlet which has been greatly enlarged by the construction of the Raleigh hall Industrial Estate which hides behind a high yew tree hedge.

Hilcote Hall, 1.25m ESE of Eccleshall, was held by the Noels from about 1600, followed by the Ansons and Dixons, and in 1960 by the First Lord Nelson of Stafford, George Horatio Nelson (1887-1962), who was the managing director of English Electric between 1930 and 1956. (The company had a large works in Stafford.) In 1987 it became a nursing home. The present Hall is probably early 19th Century, incorporating some of the previous building, but has some large, modern extensions. It stands on a wooded bank above a stream.

Horsley, 1m SW of Eccleshall, is a small, fragmented settlement. The name means 'Horsa's farm'. Horsley Old Hall, of 1611 and built by the Pershall family, no longer exists. It stood where Horsley Farm now stands. Horsley (New) Hall was built in 1883. During the Second World War it was occupied by the RAF; it then became a boarding school and has lately been redeveloped into apartments.

ECTON *0.75m ESE of Warslow, which is 7.5m ENE of Leek*

Ecton is a small, fragmented, stone-built hamlet in the steep-sided valley of the winding River Manifold. (Incidentally, the original name of the river was Hyle. Manifold is a later name which literally means 'many folds'.) The track of the old Manifold Light Railway passes by here. This has now been surfaced and is a public footpath, the Manifold Way. Above the valley towers Ecton Hill, from which have been taken vast quantities of high-grade copper and lead ore which also contained some zinc and silver. The ores were first worked commercially by German miners for the leaseholder, Sir Richard Fleetwood. These miners were the first to use gunpowder for mine excavation in Britain. By the late 1680s the mines had closed and were soon almost forgotten.

They were 'rediscovered' in 1720 and worked by a Cornish miner in association with a company of Ashbourne adventurers. They struck a rich mass of copper ore, but in 1764 their lease ran out and the mine was taken over by its owners, the Cavendish family, Dukes of Devonshire. They excavated a huge cavern in the side of the hill, which became a well-known tourist attraction. There were some 60 or 70 men underground, with many women and children on the surface washing and grading ores. Altogether, several hundred people were employed here. In about 1830 the mine showed signs of being worked out and the Devonshires leased the workings to a partnership of miners. By 1838 the seam of ore was virtually exhausted. Several companies were formed in the latter part of the 19th Century. They all hoped to find new deposits, but all failed. The Dukes of Devonshire had got out just at the right time having made several large fortunes, some of which they spent on developing Buxton as a spa town.

Noteworthy sites on Ecton Hill include: the Dutchman Mine, now covered by the huge spoil-heap (SK 098582) that looms over Ecton village; The Ecton Deep Adit, driven by Robert Shaw in 1774, which reached a depth of 1,650 feet and can still be seen (SK 096581); and the Ecton Engine House (SK 098583), which consists of a stone and tiled shelter for a Boulton and Watt steam engine of 1788, and the chimney stack, now reduced to a height of about 10 feet. Just to the north is the site of a gin-race.

At Ape Tor, a precipitous rocky cliff on Ecton Hill, adjacent to the valley road at about SK 100587, there is a stone-built projecting entrance structure that leads to a 200-foot deep vertical shaft. This connects to a 600-foot long underground canal tunnel. The copper ore and rock spoil was hauled to the surface by a horse turning a horizontal windlass (a gin) above the shaft. The entrance is protected by a strong, iron-barred gate and the land here is now in the care of the National Trust. There are other adits and spoil heaps along this stretch of road, and some people consider the charms of the Manifold exceed those of the Dove.

Ecton Low is an early burial mound, 0.25m E of Ecton Bridge, with a diameter of about 80 feet and a height of six feet. One of the farms on the Hill perpetuates the ancient Longhouse format where a man and his animals sleep under one roof. The central house is flanked by byres. A lane which runs around the east side of the hill, opposite to that which faces the valley, is called Back Ecton. There are several small farms along this lane and at the very end, in a delightful setting, is the Manor House (SK 104567). The road used to continue on down to Wetton Mill but is no longer passable in a vehicle.

The Manor House is a small stone-built house with mullioned windows which has had a varied history. It began life as an estate lodge and then, with many thirsty miners in the area, became a public house called 'The Peppercorn'. It was not officially licensed, but as the Duke Devonshire had commissioned it the authorities turned a blind eye. Nearby, the stream was dammed to provide a head of water to power a waterwheel of the copper smelting plant situated here. When the mines ceased to be worked the Manor House became a farmhouse. The farmer's wife had a sideline, namely the manufacture of lead buttons, and a workshop was created by adding a third floor to the house, which had a separate access from the rear up outside steps. When the Manifold Light Railway was being built there was an outbreak of cholera amongst the workers and the Manor House was used as an Isolation Hospital.

The Hillocks, a large house half-way up the hill at Ecton, was built in 1933 by Arthur Ratcliffe, MP for Leek. It is also known as Castle Folly; its copper spire came from a demolished chapel.

This reminds us that in medieval times Ecton was held by Tutbury Priory. After the Dissolution of the Monasteries it passed to the Earls of Devonshire.

EDINGALE *7m ENE of Lichfield*
Edingale is a compact village close to the River Mease, which meanders across its flood plain hereabouts. The most striking feature of the settlement is the tiny, mounded green at its centre, upon which stand the remains of three large and ancient elm trees. Dr Plot described this as being a Roman burial mound. Facing

the green is the Black Horse pub and several half-timbered cottages. Church Farm House is a black and white building of 1664; close by is the church of Holy Trinity, which was rebuilt by C Lynam in 1881. It is of red brick and has a short tower with a pyramid roof. The vestry east window has an Anglo-Saxon, stonework head rescued from the previous church. Opposite Rose Cottage is the old, green-painted village water pump, set into the roadside bank. There are some new houses in the village but it remains a pleasant little place. The place name Edingale means something like 'the hall of Eada'.

ELFORD *5.5m E of Lichfield*
Elford lies above a bend in the River Tame and the name could be from 'eel ford'. In 1066 the manor was owned by Earl Algar but after the Conquest it was taken by the king himself. It was a village of considerable size for its day, with 24 villagers and 8 smallholders and their families, plus all those who did not owe service to the lord of the manor and who are not, therefore, mentioned in Domesday Book.

The list of local lords reads like a litany: Ardernes to Stanleys to Smythes to Bowes to Howards to Pagets. There is an early burial mound called Elfordlow alongside the Tamworth road. The country around the village is flat but pleasant, and the settlement itself is very quiet and dignified. It is well-wooded and there are some very attractive houses.

The church of St Peter is approached along an avenue of lime trees. It has a tower of 1598 and the rest is by Salvin, of 1848, except for the south aisle and the south chapel which are by Street, of 1869. It is the monuments for which the church is best known. These were very thoroughly restored by E Richardson in 1848.

The most popular of the monuments is without doubt the effigy of the child, John Stanley, who was killed by a blow from a Real (Royal) Tennis ball, which is very hard, in about 1460. In fact, there are anachronistic details, the hairstyle and face being more in the style of the 13th Century.

Richardson was also responsible for the unsubstantiated attribution of the name of the great Sir John Spencer (who crowned Henry VII on Bosworth Field) to the splendid alabaster figure of an unknown knight, of about 1370. There are also monuments to Sir Thomas Arderne, died 1391; William Staunton, died circa 1450; Sir William Smythe, died 1525; and Craven Howard (who married the Bowes family heiress) and his son, Henry Bowes Howard, who became the 4th Earl of Berkshire and the 11th Earl of Suffolk. The church is heavy with painted coats of arms and gilded angels. The stained glass windows are by Wailes and by Ward and Hughes. The south aisle west window is 16th Century Dutch, brought here in 1825 from Herckenrode Abbey near Liege.

At the half-timbered house recently renamed Franheim, Stanley Whitehead established (in 1953) a non-profit making organisation which enables young people to participate in adventure holidays, both in this country and abroad. They use Land Rovers called 'Frams'. Fram is Norwegian for 'forward'.

In 1936 Francis Paget gave Elford Hall (1757) and 650 acres to Birmingham Corporation. The Hall was demolished in 1964 and there are now new villas in the grounds. The medieval Manor House may have stood on the moated site by the house called Elford Park.

ELLASTONE *5.5m NNE of Uttoxeter*
There are two parts to the village, Upper and Lower. Lower Ellastone lies close

to the River Dove on the road to Norbury (in Derbyshire). It is a pleasant enough place with some old stone houses. In the middle of the village is a lane running north. This formerly went on to the Abbey, but now comes to a dead-end just beyond a little stone bridge. Here are two farms and an old stone mill now used as an agricultural merchants. The mill was built in 1822. The water wheel is gone but the mill pool remains. It was still working after the Second World War. The previous mill on this site belonged to Calwich Abbey. **Calwich** is a scattered hamlet on the steep west bank of the River Dove, where there are three burial mounds: Calwich Low, a nameless mound and Rowlow. The name Calwich means 'calf-settlement'.

Calwich Abbey (or Priory) lay 0.5m NW of Ellastone. It was founded in about 1130 as an Augustian house. The monks were driven out in the late 1530s at the Dissolution, and the buildings were taken over by John Fleetwood and made into a private house. It was said that he 'made a parlour of the chancel, a hall of the church and a kitchen of the steeple'. In 1630 Richard Fleetwood was living here. He married a girl of six years of age and she had born and buried a child before she was 13. In 1611 Fleetwood bought a baronetcy (from James Stuart) and, as Sir Richard Fleetwood became a Catholic, left the Abbey and, two miles away, built himself the most splendid house in the county, namely Wootton Lodge.

His son, Thomas, stayed on at Calwich but in the early 18th century the Abbey passed to Bernard Granville. He pulled down the building and built a new house by the stream, which he dammed to form a lake. He was an eccentric and a semi-recluse who doted on his house and garden, both of which had a high reputation for their beauty. Famous people came here. Handel played the organ for Granville and gave the old man 38 volumes of manuscripts of his compositions. Local tradition has it that he composed some of his Water Music here. Jean Jacques Rousseau, the bohemian French philosopher, spent a year (1766) at nearby Wootton Hall (not Wootton Lodge) and was thoroughly miserable. One of his few pleasures were the visits he paid to Calwich, where he could speak to Bernard Granville in his own language. Indeed, it is said that when his friend went away for the winter Rousseau consoled himself by writing his now classic 'Confessions'. Granville's sister, Mrs Delaney, was at Calwich frequently, and her letters are now in the British Museum.

In the early 19th Century the house passed out of the hands of the Granvilles and was, alas, demolished. Only the delightful Fishing Temple (of about 1790) and a part of the stable block remain. The Temple has a portico of columns, tripartite windows, a copper dome and steps from the back door that lead straight to the waters of the nine-acre lake. It is approached off a track that leads from the road to Mayfield. The four stone lodges also survive. The estate is now owned by a firm of undertakers.

Upper Ellastone lies on higher ground to the north-west. The church of St Peter is mostly of the 16th Century, with a nave rebuilt in 1830, and monuments to local families - the Fleetwoods, Davenports, Bromley Davenports and the Granvilles. There are many stone houses in the village. The Old Hall is a fine, sturdy ashlar house of the late 17th Century. It stands boldly in the centre of the village and has lately been an antiques' shop. At one time it became an inn, the Davenport Bromley Arms, and as such was the model for George Eliot's Donnithorne Arms in her novel 'Adam Bede' (1859). On the road to Leek is the Adam Bede cottage. This is the house where George Eliot's uncle, Samuel Evans, lived - he became Seth Bede in her writings - and is immediately recognizable by the strange stone ornaments on the wall alongside the road. In Eliot's book Loamshire is Staffordshire, Stonyshire is Derbyshire, Oakburne is Ashbourne, Norbourne is Norbury, Eagledale is Dovedale and, of course, Ellastone was Hayslope.

On the strength of a house named 'Bioomsmithy' being mentioned in 1433, it was assumed that there was ironworking at Ellastone during the 15th Century, possibly at or near the mill already mentioned. It is known that in 1620 there was a forge and a furnace at Ellastone. There is a tumulus (SK 138442) lm NE of the village alongside the road to Mayfield. Adjacent to the bridge (1777), across the Dove on the road to Norbury, is a large, shallow depression that could have been either a mill pool or a fish pond (SK 119424). On the other side of the road is an area of disturbed ground and what appears to have been an old track that possibly led to a ford.

The film 'Blanche Fury', starring Stewart Grainger and Valerie Hobson, was shot in Ellastone village.

ELLENHALL *1.5m SSE of Eccleshall*

Ellenhall is a pleasant agricultural village in attractive rolling country. The red brick Hall, with its two 18th Century gables and round sham windows, is now a farmhouse. The church of St Mary lies alongside the Hall on sloping ground well off the road. In the chancel is a Norman window. The tower is brick, of 1757; likewise the south of the nave. The chancel and the north side are stone. The style is largely Perpendicular.

In 1086 Ellenhall was an outlier of the extensive manor of Sugnall, which was owned by the Bishop of Chester and held from him by the quaintly named Fran and Fragin. Later it passed to the Noel family, who founded Ranton Abbey, and then to the Harcourts of Stanton Harcourt. One mile north of Ellenhall, on the lane to Eccleshall, is Pyebirch Manor - gabled, ivy-clad and surrounded by trees. This was once the home of Charlotte Burne, author of 'Shropshire Folklore'.

A widespread country practice of ancient origin was the making of either a 'nursrow tree' (out of oak or ash) or a 'shrew ash' (out of an ash tree). A hole was bored into the trunk of a tree, a live shrew or mouse was placed therein and the hole sealed with a plug. As the poor creature died so its life force was thought to transfer to the tree. If a cow, sheep or horse fell lame a twig would be cut from the tree and laid against the afflicted limb. A cure was effected by transferring the life in the stick to the limb, and the malaise in the limb to the stick. The origin of this remedy was associated with the belief that lameness in animals was caused by them having been touched by a shrew.

ELMHURST *1.5m N of Lichfield*

This small, nucleated and most attractive village lies on the ancient road from Lichfield to King's Bromley. Old cottages and mature houses, a farm and a new terrace of red brick houses are served by a primary school and a red brick community centre. The little red brick mission church is attached to a house and hides away down a wooded footpath that leads off the tiny crossroads green. The whole village is embowered in tall trees, in which singing birds sing as cheerful a welcome as you can imagine.

The first Hall, home to Michael Biddulph, MP for Lichfield in 1646 and 1648, was demolished in about 1808 when it was bought by John Smith, who built a new Hall in Elizabethan style. That in turn was demolished in 1921. A quarter-of-a-mile south of Elmhurst Hall Farm is a gabled, lodge-like house of brick with stone dressings, a wide entrance gate and a low garden wall decorated with stone balls. The name Elmhurst is Anglo-Saxon and means either 'elm wood' or Elle's wood'.

ENDON *4m NE of Han/ey, Stoke-on-Trent*
The name means 'Eana's Hill'. Do not be misled by the 20th Century growth along the main road, the A53 from Leek to Stoke. The old village lies off the road at the north end of the long, main-road, modern developments. A little stream crosses Brook Lane, and next to the ford is a stone footbridge. Most of the houses are red brick though there are some older stone cottages. By the Wesleyan Chapel of 1855, which is now a pair of semi-detached dwellings, is the famous well. A spring issues here, through the mouth of a bearded man set in a stone housing of 1845. The traditional custom of dressing a well with flowers in the month of May (on Spring Bank Holiday Monday) is maintained here.

High above the village is the pretty church of St Luke. It has a tower dated at 1730 but the rest was rebuilt by J Beardmore in 1876-9. The stained glass in the east window is by Morris & Co, of 1893. Bank House stands opposite the church at Endon at the summit of the hill. It was the house of John Daniels (died 1821), who was one of the owners of the New Hall Pottery, Shelton. He and his sister, Alice, are both buried in the garden. At the bottom of the hill on which the church stands is The Plough, a late-Georgian inn with three two-storey bow windows. The groom at more than one wedding has popped in here for a bit of Dutch courage.

Half-a-mile north-east of the village is The Ashes, a good stone house of the 17th Century with two projecting wings and mullioned windows. The Ashes has vaulted cellars, and in one is a large stone coffin with Cistercian markings. In the valley below is the Caldon Canal which is crossed here by the cast-iron Hazlehurst Bridge of 1842.

Stockton Brook, 1m SW of Endon, lies around the A53 Leek to Burslem-Hanley road, where the road crosses the Caldon Canal and the Leek to Stoke railway. The attractive little timber-clad station was opened in 1896 and closed in 1956, but still stands beside the main road and is now used as a shop.

ENGLETON *1.25m SSE of Stretton near Penkridge*
In 1937 a Roman villa was found and excavated at Engleton, 500 yards south of Watling Street at SJ 894104. It had a small bath wing and was probably occupied between the 2nd and 4th Centuries. The pillar of a sundial in the grounds of Engleton Hall Farm is said to be Roman and to have come from the villa site. Other finds here include a coin of Ealdred (994-995) and a crossbow-type brooch. The name Engleton means 'English town', a settlement of the Angles. There was possibly a medieval settlement here, probably deserted by 1539. There are ponds and depressions near Hall Farm which might be remnants of the moat of the old manor house, the seat of the Moretons.

ENVILLE *7.5m SE of Bridgnorth*
The attractive village, with its red brick cottages, pink sandstone church and grey rendered Hall, lies in lovely wooded countryside near the border with Shropshire. The Hall and its estate dominate the village. The present house, though impressive, is something of an agglomeration. An avenue of lime trees leads to the entrance and to a long, regular stable block in brick with a central

arch, cupola and giant pilasters to the centre bay, of about 1750. The Hall itself has two fronts. The south front has a recessed centre and two octagonal towers of the 16th Century which were given a Gothic facade of battlements, ogee ornaments and pinnacles in the 18th Century. The north front is unadorned 18th Century classical Georgian. In 1904 there was a fire and the interior was rebuilt. At the same time the coach porch was added.

The gardens and hilly grounds were landscaped during the 18th and 19th Centuries. In the thick woods is a chapel with a round tower and a conical roof, dedicated to the landscape gardener and poet, William Shenstone, who probably worked on the gardens here. Near the chapel is a Cascade and a Gothic Gateway with three arches and castellated walls. The large lake has a fountain with a triton and four horses. Near to the Hall is a Gothic summer house (called The Museum) of 1750, by Sanderson Miller, an attractive architectural oddity. Beyond the woods, on higher ground, are the Sheep Walks and in the valley is a Temple with four columns. In various states of repair there is also a Hermit's House with thatched roof, a Pagoda in the wood and a Boathouse.

The manor of Enville belonged to the Saxon Alric, a thane of King Edward, in 1066 but by 1086 it had passed to the Norman Lord, William, son of Ansculf, who installed Gilbert as his lord of the manor. By the 15th Century it had passed to the Lowe family. The heiress of Humphrey Lowe married Robert Grey, the third son of Reginald, Lord Grey of Ruthin. The Greys later became Earls of Stamford and Warrington and had large estates in Cheshire and Leicestershire. In 1883, on the death of the 7th Earl, the family properties were divided and Enville came to Sir Henry Foley Grey, whose granddaughter is the present owner.

The church of St Mary stands on a hill overlooking the village and the Hall. It is constructed of a very pink sandstone - a striking sight when you come upon it unexpectedly. It is a Norman church but was much restored by Gilbert Scott in 1872-5. The nave is Norman, the chancel Decorated and the tower, with its elaborate 'Somerset Crown', was rebuilt by Scott. In the north arcade spandrels are two carved figures, possibly Anglo-Saxon: one of a Bishop and the other of an oriental priest with a fan. The chancel was rebuilt in the 14th Century by Roger de Birmingham, a vicar of this church, whose tomb lies in the north chancel wall founder's recess. There are also four very fine misericords. Monuments include that to Thomas Grey, died 1559, and many more to the Grey family of Enville, the Amphletts of Four Ashes and the Moseleys of Mere.

Mere Mill is a disused water mill at SO 822886. It has an overshot wheel of 11 feet diameter with eight iron arms and a remarkable number of wooden parts - shaft, sole-boards, buckets, shrouds, crown wheel and other shafts. Spittlebrook Mill is a derelict windmill at SO 845876. It has a 25-foot diameter base and some working parts. It is known to have existed by 1820.

Highgate Common near Enville was bought by the County Council about 40 years ago to preserve it as a public amenity.

Enville Common, to the west of Enville, is today covered by a wood called The Million. The area is also called Enville Heath and is haunted by the ghost of Billy Pitt and his mongrel dog. Billy had been put in Enville stocks on a cold night and died of exposure.

Morfe Hall Farm, 0.5m NNE of Enville, may be on the site of the Morfe manor house. Morfe Heath Farm, 1.5m NE of Enville, was built in 1723. In 1968 it became the club house for the Enville Golf Club. Morfe Forest was to the west, in Shropshire.

ESSINGTON *4m NE of Wolverhampton*

The name is Anglo-Saxon and means 'the homestead of Esne's people'. Essington is mentioned in Domesday Book when the property was held by William, son of Ansculf, a major landowner in the county. The manor was formerly within the bounds of Cannock Forest and there was a large oak wood here. The early lords were somewhat ruffianly and had brushes with the law on more than one occasion.

Today Essington is a place of modern houses surrounded by a landscape scarred by old coal mines and clay quarries. When the pits closed, Hilton Main being the last, the railway was dismantled and the canal (the Wyrley and Essington of 1797) became disused. In their place the M6 roars by a-quarter-of-a-mile to the east, and the M54 within yards to the north.

The yellow brick church of St John was built in 1933 to a design by Wood and Kendrick. There are interesting things to the west of the village, along Bagnop Road: Fennel Pit Farm (fennel is a yellow flowering herb used for flavourings); a small industrial estate; Essington Hall, four bays, 2.5 storeys, red brick, a small orchard and partially filled in moat (an earlier, water-filled moat exists a little to the south); Pool Farm, Elizabethan interior, red brick, a simple but handsome house with outbuildings; the Fish Ponds, maps show only one but now there are six; clay pigeon shooting ranges in an old quarry next to the pools, and on the same site a popular car-boot sale is held every Sunday; and Windmill Farm, adjacent to which are the considerable remains of an old roundhouse windmill in red brick, originally built in 1681 by Henry Vernon and reconstructed about 100 years later. It worked two pairs of stones and had four sails until the 1880s. It is the only post mill left in the county.

Downhill, to the west, are the Tarmac sand and gravel quarries and industrial units on the site of the Hilton Main Colliery. A variety of concrete blocks are manufactured here.

Hilton itself lies lm NE of the old colliery. The settlement has interesting historical associations with Essington. Hilton is best known today for the Hilton Park Service Station on the M6 motorway which was built in the well-wooded grounds of Hilton Park Hall. There is no village here. The Hall stands to the east of the suburban areas of Featherstone (where there is an open prison) and Shareshill, both of which lie on the Cannock road north-east of Wolverhampton. It is a very large and very fine house built in the early 18th Century of brick with stone quoins and dressings. The main front faces the lake. It has a five-bay recessed centre with two wings of three bays, all of two storeys with an attic storey. The pediment is curved and decorated with vases, scrolls and garlands. The modern entrance is at the side, through an impressive coach porch which was installed by the Victorians. The interior is very fine with panelled rooms and an excellent staircase.

The manors of Hilton and Essington belonged to the Swynnerton family in the Middle Ages. In 1562 they passed by marriage to the Vernons. It was Henry Vernon who built the present Hall. On raised ground, 0.5m south of the house is Portobello Tower, a battlemented folly that commemorates Admiral Vernon's capture of Portobello in 1739. Close to the house, amongst trees, is a moat, the site of the early manor house, for Hilton is an ancient settlement that had an ancient custom.

The Lord of Essington owed homage to the greater Lord of Hilton. Every New Year's Day the Lord of Hilton filled with water a brass figurine in the shape of a man who had an enlarged symbol of his manhood. The figure, called **Jack O'Hylton,** was placed on a fire and steam issued through his mouth. This fanned the fire and made it burn more brightly. The Lord of Essington then brought in a goose which was driven three times around the fire before being killed, cooked and dressed. The bird was then served to the Lord of Hilton, by either the Lord of Essington or his bailiff, and the Lord of Hilton duly granted the lesser Lord a further year's tenancy. On the authority of Dr Plot we know that the ceremony was being performed at least as early as 1650.

Hilton Hall remained in the possession of the Vernon family until some 50 years ago when it was sold. Jack O'Hylton is now with a senior member of the family in a village near Kington, Herefordshire. The Hall was taken over by a religious order and became a kind of Catholic guest house. In recent times it was sold again and has been acquired by Tarmac Construction Ltd, who have renovated the Hall, the grounds and the outbuildings, and have established their Head Office here. It is to be hoped that they might one day replace the hideous green corrugated fence that surrounds the park.

Warstone, 1.25m NW of Essington, consists of little more than two farms, old coal pits, rows of earth movers, waste disposal tips, old tile works and a tall chimney. At Upper Ryde Farm are some intricate wrought iron gates.

Essington Wood, 1m NE of Essington, has a treasure story that sounds to us like a publicity stunt concocted by a one-time landlord of the nearby pub, the Old Mitre Inn, an 18th Century hostelry. Not wishing to perpetuate the tale all we will say is that it involves a Cuban revolutionary, on an arms-buying mission, burying gold coins in the wood. We realise, of course, that this is probably more intriguing than if the whole tale had been told. However, the pub does have a history of hoaxes. One landlord exhibited two skeletons in the coach house, which he said were the remains of William Duce, the highwayman, and Jonathan Wild, the thief-taker.

At Essington Wood Methodist Church (small, red brick with round-headed windows) there are two roads to Essington: Bursnips and Hobnock, ancient names indeed.

ETTINGSHALL *1.25m SE of Wolverhampton*
Ettingshall is a flourishing industrial area centred on the crossing of the A4039 and the A4126. The name is Anglo-Saxon and probably means 'the secluded grazing land'. To the north is Priestfield, to the west is Parkfield, to the south is Lanesfield and to the east is Millfields. Most of these fields would have belonged to the ancient manor of Ettingshall which has its own entry in Domesday Book.

To the south of Millfield's Road the land is once again a field, a vast wasteland, cleared and levelled and awaiting redevelopment. Here, until 1979-80, stood the huge Bilston Steelworks and the old Bilston Quarries. In Ettingshall Road are Cables and Instruments, Dixon's Wallcoverings, Tools and Machines and the Bull's Head pub; in Spring Road (a continuation of Manor Road) are Tarmac Roadstone, Grasshopper ('the best things next to babies') and the security gated sprawl of NET Thompson. The latter is a group of concerns variously occupied in water treatment, friction welding, the manufacture of pontoon bridges for military tanks and nuclear engineering. Buyers at government level from Russia, Japan and the Middle East had been guests in the few days before we visited. Beside the main gates of this redoubtable concern stand a pair of inter-war bungalows, a solitary island of domestic habitation in a sea of industry. Other firms in the area include A & B Steel Profiles, Cozens Conveyor Belts, Banshaw Plate Rollers, Foley Metals, United Thompson Chassis and Barnett International (manufacturers of crossbows). The aptly named Forge Hammer pub blends nicely into this grim landscape.

The heaviest load ever carried by British Rail was a 122-foot-long boiler drum weighing 240 tons. It was made in Ettingshall and taken to Eggborough, Yorkshire in 1965.

At **Parkfield,** amongst the schools and houses, is the church of St Martin (1938). It stands in Dixon Street, an unashamedly modern, monument-like brick building erected in 1938-39 to a design by Lavender and Twentyman. The figure of St Martin over the entrance is by Donald Potter.

Ettingshall Park was a house and estate which dated back to 1552. It was the home of the Gibbons family. In the 18th Century it was rebuilt and was later the seat of the Feredays, ironmasters. To celebrate the defeat of Napoleon the Feredays gave a feast for their 5,000 workers, who were seated at 100 tables in a field at Ettingshall, at which 100 barrels of 'Stout Staffordshire Ale' were consumed. It is probable that the Feredays were the model for the Farringdons in the novel, 'The Farringdons', written in 1900 by Ellen Thorneycroft Fowler of Woodthorne. Today Ettingshall Park is a suburban residential area and has no connections with its parent settlement. To the south it adjoins the houses of **Cinder Hill** and the green open spaces of **Beacon Hill**.

FAREWELL *2.25m NW of Lichfield*
A tiny place. The church of St Bartholomew is most pleasantly situated. It has an early 14th Century chancel, and the rest was rebuilt in brick in 1745. There are some misericords. Farewell Hall is a handsome, brick 17th Century house of five bays, a hipped roof, a good staircase and a doorhead shaped like a shell. It is now a farm. There was a Benedictine Priory at Farewell, founded about 1140 by Roger Clinton, Bishop of Coventry (which included the diocese of Lichfield), and the church is descended from it. Nothing of the Priory remains. The name Farewell means 'the fair, clear spring' and there is, indeed, a spring on the west side of church. It is though that a hermitage existed here before the Priory and its church were built.

Spade Green, 1m S of Farewell, was called Childerend Pipe in the late 13th Century.

FARLEY *3.25m E of Cheadle*
A most pleasant, airy little place with good stone houses and splendidly romantic views of Alton Towers. Farley Hall (1609, altered 1784) was home to the Bill family from 1607 to 1957 but is now owned by Mr Anthony Bamford of JCB.

Barbary Gutter, on the west side of the road between Farley and Alton, is a wooded dell through which the old coach road was made in 1807. The name is probably from the shrub Berberis known to have grown here. A headless horseman is said to haunt the road, which was the former main drive to Alton Towers. Guarding the way is the Chained Oak, a 900-year-old tree whose roots entwine around a boulder and whose branches are bound with iron chains.

FAZELEY *1.5m S of Tamworth*

Fazeley is an industrial village located at the junction of the A5 and the A4091. It was here that Sir Robert Peel, father of the Prime Minister of the same name, built the largest of his cotton spinning mills, the giant 'Steam Mill' of 1883. This is little more than an oblong box with a chimney, but its clean lines and the technology of its construction make it one of the finest in the country and highly regarded by experts in the field of industrial archeology. It has five storeys and 29 bays and stands beside the Birmingham and Fazeley Canal on the road to Drayton Bassett. (It is best viewed from the canal.)

The church of St Paul was built in 1853 by J Stevens and paid for by Sir Robert Peel. It has an unusual clerestory with 10 small clover-leaf-shaped windows. (See Drayton Bassett.)

Two Gates, 0.75m ESE of Fazeley, is a crossroads' settlement where the A4097 crosses Watling Street (A5). The Reliant Engineering Company, manufacturers of the Reliant Robin three-wheeled car (star of the 'Only Fools and Horses' TV show), have had their works on Watling Street at Two Gates since 1935.

In 1942 Colin Grazier, born at Two Gates, was an Able Seaman on HMS Petard when his ship disabled a German U-boat. Grazier helped retrieve information from the U-boat before it sank. This information directly led to the cracking of the Enigma Code used by the Germans. Grazier and an officer died when the submarine finally sank. Both received the George Cross.

Bonehill, 0.75m WNW of Fazeley, is a hamlet near the Bourne Brook. Bonehill Mill, however, is 0.5m SW of Bonehill at SK 199021 and almost in Fazeley. It has four storeys and a giant, iron, breastshot waterwheel, 14 feet wide and 12 feet in diameter. The Peel family used it for calico printing and it was still working in 1965 grinding corn. Bonehill House was built in the early 19th Century for Sir Robert Peel's younger brother, Edmund, died 1850.

FENTON *1m SE of Stoke on Trent*

The name is Anglo-Saxon and means 'the settlement by the marsh'. The modern town includes the two ancient hamlets of Fenton Vivian (Vivian after its Norman Lord of the 1240s), which borders Stoke, and Fenton Culvert (a later daughter settlement) which lies near the junction of the A521 and the A50.

Iron ore and coal were mined here from medieval times and the many large patches of waste ground in Fenton are the sites of the former workings. It is not wise to build on such land.

The most famous potter from Fenton was Thomas Whieldon. He was born in 1719 and by 1740 he was a Master Potter with his own works at Fenton Low, 0.25m N of the town centre. In 1755 he had another works at Fenton Hall, a Georgian mansion which doubled, almost uniquely, as a factory and grand home. He made many kinds of pottery and was acknowledged at the time as the finest craftsman in the whole of the Potteries. He trained Josiah Spode and was in partnership with the young Josiah Wedgwood from 1754 to 1759. The famous cream 'Queens Ware' which established Wedgwood's reputation was developed by Whieldon. Today the Stoke-on-Trent Sixth Form College and a leisure centre occupy part of the site on which stood Whieldon's Fenton Hall works. The rest of the site has disappeared into the huge clay pit that lies between the college and the Stoke to Longton road. This pit is called the Fenton Manor Quarry and was worked by the Steetley Brick and Tile Company. It is no longer worked and is now rough, overgrown, 'brown' land.

Felix Pratt, whose old Rialto Works were on the site of the present Workshops for the Blind, made several breakthroughs in the use of colours. In about 1840 the firm of F & R Pratt of Fenton developed the first successful method of multi-colour (polychrome) printing on pottery ware.

The centre of Fenton lies off the main road in Albert Square. Here is the Town Hall of 1888, built in brick with stone dressings by William Meath Baker, to a Gothic design by R Scriviner & Son. He rented it first to the Board of Health and then the Urban District Council, who finally bought it in 1897. Mr Baker then donated land at the back of the Town Hall (in what is now called Baker Street) for a library, which was built in 1905-7 to a design by B Lawson with funds from the trust of Andrew Carnegie. On the corner of City Road and Christchurch Street was the Athenaeum of 1853. This five-bay Italiante building was first used as a literary and scientific club until 1867, after which date it became successively a National School, offices for the Board of Health (before they moved to the Town Hall), the Art School, offices of the District Bank and, finally, offices of the National Westminster Bank who demolished it in 1978-9 and replaced the old building with a plain, red brick, modern box.

The large and quite handsome red and blue brick Christ Church was built in 1890 to a design by Charles Lynam. The tower was added in 1899. Even higher than the tower is the little stair-turret. Opposite the Town Hall are modern council flats and in the central square are formal gardens and a white War Memorial. It is extraordinarily quiet here and altogether a most unusual town centre.

At Lane Delph, opposite the public toilets, at the junction of City Road and Victoria Street (which here unite to form King Street), were the famous **Mason's Ironstone Works**. Miles Mason came to the Potteries from Liverpool about 1800. He and his sons did well but in 1842 they were persecuted by the Chartists for their use of machines and their use of the 'allowance system'. Mason's house at Heron's Cross was burnt down. The machines, ironically, proved unreliable and were withdrawn, and in 1848 Mason's son, C J Mason, was declared bankrupt. However, the name was nationally known and the trademark 'Mason's Ironstone' was adopted by the firm's successors, and is still in use today. (Ironstone is a mixture of flint, clay, Cornwall stone, blue oxide, cobalt and 'scoria', which is slag of ironstone).

King Street leads to Longton. The buildings on the right-hand side of the road have been erroneously described in several current books, so to avoid confusion we will mention them all, even if of no particular interest. (This information is of 1988.) We start at Foley Place (adjacent to the Esso Garage) which is a short, but splendid, terrace of Georgian-style houses of about 1835. Adjoining them, on the main road, is the Foley Arms Hotel. Next is the modern red brick and dark glass of Precision Studio; then the red brick and white flagpoles of the Coalport works, also modern; then The Potter pub and then the Foley Pottery. This is currently owned by Coalport but was built about 1798 by Josiah Spode for Samuel, his eldest son. It has eight bays and a central arched doorway, surmounted by a Venetian window and a pediment. The brickwork is painted cream and the door is red. Next come the premises of James Kent Ltd, who occupy the Old Foley Pottery, though the old facade has been replaced with modern brick walls and blue iron gates. Parts of the works are from the late 18th Century. In the yard John Wesley preached one of his last sermons on 28th

March 1790. Next is a yard and buildings occupied by several small businesses and then the works of James Birks & Co, pottery kiln builders.

Adjacent to them is the famous Boundary Works which were built by Josiah Spode in 1819. It was a model factory in its day. There are 17 bays of two storeys, the middle five bays being raised to 2.5 storeys and contains the arched entrance. Above this is a Venetian window, a small tri-partite window and a pediment. Lastly, the Phoenix Works of 1881 - a handsome factory, much smaller but a little taller than the Boundary Works, with a similar arched doorway and pediment. However, the middle window is not Venetian and the stop-chamfered mullions are a Victorian addition. A few yards further down the road is the boundary between Fenton and Longton, marked by a council sign.

Frank Bough, the popular television presenter of topical and magazine programmes, was born in Tirley Street, Fenton, in 1933, although he was brought up in Oswestry, Shropshire. And the town has its very own spy. Michael Bethaney, born in 1950, was brought up in Wileman Street and attended Longton High School. He joined MI5 in 1974, was found guilty of spying for the KGB in 1984 and sentenced to 23 years in prison, being released in 1998.

The A50(T) dual carriageway from Stoke to Uttoxeter was completed in about 2000. It was a major work of civil engineering with numerous bridges, cuttings and a tunnel. It runs parallel with Ryknilde Street (now the A522) for almost its entire length and has given the old road some much needed respite. Now you can forego the traffic and urban charms of Fenton and Longton and whistle as you drive. There can be dangers though: there was once a spate of youths dropping bricks from the numerous bridges with potentially lethal results, and when the road is closed occasionally for repairs Stoke comes to a standstill.

FLASH *7m NNE of Leek and 4m SSW of Buxton*
At 1,518 feet above sea level Flash is reputedly the highest village in England, with the highest pub and the highest Post Office. It is a somewhat nondescript little place and is best seen from a distance. The country all around is magnificent - wild moors and long views in every direction from the A53 Buxton to Leek road. Romantic country too, for this is the setting Sir Gawain and the Green Knight, the epic medieval poem. The church of St Paul is a sombre looking structure by W R Bryden of Buxton, with a carved stone pulpit which was given by Lady Harpur-Crewe. There is also a Methodist Chapel of 1821.

It is said that in days gone by Flash was used as a refuge by criminals on the run. It was isolated and difficult to reach, especially in the winter, which deterred officers of the law from travelling here. Also, justice was traditionally handled at a local level, and if a wanted man crossed a county boundary his apprehension became legally complicated, if not impossible. The position of Flash, so close to the junction of three counties, was thus attractive to the criminal. It is said also that forgers and coiners worked here - hence the term 'Flash money', meaning it was counterfeit. There seems to be little hard evidence for counterfeiting at Flash but the primary trade here in the 18th Century was button-making, a trade with some technical similarities. It was also a magnet for pedlars, some of whom built cottages on the common land.

Mains water only came to Flash in 1989 after a reservoir was built on Oliver Hill.

Flash Bottom, 0.5m. SSW of Flash, lies in a valley and the ground here was marshy. (See Swythamley.)

Three Shire Heads (SK 009686) lies lm NW of Flash on Axe Edge. This is the point where Staffordshire, Cheshire and Derbyshire meet. It is a beautiful and dramatic spot. The River Dane is joined by a stream and at their confluence there are waterfalls, bridges, rocky cliffs, trees and stoney pools. Several tracks meet here and it is a favourite place of walkers and horsemen. It can only be reached on foot, though if approached from Knotbury a car can be taken within 0.5m of this idyllic place.

Three-quarters-of-a-mile NNE, on the Buxton to Leek road, and within a few feet of the county boundary sign between Staffordshire and Derbyshire, is the **source of the River Dove**. The river itself is the boundary line between the two counties. The spring, which is the actual source, is in a depression marked by a headstone. It is strange to think that these wild, open moors were forest-clad until prehistoric man cleared the trees. Grazing sheep have since prevented natural regeneration. There are evocative names hereabouts - Blackclough, Wolf Edge, Knar, Hawk's Nest, Wildboarclough. These moors, hills and valleys are attractive in summer, but in the grey light of winter with storm clouds on the horizon they are magnificent.

Birchenbooth, 1.25m WNW of Flash, is the site of an abandoned settlement and an early 19th Century coalmine. The house called Birchenbooth was abandoned from about 1940. The suffix 'booth' means 'both'. The house was a longhouse-style building combining a human residence and a cowshed.

FORDHOUSES *2.5m N of Wolverhampton centre*
There was a settlement here by at least the 14th Century. It lies west of the Stafford Road and south of the M54. The ford was probably across the Wybaston Brook, which runs from Moseley Pool to the River Penk. This now disappears into an industrial park - Nurdin and Peacock, Goodyear Distribution, Dana (transmissions) and the mighty IMI. South of the Wobaston Road are the houses, mature and affordable, and many council owned. There is an extensive main road shopping centre with a surprising variety of stores and services for a suburban place.

In 1970 an executive plane belonging to the nearby Dowty-Boulton Paul company crashed into a house killing both the pilots and the lady living in the house.

As one travels south from Fordhouses one imperceptibly enters **Oxley**. There are no oxen here nowadays, and the only fields are now the links of the Oxley Golf Club. It is primarily a residential area, though it could, if it wanted, claim the enormous Goodyear Tyre Factory, parts of which regularly burn down. To the west Oxley adjoins Claregate and Autherley. (See Claregate.)

FOREST OF MERCIA
This is an on-going scheme by the Countryside Commission and the Forestry Commission to develop a fragmented woodland. It covers an area from Bednall (near Stafford) in the north to Great Barr in the south, and from Coven in the west to Lichfield in the east.

FORSBROOK *0.5m NE of Blythe Bridge, which is 3m SE of Longton*
Finds of Anglo-Saxon jewellery are extremely rare in Staffordshire. The most beautiful and elaborate piece yet found in the county is the Forsbrook Pendant. It was discovered by a labourer levelling a hedge bank and was sold to the British Museum in 1879. The pendant consists of a 7th Century Anglo-Saxon ring with

an attached cord loop. It is decorated with gold wire cloisons (strips of gold soldered to a plain base) which are filled with garnets (red, semi-precious stones, probably imported from India) and blue glass. Around the rim are two strands of beaded wire with a central strand of plain wire. These wires terminate in a pair of open-jawed, snake-like heads facing each other, one on each side of the loop. The ring has a diameter of 28 mm and encloses a solid gold Roman coin, a solidus of Valentinian II (AD 375-392), which weighs about 4.55 gm.

Forsbrook lies about 0.5m N of Rickanilde Street, the Roman road from Derby to Chesterton. It is a residential area with two large modern schools, a few shops, a couple of inns and a church. St Peters (1848-9) is a modest sandstone building, with a bellcote and lancet windows by James and Edward Barr. The north aisle was added in 1912 by J H Beckers.

In 1988 Nell, a seven-month old Border Collie, was knocked down by a car. Her spine was damaged and she was paralysed in her hind quarters. Her owners, Monica and Richard Hill, made a cart to carry her useless back legs and this was harnessed to her chest. Nell now had the ability to move unaided. Her cart was similar to those available from specialist manufacturers, and, like these, had one great drawback: it had to be unharnessed by a human if Nell was tired and wanted to lie down. In 1990 Mr Hill and his son-in-law, Robert, a student of aeronautical engineering, tackled the problem. They solved it by adapting Nell's cart so that whenever she dropped the front half of her body to a resting position she pressed against a spring and the wheels moved backwards and down. This enabled her to attain a normal lying position unaided. As she stood up the wheels were pulled back into the upright position and she could trundle away again.

Nell can now spend all day harnessed to her cart. It is truly remarkable to see her running around, turning on the spot, moving backwards, lying down and getting up. She is bright-eyed and happy and wins the hearts of all who see her. Out of her cart she can do no more than drag herself around slowly and painfully.

In January 1992 Central Television showed a short film of her demonstrating the cart. Since then Mr and Mrs Hill have had numerous enquiries from owners of crippled dogs and a manufacturer has expressed an interest in taking up this marvellous innovation. What a lucky dog she was to have such loving and enterprising owners. Mr and Mrs Hill live in Portland Drive, Forsbrook, Blythe Bridge near Stoke-on-Trent

FORTON *1.5m NE of Newport*

The village lies on the A519, Newport to Eccleshall road. Just to the north of this road, and visible from it, is The Monument, a stone cone-shaped building, now in ruins. The story is that there was once a watermill on the nearby stream but the water failed and so the landowner built his miller a windmill on the ridge. This then fell into disuse and was partly demolished. What was left was converted into a monument, or folly, by the addition of a conical cap and large stone ball which has since disappeared.

At the crossroads are some houses and The Swan pub. The lane south from here leads to Forton Hall, a handsome brick house of 1665 with gables and mullioned windows.

Close by the Hall is the church of All Saints. It has a square tower, the lower part of which is of the 13th Century and the upper part Perpendicular with a crown of eight pinnacles. The 13th Century chancel has a Norman window in the north wall and a Victorian window in the east wall. The nave arcade and the south nave are of the restoration of 1723. The north nave is medieval. There is a font of the restoration and part of a Norman font with a Celtic design. The alabaster monument to Thomas Skrymsher, died 1633, is by Garrat Hollemans of Burton. In the churchyard is an old yew tree with a girth of some 18 feet

Lower down, in the valley, are several good houses in the same style as the Hall and a stone bridge, with arches askew, which carries the road (and the course of the old canal) over a head stream of the River Mease, which flows into Aqualate Mere 0.75m to the NW. The road continues on to the hamlet of **Meretown** where there is a horse breeding and fostering establishment with a national reputation.

Aqualate Hall lies 1.5m SE of Forton. The entrance is off the Newport to Stafford road - not the main entrance with wrought iron gates - as these are permanently locked, but the dirt road entrance lm E near Coley Mill farm. In the park there are deer. These used to roam in the field alongside the road, but there were several car accidents caused by drivers looking at the deer rather than the road, so the animals are now kept out of sight. Aqualate Hall is approached along the track that leads through the adjacent farm. The Hall was built by Edwin Skrymsher in the early 17th Century. Sir George Boughey bought the house in the late 18th Century and commissioned John Nash to rebuild it. The result was a spectacular, castle-like Gothic mansion. Unfortunately, this was burnt down in 1910, and in 1927 a much smaller house was built by W D Caroe. An original Nash range with gables joins the new house to the 18th Century brick stable. Ownership of the Hall and the estate changed hands recently. In the grounds there is a red brick house with stepped gables and a castle-like tower and there are two attractive Gothic lodges, probably by Nash.

The outlook from the Hall over the deer park and the great lake is truly beautiful. It was landscaped by Repton about 1800 but looks totally natural. The lake is surrounded by wetland plants, meadows and woods. The aspect is open and the country scene presented is idyllic. The mere is one mile long and 0.25 mile wide, which makes it the largest natural lake in Staffordshire. The River Meese begins in Aqualate Mere. The lake was a great deal larger than its present 220 acres and stretched westwards to the mill at Meretown. In the 1700s the Skrymshers reclaimed the shallow pool and marshes of the west end for agriculture. On the north side of the lake is Anck's Hill, and nearby large numbers of human skeletons were found in 1815. They were laid out in trenches, one above the other, and are presumed to be the slain of some ancient battle. To the east of Anck's Hill is a well, hewed out of solid rock, which has a diameter of 19 inches and is believed to be of Roman origin. As if all this were not enough, there is a heronry here and also a mermaid.

Legend has it that when the Vivary Pool at Newport became silted up the mermaid who lived there came to Aqualate. She is a gentle creature and her only concern is to prevent the destruction of her new home. On one occasion, long ago, some workmen were dredging part of the mere when the mermaid appeared. She feared that they were attempting to drain the lake and gave this warning: 'If this Mere you do let dry, Newport and Meretown I will destroy'. The mermaid has been seen many times and legend has it that whenever she is sighted calamity befalls the world. She was seen before the last two world wars. These days the gardens are occasionally used as a venue for 'orchestra and fireworks' display evenings.'

The Guild of Monks, 2m ESE of Forton, is a house. In the mid-12th Century. A hermit's dwelling here was given to Shrewsbury Abbey and later a grange was established. The present house is not old.

FOXT *1m NE of Froghall, which is 3m NNE of Cheadle*

Foxt is a substantial but spread-about village of stone and brick houses - pleasant enough but by no means pretty. There is a pub, the Fox and Goose, and close by is the charming Rose Cottage. The attractive, simple little church of St Mark the Evangelist has lancet windows and was built in 1838. The machiolated tower is a feature. (Machiolation describes an overhanging defensive gallery at the top of a tower.)

The name was originally Foxwist. The suffix 'wist' is from the Old English for 'dwelling', hence Foxt means 'fox's dwelling'.

The country around is moorland, and stone walls abound. About 1m N of Foxt, on the road to Ipstones, is Hope Stones Farm. It lies on a hillock adjacent to a tall, natural rock outcrop - a most picturesque sight.

Near Windyway Cross, a house 1.25m WNW of Foxt at the south-west end of Ipstones Edge, is a medieval wayside cross, 10 feet high, called the Long Stone (SK 058490).

FRADLEY *3m NE of Lichfield*

Fradley is a village at the junction of Ryknild Street, the A38(T), and the Trent and Mersey Canal. In 1262 it was Frodreslege. The church of St Stephen was built in 1861. Fradley Common was the venue for Lichfield Races from the 1680s until 1701, when they transferred to Whittington Heath. The Common was enclosed in about 1805. In 1939 the RAF built an airfield here, RAF Station Lichfield, which was a bomber base. Fradley Junction, 1.25m WNW of Fradley, is where the Coventry Canal joins the Trent & Mersey Canal.

FRADSWELL *8m NE of Stafford and 3m NNE of Weston*

In Domesday Book it is Frodeswelle and was a member of Great Haywood manor. The name is from the Anglo-Saxon and means 'Frod's well (or stream)'. 'Frod' was a personal name, which also means 'wise'.

The first Fradswell Hall was built in the 17th Century by Thomas Lord Cromwell, First Earl of Ardglass. The present Hall was the home of Judge Sir John Ashworth (died 1975). The small village has the church of St James the Less which is attractively set amongst trees. It has a 13th Century chancel, Victorian nave, purple brick tower of 1764, stained glass windows by Wailes and a monument to Jane, daughter of the 4th Lord Cromwell.

Fradswell Heath, 1.25m NE of Fradswell, was a 'barren' common land inhabited by an 'immoral, superstitious lot', as described at the time of the enclosure act of 1852.

FREEFORD *1m S of Lichfield*

Freeford Manor was the home of the Dyott family. The five-bay house is of at least 16th Century origin, but most of what we see today is early 19th Century Georgian. Sir Richard Dyott was the Royalist commander of the Lichfield garrison during the Civil War. On 2nd March 1643 Lord Brooke, the Roundhead general, was standing at the cathedral end of Dam Street in Lichfield when he was shot dead by 'Dumb Dyott', the mute son (or nephew), of Sir Richard. Charles I granted the wish of Dumb Dyott, that when Dyott died his body should be taken by torch-light procession from Freeford to Lichfield for midnight burial. Some 200 years later this custom was revived on the death of General

William Dyott. He lies in the Dyott chapel at St Mary's, Lichfield.

FROGHALL *3m NNE of Cheadle*

Froghall is totally dominated by the huge Bolton's brass and copper works which were established here in 1890. They lie in the lovely Churnet Valley, but though often criticised do little to disturb the countryside. The valley is very steep and narrow so the works are hidden to all but travellers on the main road, the A52. There is little more here than the works' car parks, the bridge over the river and the Railway Inn.

However, on the east bank is a turning to the north (B5053) which leads to Froghall Wharf. Here the Caldon Canal (1780) came to an end. It runs for 17.5m and joins the Trent and Mersey Canal at Etruria (Hanley, Stoke-on-Trent). It was called the Caldon because its purpose was to convey the limestone quarried at Cauldon Lowe, four miles away and high in the hills (649 feet higher). A plate-way connected the mines with the canal. The plate-way was gravity operated. The full tubs travelling downwards hauled the empty tubs back up. (Note: The essential difference between a plate-way and a railway is that the wheels of the waggon used on a plate-way had their flanges on the outside edge).

The wharves here were busy places. Old photographs show throngs of men, horses and narrow boats, and piles of stone. The old buildings have been restored, and there is a restaurant, a battery of lime-kilns and a picnic place. Horse-drawn narrow boats operate from here in the summer.

FULFORD *4m NE of Stone*

It lies high in the wooded hills to the north-east of Stone. Pleasant modern houses line the main road and cluster not so pleasantly in estates on the side turnings. They swamp the old, small village but the attractive, red brick Gothic church of St Nicholas (1825), and the Old Hall - now a farmhouse - lie at the top of the hill, away from the recent developments, in landlordly isolation. The upper side windows of the Hall have been ill-treated by blocking and butchering.

Stallington, 0.75m NNE of Fulford and 1m S of Blythe Bridge, is a small hamlet with a large hospital complex. It was formerly a manor belonging to Stone Priory. The Hall is at least early 19th Century and for many years was the home of the Hill-Child family. From 1930 to 1998 it was a hospital for the mentally handicapped. The first element of the name 'Stalling' might be from either a personal name or from the Old English for 'stoney hill'.

GAILEY *7.5m N of Wolverhampton*

Gailey is a busy crossroads where the A5 and A449 intersect. The hamlet was mentioned in Domesday Book and is not just a modern crossroads' development, as one might have thought. There are a couple of farms, a Post Office/corner shop, an AA Control point, a large caravan company and an excellent craft centre that has taken over the church as a pottery and the school as a display warehouse.

The suffix of the name is probably from 'gale', a common name for Myrica Gale, also known as Bog Myrtle. An alternative name for the settlement was Spread Eagle after an hotel that stood at the crossroads. This was rebuilt away from the road when the A449 was widened. It still stands, though public houses these days have a habit of changing their names frequently, and often tastelessly.

The church is by G T Robinson and was built in 1849 with a chancel of 1874.

Gailey Wharf lies 0.5m E along the A5. A Gothic Georgian house and a circular, battlemented tower face each other across the Staffordshire and Worcestershire Canal. The wharfs are most attractive with colourful narrow boats tied up to stone quays, and lawns and trees completing a most picturesque scene. Life here is peaceful and slow, yet only yards away lorries and cars flash by in frantic haste.

The Roman city of **Pennocrucium** lay astride Watling Street, lm W of Gailey Island at Stretton Mill (on the right if you are travelling westwards). There is nothing left to see of the Roman occupation. (For a further note on Pennocrucium see Penkridge.)

One-and-a-half miles further on is the ornamental black-and-white-painted aqueduct that carries the canal over the road. It was built by Thomas Telford in 1832. Close by are Gailey Pools - two reservoirs built as feeders for the Staffordshire and Worcestershire Canal.

GAYTON *5.5m NE of Stafford*
The name probably means 'the settlement by the gate'. In 1066 Gayton and nearby Amerton were held by Aelmar and Alric. After the Conquest they were given to the great Earl Roger de Montgomery, King William's right-hand man. Today it is a pleasant little village with a well-known pub, The Gayton Hotel, a church of the 18th and 19th Centuries but with a Norman chancel arch, some good houses and an old blacksmith's shop with a complete set of tools (now locked up and privately owned). There are several dead-end lanes.

The charming Gayton Brook is crossed by a ford at one place and a bridge at another before meandering off across the gentle meadows. South of the churchyard is Moat Farm which is surrounded by an oval moat. To the west of the house is a large moat-like feature believed to have been a fish pond.

To the north-east of the village, down a short track and close to the stream, is a building next to a small pool which has a water course leading from it. This would appear to be the site of a mill. There is a small Nuclear Bunker in Gayton, an underground structure that has an area of 162 square feet. It was built in the 1950s, during the Cold War, by the council but is now in private ownership.

Amerton, 0.75m SE of Gayton, lies along the Weston to Uttoxeter road, the A518, and is a hamlet best known for the Amerton Working Farm. Amongst the attractions are a wildlife rescue centre, a craft shop, a milking parlour, a garden centre and a bakery. The Amerton Brook runs through the settlement and to the south it adjoins the now-disused Hixon Airfield. In Domesday Book it is called Mersetone. The name is not properly understood but could be from 'ham-ton', meaning 'farm-settlement'.

GENTLESHAW *See Cannock Wood*

GLASCOTE *1.5m SE of Tamworth*
It is a part of Tamworth, an industrial suburb south-east of the town centre. The name would suggest that glass was once made here. The brick built church of St

George was designed by Basil Champneys in 1880. It has a large, low saddleback roof, a round stair turret and stained glass windows by Burne Jones. About 1943 a gold alloy torc dated at between 1BC and 1AD was found by men working at a boatyard on the Coventry Canal between Glascote and Amington.

GNOSALL *7m W of Stafford*

The name is pronounced Nose-ul. It is reputed to have the longest High Street in the county at just over one mile. However, there are really two villages, Gnosall and Gnosall Heath, joined by the A518 Stafford to Newport road. In recent years there have been many new houses built here but, for the most part, they are tucked away in medium-sized estates, well out of sight of the main road, and the old village centre remains unscathed.

The Shropshire Union Canal passes to the West of Gnosall Heath. This stretch of water in known to boatmen as being particularly attractive, with pleasant country, deep dramatic cuttings, a tunnel, some delightful private moorings and several popular canal-side pubs. On the 21st January 1879 a labourer was walking by the main road canal bridge when he was attacked by a man-monkey who had great, white luminous eyes. A local policeman had heard of similar events and said that the apparition had begun to appear shortly after the death of a man who had drowned in the canal.

In the main village there is an old timber-framed and thatched house, now a shop and newly restored. However, the great attraction here is the church of St Lawrence, thought by many to be one of the finest in the county. It is a large cruciform church with transepts and a crossing tower. It was a 'Royal Free Chapel' - a Collegiate church, with a dean and four canons, controlled by the King. This status brought great privileges. There were only 13 in the whole country and, as these churches were richly endowed with land, they were financial forces to be reckoned with. St Lawrence is essentially a Norman church but has been partly altered and partly rebuilt at various times since. The crossing arches, south transept, blank arcading and triforium of twin openings with straight heads are some of the finest Norman work in the county. The aisles were added in the 13th Century and the porch is by Lynam of 1893. The overall external style is Perpendicular.

Gnosall is essentially a dormitory town for Stafford but it did have some local industry. There were stone quarries here in the Middle Ages and these were re-opened for a time when the canal was being constructed. In the early 19th Century Stafford shoe manufacturers sent out cut leather pieces, for stitching and making up, to cottage workers in several villages around the county town, including Gnosall. There is a moated site 0.5m S of the village on the road to Haughton. It is rectangular and measures 170 feet by 180 feet. Between 1836 and 1865 there was organized horse racing at Gnosall. On the main road, at the entrance to the lane that leads to the church, is a reconstructed stone lock-up. A railway once passed through Gnosall Heath but that fell victim to the cuts made by Mr Beeching and is now dismantled.

Audmore is a lane-loop of dwellings just to the north-west of Gnosall. The name means 'old marsh land'. It is thought that the Roman defensive bank and ditch called the Limes Britannicus passed through Audmore.

The hamlet of **Cowley**, 1m S of Gnosall, bestrides the Shropshire Union Canal, Upper Cowley to the north and Lower Cowley to the south. The canal tunnel here is 81 yards long and is cut through solid sandstone. The name Cowley could mean many things but 'cow pasture' is as good as any. To the west of Cowley House Farm is the possible site of a medieval village, probably deserted in the 18th Century.

Beffcote, 2m SW of Gnosall, is a hamlet in the lee of Broad Hill. A section of the Roman road from Pennocruciam to Whitchurch was discovered in 1938, just to the west of Beffcote. On Broad Hill there is a 43-acre common, a hollow ledge called the Cavalier's Stable, and the remains of a windmill. The mill was called Beffcote Mill. It had a short working life, was derelict by about 1900 and was then incorporated into a house called The Coffee Pot in 1975.

GORNAL *4m S of Wolverhampton*

The Gornals, there arc three of them, lie on the western boundary of the Black Country. Each has its own little shopping centre. **Upper Gornal** stands on the ridge which is followed by the Wolverhampton-Dudley road, the A459. **Lower Gornal** lies downhill, 0.5m SW, and lower down still is **Gornal Wood,** 1m SW. The Gornals are the traditional home of Aynuk and Ayli, the mythical characters who are the butt of so much local humour. It is here that a man placed his pig on a wall to watch the band go by, a little incident of slight humour that is commemorated by the Pig on the Wall pub in Upper Gornal.

Most of the men used to work in the coal mines and their womenfolk were known all over the Black Country as purveyors of salt, which they sold as blocks from carts drawn by donkeys. Sand was quarried locally. It was very finely crushed and used as a scouring powder. This too was sold by Gornal women from carts drawn by donkeys.

The area of **Ruiton** is deepest Gornal. It is also the name of the street where stand the remains of a windmill, derelict since 1871. Indeed the name Gornal is probably derived from the Anglo-Saxon 'cweorn-halh' meaning 'the mill in the remote place.' There were two mills here at one time, it is said, but one was taken down because there was not enough wind for both of them! The windmill and the attached Windmill House are on an open green space. Around the green are several stone houses. It is easy to visualize the old country village it once was.

The people of Gornal are most friendly. Pigeon racing and Nonconformity are the religions of Gornal. There are many chapels of many denominations. One of the most striking is the large, red brick Zoar Methodist Chapel of 1906 that dominates the shopping centre of Gornal Wood. The Church of England is represented by St Peter's (1842) in Upper Gornal and St James (1823) in Lower Gornal, both built of yellow stone. In Jew's Lane is a Kingdom Hall of the Jehova's Witnesses.

The last of the mines closed in the late 1960s and new housing estates have been built on the reclaimed land. Indeed, terraced houses are a scarcity to be relished. Ellowes' Hall School, yellow brick and flat-roofed, stands on the site of Ellowes' Hall, demolished in 1964. This was the home of the Ellowes family for 150 years. They were ironmasters and at one time controlled the Bradley works and those at Dudley Port and Windmill End (Darby End, Netherton).

Less than 2m W of Lower Gornal, down a track off the Himley Road, is the Glynne Arms. At the road junction is a little, colour-washed toll house. The Glynne Arms is better known locally as the Crooked House (or Siden House). The south end has subsided considerably, due to settlement of the ground below caused by coalmining. All the doors and windows lie at strange angles, and coins or marbles placed on a table apparently roll uphill. It has become quite a tourist attraction. The name Glynne is that of the family who previously owned the estate on which it stands. Their manor house was Oak House Farm, now demolished. This was the centre of an iron-working and coal-mining development in the mid-19th Century, owned by Sir Stephen Glynne, the 9th and last Baronet. He became a brother-in-law to Williams Ewart Gladstone when the future Prime Minister married his sister, Catherine. The industrial venture failed in 1875, despite assistance from Gladstone, and the estate was sold. The area is still one of industrial dereliction and there is a waste disposal site nearby. Surprisingly, the locality is quite well-wooded.

Cooper's Bank is a modern residential area that adjoins the Gornal Wood Crematorium and Cemetery, south of the Himley Road. **Heath Green** is a residential area off Old Park Road, adjoining Upper Gornal and the A459 Dudley - Wolverhampton Road. Hidden away in Heath Green is the Hare and Hounds. This stands on (or near) the site of Old Lodge Farm, the birthplace of Abraham Darby (1678-1717). He was the son of John Darby, a Quaker farmer and locksmith. Abraham went on to become the leading ironmaster of his age and his perfection of the technique of smelting iron with coal was a landmark in the history of, not only England but, the world (See Dudley.)

Parke's Hall Pool, on the north side of Parkes Hall Road, Upper Gornall was built as a reservoir in about 1835. The Tipton Slasher had his first fight near the Pool. He fought Skim Skinny of Gornal and the fight lasted for two days. The Slasher won the prize, a donkey and a bag of sand.

GRADBACH *1.25m ESE of Allgreave, which is 4.5m SE of Macclesfield*
Gradbach, 'grassy brook', is a small hamlet with a Methodist chapel of 1849 that lies on the slopes of Gradbach Hill, overlooking the lovely River Dane. It is much reduced in size now but was once a flourishing industrial settlement with two factories, a mill and about 50 houses.

The strong stone mill remains. It was built in the early 1790s to spin cotton and wool, was converted to spin flax in the late 1790s, and had closed by 1868. About 1885 Sir J Harpur-Crewe acquired the mill and used it as a sawmill and joiners' shop. The waterwheel at this time had a huge capacity: each of its 96 pockets held 35 gallons. It was sold for scrap in the 1950s. After conversion the mill opened as a Youth Hostel in 1984.

A path leads from the mill beside the River Dane, over the Black Brook and into a lovely wooded valley. On the hillside above is the great cleft of Lud's Church, the Green Chapel of the Sir Gawain and the Green Knight medieval epic poem. It was by the River Dane that the beheading scene takes place. (For more on Lud's Church see Swythamley.)

Gradbach Old Hall has some 17th Century stonework but is mainly 19th Century. In 1951 it was bought by the Buxton and District Scouts' Association who use its fields as a campsite. A room in the house is said to be haunted by the ghost of a young boy, the son of an early owner, Lady Sarah Downes. The story goes that Lady Downes and her husband had a beautiful daughter who married a foreign gentleman. The daughter would inherit the Hall when her parents died. However, late in life the parents had a son who duly inherited the Hall. The jealous daughter treated the young boy cruelly and he died. It is his ghost which haunts the room at Gradbach Hall.

GREAT BARR *3m NE of West Bromwich*
The name Barr is from the Welsh 'bar' meaning 'the top, the summit'.

Set amongst what is now a suburban sea, but which used to be an idyllic setting, stands the Gothic-style Great Barr Hall. This was built for Joseph Scott in 1777, though it has been changed for the worse. It lies in a valley at the back of St Margaret's Hospital and is used by the hospital as office accommodation. Vestiges of the estate remain on the A34: Handsworth Lodge, which has a Gothic facade; Merrions Wood, a part of the park; and Fairyfield House, Gothic again, five bays, pointed windows and an ogee window over the porch.

The church of St Margaret is of 13th Century-style, built by W D Griffin in 1860, with a steeple of 1890. The Scott Arms is named after the Scott family who were the squires of Great Barr from 1618 to 1911. The town is divided into four sections by two modern roads - the M6 and the A34 - which have an intersection here.

About 1.5m north of the Hospital is **Bar Beacon**, a hill of 700 feet which, as its name suggests, was used as a place to build fires as warnings or celebratory beacons. There is a Peace Memorial, beech trees, good views and a car park. The turf-covered rectangles are water reservoirs. On the road we were surprised to see Balla Pais Bars, a restaurant with neon lights and very Continental.

At **Grove Vale,** 1m WSW of Great Barr, is Bishop Asbury's cottage. For something on this see the article on West Bromwich.

Kingstanding, 2m E of Great Barr, is in an exposed situation and has a reputation for being cold. It takes its name from the burial mound called King's Standing. Icknield Street passes close by to the east, and a hoard of Roman coins was found in 1884 when the foundations were being dug for the water pumping station. The old settlement stood around the Hare and Hounds pub but the area was developed residentially from 1928. The church of St Columba was built in 1957-60.

Pheasey, 1m E of Great Barr, is named after Simon Veysie who bought the land here in 1557. The present housing estates and two shopping centres were built from 1935 and later, and the yellow brick church of St Chad was built in 1964.

Queslett, a former settlement on the former Barr Lea Common, is now a residential suburb of Great Barr. The name is from 'queast-slade', which means 'wood pigeon dell'.

GREAT BRIDGEFORD *3m NNW of Stafford*
It was probably named after the substantial stone bridge that carries the A5013 road over the River Sow. The stones are said to have come from Eccleshall Castle when it was pulled down during the Civil War. Today this bridge has been joined by another, larger and rather ugly, bridge over the main-line railway.

Bridgeford is a residential hamlet with an estate of modern houses, a few old cottages, a service station, a village hall with tennis courts and a polythene-tunnel-riddled Garden Centre. The evergreen song 'Sailing', first popularised by Rod Stewart, was composed by the Sutherland brothers who lived at Great Bridgeford, we are informed.

GREAT CHATWELL *3.5m SE of Newport, Shropshire*
It hides in lanes east of the A41, Newport to Wolverhampton road. The name is probably corrupted from Saint Chad's Well, as in nearby Chadwell, over the border in Shropshire. The well at Chadwell was formerly of some repute. Great Chatwell is a small rural village with a pub, the Red Lion, and once had a chapel (1548), but the last vestige has probably been incorporated into the outbuildings of cottages called The Bull Ring.

Orslow, 0.75m NE of Great Chatwell, is an upland hamlet whose name is Anglo-Saxon and means 'Horsa's burial mound'. In the early 13th Century there was a windmill recorded at about SJ 818156. Orslow Manor is a square, red brick farmhouse of about 1800. The Orslow Brook runs from Orslow to Moreton where it joins the Moreton Brook.

GREAT HAYWOOD *4.5m E of Stafford*

There are two villages: Great Haywood and Little Haywood. They both lie close to the Trent and both turn their backs to the river. The long wall that runs between the two villages marks the eastern boundary of Shugborough Park, which extends over the river, although it only encloses a narrow strip of this eastern bank. Much of Great Haywood used to lie on the other side of the river close to Shugborough Hall, but from 1737 Thomas Anson began demolishing cottages as his tenants leases came to an end. He wished to improve the view from the Hall, and the villagers were first moved to another part of the estate and then moved over the river.

Some of the new cottages built by the Lords of Shugborough still stand on the lane that leads to the Essex Bridge. This handsome structure was built in the late 16th Century by the Earl of Essex, who lived in Chartley Hall about three miles to the north. Its purpose was to provide passage over the River Trent to Cannock Chase for his huntsmen, horses and dogs. It is a narrow bridge, only four feet wide, but most strongly built. There are 14 arches with cut waters on both sides, though it is said that there were originally 40 arches. The river is most attractive here with sandbanks where swans sleep and high trees at the water's edge. A few yards north of the bridge the River Sow joins the Trent. A third 'river' at this confluence (the most westerly) is actually a branch of the River Sow, which joins its mother stream after flowing over a weir.

A little further north still is the Great Haywood canal basin and junction, where the Trent and Mersey Canal is joined by the Staffordshire and Worcestershire Canal. The latter was completed by James Brindley in 1772 and crosses the River Trent here by a noteworthy aqueduct. Altogether Great Haywood has a 'meeting of the waters'. The Staffordshire Way, a long distance footpath, passes through Shugborough Park and over the Essex Bridge.

There are three churches in the village. St Stephen's is of 1840, by T Trubshaw, enlarged at a later date by H J Stevens. St John the Baptist is Roman Catholic, of 1828, by Joseph Ireland and was originally at Tixall. It was brought here in 1845 when Tixall passed to an Anglican Squire. The style of the church is largely Perpendicular. There is also a Nonconformist chapel in the village.

The main-line railway from Stone to Colwich and Rugeley follows the Trent valley and runs parallel to the Trent and Mersey Canal.

Reggie Smith, a landlord of the Coach and Horses at Great Haywood, commited suicide by hanging himself in the loft of the pub. Ever since then there have been reports of motorists swerving to avoid a man walking in the road, only to find that it was a phantom. In 1976 a girl reported that she had knocked a man down but no body was ever found.

In Main Street, between Little Haywood and Colwich, is Mount Pavilion, an old house of about 1730, remodelled and enlarged as a Gothic mansion in the mid-19th Century by Viscount Tamworth, who died before the work was completed. The house was then sold to the Benedictine Order of Contemplative Nuns who came here in 1834-5. They did not come empty-handed: amongst their possessions were the relics of 29 different martyrs, including the arm of the

Venerable Oliver Plunket. The house is now called St Mary's Abbey.

In 1066 Great Haywood was part of the ecclesiastical estate of St Chad's, Lichfield. After the Conquest it passed to the Bishop of Chester, who also controlled Lichfield. In 1086 there were 9 villagers, 5 smallholders and their families, a priest and a mill. The name Haywood probably means 'an enclosure (a "hay") of woodland', but could also mean a 'field surrounded (and so enclosed) by woodland'.

Little Haywood lies 0.5m SE of Great Haywood. It has substantial older houses with mature gardens, but consists for the most part of modern estates. The Lamb and Flag pub was home to one of the country's earliest revival folksong clubs (circa 1960). In the 19th Century the pub had its own brewery and three-storey malthouse. The village of Colwich adjoins Little Haywood to the south-west. J R R Tolkien (1892-1973), the author of the 'Lord of the Rings' fantasy, stayed at Great Haywood in 1914, 1916 (for several months after his honeymoon) and 1917, and is thought to have written 'Lost Tales' here.

GREAT WYRLEY *3m WNW of Brownhills*

The name Wyrley means 'the bog myrtle glade'. The settlement lies just south of Watling Street and today is very much a modern place of estate housing surrounded by old clay pits and coal mines. The parish church of St Mark was built by T Johnson in 1845 and lies hidden amongst the houses. Adjacent to the churchyard is the Rectory.

There is little more to say about Wyrley except to mention the Wyrley Gang Affair which remains a mystery to this day. In the last quarter of the 19th century the vicar of Great Wyrley was the Rev Shapurji Edalji, a Parsee who converted to Christianity and was married to an English woman. They had a son called George who was studying to be a lawyer in Birmingham. Between 1888 and 1892 the family received abusive anonymous letters and were the subject of hoaxes. It is likely that racial prejudice was the root cause of their problems. In 1902 a horse was found disembowelled in a field.

The day after the killing George Edalji was suspected by police even though he had an alibi. Letters arrived threatening more killings. These were signed by G H Darby, Captain of the Wyrley Gang. The police accused Edalji of being the author and he was arrested and charged with maiming and killing a horse. Another horse was killed whilst he was under arrest but this was dismissed by the Stafford Police, who investigated the affair, as being the work of his accomplices. What is more, one John Henry Green confessed to the crimes but was never charged. In October 1903 Edalji was tried and found guilty at Stafford Quarter Sessions and sentenced to seven years in prison.

The press believed that there had been an injustice and campaigned for an enquiry. Sir Arthur Conan-Doyle, creator of Sherlock Holmes, investigated the case and concluded that Edalji was innocent. He wrote to this effect in the Daily Telegraph and, shortly after, an enquiry was held that resulted in Edalji receiving a free pardon, though he did not receive compensation for the three years he had been imprisoned.

Landywood, a southern suburb of Great Wyrley, was Laund i' th' Wood in the 16th Century. 'Launde' is Middle English for 'lawn', but a lawn then was 'a natural glade in a wood'. Landywood Enterprise Park was opened by Princess Diana in 1987. The church of St Andrew was built about 1970.

Norton Canes is 1m E of Great Wyrley. In 1086 it belonged to the Bishop of Chester, as part of his Lichfield estate, but was described as waste, i.e. no-one lived there and the land was uncultivated. The village stands on rising ground, just north of Watling Street (A5), and today there are good views over countryside blighted by old collieries and industrial housing.

The church of St James has parts of 1832 but was rebuilt in 1888 after a fire. It is of dirty black stone with a red tiled roof. There are monuments to the Fowke and Hussey families of Little Wyrley Hall.

Little Wyrley Hall stands 1.25m S of Norton Canes. The Hall is a Tudor house that has been encased in brick. A long service wing was added to the west in about 1660 and extended again on the east side in 1691. It has good gables and dormer windows, some of which date from 1820 as does the staircase and stairwell with balconies below the cupola. The door furniture of the first floor rooms is highly ornate and is of 1691. With only one exception ownership of the manor of Little Wyrley has passed by inheritance from Norman times to the present.

In 1691 Dr Phineas Fowke inherited the manor and the current owner, Mrs Frank Wallace, is directly descended from him. Her husband was a big game hunter and had a huge collection of trophies. He was also an artist and an author, somewhat more worthy occupations. Little Wyrley was surrounded by coal mines, a railway and a canal. Only the canal, a spur of the Essington and Wyrley Canal, remains, but within a mile or so in every direction the housing estates are watching, with avaricious eyes.

Newtown, 2m S of Great Wyrley, is a hamlet on the A34 which developed after Lord Hay's extension of the Wyrley and Essington Canal brought the limestone-burning industry here. Just to the east of the settlement, at SK 996041, a Neolithic or Bronze Age mace-head was found.

Cheslyn Hay, 0.5m WSW of Great Wyrley, was originally a division (a hay) of Cannock Chase, of some 500 acres, and was hedged and ditched around. Much of this became common land because it was of poor quality and was wild and uninviting. The rights on it were held by the inhabitants of Great Wyrley. Cheslyn Common became a magnet for squatters and beggars, who built little mud huts and were lawless. This community was called Wyrley Bank and apparently had a national reputation. The ratepayers of Great Wyrley deeply resented having to help support the sqautters of Wyrley Bank and in 1792 obtained an Act of Parliament to enclose the common, which enabled them to legally remove their troublesome neighbours. The opening of the collieries transformed the landscape and today Cheslyn Hay is a large residential area west of Great Wyrley.

GREENSFORGE *1.5m W of Kingswinford*

There are unexplained earthworks here that are said to have been a Roman fort or a cemetery. There have been some Roman finds in the area: pottery fragments, a coin and a turf rampart. Local people call it The Churchyard, or Wolverhampton Churchyard.

What is more certain is that there was early industry here. Dud Dudley, who lived at Green Lodge, near Greensforge, mentions it as one of four which was making bar iron using coal as a fuel in about 1621. Glass was also being made in the vicinity at that time. By 1669 the forge was a part of the great Foley family iron empire. The ironworks was powered by a water-wheel. The Smestow Brook was presumably dammed to make a control reservoir, which may have been situated where the valley widens, just east of the road bridge, opposite Greensforge Farm. The farm has very grand chimneys, tall and fancy and not what a farmer normally spends his money on. This 'pond area' is now heavily wooded with tall, thin trees and dense undergrowth.

The Staffordshire and Worcestershire Canal follows the river, the Smestow Brook, in a channel cut out of the sandstone rock at a level about 15 feet above the valley floor. The hamlet is centred on the bridges over these watercourses and consists of the cream-painted, brick-built Navigation Inn, a white cottage, and a lock on the canal. It is a pretty place but spoilt by the fast traffic on the road.

GRINDON *3m N of Waterhouses, which is on the A 523, 7m SE of Leek*
In 1066 Wulfgeat held it but it was taken from him and given to Robert of Stafford. At the time of Domesday it was waste and no-one lived there. This is not altogether surprising for it is wild moorland country which may charm the summer visitor but can be a hard place in the winter.

In 1947 six RAF men and two press photographers were killed when their aircraft crashed shortly after they had dropped food and other supplies by parachute to the villages of Grindon, Wetton, Onecote and Butterton. These had been cut off for many days by snow, ice and blizzards.

Grindon is a sizeable village built on a sloping hill, near the top of which is the church of All Saints. This was constructed in 1845 by the Francis brothers. It has a screen of sycamores and is beautifully situated. The font is Norman and there is a memorial to the RAF men who died here. The spire is a landmark for many miles around.

Mycock is a very common name in the Grindon area. There are burial mounds in the hills and copper and lead were mined near the village. Less than lm E is Weag's Bridge in the Manifold valley, where motorists can park and walk along the now surfaced track of the old railway. Half-a-mile north, up the valley, is the famous Thor's Cave. There are steps up to the cave from here but it is a very stiff climb. There is a much easier route from Wetton.

Deepdale, on the west side of the River Hamps, south of Grindon, has at least 11 prehistoric burial mounds

H

HALES *2.5m E of Market Drayton*
The name Hales is from the Anglo-Saxon 'halh', meaning 'a pasture'. The hamlet of Hales lies on the northern slopes of the delightful Coal Brook valley. There is an air of timelessness here. The church of St Mary is outwardly most impressive. It was built by George Gilbert Scott in 1856. The style is Middle Pointed (late 13th, early 14th Century). On the opposite side of the road, hidden by trees, is the old rectory. Down the lane that leads eastwards is Hales Hall and the Home Farm.

Hales Hall was built in 1806, with a later wing added, and was home to the Buchannan family until 1915 when it passed to Ernest Hall. He was a founder member of the British Fresian Society. On the estate one field is known as Chapel Field.

The track continues past the turn and in the west lane-side corner of the second field, to the south, is the site of a Roman Villa (SJ 722337). It lies on a slope above a stream. The villa has been excavated and revealed a small 2nd Century house with a portico and a separate bath-house.

Between Hales and **Almington**, 1m NW of Hales, the road passes through sand and gravel quarries. To the north are disused pits and to the south are the large ARC workings, still very much a going concern as the inhabitants of Almington, who have to put up with enormous lorries thundering past their houses, will all too volubly inform you. Ready-mixed concrete is also sold from here. Almington Hall stands on or near the site of the medieval manor house but the 18th Century Hall burned down in 1900 and was rebuilt shortly after. The name means 'the settlement of Alhmund's people'.

Blore Heath lies 1m N of Hales. This was the site of the Battle of Blore Heath, the second battle of the Wars of the Roses, which took place on 23rd September 1459. The Lancastrian forces under Lord Audley were defeated and Audley was killed. A cross marks the spot where he fell (SJ 716353). It is best approached from the A53, Market Drayton to Loggerheads road, and lies in a cornfield, almost due south of Audley's Cross Farm. It cannot be seen from the road because of the way the land falls. (See Blore, near Hales.)

Clod Hall, 1m WNW of Hales, at the junction of the A53 and Pinfold Lane, is a timber-framed, thatched cottage of perhaps the 17th Century with later additions. Pet food was sold from here in the late 20th Century.

Old Spring's Hall, 1m SE of Hales, is an attractive, early 19th Century, ashlar house of five bays with a pillared porch. It lies at the end of a long drive in a small, well-kept park and is the registered office of Benfield, the house builders.

From here a lane runs to **Tyrley Locks** on the Shropshire Union Canal, which here marks the boundary between Shropshire and Staffordshire. There are five locks, covering a rise of 33 feet, a small souvenir shop and a few cottages. In the summer it is quite busy here. The bridge was constructed by Thomas Telford. One mile north of Tyrley Locks is Peatswood Hall. The black-and-white house has a large park, a lake and a handsome brick stable block of seven bays and two storeys, with a central pediment, domed cupola and three-part doorway.

HALESOWEN *4.5m S of Dudley*

With neighbours like Cradley and Blackheath you need friends. Halesowen has these in the shape of the craggy Clent Hills which lie a mile or so to the south. Indeed, hills are prominent in the area: from almost every direction the town centre is approached down an incline. Today it is very much a modern place with tall blocks of flats, steel-framed office buildings, car parks, ring roads, pedestrianised areas and shopping malls. However, tucked away in odd corners one can still find pieces of yesteryear.

The Anglo-Saxon name of the settlement was Hala, from 'halh', meaning a remote valley, or a dip. After the Norman Conquest it passed to Roger de Montgomery, Earl of Shrewsbury, and remained a detached part of Shropshire until 1844. In time Hala became Hales and in 1177 became Hales Owen when the manor was granted to David Owen, Prince of Wales. It later passed to the Bishop of Winchester and in 1214 he established an abbey, a convent for white canons from Premonstraten in Picardy. The abbot obtained a borough charter in about 1232 and a borough it remained until 1835. From 1936 to 1974 Halesowen once again had borough status but is now, ignominiously, a part of Dudley.

The modern town shuns the Monastery of St Mary, which now lies in ruins in fields just south of the busy A456. It can be glimpsed from the road, near the

Black Horse Inn. Most of the substantial remains of this once large and impressive abbey have been incorporated into the farm buildings of the Manor House. The original structures are of sandstone; the later work is in brick. The brick-built house itself is not unattractive, with steep gables, lancet windows and stone quoins. Behind it the ground falls away to a stream and to the left are earth walls, the remains of monastic fish ponds. In the garden are yew trees. The site can be approached from the Halesowen Athletic and Cycling Club Manor Abbey Sports Ground which is signposted on the A456, just east of its junction with the B4551. In 1991 the abbey ruins were uncared for, the manor house was boarded up and the farm buildings were derelict - a sorry state of affairs.

Older than the Monastery, and certainly more accessible, is the parish church of St John the Baptist. This was founded by Roger de Montgomery and stands on the site of an even earlier Anglo-Saxon church. Most of what we see today dates from the 14th and 15th centuries, but there is some original Norman work. This includes the west wall, the nave arches and the large font with pillared figures. The body of the church is constructed of red sandstone but the square, off-centre tower is surmounted by a grey, stone spire. The whole edifice was restored by the Victorians and reopened in 1884. In the churchyard lie the bones of the poet William Shenstone, about whom more later. By the main entrance is the ancient cross that once stood at Great Cornbow until it fell during a gale in 1908. In Church Lane, a steep little street that leads down to Runbow, are the delightful timber-framed White Friars Cottages, dated at 1325.

Halesowen is a watery place and the streams that rush down to join the River Stour provided power and water for the weaving and fulling of cloth. Heavy industry came to the area early. Coal was mined from at least the 13th Century and was important to the economy of the area until 1948 when the Coombeswood pit closed. The collieries at **Hawne** (hard by Belle Vue Forge) and **Witley** (on the Stourbridge road) were abandoned in the 1920s. Hawne was lost during the General Strike of 1926 when the pumps were left unmanned. An engine house has been restored as a memorial to the industry and can be seen in Hayseech Road. The name Hawne has the same origin as 'Hale' in Halesowen, and Witley mean 'Witta's clearing in the forest.'

At **Coombeswood,** which is just north of the town centre, is the Coombeswood Tube Works. Begun in 1860, it later became a part of the Steward and Lloyd empire and now answers to British Steel. Another giant of industry, Walter Somers, was early established in the town, arriving in 1866. Summers came from Derbyshire with a borrowed £100 (worth much more then, of course) and leased an iron forge. The firm has flourished ever since and still has a commanding presence on the lower slopes of Mucklow Hill. It was this works that made the long-range gun barrels for Saddam Hussein of Iraq, about which there was so much controversy in 1990. Frank Summers, one of Walter's two sons, was interested in local history and published 'Halas, Hales, Halesowen' in 1932.

However, it was nailmaking for which the area was once best known. This labour-intensive industry was run on an outwork basis. Whole families slaved in sheds behind their houses and were paid on piecework. The work was hard. extremely poorly paid, and the nailers did, indeed, lead wretched lives. In the February cold of 1852 striking nailers dragged a tub of coal from Halesowen to Bromsgrove (where the nailmasters lived) to draw attention to their plight. The coal was donated by Thomas Attwood (1783-1856), the Chartist leader and MP. He was born at Hawne House, Halesowen. As the nailers marched they sold broadsheets of a specially composed song.

Of the many old water-mills that once flourished in he area only **Lutley** Mill seems to have survived. It can be approached off Lutley Mill Road, which joins the Stourbridge Road 1m W of Halesowen town centre. The wheel, though in disrepair, is still in place. A plaque bears the date 1823 and marks the old Shropshire-Worcestershire border. North of the stream, the Lutley Gutter, are the serried ranks of suburban Cradley.

The Dudley Canal once passed through Halesowen. It came down from Old Hill and then looped round to disappear into the **Lapal Tunnel**, which closed because of mining subsidence in 1917. The name Lapal is from the Anglo-Saxon and means 'Hlappa's hollow'. Isolated stretches of the canal remain, a little overgrown but still holding water.

One such has been incorporated into the Leasowes Park, the entrance to which is off Mucklow Hill (the downhill carriageway). This park was once a part of the extensive gardens landscaped by the poet William Shenstone (1714-1763). In his day he was held in high esteem. Doctor Johnson and Oliver Goldsmith numbered amongst the illustrious visitors to Shenstone's idyll. The poet's house is now gone (the present buildings date from 1776) and with it many of his garden's noted features, such as the Niagara Cascade. Today there is a golf course, a wilderness area of scrub woodland, a lake called Breaches Pool and grassy lawns. A trail guides one to such features as inscribed seats, urns, notable trees and a 'ruined priory'. At the top of Mucklow Hill, lording it above this greenery, stands the bastion that houses the Midlands Electricity Board Headquarters, a great red brick place with flat roofs.

Halesowen's second claim to literary fame resides in the personage of the novelist **Francis Brett Young** (1884-1954). His best known story, 'My Brother Jonathan' is set in Wednesbury. It has been filmed twice and these films have been broadcast on television in recent times. Brett Young's father was Dr Thomas Brett Young, Halesowen's first medical officer. Francis also qualified as a doctor. He served with the Medical Corps in South Africa under General Smuts but caught malaria and left the army as an invalid. Between 1916 and 1918 he wrote his Black Country novels. Place names were changed but only thinly disguised: Dudley became Dulston, Halesowen became Halesby, Wolverhampton became Wolverbury and Wednesbury became Wednesford. In 1950 Brett Young was given an honourary degree by Birmingham University and in 1979 the Brett Young Society was formed.

To conclude, it goes without saying that the suburbs of Halesowen are now dominated by housing estates: **Short Cross**, **Hawne**, **Hasbury** ('hazel tree fort'), **Lapal**, **Cockshot** (probably from Cockshutt; means 'wild bird funnel-net-trap'), **Olive Hill** and **Cakemore** ('Cuafca's moor'). It is interesting to note that at **Hayley Green** the Dudley Metropolitan border dips over the A456, which here is the 'natural' barrier to the urban sprawl of the Black Country. Ignoring this boundary the Hayley Green Hospital (66 beds for the elderly) and satellite buildings have been built south of the road close to Uffmoor Woods. The foot is now in the door. How long before **Illey** ('Hilla's clearing in the wood'), 2m W of Hayley Green, is caught in the surging tide. It already has to contend with the M5. For how much longer will its mill, its Hall, its pub and football ground keep their independence?

Even **Hagley Hall** may not be safe. This has been the home of the Lyttelton family since 1564. The present house was built in 1756-60 by the First lord Lyttelton when he retired as Lord Commissioner to the Treasury. The architect was a local man, Sanderson Miller. Italian craftsmen were employed to make the ceilings and chimney pieces. The second Lord Lyttelton was one of the founder members of the infamous Hellfire Club. He once wagered the Hall against 'The Misers' in a card game. Fortunately he won, and that is how the famous picture came to Hagley. The fourth Lord had 15 children and three successive Lytteltons have been Presidents of the MCC.

The present incumbent, John Lyttelton, now Lord Cobham, can remember his uncles practising cricket in the Gallery and doing considerable damage to the fabric of the building. The Hall is a symmetrical, palladian-style mansion of 11 bays and two storeys, above a windowed basement, with a central pediment and taller, two-storey, protruding end bays capped with pyramid roofs. Steps lead to the central entrance. Inside there are many fine pieces of 18th Century furniture (collected by the first Lord on his Grand Tour of Europe) and family portraits by Van Dyck, Reynolds and Lely. There is a nature trail in the 350 acre Park. Hagley Hall is open to the public on Bank Holidays and daily between 12.30 pm and 5.00 pm in July and August. The name Hagley, by the way, means 'the wood where haws are found'. Haws are the fruit of the hawthorn bush.

HALMER END *4m NW of Newcastle-under-Lyme*
A small mining village on the B5367. It lies on the edge of a bluff and looks down on coal mines, old and new. There is little in the way of a centre, but terraced houses abound, many of which have been affected by settlement. In the 1980s there was a problem with earth tremors caused by blasting at the huge open-cast coal pit at Bateswood, which adjoins the built-up area.

It was an underground explosion at the Minnie Pit on 12th January 1918 that put Halmer End on the front pages of the national press. The Malloch (death roll) was 155 men and boys. It was, and still is, the worst mining disaster to have occurred in the North Staffordshire Coalfield. Wilfred Owen wrote a poem:

And I saw white bones in the cinder-shard
Bones without number;
For many hearts with coal were charred
And few remember ...

Actually the tragedy is well remembered, with plaques in most of the local churches and a monument by the pit-head mound that caps the old shaft. The mound itself is a memorial and is fenced around. To reach the site leave Halmer End on the road to Shraley Brook. At the bottom of the hill the road bears left past The Railway pub, through the brick abutments of the now-demolished railway bridge, past the station master's house (on the right of the bridge), and about 100 yards down the road there is a dirt track to the left. The Minnie Pit shaft mound is about 50 yards down this road, on the left. Opposite are spoil banks and the brick foundations of the steam engine house, and behind them is the engine pool. Behind the shaft-pit-mound and stone memorial, and running parallel with the dirt track (which is itself an old mineral tramway route), is the embankment of the disused branch line. On the other side of this is the site of the open-cast Bateswood Pit which was worked out by about 1990.

Podmore Lane (which starts opposite the rendered Methodist church of 1867), leads to a Nature Reserve, which incorporates the spoil banks of the old Podmore Colliery. The main road to Shraley Brook passes a brick built Congregational Chapel of 1900, which is being used as a hay barn.

Shraley Brook consists of little more than the Rising Sun pub and a handful of cottages. The hamlet was devastated by the Minnie Pit explosion because most of the men and boys who lived there worked at the pit and many were killed. Two whole generations were virtually wiped out in a few minutes. At SJ 780503 there is a toll-house.

Miles Green, 0.5m NNE of Halmer End, is a fair-sized hamlet which, until the mid-19th Century, was called Meer Green, probably after the Mee family. Thomas Mee was the major landholder here in the early 16th Century.

HAMMERWICH *1.5m E of Brownhills and 2.5 WSW of Lichfield*

A most pleasant village close to the depressing estates of Brownhills and Burnt-wood, but still very rural. The church of St John the Baptist stands on a hill. It was built in 1872 of red sandstone, but there has been a church here for over a thousand years. There are good views from the churchyard: over rich arable farmland in one direction and over part of the village and a white, embattled windmill, now converted into a dwelling, in the other.

To the south-east of the church is a lane called The Lion's Den. We have come across this unusual name in several places but can find no satisfactory explanation as to its origin. There is a duck pond here and another lane runs from this junction to a very substantial and very ugly footbridge over the railway that leads to a field. Someone, it seems, insisted that their right of way be honoured, come hell or high water. There are new houses in Hammerwich but they have been very carefully integrated.

The village is undoubtedly of ancient origin, and the Lichfield Morrismen perform an old dance called the Vandals of Hammerwich to a very good and brisk tune. This is also used for another dance called The Lichfield Greenhill Bower Processional. There is a cottage hospital here named after Thomas Barber Wright, the originator of Hospital Sunday.

HAMSTALL RIDWARE *See Ridware*

HANBURY *7m ESE of Uttoxeter and 2.5m WSW of Tutbury*

From the Uttoxeter to Tutbury road in the Dove valley the village of Hanbury looks splendid, set on a bluff beyond emerald green fields. One drives up the hill with great expectations only to meet with disenchantment. The village must once have been a charming place. The venerable church has ancient yews and several old buildings set around it, including a good black-and-white cottage. The colour-washed water tower vies with the church for dominancy of the skyline, and from some angles gains the day. That is acceptable; what is not is the mass of tidy, orthodox, but oh so ordinary, modern housing that has destroyed the ancientness of the place.

The Victorian School of 1848 is neo-Tudor with a quaint turret, and although not an attraction does little harm. (Queen Victoria made a personal contribution to the cost of building it.) The church of St Werburgh is beautifully positioned on the on the edge of the bluff that overlooks the broad plain of the River Dove. It has several treasures including three fragments of 14th Century glass, by Coventry craftsmen, displayed in the south aisle window. The centre piece depicts Christ crucified and wearing a purple robe.

There is a fine monument to Sir John de Hanbury, believed to have died in 1303. If the tomb sculpture was made shortly after his death this would make it the oldest alabaster figure in England. The crossed legs indicate that the knight had been on a crusade to the Holy Land, and the dog at his feet shows that he died in peace. In the sanctuary, to the left of the altar, is a tomb to Ralph Adderly, Knight, who died in 1595. His likeness is engraved in line on the top slab, along with that of his two wives, and on the sides are sculptures of their children.

Opposite is a monument to Sir Charles Egerton, Axe Bearer in the Forest of Needwood, who died in 1624. He reclines on one elbow, dressed in armour, for he was a soldier and commanded Queen Elizabeth's armies in Ireland. In the north-east corner of the Sanctuary, above the vicar's desk, are the stern busts of two Puritan Ladies in typical dress. They are Katherine Agard, died 1628, and her daughter Anne Woollocke, died 1657. Statues of Puritans are rare because they normally despised such imagery. Sir John Egerton, son of Sir Charles, is buried at the east end of the north aisle. He died in 1662 and wished to be buried in the chancel, but legend has it that his sister could not bear the thought of him lying within the gaze of Puritan Ladies, and so had his tomb placed around the corner, out of their sight.

St Werburgh, to whom the church is dedicated, was the daughter of Wulfere, King of Mercia (657-74). The King was pagan but his Queen, Erminhilde, was Christian and she brought up her children as Christians. After the King's death Werburgh became a nun. At the request of King Ethelred she founded four monasteries - at Trentham, Repton, Weedon and Hanbury. The nunnery at Hanbury, founded in 680, was her favourite and it was here that she requested to be buried. She actually died at Trentham and the nuns there wished to keep her body. However, legend has it that they were overcome by a deep sleep and the nuns from Hanbury stole the body back. Hanbury became a place of pilgrimage. The well behind the church is still called the Pilgrim's Well and miracles were said to occur at Hanbury. At the end of the 9th Century the Danes invaded the area. The saint's remains were removed to Chester for safety and her shrine is in the Cathedral to this day.

In 875 the Danes looted and burned both the church and the monastery at Hanbury - both were probably made of wood - and there are now no remains of either building. The church we see today was begun by the Normans. The massive columns of the north arcade, the slender columns of the south arcade and the base of the tower are of about 1100, but the church was virtually rebuilt in the 14th Century with further alterations and additions in the 15th and 19th Centuries. The chancel was rebuilt in 1862. There is much decoration around the altar. The walls have painted scenes and the ceiling is intricately patterned. The reredos, font and pulpit are all of alabaster, as are the central floor tiles. The 14th Century glass already mentioned was dedicated as a memorial to those who died as a result of the Great Hanbury Explosion.

During the Second World War bombs were stored in the disused underground workings of the **Fauld** gypsum mine, 0.5m to the east of Hanbury. In 1939 the RAF opened up part of the old, disused alabaster underground workings to store bombs. In November 1944 a workman accidentally caused some 3,000 to 4,000 tons of this ammunition to explode. It was, and still is, the world's greatest non-nuclear man-made explosion. The village suffered considerable damage and 62 people were killed. The huge crater is still there (SK 183278) and is about 140 feet deep. There is an Italian marble memorial stone and there is public access.

Tutbury alabaster is well known, but most of the workings are, in fact, closer to Hanbury. There has been a long history of gypsum and alabaster mining in the area. The relationship of gypsum to alabaster is this: anhydrite plus water creates gypsum; gypsum plus more water creates alabaster, and even more water dissolves the alabaster away i.e. the beds are 'washed out'. Alabaster is hard, fine-grained, takes a polish, can be easily carved and is usually found near the surface. Small open-cast pits were worked from at least the 14th Century. In 1374 John of Gaunt ordered six cartloads from his quarry at Castle Hayes Park, 1.25m ESE of Hanbury. (He wanted it for the building of his wife's tomb at St Paul's Cathedral in London.) The quarry was extensively worked during the 15th Century and was described by Dr Plot as 'incomparably the best'.

Alabaster was quarried right up to the late 19th Century when, in about 1880, mining with a shaft and tunnels commenced. Today the only mine operating in the area is that of British Gypsum at Fauld. The blue sheds (SK 182286), that cover the surface machinery, and the processing works can be seen quite clearly from the Uttoxeter to Tutbury road. What is not evident is the extent of the workings which cover an area of 10 square miles, mainly in the south of the mine-head. The rock is blasted and moved by mechanical diggers. Pillars about 20 feet square are left to support the ground above. They represent a quarter of the seam - three quarters is extracted. It is a huge concern with an output of between 500,000 tons and 750,000 tons per year. The gypsum is used almost wholly for the manufacture of plaster.

There are still a very few areas, mostly near the surface, where alabaster can still be extracted, but these are nearly worked out. Alabaster is cut by sawing. It is not an economically viable business and there is only one local customer, who has an occasional block specially cut for him on request. At the entrance to the mine is a red brick house with stone dressings, leaded lights and black-and-white gables. This is known locally as The Manor and was built in 1903 by the owner of the nearby Manor Farm. Some of the roof timbers are of 1680, but where they came from is not known. The drive is lined with pieces of gypsum rock.

A quarter-of-a mile east of the mine is a large, red brick farmhouse with a half-timbered, jettied gable and porch, and good brick barns, of 1875. There are moated sites at Moat Farm, 2m NNE, on the A515 Sudbury road (fragmentary 240 feet x 210 feet), and at Woodend, lm S of Hanbury (rectangular 19O feet x 2l0 feet). Both are marked on the 2.5 inch Ordnance Survey map. One mile south-west of Hanbury is New Lodge where both George III and William IV were frequent guests. Here also, in 1849, died George Edward Anson, Keeper of the Privy Purse to Queen Victoria.

HANCHURCH *2m S of Newcastle-under-Lyme*

Hanchurch is a small, unspoilt settlement of substantial houses and bungalows that lies on high ground, close to the junction of the M6 and the A500, just beyond the southern suburbs of Newcastle-under-Lyme. It is a very mature little place with a smattering of black-and-white, timber-framed properties but with no services. The prefix 'han' in the place name could be either from the Welsh 'hen', meaning 'old', or 'han', the Anglo-Saxon for 'high'.

As to 'church' there is something of a mystery. There is no documentary record of a church here but there is evidence that this is an ancient site of religious significance. In Peacock Lane there is an irregular, white-stuccoed house called Hanchurch Yews. It stands in an enclosure of about 200 yards square, lined with yew trees believed to be about 1,000 years old. Since pagan times yews have had a religious significance. In the past ploughing has turned up human bones and fragments of grave stones, and there is a strong local folk memory that there was a church here but that it was moved to Trentham by four white swans or mice or oxen. If the church (early churches were usually timber-framed) had been abandoned the holy furnishings would have been taken away, and Trentham is the parish seat. The church at Trentham has two dedications: to St Mary and All Saints. Ancient artifacts found in the yew-lined enclosure include a prehistoric stone hammer and shards of Roman pottery. The present chapel at Chapel House was built in 1888.

However, Hanchurch has a surprise. This is the Hanchurch Christian Centre, which was constructed in 1992 on the site of the Hanchurch Residential Open Air School for 'delicate children'. Since 1993 it has housed the United Christian Broadcasts' World Headquarters. This has some 100 staff and broadcasts worldwide on both radio and satellite/cable television. Their programmes include interviews, reviews, news and music and they also publish a paper magazine that has a one-million mailing list. UCB occupies a large, irregular black-and-white building and has its own sound and TV studios.

Below the village is the large yard of a transport company, and to the south is Hanchurch Manor, an attractive Victorian ensemble with a notable fountain and fishing pools, which is a little too close to the M6 for comfort. One mile south-west of the village are the conifer-clad Hanchurch Hills, a long, dark line on the horizon. These were once owned by the Duke of Sutherland (who built a palace at Trentham lm E) but were given to the public by later owners, the Fitzherberts of Swynnerton (now Lords of Stafford). The hills are a favourite haunt of walkers, joggers and fading-light lovers. Pine marten and deer are said to frequent the woods but we have had to content ourselves with sightings of foxes, grey squirrels, rabbits and a grass snake.

In recent times another breed of animal has roamed these woods, namely the press photographer. The reason is that Mr Tony Latham lived at the Duke's Hunting Lodge (SJ 839400), which stands beside the lane to Stableford on the highest point of the ridge. Mr Latham was the originator of the notorious Pindown punishment (solitary confinement combined with enforced mindless boredom) inflicted upon misbehaving children in the care of Staffordshire County Council Social Services. The scandal did not end there. Mr Latham was later found to have owned several private companies - the Fundwell firms - which had contracts with the local government department that he headed. Not only that, these companies failed with substantial debts. And worse still, these young people were frequently obliged to work for Mr Latham's private gain, in an unpaid capacity and against their will. The newspapers called it slavery.

Less than a mile to the north-west of the Duke's Hunting Lodge, along the public footpath, is Hobgoblin Gate (SJ 831407). Perhaps it was these magical little men who cursed this place, who stole away the church, and who brought the motorway and Mr Latham.

HANLEY 2.75m ENE of Newcastle-under-Lyme

Waterloo Road at Cobridge, on the outskirts of Hanley, has some large Victorian houses - the old homes of master potters and businessmen - though today they are mostly in a bad way. Many of the houses have been sub-divided into bedsits and rented out to students and the unemployed; others stand empty and derelict. From the crossroads at Cobridge there is a good view of Hanley, standing atop its hill with skyscraper flats and other tall buildings, pronouncing that this is now the unchallenged centre of the Potteries.

The name Hanley is Anglo-Saxon and means 'the clearing in the high wood'.

Today it is a bright, modern shopping centre. As well as the usual chain stores there is a department store (very much a dying breed) and many individual, privately-owned shops, not mention the three theatres-cum-concert halls, two of which have recently been lavishly renovated by the Council at a cost of many millions of pounds. The central area is now largely pedestrianised and adjoining it is a huge new shopping cerure. The shops dominate the town. Many a visitor must have come and gone and never seen the churches, the local government offices or the handsome new art gallery and museum.

The Victoria Hall, which adjoins the back of the Town hall, is known throughout the North Midlands as a concert hall. Delius, Elgar and Beecham have appeared here but in recent years it has become a place at which you are more likely to see popular singers and rock groups. The Hall was designed by the borough surveyor, Mr Joseph Lobley, and opened in 1888. The Town Hall itself was originally built as a hotel - the Queen's Hotel - in 1869 to a design by Robert Scrivener. It is in a French style, built of brick with stone dressings. The modern block of Unity House is the present centre of administration.

Hanley has been so much redeveloped that there is very little that is old, and even less that is especially attractive; signs of the pottery industry that flourished here are almost non-existent. In the centre the only buildings one feels obliged to mention are the Old Library of 1818 in Pall Mall, which used to be the British School and Art School, with an unusual attic storey added in 1880; the new library which is truly awful; the new museum and art gallery which is superb both as a building and as a museum - the spitfire museum is here also; the Post Office in Tontine Street of 1906 by John Rutherford, a good, old-fashioned classical building; the Market Hall, also in Tontine Street, now shared between a bookshop and a pub; the new law courts; the Italianate Bethesda Chapel of 1819 in Albion Street with a facade of 1859; the brick parish church of St John in Tower Road of, 1790, with a polygonal apse of 1872 and pedimented doorways with Tuscan columns; and, finally, St Mark's in Snow Hill, of 1832, which is possibly the largest and finest Commissioners' Church in Staffordshire. Near the church, at the corner of Hope Street and Hanover Street, once stood the Five Towns Restaurant, on the site of the birthplace of Arnold Bennett.

The landmark building in Hanley is Unity House, a tower block of offices built near the centre of the town by the Stoke City council in 1973. The council abandoned the building in 1993 as part of their decentralisation plan. It has remained empty ever since and the waste of money involved has been a matter of public concern well aired in the local press and on the radio. In 2004 I was told by an official in the Property Department: "A decision as to its future has yet to be made."

John Smith, the Commander of the ill-fated 'Titanic', was born in Hanley. In 1910 Lady Scott, the wife of Captain Scott of the Antarctic, made a bronze sculpture of John Smith and offered it to the town of Hanley. It was refused and now stands in the Museum Gardens in Lichfield. In recent years the Commanders' family have endeavoured, without success, to obtain the bronze for Hanley.

Sir Stanley Matthews was born in 1915 in Seymour Street, Hanley, the son of a barber. He played for Stoke City and Blackpool as outside right, and was known internationally as a brilliant dribbler of the ball. He was the first footballer to be knighted whilst still a player and played for England 54 times. He retired in 1965 after 38 years as a professional footballer. In 1987 he unveiled a statue of himself, sculpted by Colin Melbourne, in Market Square,

Hanley. He spent his final years at Penkhull and died at Nuffield Hospital, Clayton, Newcastle-under-Lyme, in 2000.

Perhaps Hanley's most famous son was not born here but was adopted. Josiah Wedgwood came to the town in 1769 and founded the industrial estate he called **Etruria**. The Trent and Mersey Canal was in the course of construction and to take advantage of it he built a large new factory, and a large new house for himself, in what was then a rural area on the edge of the town. The house, Etruria Hall, stands on a hill and overlooked the works and the cottages he built for his workers. The Hall still stands: a five-bay, pedimented mansion of 1770, designed by Joseph Pickford, with wings added at later date, although it is now only a part of a large new hotel, The Moathouse

He sited the factory at the point where the newly turnpiked Leek to Newcastle-under-Lyme road crossed the course of the canal. Wedgwood had been chief advocate of the canal and it was he who drummed up enough support to make it possible. He was a major investor and also the treasurer of the canal company. The Grand Trunk Canal, as it was originally called, joined the River Trent at Wilden Ferry, near Burton on Trent, crossed the county and left through the Harecastle Tunnel to the Cheshire plain and thence to the River Mersey. Wedgwood had already been largely responsible for the turnpiking of several roads in North Staffordshire, and through his energetic championing of improvement in transport became the accepted leader of the Master Potters. The new factory was something of a landmark because it was the first large, modern factory dedicated to the production of quality prestige ware.

Wedgwood himself was an extremely industrious man, full of ideas, both technical and commercial. For example, he invented new glazes (several of which involved the use of poisons such as lead and chlorine and which killed many of his workers) and had a London showroom in Greek Street, Soho run by his friend Thomas Bentley. After many successful years at Etruria the company moved to another green-field site at Barlaston in 1939.

The Etruria factory was sold to the **Shelton** Iron and Steel Company which later became a part of British Steel. The 2nd Earl Granville had established an ironworks here in 1841. In 1871 a blast furnace stone breaker commited suicide by throwing himself into the furnace. This gruesome event, inspired H G Wells's story 'The Cone'. British Steel demolished Wedgwood's works in the 1960s without any objection from the local council. All that remains is the enigmatic Roundhouse; no-one knows what purpose it served. The last Shelton Bar Steelworks' furnace was fired for the last time in 1978 and retracted to a small rolling mill. After a long battle to keep it open, the works closed in 2000.

Some of the derelict land was cleared and landscaped in the 1980s, and in 1986 the National Garden Festival was held there. Millions of pounds were spent on the venture and most of these millions were not recovered because attendances were so low. Etruria Hall and the steel mill lie just north-east of the junction of the A500 (Queensway) and the A53, Hanley to Newcastle-under-Lyme road. Most of the ruins there are of the conveyor belt system which was used to bring in coal from the colliery on the other side of the A500.

Between the Shelton works and the centre of Hanley are the new offices of the Evening Sentinel, and past them the handsome canal marina around which have been built some good brick houses, a pub and a waterways' office. Shelton Hall, by the way, was built in 1782 by Ephraim Chatterley and demolished in 1958. It stood between Cemetery Road and Caledonia Road.

Hanley has two parks. South of the town is the orthodox Victorian park of

1894, by T H Mawson, with a pavilion by Dan Gibson, and north of the town is Central Forest Park of 1971. The latter was created out of 80 acres of derelict colliery workings and 15 acres of old clay pits (called marl pits locally). The park will need some time to mature but it is a brave effort. At the entrance is the winding wheel of the Deep Pit.

Other reclamation schemes include the 49 acres of Monks-Neil Park at **Fegg Hayes** and the Grange Scheme which stretches from Etruria to Burslem.

A mile or so west of Hanley is **Bentilee**: a large housing estate developed between 1952 and 1955. It was designed to be self-suffient with its own library, health centre, shops and churches: St Stephen, and St Maria Goretti (1890-1929).

Cobridge, 0.5m NNW of Hanley, is on a ridge above the Fowlea Brook, hence its name: 'cob' (meaning 'big') ridge. It is a mixed area of terraced housing and industry, a part of which is now the Red Light district of Hanley. Cobridge Station, on the Loop Line, closed in 1963, and Cobridge Park, in Elder Road, opened in 1911. Christ Church was built in 1839-41.

The Brownfields Vase, 11 feet high and six feet in diameter, was sculpted by the Frenchman Carrier in Louis XV style and was reputed to be the largest piece of china ever made. It was manufactured in about 1878 and exhibited at Crystal Palace in 1889. The Brownfields Pottery Works were at the junction of Waterloo Road and Elder Road, Cobridge and were later partly occupied by Messrs Myott. The vase was destroyed in a fire at the works in 1894.

Sneyd Green, 1m NNE of Hanley, is now a suburban area but pottery was made here from the 13th century and again from 1650. At the junction of Sneyd Street and Crossway Road two medieval pottery kilns were discovered by school children. One of these kilns is "probably the most perfect example of a medieval pottery kiln known in England". The church of St Andrew was built in, or by, 1962.

The Stoke-on-Trent Municipal Airport was at **Meir**, 2m SE of Hanley, but in 1979 the runway was taken up and Meir Park housing estate now covers the area.

Northwood, 0.5m E of Hanley and now a suburb of Hanley, was formerly a separate settlement and became a parish in 1845. The Commissioner's Church of Holy Trinity was built in 1848. The Cat Inn, Mount Street, Northwood was a regular cock-fighting venue and the blind Duke of Chatsworth came here from Chatsworth to attend the mains. By 1910 the pub had been rebuilt.

HARLASTON *7m E of Lichfield*

Harlaston lies in the gentle green valley of the meandering River Mease. There are some good houses in the main street. Harlaston Manor Farm lies next to the parish church. It is a timber-framed house dated at 1540 and has been restored in recent times. The church of St Matthew has an early 13th Century tower but the rest is of 1882, when it was rebuilt. Inside is an early 18th Century marble tablet to Ann, Lady Egerton.

The jewel in Harlaston's crown is Haselour Hall, 0.5m WSW of the village. In fact, the exterior front, with the exception of the small, central 'old porch' gable, was restored-rebuilt in 1885. The core of the house is original and is dated at about 1600. The large mullioned and transomed windows, the elaborate but not uniform decoration in the studding, and the maze of chimneys give this mansion great charm. It stands at the end of a drive, in park-like grounds, with oak trees before and a small wood beyond. To the right and rear, and attached to the house, is a medieval stone chapel of about 1370, although the thin turret and spire are of an earlier 13th Century style. On the roadside is an entrance lodge of the late 19th Century by Sir Edwin Lutyens.

Haselour Hall had many owners in the Middle Ages. The house passed to the Arderies, the Stanleys, the Smythes, the Huddlestones, and the Brookes who took possession in 1557. It was probably the Brookes who built the Hall that we see today. In the 16th Century it had a double moat, now filled in, and a guard-house, now demolished. By the 18th Century it had become a farmhouse and the chapel was used as a cowshed. In the early 19th Century Thomas Neville began to restore the Hall and this was completed in the 1880s by a Mr A H Trafford. At this time the left-hand gable was added and the chapel richly restored in high Victorian, Roman Catholic style.

At the time of Domesday Book Harleston was a substantial village with 21 families, two serfs and two mills. Before the Norman Conquest the manor had belonged to Earl Algar (or Aelfgar). This was only one of several properties he held in Staffordshire so perhaps a few words about him would not be out of place.

His father was Earl Leofric of Mercia. The House of Leofric was one of the two leading families in England. The other was the House of Godwine, Earls of Wessex, to which Earl Harold (who was to be killed at the Battle of Hastings) belonged. Algar was the Earl of East Anglia. In 1055 he was charged with treason and stripped of his title and lands by the Witan, the powerful 'Council to the King'. Exactly what he had done we do not know. Algar left England and went to Ireland where he raised 18 ships' companies of Vikings. He then joined Gruffydd ap Llewelyn, the King of Gwynedd and Powys, the two largest kingdoms in North Wales. Together they raided and captured Hereford. Earl Harold was given 'the militia of all England' and drove the invaders to the Black Mountains. At a meeting in the hills above the Wye a treaty was made and Algar was reinstated as Earl of East Anglia.

In 1057 Algar's father, Leofric, died. Algar inherited his father's estate but shortly after, in 1058, was outlawed for a second time. Again, for what reason we do not know. He returned to Wales and it was probably at this time that his daughter, Aldith, married Gruffydd ap Llewellyn. Algar and Gruffydd then allied themselves with Harold Hardrada, the Viking chief from the north, and together they rampaged through England. Little is known of this attack but shortly after Algar was once again restored as Earl of East Anglia. Four years later, probably in 1062, he died. In 1063 Earl Harold and his brother, Tostig, attacked Wales and won many victories. Gruffydd was killed by his own men and his head given to Harold, who in turn gave it to King Edward. Harold was now the first nobleman of England and began to seriously consider his claim to the throne.

HARTSHILL *1m E of Newcastle-under-Lyme, and 0.75m WNW of Stoke*
The suffix 'hart' probably means 'female deer' and in medieval times there was indeed a deer park in the vicinity. Hartshill stands on high ground between The Lyme and Fowley Brook valleys. The early centre of the settlement was around the junction of Hartshill Road and Stoke Old Road. There was a windmill at Hartshill but it was demolished in the early 19th Century, and Holy Trinity church now stands on the site. The church was built 1842 by the celebrated architect, Gilbert Scott, at the expense of the Minton family. They also built the attractive Gothic style cottages opposite the church, a little downhill. These were

occupied by important overseer craftsmen employed in the Minton works in Stoke. (One of the old Minton work' buildings is now occupied by John Caudwell and his mobile phone business; Sainsbury's in Stoke is on the site of another.

Today Hartshill is a suburban area of Stoke but has its own range of shops and services. Many of the small terraced house are tenanted, especially by overseas nurses who are employed at the North Staffordshire Hospital. There are, in fact, three establishments: the Royal Infirmary, the City General and Central Outpatients, though they are presently administered centrally as the University Hospital of North Staffordshire.

The Royal Infirmary in Princes Road was previously called the North Staffordshire Infirmary and moved here to purpose-built premises in 1869. Plans and advice on its construction to the new 'pavilion' layout were provided by Florence Nightingale. The City General, situated alongside the London Road, started life as the Stoke Parish Workhouse, built in 1832-4. This building still stands. Today the City General is being greatly extended and has become a teaching hospital in association with Keele University.

Hartshill Hall, on the north side of Princes Road, opposite the hospital Accident and Emergency entrance, was built in 1881 by Thomas Aidney, a colour manufacturer. When he died Robert Nicholls, a local historian, bought the Hall. He offered marriage to Aidney's widow but she refused him. Out of pique Nicholls built a high brick wall to block her view of the Hall gardens from the house by the Hall that she had moved to. Hartshill Hall hides behind a screen of tall, mature trees and is a large, irregular brick house with a shaped Dutch gable on the garden side. One says garden side, but as we write Barratt, the builders, have cleared the grounds and are raising a large block of apartments on the site. In recent times the Hall itself has been used as a school but is now being renovated as a private house.

Opposite the Noah's Ark Inn on Hartshill Road there was once a house called Longfield Cottage, which was the centre of a small estate. This was the early home of the novelist, Dinah Maria Mullock, who was born here in 1826. In 1918 the Cripples' Hospital moved to Longfield Cottage. There were extensions and a change of name to Hartshill Orthopaedic Hospital. In 1948 it was incorporated into the NHS. By the late 1990s the buildings had been demolished. Longfields House, close by the Cottage, was also demolished and the present North Staffordshire Medical Institute was built on the site.

HATHERTON *1.25m W of Cannock*

Today most of Hatherton lies adjacent to Watling Street, the Roman road we now call the A5. Here is the striking Four Crosses Inn, half black-and-white with gables and heavy studding, and half 2.5-storey red brick. The author remembers recording some guitar music here for an ATV Christmas programme. There was a roaring open fire and by the time we had finished I had all but melted and my guitar was all but incinerated.

Carved on a beam at the front of the Four Crosses was the following inscription dated '1636N'. It is in Latin but in translation reads:

You'd weep, if doomed but for a month to stay;
You laugh, uncertain of a single day.

Dean Swift (1707-1783), author and cousin of Jonathan Swift, always stayed at the Four Crosses when travelling from London to Ireland and is said to have scratched this witticism on a window pane:

Thou fool! To hang four crosses at thy door;
Hang up thy wife, there needs not any more.

The sign of the Four Crosses represents the arms of the See of Lichfield, which has four forme crosses, one in each corner.

On the other side of the road is a brash newcomer, the red brick Tumbledown Farm pub, and a few new houses. A lane leads north from here and after a short distance one comes to a 'Y' junction. Here is the very small, fresh-looking, red-brown brick church of St Saviour (1876) which has lancet windows. Turn left at the fork and just down the road is the splendid new red brick clubhouse of the Cannock Cricket and Hockey Club.

Hatherton Hall lies 1m N of Four Crosses. It sits on a slope above a lake embowered in trees, in its neat little park protected by a sandstone boundary wall, beyond which are a few cottages. The present Hall is a late Georgian stuccoed house of 1817, in Tudor Gothic style, of five bays with an ornate central porch. It was the home of the Walhouse family, one of whom married the Littleton heiress of Pillaton and Teddesley (both near Penkridge, three miles away) and who became Lord Hatherton.

In 994 Lady Wulfruna gave Hatherton to the monastery in Wolverhampton. In Domesday Book it is called Hagerthorndun, 'the hill where hawthorns grow'. There was a Norman manor house on the site of the present 19th Century Hall, occupied by the de Hatherstones. The body of Sir Hugh de Hatherstone was found in the mid-19th Century at a spot where there had been a medieval chapel. The head was separated from the body and Lord Hatherton had the skull made into a goblet encased in silver. One evening at a dinner party the goblet was being passed around when the ghost of Sir Hugh appeared, snatched the goblet and disappeared with it. The next day a ball of silver was found in the grounds. All Sir Hugh had wanted was his head back.

HAUGHTON *4m WSW of Stafford*
The village lies along the A518, Stafford to Newport road. There is a lay-by with a small shopping centre, a village hall and a garage. The church of St Giles has a 13th Century tower, north wall and north-east chantry. The rest was mostly rebuilt in 1887 by J L Pearson for the vicar, the Rev G T Royds. There is a stained glass window in memory of Clement Fletcher Royds, an RAF fighter pilot, who was killed in action in 1945. Four Royds have been vicars here. Engraved in alabaster is the likeness of the Rev Nicholas Graviner, died 1520.

Close to the church, on the main road, is Haughton Old Hall, a delightfully lopsided black-and-white house of the 16th Century. Nearby, on the other side of the road, there used to be another very good timber-framed house but this was burned down several years ago. The owner had applied for permission to demolish the listed building on several occasions and had been turned down. His dog died in the fire.

The Moat House is a medieval open hall house, of about 1430, which was much modified in the 17th Century and restored in the 1990s when the name was changed from Moat House Farm. The moat no longer exists. There are three moated houses in the area which might have been the manor house of Haughton: Moat House, Booden Farm and Woodhouse Farm.

Two fields, each called Windmill Piece, may have been the sites of two windmills. The railway station at Haughton opened in 1849 and closed in 1966.

The Reverend John Darwell (1731-1789), hymn composer, was born at Haughton in 1731. His best known work is Darwell's 148th, the tune for psalm 148, which begins 'Ye Holy Angels Bright'. His wife was a published poet.

On the edge of the village, in the Newport direction, is a tiny cruck cottage. This has been very much restored and a large new bungalow attached. The whole is quite acceptable. Almost all the new development in the village has taken place on the north side, where considerable numbers of middle-market dwellings provide accommodation for commuters to the county town.

Upper Reule is a farmhouse 1m W of Haughton. Remnants of a moat stood close by and were likely to be of the old house, early home of the Chetwynd family from the end of the 13th Century until 1612, when Sir Walter Chetwynd moved to Ingestre. Subsequently, the house became ruinous and was quarried for stone.

HAWKSMOOR *1.5m ENE of Cheadle*
Hawksmoor is not a village. It is a National Trust Nature Reserve of 250 acres and lies adjacent to the B417 between Cheadle and Oakamoor. On the Bunter pebble beds and sandstone there are bilberry, dwarf oaks, bracken, scrub and birch, as well as Forestry Commission plantations of sycamore, beech, pine, fir cypress and hemlock. The Crabtree coal seam outcrops near the River Churnet. In Lightoaks Wood, just south-west of Oakamoor, is a hut which was once the home of 'Charcoal Jack', one of several charcoal-burners who were employed right up to the end of the last century by Bolton's copper works. At East Wall Farm (SK 036448) iron slag has been unearthed, which suggests that there was probably a furnace here. East Wall was called Heystiswell in the 12th Century. There are three nature trails, of 2.5m, 1.5m and 1.5m in the Nature Reserve.

HEDNESFORD *1.5m NE of Cannock*
Hednesford (pronounced Hensford) is a place of old coal pits and miners' terraced houses; yet in the centre of the town is the Anglesey Hotel. This most attractive house was built in 1831 for Edmund Peel of the Fazeley family that produced the Prime Minister, Sir Robert Peel. He used it as a summer residence and trained his racehorses on the Hednesford Hills. (Racehorses are still trained at Upper Longdon, 3m to the north-east.) It is very doubtful that anyone would build a holiday home in Hednesford these days, but at that time it was a little country village in the foothills of Cannock Chase, and no-one could foresee that from about 1850 onwards it would be vandalised both above and below ground.

The parish church of St Peter is of 1868 by T H Rushworth, but without the tower he meant it to have. Today the parish church is upstaged by the dramatic lines of the Roman Catholic church of Our Lady of Lourdes, designed by G B Cox of Birmingham and built between 1927-33. Architects are scathing but it certainly jollys up the place a bit. The style is very Continental, a feeling enhanced by the tall pine trees to the front and the grotto to the side. In the evening sunlight the stone fairly glows.

The Cross Keys Inn at Old Hednesford is timber-framed and dated 1746. Hednesford Raceway, 0.5m NE, lies high in the Hednesford Hills. Here is a large, circular water reservoir. It was built in 1878 and abandoned because of settlement fractures in 1916. Today it has service buildings and caravans, and a motley array of fences which have been erected to protect a venue now devoted to stock car racing. The area around is a heathland common with long views over violated landscapes. Cock-fighting was practised at Cockpit Hill, and prize fights took place here. There was a horse-race track and several stables operated locally.

At **Hazelslade**, 1.5m ENE of Hednesford, three Grand National winners - Ereman 1907, Jenkinstown 1910, and Grakle 1913 - were trained by Thomas Coulthwaite, who came here from Manchester because of its central location and springy turf. Hazelslade is a substantial village. It has a pub called The Hazelslade which for many years had a successful folk club. The church of All Saints was built in 1884. The name Hazelslade means 'the vale where hazel trees grow'.

In 1873 a vast army excercise was held between Etching Hill at Rugeley and the Hednesford Hills, which was watched by some 150,000 spectators assembled on Rawnsley Hill.

Wimblebury, 1m ESE of Hednesford, developed as a mining community in the mid-19th Century. By 1871 it had a population of some 700 and apparently had such numbers of churches and chapels that it was called The Holy City. By the 1950s mining subsidence had made many of the buildings unsafe and the area was cleared and redeveloped with modern housing. For a photograph of Wimblebury Colliery during a strike in the 1920s see Cannock Chase Past by Sherry Belcher (Phillimore), p 114. The church of St Paul was built in 1889-90. The name is from a local farm and means 'Wimbald's fort'.

Rawnsley, 1.5m ENE of Hednesford, is a former coal mining settlement in a marshy valley amongst the dales of Cannock Chase. The name is thought to mean 'the raven's woodland glade'. Rawnsley adjoins Littleworth to the south-west and here is the church of St Michael and All Angels, built about 1990. Apparently, there is no better explanation of the name Littleworth than 'a place of little worth' - charming.

HELL LANE *1.5m SE of Wolverhampton*

Hell Lane was the most notorious area of the Black Country. The amount of criminality associated with this place is quite amazing. Highwaymen and brigands operated from here throughout the 18th and 19th Centuries and into the early 20th Century. The name Hell Lane was applied to both a road and an area. Neither now exists, having been developed in the later 19th Century. The road lay on ground now occupied by the present Monmore Park Industrial Estate of Ettingshall Road, 1.5m SE of Wolverhampton, near the Birmingham Canal Old Cut Main Line. The settlement lay south of what was then called Ettingshall Lane, and ran from the present day Bilston Road through Catchem Corner (the name is no longer current) to Sodom (now called Hurst Hill).

To quote John Freeman, "Hell Lane was a resting spot of sheep stealers and highwaymen, who have been known to stop coaches, relieving travellers of their valuables and hold up menageries while they selected and led away some of their best horses." In Benjamin Disraeli's novel 'Sybil' (1846) Hell Lane is Hell House Yards. Here are some of the infamous characters who lived in Hell Lane:

Devil Lees, a highwayman, and his gang; Dick Evans, a well known fighter; Billy Moore, a leader of the Hell Lane Gang; The Brett family, infamous in Hell Lane, who frequented The Duke of York in the 1920s and 30s; Kat Rhodes, a wizard (wise man), who dressed gaudily in red and yellow and wore his hair in pigtails; and Nell Nicholls, the White Rabbit Witch, who lived in an old cottage close to a rickety wooden bridge that crossed the Black Stream. She could cast spells and if anyone spoke badly of her they would have a mishap.

Not surprisingly, there are stories of hauntings in the area. A Black Dog Spectre followed a man to his home. As the man went to open the door of his cottage the dog howled, the house collapsed and the man died. Another story has one Dick Ormes seeing the form of a headless woman - the ghost of a woman murdered by the Hell Lane Gang. Later, the ghost was seen by others to enter Ormes's cottage. Shortly after, he was found dead in his bed with a pipe in his mouth. His dog, pig and cow had disappeared.

Several attempts were made by Methodist missionaries to convert the heathen miscreants of Hell Lane and in 1802-6 a Methodist Chapel was built in Hell Lane, near Ruffian Lane. There are those who would say that today Heath Town, Wolverhampton, has a similar reputation to the Hell Lane of old.

HIGH OFFLEY *See Offley*

HILDERSTONE *3.5m E of Stone*
Hilderstone is a linear village in attractive undulating country north of the county town. In 1762 an alternative road from Stafford to Manchester, by way of Sandon and Hilderstone, was turnpiked - that is, was greatly improved and paid for by the charging of a toll.

The charming church of 1827, by Thomas Trubshaw, is set in a most attractive church yard with clipped yews and a variety of other trees. It is built of stone with lancet windows and a short spire. There are monuments to the Bourne family of potters, who paid for the church. They lived at Hilderstone Hall, a rendered Georgian house set in a small park, which Ralph Bourne built in about 1750. The family stayed there until 1950. In the grounds is an 800-year-old Cedar of Lebanon, a memorial to the medieval house.

Just south of the Hall, by a wood with two small pools, is a moated site. It is rectangular, 400 feet by 320 feet, with an extra bank on the north side and altered on the south side. The Manor House lies by the road, 0.25m NE of the Hall.

Most of the village cottages are of red brick and lie on a hill, at the bottom of which is Lower Farm, an 18th Century, four-bay house. At the back of the farm are fields laid to pasture. One of the meadows covers a gentle rise and here are some of the best preserved **medieval field strips** one could ever hope to find. They can be seen quite clearly from the road. In fact the Sandon/Hilderstone area is well known as a place where the old three-field strip system lingered long, even into the 19th Century. They were known as the Hilderstone Doles and the strips were individually owned, although in one tenancy. The deeds were kept by a local firm of solicitors (Walters & Welch of Stone) until the 1980s. Bearstakes, the name of a field at Hilderstone, has obvious implications.

The Spot and Spot Grange are in an area by Spot Farm, 1m NNW of Hilderstone, and Spot Acre is 1.75m NNW of Hilderstone. The name 'spot' is probably from the Old English 'splot', meaning 'a piece of land'. It is possible that Wulfric Spot, the founder of Burton Abbey, took his name from here. In old deeds the area is referred to as 'le spot grange', indicating an abbey connection.

Blithewood Moat, 0.5m W of the River Blithe and 2m ENE of Hilderstone, at SJ 991363, is a large, concentric, square moated site. The spoil from the ditches forms banks higher than the house platform in the middle. The medieval house no longer remains. The Channel Four TV Time Team was scheduled to investigate the site some time after 2000.

At **Hollywood**, 1.25m SW of Hilderstone, there is an earthwork in Campfield Coppice thought to be a Roman camp on the Roman road from Blythe Bridge to Stafford.

Smallrice, 2m S of Hilderstone, is a scattered hamlet in undulating country. The named is a corruption of 'small rise'. Smallrice Farm has a horse gin - a central upright power shaft, turned by a horse walking round in circles pushing a bar connected to it. Horse gins were often covered, with either a roof supported by pillars or as separate enclosed buildings.

Cotwalton, a hamlet on high ground 1.25m W of Hilderstone, was Cotewaltune in the will of Wulfric Spot, Earl of Mercia and son of Lady Wulfruna. The name might mean 'the cottage of the Welshmen'. The Old British, or Welsh, were called 'walhs' by the Anglo-Saxons. Cotwalton Drumble is an attractive wooded valley with a waterfall in the Hilderstone Brook.

HILL CHORLTON *See Chapel Chorlton*

HILL RIDWARE *See Ridware*

HILL TOP *1m NNW of West Bromwich*
It stands on a windy hill mid-way between West Bromwich, to the south, and Wednesbury, to the north. This is no fringe suburb but a place in its own right. A few of the grander Victorian houses survive but new houses proliferate. There is a handful of shops, the Sow and Pigs, the Hen and Chickens (is that a coincidence?), a car sales yard, a rather grand Police Station and Sergeant's House of 1897 with gables and a clock, and the ever-so-humble parish church of St James which has a colour-washed rendered facade and a side view best forgotten. It is a simple oblong and does not appear to have been built as a church. To the north are excellent views of Wednesbury and its two churches standing clear on the horizon and showing that place to be a real hill town

Hateley Heath lies to the east of Hill Top - the Millfield pub, big, of yellow brick; a handful of shops; acres of council houses; and the wide open grassland where once stood the Millpool Colliery. Part of the pool remains, now fringed around with small trees.

Gold's Green is 0.5m W of Hill Top centre. It is an industrial area on the slopes of the valley of the River Tame. Here are the gleaming new buildings of an abattoir of the Barrets-Baird group of companies. We went around the back to photograph the Steel Sections works over a field of golden dandelions. As we waited for the sun to emerge a large lorry drove into the Barrets Baird yard. It docked at the slaughter house gate and the screams of the pigs within brought tears to our eyes. They could smell the blood. We spoke to a man with a cadaverous face and cold, sunken eyes. It was a lovely spring day outside but here was a place to chill the heart. Those screams live with us still.

Along **Harvills Hawthorne** road are some terraced houses and behind these are modern estates. At the junction with Bagnall Street is the tiny, white-painted Triumphant Church of God Chapel. Travelling down the hill one passes the Miners Arms, a traditional little pub; the cosy looking enclave of the parish church of St Paul, brick, with a bellcote and rectory beside; and a variety of industrial units. At the bottom of the hill there is a railway crossing, bits of dismembered canal, derelict land and Ratcliffe's No.1 Works in Eagle Street. But now we are in Great Bridge, Tipton.

Down Holloway Bank is **Balls Hill**, a low rise on the edge of the Tame River valley. An old iron works now houses smaller and varied businesses. Amongst the facilities are a service station and a health club, but new houses now dominate the scene. Beyond the Tame Valley Canal (1844) is Woden Road South. The name tells us we are now in Wodensbury (Wednesbury) but drive down, past The Bridge Foundry and the Sandwell College, and you will see the River Tame in as pretty a setting as that misused waterway ever sees in the Black Country. (See Wednesbury: Mesty Croft.)

HILTON *(near Wolverhampton) 5.5m NE of Wolverhampton*
Hilton is best known today for the Hilton Park Service Station on the M6 motorway, which was built in the well-wooded grounds of Hilton Park Hall. There is no village here. The Hall stands to the east of the suburban areas of Featherstone (where there is an open prison) and Shareshill, both of which lie on the Cannock road, north-east of Wolverhampton. It is a very large and very fine house, built in the early 18th Century of brick with stone quoins and dressings. The main front faces the lake. It has a five-bay recessed centre with two wings of three bays, all of two storeys with an attic storey. The pediment is curved and decorated with vases, scrolls and garlands. The modern entrance is at the side through an impressive coach porch which was installed by the Victorians. The interior is very fine with panelled rooms and an excellent staircase.

The manors of Hilton and Essington belonged to the Swynnerton family in the Middle Ages. In 1562 they passed by marriage to the Vernons. It was Henry Vernon who built the present Hall. On raised ground, 0.5m S of the house, is Portobello Tower, a battlemented folly that commemorates Admiral Vernon's capture of Portobello in 1739. Closer to the house, amongst trees, is a moat, the site of the early manor house, because Hilton is an ancient settlement that had an ancient custom.

The Lord of Essington owed homage to the greater Lord of Hilton. Every New Year's Day the Lord of Hilton filled with water a brass figurine in the shape of a man who had an enlarged symbol of his manhood. The figure, called Jack O'Hylton, was placed on a fire and steam issued through his mouth. This fanned the fire and made it burn more brightly. The Lord of Essington then brought in a goose, which was driven three times around the fire before being killed, cooked and dressed. The bird was then served to the Lord of Hilton, by either the Lord of Essington or his bailiff, and the Lord of Hilton duly granted the lesser Lord a further year's tenancy. On the authority of Dr Plot we know that the ceremony was being performed at least as early as 1650.

Hilton Hall remained in the possession of the Vernon family until some 40 years ago when it was sold. Jack O'Hylton is now with a senior member of the family in a village near Kington, Herefordshire. The Hall was taken over by a religious order and became a kind of Catholic guest house. In recent times it was sold again and has been acquired by Tarmac Construction Ltd., who have renovated the Hall, the grounds and the outbuildings, and have established their Head Office here. It is to be hoped that they might one day replace the hideous green corrugated fence that surrounds the park. One mile SW of the Hall, close to the main road, is the site of Hilton Main Colliery.

HIMLEY *5m SSW of Wolverhampton*
The name means 'the glade where hymele grows'. It is a small village on the A499, Wolverhampton to Kidderminster road. Himley House Hotel is the building that catches the eye. It was built as the dower house to Himley Hall, the

entrance to which is off the B4176 to Dudley. Himley is an ancient manor but it is as the home of the Wards, Lords of Dudley, that it achieved a degree of fame.

After a fire had destroyed their house at Dudley Castle in 1750 the family moved to Himley. Dud Dudley, the illegitimate son of the 5th Lord, had operated one of the first iron furnaces in the country to be fuelled by coal at Himley some 100 years before. On taking residence at Himley Hall the family set about exploiting the countryside around. Between 1776 and 1807 the Wards of Dudley promoted five Enclosure Acts by which they obtained over 2,000 acres, supposedly for agricultural improvement but in practice carefully chosen for their mineral wealth - ironstone, coal, limestone, fire-clay and glass house pot-clay. What is more, these Acts enabled the family to avoid paying compensation for settlement damage caused by underground mining operations. Much to their shame they continued to shun their responsibilities into the 20th century. Unbelievable when you consider that William Dudley, 11th Lord Ward, later to become the 1st Earl of Dudley (1860), was the second richest (some say the richest) nobleman in England.

Himley Hall had been rebuilt about 1720. Of this time is the west front of seven bays and a tall central pediment. The three-bay wings of this facade were added in 1824-7 by William Atkinson, who also built the long, nine-bay south facade and its giant Ionic portico. The grounds were at least partly landscaped by Lancelot Brown who dammed the stream to create five pools. The Great Pool is a major feature of the gardens around the house, now the haunt of fishermen.

In 1836 Sir Stephen Glynn, Gladstone's brother-in-law, opened his Oak Farm Ironworks within a mile to the south-west of the Hall, which was soon 'rendered uninhabitable' by the smoke and fumes. The Dudleys were getting a taste of their own medicine. The family decided to move and bought Witley Court in Worcestershire in 1845 which they turned into a veritable palace.

In 1937 the Duke of Kent and Princess Marina stayed at Himley for their honeymoon. The Hall was finally sold in 1947 to the National Coal Board who used it to house their Regional Offices. In the 1960s they moved out and the Hall was bought jointly by the Borough Councils of Wolverhampton and Dudley, who used it as an extension of the Wolverhampton Polytechnic, as a Teachers' Resource Centre (not training college) and as a library book store. In the grounds is a country park and golf course, and in the high walled garden is a model village and a miniature railway. Public events are often held in the grounds which remain an oasis of green surrounded on almost all sides by the industry and suburban housing of Kingswinford, Gornal, Sedgley, Gospel End and Wombourne.

The church of St Michael (1764) has been spoiled externally by the application of cement rendering, but still looks well standing amongst the clipped yew trees in the churchyard. Inside is a lovely curved parapet on the west gallery and a monument to Rosemary, Viscountess Ednam, who was killed in an air crash at Meopham, Kent. On the right-hand side of Himley Hall Hotel, is a private Garden of Remembrance. It is a secret garden with a stream; a small stone temple with plain columns and a hipped roof; and four gravestones by Eric Gill to John Jeremy Ward (died 1929 aged 9), Georgina Countess of Dudley, Rosemary Viscountess Ednam (both of whom died in 1930) and the 2nd Earl of Dudley, died 1932. In 1987 the body of the 2nd Earl, William Hamble Ward, was brought back from Paris where he had died and been buried. He was interred in the garden here. If he had been brought back any earlier Death Duties would have been payable.

The 2nd Earl had been Viceroy of Ireland (1902) and Governor-General of Australia (1908). In 1918 he divorced his wife, Rachel, and two years late she drowned whilst swimming in County Galway. In 1924 the 2nd Earl married the musical comedy star Gertie Millar, widow of popular composer Lionel Monckton. They lived mostly in their villa at Le Touquet. The Earl died in 1932 and 20 years later his widow passed away. She was buried at Himley but her grave was desecrated by thieves searching for the Countess's jewels which they believed had been interred with her.

The Glynne Arms, better known as the Crooked House, can be found down a lane off the road from Himley to Dudley. About 0.75m S of Himley House Hotel (on the left-hand side if heading south), is **Holbeache House**, an early 17th Century brick house, much altered in the 19th Century. Here lived the Catholic recusant, Stephen Littleton, and here on the 17th November 1605 Guy Fawkes's fellow conspirators, Catesby, Winter, Digby et al, were besieged. Some were shot dead and others captured, taken to London and executed.

HINTS *2.5m WSW of Tamworth*
The village lies 0.25m S of Watling Street (the A5). It is a charming and ancient place set amongst rolling timber-clad hills. The name is Celtic, derived from 'hynt' meaning a road. The lane to the village leads downhill and forks right and left at a large farm. The right fork, which has 'no access' signs, is the old road to Canwell. It leads down to a ford across the Bourne Brook, which upstream from here is called the Black Brook.

On the right-hand side of the lane, at its junction with the stream, is an area of very much disturbed ground. Here are the remains and waterfalls of the old Hints Hall water gardens. The old Hall was pulled down after the Second World War and has been replaced by a more modest modern villa. Just uphill from the rough ground, at the bottom of the adjacent field, is an area in which Roman coins have been found by the local metal detecting club. This is the likely site of a Roman hostelry or mansio.

Downstream is the site of a late medieval ironworks and forge that was powered by a watermill (SK 167023). There was another forge in Rookery Lane (SK 155029). Local people have noticed that the tracks near Bangley Farm are magnetic; they were partly constructed with material taken from the furnace slag heaps which still contained quantities of iron. A pasture at the site of the forge is called Hammer Mill Close. Iron was worked at Hints from the end of the 16th Century to at least the middle of the 18th Century.

The left-hand fork of the lane from the A5 leads to the village. Here are a variety of houses, both old and new, and the church. There is no pub and no shop. The present church of St Bartholomew was built by Oldrid Scott in 1832. It is of yellow stone with red stone dressings and has lancet windows. Inside are monuments to Sir Thomas Lawley, died 1779, Robert Lawley (Lord Wenlock), died 1834, and Sir Francis Lawley, died 1851, all of Canwell Hall, which stood 1.5m SSW of Hints. Below the church the lane comes to an end at the bridge over the brook that leads to a farm. The valley is delightful here. Sheep graze in meadows surrounded by wooded hills. Joining the stream by the bridge is an overgrown drainage channel. This was dug out by Italian prisoners of war.

In the grounds of the old Hall are some very superior modern houses. It is little wonder that this charming spot has been inhabited since Iron Age times.

There is a large circular prehistoric burial mound called the Gold's Clump (60 yards in diameter) on the land of Elford Low Farm, close to the A5, just west

1. Cannock Chase: a Deer Leap near Rugeley and a County Ranger. The deer leap is designed to let deer get into an enclosed area but not to get out. Beyond the pale is a trench. (1988, pkt 35 neg)

2. Bradeley in the Moors, Rock Farm, near Alton. The farm is on the right of the picture. The remains of Croxden Abbey lie 1m S. Lord Willoughby de Broke was once the local squire. (1988, slide 4229)

3. Dudley Zoo, a Himalayan bear paces in his concrete prison. Animals should only be confined for good reason. Our casual delight is not one. (1991, slide 7658)

4. Dudley: the Merry Hill Centre aerial carriageway. This out-of-town shopping centre had a dire effect on Dudley town centre. No more is she Queen of the Black Country. (1991, slide 7521)

5. Lichfield Cathedral over Minster Pool. Founded by St Chad, it was a place of pilgrimage by the 9th century. The present building dates from c. 1330, though it has since been modified. (1987, slide 91)

6. Seighford: St Chad's church, has a Norman north arcade and a 17th century brick tower. The Doomsday name of Seighford was Chesterford, implying a Roman connection. (1989, slide 3742)

7. Hanley, Stoke-on-Trent, Shelton from the woods of Hartshill. The old steel works, top of the picture, have been demolished. The 'D' road is in the middle ground. (1987, slide 57)

8. Newcastle-under-Lyme, the northern reaches viewed from and over Apedale, an old industrial area traversed by a rough road that leads from Halmer End to Newcastle. (1988, slide 3811)

9. Cradley Heath: Noah Hingley's chain shop - the last hand-made chain makers in the Black Country. It was a true 'sweat shop', though it was worked in with pride. (c. 1965, slide 8057)

10 Leycett: Miners at Podmore Hall Pit, near Newcastle-under-Lyme. It is not signed off the road. There are several small private drift coalmines in the area still in production. (1992, pkt 116 neg 14)

11. Penkhull, Stoke-on-Trent: a Zimbabwean wedding party. I video weddings professionally and on occasion do the stills as well. The parties here are doctors, and a jovial crew to boot. (2002, off print)

12. Keele Hall, built for the Sneyd family in 1856-61 by Salvin, is now the nucleus of the University of Keele. Between 1901 and 1910 it was rented by Grand Duke Michael of Russia. (2003, digital).

13. Broughton Hall, near Eccleshall, is now the home of John Caudwell, the multi-millionaire mobile phone entrepreneur. The stone part of the house dates from only 1926. (1987, slide 236)

14. Eccleshall: Bishop's Wood was the site of a medieval glass works. This hut protects the reconstructed remains of one of the furnaces, SK760312, used to melt the sand. (1987, slide 345)

15. Hoar Cross Hall: the Long Gallery. The present house was built for the Meynell family in 1862-71 but has recently become a Health Centre with unsympathetic extensions. (1997, pkt 168 neg 7)

16. Hoar Cross: one of the Stations of the Cross which grace the Roman Catholic church of Holy Angels, 1872-6. They are the work of Wint and Boeck of Antwerp. (1992, pkt 151 neg 8)

17. Hilton Main Colliery, near Wolverhampton, had closed shortly before this picture was taken. A redundant miner stands before the winding gear. (c. 1965, slide 8049)

18. Hilton Main Colliery awaiting demolition. It stood about 1m SW of Hilton Hall, now the headquarters of Tarmac Constructions Ltd., and formerly the home of Jack O'Hylton. (c. 1965, slide

19. Oldbury: Tat Bank Railway Sidings. You do not have to be an enthusiast to appreciate the latent romance of a railway goods yard, even in these days of electrification. (1991, slide 7193)

20. Coseley: a horse on Ladymoor. The Black Country has several 'commons' of rough grazing land stocked with delightfully 'nondescript nags', some better cared for than others. (1991, slide 7349)

21. Thor's Cave, near Wetton, overlooks the Manifold Valley in dramatic Peak District country. It was inhabited in pre-historic and Roman times. Not for children or dogs. (2004, digital)

22. Stone: Mosty Lea Mill, in the narrow valley carved by the Scotch Brook, which drives nine water mills. Built to grind corn, it was later used to crush flint for the pottery industry. (1997, slide 1023)

23. Wolverhampton, Heath Town: high-rise flats and the dual carriageway on the Wolverhampton-Wednesfield road, developed in the 1960s. (1991, slide 993)

24. Wolverhampton, Springfield: the view north from the A4124. The canal locks, gasometer, sheds and steelworks are the Black Country personified. (1991, slide 7957)

25. Alton, Threapwood near Old Furnace: the lovely woods that lead down to the River Churnet and the Ramblers' Retreat at Dimmingsdale, a walkers' paradise. (2004, digital)

26. Netherton: Warren's Hall Park is old coal mining land that has been landscaped. Cobbs Engine House was built in the 1820s. Close by is the Netherton Canal tunnel. (1991, slide 7770)

27. Three Shires Head: a remote spot near Flash, north of Leek; a place of waterfalls and misty hills, where Staffordshire, Cheshire and Derbyshire meet - a place of wild beauty. (1992, pkt 114)

28. Kinver: Marion Raven, the author's mother, at Holy Austin Rock, a spectacular settlement of cave dwellings. In summer Kinver is a resort town. (1987, slide 627)

29. Knutton Cemetery Chapel. Such tin chapels and churches were once not uncommon. Simple and dignified they are most charming. The dogs, from left, are Tess, Poppy and Bruno. (2002 slide 8852)

30. Knutton, near Newcastle-under-Lyme: the Whalley Clay Quarry. There were many of these great pits in the Stoke area. Today, this one supplies a roof tile company. (2003, digital disc 9)

31. Hanley: the Caldon Canal near the town centre. The canal builders were supported by pottery manufacturers because the smooth ride by narrow boats caused fewer breakages. (1987, slide 159)

32. Longport Boatyard, Stoke-on-Trent, lies adjacent to the Trent and Mersey Canal. The immediate area is the most picturesque in the conurbation. Close by is a surviving bottle kiln. (2003, dig disc 2)

of the lane that leads to Hints, and in the hills around are likely sites for others. South-west of the ford, at SK 147026, is a circular clump of trees on a hill ridge. Such features were often deliberately cultivated in more recent times as route landmarks for livestock drovers, but they can also indicate ancient burial places or areas of religious significance. Even though the trees in such groupings may only be some 100 years old, farmers and local people often plant new trees when the old ones die and so keep such living memorials alive for many centuries.

One mile NE of Hints, on the road to Hopwas, is the quarry from which the stone for Tamworth church was taken. It is now embowered in trees and is called The Devil's Dressing Room.

In Alder Wood, **Bangley**, at about SK 176013, heat-shattered pebbles from a probable Middle Bronze Age burnt mound were found in 1981. (Heated pebbles were dropped into a container of cold water to heat it.) In the vicinity Romano-Iron Age pottery was also found, but not connected with the pebbles. Great Bangley Farm is 1.5m S of Hints and Bangley Farm is on Watling Street, 0.75m ESE of Hints. Tracks near Bangley Farm are magnetic, having been metalled with iron slag from the furnaces. Bangley Farm was also probably the lodge to the medieval Bangley Deer Park before becoming a farmhouse.

HIXON *2m SE of Weston, which is 5m NE of Stafford*

Hixon is a village on a hill east of the busy A51. In recent times the settlement has acquired much new housing, mostly occupied by commuters to the county town. The church of St Peter was consecrated in 1848. Hixon Station, on the North Staffordshire Railway, opened in 1849 and closed in 1947. There is a scruffy industrial estate and a church of 1848 by Gilbert Scott.

Between the village and the main road is a disused wartime aerodrome, the old buildings of which are used as warehouses. This airfield opened in 1942 and closed in 1962. During the war Wellington III bombers flew from here. To the south-west of the village are two delightfully named farm-hamlets: Swansmoor and Tolldish.

HOAR CROSS *2.5m ESE of Abbots Bromley*

There is no village at Hoar Cross, only scattered cottages and farms. The area lay in the medieval Forest of Needwood and is still well-wooded. It has been suggested that the cross in the name may refer to an old boundary marker between the parishes of Yoxall and Ridware. The Hall belonged to the Talbots, Earls of Shrewsbury, but was purchased by the Meynells who rebuilt it in 1862-71 to a design by Henry Clutton. It is a large house built of brick in Jacobean style. The front has a symmetrical main block with a coach porch to the right and a chapel to the left. The garden side has three gables and big mullioned and transomed windows.

In the 1950s the Hall was abandoned and the Meynells moved to a smaller house nearby. (The kennels of the Meynell Hunt had already been moved from Hoar Cross to Sudbury.) In the 1980s Medieval Banquets were held at the Hall on a commercial basis and it was sometimes rented out for antique fairs and the like.

The Meynells finally put the Hall up for sale and it was bought by Steve and Janet Jones, who spent a small fortune on restoration and added very substantial brick extensions to accommodate an 80-bed Health Spa and Health and Beauty Resort which opened in 1991. Clients can choose from 57 different treatments.

The church of Holy Angels is the great attraction at Hoar Cross. It is a lavish

Roman Catholic extravaganza, commissioned by the widow of Hugo Francis Meynell Ingram of Hoar Cross Hall as a memorial to her husband who died in 1871. The architect was G F Bodley and he was given a free hand with no financial restrictions. Work began in 1872 and the church was dedicated in 1876. At a later date the nave was extended by one bay and the chapels added. The church has nave, chancel, transepts, central tower and chapels in Decorated style. It is oppressively dark inside, more like a mausoleum than a church. This is largely due to the stained glass windows by Bullison and Grylls.

It is the sumptuousness of the decoration and the furnishings that is so remarkable. Outstanding amongst these are the carvings of the Stations of the Cross, by the Dutch carvers, Wint and Boeck of Antwerp. They must be priceless. The money spent here was phenomenal - the marble floors, intricately carved walls, the statues of the saints, the embroidery and vestments (which include a Chasuble said to have belonged to Pope Gregory XI, died 1378), and the lavish tombs and monuments to the Meynell family. Most of the furnishings and decorations were also designed by Bodley and this church is one of his two most-highly-thought-of works. The key to the church is held at the cottages opposite. The Parsonage was also probably designed by Bodley.

HOLLINGTON *4m NW of Uttoxeter*
Hollington lies on the southern hills of the Staffordshire Moorlands and is famous for its stone quarries. The sandstone obtained from here is soft and easily shaped when freshly quarried, but quickly hardens and becomes very durable on contact with the air. There are three varieties of stone - red, white and mottled - which has been used in the construction of many notable buildings, such as the medieval Croxden Abbey, 1m NE of Hollington; the Town Hall, Derby (1828); Drayton Manor (1835); Trentham Hall (1838); the County Buildings, Stafford (1895); the Town Hall, Walsall (1904); and Coventry Cathedral (1962). It has also been used for restoration work on the Cathedrals at Worcester, Hereford and Lichfield. The quarries still operate. At the Ground Hollow Masonry Works the stone is cut and shaped.

Hollington village church is St John's, of 1859-61, by Street. He tried hard here and the church has rock-faced walls and lancet windows, but has several original features (especially the relationship of the apse and its three-light window) which have not met with universal approval.

A Roman road leads to the village from Rocester, three miles to the east. From the village a steep lane leads down to the Raddle Inn and on to the hamlet of **Great Gate,** which lies in a lonely valley with woods and meadows. In the hills beyond are the red and white cliffs of old stone quarries. Time stands still in such places.

HOLLINSCLOUGH *6m S of Buxton and 2m NW of Longnor*
Hollinsclough is a stone-built hamlet in magnificent Moorland country with hills all around. The River Dove flows by, less than 0.25m to the north, and here marks the boundary between Staffordshire and Derbyshire.

The church of St Agnes is attached to a house - as at Lordshill, Snailbeach in Shropshire - and has curious obelisk ornaments on the chancel and porch. It was built in 1840 but is now a residential educational centre. The Methodist chapel was built by John Lomas, a pedlar, who spoke in a debate in the house of Commons in 1785. He raised the chapel in his garden. Hollinsclough was the setting for the film 'Murrain', produced by ATV.

There is a prehistoric burial ground, 0.25m SW, near Coatestown, on Hollinsclough Moor. On the other side of the Dove are the distinctive limestone outcrops of Chrome Hill (the larger one) and Parkhouse Hill (the smaller, conically shaped one). Together these are known locally as the Dragon's Back.

Between these hills runs a track to Dowall Hall. The track continues up a rocky valley, at the entrance to which is a prehistoric burial cave. This is a narrow fissure, in which were found the remains of 10 people ranging in age from a baby to a old man. Buried with them were flints, pottery fragments and the bones of domesticated animals including those of sheep (or goat), pig and the headless body of a dog. These were early Neolithic farmers, and a lovelier spot they could not have found. A spring issues forth from the rocks and gently meanders across the level meadows, which are encircled by the hills. The entrance to this delightful, hidden place is at Glutton Bridge on the road between Longnor and Buxton, the B5053. If heading northwards, turn left immediately after having crossed the River Dove. All of this, of course, is in Derbyshire but we make no apology for mentioning this enchanting spot.

Tenterhill, 1m WNW of Hollinsclough, is a tiny hamlet in a tiny dale. The name suggests that cloth working/dyeing was carried out here. A tenter is a frame on which cloth is held by tenter hooks to stretch it so that it will dry in shape.

HOPTON *3m NE of Stafford*

Hopton is mentioned in Domesday Book of 1086 when there was a village of at least 13 families. The village is most attractive despite the large number of modern houses. It is spread about on irregular, sloping ground. Some houses are on the sandstone edge and have long views to Wales, whilst others shelter in little nooks. Deep lanes and rock outcrops add to the charm, and the village church is notable for having been adapted from an old brick barn in 1876.

Hopton Heath lies on the ridge 0.25m NE. Here is a mobile home park, some scattered cottages and warehouses belonging to the enormous and extensive RAF supply depot that virtually surrounds the village of Hopton. The Battle of Hopton Heath took place on 19th March 1643 and was the only major Civil War battle to be fought in Staffordshire. Cannon balls and musket shot still occasionally turn up in the fields hereabouts. The Royalist army under the Earl of Northampton (who was killed), defeated the parliamentary forces under Sir John Gell and Sir William Brereton. The dead of both side were buried at the churches of Sandon and Weston (on Trent).

HOPWAS *3m W of Tamworth*

At the time of Domesday Book Hopwas belonged to the King. There were at least 13 families living there and a mill. The village lies beside the River Tame on the road to Lichfield, just beyond the westerly reaches of Tamworth's suburbia. Hopwas Bridge has five round arches and is of the late 1790s. Hopwas Hays is a large wooded hill, to the north of which are army rifle ranges.

The church of St Chad (1881) stands to the west of the village against the hill. It is by John Douglas and is quite delightful - such a change from the ubiquitous Gothic. In essence it is red brick in the lower part and black-and-white in the upper, with a varied roof line and an amusing little spire. There are many features that should be incongruous but somehow are not - the chimney stack, the dormer window and a tiny buttress. If the spire was removed it could easily be taken for a mock-Tudor house.

At the end of the 17th Century the villagers of Hopwas adopted and brought up a baby that had been abandoned in the village at night. They named him Thomas Barnes - he was found in a barn. Thomas became a wealthy London merchant and in 1717 he endowed a school at Hopwas as a gesture of gratitude. The original school was replaced in 1909 but carries Thomas Barnes's name.

In 1999 nine Limousin cattle escaped from a farm at Hints and took refuge in Hopwas Wood. There was TV and press coverage and an army of 100 soldiers, marksmen and mounted police hunted the cattle. Four were shot dead but there was a public outcry and the remaining five were caught and taken to Hillside Animal Sanctuary.

HORTON 3m WNW of Leek

The hamlet lies on high ground west of the southern tip of Lake Rudyard. The name means the 'muddy settlement'. Horton stands above the Horton Brook. This is not the Horton in Domesday Book, which describes the one near Tamhorn, Tamworth. Our Horton was a manor by the mid-12th Century, and in the 13th Century it included Endon, Bagnall Stanley, Longsdon and Rushton James. The church of St Michael almost certainly stands on the site of a chapel known to have been here by the 1220s.

The present church is mostly Perpendicular with a pinnacled tower and was restored in 1864 by Sugden. The east window and south arcade are by him. There are monuments to the Wedgwoods, including John, died 1589; John, died 1724; John, died 1757; and John Fowler, died 1827. In the churchyard is an old yew tree some 20 feet in girth, and the grave of Mary Brooks who died in 1787 aged 119 years.

Below the church is Horton Hall, a very good 17th Century house with gabled wings, dated, 'R. E. 1647 and T E 1668'. It was built in fine stone by the Edge family. The centre is recessed and the wings slightly project forward. The gables are topped by decorative balls. The windows are 18th Century sashes, but look well enough. The Vicarage lies to the right of the Hall. It has an early 18th Century brick facade, five bays, two storeys and a parapet. The Dairy House lies 0.75m NW of the hamlet, a charming stone house of 1635 with a recessed centre, three small gables and projecting wings with larger gables.

The Horton Gap is a dry valley that runs from south of Horton to the southern end of Rudyard Reservoir, and is thought to be the original course of the River Churnet.

Gratton, 0.75m SSW of Horton (near Lake Rudyard), is a tiny hamlet which was home to George Heath (1844-1869), known as the Moorland Poet. He was born at Hall Gate Farm and his collections include 'Simple Poems', 'Heartstrings' and 'Tired Out'. He died of consumption at the age of 25. Hall Gate Hall is a cruck house. There must be something in the air in this little place because Gratton Hall was the birthplace of the philosopher, Thomas Ernest Hulme (1883-1917).

Harracles Hall is 0.75m E of Horton. It is a Georgian brick house of seven bays, a garlanded pediment and a hipped roof. The mansion, now a farmhouse, stands at the end of a long track off the Rudyard to Longsden road. Harracles Hall was the house of the senior branch of the Wedgwood family which first came here in the 14th Century. John Wedgwood, died 1494, married the heiress of Harracles. His grandson married a Bowyer (of Knypersley). His great grandson married an Egerton and was granted a crest and coat of arms in 1576. From him descended the senior line. A grandson of the Wedgwood who married the Bowyer girl became Master Potter in Burslem and was so described in 1640. Three generations of Master Potters of Burslem later Thomas Wedgwood begat a 7th son. This was Josiah, born in 1730 and destined for greatness.

HULME *(near Longton) 1.5m NE of Longton and 1.5m SW of Werrington*
Hulme is a small village in open country situated between Weston Coyney and Park Hall Country Park to the south, and Werrington to the north. The houses and farms are of brick and stone and are dominated by a large, brick stables-cum-store building with a cupola and diamond pattern ventilation openings, which is now host to an animal foodstuffs' business. There are ponies in the fields and chickens and ducks in the muddy back lane. Altogether, it is quite charming in a bedraggled kind of way and something of a time capsule considering the proximity of Longton.

In Old Danish Hulme means 'a piece of land beside a stream'. In medieval times it was also known as Hulm Sub Kevermund. Kevermund might be from the French 'Queremont', meaning 'hill where goats are kept'. In the 13th Century Kennermont Hay, in which Hulme was located, belonged to the Abbots of Hulton Abbey.

HUNTINGTON *1.75m N of Cannock*
Huntington is a small mining village on the A34 that has become a northern suburb of Cannock. It is a work-a-day place once centred on the now-abandoned coal mine. A huge conical spoil heap (not slag, which is the molten waste from a furnace) dominates the village. There is a row of brick miners' cottages just to the north of the mine - quite quaint in a drab kind of way - but they are on a dangerous bend close to the road and have virtually no back gardens. The Coal Board was never a good landlord here. There are several sizeable estates of more modern miners' houses in the area, but these were skimped, prefabricated structures which were recently sold off very cheaply.

Huntington is now on the fringe of Cannock Chase but in medieval times was well within the boundaries of the Royal Forest of Cannock, a place used for hunting by the king and his lords. Possibly there was a lodge here or even a small settlement (implied by the 'ton' ending) of foresters and houndsmen.

Plot (in the 1680s) mentions that stone quarried at Huntington was highly prized for constructing the hearths of iron furnaces. The redundant Water Pumping Station that stood by the main road was demolished in the mid-1980s.

I

ILAM *4.5m NW Ashbourne*
The name may have been from an earlier name of the River Manifold 'the Hyle', on which it stands. The village lies west of the Thorpe Cloud entrance to Dove Dale, one of the most beautiful and varied landscapes in Britain. However, Ilam lies on the River Manifold which has pleasures and mysteries of its own. In the summer months the river disappears just south of Wetton Mill, some 5m N of Ilam, and travels underground to re-emerge at the 'boiling holes' at the foot of the rock on which stands Ilam Hall, a most striking phenomenon and one which

must have deeply impressed the early, primitive inhabitants of the area.

In the 11th Century Ilam estate belonged to the Benedictine Abbey of Burton upon Trent. After the Dissolution of the Monasteries it was bought by John Port whose family lived here for 250 years before it was sold to David Pike-Watts in 1809. The Hall was rebuilt in 1821-6 by John Shaw for the then owner, Jesse Watts-Russell, a wealthy manufacturer. It was a large Gothic mansion with turrets, battlements and ogee-shaped windows. The old village was demolished by Jesse Watts-Russell when he rebuilt the Hall, and between 1840 and 1850 he built a new model village at the gates to the Hall. In 1875 Jesse Watts-Russell died and the Hall passed to the Hanbury family. In 1927 it was sold to a restaurateur who got into financial difficulties and duly sold it to a demolition contractor - the stone was valuable. It was three-quarters demolished when Sir Robert Dougall bought what was left and gave it to the National Trust. (This gentleman also gave the nation much of Dove Dale.)

Only the coach porch and the main hall have survived, along with the stables and an octagonal tower by the entrance drive called the Pepper Pot. Since 1935 the Hall has been used as a Youth Hostel. The tower is a toilet and the stables house the National Trust Estate Office and workshops. The Italian formal gardens are but a remnant of the originals which stretched down to the river.

The houses of the rebuilt village are rather over-embellished with steep boarded gables, hung tiles and half-timbering. The school is of a similar style. Close to the bridge over the River Manifold is the 'Eleanor Cross' designed by Gilbert Scott and erected in 1840 to the memory of Mrs Watts-Russell.

The church of Holy Cross is 13th Century but was restored-rebuilt by Gilbert Scott in 1855. It is spoiled externally by the addition to the north side of an octagonal mausoleum, built in 1831 in memory of Mr Watts-Russell's father-in-law, David Pike-Watts. The south chapel was rebuilt in 1618 and contains the shrine of St Bertelin, an Anglo-Saxon saint much venerated in Staffordshire. A 20-foot section of the church wall is of Anglo-Saxon origin. In the churchyard are two Anglo-Saxon crosses: one round at the base; the other rectangular for its full length. In the church are monuments to Robert Meverell, died 1626, of Throwley, and Jesse Watts-Russell. The font is most handsome - Norman with 'primitive' carved figures and beasts.

Between the church and the river is a well within a wall, said to have been used by St Bertelin when he was a hermit living in the Grotto near the Boil Holes. At Congreve's Grotto is a stone desk and seat where William Congreve (1670-1729) is reputed to have written 'The Old Batchelor'. Samuel Johnson knew Ilam well and was very fond of the place. He wrote his only novel, 'Rasselas', within a period of one week whilst staying here.

St Bertram's Bridge over the River Manifold used to carry the old road to Blore before a new road was made that kept village traffic away from the Hall. It was restored in 1839. Paradise Walk may have been worthy of the description once, but now it is very ordinary. On Ilam Tops are disused mine shafts and quarries.

Castern, 1.25m NNW of Ilam, lies remote in the hills in an isolated position at the end of a track and is hardly big enough even to be called a hamlet. It was formerly a manor belonging to Burton upon Trent Abbey but was bought by Nicholas Hurt, of Alderwasley in Derbyshire, in 1617. It was his family that had the early 18th Century Hall built, probably to designs by the Smiths of Warwick. It is a stone house of five bays with stone window surrounds and a pediment over the middle window. Prehistoric finds in the area include: a Neolithic or

BronzeAge axe; a bronze armilla; Roman pottery and a fibula in a burial mound; and several other burial mounds. The name Castern probably means 'Catt's thorn bush'.

In the hills north of Ilam are 'Celtic' fields, probably Iron Age or Romano-British. The moorlands were once covered in forest but this was cleared in prehistoric times and the land used for grazing as well as for the growing of crops.

There are also Bronze Age burial mounds, some of which were excavated in the 19th Century. Pottery of the Beaker People and Food Vessel periods were found amongst the grave goods.

INGESTRE *5m ENE of Stafford*

Ingestre is an estate that contains an estate village. It lies on a flat promontory with water on three sides - the River Sow to the south and the River Trent to the north and east. To the west is the high ground of Beacon Hill, Hopton Heath and Weston Bank.

The Chetwynd family built the Hall, but in 1768 it passed by marriage to a junior branch of the Talbots who took the name of Chetwynd-Talbot when they became Earls Talbot in 1284. In 1856 they became Earls of Shrewsbury. The magnificent south front of Ingestre hall was built by Sir Walter Chetwynd (died 1638). The Hall must be the finest brick house in the county and is certainly the finest Jacobean brick house. The south front has two shaped gables and a recessed centre with projecting porch capped by a cupola, all of two storeys, with mullioned and transomed windows.

In 1882 there was a fire and the interior of the house was destroyed. John Birch was employed to reinstate the Hall. The old 17th Century stables are next to the church. The new stables by Birch are a huge and impressive courtyard block with Lion Gates. They have now been converted to apartments.

The church of St Mary was rebuilt in 1676. The architect is believed to have been Sir Christopher Wren and this is probably the case. However, did he realize that his design was for a country church? No matter how fine a design may be it has to fit its surroundings, and this is most emphatically a classical town church. The doorway has Tuscan columns and a pediment, the tower top is balustraded and has corner urns, and the clerestory windows are circular. Inside there is some fine plasterwork and wood carving. There are numerous monuments to the Chetwynds and the Talbots.

The stone used in the church came from the once extensive quarries at Weston Bank on the A518, Stafford to Weston road. At the top of the steep hill, just over 1m from Weston, is a turning north-west on to a dirt track. After a few yards the track splits. If you follow the right-hand fork this leads to a row of estate cottages. Opposite these is part of the old quarries, now covered in trees They used to stretch over to the other side of the main road but have now been levelled.

Behind the cottages, against the wooded hillside, is the substantial ruin of the old Water Pumping House (SJ 960267) which supplied water to the whole of Ingestre Estate. The engine was coal-fired.

The lane continues on downhill to Tinker's Borough, a house named after the old cave dwellings (SJ 956272) that lie across the fields just west of the footpath from here to the village of Salt. They are now in ruins, are well camouflaged and difficult to see from a distance.

There are, in fact, quite a lot of houses on the Ingestre estate around the Hall.

The two large Lion Lodges are now homes, guarding the long-abandoned, grand approach drive. **Little Ingestre** is now the Balmoral Hotel and Restaurant. Further along the approach road is Ingestre 'village', comprising a few houses and the Old Rectory. At the Home Farm and the Old Stables close to the Hall various buildings have been converted to flats. Within the grounds, landscaped by Capability Brown, there is now a golf course. The Hall itself was abandoned by the Earls of Shrewsbury in 1960 and sold to the Borough of West Bromwich (now Sandwell), who use it as a Residential Arts Centre.

At **Hoo Mill** Locks, in 1839, Christine Collins was murdered by three canal boatmen. They were conveying her, together with other cargo, from Liverpool to London along the Trent and Mersey Canal. Her body was found near steps (now called The Bloody Steps) at Rugeley. The boatmen were caught, tried and hanged. This true story was the basis of the Inspector Morse series episode called 'The Wench is Dead', first televised in 1998.

IPSTONES *4m N of Cheadle*

The village lies on the dramatic road from Froghall to Warslow to Longnor (the A5053) which passes through some fine Moorland scenery. It stands, somewhat bleak, on high ground with good stone houses, such as the 18th Century The Grove, a village shop and an agricultural Country Store. The settlement is somewhat elongated and has three centres: Stocks Green, where the stocks once stood and the church still stands; Ipstones Green, where the manor house once stood; and Schoolhouse Green, where the schoolhouse once stood and there is now some commercial activity.

St Leonard's church, of 1790, was built of stone by John Sneyd. A Norman tympanum, from the previous church, with a carving portraying two dragons, has been built into the inside south wall. The chancel is by Gerald Horsley of 1902. There are monuments to the Sneyd family, including one in the form of a family tree in black and white marble.

About 0.25m WSW of the church, and near the concrete obelisk which marks a survey triangulation point, is Odda's Hall. This is an attractive small house of three bays and three storeys, built of ashlar stone with a pitched roof, irregular quoins and a Venetian window on the first floor above the door.

A short distance past the church, to the north-west on Church Lane, is a group of cottage and the unusually named **Above Church House** (originally Farm), a modest but attractive 16th Century, two-storey, stone-built house with mullioned and transomed windows in the gable-end wall. The barns and cottages adjacent once belonged to it, but the house behind - misleadingly now called Above Church Farm - is a later dwelling erected by a builder who worked on churches, hence the patterned tiled roof and rock-faced walls. The grey stone cottages were once occupied by workers in the iron ore mines, about 0.5m NW along Church Lane. The adits can still be seen. This is a common land area with a scatter of squatter cottages and the later enclosure strips.

Ipstones Park, 1m E of Ipstones, was a medieval deer-park which existed as such until 1867, when it belonged to the Earl of Shrewsbury.

The road west to Cheddleton passes through **Noonsun Common** to Belmont Hall. The hamlet of Noonsun Common has a SW-NE alignment with standing stones at Sexton Farm which some think has an ancient astrological significance.

Belmont Hall was the 18th Century home of the Sneyd family. In the early 19th Century the gardens of Belmont Hall were considered to be one of the top seven in the country. By 1806 the Hall had been much reduced in size, although it is still haunted by the ghost of a beautiful young melancholic woman. On the roadside by the Hall is the Chapel house, a house that looks like a church. The story is that John Sneyd, who had just paid for the village church, fell out with the vicar, so Mr Sneyd decided to build his own church. It was well under way when the quarrel was patched up and the new church was altered to become a house.

A little further along this lovely road are some pools and woods, and beyond these is Moss Lee Hall, a good, irregular, stone house of 1640, now an isolated farmhouse. Other houses worthy of mention are Whitehough, 0.5m N of Ipstones, which was probably two houses originally, dated at 1620 and 1724; and Sharpcliffe Hall, 1.25m NW, a large gabled 17th Century house.

There has been a house at **Sharpcliffe**, 1.25m NNW of Ipstones, since at least the 1280s; there are two burial mounds (one now destroyed for gravel) and two stone implements have been found on the estate. The present Hall is of about 1630. The Sharpcliffe Rocks, which lie on a ridge just to east of the Hall, are a pebble and sand conglomerate of Triassic age.

There are tales hereabouts of a witch who could change herself into a white rabbit, and it is said that in the 1650s the Wandering Jew was in the Ipstones area. The Jew had refused to give Jesus a drink of water and was cursed to spend his life as a wanderer until Christ's second coming. The Jew is said to have cured a lame man in the area by instructing him to put two or three bay leaves in his beer and serve God zealously.

On the eastern side of Ipstones' Edge is a ravine-like valley called Coombs Valley. Features of the Coomb have given rise to evocative names such as Ghost Ridge, Spirit Hole and Devil's Hollow; a large black boulder is called the Hasley Stone. Thereby hangs a tale (collected in 1944 and passed to me by Roy Palmer): There were two brothers and they were both enamoured of the same lady. One poisoned the other and threw his body into the Coomb Brook, but the ghost of the dead man rode up and down Ghost Ridge on his horse. Seven priests were called to lay the spirit, which was finally caught and trapped beneath the Hasley Stone. However, the spirit escaped and had to be caught again, and was buried beneath a hawthorn tree. Once more he escaped and became a bird. He can be heard to this day singing in the Coombs Valley at evening time.

At **Greenhills**, 1.25m ENE of Ipstones, is The Moorlands Farm Park where rare breeds of farm animals are held. Here, too, is Upper Greenhills Farm where Tamworth Pigs are kept.

KEELE *2m W of Newcastle-under-Lyme*

In the early Middle Ages Keele had associations with the Knights Templar, but very little is known of their activities here. The modern village is a pleasant enough little place, which lies by the western gates to the park of Keele Hall and consists of a shop, a pub, a church, some old estate houses, a clutch of bungalows and a few modern houses. To these have been added incongruous blocks of flats, built by Keele University to house students.

The large stone church of St John lies on high ground beside the main road. It was built in 1868 and is singularly uninviting. Inside are the tombs of William Sneyd, died 1613, and Ralph Sneyd, died 1703. The Vicarage and the School are of red brick patterned with blue brick.

Keele Hall lies to the west of the village and can be approached from one of two entrance drives, both of which pass through the awful agglomeration of buildings erected by the University, which came here in 1949. The Hall was built by the Sneyds, an old country family who had held land at Wolstanton since at least 1400. They had made their fortunes as lawyers in Chester during the early and middle 16th Century. In the late 16th Century they acquired the Keele estate and in 1580 Ralph Sneyd built the first Hall. During the Civil War the Sneyds were Royalist. In the 18th Century they made further fortunes in coal mining and iron manufacture, and in 1856-61 Keele Hall was rebuilt for them by Anthony Salvin. (The stables had been rebuilt some 20 years earlier by Blore. Today they are known as the Clock House).

Salvin's Hall is of red sandstone, with mullioned and transomed windows and gabled roofs in Jacobean style. It is 'L' shaped with a staircase tower at the junction of the wings. In keeping with the old house that preceded it there is a Great Hall. The ornate State Rooms are most attractive with their columns and carvings, 18th Century chimney pieces and beautiful views over the gardens and laurel-shrouded lakes. The front entrance faces a courtyard close to high ground.

The fortunes of the Sneyd family declined, and for 10 years in the early part of the 20th Century the Hall was rented out to the Grand Duke Michael of Russia. In 1901 he was visited here by Edward VII. After the First World War the house was empty for some years, and during the Second World War it was occupied by the Army.

In 1947 Colonel Ralph Sneyd sold the Hall and 154 acres, and two years later the University College of North Staffordshire was established. In that same year, 1949, the Colonel died and with him the senior line of the Sneyd family. (Apparently, it was Colonel Sneyd, as DAPM in Paris during World War One, who arrested the notorious female spy Mata Hari.)

The Hall has survived and is well cared for; not so the Park, which has been littered with such an ill-assorted collection of buildings that they need to be seen to be believed. Individually some have undoubted merit, but together they are an unholy mess. The early college had literally been housed in Nissen huts and other old army buildings. They were ugly but at least they were commercially worthless and easily removed. What Keele has today cost enormous sums of money and will, therefore, be here for many years to come.

These buildings include the plate-glass Library, by Sir Howard Robinson, which clashes very nicely with the blue engineering brick chapel by G G Pace, and the red brick box dedicated to Walter Moberley and designed by J A Pickavance.

The rest are best forgotten. In 1962 the University College of North Staffordshire was upgraded and became Keele University. The latest addition to the University estate is the development of a commercial Science Park which is attracting research-based and hi-tech companies.

Ernest J D Warrilow, MBE (1910-2000), was a documentary photographer of the Potteries. Many of his photographs comprise the Warrilow Collection held at Keele University. He was born at Etruria, Hanley, and died at Horton.

KIDSGROVE *5m NNW of Hanley*
From the railway station at Kidsgrove a path leads down steps to the murky

orange water of the Trent and Mersey Canal, which emerges here from the Harecastle tunnels. The small tunnel (2,880 yards long) was constructed by James Brindley in 1766-77 but is no longer used. The larger tunnel (2,920 yards long) is the work of Thomas Telford, built in 1824-7, and is still very much in use. The Harecastle Railway Tunnel of 1848 (accessed from Boathouse Lane) has been bypassed.

The town is in an old coal-mining and industrial area with rows of dull Victorian terraced houses and estates of modern houses. The blue brick church of St Thomas was built in 1837 and is said to have been designed by Mrs Kinnersley of Clough Hall. The chancel was added in 1853 by Sir George Gilbert Scott. There are monuments to the Kinnersleys. Close to the church is a remnant of the Park of Clough Hall, which was pulled down between the Great Wars. East of the church, on the hill above the railway, is an 18th Century stone tower folly. The Victorian Hall in Liverpool Road is of 1897. It has a steep pediment, short columns, a portal arch and was designed by Wood and Hutchings.

Bath Pool, 0.75m S of Kidsgrove, appears to be a natural lake, but by 1812 it was a reservoir for the Trent and Mersey Canal. It lies in a glacial melt-water channel between the Cheshire Plain and the Upper Trent Valley. By 1641 Clough Hall had been built in the Bath Pool valley by the Unwyns. In 1890 it had been neglected and was sold to a Manchester company who developed the 120-acre estate as a pleasure garden. This closed in the 1920s. The Hall had become an inn but was demolished in 1927 by the local council. The Clough Hall housing estate, 0.55m SW OF Kidsgrove, was built in the grounds of Clough Hall. There are woods of mature trees in the valley.

The Kidsgrove Boggart is the headless apparition of a woman murdered in one of the canal tunnels by the narrow-boat man with whom she was travelling. Her shrieks of anguish have brought terror to many who have walked in the woods hereabouts.

More chilling is the true story of the Black Panther, Donald Neilson, a serial killer who kidnapped Shropshire heiress, Lesley Whittle, in 1975 and held her to a ransom of £50,000. He hid her in a shaft that serviced the now disused railway tunnel beneath Harecastle Hill. She died there. Neilson was tried and sentenced in 1976.

Mow Cop stands on high ground, 2m NE of Kidsgrove. It lies on the border between Staffordshire and Cheshire and the mock ruin was built as an eye-catcher for Rode Hall, Cheshire.

Birchen, 1m E of Kidsgrove, was the site of the Birchenwood Coke Works, built in 1896 by the ironmaster, Robert Heath.

Rookery, 1.25m NE of Kidsgrove on the edge of suburbia, has a mission church dedicated to St Saviour and at least three wells.

KING'S BROMLEY *5m N of Lichfield*

One of the most beautiful cottages in the county is Manor Thatch in Manor Road, King's Bromley. Originally two dwellings it has recently been made into one. The walls are white-washed and the thatched roof hangs low over the top windows. The gardens, too, are beautiful and a credit to their owner.

The old Manor House used to stand nearby but it is long gone. All that remains is a four-storey brick tower, probably of Victorian origin, and a hexagonal garden house. The Manor House used to be the home of the Lane family, descendants of Colonel John Lane, Protector of King Charles II. They had moved here from Bentley Hall in Wolverhampton during the 18th Century.

The village has charming areas but is spoilt by the relatively heavy traffic on the A513 and its position at a road junction. The church of All Saints is mostly Decorated but has a Perpendicular tower and clerestory, and a handsome Victorian porch. The lower part of the south nave wall is all that remains of the original Norman church.

The village is prone to flooding and, as though an offering to the water gods of the River Trent, there is an annual race of hundreds of plastic ducks on the river. This 'custom' began in the 1990s and is organised by the local Parent Teacher' Association. The King's Bromley Wharf on the Trent and Mersey Canal is 1.5m SSW of the village.

The 'King' in King's Bromley means what it says. The manor was originally owned by the Kings of Mercia and after the Conquest by King William. Leofric (Earl of Mercia) died at King's Bromley in 1057. Bromley is derived from broom (a yellow flowering shrub found on poorish sandy soil) and ley (meaning a field or clearing). The name probably means 'a field made by clearing broom'.

The area is rich in ancient earthworks. These include: two enclosures at SK 140171; two ditch lines, pits and a circle at SK 116162; and part of a rectangular enclosure, a circle, pits and a ditch at SK 110169.

KINGSLEY *6m E of Hanley*

Kingsley is a stone-built village on the relatively busy A52, Hanley (Stoke-on-Trent) to Ashbourne road. It is on rising ground and has good views over the surrounding country.

There is a back road here well worth the diversion. It leads from the centre of the village northwards to Hazelcross. At Hazelcross turn right and the lane leads back to the main road along a lovely stretch of the Churnet Valley. There are superb views over the river and the Caldon Canal to the Ruelow Woods. There is a bungalow on the right-hand side of the road that stands on the site of an old lemonade works. It has its own private spring of water. In recent times it became the nucleus of a Wildlife Sanctuary.

The church of St Werburgh at Kingsley has a tower, which is 13th Century in its lower part. The rest was much rebuilt in 1820 by James Trubshaw (Junior), and in 1886 by Charles Lynham, who remade the chancel.

KINGSTONE *3.5m SW of Uttoxeter*

The village has been very much developed in recent years and the school is most unfortunately sited on what should be the village green. The church of St John (1861) looks somewhat severe. It stands on a rise facing the village, over the road and a small stream. This could have been a quaint place but is not. The red brick, ivy-clad Kingstone Hall, with its two large projecting gables of applied plaster and timber facings in mock-Tudor style, stands with its large red brick barn along the lane that leads south-west past the church. Behind the stucco of Kingstone Hall lies a timber-framed house. This lane comes to a dead end at the edge of Kingstone Wood. Near the top of the hill is the Shrewsbury Arms and opposite is the old black and white Manor Farm. Near here is the village shop with an approach road that takes one through a housing estate.

Kingstone Manor House is no more but its moat remains near the yew trees which mark the site of the old church.

One wonders about the name Kingstone. Does it perhaps refer to an old boundary marker or perhaps a monolith from an ancient burial mound? To the south are the forests of Kingstone Wood and Bagot's Wood, modern coniferous re-plantings of the medieval Needwood Forest.

The Blythe, 1m SW of Kingstone, is a tiny hamlet on the River Blithe (sic). Here, at the end of a short lane to the north, and protected by a pack of howling dogs, is a delightful, tumble-down, red brick mill and the black-and-white mill-house. They stand amidst a tangle of overgrown stream-side trees and bushes. The river meanders around the meadows hereabouts in a wide, stony bed. The fields are laid to pasture but the old, probably medieval, plough marks can be seen quite clearly. The area has a timeless feel to it despite the unexpected vehicle workshop at the crossroads. The Blythe Inn, a little ways south, is owned by the youngest landlady in England; at least she was a few years ago.

Wanfield Hall (SK 049292), 0.75m WSW of Kingstone, is a grey rendered farmhouse of modest proportions with recent red brick extensions. Most of the windows are modern but two old stone mullions have survived and speak of an ancient fabric. The house stands behind a small copse surrounded by fields of stoney clay and pastures filled with horses. Wanfield is the home of Charles Chetwynd-Talbot, Earl of Shrewsbury, the oldest existing earldom in England. He came here in 1960. Before that his family resided at the magnificent Ingestre Hall.

KINGSWINFORD *3.5m WSW of Dudley*
Kingswinford is the first entry in the Staffordshire Domesday Book. There it is called Swinford, although even before the conquest it had belonged to King Edward. After the Conquest the manor passed to King William and sometime after 1086 it acquired the prefix 'King' to differentiate it from other Swinfords, much in the same way that many of the Astons and Actons were qualified by the addition of the name of their new Norman Lord. Swinford means 'swine-ford', in this case presumably the ford across the stream that runs through the old village centre near the church. Part of the old centre still remains, and it comes as something of a surprise to find a village green, a row of cottages, an old pub and a high grey house with Gothic windows astride a busy main road (the A4101) in the middle of suburbia.

The medieval church of St Mary has a Norman tympanum carving of St Michael slaying the dragon and a Norman Tower, restored in the 17th Century. The building was much enlarged in the late 18th Century. It has a Breeches Bible - which has Adam and Eve fashioning breeches from leaves to protect their modesty - and a font with a gilded canopy by Sir Ninian Cowper. There are monuments from the 16th and 17th Centuries to the Corbyn family. The church had a large parish in the Middle Ages, but in the 18th and 19th Centuries it lost much of its territory to the new parishes which were created in response to the great population increase that came with industrialisation

In the churchyard is a stone pillar believed to be the shaft of a medieval preaching cross. At this cross the decisions and sentences made and passed by the Court Leet at the Old Court House were publicly announced. The Old Court House is on the other side of the main road and is now a pub of the same name. Just west of the Old Court House, along the A4101, is the Pensnett Trading estate, at the entrance to which is an old pit-head winding gear scaffold.

Scattered around the town are some of the elegant villas built by the 18th Century glassmakers and ironmasters, such as Somerhill House, of 1756, in Somerhill Road. This is a brick mansion of five bays and 2.5 storeys with a grand facade. It is now a hotel and the front garden has been turned into a car park. Broadfield House in Compton Drive is another large house of the period - again brick, of five bays and 2.5 storeys, with a porch of Ionic columns and a three-part lunette window. This now houses a museum of glass, which has exhibits from all over the world as well as examples of ware from local manufacturers.

For the rest, Kingswinford is very much a modern place with acres of estate houses and shopping precincts. New houses have even intruded into the large gardens of the few old houses that are left. The new centre of the town of Kingswinford is at the crossroads of the A491 and the A4101. Here is The Cross pub, the circular concrete dome of the MEB showroom and many shops. In Standhills Road is the monstrous white concrete building with pink pillars that houses the Central Accounting Unit of the M E B.

The 16th Century, timber-framed Bradley Hall was dismantled in 1924 and rebuilt at Stratford-upon-Avon. Kingswinford could ill afford such a loss. The modern Bradley Hall is an old people's home and is on a different site. One mile north-west of the town is Holbeche House, a 17th Century house with secret priest holes that has a 19th Century brick facade. This is where Guy Fawkes' accomplices were killed and captured. (See Himley.)

Wall Heath, 1m NW of Kingswinford, was a hamlet on the edge of Kinver Forest by the early 13th Century. Wall Heath and Ashwood Common were enclosed in 1776. Today Wall Heath is a northern suburb of Kingswinford.

Now here is a curious story, and from all accounts a true one. The British Oak Inn in Stallings Lane, Wall Heath, was formerly a farmhouse of 1684. The farm was called Duncalf's Barn because it was built on the site of a barn in which John Duncalf died in 1677. Duncalf, who was born in about 1655, stole a bible from a Mr Babb and sold it to a maid living near Heath Forge. The maid's bible came to the attention of Mr Babb and Duncalf was accused of the theft. Duncalf strongly denied the crime and swore that if he was lying his hands would rot off. After two weeks his wrists turned black and the flesh of his hands started to rot. He was committed by the Justices of the Peace to the care of John Bennet of Wall Heath, who put him up in his barn. On 21st June 1677 Duncalf died, both his hands and legs having rotted and then gone hard. The facts of this story were recounted in a pamphlet published by the Rev J A Illingworth in 1678.

KINGSWOOD COMMON *2m SE of Albrighton*
It lies astride the A41, Newport to Wolverhampton road, the kind of place you associate with highwaymen. It is an area of scrub and malnourished trees and is pock-marked with small sand and gravel pits. There are a number of old squatters' cottages around the edge. These have been extended and modernised to provide modern homes of character. Illegal boxing matches took place on Kingswood common because the nearness of the Shropshire border allowed those involved to escape the Staffordshire authorities with ease.

KINVER *3m W of Stourbridge*
The name Kinver is one of the oldest place names in the Midlands and is probably of Celtic origin. Prior to 1066 Earl Algar owned Kinver and its two mills, but they were taken from his estate and kept by King William. In 1086 there were 24 families, a priest and two slaves in the village. King William either created or extended the Forest of Kinver; that is, he fixed the boundaries. Even today the area is quite heavily wooded and from a distance the settlement

looks to be surrounded by forest.

Kinver Edge, rocky and tree-clad, stands high above the village. Today it is a country park of some 300 acres, owned and maintained by the National Trust. Here is the seven-acre hill fort constructed by prehistoric settlers and lower down are the caves of other early peoples. These caves were hewn out of the red sandstone and at a later date were extended by the addition of brick fronts. Indeed, they were occupied as houses into the early years of the 20th century. The best-known and most easily accessible are on Holy Austin Rock. From the top of this bare, rocky, red crag are superb views over the forests. The highest cave house reminds one of an American Indian desert dwelling. Nanny's Rock, 0.75m SW of Holy Austin Rock, has five cave dwellings. One of these was occupied by Nanny, a herbalist and maker of potions with a local reputation as a healer. Highwaymen are also said to have used the caves as a refuge as late as the early 20th Century.

The village of Kinver was an ancient borough but has not had a market for many years. The long, winding High Street is quite charming with its half-timbered cottages, old pubs, Georgian houses and a variety of shops. In Dark Lane is the 16th Century, timber-framed Old Grammar School, a most handsome building now converted to a house.

The church of St Peter stands high above the village of Kinver Edge. There has probably been a church here since Anglo-Saxon times but most of the present building is of the 14th and 15th Centuries. The north aisle was rebuilt in 1856 by Thomas Smith. Inside there is a Norman rood staircase, which is very rare, a 14th Century font and a 17th Century pulpit. In the south chapel is the altar tomb of Sir Edward Grey of Enville, died 1528, who has for company his two wives, seven sons and 10 daughters. In the north chapel is the effigy of John Hampton of Stourton Castle and monuments to the Foleys of Prestwood. The east window glass is by William Wailes, of about 1853.

Potters Cross, 0.75m NNW of Kinver, is now a suburb of Kinver but was formerly a separate settlement. It is said that in medieval times a minor aristocrat was caught poaching the King's deer in Kinver Forest. He was brought to Potters Cross, where he was killed by being flayed alive and his skin left on public view as a warning to others.

The Gallows Elm Tree once stood opposite from where the Elm Tree Inn now stands (SO 842853), at the top of the hill north of Potters Cross, Kinver. A Cavalier was reputedly hanged from it in 1651. In 1975 a human bone of a gallows' victim was found here. In the novel 'Bladys of the Stewponey' Captain Kidson (based on the real life highwayman, George Baxter) was hanged on the Gallows Elm Tree.

One mile east of Kinver at **Whittington** is the timber-framed, 16th Century Whittington Inn, and south of the Inn is Whittington Farm, an 18th Century brick house of seven bays, two storeys and a parapet.

At **Greensforge** three Roman forts have been identified from aerial photographs. The most important measures 550 feet by 450 feet and has a turf rampart and two ditches. South of this is a larger fort of a different date enclosed by a single ditch. These forts were occupied in the 1st Century. A large marching camp of 35 acres lies 1m NW. (Greensforge has its own article, p154.)

The following metal working sites are known in the parish of Kinver. They are all in the valley of the River Stour.

Kinver Water Mill (SO 848833), is probably the site of a medieval mill which produced iron and steel wire in 1868. Now it is part of a pumping station.

Prestwood Wire Mill (SO 868861), about 3m NE of Kinver, may also be the site of Halfcot Mill.

Gothersley Mill (SO 862870), about 3m NE of Kinver, was a blade mill until about 1743. It was then possibly a forge and, before 1970, a slitting mill, which finally closed in the 1870s.

Old Hinksford Mill (SO 867900), about 35m NNE of Kinver, was a blade mill from about 1650. There is another mill known by this name.

Walke Mill Ironworks (SO 851843), at **The Hyde,** 0.5m NNE of Kinver, on the west side of the River Stour, was a fulling mill of about 1590, which was taken over by Richard Foley (1580-1657) and converted to a slitting mill. Iron sheets from his various ironworks were rolled and cut into bar rods – strips suitable for nail making. This was the first time a mechanical process had been used in England. There is a strong tradition that Foley brought this invention from Holland, where he is said to have posed as a fiddler to spy on the Dutch developers of the process. The mill flourished and by the late 1630s was worked by George Brindley of Hyde House. Brindley's great grandson was still operating it in the early 18th Century. It finally closed in 1919.

The hamlet of The Hyde (SO 850844) is a delightful little place on the wooded banks of the River Stour and the Staffordshire and Worcestershire Canal, 0.5m NE of Kinver. It can only be approached in a vehicle down a rough track signposted off the Kinver-Stourton road. However, it is but a short walk from Kinver along the canal towpath. There is little more than an old farm, a few cottages, summer chalets, a couple of bridges and a clutch of narrow boats, but the Hyde does have an unspoilt charm. In the hillside, east of the late 19th Century lock keeper's cottage, there was a rock house in 1830.

KINVER FOREST

This was a royal hunting ground from the 11th to the 16th Centuries. It stretched from Seisdon, Lower Penn and Tettenhall Wood in the north to Kinver Edge and Kidderminster in the south. Royal visitors included William II, Henry II (probably), King John and Henry III, who was at Bobbington on at least two occasions. There was a royal hunting lodge at Stourton, which later became Stourton Castle, and there might have been one at Bobbington.

KNIGHTLEY *3m NNW of Gnosall, which is 7m W of Stafford*
A small, scattered hamlet with a strange little yellow brick church of 1840, by Thomas Trubshaw, which has a stained glass window by Kempe of 1900.

Knightley Grange lies 1m S of the church. It is a red brick mansion with stone dressings in a neo-Elizabethan style. The house stands on a bluff and has superb views over the white-painted Gamekeeper's Cottage towards the Wrekin. In the park there is a deer farm surrounded by high wire netting.

Knightley Dale, 0.5m SE of the Grange, is a hamlet with a substantial moated site in the field just north of the junction of the lanes. Down a track at the foot of Prospect Hill is Knightley Hall, which has an enormous chimney stack and a large, yellow brick barn. The Knightley family now live at Fawsley, Northamptonshire. At Knightly Dale, 1m SSE of Knightly is a field called Moat Meadow. This might be the site of the old manor house. In early medieval times there was a deer park in the vicinity of Knightly.

KNIGHTON *See Adbaston*

KNUTTON *See Newcastle-under-Lyme*

KNYPERSLEY *6m N of Hanley on the A527*
Knyper is probably from the Norwegian 'griper' meaning 'rocks'. Knypersley is a dour southern suburb of Biddulph which, like the country around it, bears the scars of its industrial history. The smoke-blackened church of St John the Evangelist was built in 1848-51 and paid for by James Bateman, who also financed the large neo-Jacobean parsonage, complete with stables and coach-house, and the school of 1850. All were the work of the architect, R C Hussey.

James's father John had lived at Knypersley Hall and James kept the walled garden in which he cultivated plants for his famous gardens at Biddulph Grange, 1.25m to the north. Most of the grounds of the old Knypersley Hall have been sold and built upon, but the back garden remains and is now, fittingly, a garden centre.

One mile to the south-east is the **Greenway Bank** Country Park, which includes the last 110 acres of the 19th Century landscaped park of Greenway Bank Hall, which was demolished in the early 1970s. There are dramatic stone outcrops, an arboretum of native British trees and two pools. The Serpentine Pool is set in a delightful wooded valley where there is much bird life, including redstart, kingfisher and dipper. In the wetland areas are many species of plants, such as marsh marigold, marsh violet and water avens. The other pool is the Knypersley Reservoir, a canal feeder reservoir, at the southern tip of which is the source of the River Trent, one of England's longest rivers. In the spring the azaleas and rhododendrons flower in profusion. There are public toilets and a car park.

L

LAPLEY *3.5m WSW of Penkridge*
Lapley is an intriguing little village with a lot of character, which lies just off the old Roman road that ran from Stretton (Pennocrucium) to Whitchurch. Lapley Priory was founded by Earl Algar, between 1061 and 1086, on land he gave to the Benedictine monks of Rheims. Earl Algar's son had died at Rheims and was buried there by the monks. The Priory buildings adjoined the church on the north side and on part of the site now occupied by the Old Manor House.

The church of All Saints survives. It is an imposing building with a high, strong central tower which is Norman in its lower part and Perpendicular above, with a parapet and eight pinnacles. The nave and chancel masonry is also Norman, with a perfect Norman window in the south chancel wall. There are two Perpendicular windows in the north nave.

Next to the church is an attractive old house with good gardens. South of the church is Park House, a large, pleasing building with crenellated walls and a turreted gatehouse. It dates partly from the 18th Century and partly from about 1867.

Across the fields once stood Fort St George, a conceit constructed by Colonel Tudor of Park House between 1858 and 1870. It was an imitation of Fort St George in Madras, India, and was used as the HQ of the Lapley Rifle

Volunteers. It was demolished in the 1980s and the site is now farmland.

Lapley Hall (House) was built about 1600 but much restored and enlarged in 1875 when the Gothic arched garden wall was probably built. In 1643, during the Civil War, the Hall was held for the King and a Parliamentary attack was beaten off.

The inheritance custom of Borough English lingered late here. There is a record that morris dancing took place in the area in 1655.

LEEK *11m NE of Hanley (in the Potteries)*

The name derives from 'lock', Old Norse for 'stream', possibly the stream that once emerged in the parish churchyard called Spout Water. Leek was one of the many important manors owned by the great Anglo-Saxon Earl Algar, whose estate was dispossessed after the Norman Conquest. As with most of his lands Leek was usurped by the new king. The old borough lay at the top of the hill around the Market Place and the parish church. It was the creation of Earl Ranulph de Blunderville of Chester, and his grid pattern of streets is still evident. Later, the borough was developed by the Abbots of Dieulacres Abbey which lay lm N of the town.

At the centre of Leek, roads from Buxton, Ashbourne, Uttoxeter and Stone, Burslem and the Potteries, and Macclesfield all meet. Around the town is the magnificent countryside of the Staffordshire Moorlands - their hills and dales, rivers and reservoirs.

The old stone market town began its transformation to a place of industry in the 18th Century when silk spinning and weaving, ribbon weaving and button making became substantial cottage industries. In 1762 the road between Stockport, Macclesfield, Leek and Ashbourne was turnpiked and improved, so providing the town with easy transport to the major markets of the south and the north. The first silk weaving factory, the Wellington Mill in Strangman Street, was not built until 1853 and even then the cottage industry continued in purpose-built houses, such as the early 19th Century, three-storyed terraced houses with their long, top-storey windows, that still survive in London Street.

In 1860 the huge six-storey mill of Wardle and Davenport was built in Mill Street, one of many similar factories that brought great prosperity to Leek. The waters of the River Churnet, which curve around Leek in a large meander, were found to be suitable for silk dyeing and this trade flourished as a complimentary industry to the weaving process.

During the 19th Century much of the town was either built or rebuilt. There are comparatively few early buildings. Amongst them are the timber-framed and gabled Roebuck Inn of about 1626; the Ash Almshouses in Broad Street of 1676, stuccoed and renovated about 1987, making a pretty sight; and several 18th Century houses such as the Vicarage, Foxlowe (east of the church), the former Grammar School at Overton Bank, and in the Market Place the Red Lion.

The second half of the 19th Century in Leek was dominated by a local architect, William Sugden (died 1892) and his son, William Lamer Sugden (died 1901). One of their most notable buildings is the red brick Nicholson Institute of 1882-4 which houses the School of Art, the museum and the library. It lies largely hidden behind the splendid 18th Century stone house called Greyfriars in Stockwell Street. Together they make a delightful group. The Sugdens built many of the public buildings: the County Police Station; the former Black's Head, now Woolworths; the District Bank, one of their best; the Memorial Hospital in Stockwell Street; the Congregational Chapel in Decorated style; and many, many more public and private works.

They did not, however, have a hand in constructing the parish church of St Edward the Confessor, a large, but not very attractive, stone building which was rebuilt after a fire in 1297. In 1556 and 1593 the south and north aisles were removed and irregular windows inserted in the new walls. The porch is of 1670. The chancel was rebuilt again and furnished by G E Street in 1865. There are some good examples of the Leek School of Embroidery, founded by Lady Wardle in the 1870s and a stained glass window by William Morris in the Lady Chapel. In the west of the nave is a striking 18th Century gallery of many tiers. The monuments include a brass plaque to John Ashenhurst, died 1597, and a memorial to William Trafford of Swythamley, died 1697. In the churchyard are two Anglo-Saxon crosses probably of the 11th Century. There can be little doubt that an Anglo-Saxon church preceded that of the Normans, and there are records of carved Saxon stones being seen inside the church early in the 20th Century.

On the 20th, 21st and 22nd June it is possible, weather permitting, to see a double sunset from Doctor's Corner (where eight doctors are buried) in the churchyard. The sun sets over Bosley Cloud, 7m NW, beyond Lake Rudyard, disappears and re-emerges to set a second time over the Cheshire plain.

All in all, Leek is a most pleasant town. It has a variety of buildings, a good selection of shops, a flourishing market, a busy atmosphere and a superb situation. However, it has very few specific tourist attractions About the only place that could be so called is the James Brindley Mill at the bottom of Mill Street, which was probably built by the great canal engineer in 1752 and now houses a small museum. However, Leek is the ideal centre from which to explore the Staffordshire Moorlands.

The suburb of **Compton** has some early 19th Century areas, such as King Street and Albion Street, where there are three-storey weavers' cottages, the impressive church of All Saints (1885-7) by Norman Shaw, and St Mary's (Roman Catholic, 1886) by Albert Vicars.

Before leaving Leek perhaps we should mention at least one of the town's witches. At Gettliffe's Yard in Derby Street there is reputed to have lived an old crone who owned a black cat. The witch had a neighbour who noticed that whenever the witch's cat came near to her her baking turned out badly. One day the neighbour threw a hot oatcake at the cat and chased it into the witch's house. Inside the house she found no sign of the cat but the witch was howling in agony from the pain of a bad burn on her back.

Birchall, 1.25m SSE of Leek, is an amalgamation of Big Birchall and Little Birchall. It was probably at Big Birchall that Dieulacres Abbey had its Birchall Grange, established by 1246. At Little Birchall there is a Plague Stone on the west side of the A520.

Bradnop, 1m E of Leek, is a small village which lies on high ground just off the A523(T), Leek to Ashbourne road. The name is from the Old English and means 'broad enclosed valley'. The suffix 'nop' is from 'hof' or 'hope', meaning 'valley'. By the mid-14th Century Hulton Abbey had a grange at Upper Bradnop. The manor later passed to the Astons and the Sneyds. The medieval Earls' Way (the Earl of Chester's route to his Midland estates) passed through Bradnop, and in 1745 the Young Pretender and his Jacobite army passed through the village. The school served as a mission church between 1862 and 1990, at which time services were moved to the Methodist church. The school closed as a school in 1978. The station opened in 1905 and closed in 1935. A troublesome ghost at Bradnop was laid by being lured into a cupboard in Leek and the doors nailed up to trap him.

Oxhay Farm, Bradnop, was the Red Lion in 1745 when the Jacobite army passed through. Two of the soldiers had a fight and one was killed. He was buried behind the farm and ever since a phantom black dog has been seen here.

One mile north of the town, at Abbey Farm (SJ 982578), are the remains of **Dieulacres Abbey** which was founded by the Earl of Chester in 1214. It was a Cistercian house that moved here from Poulton in Cheshire. Very little remains of the Abbey. The Early English bases of the crossing piers of the church are in situ and there are many fragments of sculpture built into the outbuildings and walls of the farm. The best pieces are in the garden arch, attached to the house at the end of the entrance drive, and include a fine mid-14th Century king. The farmhouse itself is black and white on a stone base, dated at 1625. The stone archway at the back, with tracery in the spandrels, almost certainly belongs to part of the original Abbey buildings. The house was built by the Rudyard family who had acquired the Abbey soon after the Dissolution of the Monasteries. The stone outbuildings have Gothic doorways and the windows were built about 1820.

By the site of the Abbey there is a cave in the rock cliff. This may have been a hermit's dwelling before the 12th Century and (or) an anchorite's cell in the 14th or 15th Centuries. Certainly it was later used as a habitation because it has signs of a fireplace, door jambs and a projecting building. Deiulacres Abbey was second only to Burton Abbey for wealth in Staffordshire.

One mile west of Leek, by the River Churnet, is **Westwood Hall,** a large neo-Elizabethan gabled mansion of 1850-3, built by John Davenport of the pottery manufacturing family. The south and east fronts are of red sandstone but the rest is brick. The house is pleasantly irregular but has not been well treated; one of the two original courtyards has gone, as have many of the leaded glass windows, and the chimneys have been drastically reduced in height. In the grounds is an attractive, modern Summer House, the Old Stables and an Entrance Lodge with a large arch.

Two miles north-east of Leek is Lake Rudyard, a large and long-established reservoir after which Rudyard Kipling was named. It can be seen to its best advantage from the special lay-bys on the A523, Leek to Macclesfield road. (Rudyard has its own article.) At Tittesworth, 1.25m NNE of Leek, in the fields of Tittesworth Farm, are the remains of prehistoric camps. The old packhorse salt road from Cheshire passed through Meerbrook (at the northern end of the Tittesworth reservoir), and then to Middle Hulme, Blackshaw Moor, Stonycliff and on to Blackmere House (now called The Mermaid Inn) on Morridge Hill.

LEEKBROOK *1m S of Leek*

Leekbrook is a hamlet on the A520, at the confluence of the Cartledge Brook and the River Churnet. It is named after a stream which joins the River Churnet. Joshua Wardle's original silk dyeing works was first sited on the banks of the River Churnet in 1830. In 1974 most of these buildings were demolished. A new works was built on an adjacent site in the 1930s and production is now carried out there. Leek sausage works are at Leekbrook and from the 1970s the valley has been developed as an industrial estate. Leekbrook has had a busy railway history: the Leekbrook-Waterhouses line opened in 1905; the Leekbrook-Oakamoor line closed in 1960 but a single track remained open as a mineral railway to Moneystone; the Leekbrook to Cauldon line closed in 1935; The Churnet Valley Line, which ran from Macclesfield to Uttoxeter and passed through Leekbrook, opened in 1849 and closed in 1960; the Stoke-Leek line, which joined the Churnet Valley line at Leekbrook, opened in 1867 and closed to passengers in 1960.

LEAMONSLEY *0.5m W of Lichfield*

Leamonsley is a suburb of Lichfield located in the triangle at the junction of the A52 and the A461. The name is probably from the Celtic 'lemo', meaning 'elm tree' and the Anglo-Saxon 'leah', a wood or a clearing in a wood. The settlement developed around a fulling mill which was opened in the 1790s. The church of Christ Church was consecrated in 1847.

Maple Hayes, 0.5m NE of Leamonsley, is a late-Georgian house of five bays, 2.5 storeys, a hipped roof and one-bay canted wings which were added in about 1885. The house was rebuilt in 1796 by a Lichfield wine merchant. It later became a boarding house for King Edward VI Grammar School, and from 1982 a special school. To the north of the house, in a hollow by a stream, Erasmus Darwin created his botanical garden, near Darwin's Bath, a popular bathing place from about 1700 (SK 096099). He bought the land here in 1777. The Bath house was restored in 1890. There was a conduit head that supplied water to Lichfield Cathedral Close from the mid-12th Century. The last conduit in the Close only closed in 1969. There is a moated site alongside the access lane, 0.5m NE of Maple Hayes House.

LEYCETT *2.5m WNW of Newcastle-under-Lyme*

The name Leycett means 'the clearing in the wood'. It lies in quite hilly country, a landscape of old coal and clay workings now healing over. Coal has been mined in the area since the 16th century. The settlement was planned by the Leycett Colliery who built rows of terraced brick houses for their miners in 1869. When the mine closed there was little need for the houses, and most were demolished by the Coal Board between 1968 and 1969.

Firmstone's Mineral Railway opened in 1838 and ran from Leycett to Madeley Heath, 1m SW of Leycett, where there was an ironworks. It closed in 1957.

In medieval times there was a deer park at Leycett, probably made by the Knights Hospitallers of Keele. Today Leycett is best known for its 'Amenity Site', or rubbish dump. For something on the small, privately-owned drift mines still operating in the area, see Silverdale.

LICHFIELD *12m SE of Stafford*

Lichfield is the only Cathedral in England that has maintained its medieval outline. Its three spires - the 'Ladies of the Vale' - are unique, instantly recognisable and a landmark on every approach to the city. The town itself is handsome and largely unspoilt, though very little is left of the medieval settlement and much of what we see today is Georgian.

Its early history is loosely connected with that of the Roman town of Letocetum, less than one mile to the south-west at Wall on Watling Street (the A5). One explanation of the name Lichfield means 'open land near Letocetum'. (The root of the Roman name is Celtic.) The Lichfield coats of arms include one which depicts three British kings lying dead killed in battle with the Romans. They are said to lie in the burial mound on Borrowcop Hill to the south of the town. An alternative derivation of the name Lichfield is 'death's field' from 'lych' meaning 'death', a reference to the legend that Christian's were slaughtered here by the Romans on an order from the Emperor Diocletian.

There was a Christian settlement at Lichfield by at least the early 600s. In 655 a local prince called Morfael of Luitcoet joined with the great British prince, Cynddylan, and won a victory over the invading pagan Angles at Caer Luitcoet, which was either Lichfield or close to it. Shortly after, however, Cynddylan was killed, Morfael fled to Somerset and the Angles took Lichfield, though they had in the meantime become Christians themselves.

About 670 Lichfield and a large estate around it were given to St Chad. He established a Ministry here - a large church from which priests went out and preached under trees (often yew trees because of the all-year-round shelter they provided), at specially erected preaching crosses and not infrequently in the old pagan temples. The ordinary people had become Christian largely because their King decreed it, not because they believed in the new gospel, and for many years they worshipped the old gods along with the new.

In 672 St Chad died, and in 700 the first 'Cathedral of all Mercia' was built at Lichfield, and the remains of St Chad were buried there. The Cathedral, probably made of wood, became a place of pilgrimage and in the 9th Century was, for a short time, the seat of an Archbishopric. By late Anglo-Saxon times the Diocese stretched from Warwickshire to the Ribble - a huge area.

At the time of Domesday the church at Lichfield owned two extensive estates: one around Lichfield that stretched from Norton Canes in the south-west to Hints in the south-east, and to Rowley and Yoxall in the north; and the other around Eccleshall that stretched from Doxey near Stafford westwards to the Shropshire border. These properties were probably Anglian, or even possibly Romano-British estates which had been handed over intact to the church.

After the Conquest the Normans transferred the seat of the diocese to Chester (1075). It then went to Coventry, and then to Coventry and Lichfield jointly. The church chapter was reconstituted by Roger de Clinton in 1130, and at about this time the Cathedral was rebuilt. It had a nave, choir and apse. Roger de Clinton also fortified the Close around the Cathedral and cut a moat around the settlement. About 1220 the third and last, and largest, Cathedral was begun and was substantially complete by about 1330 when the great apse at the east end was finished.

In 1290 the estates of the Bishopric were greatly extended by the acquisition of Cannock Chase from the King. The Cathedral was savagely mutilated during the Civil War and was besieged three times by the Roundheads. In 1646 a spire collapsed and badly damaged the building. It was rebuilt by Bishop Hacket in 1661-69 and re-consecrated in 1670. In the 18th Century there was further substantial rebuilding, both inside and out, and again in the 19th Century when, from 1857 to 1901, Sir George Gilbert Scott and his son John Oldrid Scott created much of what we see today. How much was faithful restoration or accurate replacement of older work is not known.

The great sandstone west front is quite spectacular. The mass of ornament is bewildering - statues, cinqfoils, quatre-foils, trefoils, arcading and carved porches. The interior is equally impressive and finely wrought. Amongst the monuments are busts of Samuel Johnson and David Garrick by R Westmacott; Bishop Ryder by Chantrey; Bishop Woods in bronze by Epstein; and Bishop Lonsdale by G F Watts. Perhaps the most outstanding feature of the Cathedral is the Lady Chapel, begun about 1320, with its nine huge traceried windows, its arcaded wall and the 19th Century Oberammergau triptych altar piece.

The Cathedral is fronted by a lawn and surrounded by a charming close. This was the cultural and social centre of the town, even the county. Stafford was the administrative centre of the shire but it was to Lichfield that men who cared for more than business tended to gravitate. Paradoxically, the Bishops, the figureheads of sophisticated life, lived not in Lichfield but in Eccleshall, and did so from the early Middle Ages to the last half of the 19th Century.

The Bishop's Palace in the Close was a town house of convenience. The elegant stonework of the Palace is by Edward Pierce, who was one of Christopher Wren's most favoured stonemasons. It is now a school, predictably called St Chad's. The close was re-enclosed and re-fortified by Bishop Langton in about 1300 and he it was who built the two causeways across the pool, Bird Street and Dam Street, which brought the growing town and the Cathedral closer together. The main approach to the Close is off Beacon Street, down a lane of great character. Here are the remains of the West Gate.

In the Close are various buildings of interest: the timber-framed houses around the lawns of the hidden Vicar's Close (approached through a narrow passage through a private house); St Chad's School House in Victorian brick; the handsome Deanery of seven bays with a central pediment; the mid-Georgian Selwyn House by itself to the east of the Cathedral; and St Mary's Vicarage whose east and south walls are mostly the medieval guard wall. Much of the south side of the Close has been developed in recent years.

The Bishop's Fish Pool, below the Cathedral, was originally much larger and extended considerably further west beyond the main-road bridge. The Stowe Mere Pool, north-east of the Cathedral, was also much larger at one time. These reductions in size took place in 1855 when the pools began to be used by the Staffordshire Waterworks Company as reservoirs. They were used as such until 1901.

The town was largely the creation of Roger de Clinton, who laid out the regular grid pattern of streets that have survived to this day. His work was carried on by Bishop Walter Durdent (1149-59), who obtained a market and borough status for the town about 1150. In the 14th and 15th Centuries the town was the largest in the county with a population of about 2,000. (Wolverhampton was the second largest and Stafford was third). Nationally, however, Lichfield was something of a backwater, but then came the coaching road from London. It entered the county at Basset's Pole (A51) and passed through Lichfield to Darlaston near Stone, where the route branched to Newcastle under Lyme (A34) for Carslisle, and to Nantwich (A51) for Chester.

The town continued to prosper and in the Georgian period was largely rebuilt in red brick, a material which had been used very early here because of a shortage of timber. The Hospital of St John in St John Street, was rebuilt in brick in 1495 by Bishop Smyth, and the eight impressive chimneys we see today are probably from that date.

In the 19th Century the town turned its back on industry, and the canals and the main-line railway bypassed it. This disdain for commerce and the concomitant lack of prosperity saved Lichfield from the drastic redevelopment that occurred in the nearby towns of the Black Country, and preserved its Georgian elegance to a time when people began to care about conservation. Today Lichfield even has a road bypass, built to protect the old town and its new and increasing tourist trade from the ravages of large lorries and the clutter of small cars.

Lichfield really is a most pleasant town. It is probably best approached from the Cathedral Close by the back road, Dam Street, a charming pedestrianised lane, lined with Georgian houses faced in brick and stucco, that leads to the Market Place. Quonians Lane is a delightful little thoroughfare which leads off Dam Street. The name could be from the Latin Quoniam, meaning 'since' or 'seeing that'. Samuel Johnson attended Dame Oliver's School which was in this lane. Bridgeman and Sons Ltd, architectural and ecclesiastical craftsmen in wood and stone, have been in business in Quonians Lane since 1879.

Markets are still held in the Market square, crammed in-between the road and St Mary's church, which now houses a craft and tourist trinket shop. Dr Johnson was born in 1709 at a house (of 1707) in the Market Place. It is stuccoed on the outside, but inside is full of polished wood and houses a museum to the literary wit who overcame such terrible physical afflictions. His statue, of 1838 by R C Lucas, also stands in the Market Place and is highly regarded as a work of art in its own right. Close by is the bronze statue (1908) of Dr Boswell by P Fitzgerald.

Along the other side of St Mary's is Bore Street, which has the handsome Tudor Cafe, timber-framed with gables, jetties and herringbone masonry; the 18th Century Donegal House (now called the Guildhall), the town house of the Donegal family of Fisherwick, with five bays, three storeys, a parapet and a Tuscan columned doorway; the Gothic Guild Hall of 1846; and many offices and shops, a few too many of which have plate-glass windows.

The mundane 20th Century shopping precinct has been hidden out of sight of the more civilized old town, and with a little luck the casual visitor may come and go in ignorance of its existence. In Stowe Street, amidst modern houses, is an old cruck cottage, of which there were once a great number in the town. In Stowe Hill are two good detached houses of about 1750 - Stowe Hill House and Stowe Hill Mansion.

Close to the stone bridge (1816) over Minster Pool are the Library and the Museum of 1857-9. Uphill, on the same side of the road, is the mid-18th Century, stuccoed West Gate House and the Angel Croft Hotel. Both have good iron gates and railings. On the other side of the road is the house of Erasmus Darwin (father of Charles Darwin), a tall, brick, late 18th Century building of five bays and two storeys with Venetian windows. The doorway has a pediment supported by Tuscan columns. The George Hotel is of the late 18th Century and has a fine ballroom integral to the building, which is quite rare.

Milley's Hospital in Beacon Street is named after Dr Thomas Milley, who built the present 15 homes and a chapel for poor women in 1504. One of the seven Lichfield morris dances is called Milley's Bequest.

In Trent Valley Road is the former workhouse of 1841 by Scott and Moffatt, now St Michael's Hospital. This is in Gothic Tudor brick with battlements and gables, and is interesting because it is an early work of Sir George Gilbert Scott, who was later to restore the Cathedral so splendidly.

The church of St Chad is, if anything, a more holy place than the great Cathedral. It stands by the east end of Stowe Mere Pool where St Chad had his hermitage. ('Stowe' means 'holy place or hermitage'). Much of the church is Early English with a Decorated tower and some Victorian restoration. St Chad's Well lies close by across the stream. The spring is covered by a pyramid tiled roof supported by four posts. Steps lead to the water and then to the stone on which St Chad is said to have stood when he baptized new converts.

To the south of the town is the modern Lichfield Trent Valley Railway Station, and 0.75m. SE of this is St Michael's church which has good views over the town and the Cathedral. The church is Early English with a Perpendicular tower but was mostly rebuilt in 1842 by Thomas Johnson. The parents and brother of the great Samuel Johnson are buried in the seven-acre churchyard, in which Mesolithic flints have been found. It was also an important Anglo-Saxon burial ground.

One of Lichfield's lesser known sons was Henry Salt (1780-1827), who was one of the early English Egyptologists. It was he who brought to England the huge bust of Rameses II, now in the British Museum, and the sarcophagus of Seti I, now at Sir John Soane's House in Lincoln's Inn Fields. He also had dealings with the now-slightly-notorious, Belzoni, the giant adventurer who carved his name on monuments all over Egypt.

In the park, near the Museum at Minster Pool, is a bronze statue of Commander John Edward Smith, the Captain of the Titanic, by Lady Scott (1910). The statue had been offered to the Potteries town of Hanley where Smith was born, but was rejected.

Lichfield has an almost unique set of Morris dances for eight men (rather than the usual six). They are virile dances and possibly very old. There had been a strong tradition of Morris in the town until 1907 but it finally died in 1936. During the 1960s folk revival, public requests were made for information about the dances and their music. The responses came anonymously, by telephone and post, the reason being that the last dancers had been a group of boys from 'The Midland Truant School'. Today the dances are widely performed and much admired. (They are reprinted in '1,000 English Country Dances', by M. Raven)

Every Whit Monday Lichfield has a well known carnival which commences with the Greenhill Bower Procession. The Greenhill is a small, triangular green on a sandstone bluff. Just to the east of this is St Michael's church The procession used to be a most spectacular affair notable for its display of morris dancing and medieval armour.

An ancient spring fertility rite had become intermingled with the medieval Court of Array. Once a year the local lord had to array his quota of able bodied and properly equipped men, ready to serve should their king call upon them. The modern Beauty Queen is a survival of the Carnival Queen. She, in turn, is a survival of the May Queen who was originally a ritual prostitute, with whom lusty young men had their way in order to encourage the crops to grow.

There is another custom for which Lichfield is well known, namely the Sheriffs Ride. In 1553 Queen Mary Tudor gave Lichfield the rights of a county, including the right to nominate a sheriff. Every year on the 8th of September, the 20 or so miles of the boundary of the 'county' were walked by at least one member of every family in the town in a light-hearted procession, led by the sheriff on horse-back.

This custom had a practical importance because boundary disputes were not uncommon. Small boys were often bumped against boundary marker stones to impress their position upon them. (During the Civil War some of the town archives were destroyed, and in 1656 the civic authorities won a boundary dispute with Lord Paget on the strength of the evidence of an old man who had 'beaten the bounds' as a youth.)

The ritual continues to this day, although the date has been changed to the Saturday nearest the 8th of September, so that the local pony club can participate.

Streethay, 1.5m ENE of Lichfield is a hamlet on Ryknild Street, hence its name 'enclosure on the street'. There was a settlement here by the 13th Century and the medieval manor house had a double moat. The house was rebuilt in 1620 by Richard Pyot and remodelled in the later 20th Century.

LIMES BRITANNICUS

The Limes Britannicus was a defensive earthen wall fronted by a ditch, which was constructed in about 50AD by the Romans, and ran from Doncaster to Gloucester via Sheffield, Buxton, Leek, Stone, north-west of Gnosall, Shifnal, Worcester and Tewkesbury. After the construction of Hadrian's Wall it became of little importance, fell into disuse and has subsequently all but disappeared.

LITTLE HAYWOOD *See Great Haywood*

LITTLE WYRLEY *See Norton Canes*

LONGDON *4m NW of Lichfield*

There are three Longdons - Upper Longdon, Longdon and Longdon Green. **Longdon Green** is an attractive village, most unfortunately divided by the Rugeley - Lichfield road. To the west is the old village green with a pub and some large brick houses. To the east are a few more cottages along a wooded lane that leads past Lysways Hall (now rendered in two by the removal of its centre block) to **Hanch Hall**, a mile east of the main road. From the road only the Victorian additions to Hanch Hall are visible. The main house has a superb Queen Anne facade of seven bays. The staircase is very fine and parts of the fabric of the house are of the 15th Century. To complete the picture it has a wood-fringed lake with swans.

Seedy Mill Farm is 0.5m SSE of Hanch Hall. Seedy Mill, on the Bilson Brook, south of Seedy Mill Farm, was a township in the 13th Century. Today the dominant structure is a very large and not very beautiful SSWWC Water Treatment Works (1939-43). Close by is the Seedy Mill Golf Club which welcomes non members to its restaurant. In 1999 Greg Peters, aged 11, made two 'holes in one' on the same day on this course.

Longdon itself lies on the Rugeley to Lichfield road, on high ground, 0.5m. NW of Longdon Green. The church of St James has a Norman south porch, nave and chancel; a south chantry chapel of about 1500, built by John Stoneywall who was born at Longdon and later became Abbot of Pershore; and a Victorian north transept. Here are monuments to Thomas Orme of Hanch Hall, died 1716, C S Foster, died 1854, and John Foster, died 1860.

Upper Longdon is quite a separate village, 1m E of Longdon. Nowadays, this is very much a place of upmarket houses. On the main street are the stables of Reg Hollinshead, where racehorses are trained, and it is a common sight to see them being ridden out. Mr Hollinshead also runs a school for apprentice jockeys here.

Upper Longdon had a windmill. It is first mentioned in 1806 and is thought to have ceased working in about 1900. In 1973 the tower was converted into a house called Cosy Cottage by the addition of a circular brick bungalow around the base.

Here is an intriguing little tale. Sir William Wolseley, 3rd baronet of Wolseley Hall, Colwich, had his fortune told by a Persian fortune-teller who said that he and the four Arabian horses he had just purchased would be drowned together.

As a precaution Sir William sent the horses home to England on four different ships and took a fifth himself. Years later, on 11 July 1728, Sir William entertained Charles Wedgwood at Wolseley Hall and, out of courtesy, as it was a dark and stormy night, accompanied his guest part of his way home. However, on the return journey there was a heavy thunderstorm and, as Sir William was crossing an otherwise small and placid stream, the Longdon mill dam burst and a raging torrent swept Sir William's carriage away and he and his horses were all drowned.

The forests of Cannock Chase adjoin the village to the west, and about one mile into the woods is Beaudesert Old Park. The entrance to the **Beaudesert** estate lies lm SW of Longdon (not Upper Longdon), down a lane that leads to the brick-built Grand Lodge. This is probably by John Shaw, about 1814. The lodge stands at the foot of the hill, on which is a ruined fragment of the great Tudor hall of the mansion built by the Pagets. The house was demolished in 1932 and all that is left is a wall with three late Perpendicular windows.

Beaudesert originally belonged to Lichfield Cathedral and the Bishops had a palace here. In 1546 Sir William Paget (died 1568), Secretary of State to Henry VIII and later the First Lord Paget of Beaudesert, acquired the estate. A most handsome Tudor mansion was built on to the old bishop's palace and here the Pagets lived and in time became Earls of Uxbridge and Marquisses of Anglelsey. It was they and their lessees who stripped Cannock Chase of its ancient oak trees to burn for charcoal, with which to smelt iron. After Beaudesert was demolished in 1934 the family moved to Plas Newydd near Anglesey. Today the park is used partly as a Golf Club and partly as a camping ground for Scouts and Guides.

Henry William Paget (1768-1854), Tenth Baron Paget and Second Earl of Uxbridge, eloped with Lady Charlotte Wellesley, the wife of the Duke of Wellington's brother, and later fought a duel with pistols with her brother. At the Battle of Waterloo Paget was the Duke of Wellington's cavalry commander. He was shot in the right leg and his leg was amputated without anaesthetic. He showed remarkable fortitude and this small event became nationally known. After Waterloo he was rewarded with the title Marquess of Anglesey.

LONGNOR *6m SSE of Buxton*
Longnor is a sturdy little market town of great character on a hill in the upper Manifold valley. It is a quiet place built of stone with several inns, including the Crewe and Harpur Arms near which is a two-piece, stone market cross of about 1500. There is a cobbled square and a Market Hall of 1873 that is now the workshop of a sculptor. To the left of the Market Hall is a delightful cobbled passage called Chapel Street, where there are little stone cottages and Parrot's Tearooms.

The church of St Bartholomew is of 1780 in a Georgian classical style but with a Gothic pinnacled tower. It has a Venetian east window, and a lowered ceiling which, from the inside, hides the upper windows. The font is probably Norman. In the churchyard lies William Billings, died 1791, a soldier who escaped death many times and is reputed to have reached the age of 112. The last two lines of his old epitaph (which have been replaced) read:

Let me alone awhile,
Asleep, not slain
And when the trumpet sounds
I'll march again.

All around the town are the wild Moorlands. The upper Dove Valley lies 0.5m E, and at Crowdecote is most attractive. Broadmeadow Hall lies 1.25m SE of Longnor, and 0.25m N of the Hall is a motte and bailey castle, close to the River Dove.

Near the bridge over the Manifold, on the road that runs south-west of Longnor to **Hardings Booth**, is a working watermill (SK 085646). Longnor Mill was the workshop of the Harpur-Crewe estate and the iron waterwheel (14 foot 6 inch in diameter), fed by a leat from the river, drove two circular saws, a planer and a morticing machine. It has been renovated and restored and continues to be a wood-working mill. A hoard of 14th century silver coins was found in Boosley Folly Meadow in 1867.

The Longnor area has many folk customs and superstitions. A few hundred yards up the road from Dunbrook, Longnor is a little hut called Doctor Trees. This was formerly used by a man who helped injured and sick animals. It is now haunted by a big black dog, a benign spirit drawn to a place where he found care and kindness.

LONGSDON *2m SW of Leek centre*

The village lies astride the A53, Leek to Burslem road. Four prehistoric burial mounds have been identified from aerial photographs, 0.5m SE of the church. In 1242 the manor of Longsdon, together with Rushton and half of Ipstones, was held by providing one knight to help garrison Chester Castle for 40 days a year.

The parish church of St Chad opened in 1905. In 1990 Anthea Turner, the TV presenter, was married at St Chad's. Water from St Caena's Well at Wall Grange, Longsdon was pumped from the waterworks, built in 1848-49, to a reservoir at Ladderidge. It was then piped to the Potteries.

Stonelowe Hall, 0.25m W of Longsdon, is probably of the 17th Century, though the Stonelowe family were here in an earlier house by the early 13th Century. From them it passed to the Sherrards, to the Buckleys and in-between times to possibly the Britles and the Breretons. It was restored in 1866 by Editha Pigot. Stone Lowe, an Anglo-Saxon burial mound on a promontory west of the Hall, is a pile of stones against a natural sandstone outcrop.

Wall Grange, 1.25m ENE of Longsdon, is a hamlet in a bend in the River Churnet. 'Wall' is probably from 'well', a reference to St Caena's Well, and by the early 13th Century Trentham Priory had a grange here, hence Wall Grange. After the Dissolution, and until 1911, the estate was owned by the Leveson Family. There may have been a medieval village at Wall Grange Farm, which has since been depopulated. In 1849 the newly-formed Staffordshire Potteries Water Works' Company (SPWWC) started pumping water from springs by St Caena's Well. Their waterworks was at Horse Bridge; it closed in the 1980s. The same company built pumping stations at Hatton (1891), Meir (1868), Stockton Brook (1884), Millmeece (1914) and Cresswell (1928-32).

LONGTON *2.25m SE of Stoke on Trent*

There was a manor of Longton by at least the 13th Century, when it was held in return for providing guard duties at Newcastle-under-Lyme Castle and for escorting the king as far as Wrinehill in time of war. By the 17th Century there was a manor house, home of the Foley family. In the 1770s the house, which stood 0.75m SW of modern Longton, was rebuilt as an imposing Georgian mansion. It was demolished in 1939.

The name means 'long-town', and it lies along the A521, the main road from Derby to Newcastle-under Lyme, which was turnpiked in 1759. Between Lane End and Fenton this road was laid down on the old Roman road from Tean to

Stoke on Trent. The town developed late, and because of this many of the old pottery works have survived. It is a poor area, the poorest in the Potteries, and even now has some very mean housing. Paradoxically, this is the place that specializes in the finest wares, such as porcelain and the delicate bone china of Spode.

The centre of the town is Times Square and is unforgettable. It is actually a part of the main road, and a busy bottle-neck junction, which is here crossed by a huge, ugly railway bridge. On one side of the Square is the Town Hall and on the other was the church. The Town Hall was rebuilt in 1836 to a design by Burrill. It is of ashlar, in Classical style and has 13 bays with coach-porch and pediments. The extension is of 1912. The Market Hall lies behind - a great barn of a place, ill-lit and inelegant. The front facade is dirt-blackened and the rear, which faces a street, is very dull.

The church of St John the Baptist was built in 1761 and paid for by John Bourne. However, mining settlement caused structural damage and it was rebuilt in 1792-5. It was further restored in 1889 and finally demolished in 1985 because the settlement could not be halted. The church stood on the green mound adjacent to the red brick Crown Hotel.

The shopping centre lies on the hill beyond Times Square. It is a brisk, busy place, and there is a new shopping precinct, named after Arnold Bennett and opened in 1965.

There are more pottery works in Longton than in any other town in the Potteries and more china factories than in the other five towns put together. There are no dynasties of famous manufacturers but there are a number of firms who were established in the late 19th Century and are still in business. Several of the works exhibit variations of the Classic Georgian facade of central arch surmounted by a Venetian window and pediment. The Portland Works (Aynsley Pottery) in Sutherland Road has exactly this arrangement and was built as late as 1861.

Longton Hall is now no more, which is a shame because it was here in about 1749 that the first pottery works in Longton was opened. William Littler was the Master Potter and the factory made the first soft paste porcelain in Staffordshire. 'Littler's Blue', a brilliant blue ground colour was widely used by many later pot works. In 1760 finance was withdrawn, the Longton Hall Works closed and Littler left for Scotland.

The remarkable 19th Century townscape of the Potteries has now long gone. The hundreds of graceful bottle-shaped brick kilns have almost totally vanished. Actually, they were incredibly inefficient and only one per cent of the heat generated was actually used to fire the pots. The rest was absorbed by the kiln walls or escaped up the chimney. A few more slender versions are still used for calcining flint, but as furnaces for firing pottery commercially they are extinct and only a handful of old kilns have survived at all.

The best known are those at the Gladstone Museum, which is situated in Longton, just off the main road to Uttoxeter, on the corner of Chadwick Street. The site is on land that was once owned by the Foley family, one of whom became Baron Foley of Kidderminster in 1712. About 1790 the Gladstone Works was constructed and had a succession of owners. The kilns were fired for the last time in 1960 and the premises then used as a warehouse until they were put on the market. In 1971 they were about to be demolished when H and R Johnson, the ceramic tile manufacturers, bought the works and a Trust was formed to make a living museum of the pottery trade. Pottery is made and decorated here and all the processes can be seen at close quarters. The buildings lie around a courtyard - the slip house, the clay preparation rooms, the casting shop, the bottle kilns and the engine house. In addition, there are now two shops, a tea room and displays of tiles and sanitary ware.

In Heathcote Road were several collieries and iron works known as the Lane End Coal and Iron Company. Beyond these is the site of Longton Hall, for long the home of the Heathcote family who were major landowners in Longton and Chesterton. The kiln bases of Littler's pottery have been found under the stables.

To the south-west Longton comes to an end at **Normacot** (meaning 'Norseman's cottage') a suburban area first developed by the Duke of Sutherland. Behind the church of Holy Evangelists is Furnace Mill.

Perhaps Longton's most famous son is Reginald J Mitchell, the designer of the Spitfire which first flew in 1936. He was actually born in Talke, near Kidsgrove, but grew up in Normacot where his father was a schoolmaster. They lived in the school house, which still stands opposite the church of the Holy Evangelists. (The school has gone.) He was a student at the Technical College, College Road, Shelton, which became the Polytechnic.

The suburban sprawl continues from Normacot on to Meir and from there to Blythe Bridge. These places will soon have to be included in the Potteries as there are not a few manufacturers here with strong pottery trade connections. To the south of Longton the suburbs of Dresden and Florence are to be found.

Florence is named after the eldest daughter of the 3rd Duke of Sutherland. The Duke and his father laid out many of the streets of the area in the 1860s and the 1870s. Queen's Park, opened in 1888 and was a gift of the Sutherlands to the town. The Duke, who was forced to leave his palace at Trentham because of the smell of sewage in the River Trent, was careful to provide the houses he built with the proper facilities, and gave 250 acres at Blurton Waste for the construction of a sewage farm. There was a large coal mine at Florence and beyond the pit-head workings, in the direction of Cocknage, is some very pleasant country.

Dresden, 0.75m S of Longton, was largely the creation of a local building society which began constructing houses there in 1854. Their terraces had a bow-windowed house at each end. They also built detached and semi-detached houses. The church of The Resurrection was built in 1853. Havergal Brian, the composer of more than 30 symphonies, was born at 35 Ricardo Street, Dresden in 1876, He died in 1972.

The old Park Hall sand and gravel quarries lie just north of **Weston Coyney,** which is 1.5m WNW of Longton. In 1981 this extensive, 47 acre, hill wilderness was opened as a Country Park. There are long views over the surrounding countryside and dramatic views within the park itself. The Play Canyon is a splendidly romantic place with a misleadingly mundane name. Kestrels and Little Owls live on the rocky ledges above the sandpits and the organized cyclo-cross course. Altogether, there are five species of owl in the park: Little Owl, Tawney Owl, Long-Eared Owl, Short-Eared Owl, and the increasingly rare Barn Owl. There is a moorland area frequented by dotterel, golden plover and redshank during the migrating season, and in Iron Wood and Pump Tree Wood there are fungi (150 species in the park as a whole). In the marshes at Lady Corner, near the gasholder at Dividy Road, there are bog myrtles and acres of orchids which blossom in early June; and the sheltered pools of Skinner's Canyon are a haunt of butterflies and dragonflies. Of larger animals there are foxes, rabbits, hares, weasels and stoats. For the comfort of humans there is a smart new Visitors' Centre, a Golf Club, several car parks and a pleasing absence of restrictions notices. Watch out for flying joggers though.

Hulme, 1.75m NE of Longton, is a village in open country. (See page 181)

Lightwood, 1.5m SE of Longton, is now a newly-developed residential area of pleasant detached houses with access roads that are too narrow for two and three car families – a not uncommon problem in modern housing estates. In 1960 a hoard of some 2,500 roman coins and two silver snake bracelets were found at No 698 Lightwood Road. The coins mostly dated from 253-274 AD. The hoard is on display at the Potteries Museum, Hanley.

LYE *1.5m E of Stourbridge*

Lye stands high on the southern banks of the River Stour to the east of Stourbridge with which it is associated. It is most easily approached along the road from Stourbridge to Halesowen and Birmingham. This road passes beneath the 10-arch brick and stone Stambermill Viaduct of 1882 that carries the railway over the river Stour. The river has been deepened and channelized here so that it now lies several feet below the green meadows of its flood plain. Nearby, the Stepping Stones pub keeps alive the memory of a mode of crossing now superseded by a road bridge. The Birmingham road continues beyond the viaduct, rising to higher ground and the town centre of Lye which begins at the Lye Cross crossroads. It is sad to see so many shops empty - we counted eight in a space of 50 yards. However, there is still a good selection of services and retail outlets and the place has maintained its traditional and separate character.

Four buildings catch the eye: Mount Sion, 1827, of gaunt grey stucco; a pair of shops with shaped 'Dutch' gables; a yellow and red brick block of Victorian shops with end gables and dormers; and Christ Church, of mature red brick to a cruciform plan, which stands back from the road behind yews and broad-leaf trees. Opposite the church is a small courtyard, which has been decorated with painted murals depicting contemporary work and leisure activities. Here, too, is a little green tower clock. Behind the church is a car park, an area of grass much favoured by the dogs of Lye, and a small-windowed, modern box that proclaims itself to be the "World Headquarters of Firtakleen, manufacturers of Ergonomic wringers and Combine Snappers". The shops stop at the Old Bell and a new housing estate takes over as the road heads on, uphill, in the direction of Birmingham.

The name Lye is from Leigh, which in turn is from the Anglo-Saxon 'leah', a glade or natural clearing in a wood. Traditionally the area has been derided by its neighbours as being backward and desolate. Indeed, it seems to have been 'waste' well into the 19th Century. A local poem of 1878 is titled 'The Lye Waste Soup Shop'. And what nicknames these waste-landers had: Wokum, Pongey, Tuckey, Figup, Shaggsby, Tinkey, Gourge, Wobber, Crackback and Firelock.

Industry at Lye seems to have first come to the valley in the last years of the 17th Century. By 1699 there was a water-driven iron forge and the owner, James Folkes, began an industrial line that continues to this day. The Old Forge Trading Estate commemorates this early industrial activity. Fireclay was mined locally and worked to produce bricks and pots for the iron and glass trades. Nails and chains were also made here.

Lye's claim to artistic fame is that the actor, Sir Cedric Hardwicke (1893-1964), the son of a local doctor, was born at Lye Cross. Sir Cedric once described the area of his birth thus: " . . . slums and backyards which always seemed without sunlight, families of more than a dozen living in one room, ragged children slaving next to parents in grim chainshops."

It seems quite in character that the first church here was a Unitarian Chapel (1806). Before that visiting clerics preached in public houses.

Grange Estate is a residential area, south-west of Lye centre, approached from Grange Lane. **Ludgbridge Brook** runs through Stevens Park and has given its name to the surrounding area.

Chawn Hill is a residential area south of Lye between Grange Lane and Stevens Park. The name is probably from the Anglo-Saxon and means 'the hill where calves are kept.' Just as today calves are quickly weaned, separated from their mothers and kept together in special fields.

Netherend is an old industrial-cum-residential area that lies north of the Stourbridge-Halesowen road between Lye and Cradley. 'Nether' means 'lower'. Netherend was perhaps the 'lower-end' of the Wollescote Hall estate.

LYME FOREST *North Staffordshire*
This large primeval forest was probably named by the Gaelic Celts about 1000 BC with their word for 'elm tree', but it may be older than that. It was still heavily wooded in medieval times. Its extent is indicated by place names. Several towns formerly had 'under-Lyme' affixed to them, like Newcastle-under-Lyme, but have since dropped it. These are Chesterton; Madeley; Whitmore; Ashton (Lancashire), Betton and Norton (Shropshire); Newbold now Astbury, and Laughton (Cheshire). Lyme, or a corruption of it, occurs in Burslem, Lyme Handley (Lancashire), and Lyme Park (Cheshire). It probably stretched up into Yorkshire and Derbyshire, and was a very large forest indeed

MADELEY *5m W of Newcastle-under-Lyme*
Madeley is a pleasant place on a summer's day with the ducks and geese on the broad mill pool beside the main road. A brick-built mill, now painted white, stands at one end. There is a wide variety of housing from the humble to the high, old and modern, and a range of shops, a fish and chip shop and a police station.

The Old Hall is a handsome half-timbered house of 1647 and bears the inscription, clearly visible from the road: 'Walk Knave; what lookest at?' Actually, it never was a hall but a farmhouse. By way of contrast there is a drab modern council estate further north, on the far side of the pool.

To the west of the village the main-line railway scars the countryside. It is not the railway as such that does any visual damage, but the gantries and cables that enshroud it. Apparently, Madeley is on a 'speed section', where records were broken in the days of steam.

Just north of the village there used to be a teachers' training college, Madeley College of Education. The M6 crosses the main road nearby. As one moves north-east Madeley becomes **Middle Madeley** and then **Little Madeley**, for no apparent reason, and finally arrive at Madeley Heath. At the crossroads here a lane leads past a row of semi-detached houses to the huge and unexpected brick and tile works. Steetly, now called Eternit, produce the traditional thin, hard Rosemary roofing tiles. Ibstock, the brick manufacturers, also have a presence.

The large church of All Saints is to the south of the village of Madeley on a raised mound. The arcade is late Norman and has rare, many-scalloped capitals; the nave is Early English; the north doorway and north windows are Decorated; the transepts, south arcade, north chapel (now the vestry) and tower are Perpendicular; and the chancel is Victorian, of 1872, by Charles Lynam. The glass in the south-aisle west window is by William Morris (St Peter), Ford Madox Brown (St Philip and Noah) and Burne-Jones (Christ).

South-west of the church are brick almshouses of 1645. The porches are Victorian. The School and Master's House are of 1875 and were paid for by Lord Crewe. There was a colliery at Madeley but this is now closed.

The Madeley deer park was called the Great Park, being the largest of the Madeley Manor parks. The other parks were Leycett and Netheret. The Great Park covered some 840 acres and Dr Plot said that the timber here surpassed in quality that of the renowned woods of Bagot's Park, Abbots Bromley.

Plot also mentions that in the park was the household oven of the Manor house; it was not uncommon to place the oven away from the house in case of fire or explosion. Keele University has done a study of the Madeley Great Park.

The Old Manor was built by Ralph de Stafford, First Earl of Stafford (died 1372). It then passed to the Offleys. John Offley was a good friend of Isaac Walton and the two men often fished the lake here together. Indeed, Walton dedicated 'The Compleat Angler' to John Offley. The Manor then passed to the Crewe family and in 1793 it was demolished.

In the valley today is a stream and the remains of two large moats. The land around is disturbed over an area of about three acres. In the shade of a tree is a fragment of a sandstone wall, some five feet thick. South of the ruin is the outline of a low earthen bank, running roughly parallel with the stream.

This mound is the remnant of a deer park trench and bank, and the sandstone ruin is all that is left of the large and most handsome 16th or 17th Century Manor House (depicted in Dr Plot's 'Natural History of Staffordshire'). This was mostly timber-framed. The sandstone fragment formed part of the entrance block and was quite probably part of an earlier defensive structure. The moats are thought to have been largely ornamental. The stream was once dammed and formed a lake between the mansion and the road.

After the demolition of the old Manor House a new house was built on high ground to the north. This is called Madeley Manor Farm, and stone from the Old Manor was used in its construction. Manor Farm is a brick, three-storey farmhouse, the back of which forms one side of a large cobbled courtyard with barns and cowsheds around the other sides. It stands high on a hill and faces south over the valley and the ruins of its predecessor

At **Hieghley**, 1.25m N of Madeley, are the meagre ruins of Heighley Castle (SJ 273467). The Castle stands on a high hill and a section of red sandstone walling can be seen from the main A531, about 0.25m W of the motorway bridge. The access lane dips steeply downhill to the north, off the main road. It passes Castle Farm and is joined by a forestry track on which is a sign marking the entrance route to the castle.

The castle was once a very substantial and strong place and the 'moat' was hacked out of the rock. Today only one small piece of walling still stands. The hill is totally overgrown and very rough underfoot, with old logs and stones obscured by brushwood, making the going very hard. We nearly came to a nasty end up here, victims of a precipice that was hidden by man-high nettles and ferns. There seems to be quite a lot of stonework in the undergrowth. There are superb views from the castle, but it is a dangerous place. This was the home of the Audley family in the Middle Ages (see Audley) and was later held by the Gerards. The Castle was pulled down after the Civil War.

At **Wrinehill**, 1m further along the A531, towards Betley, is The Summer-house, of about 1710. It only has three bays but, nevertheless, displays a grand facade with giant pilasters, pediments and segmental headed windows. The village was divided between Staffordshire and Cheshire until 1964. The Hall was the seat of the Hawkestones until about 1400 when it passed to the Egertons. The Egertons disposed of The Summerhouse, the Hall and the Red Lion pub in 1815. The Hall has since been demolished.

MAER *6.25 SW of Newcastle-under-Lyme*

Between Stableford and Blackbrook the A51 passes through a beautiful valley of curving, wooded hills. These are the Maer Hills. Half-a-mile west of Hill Chorlton the road bends around the tree-clad Berth Hill, on which are the single ditch and bank earthen defences of a nine-acre prehistoric fort. The road is joined here by a lane that leads south to the village of Maer. At this junction is a War Memorial and a lodge. From the lodge a parallel grand entrance drive leads to Maer Hall. The approach to the village is quite dramatic. The lane passes through a deep sandstone-lined cutting and under a small bridge to the stable block with its imposing 18th Century gatehouse. The church is perched on rocks high above. Further along the red brick village appears, largely unspoiled. All in all, a delightful little place.

The Jacobean Hall was built by the Bowyer family, then passed to Josiah Wedgwood II and then to the Harrisons, a shipping family from Liverpool. The Harrisons added large Victorian wings, but these were pulled down about 30 years ago and the Hall restored to its original size. The house is very handsome and has a superb hall. The long, gravelled approach drive from the main road passes through the well-kept and well-wooded park (in which is situated the village cricket field), skirts the large lake and brings one to the gabled front of the Hall. The lake, by the way, is a remnant of a huge Ice-Age lake that covered the whole of the Maer Valley.

The church of St Peter has a south porch of about 1200 and most of the rest is early 17th Century, restored by the Victorians. There is some modern stained glass by Shrigley and Hunt, and in the chancel are the effigies of Sir John Bowyer, died 1604, and his wife. In the churchyard are yew trees and sycamores. Charles Darwin often stayed at the Hall whilst he was courting.

The River Tern begins in the Maer Lake. For the first three miles, from Maer to Willoughbridge, its course has been straightened and deepened because it is used here as a strine, to drain the bogs and other marshy land along its course.

In the Dark Ages a number of battles are said to have been fought in the Maer area: 635, Penda, King of Mercia, killed Oswald, King of Northumberland; 642, Penda killed Maserfield; 642 Oswy, King of Northumberland, killed in battle and is buried at King's Bank in the Maer Hills; 705 Kenned, King of Mercia, battled with and beat Osrid, King of Northumbria. On the ridge of the Maer Hills are earthworks of the Iron Age/Anglo-Saxon period: a fort on Berth Hill (already mentioned) and unexplained, man-made mounds on Berth Hill and King's Bank.

During the period when boxing was against the law, illegal fights were held in the Maer Hills.

MALBONCK FOREST

Malbonck (Malbank) Forest, also known as Alstonefield Forest, took its name from the Malbank family, lords of Alstonefield until 1176. The forest lay along the top of the ridge of Morridge and to its east covered the settlements of Fowfield, Heathylee and Quanford (Flash) and down to the River Dove and to the northern boundary of Cheddleton parish.

MARCHINGTON *3.5w ESE of Uttoxeter*

It lies on the edge of Needwood Forest in hilly country. To the south are woods and to the north the River Dove, with attractive country all round. This is a very mature village with substantial red brick houses set in high-banked lanes. Only the school of St Peter strikes a discordant note with its skinny white window frames and pale yellow bricks.

Marchington Hall in Green Lane is a striking 17th Century brick house with iron gates and steps to the front door. It has two gables, connected by balustrading, and stone mullioned and transomed windows in the proportions of a Christian cross. To the right is Tetley House, another fine building of red brick with 2.5 storeys, three bays and a hipped roof. There are several black-and-white cottages, and near the Bull's Head is a house with a well-decorated, timber-framed gable end. At the bottom of the hill are some old cottages, the Dog and Partridge pub by the stream, and beyond them the red brick church of St Peter.

The church is at the end of a short avenue of pollarded trees, quite elegant and older than it may look. It was built in 1742 by Richard Trubshaw. The octagonal tower is topped by a small dome. The inside was harshly treated in 1892 when most of the old furniture was removed and a Gothic chancel added. There is a monument of 1592 to Walter Vernon and his wife of Hound Hill. It is curious to find the church of an old hilltop village so low down. Was it always here?

To the south-west are the olive-green ranks of Marchington Camp. This was an Army depot but is now an Industrial Park and an EEC Grain Store. A little further east, on some rough scrubby ground that could have been an aerodrome, is a Gliding Club.

Near the camp and 0.25m SSE of the church is Hound Hill. Gypsum and alabaster (a good quality gypsum suitable for carving) was mined on the hill from at least the late 18th Century. The mineral outcrops here and can be open-cast mined. Alabaster is actually sawn by a special machine. In the early 19th Century production ceased but commenced again in 1920 when the Agatine Mining Co Ltd worked the hill. They had left by 1925. The outcrop can still be seen. In the quarry are animal burrows and what looks like a double garage. At the top of the hill the overgrown wall that runs alongside the road is made of sub-standard alabaster and gypsum.

Smallwood, 1.5m WSW of Marchington, is an estate and hamlet first mentioned in 1382. The wood would be a detached part of Needwood Forest. Small meant 'narrow', rather than 'little'. Smallwood Hall (SK 109295) is a Georgian-style house which took over as the 'big house' from Marchington Woodlands Manor. In the 19th Century the Webbs of Tutbury Cotton Mill lived here.

In turn Smallwood Hall was superseded by Smallwood Manor, built in 1884 by R W Ellis for the Hodgson family in the style of an Eastbourne villa, where Mrs Hodgson took her holidays. In 1937 it was leased to Denstone College for use as their preparatory school.

MARCHINGTON WOODLANDS *1.25m SW of Marchington*
Lovely country. In the evening light there is a timeless air here. The village huddles against Forest Bank, a remnant of Needwood Forest spread over a long, steep edge. There is a scatter of old cottages and farms - not prettified, but working places. The Forest was a hunting ground and here is a cottage called Newfield House, which has the antlers of a stag from Bagot's Wood nailed to the front wall between the upstairs windows. Attached to the house is a timber yard trading as Jane Lawrence.

In the plain below are farms and isolated cottages linked by a network of twisting lanes. The land here was cleared slowly and haphazardly by unorganised individuals during the late Middle Ages. It still has a frontier feel to it.

On a hill 0.75m NE is the striking church of St John. This was built in 1859 by A D Gough of London and paid for by Thomas Webb of Smallwood in memory of his wife.

Two hundred yards north of the church is Woodroffs - a true delight. It is a superb timber-framed Jacobean yeoman's cottage built to a 'T' plan with simple but very effective vertical studs. There is a central chimney, some original glazing and internal panelling. Smallwood Manor lies 0.25m W of Woodroffs. It was built in 1884 by the Hodgson family in the style of an Eastbourne villa.

Off Tinker's Lane, at SK 108289, is a four-sided, 3,600 square metre enclosure surrounded by a moat.

MARSTON *3m N of Stafford*
In 1066 the manor was held by the Anglo- Saxon freeman, Wufgar. By 1086 it was owned by Earl Roger of Montgomery and held from him by the church of St Evroul, Lisieux, France. (This church also held High Onn and at Sheriffhales had a priest with one plough and two oxen). Today Marston is a scattered hamlet of farms and cottages.

The little church was rebuilt in 1794 by William Dudley. The nave is of stone, the chancel of brick and the stained glass windows are by Pearce of Birmingham.

Wodehouse, a large brick house with tall, diamond-shaped chimneys, is embowered in trees near the A34. It was built about 1900 for a solicitor but later became a local authority school. About 1960 it was reinstated as a private house.

MAVESYN RIDWARE *See Ridware*

MAYFIELD *1.25m SW of Ashbourne*
Mayfield is on the A52 Ashbourne to Leek road. It lies on the banks of the River Dove, which is crossed here by the Hanging Bridge. This is a five-arched, stone-built, medieval packhorse bridge which has been widened in later times. The white-painted Queens Arms pub stands opposite the bridge.

The road to Leek forks right, and near the top of the hill is a Toll House. The left fork at the pub leads to the village of Mayfield.

On the right-hand side of the road are the ruins of at least one cliff-side cave house. At the top of the hill a lane to the left, Congreve Lane, leads past some sturdy Victorian stone-built workers' cottages, with raised foregardens and good iron railings, to more of their kind and on down to the mills by the river. Altogether, there are 41 houses in five terraces, the oldest being Mayfield Terrace of 1856.

There were four mills here but now there are only three. The oldest is that by the mill stream, built mainly of brick with iron columns and iron beams. The other two mills are partly of stone and are separated by an office block dated at 1871. The stone-built Owners House is an Italian Classical style of about 1850. It is now used as a canteen and works club.

Birds Grove, a house at the junction of Birdsgrove Lane and the A52, was built in about 1850 and occupied by the Greaves family. After the Second World War it was purchased by the Pharmaceutical Society and used by them as convalescent home.

Wallash is a south-west area of Mayfield. Number 22 Wallash was a working blacksmith's shop until 1964. Sometime after 1974 the interior of this shop, called the Woodward Smithy, was removed to the Staffordshire County Museum at Shugborough.

The church of St John the Baptist at **Church Mayfield** lies on the edge of the village, just to the west of the mills, in something like the village setting one had expected to find elsewhere in the settlement. The church has a late Norman south doorway and south arcade; a Decorated chancel with Georgian Gothic crenellation and Decorated south aisles; a Perpendicular tower of 1515; and 18th Century pulpit and benches.

The lane on which the church stands continues westwards for 0.25m and joins the main road at **Middle Mayfield**, which lies around a crescent-shaped lane. Mayfield Hall is a seven-bay, Georgian mansion of ashlar with a three-bay pediment. The entrance to the stables has a dome and lantern. Opposite the stable entrance is a handsome red sandstone house of three bays and three storeys with two gables and mullioned windows. Beneath the Hall are cellars and passages cut out of solid sandstone. They are thought to date from the 12th Century and the extent of the tunnels is unknown, but they are wide enough to take a cart down. In the 1920s the Hall was occupied by two families, the Wardles (Rear Admiral T E Wardle is of that line) and the Barbers. There is a Wellingtonia Sequoia tree in the grounds. Along the lane are two more handsome stone-built houses: Brook Farm and Old Hall Farm, which has a central porch and round chimneys. A charming enclave.

The main road continues westwards to Ellastone, on high ground, and provides some good views over the River Dove. On the north side of the road is Calwich Bank Farm, yet another handsome stone-built farmhouse of five bays and two storeys, with trimmed ivy on the walls and clipped yews along the path to the front door.

Signs of early man in Mayfield include: strip lynchets at SK 143453 at Middle Mayfield (now a listed monument); a Neolithic or Bronze-Age battle axe found at SK 151464; a burial mound at SK 155460; and a Roman urn found in Church Townfield.

Mayfield Cottage, now called Stancliffe Farm, on the north side of Slack Lane (SK 152457) was the home of the illustrious Irish poet Thomas Moore from 1813 to 1817. He is believed to have written 'Lalla Rooka', 'The Woodpecker' and 'Twopenny Postbag' whilst here. His daughter, Olivia Byron Moore (1814-15), died at the age of about six months and is buried in Mayfield churchyard. It was at Mayfield that he immortalized the sound of the bells from the Cathedral of the Peak at Ashbourne, just over the river:

Those evening bells, those evening bells,
How many a tale their music tells.

MEAFORD *1.25m NNW of Stone*

Meaford is a small village on the north side of the A34, at its junction with the A51 at the Darlaston (Stone) roundabout. Like Darlaston it was never more than a hamlet consisting of a few houses and an inn. These were demolished and the present buildings constructed by Lady Forester of Meaford Hall in the 1880s. They all lie alongside the old road, now bypassed by the new A34, and consist of the butler's house (1884), detached and set back; a block of cottages (1889) for the gardeners and cooks; the George and Dragon pub (1887); a cottage (1884) near the pub, which was joined to it until recently by a range of stables that had survived from the old coaching inn (they were mostly demolished in 1987 by the new owners of the pub); and the school (1880) which was used as a church on Sundays.

Meaford has been variously called Mepford, Metford and Mayford. It belonged to the Abbey of Burton until the Reformation, and there was a building of some kind here when the Jervis family built Meaford Hall in 1686. In the cellars of the Hall there are parts of a crypt, a benitier for holy water and an ancient doorway.

Admiral John Jervis (1735-1823), who became Earl St Vincent, was born in the Nursery House which is the oldest surviving part of the Old Hall. It is made of sandstone, has two storeys, shell ornament on the cornice and a reconstructed porch with original pilasters and their foliated capitals. The Admiral's title reflected his defeat of a superior Spanish fleet off Cape St Vincent in 1797. He went on to become First Lord of the Admiralty and there is a monument to him in the crypt of St Paul's Cathedral, London.

That part of the main Hall which stands today was built in the mid-19th Century and altered and restored in 1874-87. It is of Jacobean style and constructed of sandstone. There is some elaborate ornament, especially the strapwork entablatures. To the garden side there is a canted bay and a convex bay, both of two storeys, with recessed stepped gables behind a pierced parapet that runs the whole length of the building. The 'U'-shaped and very substantial stable block, built during the same period, still stands in very good order at the rear of the Nursery wing.

Lady Forester (Mary Ann Jervis) had received a huge inheritance of some two million pounds - a great fortune in those days - and it was with this that she financed her building. She died childless in 1893. In 1943 the estate was bought by the Roden family who demolished the East India Wing (which had been constructed in 1874-87 by Lady Forester).

The Hall and gardens were used as a market garden and plant nursery until 1963 when Percy Bilton Ltd (Builders) bought the premises and used them as offices and as a heavy plant depot before developing the site for housing. There is an attractive small park which has two ornamental pools and good views of the Bury Bank hill with its tree-clad Iron Age fort. The main Hall and the Nursery Wing are Grade II listed buildings and the whole estate is under consideration as a Conservation Area.

Meaford Old Hall, a restored timber-framed house on the other side (east) of the canal and the railway from Meaford Hall, was the home of John Joule of Joule's Brewery in Stone and he died there in 1858.

North of the Darlaston island and 'Yesterdays' inn is a row of old brick cottages, squashed between the road and the River Trent. They lie low, only the roof tops showing. Behind them once loomed the cooling towers of the Meaford Power Stations. Meaford Power Station A was opened in 1947 and closed in about 1976; the B Station closed in 1990 when it was demolished with explosives.

MEERBROOK *3.5m N of Leek*

The A53 Leek to Buxton road swoops down to the army camp at Blackshaw Moor, where a lane leads westwards to Middle Hulme and Meerbrook. To the north of this lane are the dramatic, jagged rocks of the Roaches. Hen Cloud is the nearest, most southerly hill, and the Five Clouds form a ridge behind, running north-westerly. At **Middle Hulme** the lane crosses the infant Churnet which has its primary source at Tittesworth Reservoir. Here is the access to the Fishing Lodge which has a cafe, parking and a picnic spot. The old packhorse route passed here. The track across the valley now lies beneath the waters of the reservoir. A causeway carries the modern road over the lake. North of this is probably the site of the original mere.

The village of Meerbrook is a pleasant enough place, unspoiled, with a pub and a church. St Matthew's was designed by Norman Shaw and built in 1868 with a nave of 1873. It has a squat central tower and inside is good ironwork and woodwork. The name of the village is from the Meer Brook.

There was a settlement and a grange of Dieulacres Abbey at Meerbrook from at least the 13th century. Strange as it seems today, this moorland country place was once a mining village. The Meerbrook Coalfield lies between Axe Edge and The Roaches and extends for four square miles. It is no longer worked. The lane continues west, climbs The Gun, turns north to Gun End and from there proceeds to Swythamley. Swythamley is the site of the Green Knight's castle in the medieval epic poem, 'Sir Gawain and the Green Knight' - beautiful, romantic country.

Blackshaw Moor, 1.5m SE of Meerbrook, is a hamlet and a moor on the A53, Leek to Buxton road. A stone causeway was constructed in about 1710 from Blackshaw Moor to the Mermaid Inn, on the Morridge (a long, high hill), for pack horses carrying salt. In 1943 a transit camp for USA anti-aircraft units was constructed. In 1945 this was taken over by Polish troops. After the war it became a Polish resettlement camp, until 1964 when the residents were settled in purpose-built accommodation half-a-mile north. In 1983 the camp opened as Anzio Camp, a training centre for both the Regular and Territorial Army and for Boy Scouts.

MEIR HEATH *4.5m NNE of Stone*

Suburban houses line the main road. At the crossroads at the top of the hill are some shops, a garage and a disused windmill, after which the pub next door is named.

The Church of St Francis is modern, built of brick with stone dressings and has steep roofs topped by a bellcote. There was a furnace, or furnaces, at Meir Heath from the late 17th Century to the mid-18th Century which smelted locally mined iron-ore. The works were owned by the Foley family who controlled a small empire of ironworks in North Staffordshire. The crude pig iron, full of slag and impurities, was sent from here to Consall Forge where it was refined by being reheated and beaten by hammers powered by water wheels. It was then cut into rods about one inch square at the slitting mill and sold to the South Staffordshire nailing trade. (See Consall.)

The main road leads from Meir Heath northwards, downhill, passing the Roman Catholic church of St Augustine, to the Meir crossroads and the imposing Kings Arms, a large brick-built pub with stone dressings and tall chimneys.

MILFORD *See Walton-on-the-Hill*

MILLDALE *1.5m SE of Alstonefield, which is 7m NNW of Ashbourne*
Milldale is a beautiful, tiny hamlet of stone at the northern end of the spectacular Dove Dale Gorge. Here the River Dove is crossed by the twin-arched packhorse bridge called Viator's Bridge - a totally delightful little place. In the summer there is a small tea shop and an information centre in the old mill. The main access road leads down the steep hill from Hopedale to the west, and here on Sunny Bank is a perfect moorland cottage. Another road leads northwards, alongside the river to Lode Mill and Shining Tor. (See *Dovedale.*)

MILTON *2m E of Burslem*
Milton is a substantial village-cum-town on the north-east of the Potteries' conurbation, to the east side of the A53 road to Leek. The Caldon canal (1777) passes through the settlement, and in 1867 the Milton to Cheddleton railway opened. There was a well on the site of the present TSB bank and this was ceremonially dressed. There is a full range of services and shops in the settlement. The Leigh Memorial Methodist Church (1865) at Milton is named in honour of Samuel Leigh, the first Methodist missionary to venture to Australia and New Zealand. He was born in about 1790 and sailed to the colonies in 1815. Alan Lake, the last husband of film star Diana Dors, was born in Milton.

MILWICH *4.5m ESE of Stone and 6.5m ESE of Stafford*
In early Norman times Milwich was part of the King's estates. Today it is a small, unspoiled, brick-built, nucleated village in the midst of rolling, well-wooded and well-watered country east of Stone. The church of All Saints lies on rising ground on the road to Sandon. It has a Perpendicular tower and the rest is purple brick, dated at 1792, with a Victorian east window. There is a bell here with the date 1409, which is reputedly the oldest bell in Staffordshire. Below the church is the black-and-white gabled Hall which was a farm but is now a private house. The Vicarage is of 1852 in Gothic style by Ward and Son of Hanley, and lies adjacent to the church. In the village is a beautifully restored, timber-framed and thatched cottage called Ivy House. The right-hand gable end is 13th Century post and cruck, and the brickwork is laid to a herringbone pattern. On the outskirts of the village is a similar cottage called Grimblebrook Farm. The pub is called The Green Man (an ancient name), and opposite is a Toll House of 1793 on the turnpiked Stone to Uttoxeter road. The stream that flows through the settlement has several names. It meanders over a stony bed with trees overhanging - a pleasant sight. A public footpath from the pub car park leads along the bank, from where the Hall is seen to its best advantage with the church high above on the ridge behind. There are a handful of new, large houses on the road from the church to the village, which, though desirable in themselves, are out of proportion to the older dwellings in the settlement.

  Coton, 0.5m ESE of Milwich, is in the Domesday Book of 1086 as Cote, the Anglo-Saxon for 'cottage'. In later medieval times it was a sizeable village but then became deserted. It is now fragmented, the separate parts of Coton Mill, Coton, Coton Green, Coton Hill and Coton Hayes being considered as one scattered village. Along the lane from Coton to Beacon Bank (a dead end) is

Coton Mill. This is a small derelict building, but inside is most of the old machinery; it still has its iron water-wheel and two pairs of mill stones. There is also a kiln in the north-west corner, which has been there since at least 1833 when the machinery was new.

Garshall Green, 1m N of Milwich, is a spread-about hamlet on high ground, and was once a part of the Manor of Milwich. In the 14th Century it was Geringeshaigh, meaning 'the meadowland of Gering (or Garing)'. 'Garing' is Old French for 'moustache'.

In the early 19th Century there is mention of a windmill just south of the chapel. It was called Milwich Mill and stood at SJ 969340. From about 1860 to 1940 the Snape family ran a pottery at Garshall Green. The castle or castellated house, known as Garshall Castle and owned by Hervey Bagot (or Hervey de Stretton), may have been at the moated site at SJ 965335, between Garshall House and Oulton House.

MIXON *1m NNW of Onecote, which is 8m NNE of Cheadle*

Mixon is a moorland hamlet, in the valley of the River Hamps, at the end of a dead-end track. Mixon in Old English is 'a dunghill'. The settlement as we see it today existed by 1775 and was occupied by miners in the early 19th Century. They worked at the now-disused copper mine at Mixon (SK 096584). To keep the mines clear of water there were two 40-foot-diameter waterwheels as well as stream engines. The mines closed in 1858. Hustings Farm used to double up as an inn.

The original settlement of Mixon appears to have been the hamlet of Old Mixon Hay, 1m WNW of Mixon. Hulton Abbey had a grange here by 1237. It lies on the slopes of The Morridge ridge. New Mixon Hay lies 0.75m SW of Old Mixon Hay.

MODDERSHALL *2.5m NE of Stone*

The village lies in a sheltered valley, high in the wooded hills south of the Potteries and north-east of Stone. Without being pretty this is a fine, pleasant place. The stream that tumbles down the valley is dammed by the road and has formed a small lake. There is also a duck pond by The Boar Inn, a red brick inn. The pool is actually a mill pool but the old flint mill, Boar Mill, closed in 1954 and was subsequently demolished.

It is said that The Boar Inn is haunted by the ghost of a soldier who hanged himself in an out-building rather than return to service during the Second World War.

On higher ground near the lake is the rock-faced mission church of All Saints. It was built in 1903 by the Wedgwood family, but was later affected by mining subsidence and was dismantled and rebuilt in 1993. The furnishings and fittings are all modern and very good.

Moddershall Oaks, a long, South-African-style, ranch-like house constructed of wood with an open verandah, was built for Josiah Wedgwood III.

MODDERSHALL VALLEY *NW of Stone for a good 2m*

This is really the valley of the Scotch Brook. It is a lovely wooded dale, followed by the A520, Stone to Leek road. From a point about one mile outside Stone, for a distance of about one mile up the valley, there are nine water-mills and the derelict remains of a tenth. This is quite extraordinary. Most of the mills had originally been built to grind corn, but in the first half of the 18th Century powdered flint was found to improve the clay used for white crockery ware, and to satisfy the demand watermills were converted to crush the flints.

Several of the mills today still have their waterwheels and are being renovated. Of these the star has to be Mosty Lea (SJ 916362) near the top of the hill. At the time of writing all that is apparent from the road is a dark-coloured shed, but behind this is an almost perfectly-restored working flint mill. The mill pool and the woods around provide an idyllic setting. The County Council, who bought and restored the building, are to be heartily congratulated Much of the work was done by unemployed people from the Manpower Services Commission.

Ivy House is the most spectacular and picturesque of the mills with its tall chimney (the flints were calcined by heating before being crushed), mill house, mill buildings, and a crane with a long derrick. It can be seen from the road, as can Coppice Mill in its charming wooded dell. Coppice Mill was first a corn mill, then a paper mill and lastly a flint mill. Both these mills have had their wheels restored.

It was at Coppice Mill that Henry Fourdrinier established a paper-making business using machinery invented by Henry and his brother Sealy. This was patented in 1901. They were of a French Protestant family who had emigrated to England in the 18th Century. The Fourdrinier family made several important inventions and could produce endless continuous sheets. Later, at their Ivy House Works in Hanley, they produced the tissue paper used by potters to carry the transfers used in their printing process. By 1840 Henry lived at Burston Hall. He died at Mavesyn Ridware in 1854.

Possibly the prettiest of all the Moddershall Valley mills is Splashy Mill, on the lane that runs directly west from Moddershall to the A520. A modern house lies adjacent but does no harm.

Here is a complete list of all the mills and their alternative names: Boar Mill, Coppice Mill (Shardlow's Mill), Hayes Mill (Oulton Mill), Ivy Mill, Mosty Lee Mill, Ochre Mill, Splashy Mill (Top Mill), Wetmore Mill, and Weaver's Mill in Stone which was named after a former owner, Mr Weaver. There were water-mills in the valley from the 12th Century. Many started as either fulling or corn mills.

The Hayes, on the eastern side of the A520, is a large multi-bay, two-storey Georgian house with an offset porte-cochere, an elongated cupola and a hipped roof. In the 1870s it was enlarged by the master potter, James Meakin. In about 1900 the Hollins family (of the Minton Hollins' pottery) came here.

MORETON *4m SE of Newport*
Moreton is a fragmented village in good, Shropshire-type country on the Shropshire border. The neo-Norman church of St Mary was designed by Thomas Trubshaw and built in 1837. The Vicarage and the School are of 1839-40, in the same style. One mile north-west is the pleasant village of Outwoods. This is nice country to get lost in.

Domesday Book records the occupants of Moreton in 1086 as being: 'Benedict who has one slave, one man at arms with one Englishman and four smallholders.'

Charlotte Sophia Burne (1850-1923), author of the classic 'Shropshire Folk Lore' (1881), the standard work on the subject, was born at the Vicarage in Moreton.

MOSELEY OLD HALL *4.25m NNE of Wolverhampton town centre and 0.5m from Featherstone on the A 460*
Moseley Old Hall can be difficult to find. It is most easily approached off the A460, Wolverhampton to Cannock road, at Featherstone, but the signs are somewhat wayward. The Hall is far from impressive, but beneath the casing of Victorian brick is the timber-framed and gabled manor house at which Charles II stayed for two days and one night whilst on the run after his defeat at the Battle of Worcester in September 1651. The house was built by Henry Pitt of Bushbury in 1600. His daughter married Thomas Whitgreave and they had a son, also called Thomas. It was this mother and son who sheltered the King. Inside, the Hall is very much as it was when Charles II stayed here. There is a timbered hall, a good staircase leading to the King's room and the bed in which he slept. To the right of the fireplace in this room is the entrance to a priest hole. Apparently, the King had very fond memories of his short stay here, and even as he lay dying his thoughts were of Moseley and 'an ancient altar'. Father Huddleston, who had been Chaplain to Thomas Whitgreave, gave Charles the last rites. The National Trust now administers Moseley Old Hall and it was they who laid out the formal gardens. Ironically, this house, which partook in one of history's great escapes, is only about 300 yards away from Featherstone Open Prison.

MOXLEY *1m ESE of Bilston*
Moxley lies mid-way between Bilston and Wednesbury. If it has a centre it is at the forked junction where the Darlaston road meets the A41. Just east of the canal bridge is the red sandstone parish church of All Saints with its short tower topped by a spire. It is a Commissioners' church (see Bilston), built in 1851 to a design by W Horton. Opposite are the galvanising works of Frost & Sons. Down Bull Lane is Wasson's Hot and Cold Rolled Steel Works. Here, too, is a wooded wasteland wherein lie a most peculiar agglomeration of buildings collectively called the Moxley Hospital. At the junction of the A4037 is the Fiery Holes Inn. This faces a canal-fringed industrial desert. Behind the pub is the residential desert of Old Moxley - council houses, blocks of flats and cars parked everywhere. Tucked away in Castle View Road is Black Country Grains, suppliers of pigeon food and bird seed. Great Bridge Road leads one past a recreation ground and a row of strange red brick semis, looking like little castles, to the Holyhead Road, here called Moxley High Street. High Street? The place is boarded up. The Moxley Arms stares gloomily across the road at the Moxley Wire Rope Works and a sign directs the traveller to the Darlaston CPA Urban Farm. Moxley is home to George Ward (Moxley) Ltd, probably the country's largest manufacturers and importers of clay and plastic flowerpots. In the 19th Century the landlord of the Britannia Inn kept a pen of fighting cocks at the back of his pub. It was here that 'Cockie' Potter began his career as a trainer of fighting cocks. He went on to become Cock-master General to Lord Derby in charge of more than 2,000 birds and the leading expert on this 'sport' in Britain. (See Bilston.)

MOW COP *2m NNE of Kidsgrove, which is 7m N of Newcastle-under-Lyme*
Mow Cop lies half in Staffordshire and half in Cheshire. It is a large rocky hill nearly 1100 feet (335 metres) above sea level. To the south-east are the Staffordshire Moorlands and to the north-west is the great flat plain of Cheshire. It is known for two things: the ruined castle-folly, built in 1754 by the

Wilbraham family of Rode Hall as a decoration to the view from their house; and as the birthplace of Primitive Methodism, which originated at a camp meeting organised by Hugh Bourne, a wheelwright from Stoke, in 1807.

Bourne, his brother and William Clowes (the champion dancer of Burslem) wanted a simpler religion with less of the pomp and ceremony of other organized faiths, including their own Methodism. At the height of their popularity they had some 5,000 churches and 100,000 members. In 1932 they were reunited with the Methodists. Bourne is buried in Englesea Brook in Cheshire.

Mow Cop is on the carboniferous Yoredale Rocks, the oldest in the area. These were quarried for coal on the eastern flank of the hill and for limestone on the western flank. A row of terraced houses called Welsh Row was occupied by Welsh miners brought here in about 1862. Millstone was quarried here from 13th Century. There are many springs on the hill.

The Old Man of Mow is a tall rock pinnacle that had religious significance to prehistoric man, although it is possible that the pinnacle itself was created by miners quarrying around it out of respect for the holy ground on the top surface. The hill is now owned by the National Trust. Mow Cop village is largely stone-built and somewhat untidy. St Thomas's is a Commissioners' church of 1841 and looks like a Gothic barn. The school is of 1843, St Luke's of 1875 and the Wesleyan Chapel of 1865. There is a car park and the views are tremendous.

Harrisehead is a settlement which straggles along the road between Mow Cop and Newchapel to the south.

MUCKLESTONE *4m ENE of Market Drayton*
It is a very small village comprising a few red brick cottages, a red brick farm with substantial lower parts of sandstone, a couple of new houses, a chapel-like school (now a dwelling), a modern school in the usual modern bad taste, and the church. From the tower of St Mary's church Queen Margaret, wife of Henry VI, is said to have watched the Battle of Blore Heath (23rd Sept 1459) which was fought 15 miles to the south-west. Lord Audley of Heighley Castle was killed and a cross marks the spot where he died. (It is in the field opposite Audley's Cross Farm, on the A53, half way between Loggerheads and Market Drayton.)

St Mary's is the parish church. It has a medieval Decorated tower but most of the rest was rebuilt in 1883 in a matching style. The interior is dark, due mainly to the stained glass windows designed by Kempe. In the churchyard, alongside the road, is a blacksmith's anvil. This came from the cottage opposite, which stands on the site of the old forge where William Skelhorne, a smith, is reputed to have reversed the shoes of the horse ridden by Queen Margaret before she fled after the battle of Blore Heath.

Mucklestone Wood Farm, 1m SE of Mucklestone, was formerly called White House Farm and has a terrible tale to tell. On 28th January 1826 two magistrates, Henry Delves Broughton JP and Mr Eld JP, called at the farmhouse and demanded entry. They had heard rumours that William Smith and his sister were keeping their brother, George Smith (born about 1781), an alleged lunatic, in appalling conditions so that they could receive £50 a year for keeping him. The magistrates searched the house and found George Smith locked up in the attic, emaciated, naked and filthy. He was taken to Stafford Lunatic Asylum but died there three years later in 1829. His body was returned to the farmhouse and his previous 'captors' who buried him in Mucklestone churchyard. However, in 1883 a workman accidentally struck George Smith's coffin with his pick and it was found to be empty.

Oakley Hall, 1.5m W of Mucklestone, is a mansion of 1710, built for Sir John Chetwode, 1st Baronet. The handsome east facade of 11 bays is of brick with stone dressings. It is two storeys high, has giant pilasters on either side of the centre three bays, and a highly ornamented central pediment. Field Marshall Lord Chetwode, the 7th Baronet, lived here. In Recent years it has had several owners and we understand the present incumbent is a financier.

To the left of the Hall are some outbuildings now let out to a handful of small businesses. Parts of the Hall itself are hired out for wedding receptions and the like. The River Tern runs in a valley to the rear of the house and has been dammed to form a lake,

The Home Farm still functions commercially and a large agricultural park adjoins the River Tern, which here marks the border between Staffordshire and Shropshire. An Iron Age dugout canoe was found in the mud of the Tern hereabouts. About 0.25m NW of the entrance lodges to Oakley Hall estate are the Devil's Ring and Finger (SJ 707378). These are two large stones, some six-feet high, that have been dragged out of the adjoining field and built into a low stone wall by a tree. One stone is pillar-like and the other is round with a central hole, 20 inches in diameter. They probably formed part of the main burial chamber in a prehistoric tomb which has been destroyed by ploughing.

To the south of the Hall, just over half-a-mile along the A5415, north-west of its junction with the A53, is a splendid Georgian-style house of the 1970s called Daisy Lake (SJ 708357).

About 0.5m further along is a wood called The Folly and on the northern edge of this wood, and visible from the road, is a curious ruined building. This consists of an old rectangular sandstone structure with arched doorways, believed to have been built as a coaching station, on a now-abandoned coaching road. To this has been added a castellated, three-storey brick tower. The tower (SJ 714364) was built by Colonel D'Avenent, probably in the 1770s, as a viewing point from which to watch his racehorses being exercised in the fields on the other side of the road. After he died the land and tower went to Sir John Chetwode and formed part of the Oakley estate. A later Chetwode also used it for viewing his racehorses. The whole building was later converted into a house and lived in by a gamekeeper. The field between the house and the highway is still called the Rearing Field. Then, in the 1960s, lightning struck, literally. The lead pipes and taps melted, the timbers caught fire and the house burned down. The gamekeeper and his wife and child were inside at the time and barely escaped with their lives. The building was abandoned and is now in the process of being destroyed by young boys.

Winnington, 0.75m N of Muckleston, is a crossroads hamlet in rolling country. In Domesday Book it is Wennitone which means 'the settlement of Wenni's people'. The 'ing' middle syllable means 'the people of' in Anglo-Saxon place names. Grange Farm is quite probably the grange farm which the Cistercian monks of Combermere Abbey had here in medieval times. It is a large white-rendered, six-bay, two-storey house with a slightly projecting two-bay centre. The extensive farm buildings are red brick but The Grange no longer operates as a farm. For the rest there are two or three cottages.

Napley, 0.75m NNW of Mucklestone, is a farming hamlet strung out along a narrow, dead-end lane. Here are Quarry Farm, Bank Farm, Napley Cottage, Napley Farm, pastures and black-and-white cattle. Napley Heath was enclosed in 1807.

N

NEEDWOOD *3.5m W of Burton upon Trent*

Needwood is a tiny hamlet at the centre of the former Needwood Forest. It was originally called Five End because it developed at the junction of five straight roads. These were made at the time of the enclosure of the forest in about 1811. The New Inn is also probably of this time. The name Needwood is unexplained, the prefix probably being of British origin. The forest was a natural woodland-cum-chase. After the Norman Conquest it became the hunting ground of the Ferrers family. From 1399 to 1801 it was a Crown estate and was officially a Forest.

Before the Enclosure Act of 1801 it was nearly 10,000 acres in extent, had a circumference of about 24 miles, covered the high plateau between the Rivers Trent, Dove and Blithe and included the settlements of Barton, Hanbury, Marchington, Tutbury and Yoxall. There are several local legends placing Robin Hood in Needwood Forest, in particular the ballad of 'King Edward and the Tanner of Tamworth', where the battle is said to have taken place at Marchington Cliff. There were between eight and 12 separate deer parks within the forest.

NETHERTON *1.5m SW of Dudley*

The name is Anglo-Saxon and means 'the lower settlement.' What we see today is an old industrial village with a busy main-road shopping centre that lies between Dudley and Halesowen. Netherton is famous for Jews harps, Real Ale and the Netherton canal tunnel, not to mention the Nailmakers' Strike of 1862 and the scenic charms of Warren's Hall Park.

The settlement nestles on a hillside below the church and is a cheerful place with a little village green. Facing the green is the Old Swan public house at which Ma Pardoe sold her own beer, brewed on the premises. She died in 1984 but the Campaign for Real Ale bought the premises and continues the tradition.

Another publican of note was Joseph Darby, who kept the Albion in Stone Street, Dudley, but who was born at Windmill End in Netherton in 1861. He was the World Champion Spring Jumper, a sport popular in Victorian times. All manner of strange jumps were made: leaping off and landing on eggs without breaking them; jumping over canals with an intermediate spring, apparently off the surface of the water (probably a kind of hitch kick); and jumping over 12 chairs with a leap taken from a glass of water from which none was spilled. Darby died in 1937.

Netherton grew on coal and iron. Perhaps the most famous works was that of Noah Hingley and Sons who, besides other things, made ships' anchors, including that of the ill-fated Titanic. They also made chains with links up to 40 inches in diameter. Grazebrooks, another iron founders, made bomb casings during the war; Samuel Lewis made hand-made nails, chains and barrows; and John Barnsley, who now make lifting gear, were famous in late-Victorian times for their Jews Harps, many of which were exported to the USA. Nailmaking was an important trade in the area. It was a cottage industry, and the workers were little more than the slaves of the nailmasters who supplied the iron rods and bought back the finished nails. In 1862 the nailers went on strike and marched from Netherton to Bromsgrove hauling a tub of coal. A song was written, printed on broadsheets and sold on the journey. They achieved their purpose and gained an increase in their wages, but it was short lived because machines were soon to be developed that made their craft all but redundant.

St Andrew's church is a landmark for many miles around. It stands embowered in trees on top of the hill, one flank of which appears to be virgin moorland. There was almost certainly an Iron Age fort here and later an Anglo-Saxon church. The present building dates from 1827-30 and is the work of Thomas Lee. It is a Commissioners' Church with a tower and lancet windows. Inside there are three galleries. Victims of the cholera epidemic of 1832 are buried here in extensive, unmarked, common graves which were dug especially deep. In 1844 Netherton became a parish, and a very large one, but in 1865 it lost this status and became a part of Dudley.

At **Darby End**, 0.66m E of Netherton, is Warren's Hall Park and the Bumble Hole - 80 acres of old mines and ironworks which have been made safe and landscaped. Here is the much photographed Cobb's Engine House, which was built about 1877 to pump water out of Pit Number Three of Windmill End Colliery. It was operating until about 1928 and was then neglected until restored in 1974. It is now an Ancient Monument. It is built of brick, has a 90-foot chimney and stands near two canal bridges.

Close by is the entrance to the 5,027-yard Netherton Tunnel of 1858 which, unlike the Dudley Canal Tunnel, has a towpath on both sides of the waterway. It is reputed to be the widest canal tunnel in Britain. Near to Cobb's Engine House (in Vale Road, off Darby End Road) is the gaily painted Dry Dock pub, where huge meat and potato pies, bedecked with pastry cows' horns, can be purchased from the Irish landlord. Anyone who can eat a whole pie gets a medal. Just off the main road is the Hilly Piece, recently reclaimed land cut through by murky streams that emerge from sinister culverts.

Baptist End adjoins Netherton to the north-east. It is a largely residential area - some Victorian terraces, modern houses, 15-storey blocks of flats, the White Lion, the White Swan and well-tended allotments. In St Peter's Road is The Willows, a pub restaurant, behind which is a delightful little marina. Willows abound and there is an old canal-side swing crane and an amusing (and solidly built) little folly windmill.

Primrose Hill adjoins Netherton to the south-east. It is a mixed industrial-residential area: Noah's Ark Methodist Church; Primrose Hill Trading Estate, very new and very smart; Andover Tool and Engineering Ltd; the White Swan; a Congregational church; an overgrown canal basin on the Dudley Canal (1779); and long views from the hill top over estates of houses towards Cradley Heath.

Saltwells lies 0.66m S of Netherton church. Here are woods, streams, springs, cliffs and marshes. Saltwells is not a town or a village. It is an old mining and metal working area that in the 1980s was partly reclaimed and which now includes a 100-acre Nature Reserve. It lies in the Blackbrook Valley, just east of Brierley Hill and to the north of Quarry Bank. The Nature Reserve is best approached off the A4036, turning east at the Merry Hill island. There is a free car park by the Saltwells Inn. Many of the oak, beech and lime trees in Saltwells Wood are long established, some over 200 years old. However, much of the area was a dangerous wasteland - coal mine spoil heaps, open shafts, disused quarries, the ruins of brick works and forges, and abandoned canals and railway tracks. There is a collection of old photographs illustrating these industries in the Saltwells Inn, a large hostelry with a reputation for friendliness and traditional Sunday lunches. Today, there is a wide variety of wildlife in a wide variety of habitats.

The most dramatic feature is the **Doulton Clay Pit**. This is entered down a steep slope, past a red stained rock spring. Cliffs of many colours rise sheer above delightful woods, pools and marshes. China clay was mined here from 1870 to 1947 when extraction ceased because of flooding. The exposed geological successions are of great interest to students and in 1981 it was designated a Site of Special Scientific Interest. Rare orchids and some less common birds such as redwing are found here. There are three signed walks in the area as a whole and a permanent field centre, from which guided tours are available for groups. (For further information contact the Chief Warden, Dudley Education Dept, Westox House, Trinity Road, Dudley).

But what of the saltwell which gave its name to the area? This was formerly called the Ladywood Spa. The waters were reputed to have healing qualities and were sold commercially until the company collapsed in the 1920s. Parts of their old buildings remain and these have been investigated by the Black Country Society. Incidentally, the large lake at the top of the hill is not part of the Nature Reserve. This is the Lodge Farm Reservoir, known locally as Netherton Reservoir. Here there is a boat club, and both sail and power vessels sport and play, forcing the ducks to the safety of the tree-fringed margins.

NEWBOROUGH *6m SE of Uttoxeter*

Newborough lies on the edge of Needwood Forest The countryside is not spectacular but is certainly most charming and in places has a strong medieval atmosphere. The numerous woods and plantations, especially to the east, give one the feeling of being in a forest.

Newborough was originally called Agardsley. (Agardsley Park, 1.5m. N of Newborough, preserves the original name of the settlement.) However, in 1263 Robert Ferrers, Earl of Derby, converted the village into a town almost overnight. Long, evenly-spaced plots called burgage plots were marked out and settlers encouraged to come in and build houses. They were enticed by offers of rights to graze their animals and collect firewood in the woods of Needwood Chase. (Needwood did not technically become a Forest until some time later when ownership passed to the King.) The name of the old village was changed to New Borough to reflect its new, higher status.

The Earls had established Uttoxeter in a similar fashion in 1140 and that new town had flourished; not so Newborough. Today it is a tiny village at a crossroads, with an inn and a Post Office. The burgage plots are still there, however, traceable in the regular lines of the long gardens at right angles to the road. Newborough Hall Farm, 0.25m NNW of Newborough, lies just south of the moated site of the now-demolished Hall, a complex of moat, millpond, two fish ponds and connecting channels at SK 133259 and SK 134259.

The church of All Saints is of 1901 by J Oldrid Scott. It is a church of some distinction, except for the 120-foot octagonal tower and recessed spire, which some find refreshing and others abhor. It seems likely that this is by a hand other than that of Oldrid Scott.

Will Willet, who is buried in the church graveyard, danced non-stop from the evening of 2nd September 1752 until the morning of 14th September - 12 days. Actually, he only danced for a few minutes because at midnight, 2nd September the calendar was changed and 12 days were lost.

On May Day (or the Saturday nearest to it) there is a well dressing. The three wells of Newborough are decorated with flower pictures - petals pressed into panels of clay. There is a dressing ceremony, displays of traditional dancing outside the Red Lion, a show of flowers in the church, games, stalls and re-freshments, and the ubiquitous fire engine. A general good time is had by all. It is a low key affair and even the police are engagingly disorganized.

Holly Bush Lane leads past the Post Office to **Holly Bush Hall**, 0.5m N of Newborough. This is a most attractive three-bay house with rendered elevations and a columned portico. It is most pleasantly situated in parkland complete with specimen trees and a lake. In recent times, however, the estate has been blighted by a small housing development through which one has to drive to reach the Hall. Holly Bush is now the home of the Meynell-Ingram family who used to live at the much grander Hoar Cross Hall, less than two miles to the south. The Meynells started the local fox hunt.

NEWCASTLE-UNDER-LYME *14m NNW of Stafford*

Newcastle-under-Lyme was historically separate from the Six Towns of the Potteries, but so were the Six Towns historically separate from each other. They all grew together at roughly the same time, and Newcastle with them. Having said that, there is no doubt that the centre of Newcastle has the air of a country town and, indeed, it became a borough when Hanley, Burslem, Longton, Tunstall, Fenton and Stoke were only villages.

That borough status was granted in 1180 when the town was established around the new castle that the Normans built to the north-west of the present town centre. (The 'old' castle was at Chesterton, where there had been a fort since Roman times.) The motte of the castle still exists, a mound with trees atop. It lies in the Queen Elizabeth Gardens with a bowling green to one side and a factory to the other. Nearby, in John of Gaunt's Road, are some stone foundations, believed to be part of a curtain wall. The main defence of the castle was the large lake that almost surrounded it, caused by damming a stream.

The 'Lyme' in the town's name is from the great Forest of Lyme that covered much of North-West Staffordshire in medieval times.

Newcastle still retains the original grid pattern of streets established at, or soon after, its foundation. The town prospered in the 14th and 15th Centuries from the wool trade, and later became an important staging point on the coach routes to the north and north-west. Today the town has a flourishing market which operates several days a week and has large numbers of pubs and several nightclubs, one of which is the mammoth Zanzibar.

Newcastle town (as distinct from the borough) is predominantly a residential rather than an industrial town because it was not situated on coal-bearing beds. Early industry was based on wool and iron-working. In the 19th Century a variety of trades flourished, including the making of hats, clocks, smoking pipes, silk goods, ironware, pottery, and cables and wires. There was also leather tanning and a range of light industries.

Today, because of its central location, there are a number of distribution companies and carriers, especially on the northern industrial estates off the A34. The heavy industries such as iron smelting furnaces, coal mines and clay quarries were within the borough but in areas such as Knutton, Chesterton and Apedale.

In the mid-1770s Sir Nigel Gresley constructed a two-mile canal from his mines at Apedale to Carry coal to Newcastle-under-Lyme. It terminated alongside the present Liverpool Road. In 1799 it was connected to the Newcastle Canal by the Newcastle Junction Canal, which ran alongside Water Street and Victoria Road.

It was the prosperity brought by these industries that paid for the many large houses in the leafy suburbs, and for the redevelopment of the town centre that effectively removed almost every building of historical or architectural interest.

As a brewery town Newcastle-under-Lyme was second only to Stone in North Staffordshire. Bents were here between 1799 and 1836 before moving to Liverpool. Their brewery was on the site now occupied by the Borough Arms Hotel in King Street. In nearby Water Street (accessed off Brunswick St) were the breweries of Baker and King (1839-1886), and the Waterloo Brewery (1860-1880). The sites of these breweries were later occupied by the Magistrates Courts. (The courts were later moved to Rycecroft.) Ridgeways' brewery (1850s-1900s) was located in Lower Street. Today the brewery trade, like the clothing and textile industry, is non-existent.

The church of St Giles stands on a medieval site but only a little of the masonry in the tower (c 1290) is of that period. The rest was rebuilt in 1873-6 by Sir George Gilbert Scott, and even the tower was encased in Victorian stone in 1894. The style of the rebuilding is late 13th Century. The overall impression is of a large but unimpressive parish church. Close by there is a little Unitarian Chapel of 1717 with an upper floor of 1926.

The most prominent building in the town centre is the brick and stone Guidhall of 1713, which stands in the middle of the High Street. The ground floor was originally open, and the rounded north end and the giant portico of two Tuscan columns were added in 1860-2. Iron Market was just that in medieval times. It is a pleasant, wide street and here is one of the few old buildings in the town, the ancient pub now called The Boozy Dog in which is played very loud popular music.

Perhaps the most memorable building in the town is in London Road (A34) at the southern end of the centre. It is the Roman Catholic church, designed by the Rev James Egan, faced entirely in blue engineering brick and decorated by a host of blank arcades. Save for a few Georgian facades over plate-glass-windowed shops, that is the architectural heritage of Newcastle.

Here are a few buildings and their dates: St George's, a Commissioners' church, 1828; St Paul's, 1905-8; Ebenezer Methodist church, 1857; Municipal Buildings, Merrial Street, 1967; Police Station, 1936; Market Cross, 18th Century on medieval steps; the Conservative Club, 1769; St Michael's by Austin and Paley, 1938; The Barracks, a superb brick-built army barracks arranged around a central courtyard and positioned opposite the bus station.

Westlands, 1.25m S of Newcastle, is a large estate of good-class, private houses that was built on the land of Westlands Farm from the 1920s. It is now a separate ecclesiastical parish and its church is dedicated to St Andrew (1962). A Roman coin of the rule of Claudius was found in Sutherland Drive.

Clayton is a suburb 1.5m S of Newcastle. It was formerly two separate settlements called Clayton Culvert (or Great Clayton) and Clayton Griffiths (or Griffin), after the Griffiths family who were the 13th Century lords of the manor here. Chetwynd House in Northwood Lane is a house of the early 20th Century, around an irregular courtyard, with rows of small leaded windows, long roofs and capped chimneys. Clayton Hall in Clayton Lane is probably Georgian, rendered, with giant pilasters on the central block, a tower and some additions of the 1840s. In Beresford Crescent lives Charles Castriot de Renzi, a direct descendant of the Albanian national hero Alexander George Castriot, also known as Skanderburg, who rescued his country from the Turks in the early 15th Century.

Seabridge, 1.75m SSW of Newcastle, was, as late as the 1960s, a separate hamlet. It has now been heavily developed for housing and is a suburb of Newcastle. The old hamlet lay somewhere near the present Seabridge County Junior and Infants' School. The name in the 13th Century was Sheperugge and in the 17th Century it was Shea Bridge. It means either 'sheep ridge' or ' sheep bridge'. The Park Brook flows here. William Boulton (1825-1900), a pioneer in ceramic engineering, was born in Seabridge. His eldest son was engaged to Arnold Bennett's sister, Tertia, but he was drowned whilst on holiday with her at Barmouth. Seabridge Hall, "a respectable old mansion" was occupied by John Wedgwood in 1843. A previous owner was Lady Pilkington.

Basford ('Bassa's ford') is an attractive, residential, north-eastern suburb of Newcastle with some good detached houses and a Gothic church of 1914 by Austin and Paley, with a new west end of 1969. In Etruria Road is the New Victoria Theatre The theatre has a bland facade but is functional and pleasant inside. Live theatre struggles these days to compete against television and cinema and has to be subsidised to a high degree.

The original Victoria Theatre was founded in Hartshill by Stephen Joseph in 1962. His company converted an old cinema on the corner of Victoria Street and Hartshill Road to a theatre in the round. This old building still stands, now fronted by the Britannia Building Society. Subsequently, a new company took over the administration, and between 1984 and 1986 a purpose-built theatre in the round was constructed on the tennis court and gardens of Stoneyfields. This is a mansion built in 1780 and is now a pub called The Polite Vicar. Peter Cheeseman had been the theatre director since 1962 and is remembered for the 11 locally-based documentaries he produced. Cheeseman retired in 1998.

H G Wells stayed with a college friend at his terraced house, 18 Victoria street, Basford, and is said to have written his story 'the Cone', set in Shelton steelworks. He wrote of his stay at Basford in 'How I Died' (1898). Basford is Pineford in Arnold Bennett's novels.

Milehouse, now a suburban area, 1m N of Newcastle-under-Lyme, probably took its name from an inn called The Milehouse, which once stood on the Liverpool road at Cross Heath. The name is preserved in Milehouse Lane. In 1945 Rolls Royce manufactured the Derwent, the first jet engine ever made in Britain, at 'Factory 81', Milehouse.

Chesterton, 2.5m NNW of Newcastle centre is now a suburb of the borough town. On a flat-topped hill at Mount Pleasant there was a bank and ditch earthwork that enclosed some 20 acres. This was probably the site of an Iron Age settlement and later the site of a Roman fort occupied in the 1st Century. Some sandstone foundations were also found here.

In Springwood Road, Chesterton are the substantial remains of The **Partridge Nest Ironworks** (SJ 823499), a very early, coke-fuelled, blast furnace used for smelting iron from iron-ore. It was built by Sir Edensor Heathcote in 1790. The furnace is a short, solidly-built tower with sloping (battered) walls, made from locally manufactured bricks. It is on a hillside, and has been partly renovated with the aid of a grant. There is an arched furnace mouth and fire wall to a square fire chamber gathered above into a funnel-shaped shaft. Originally it also had an engine house. This contained the engine which made the air blast.

There was also a casting shop in which anvils, vices, irons and smithy tools were made. In 1833 the furnace lining was removed, the engine house pulled down and the casting shop converted to four cottages, which were later demolished. The present cottages, to the left of the furnace, are later, 19th Century buildings. The Partridge Nest Ironworks lies down a short lane called Springwood Road, off the B5500. This is in square C1, page 50, in the W H Smith Street Atlas. The valley is quite rural and must look much like it did when the furnace was operating.

At **Holditch**, just south of the Mount Pleasant site, was a large civilian settlement of the Roman period with buildings of wood, stone and brick, and roadways but no defensive works. It was occupied from the late 1st to the 3rd Centuries. Today the area is covered by an industrial estate and a school. The modern village consists largely of Victorian terraces. The church of Holy Trinity is of 1851, by H Ward and son of Hanley, with stained glass by William Wailes.

Crackley, 2.5m NNW of Newcastle, is a large area of modern housing. To the south it adjoins Chesterton. The church of St Chad has an adjacent Church of England school and there is another school on Crackley Bank. Adjoining Crackley to the north is **Red Street**. Red is probably a corruption of the Celtic 'roed' meaning 'forest-road'.

Waterhayes Village, NW of Chesterton, is an estate of modern houses, started about 1980, on the site of the old Glasshouse colliery and Glasshouse Farm. The name is from another farm now obliterated.

Knutton, 1m NW of Newcastle town centre, is now a residential suburb with a Gothic church of 1827 and a few shops.. The name means 'Canute's Town', that is, it belonged to King Canute. At the time of Domesday it belonged to Richard Forester, a major landowner in the county. It developed during the late 18th and 19th Centuries on coal, iron and clay. In the later 19th Century Francis Stanier had control of the huge Silverdale and Apedale furnaces and had a forge at Knutton. In his day he became a millionaire on the proceeds of these enterprises. A huge clay pit, Whalley's Quarry, still operates at Knutton.

Wolstanton lies 1.5m NE of Newcastle, beyond Basford. It stands high, with views over Hanley and Burslem to the east. The name Wolstanton is from St Wolstan, Bishop of Worcester from 1062, who founded the church at Wolstanton.

The Roman road from Derby to Chesterton passed through Wolstanton. Paved sections have been found in the large green called Wolstanton Marsh and in the garden of a house in Links Avenue at SJ 84693792.

There was glassmaking in the 17th and 18th centuries at the Glasshouse in Red Street. There are some good houses such as the brick-built Moreton House, dated at 1743, with five bays, 2.5 storeys and a parapet. It is now an old people's home and greatly extended at the back. The Archer pub is close by.

The church of St Margaret was rebuilt by Ward and Son in 1859, and the chancel was designed by Salvin shortly after he had finished rebuilding Keele Hall. There are monuments to the Sneyd family, including Sir William Sneyd, died 1689, and John Sneyd, died 1710. Opposite the church is the highly original school of 1871 by James Brooks. There are two Methodist churches, one in High Street, of 1894, and the other in Bradwell Lane, of 1966.

In about 1693 the Dutchman, John Philip Elers, leased **Bradwell Hall**, in the parish of Wolstanton, from the Sneyd family. He made excellent china services and brought new standards to the refinement of clay and to the decoration of the finished ware. He guarded his secrets closely and is said to have only employed half-witted labourers in his workshops. He lived at Dinsdale Hall but in 1700 was declared bankrupt and went to Dublin with his new wife, Elizabeth Banks of Uttoxeter, and there he died in 1738. His contribution to the pottery industry in North Staffordshire was primarily the example he set by the quality of his ware, which forced his competitors to emulate him. There are examples of his work at the Newcastle-under-Lyme town museum at Basford, on the Newcastle to Tunstall road. One of Newcastle's most famous sons was Thomas Harrison, son of a butcher and grazier in the town. He became one of Cromwell's generals and was one of the judges at the trial of Charles I. After the Restoration of the Monarchy, Major General Harrison was himself tried for his involvement in the death of the King. He was found guilty and on 13th October 1660 was hanged, drawn and quartered before a cheering crowd.

Cross Heath, 1m NW of Newcastle, is a suburban area with an industrial surprise. In 1797 Richard Thompson built a mill in Liverpool Road for the spinning and weaving of cotton, not a trade associated with the area. It continued operating as a cotton-doubling mill into the 1960s, in the ownership of A & S Murray. It was later called Swift House. The church of St Michael and All Angels is said to be haunted by a lady in white.

Springfields, 1m SE of Newcastle-under-Lyme, is a suburban area with a large brick pub, The Springfield, and an estate of out-of-town stores including Focus and Comet. This was built on the site of the large Wheatley brick and tile works (SJ 860444), the clay pit of which still exists behind the McDonalds and Aldi outlets. In the Springfields-Trent Vale area there was a Roman fort.

Porthill, 1.5m N of Newcastle-under-Lyme centre, is a former small village which is now a suburban residential area with some mature, good-class houses. The parish church of St Andrew was built in 1886. Porthill is Hillport in Arnold Bennett's novels. In 1953 an RAF Meteor crashed in flames on the Porthill Park cricket ground killing the pilot. The BBC Radio One disc jockey, Bruno Brookes (born 1960), lived at Rhodes Court, Porthill whilst broadcasting on BBC Radio Stoke.

Rather more significantly, the founder of the modern circus in England, and Master Horseman, Philip Astley, was born at Porthill in 1742. In the 18th Century he was a household name throughout the country. He became apprentice to his father, a cabinet maker, but at about the age of 17 joined the cavalry and quickly gained a reputation as an outstanding horseman.

He left the army and set up as a trainer and trick rider. To add variety to his performances he employed clowns (he called them Merrymen), jugglers, acrobats and other troubadour acts who normally worked on the streets and in fairgrounds. For the first time they performed collectively in specially-built, circular, wooden arenas. The circus was born. It was immensely popular, both with the ordinary man and with royalty: George III and Marie Antoinette were amongst Astley's admirers.

The English country dance tune called Astley's Ride is 18th Century in style and was almost certainly named after Philip Astley, if not specially composed for his circus musicians. (The music is printed in Midlands Digest, Volume 3, page 48.)

In **Trent Vale** there is a large estate of semi-detached houses, built and rented out by the William Sutton Trust, who are dedicated to supplying 'affordable housing'. Springfield and Trent Vale are technically in Stoke-on-Trent, but in character and spirit belong to Newcastle.

Jackie Trent, real name Yvonne Burgess, the singer and songwriter and husband of Tony Hatch, was born in Newcastle-under-Lyme in 1940. They wrote several songs for Petula Clark, including 'Don't sleep in the Subway'. They also wrote the score for Cameron Mackintosh's West End production 'The Card' (1972), a musical adaptation of Arnold Bennett's novel; and the theme tune for the popular television soap opera 'Neighbours'.

NEWCHAPEL *1m E of Kidsgrove, which is 6m N of Newcastle-under-Lyme*
Newchapel is a grim village on a ridge in the industrial moorlands north of the Potteries. Coal was mined here. The church of St James is Victorian red brick, of 1887, by T Lewis and Son of Newcastle. It is large but with a bellcote only and lancet windows. It is known as the last resting place of James Brindley (1716-1772), the great canal engineer, who is buried in the churchyard to the south of the east wall of the church. Brindley had no formal education and an apprenticeship to a millwright was all the training he ever received, but he had a natural aptitude verging on genius. He applied this to canal building, a new trade of which established engineers had no previous knowledge. He completed 365 miles of canal, and the enormous number of calculations involved in building bridges, tunnels, aqueducts, embankments and cuttings was all done in his head. He was almost illiterate and could barely sign his name.

The Grammar School at Newchapel opened in 1714 and closed in 1877. The present Wesleyan Methodist Chapel opened in 1987. By 1968 the small, privately-run Newchapel Natural Science Centre and Astrological Observatory was in existence. It was founded by Michael Pace and hides behind a row of terraced houses. They have a small wind turbine to generate electricity. This whirls round at very high speed, so fast that it becomes invisible. It is not protected by a wire mesh cage and many of the homing pigeons of a local fancier have been killed by the blades. No-one showed sympathy for the concern I expressed: "Anyway, they provide a good dinner for a local fox," I was told.

Westcliffe, 1m SSE of Newchapel, is sometimes called Turnhurst and is a residential area. The present Westcliffe Hospital stands next to the site of the Wolstanton and Burslem Workhouse, of 1841, but was demolished in 1993. It was looked upon with horror by Arnold Bennett who called it 'Bastille' in his novels. The Claybourne Centre, opened in 1977, next to the Westcliffe Hospital. It was purpose-built for the care of dementia sufferers.

Packmoor, 0.25m E of Newchapel, is a substantial modern hamlet on high ground. In 1917, during the First World War, John Harold Rhodes (1891-1917) of Mellor Street, Packmoor, stormed an enemy pillbox and captured nine Germans single-handedly. He was awarded the Victoria Cross and the Croix de Guerre. Later, he was wounded in action and subsequently died. In civvy street he had been a miner.

Oxford, 0.75 SE of Newchapel, is a modern housing estate built on the site of the old hamlet of Wedgwood. It probably takes its name from the long-gone Oxford Colliery.

NEWCHURCH *6m W of Burton on Trent*
Newchurch is a tiny place, with a church and a telephone box, on the A515 between Yoxall and Sudbury. Christ Church of 1809 is brick and was reputedly built for disafforested parishioners after the enclosure of the forest. It was altered in 1880. There are monuments to the Bass brewing family and one of their old homes, Byrkley Lodge, now demolished, is depicted in a stained glass window. Just to the north-east of Newchurch is Tatenhill Airfield, an old wartime

aerodrome now used by private fliers. The entrance is off the B5234. (Tatenhill village is 4m SE.) A farm at Newchurch breeds guinea pigs for vivesection.

Byrkley Lodge, 1m ENE of Newchurch, was a medieval hunting lodge and former home of the Bass family. It was demolished in 1952 and in 1986 Byrkley Park, a garden centre, was developed on the site. The large parkland still exists.

NEWTOWN *2m SW of Longnor*

It lies in the Peak District National Park. The farms around here have delightful names, such as Boarsgrove, Badger's Croft, Oakenclough Hall and Shining Ford. There are two churches at Newtown: the Methodist chapel of 1821 with a Georgian facade, and an Anglican church of 1837 with a battlemented bellcote and good views over the moors. There is also a public telephone box.

NEW INVENTION *1.5m N of Willenhall.*

New Invention lies mid-way between Wednesfield and Bloxwich. Neither neighbour is anxious to claim it. In fact that honour goes to Walsall who have installed one of their nasty, black-painted wooden huts called Neighbourhood Offices in the functional, flat-roofed shopping centre. Opposite stands the unlovely, ragamuffin works of Squire Padlocks, established in 1780. New Invention stands around a busy crossroads, and is essentially a residential area. What the New Invention was no-one knows, or, it seems, cares. The northern boundary is Sneyd Lane, a pleasant wooded avenue with pleasant modern houses.

NORBURY *3.5m NE of Newport*

Norbury lies just off the A519, Newport to Eccleshall road, in gently rolling country. The village is compact and there are some attractive cottages and a few farms.

The church of St Peter has a solid Georgian, Gothic, brick tower of 1759 and a fine nave and chancel in one of the early 14th Century. The east window of the chancel was designed by Miss C S Burne, the folklorist, in 1873. The monuments include the effigy of a cross-legged knight (meaning he had been on a crusade), believed to have been either Ralph Butcher, died about 1310, or Ralph Butcher, died 1342; several unknown effigies; Lady Hawys Botiller, late 14th Century; Ralph Botiller; and a wall monument to Rupert Skrymsher, whose father was Adjutant General to Prince Rupert.

Richard Barnfield (1574-1627) was baptized at Norbury and was probably born at Norbury Manor. He was a poet of high standing and for long two of his pieces were attributed to William Shakespeare. (See Darlaston near Stone.)

Norbury is best known for the canal junction that lies 1m SE of the village. It is a junction no longer, the Newport Canal being long disused and the locks concreted over, but **Norbury Junction** is still a busy place. A holiday hire boat company operates from here and there is a British Waterways Maintenance Yard. It is a place of great character with a small inland dock, a chandlers, a pub and a few cottages.

The road to Gnosall from here passes through two tunnels under the huge embankment that carries the canal.

Just a short walk from Norbury Junction are the remains of the once spectacular Norbury Manor (SJ 797233). The house platform has survived. It is an irregular quadrangle, with sides averaging 50 yards in length, and the sandstone retaining walls are surrounded by a moat fed by a stream. The first house on this site was built by Ralph Butler in about 1300. It passed to the Skrymshers in 1521 and to the Ansons (of Shugborough) in 1775. The manor fell into decay and was demolished in 1838 when a new house was built a few yards to the south.

Half-a-mile north-east of Norbury Junction is the southern entrance to the 1.25 mile **Grub Street** canal cutting. The settlement of Grub Street lies on both sides of the Shropshire Union. The deep cutting gave Thomas Telford great problems because the sandstone kept slipping into the trench. The work took from 1829 to 1834.

Loynton Hall (House), 0.75m NW of Norbury, is a red brick house of three storeys, five bays, a doorway with columns and a pediment of about 1800. It was the home of the Higgins family and then of the Burnes; Charlotte Burne, the folklorist, was of this family but was born at Moreton, Gnosall.

Loynton Moss is a much-reduced area of old marshland, of about 32 acres, now in the care of the Staffordshire Wildlife Trust. It lies adjacent to the Shropshire Union Canal. The author used to walk his dogs by Loynton Moss. It is a wild place with small, murky pools and small, woebegone trees and brushwood. Most of this moss area is the remnant of a substantial pool called Blakemore, which seems to have been the uppermost of several pools in the watercourse that supplied Norbury Mill, 1.25m SSE of Loyton Moss.

Moss Pool, a former lake, 0.5m SW of Norbury church, and mentioned by Dr Plot as the 'old Peewit Pool' in the 17th Century, had been drained and lost by the mid-20th Century.

There is a burial mound 1.25m NNE of Norbury village church; and a square moat, 0.25m NNE of Norbury Junction, in a wood adjacent to the track that leads on to Knightley Grange.

Weston Jones, 1.5m WNW of Norbury, is a rural hamlet to the east of the Lonco Brook. The settlement lies on the western boundary of Norbury parish, hence 'West-town'; John de Weston held the manor in 1316. Weston Jones Mill lies on the Lonco Brook, 0.5m W of the hamlet. Gregory, 0.25m NE of Weston Jones, is a flat-topped, oval mound, 180 feet by 150 feet and eight feet high, which stands near a stream. Its origin is debated: it could be either a burial mound or the motte of a local 12th Century Norman lord.

NORTON CANES *2m NW of Brownhlls and 3m SE of Cannock*
The name Norton means 'north settlement' and Canes could be a corruption of Cannock. In the 13th Century it was recorded as Norton super le Canock. However, Canes might be from Gains, as in Gains Brook and Gains Lane which are local names. These could be corruptions of Cahaines in Normandy and have come here as the name of a local unrecorded lord.

In 1086 the settlement belonged to the Bishop of Chester, as part of his Lichfield estate, but was described as waste, that is to say no-one lived there and the land was uncultivated. The village stands on rising ground just north of Watling Street (A5), with good views over countryside blighted by old collieries and industrial housing.

The church of St James has parts of 1832 but was rebuilt in 1888 after a fire. It is of dirty black stone with a red tiled roof. There are monuments to the Fowke and Hussey families of Little Wyrley Hall, which stands 1.25m S of Norton Canes.

The Hall is a Tudor house that has been encased in brick. A long service wing was added to the west about 1660 and extended again on the east side in 1691 It has good gables and dormer windows, some of which date from 1820, as does the staircase and stairwell with balconies below the cupola. The door furniture of the first-floor rooms is highly ornate and is of 1691. With only one exception ownership of the manor of Little Wyrley has passed by inheritance from Norman times to the present.

In 1691 Dr Phineas Fowke inherited the manor and the current owner Mrs Frank Wallace is directly descended from him. Her husband was a big game hunter and had a huge collection of trophies. He was also an artist and an author, somewhat more worthy occupations.

Little Wyrley was surrounded by coal mines, a railway and a canal. Only the canal, a spur of the Essington and Wyrley Canal, remains, but within a mile or so in every direction the housing estates are watching, with avaricious eyes. One mile to the east of Norton Canes is the huge Chasewater reservoir, a Railway Museum and a Raceway. Chasewater is used for many water sports - speed boat racing, sailing, canoeing, water skiing and sail-boarding.

NORTON IN THE MOORS *1.5m NE of Burslem*
Today it is a suburban area of Burslem and lies astride the A5051, Burslem to Endon road. Norton means 'north settlement'. In medieval times it developed as a crossroads settlement. Coal was mined here from at least 1598. The Camp Meeting held at Norton by the Primitive Methodists in 1807 led to Hugh Bourne and his brother, James, being expelled from the Wesleyan Methodists. Anthea Turner, the TV presenter, was born in Norton in the Moors in 1960. At Norton Green, 0.75m NE of Norton in the Moors, the firm of T Cope made the massive chains that support the Menai Suspension Bridge (1826).

Bemersley Green, 1.5m N of Norton-in-the Moors, is a hamlet on a ridge. The name is from the Anglo-Saxon and means 'the trumpeter's clearing in the wood'. Hugh Bourne (1772-1852), the co-founder of Primitive Methodism, was born at Ford Hayes but from the age of 16 lived at Bemersley Farm. It was from here that he organized his movement and where he set up his printing press. He died at Bemersley Green and was buried at Englesea Brook, Barthomley, Cheshire. (See also Mow Cop.)

Whitfield, 1m NNW of Norton, is known for its coal mine, the Chatterley Whitfield Colliery. The lease on the Whitfield Colliery was acquired by the Chatterley family in 1872. There was a disaster here in 1881 and 25 miners died. In 1977 the mine closed and became a mining museum, the first in Britain, but this closed in 1993. However, the buildings and winding gear are now in the care of English Heritage and are listed for preservation. (Note: Chatterley, the place, is just to the west of Tunstall and is an area rather than a settlement. It has nothing to do with the Chatterley Whitfield Colliery.)

O

OAKAMOOR *2.5m ENE of Cheadle*
Oakamoor is in the lovely Churnet valley, 2m NW of Alton, from which it can be reached by a lane that runs along the banks of the river. The village is a most

pleasant place, surrounded by woods and steep hillsides. There is a pub, a Post Office and long walks by the river. Strange to think that until recently there was a factory and a railway here. In fact, there was industry at Oakamoor from at least 1572 when George, Earl of Shrewsbury, built an iron refining forge. This had ceased production by 1590 but in 1592 Sir Francis Willoughby built a furnace and a forge, selling the iron produced at Newcastle-under-Lyme and Leek amongst other places. By 1692 there was a slitting mill in the valley and in 1717 a forge is recorded as being here. Most of these forges and furnaces are believed to have been in the vicinity of Ordnance Survey map ref SK 053452. In 1777 a tinplate works was built at Oakamoor, the only such 18th Century mill in Staffordshire. It consisted of a water-driven rolling mill, in which iron bars were rolled into sheets, and a tinhouse where the sheets were coated in tin by being dipped into a series of baths. The mill had probably ceased tin production by 1800 and converted to copper manufacture. Thomas Boulton took over the Patten & Co metal rolling mills in the early 19th century and produced cable and tubes amongst other things. In 1857 the copper wire for the first transatlantic underwater communications' cable between Valencia and Newfoundland was made at Oakamoor. Sad to say, it broke several times. The first successful cable was laid seven years later in 1864. The Oakamoor works (SK 053446) were closed in 1962 and the building demolished. Production was then concentrated in the company's Froghall works, three miles north-west, which had been opened in 1890. The firm of Thomas Bolton and Sons is still very much in business there. In 1868 the firm owned a silk mill in Oakamoor but little is known about this works. The attractive barge-boarded and gabled house called Lightoakes was home to one of the Bolton brothers. The other lived at the gabled, neo-Jacobean Moor Court. There is a Bolton Memorial chapel of 1878 and a Free Church designed by Edward Clarke. The church of Holy Trinity is of 1832, by J P Pritchett, and is built on very steep ground. An unusual feature are the three-light, straight-headed, Perpendicular windows. (See Hawksmoor.)

OFFLEYBROOK *See Offley*

OFFLEY HAY *See Offley*

OFFLEY MARSH *See Offley*

OFFLEY ROCK *See Offley*

OFFLEY *3.25m W of Eccleshall*
Offley is an Anglo-Saxon name and probably means Offa's field. About 1.75m N of High Offley are Bishop's Offley, Offleyrock, Offleymarsh, Offleybrook, and Offley Hay. Whether this Offa was the great King himself, a relation or simply an Anglo-Saxon with the same name, we shall probably never know. Many of the place names in this area are of Anglo-Saxon origin: Horsley, 'Horsa's farm'; Tunstall, 'Tuna's nook'; Garmelow, 'Garma's grave'; and Copmere, 'Coppa's lake'. The brook called Lonco, like most river names, is probably an earlier Celtic name.

High Offley lies on a hill about 1m NW of Woodseaves, which is on the Eccleshall to Newport road. When approached from the west it has the appearance of a medieval hill town, with the church a landmark for several miles around. The village is small and well preserved. We could see no new housing, only farms, brick cottages, the old manor house, the Royal Oak (now closed and converted to a house) and a school (also now converted to a dwelling).

The medieval church of St Mary has a porch dated at about 1200. Most of the rest of the building is of the 12th and 13th Centuries, except for the upper part of the tower which was rebuilt in 1667. Inside there are monuments to the Skrymsher family. On a hill to the south of the churchyard at High Offley Roman finds have been made including, in large numbers, tiles, armour and pottery. These are reported by Dr Plot. They probably mark the site of a villa or small settlement, though Dr Plot suggests that High Offley may be the location of the lost Roman town of Mediolanum.

The characterful Manor House has looked faded and run down for many years now. It is built of rendered red brick with three clusters of tall chimneys with three in each group. The porch has a crusader cross slit window and unusual lintels. As we write (2004) the house is being renovated and the large red brick outbuilding to its left has been converted to a terrace of homes.

Grub Street lies 0.5m S of High Offley. The hamlet clusters around the bridge that carries the Offley to Norbury road over the Shropshire Union Canal, which emerges from a deep, wooded cutting here. This stretch of the canal is well known to both boatmen and fishermen.

The northern Offleys are set in most attractive country - rolling, wooded and well-watered. The River Sow is dammed in several places creating small lakes, the largest of which is Copmere, near Eccleshall. There is a maze of lanes joining scattered cottages, a feature of late medieval forest clearance.

Bishop's Offley would have belonged to the Lichfield Cathedral estate which, for some years after the Norman Conquest, was transferred to Chester. Once again we have to report that the pub has recently closed and is being converted to a dwelling. There is a garage but no other facilities yet this is a most charming village with mature houses and farms, one with a yard full of very happy free-range chickens.

Offley Marsh, 0.25m SE of Bishop's Offley, is a small scattered settlement centred on a triangle of lanes. There are brick and stucco cottages and some mature houses and farms, but it is considered locally to be a part of Bishop's Offley. Here you will find the Bishop's Offley Primitive Methodist Chapel of 1875, a neat and well kept building of red brick with blue brick dressings and round-headed windows. Also at Offley Marsh is the Bishop's Offley Millennium Green 2000. This is actually a field which is kept mown and has been provided with a bench, a megalith and a handful of newly planted trees. It measures about 100 yards by 50 yards. The only non-agricultural industry we found at Offley Marsh was Eabon Stoneware, manufacturers of garden ornaments, who operate from a motley collection of wood and block sheds.

At Offley Marsh there is a substantial area of unfenced, common-like scrub woodland and disturbed ground full of humps and hollows, part of which is marshy with standing pools. Deep drainage ditches proclaim the land hereabouts to be ill-drained.

At **Offleybrook,** on the lovely lane to Outlands, is a working mill (SJ 782301) which is not marked on the 125 inch Ordnance Survey map. It is used to grind and mix animal foods and the owner installed a new waterwheel about 12 years ago. The old one is still in place but has not been used for many years. The wheels cannot be seen from the road.

At **Offley Hay** is the delightfully positioned Walkmill House with lawns that run down to the large mill pool. On the opposite side of the road is a derelict corn mill with most of the original machinery. Sadly, it has been badly neglected and the roof and floors have collapsed. The machinery lies all-a-jumble but there are plans to restore it. Adjacent to the mill is a long, low, single-storey brick building. This was part of the mill which, though originally used to grind corn, became a fulling mill. In this building was a long table on which was placed urine-soaked woollen cloth, which was then literally walked on to remove the oils from the wool. In an adjacent farmyard there was a pit with stone steps which contained the urine, and a series of rods above on which were hung the cloth pieces to be soaked. The farm building near the 'T junction is partly of stone, and this is believed to be the remains of an earlier mill, possibly the one known to have been here in the 15th Century. The long, low shed previously mentioned has stone lower parts and was probably also part of the earlier mill. Above the doorway to the shed is a stone lintel, which seems to have been inserted after the building had been completed. This lintel came from Gerard's Bromley Hall, the magnificent stone house described by Dr Plot as one of the finest in the county. On the lintel are the initials 'J. D.' and the date 1830. 'J. D.' is Josiah Deakin who used to live at Walkmill House, and 1830 is probably the date he inserted the lintel into the fulling shed. In Offley Hay there is a sycamore tree, which is said to have grown from the stake that was driven through the body of a giant in an attempt to keep him down.

Between Bishop's Offley and High Offley is the hamlet of **Tunstall**. Here is a farm house called The Tunstalls which catches the eye. It is of brick, painted white, and has four bay, two storeys and a hipped roof, as well as two tall 'spider' trees. From here there is a very good view to High Offley on its hill.

OFFLOW

Offlow was one of the five Hundreds of Staffordshire. It covered the south-east of the county and took its name from a burial mound near Whitehouse Farm at SK 123059, which is 1.75m NW of Weeford. This grave has always been thought to be that of a notable person, who is as yet unknown. The mound has all but been ploughed out.

OKEOVER *1.5m NW of Ashbourne*

Two miles south of the Dove Dale gorge the River Dove flows in a broader valley. On its western bank the oak trees of Okeover Park still stand in their 200-acre park, as they and their forebears have stood for centuries, longer even than the lords of Okeover Hall and they have been there in unbroken line for 800 years. The Okeovers of Okeover (the family took its name from the manor) are one of very few families in the country to have maintained a presence at their ancestral home from early Norman times to the present day. The estate was passed from eldest son to eldest son until 1955 when Mr Haughton Ealdred Okeover died without having produced a male heir. However, Mr Okeover's nephew, Sir Ian Walker-Okeover, succeeded to the property and so the family presence continues.

There was a village here from before Domesday when the manor was held by Burton Abbey. Today the church and Hall stand all alone, but at SK 158482 there are signs of a medieval village which was deserted before the 16th Century. In about 1100 the manor went to Orm who changed his name to Okeover. The first Hall was a moated manor house, possibly the one depicted by Dr Plot in his 'Natural History of Staffordshire' (1686), though that may have replaced an even earlier house. In 1745 Leak Okeover started to rebuild the Hall in brick but his plans were never fulfilled. He built the nine-bay west wing, with its handsomely carved pediment, the north wall of the east wing and the imposing stable block, but only made a start on the higher south range and the rest of the east wing. These were finished 200 years later by Marshall Sisson (between 1953-60), who restored and completed the house in the fashion intended by Leak Okeover. Inside are some good plastered ceilings and a fine wrought-iron staircase rail. There are three sets of iron gates - the outer (with obelisks) and inner entrance gates and those between the house and the church.

In the garden is The Temple of Pomona, inside which is a white marble statue by Giuseppe Gorganzoli of a young girl with a rosebud at her breast called The Dawn of Love. There is also a lavatory called the Necessary House with an arched entrance and a broken pediment. In the Park is an old tree called the 'Wishing Oak', which has a girth of some 30 feet.

The medieval church of All Saints stands a mere 30 yards or so from the Hall. The tower is Perpendicular but the rest is Decorated with a restoration by Sir George Gilbert Scott in 1856-8. In the chancel window are figures and fragments of the original 14th Century stained glass. The Victorian glass in the nave is by William Warrington. There are monuments to Humphrey Okeover, died 1538; Leak Okeover, died 1765, and his wife Mary, died 1764, by Joseph Wilton, which are especially beautiful; and a palimpest (a brass plate reused by engraving on the back) of the wife of William Lord Zouch, of about 1447.

OLDBURY *3m ESE of Dudley*

Oldbury has been a bit of a wanderer. It was first a detached part of Worcestershire, then of Shropshire and is now part of the West Midlands. Even today the town is something of a secret. To many it is the **Birchley Roundabout** on the Birmingham-Wolverhampton New Road, an island noted for the electricity sub-station so discreetly set at its centre. To others it is Exit 2 on the M5 motorway, which here has taken to walking on stilts. In fact the settlement lies a mile to the north on a low hill, site of the prehistoric fort of its name. The old fort is long gone, of course. Every square foot hereabouts has either been dug up or built upon, often several times.

In recent years the town centre has been almost completely redeveloped. Around a central island stand car parks, a bus station and a Sainsbury's 'hypermarket'. This is constructed of a curious mixture of red brick and cream tiles with an ogee capped tower. The Victorian red brick library, now a Voluntary Services Centre, clings on to one corner of the new edifice. In a word, the town centre is bleak, as bleak as the quarry-ravaged Rowley Hills that dominate the horizon to the west. In about 1992 a new office complex arose, huge and steel-framed, to be the future administrative centre for the Sandwell Metropolitan Council.

Only Birmingham Street has been spared. Small, traditional shops in great variety tumble down the hill, past the almost handsome Lloyds Bank building and the ghastly shack that houses the Co-op Funeral Services office; past the red brick of Christ Church, set in its delightful Georgian square complete with lawns and trees; past the tall, narrow house of another undertaker, to Hill's End. Here, facing the new ring road, are the new police station and magistrates' courts, low, squat and barracks-like. Behind them is a vista of skinny chimneys belching white fumes, even on a Sunday. Almost all the terraced houses have gone at Oldbury, replaced by pleasant, modern courts. The substantial red brick Methodist Church (Wesley 1853) and a few large 19th Century warehouses still stand but one wonders for how much longer.

An industrial estate with patches of scrub wasteland lines the road from the town centre to the Birmingham New Road. There is a curious mixture of enterprises - ToysRus, Judd Papers etc - but it is the chemical industries that have the most notable presence. The huge British Industrial Plastics Company was originally set up in 1894 to produce cyanide for use in extracting gold from low grade ore. Another major company founded in Oldbury is Accles & Pollock, established in 1902. They are a leading producer of tubes.

One of their directors was Walter Hackett CBE (1874-1964) who, under the nom de plume of Khanyer Whackett, wrote of topical events in verse and collected local stories and humour. Indeed, Oldbury has its fair share of 'street literary credits'. The eponymous hero of the folksong 'Jolly Joe the Collier's Son' (recorded by the Black Country Three) was born in Oldbury, and then there is the 'Oldbury Chant' (a local version of a Music Hall poisoning song); 'The Ol'bury Mon' and 'The Oldbury Wake and Races' (both by W. Morgan 1909); and 'Old Sam' (Peter Dodds).

One mile south of Oldbury town centre is Langley. At **Langley Green** there is still an actual green. If it were not for the looming sheds and chimneys of Albright and Wilson one could think this a country place, complete with pub (the Queen's Head), trees and terraced cottages. Just up the road is Holts famous pub and brewery: very Victorian, very cared for and very nice indeed. Opposite, are the Langley Maltings, a large brick building with a distinctive roofline. The canal and old forge and furnace buildings give the area great character.

From the residential area of **Rood End** (a rood is a cross of crucifixion) the road to Oldbury is called **Tat Bank**. Here, from the bridge over the canal, there are good views across the railway marshalling yards and the large British Industrial Plastics factory (already mentioned).

North-east of the town centre the road to Tipton follows the canal into **Brade's Village**. Here there are some well-fenced allotments, complete with a scarecrow who sports an industrial protective helmet; a wall of furnace slag; the Blakeley Special School; Brade's Hall Farm and Public Open Space; locks on the canal; blocks of plain, brick modern houses playing hide and seek amongst the landscaped mounds of industrial waste; and the Oldbury Congregational Church with a strange winged roof.

If you leave Brade's Village down Brade's Road and follow it to its junction with the Birmingham New Road you will have passed through the industrial half of **Round's Green,** which is dominated by the Babcock Robey works. You get a good view of it as you await your turn to negotiate the lethal entrance on to the New Road. Residential Round's Green lies on the other side of the road, along Newbury Lane, the entrance to which is watched over by the Methodist Church. There is a Leisure Centre, where Oldbury Football Club plays, the White Horse, the light grey mud of landscaped spoil mounds being coaxed into open greens, allotments, a couple of shops, semis and a tower block. Oldbury has a station but, somewhat misleadingly, it is called Sandwell and Dudley. More than one stranger has been not at all pleased to find that Sandwell really means West Bromwich and is more than a mile to the north, and that Dudley is three miles to the west.

Like Tipton, Oldbury is virtually an island, surrounded almost entirely by canals. An area of pools and canals at **Tiford** was landscaped in the 1970s. This interesting and attractive spot is approached off the Birmingham New Road at the New Navigation Inn, close to its junction with the M5. Finally, we must mention the Music Hail artist Jack Judge (1872-1938) who was born at Oldbury. He was the author (though this is not undisputed) of 'It's a Long Way to Tipperary'. He was certainly the first to perform this famous song - on 31st January 1912 at Stalybridge, Cheshire. He had a fishmonger's shop at Low Town, and died at 30 Harold Road, **Whiteheath Gate**, 1m SSW of Oldbury, in 1938. His mortal remains lie in Rood End Cemetery.

OLD HILL *2.5m SSE of Dudley*

If there is a centre to Old Hill it lies around the offset cross of the A459 and the A4100. Here there are car parks, red brick roads, new houses, old shops, an area of waste land, a burnt-out restaurant and a garish red market hall. The church, with its strong tower, was once red but the sandstone is now black and hugged around with holly bushes. There are schools, a low-roofed health centre, several Nonconformist Chapels, the Plaza Bingo Hall, some rows of well-kept Victorian terraced houses, tall blocks of flats and a clockmaker called Marie Micklehurst, established 1969.

The settlement lies in a broad valley, almost a bowl. Which of the nearby slopes is the original hill of the place name is anybody's guess. To confuse the matter, the locals used to call the settlement Old Dell - a more logical name. To the west the Dudley Canal meanders through industrial estates; to the south are the old Council offices and the imaginatively named Beauty Bank. On the A459, Halesowen Road, is the Rose and Crown pub, the core of which was the home of Stan Edge. Mr Edge worked as a draughtsman at the Austin Motor Works in Longbridge, Birmingham. He and Herbert Austin designed the legendary Austin Seven, first produced in 1922.

Opposite the Rose and Crown is **Haden Hill Park**. This was for long the home of the Haudene family. In 1876 this family died out with the passing of its last member, an elderly spinster. In recent times the 16th Century Hall has been renovated and in 1922 the landscaped park, which falls away down the hill in the direction of Halesowen, became a public amenity area.

Haden Hall has a ghost, the distraught spirit of a girl called Elaine who fell in love with a young priest from Halesowen Abbey. The couple eloped but were caught and as punishment were imprisoned in the tunnel that reputedly led from Haden Hall to the monastery. The entrances to the tunnel were bricked up and they were left to die. Adjacent to the Hall is Haden Hill House, of 1878, and near that is an artificial ski slope. The Haden Hill Leisure Centre, complete with swimming pool and gymnasium, faces Bans Road. Ban is from the Ban family who married into the Haden family.

In Hayseech Road is a group of restored industrial buildings called the Gun Barrel Industrial Centre. This developed around a farmhouse of 1770. The gun barrel factory itself is dated at 1801.

In 1919 an Old Hill nut and bolt manufacturer and cinema owner, the handsomely named Benjamin Priest, made a feature film of 'Bladys of the Stewponey', from the novel by Sabine Baring-Gould. He filmed in and around Kinver. Alas, but for a few frames, the epic is no more. But the firm of Benjamin Priest and Sons soldiers on, still making nuts and bolts.

Bowling Green adjoins Old Hill to the north-west. It is a residential area with its fair share of council houses. Pubs include The Bunch of Bluebells and The Woodman. The latter is well known for its folk club. At the back there is a small bowling green. The Guild Factory Shop (glass products) demands attention - a big shed with a red-framed, dark glass front.

On the other side of the Halesowen Road is **Mouse Sweet**, such a delightful name that the ordinary houses and works that it addresses can only come as a disappointment. Down Saltwells Road are the **Dudley Wood** residential estates. Hidden behind these is the Greyhound Stadium, home to the Cradley Heathens Speedway Club. This area is also called Newtown.

Cherry Orchard adjoins Old Hill centre to the south-east. It is a mixed residential-industrial area. Waterfall Lane Industrial Estate, Temple Meadow School, Beauty Bank and Cherry Orchard Drive speak of the influence of the landscaped gardens of Haden Hill, a little to the south.

ONECOTE *8m NNE of Cheadle*

Onecote lies on the B5053 between Cheadle and Longnor. It is a tiny place in the high moorlands on the banks of the River Hamps, which here is little more than a stream. Our memory of the place is of the colourful sunshades in the riverside garden of the Jervis Arms. The name means something like 'the solitary cottage'. To the north is Butterton Moor. To the east is Grindon Moor, stone wall country. The few trees here remind us that bleak though it may be in winter, these hills were once forest-clad.

The church of St Luke is of 1753-5. It has a tower, a nave and a low chancel with a Venetian east window. At the west end is a huge Commandment Board with painted figures. Onecote Grange, 0.25m NW of Onecote, stands at the confluence of the River Hamps and the Onecote Brook. The present house dates from 1884 but stands on or near the site of a grange of Croxden Abbey, which existed from at least 1223.

Folk-tales have lingered long in the Moorlands. One tells of an Onecote farmer who was returning from Leek market after nightfall when he was plucked from the ground by a headless horseman. He was taken for a terrifying ride with the horse flying through the air, leaping not just over hedges, but whole fields. He was deposited near his home and died a few days later. Another farmer saw the phantom horseman and though he lived, his horse and dog died shortly after. The horseman is said to be one of four evil spirits cast out of heaven to await the 'crack of doom'.

Onecote Lane End, 1m WNW of Onecote, is a mid-17th Century house which has a footnote in history. In 1844 Joseph Cook, the occupier of the house, went to Chancery court in an attempt to obtain the £300 bequeathed to him by his father. The case became protracted and Cook's solicitor, William Challinor of Pickwood Hall (0.5m SE of Leek), wrote a pamphlet based on this case urging Chancery reform. He sent a copy to Charles Dickens, who used it as the basis of the case of Gridley in chapter 15 of 'Bleak House'.

Bottom House, 1.5m SSW of Onecote, is a crossroads' hamlet in a broad valley with sheep in the fields and stone walls in disrepair. The settlement consists of a couple of cottages, the Standing Stone Farm and a pub. It takes its name from a house of about 1680, formerly called Botham House. Botham House Inn, probably the white rendered inn now called the Old Green Man, was where the counterfeiters George and Thomas Fearne brought their forged notes. From here they were taken on the turnpike road to Birmingham. The Fearnes were caught by Joseph Nadin, a noted thief-catcher, and George Fearne was hanged at Stafford Gaol in 1801.

Fair View is a house 1.5m S of Onecote and was the home of the admirable but eccentric Tunstall Sneyd. He was of the leading county family but married against his father's wishes and was disinherited. Tunstall Sneyd was interested in

Druidism and built a temple in the garden; he had two genuine Egyptian mummies in a chapel in the house. During the Second World War he built a wall around the grounds, complete with towers and battlements in case of invasion by the Germans.

ONNELY *1.5m SW of Madeley*
It is a small village on the road between Madeley and Woore. In 1998 animal rights' activists broke into the Kelbain Farm premises and released some 2,500 mink which were being bred for their fur.

To many Onnely means the Wheatsheaf Inn, the big white pub on the main road. However, most of the settlement lies on a back lane. It has pleasant houses, both old and new, and a small, derelict stable-cum-workshop that the owners have decided should be allowed to sleep peacefully in its mellow-brick old age. But the Victorian village school is a working pensioner and is now the Village Hall. For its sins it is stuck on the fast main road.

By way of contrast, a well-endowed upstart has arisen on the north side of the road on the way to Woore. This is a brick dwelling of country house proportions, that stands on a rise well behind a high brick wall. Nearby are the sheds of TT Pumps

ORGREAVE *1.5m WNW of Alrewas*
Orgreave is a tiny, red brick hamlet straggling along the A513, in the very flat country of the Trent valley, between King's Bromley and Alrewas, near Lichfield. The Hall was once the home of the poet Samuel Winter (died 1847). It was last privately owned by Colonel Harrison and is now an old peoples' home. The main approach is along a wide, double avenue of lime trees - a nice touch because the 'greave' element of the place name is from the Anglo-Saxon for grove. (The medieval name was Ordegrave.) It is a small, 'L'-shaped house, built about 1668, with additions over the following 60 years and some Victorian embellishment. The south and north fronts are in different styles. It has a fine door case with fluted Corinthian pilasters and a swan's-neck pediment. There is an early 18th Century stable block.

Just down the road, travelling east, is a grim spectre indeed, namely the British Gas Alrewas Compressor Station. Several acres of blue and grey sheds, pipes and pumps are protected by floodlights, video cameras, and two rows of security fencing with a 'killing zone' between them. All this was designed to deter more than adventurous schoolboys. It really is quite a fortress.

At Lupin Farm farmer Arthur Tipper has a most attractive dog kennel which he had made for his dog Jessie. It is a converted 50-gallon whisky barrel with a thatched roof, the work of master thatcher Dave Wood. (For a photograph see Midlands Digest, Book 4 page 39)

OULTON *1.25m NNE of Stone, which is 7m N of Stafford*
An unassuming but most pleasant village which has not been helped by the 20th Century houses; neither, however, has it been ruined. It lies on a hill, just to the west of the delightful Moddershall Valley.

At the heart of the settlement is St Mary's Abbey, which is a Benedictine convent for nuns. It was founded in Ghent in the 17th Century 'for young English Ladies of Catholic families' and moved to England in 1794. The Abbey buildings are based around an early 18th Century brick house, which was remodelled in 1822. In 1835 it was bought by the Duke of Sutherland, who lived here for three years whilst alterations were being made to Trentham Hall. In 1938 it became a private asylum and in 1853 it was bought by the Benedictine nuns. In 1854 the chapel was built by E W Pugin, who was only 19 years old at the time and had just taken over his famous father's business. It is large and the style is Decorated. Inside is a good iron screen. The chapter house, sacristy and presbytery are all of 1892.

The church of St John the Evangelist lies on the edge of the village, down a lane that leads on to the Moddershall Valley. It is rock-faced, with bellcote and lancet windows, and was designed by R Scrivener and Son (1894). Old Hall is a sandstone house built in 1613. Past residents include Lord Kitchener's brother and two local pottery families, the Sebhouses and the Woods.

In 1795 a large hoard of Anglo-Saxon treasure was found by a gardener in the grounds of the Abbey but it was not properly recorded and disappeared amongst the local population. Also found at Oulton was a very rare Roman die used for stamping metalwork such as armour. In later times the village had a reputation as a centre for cock-fighting.

At **Oulton Cross**, 0.5m. SW of Oulton, there was a plague cross and a large sandstone trough used for washing.

The **Downs Banks**, 0.75m NW of Oulton, are sometimes called Barlaston Downs. This is high moorland which was once common land and was then enclosed. In 1950 it was given to the National Trust by Joules Brewery. Hops were once grown on the lower land. In the past Potteries' people came here for picnics and walks.

Kibblestone, 0.5m NE of Oulton, is a tiny fragmented settlement but was probably somewhat larger, being deserted in the 18th Century. In 1284 Roesia Trussell held Kibblestone from the Barony of Wem, on condition that she found one soldier armed with a bow and arrows to serve for eight days at Tyreley Castle, near Market Drayton. In 1868 (some say 1876) Richard Pine Copeland, of the Spode pottery family, came to Kibblestone. He built Kibblestone Hall, a six-bay mansion complete with ballroom, around the nucleus of a farmhouse.

Ronald Copeland was born here in 1884. He was a friend of Lord Baden Powell and formed one of the first scout groups in the country at Oulton. He also leased land on his picturesque estate for a permanent camp site. This continues, and is famous throughout the world. It is situated in a wooded valley with several permanent brick and stone buildings, rocky outcrops, a plunge pool, flowery dells and stands of specimen trees. In 1935 Ronald's mother, Emily, died and the Hall remained empty until it was demolished in 1954. However, the family is still resident on the estate; Spencer Copeland lives at Kibblestone Park, close by the site of the old Hall.

P

PATSHULL *2m S of Albrighton, which is 8m W of Wolverhampton*
Some large, old country houses have an air of melancholy. They were designed for perfect summer evenings - any self respecting squire went abroad for the winter - to be filled with light and laughter, to be the setting for the hunt ball and the weekend retreat of visiting gentry. When they become hotels, homes for the

elderly or company headquarters, and accumulate cheap and unsympathetic satellite buildings, they almost physically wilt. Although one regrets the demolition of so many of our great houses one can be consoled by remembering that there are fates worse than death.

Patshull Hall, a large rambling place, was owned first by the Astleys, then the Pigots (who bought it on the proceeds of the sale of the famous Pigot diamond) and then by the Earls of Dartmouth. During the First world War it became an Orthopaedic Hospital. In about 1990 it was sold to a developer, who sold it on again, and in recent years it was partly renovated as a private house.

The Hall was built about 1750 by James Gibbs for Sir John Astley, 2nd Baronet, and altered and enlarged in the 1880s for the 5th Earl of Dartmouth by William Burn. The approach was designed to impress - gate posts, a forecourt with two pedimented gateways, a substantial gatehouse of five bays with giant pilasters, and an archway with Tuscan columns and a central cupola. Beyond all this is a second forecourt with two arches. The front facade is of seven bays with a three-bay pediment and angle towers. The land falls away from the front of the house and this has been terraced with steps down to the gardens.

The church lies some 200 yards from the house, in the direction of the lakes, down a track The lane is wooded, as is the churchyard. St Mary's was also designed by James Gibbs and built in 1743. In 1874 the north aisle was added. It is ashlar with a west tower, a Victorian cupola and a Venetian east window. There are monuments to Sir John Astley, died 1532; Sir Richard Astley, died 1687; Lord Pigot, died 1795; Sir Robert Pigot, died 1796; and others to the Earls of Dartmouth. In the churchyard, against the north wall, is the statue of a man in armour with long curly hair. This is thought to be the Duke of Monmouth, brought here from Sandwell Park (West Bromwich), the former home of the Earls of Dartmouth.

The Park is largely to the south of the Hall. In recent years it has been developed as a sports and leisure centre by a company that has no connection with the owners of the Hall. There is a golf course, a hotel and fishing in the Great Pool. The setting is splendid and the facilities excellent. The entrance to Patshull Pool, as it is known locally, is from the south, 1.5m W of the village of Pattingham

PATTINGHAM *7m W of Wolverhampton*
To the west of Wolverhampton is a new housing development at Perton. The old, small hamlet is now called Old Perton, which is near Wightwick Manor. From Old Perton a lane leads westwards along Perton Ridge to Pattingham. Here are many fine and very expensive modern villas, largely owned by the well-to-do of Wolverhampton.

Pattingham is an old village, once held by the great Anglo-Saxon thane, Earl Algar, and after 1066 by King William. It is a compact, nucleated settlement with some good Georgian houses, one of which is the large brick-built Vicarage It has five bays and three storeys with large angle pilasters and wooded gardens. The pub near the church is one of the most popular in the area.

In 1700 a Middle Bronze Age gold torc, said to be four feet long, was found north of the church in a field called Fantley Field. In 1780 a 'D'-shaped gold ingot – worth in those days £152 - was found in the parish by a ploughman. Pattingham once had the following but has them no more: a market, a fair, a bull ring, a gallows, a pillory, stocks, a pound and a curfew bell.

The church of St Chad has an Early English (restored) south arcade and a large tower of the 14th Century. The stained glass is by Kempe, and Kempe and Tower and the reredos is by Oldrid Scott. The church was restored by Gilbert Scott in 1871 and the spire dates from then. His son Oldrid later added the pinnacles and flying buttresses.

Nurton, 1.25m ENE of Pattingham, was recorded in 1312 as Noverton, probably from 'atten-overton' meaning 'upper town'. Nurton Hill, 0.5m NW of Nurton, is a small hamlet with a windmill, built in 1811, and is now part of a house called Mill House. The Staffordshire Way long-distance footpath crosses the Old Perton to Tettenhall road near Nurton. The country all around is pleasantly agricultural and the Shropshire border is only 0.5m to the west.

Westbeech, 0.75m NNE of Pattingham, developed on former common land from at least 1682 and there was a windmill here from then which operated into the early 19th Century.

PELSALL *3m N of Walsall centre*

It is a northern suburb of Walsall, full of modern houses and large, unexpected greens. The church of St Michael is a Commissioners' Church of 1843 with a tower of 1875 and a chancel of 1889. Pelsall is an Anglo-Saxon name. The 'all' ending means a 'nook', a secluded place in the country. How times change.

Today the settlement is bounded by the Wyrley and Essington Canal to the north and a railway line to the west. It lies on the edge of the Cannock coalfield, and from the 18th Century until recently iron and coal were mined here. Up to about 1880 nails were made by 'sweated' labour in small forges attached to the workers' cottages. At Moat Farm there is a moat, 168 feet by 80 feet. To the south of Pelsall, at Heath End, is a large sewage works.

High Bridge is 1m NNE of the church. The bridge carries the Lichfield Road over the canal. This is a no-man's land of scrub between the country pastures of the Ford Brook to the south, suburban Pelsall to the west, new industrial estates to the north and old industrial land to the east. Note the rather nice cast-iron sign post with cast-iron fingers at the crossroads, where the B4154 and the A4124 meet.

PENKHULL *0.75m SE of Stoke-on-Trent town*

Penkhull lies somewhat lost on high ground in the suburban sprawl between Stoke (the town) and Newcastle-under-Lyme. Actually, it is almost certainly older than both of them and even today the centre of the village retains its identity as a separate settlement.

Finds indicating the presence of early man at Penkhull include two Neolithic flint arrowheads; a Neolithic polished stone axe; another stone axe, Neolithic or Bronze-Age; and a small, Middle Bronze Age incense cup.

It is very likely that Penkhull originated as an Ancient British settlement and that its name derives from the British (Welsh) 'pencet', meaning 'end of the wood', and 'hyll', meaning hill, hence 'the hill at the end of the wood'

During and after the Civil War the Newcastle-under-Lyme manor court was held at what is now called the Greyhound Inn, Penkhull, because Newcastle Castle, the former Courthouse, was by then ruinous.

The Old Manor House was probably on the site now occupied by The Views, in Penkhull New Road. The Views was built in 1780 and was the birth place of Sir Oliver Lodge, the pioneer of wireless telegraphy and inventor of the spark plug for the internal combustion engine. Deaconess Smee is of the opinion that this was the site of an Anglo-Saxon fortress and that Lady Godiva was born here.

At the centre of the village is the church of St Thomas the Apostle, a substantial edifice of red sandstone, built in 1842, quite possibly on the site of an earlier church. It stands at one end of what can only be called the 'village green', a large lawned area with tall trees. The green and the church are encircled by a road, on the other side of which are some modern terraced houses, a variety of shops, two pubs – the Marquis of Granby, and the gabled Greyhound – and the Christian Fellowship Church, which has round-headed windows. Five roads meet at the church green. One of these is the charming little Garden Street, and lurking here are the remains of the red brick Penkhull Farm, guarded by high gates and barbed wire and in a sorry state.

Some 200 yards from the centre of the village, hidden away behind a block of four garages in Franklin Street, is the Nissen-hutted Pentecostal Church. The author, as a videographer, covered the wedding of two Zimbabwean doctors in this church The ceremony was memorable for its jollity and for the fact that it was conducted by four preachers, with music supplied by a rock group. It was raining outside but in this humble church was all the warmth and infectious lust for life of Africa.

Also hidden from view is the front facade of The Mount, a large, rambling, red brick mansion built for Josiah Spode II in 1803-4. The entrance today is from the rear, off Greatbatch Avenue. The front has seven bays and two storeys, with a big, stone-clad entrance bow with attached Roman Doric columns in the middle. In 1897 it became the North Staffordshire Deaf and Blind School and remained a Special School for 100 years. It is currently used as offices for the Education Department of Stoke City Council. Much of the garden has been built upon and all that is left now is a small area of woodland and two tennis courts.

In fact, the estate of The Mount was quite extensive and the present North Staffordshire Infirmary at Hartshill was built on part of it. Adjacent to The Mount is the brand new, sparkling Willows Primary School, a large brick building with blue-painted framework and a big white roof. It replaces two old Victorian schools and the cheerful chattering of little children at break times is both enormous and heart-warming.

PENKRIDGE *6m S of Stafford*

In Anglo-Saxon times the manor belonged to King Edward and after the Conquest it passed to King William. In 1086 it was a substantial village of at least 30 households and the manor also included land at Wolgarston, Drayton, Congreve, Dunston, Cowley and Beffcote. The name Penkridge is derived from the name of the river that flows through it - the River Penk - which is an ancient Celtic name.

Today there is a flourishing Wednesday general market and an important livestock market. In the late 17th and early 18th Centuries there was also a very famous horse-fair. In the 1720s Daniel Defoe attended it and said he thought that it was 'the greatest horse-fair in the world', and that 'an incredible number of gentlemen attended with their grooms to buy gallopers, or racehorses'. Horse races were also held here from about 1680 to 1734 and again in the 19th Century.

The village flourished on several trades: brick making, stone quarrying (from the 13th Century until 1940) and iron working (at Slade Pool, just south of Bednall in Teddsley Hay, from at least 1585).

It was well served by communications and was a coaching station - see the huge, white-painted Littleton Arms in the centre of the village on the A449, the main road between the Black Country and the Potteries. Here too, on the other side of the road, is the handsome timber-framed White Hart Inn, obviously restored but probably of 16th Century origin. Another good old house is the Old Deanery of about 1600, with a stone-built centre and timber-framed wings.

To the east of Penkridge the M6 sweeps by, surprisingly silent, probably because it is in a deep cutting. To the west is the main-line railway and the trains clatter by, surprisingly noisily, probably because the line passes over a long, raised viaduct. This viaduct has seven arches, each of a 300-foot span, and is 37 feet high. It is the most important engineering work on this line in Staffordshire. (It was built for the Grand Junction Railway which opened in 1837.)

The village centre is on the main road but there is another, much pleasanter and possibly older, centre at School Square which has some good houses and cottages in stone, brick and half-timber. The Schoolhouse itself is of brick with pointed windows, designed by Joseph Potter and built in 1818. Along the road to Cannock from this square are more good houses and the Haling Dean Centre.

Just over the motorway bridge on the road to Cannock is the famous Veterinary Surgery of Eddie Straiton, one of the finest establishments of its kind in the country. For many years after he retired to Minorca Mr Straiton continued to write and broadcast on radio and television.

Another illustrious name associated with Penkridge is Percy Thrower, if only for a tragedy in his life. For 1.5 miles south of Penkridge the main-line railway runs within a few yards of the A449. In about 1970 Percy Thrower, the TV gardening expert, was at the height of his fame when his teenage son took Mr Thrower's E-type Jaguar, without permission, drove off the road on to the railway track south of Penkridge and was killed.

The great Roman forts on Watling Street around Stretton Mill, 3m SW of Penkridge, were collectively called **Pennocruciam**, a Romanisation of the name Penkridge. From the ground there is nothing to see of the Roman camps and defences because they have been systematically ploughed out. Only in comparatively recent times have they been located by the study of aerial photographs.

The church of St Michael at Penkridge is of extreme antiquity. The present building was almost certainly preceded by an Anglo-Saxon church and that in turn preceded by a Celtic temple. In medieval times it was a 'royal free chapel', i.e. a Collegiate church, of which there were only 13 in the whole country. (Five of the others were also in Staffordshire, namely Wolverhampton, Tettenhall, Stafford, Gnosall and probably Tamworth.) A Collegiate church owed allegiance to the King alone, had great financial privileges and was usually endowed with extensive estates. St Michael's lost its Collegiate status and was stripped of its lands in 1548 after the Reformation.

The church is built of local red sandstone. The exterior is Perpendicular. The interior is earlier, with a chancel of about 1225 and a nave of about 1250. The tower is Decorated below and Perpendicular above. It has a 14th Century east window, Early English arcades and overall is a high, spacious church with a most pleasant and inviting atmosphere. The fine chancel screen is Dutch wrought iron dated at 1789. (It had been used as a gate on a Boer farm in South Africa and was rescued by the Hon William Littleton, who was aide to the High Commissioner there). There are six misericords and 15th Century stalls, some with original carved fronts. The stained glass is mostly Victorian.

The monuments include: an alabaster portrait group of William of

Winnesbury, Chief Forester of Cannock, died 1502, and wife and daughter; an alabaster effigy of Sir Edward Littleton (died 1558); and memorials to Sir Edward Littleton, (died 1574), Sir Edward (died 1610), Sir Edward (died 1629); and Richard Littleton (died 1518). The Littleton family lived at Pillaton, 1.5m ESE of Penkridge, and later at Teddesley Park, 2m NE of Penkridge.

At **Teddesley** they built a large brick Hall designed by William Baker. This 18th Century mansion was demolished after the Second World War. The Snetzler organ (1769) from Teddesley Hall is now at St Andrew-by-the-Wardrobe in the City of London. The stable blocks still stand, large and handsome and, rather bizarrely, in the middle of a field. They were used for the purposes of agriculture but the estate is in the process of being developed and imposing entrance gates have been installed on the Stafford to Cannock road. The Flume Farm at Teddesley still flourishes, and amongst the outbuildings is the largest diameter waterwheel in Staffordshire. It measures 38 feet by 2 feet 8 inches wide and has 13 arms. The mill was primarily designed to power a threshing machine and secondarily to power a sawmill, a kibbling machine and a cutting machine. It was made by James Bate of Himley and was installed in 1838. The main entrance to the Park is from the village of Bednall, 4m NE of Penkridge.

Parts of the Park have a distinctly medieval feel to them. In fact, Teddesley Hay was one of the eight early medieval hays of Cannock Forest. (The others were Alrewas, Bentley, Cheslyn, Gailey, Hopwas, Ogley and Rugeley.) Each Hay was in the control of a Forester and they were responsible to a Chief Forester, the first of whom was the son of an Anglo-Saxon thane called Richard Chenven. The Chief Forester was appointed by the King. There is a surprising amount of information about the early forest and its foresters, obtained from Court and Inquisition records, and this is given at some length in the Victorian History of the County of Stafford, Volume II, pages 338-343.

On the north-east fringe of the village of Penkridge, between the road to Acton Trussell and the River Penk, is the Rolling Mill (SJ 925145), an old watermill that is now powered by electricity but which still grinds corn. The river used to flow close by the mill but has been diverted to its present course as part of a flood prevention scheme, although the river still floods on occasion and makes a huge lake hereabouts. The name Rolling Mill refers to its previous use as a mill for rolling iron. Other metal working mills in the Penkridge area were at: **Bangley Park** (SJ 947143), site of Hazel Mill - pond bay, mill pond, slag, brick building on stone base, iron wheel with hexagonal shaft; **Wolgarston** (SJ 937144) site of Newtown Mill - marshy areas where mill pools were, stone dam, causeway between pools, iron slag mound to south, a mill here since 1532 at least, used for grinding bone in 19th Century and corn also; **Congreve** (SJ.904. 132) - site of Congreve Mill on Manor Farm, was a forge until about 1830, then a cow shed and demolished in 1977 as part of a flood control scheme.

The hamlet of Congreve, 1m SW of Penkridge, is the old home of the Congreve family. The grand mansion has gone but the present attractive brick manor house is still quite old at about 1700. The family also owned Stretton. Of this family was William Congreve (1670-1729), the playwright, who was born at Bardsley, West Yorkshire. In this century two of their number have received the Victoria Cross for gallantry. (They are commemorated at Stowe by Chartley church.) Sir Geoffrey Congreve was created a baronet in honour of his father but was himself killed after having won the DSO in World War Two. He is commemorated in Penkridge church. (See Pillaton.)

Cuttlestone Bridge, 0.5m. SW of Penkridge, is mostly of about 1700 and has five arches and cutwaters. It carries King Street, an ancient route that led from Penkridge to Newport, Shrewsbury and Chester.

Levedale, 2m NW of Penkridge, is a tiny hamlet. There was a medieval chapel here, probably in Chapel Field. The present mission church was built in about 1920. Levedale Hall is no more.

Water Eaton, 2m WSW of Penkridge, and just north of the site of Pennocrucium, is a hamlet close to the River Penk. The site of a large Roman fort lies to the north-east of Water Eaton. The name means 'farm by the river'.

PENN *3m SW of Wolverhampton town centre*

Penn is a Celtic name, one of the oldest in the county. It means 'hill'. There are two settlements - Upper and Lower. Upper Penn is a residential suburb of Wolverhampton that lies astride the A449, Wolverhampton to Kidderminster road, and Lower Penn is a small village, 1.25m W, in open country close to the Staffordshire and Worcestershire Canal.

In Domesday Book both settlements have individual entries. Before 1066 Upper Penn was held by Earl Algar and Lower Penn by Lady Godiva, wife of Earl Leofric. Lady Godiva erected a Preaching Cross at which Christian services were held by the priests from Dudley Priory. After the Norman Conquest both manors passed to William, son of Ansculf, and both were included within the boundary of the Forest of Kinver.

About 1200 Sir Hugh de Bushbury built the church of St Bartholomew at **Upper Penn**. It lies on a hill, very probably the site of a prehistoric fort. Of the church we see today a blocked north window may be Norman; two bays of the north arcade are 13th Century and two bays west of these are Perpendicular; the tower is 15th Century encased in Gothic brick of 1765; the brick north-west annex is of 1826; the west half of the south side with lancet windows is of 1845; and the ashlar faced east end is of 1872, by Parley of Lancaster. The font is Perpendicular and there is a monument to John Marsh, of 1802, by John Flaxman. In the churchyard, against the south wall, is the base of the Godiva Preaching Cross which was found buried near the church in 1910.

Penn Hall, at Upper Penn, lies west of the church. It is a 17th Century house, encased within 18th Century walls, with six bays to the entrance side and a round-headed doorway, above which is an Art Noveau sundial. On the garden side there are seven bays with a central doorway surmounted by a pediment. Inside is some 17th Century panelling and plasterwork, and upstairs are some unusual doors with one large panel over four smaller panels. In the grounds there is a barn of 1779 and two summer houses.

South of the village is **Penn Common,** an open grassland with some scrub. By the Turf Tavern is the site of the Old Racecourse, now a part of Penn Golf Course. The Common lies on the slopes of the Penn Brook valley. Near the road bridge are the Lloyd Roberts Buildings, a block of cottages with a tower to the right.

Lower Penn is a pleasant village that lies on the slope of a hill with a pub, The Greyhound, and a charming half-timbered cottage called The Walnut Tree, which is now attached to a boarding kennels for cats and dogs. Higher up the hill is the old forge, now a dwelling, and almost opposite is the rock-faced church. Higher still is the village green and the stuccoed Charlton House. Dirtyfoot Lane leads off the green and a few yards along is the good, mellow brick house called Lower Penn Farm. (The sign outside simply says The Farmhouse.) This looks to be the most important building in the village and was probably the manor house. The brickwork is thought to date from the 1670s. It is an irregular building of two storeys, with five bays, two front-facing gables and extensions of a lower height to the right-hand side. Together with the farm buildings it forms one side of a 'U'-shaped courtyard. To the left of the house is a mature yew tree.

At the very top of the Hill are some fine, modern villas, one of which is The Ridgeway, a neo-Elizabethan timber-framed house, with herringbone masonry, on a superb wooded site with far-ranging views over the surrounding countryside. The road follows the ridge south-east to Spring Hill and the A449.

There are two Pear Tree Farms, one on Penn Common and the other at Lower Penn. Both have specimens of the Tettenhall Pear tree.

Bradmore, 1m N of Penn, is now a suburb of Wolverhampton but was once well known for the manufacture of guns. The industry continued up to the 1950s and is remembered in the name of the Gunmakers Arms in Trysull Road.

Warstones, a large housing estate built by Wolverhampton council in the 1930s, is named after the Warstones Farm, which stood opposite Warstones Inn. Warstones Green is a park at Warstones. The name means 'boundary stone'.

PENSNETT *2.5m SW of Dudley*
The name is from the Celtic 'pen', 'a hill', and the Anglo-Saxon 'snaed', 'a piece of woodland'. In the Middle Ages Pensnett Chase spread for several miles around the hamlet.

In 1619 Dud Dudley, one of the 11 illegitimate children of the Earl of Dudley, came down from Oxford University to manage his father's furnace and two forges on Pensnett Chase. Soon after he was experimenting with coal as a fuel for smelting iron. There is some doubt as to whether he succeeded, but he certainly said that he had done so.

In 1787 the Pensnett Chase Act was passed, enclosing much of the Chase and giving the Lord of Dudley both agricultural and mining rights on the old common land. Not only was coal and iron mined there, but also special clays used for the manufacture of fire-resistant tiles and pots. On the western edge of the village, on the A4101, Pensnett to Kingswinford road, is a large clay pit that is still quarried by Hinton, Perry and Davenhill. They make Ketley Bricks and Dreadnought Tiles at their works in Dreadnought Road, **Tansey Green**, on the other side of the main road. Opposite the quarry is the entrance to the Pensnett Trading Trading Estate, where an old coal-mine engine house and pit-head winding scaffold have been re-erected.

It is a large estate and extends northwards to **Shut End**. This old mining area was once connected to the Staffordshire and Worcestershire Canal (1772) at **Ashwood**, 3.5m W, by one of the first steam railways in Britain, namely the Kingswinford Railway of 1829. (See Kingswinford.) North of the main road, in the direction of Dudley, are the woods of Barrow Hill, one of the many unexpected green areas in the Black Country.

Here is the large, almost imposing, church of St Mark, designed by J M Derick and built in 1896-9. It is constructed of ashlar stone, has lancet windows, a high nave with clerestory and a high chancel. Inside is a sword once owned by William Ewart Gladstone (1809-98), four times Prime Minister of Britain. The sword was made at the ill-fated Oak Farm Ironworks. (See Gornal.)

Between the church and Gornal Wood, and Lower Gornal to the north-east, is a stretch of wasteland and poor pasture that has a great deal of character, with donkeys grazing and huts made from old railway sleepers. The land rises up to the heights of Upper Gornal and the ridge road between Sedgley and Dudley.

In Bryce Road is **The Dell** athletics stadium. It has an all-weather track and facilities for field sports, tennis, netball, football and bowls.

Bromley, 0.5m. S of Pensnett, lies on the road to Brierley Hill. Here there are bush-fringed pools in old clay pits, an arm of a derelict canal, the Queen's Head, a Senior Citizens' Club and ubiquitous modern housing estates. The name Bromley means 'the clearing in the broom'. The use of mules as packhorses to carry coal lingered until about 1900 in the Pensnett area. A rhyme about Sally Smith, of Moor Lane, goes:

When the donkey died old Sally cried:
"Whatever shall I do?
To carry coals from Old Bog Hole
To the folks in Tackeroo."

PERTON *2m WSW of Tettenhall, near Wolverhampton*

Perton, now called Old Perton, lies along the ridge followed by the Tettenhall Wood to Pattingham road. It is an old manor, first mentioned in 11th Century charters when it belonged to St Peter's, Westminster. It is thought that the name is from 'perigtun', meaning 'the place of the pear tree'. In 1332 John de Perton held the manor by supplying the king with one chain-mail-clad soldier when he was at war with the Welsh. The manor's most illustrious son is Sir John Wollaston (1595-1658), who was Lord Mayor of London in 1643-4. Perton Hall was demolished by the early 19th Century, but a fragment of its moat exists at what is now called Perton Court, in Jenny Walker's Lane.

South Perton Farm, also in Jenny Walker's Lane, is the home of the famous and much admired Tettenhall Horse Sanctuary. From 1996 an annual Tough Guy competition has been held here to raise funds.

Perton airfield opened in 1941 and closed in 1947 when the RAF moved out. After strenuous local opposition a new residential village, New Perton, was built in the 1970s and 1980s. The church was built in 1983.

PILLATON *1.24m ESE of Penkridge*

In the flat land west of Penkridge, over the motorway and on the edge of Cannock Chase, is the hamlet of Pillaton. A track to the south of the cricket pitch leads past the old manor farm to Pillaton Hall. The modest three-bay, red brick, ivy-clad Pillaton Hall Farm is signed off the road because it now offers coarse and trout fishing and has a clutch of small businesses ensconced in an out-building

The Hall is one of those unsung and largely unseen romantic relics of which there are so many in England. The manor belonged to the Monastery of St Mary and St Modwena at Burton upon Trent at the time of Domesday. It was then held by a succession of local lords until 1502 when William of Winnesbury died. He had been Chief Forester of Cannock Chase, and by virtue of that appointment was also Lord of Huntington and Teddesley. His heir was his daughter, Alice, and she married Richard Littleton (died 1518), a lawyer in Royal Service. The Hall and the chapel that we see today were built by the Littletons. Originally, it had four ranges forming a quadrangle. Today, all that remains is the front gatehouse block and the chapel, a little brickwork of the east range, a chimney of the west range and the stone base of a fireplace of the main hall range. The gatehouse has four round angle turrets and an arched entrance. On either side are wings with mullioned and transomed windows, probably inserted later in the Jacobean period. The moat still exists. In 1488 the stone chapel of St Modwena was mostly rebuilt and is still well maintained and well furnished. Amongst the furnishings is a very rare, Early English, carved wood statue of a seated saint, probably of the late 13th Century. (See Penkridge.)

QUARNFORD *It is a Moorland parish now based on the village of Flash*
It is a parish - the highest in England - but there is no settlement of that name. The centre of population is at Flash, which has the Quarnford Post Office. Manor Farm was formerly Quarnford House and is situated near a crossing of the River Dane. This is possibly the ford over which querns (millstone wheels) were carried, as suggested by the name. Quern is from the Old English 'Cwearn'. Alternatively, it could mean 'the mill by the ford'. In 1918-19 Sir George Crewe, Lord of Alstonfield, paid his first visit to his estates at Quarnford and described them as "the very end of the civilized world". There may have been a medieval village at Quarnford, deserted in the late Middle Ages. (See Flash.)

QUARRY BANK *1m SE of Brierley Hill*
The traffic is unbelievable. It is, of course, all heading to or from Moon City, that exercise in extreme bad taste officially called the Merry Hill Centre. If you are approaching from the north down the A4036 do not expect to see a sign, not for Quarry Bank anyway. Instead, take the road, the A4100, to Cradley Heath and Old Hill. Within a few yards you are in Quarry 'Bonk', as the locals call it. This a proper place: a long, steep hill lined with a good variety of traditional small shops, professional services, churches, schools a community centre and fish and chip take-aways.

Christ Church stands near the top of the hill, a not unhandsome building of yellow brick with lancet windows, a bellcote and a hammer-beam roof. Somehow one doesn't expect to find a hammer-beam roof in Quarry Bank. North of the high street is a sad sight, a shamefully neglected cemetery. Many of the tombs are carefully tended but the graveyard itself is overgrown and quite forlorn. South of the high street is a happier place, namely Stevens Park. This was the gift of a local industrialist, Ernest Stevens. He gave another park to Stourbridge, also called Stevens Park.

Quarry Bank was once famous for its nails and chains. Both trades were labour intensive and poorly paid. The people likened themselves unto slaves. One of the last of the hand-craft chain makers was George Dunn (1887-1975). He was born and brought up in Sheffield Street and first worked as a 'blower', that is, he worked the bellows of the fire in a small craft workshop, before moving up to Noah Bloomer's Chain Shop in Oak Street. However, George Dunn is remembered not as a chain-maker but as a singer. He was a part-time entertainer and had a varied repertoire of operatic airs, music-hall songs and, above all, traditional English songs and ballads. He was the last true, traditional folksinger in the Black Country. Almost all his country songs were learned from his father, Sampson (1858-1932). George Dunn was 'discovered' in 1970 and shortly after recorded an LP, *George Dunn,* for Leader Records (Lee 4042).

R

RANGEMOOR *5m W of Burton upon Trent*

It is a small village in Needwood Forest with oaks in the hedgerows and ferns by the roadside. Many of the roads are long and straight, a sign of post-medieval enclosure of waste and common land by big landowners whose field boundaries were fixed by lines drawn on maps and not governed by the lie of the land.

The name Rangemoor is a corruption of 'Raven's Moor'. Most of the village is Victorian with a church, club, school and cottages built by the Bass brewing family, Lords of Burton. The church of All Saints was designed by Butterfield and built in 1866 with a south aisle of 1886 and a no-expense-spared chancel by Bodley, of 1895.

Byrkley Park lies 1.75m NW of the village. Here was the house, now demolished, of Lord Burton's brother. It is now a garden centre. Lord Burton lived at Rangemoor Hall, now Needwood School, 0.5m SW of Rangemoor. The original small Georgian house was greatly enlarged by the architect R W Edis in 1879 and further extended in 1900. It is part ashlar and part rendered, and though large has little character. The gardens however, are most attractive. They lie in a hollow to the east of the house with pools, lawns and trees, and even the Drakelow power station looks quite in place in the far distance. There is a stable block of 1895 and a brick-lined ice-house, 18 feet deep, approached through a long tunnel. The East Lodge, lm N, is a five-bay Georgian house of ashlar with a Tuscan column porch and Grecian decoration to the window pediments.

Half-a-mile east of Rangemoor on the road to Tatenhill, is the romantic looking Needwood Manor Hotel, a red brick Gothic house in the style of a Scottish Baronial castle.

RANTON *4m E of Stafford*

The village is most easily approached by a lane leading south, off the B5405, the Woodseaves to Great Bridgeford road. It is a scattered settlement with a small nucleus of old cottages and a small medieval church. All Saints is 13th Century Early English with mainly Perpendicular windows. The chancel is of brick and is of 1753. In the village there has been some new development in recent years of mainly large detached houses, desirable in themselves, perhaps, but totally incongruous to their surroundings. They benefit from the country but give nothing in return. There is a village hall in which local rock groups practice.

In the country around here there are three moated sites: at Hextall (SJ 858250), just over 0.5m N of Ranton - three sides remain, 230 feet by 210 feet; at Ranton Hall (SJ 846244), 0.5m NW of the village - rectangular remains, 340 feet by 280 feet; and at Ranton Abbey (SJ 839243).

Ranton Abbey was founded by Robert and Celestia Noel of Ellenhall, about 1150, for Augustinian cannons from Haughmond. In 1820 Thomas, 1st Earl of Lichfield, built a large house, a hunting lodge or weekend retreat, adjacent to the

Abbey. Alas, he was a reckless gambler, spent a fortune exercising a terrible blood lust on killing game birds, and put the family into a huge debt of £600,000 from which it has never really recovered. All that remains of the Abbey is the large, imposing tower (of the 15th Century) and a little of the nave wall with a Norman doorway decorated with roll moulding. The house, also called Ranton Abbey, is now in ruins though most of the exterior walls are still standing. It was accidentally burned down in 1942, during the Second World War, when troops of Queen Wilhelmina's bodyguard were quartered here.

When we visited in 1988 we found the timbers and water tanks lying as they fell and the whole house totally smothered in ivy. It was an eerie place and there are tales of witchcraft being practiced here. It is even said that the medieval monks were involved in far-from-Christian rites, and torch-light processions at midnight have been seen in recent years.

The agricultural park is most attractive and well wooded. Game birds were once bred in the outbuildings of the house. It was owned for many years by the Wedgwood pottery company, but in 1987 Patrick, Earl of Lichfield, bought the estate and plans to restore the abbey tower, rebuild (or replace) the house, re-make the lake, which has been drained and planted with trees, and stock the woods with game birds.

There are two entrances to the Abbey off the B5405 Woodseaves to Great Bridgeford road. At one entrance is a delightful lodge. The Hall and Abbey lie at the end of the track, one-third-of-a -mile long, embowered by trees, but the top of the church tower is usually visible from the road.

One mile east of Ranton is Vicarage Farmhouse, a timber-framed house with close-set vertical studs. Inside is some good Jacobean wall panelling.

Frankville, 0.5m NNE of Ranton, is a lost Norman settlement, situated between Ranton and Ellenhall at SJ 844253, which was deserted in the 16th Century. Finds in the area include: a prehistoric quern and axe; a cobbled pavement known locally as 'the market place'; the remains of a wooden drain system, 20 yards long and about five feet wide, perhaps a fulling mill; local memory of the presence of a row of cottages in a field; the nearby St Anne's Well; and an unusual bulge in the parish boundary, as though bent to allow inclusion of the village. In medieval times it is recorded that John de Frankville gave the vill of Frankwell to Ranton Abbey.

RAVENSCLIFFE *1m NW of Tunstall in the Potteries*
Ravenscliffe is a small country park with a car park in a valley. The wilderness area opposite the entrance has been allowed to green over. Ten years ago it was derelict industrial land with a long lost watermill. We took Boathorse Road, which runs along the top of the east side of the valley. Half- way up the hill earth moving was going on apace to make a motorbike racetrack.

If this sounds out of keeping then hold your breath, for near the top of the hill is a large, sprawling gypsy encampment courtesy of the council. Huge numbers of cars, trucks, caravans and Portacabin-style huts litter both sides of the road. Irish accents prevail. Indeed, the man in charge here is a Mr Doherty, a red-faced, ill-tempered man who had two donkeys standing in a small, muddy enclosure that had not seen grass for many a long year. There was a heavy mist and it was raining steadily, which added to the dismal atmosphere of this miserable, forlorn and God-forsaken place.

If you continue north, through the moorland, the narrow lane changes its name to **Acres Nook**, a residential area of Kidsgrove, and then back to

Boathorse Road as it dips down through the woods of the old Clough Hall estate to First Avenue at Kidsgrove. On this little journey, by the way, you crossed over the Harecastle tunnels.

REAPS MOOR *2m S of Longnor*

Reapsmoor is a hamlet in the North Staffordshire Moorlands comprising a scatter of small farms with small fields enclosed by stone walls, a pub and a church-cum-house-cum-village hall, all under the same roof. This kind of eminently practical arrangement is occasionally found in remote country places. The village hall is on the ground floor and above it is the mission church of St John (1842). The house is attached to the end. There was a cheese factory here from the 1870s to the 1950s that produced Derby cheese.

RIBDEN *1.5m S of Cauldon*

Ribden is a hamlet on the southern slopes of the Weaver Hills, best known for its now-disused lead mine (SK 076470). Both lead and copper have been mined here since at least the 17th Century, and quite probably since Roman times. Mining ceased at Ribden in the 1860s. An engine house, which became ruinous, was pulled down and the stone used to construct a lime kiln at Ruelow. Prehistoric finds include a polished flint axe and a perforated stone axe-hammer. At SK 076471 there is a moated site thought never to have held water. On Ribden Low there is a burial mound at SK 076477. It measures 28 yards in diameter and is seven feet high. It was plundered by Carrington in 1847 and he found a crouched skeleton.

The name Ribden is thought to be from the Anglo-Saxon 'Wrybba's hill', Wrybba being a personal name.

RIDWARE *2-4m E of Rugeley*

There are four Ridwares: Hamstall Ridware, Pipe Ridware, Mavesyn Ridware and Hill Ridware. They lie between the River Blithe to the east and the River Trent to the west, close to their confluence. The name Ridware has Celtic and Anglo-Saxon roots and is interpreted as 'dwellers by the ford' and also as 'river folk'. It is thought that the original settlement was at the ford of Hamstall Ridware. Hamstall means 'home farm' or 'homestead' and was added to the name Ridware when the later daughter settlements were established. The dedication of the church at Hamstall Ridware is to St Michael, often a sign of antiquity. It is suspected that the territory of the Ridwara (who were Angles) extended beyond these four villages and probably included Yoxall, 2m E of Hamstall Ridware, and Hoar Cross, 2.5m to the north. The country of the Ridwares is flat and agricultural, but the cooling towers and chimneys of Rugeley power station dominate the skyline.

Hamstall Ridware, 4m E of Rugeley as the crow flies, is a place of some character. The village lies just to the west of the River Blythe, close by the bridge. Meadows stretch to the water's edge. The Hall and church lie on higher ground to the north.

Today the Hall is in ruins hut the quadrangular outbuildings have been developed as an arts and crafts centre, and a very good one too, with a wide variety of quality merchandise and a coffee shop. The old Hall is built of brick with stone dressings and lies behind the coffee shop, which is adjacent to the farmhouse. The Hall was also based on a quadrangle. It was a manor house of the Fitzherberts, built in the 16th Century. The gatehouse is more or less complete, with its twin-capped turrets and an arch built between and decorated on top with stone strapwork (interlaced ornament similar to fretwork). The watchtower is in ruins but substantial. There are many walls still standing, some of which are incorporated into the coffee shop and the farmhouse. Inside the farmhouse are some reset linenfold panelling and some medallions of about 1530-40. The path from the farm courtyard passes another part of the old Hall, a quaint recessed stone colonnade and balcony with strapwork. This is a delightful little structure that really ought to be preserved. Ruins can be most attractive but when they degenerate beyond a certain point they can become shapeless, ugly and dangerous. This loggia faces what is now a large, walled vegetable and flower garden. A side door to the farmhouse is most attractively festooned with flowers in the summer.

The church of St Michael lies only yards away from the Hall and the farmhouse. Nothing of the Anglo-Saxon church remains and almost all of the Norman work has been rebuilt: 14th Century chancel and north chapel; Perpendicular north aisle and clerestory; 18th Century north chapel walls; and 14th Century tower, small and squat. There is a Norman font and part of the upper window in the west wall of the nave is Norman also. There is a monument to Richard and John Cotton of 1502. (The Fitzherberts acquired the manor of Hamstall Ridware from the Cotton family by marriage.) There is also an inscription to Thomas Strongintharme, died 1778.

Pipe Ridware A lane leads south and then west from Hamstall Ridware to Pipe Ridware, a tiny hamlet close to the River Trent. The church of St James was built in 1840, probably on the site of an earlier church. The chancel was added by Oldrid Scott in 1899. Inside is an interesting stepped triple arcade separating the chancel from the nave. The font is genuine Norman; the front facade of the church neo-Norman.

Hill Ridware The largest of the Ridwares with houses, a pub and a Post Office. Here is the 18th Century brick Rectory of five bays. The church is in Mavesyn Ridware.

Mavesyn Ridware The name Mavesyn is a contraction of Mal-voisins, meaning dangerous neighbours, and there are snippets of history that seem to justify this description of the Norman lords who settled here. In 1403 Sir Robert Mavesyn rode out of his fortified manor to join Henry IV at Shrewsbury. A neighbouring lord, Sir William Handsacre, set out at the same time but to join the rival army of Harry Hotspur and Owain Glyndwr. The two knights met near Mavesyn Ridware at a place marked by two great oaks called Gog and Magog. They fought their own private battle and Sir William was killed. Sir Robert Mavesyn then continued on to Shrewsbury where at Battlefield he met his death in the Battle of Shrewsbury.

The Hall from which he set out is now gone but the gatehouse remains and is in very good order. The original Hall and stables probably formed a quadrangle behind the gatehouse, which is stone in the lower front but for the rest is timber-framed, though this was enclosed in brick until about 1718. The gate arch has 14th Century mouldings and in the windows are loop holes. After the Battle of Shrewsbury the manor passed to the Cawardens and then to the Chadwick family. In 1718 the house was rebuilt by Charles Chadwick, a handsome place of brick, five bays, two storeys and a hipped roof.

The church of St Nicholas is something of a curiosity. In 1782 all but the Perpendicular tower and the Early English north aisle were pulled down and the large brick Mavesyn Chapel added. It is a very clumsy arrangement, curious but inelegant. The chapel houses the monuments to the dead of the families who owned the manor. These include two effigies of unnamed knights: one of the 13th Century and one with his legs crossed (meaning he had been on a Holy Crusade). Here, too, is the tomb chest of Sir Robert Mavesyn. There are also monuments to Thomas Cawarden, died 1477; Hugh Davenport, died 1473; and three small reliefs of recent origin depicting the Mavesyns at war.

The village is small but most attractive and in the main street is a superb and beautifully preserved Tithe Barn. There is also a most handsome little thatched timber-framed cottage. To the south, by 400 yards, is the High Bridge over the River Trent. It has a span of 140 feet and was made at Coalbrookdale in 1830.

ROACHES *See Upper Hulme*

ROCESTER *3.25m NNE of Uttoxeter*

Rocester is pronounced locally as 'Roaster'. The town lies between the River Churnet and the River Dove, about a mile north of their confluence. In a field to the north-east of the church is the site of a Roman fort which was excavated in1988. There have been many finds of pottery and a beautiful enamel brooch, depicting a man on horseback, which is probably of Celtic origin. There are believed to be four forts here in all, the first dating from about 70 AD.

Rocester Abbey, dedicated to St Mary, was founded by Richard Bacon, nephew of the Earl of Chester, in or about 1140. It was a small Augustinian house and lay to the south-east of the present church of St Michael, which retains some of the abbey church and fragments of stained glass from it. In 1539, after the Dissolution, the Abbey site was leased to Edward Draycott,

The church of St Michael has a medieval fabric but was much rebuilt and restored in 1870 by Ewan Christian who added the spire to the tower. Inside, there are polished marble columns and the east window is by William de Morgan who is renowned for his ceramic lustre tiles. In the churchyard is an extremely well-preserved cross of at least the 13th Century. In the pasture field to the south of, and adjacent to, the church is much disturbed ground. Here stood the Abbey already mentioned.

Rocester is set in attractive country but the village is most disappointing. The western approach, off the B5030, is pleasant enough with a weir on the River Churnet, the modest stone mill and the bridge, but the town centre is spoiled by modern flats and there is no sense of a village centre.

To the east, near to the River Dove, is the giant Tutbury Mill, built by Richard Arkwright in about 1782 as a cotton mill. It is four storeys high and 24 bays long. Parts of the roadside entrance are stone-built.

Today Rocester is best known as site is the new factory of J C Bamford, the manufacturers of earth moving equipment with a worldwide reputation. The building is long, low, windowless and constructed of a green material. The grounds have been landscaped and small lakes created. If one must have a factory in the country this is the way to do it. All in all, it is very praiseworthy. It is a pity, however, that the smoked glass section was added in 1987. . Near the front of the factory is a raised helicopter landing pad. However, as a landlord and neighbour the firm has upset many local people. Old cottages stand empty and large tracts of land are used as noisy testing and training grounds

Banks Farmhouse lies on a hill, 0.5m W of Rocester, and can clearly be seen from the main road. It is a large, 'L'- shaped, red brick folly of two storeys with a five-sided tower, probably of about 1700. It was almost certainly designed as an 'eye-catcher' for Woodseat Hall, which now lies in ruins a little to the south.

Barrow Hill lies 1m N of Rocester. The B5030 to Ellastone climbs the hill. On the left-hand side, heading north, is an ancient burial mound. The occupants of the nearby house (approached along the track that leads to Barrowhill Hall) told us that when Birmingham University archaeologists examined the site they found fertility figures that left little to the imagination. The barrow lies within a 675-acre camp of uncertain age but was probably used in the Iron Age. Roman coins and pottery were found here in 1872

Barrowhill Hall was built about 1780 and was a home of the Sneyd family. By 1978 the Hall was the training school and clubhouse for JCB Excavators Ltd. It is now privately occupied.

ROLLESTON BY DOVE *2.5m N of Burton on Trent*

The centre of this large village is truly most charming. The Alder Brook is entrenched and runs through the centre of the settlement. It is fringed with willows and crossed by an old bridge with a cascade. Next to the church is the old and very large Spread Eagle pub, which has a riverside car park and an embowered beer garden. The houses are from an age when space was not at a premium, and wear their maturity with quiet dignity. There are worse places to live than Rolleston. The village is far enough from Burton to be able to disown it with disdain, yet close enough to partake of its wide range of services and amenities. There are good older houses but there has also been much characterless modern development on the fringes. The School is of patterned brick and is of about 1640. The almshouses are of single-storey brick with quoins and a broken pediment, dated at 1713.

From the 17th Century Rolleston Hall was the home of the Mosley family, a member of which was Sir Oswald Mosley, founder of the British fascist party distinguished by the brown shirts they wore. The gabled Jacobean mansion was enlarged in Georgian style in the late 18th Century, damaged by fire in 1870 and rebuilt in 1871 in an Italianate style. Most of the Hall was demolished in the 1920s.

The church of St Mary is a largely rebuilt Norman building. The south porch and room adjoining are 13th Century; the north aisle and south aisle are Decorated; the tower is 14th Century with a later spire; and the north chapel is of 1892 by Sir Arthur Blomfield. There is stained glass by Kempe and monuments to Bishop Sherburne of Chichester, died 1536; Thomas Caldwell, died 1554; Sir Edward Mosley, died 1638; and other Mosleys. In the churchyard is a very large Anglo-Saxon, wheel-style Cross Head, believed to be of 9th Century origin and brought here from Tatenhill.

By the church is a schoolroom which once housed the free Grammar School, founded in 1520 by Robert Sherbourne, Bishop of Chichester. The almshouses beside the Alder Brook are of 1712.

The name Rolleston is probably from the Anglo-Saxon 'Hrothwulf's town (settlement)'. Rolleston Park was a medieval deer park enclosed out of forest, 1.5m WSW of Rolleston, near Tutbury Castle, and was created by Robert de Ferrers, First Earl of Derby (died 1139).

ROWLEY REGIS *2.5. SE of Dudley*

It lies high on the Rowley Hills, midway between Dudley and Blackheath. Despite being in the heart of the Black Country it has the air of a country place. There is a church, a pub, a village green and a few old villas. The sea of modern houses and schools that surround it only enforce the impression. In fact, the green is a recent creation, made by the removal of old cottages.

The name Rowley is thought to derive from the Anglo-Saxon 'ruh-leah' meaning 'rough clearing' or 'a clearing in rough scrubland'. The Regis, meaning Royal, seems to have been added in the 14th Century, presumably to differentiate it from another Rowley. The Pipe Rolls show that in the 12th Century it did indeed belong to the king. (King Charles II had a horse called Rowley). There used to be a borough of Rowley Regis and together with Tipton it returned a member of parliament, one of whom, Arthur Henderson, became first a cabinet minister and then Lord Rowley.

The area is probably best known for the hard ,dolerite-basalt laccolith used as a road stone and known as Rowley Rag. It was not worked until the 19th Century but is still mined in two large quarries. There were collieries too: in 1827 there were more than 50, but by 1854 there were 13 in the Rowley area. Now there are none. As everywhere hereabouts, nail-making was once an important industry in Rowley.

The Church of St Giles was founded in 1199 as a chapel-of-ease for the church of Clent. A 19th Century vicar, the Reverend George Bans, described the old Norman Church as a cold, damp, ruinous and gloomy dilapidated dungeon', and in 1849 he had it rebuilt. However, by 1900 it had become unsafe because of settlement caused by mining, and was rebuilt once again in 1904. Then it was destroyed by fire in 1913 during the Suffragette Riots, and the Gothic red brick church we see today is of 1923.

At **Turner's Hill**, nearly a mile north of Rowley Regis, two tall aerial masts and a concrete 'mushroom' water tower stand guard over the ARC Edwin Richards Quarry and the Rowley Olympic Sports and Social Club. Head south-east, down Portway Hill and one passes a half-timbered farm house which still operates as a smallholding. There are splendid views north-east, over the tower-blocks of Oldbury to the sprawl of the Black Country beyond.

Portway is a crossroads' settlement with a few shops, the Four Ways pub, the Rowley Village Tandoori and many acres of council houses. Follow Portway Road southwards, through the clouds of dust that emanate from the entrance to the ARC Quarry, and the street name changes to the delightful **Tippitty Green,** which developed around the Manor Mill. Here is the Tarmac works and quarry landfill site which you have time to savour as you sit in an unexpected traffic jam and await your turn to enter Haws Lane opposite the Bull's Head. On your left is Allsops Hill Quarry and on your right Hailstone Hill Quarry.

Hailstone is at **Cock Green.** Here there are estates of modern houses, several schools, a few Victorian terraces, the Hailstone pub, a handful of shops and **The Knowle** Methodist Church - red brick with tall lancet windows. Down Doulton Road is an industrial estate and a brickworks. (Note: The Knowle and Cock Green are really one and the same.)

Springfield lies a little further along the Dudley Road (B4171), a place of yellow brick council houses. Behind them is Rough Hill, and rough it is with hummocky ground, gorse bushes and quarry-cliffs; and before them is the preserved industrial landscape of Warren Hall Park and the Bumble Hole. (See Netherton.) Rowley Regis has a station, but it is lm SE at Blackheath.

RUDYARD *2.5m NW of Leek*

The name Rudyard may mean 'the place where rudd (a type of fish) are kept' or alternatively, 'lake near a garden in which rue is grown'.

Rudyard is famous for its lovely lake, the 'silver lake', which was greatly enlarged as a reservoir to feed the Caldon Canal. (Authority to make the reservoir was granted by Act of Parliament in 1797.) Today it looks totally natural and is most conveniently seen to its best advantage from lay-bys on the A523, Leek to Macclesfield road. Fishermen and sailors frequent its shores and silver waters. It is wooded all around and is a beautiful sight.

The village of Rudyard lies at the south-western tip of the 1.5-mile-long, but narrow, reservoir. There are hotels and guest houses and it is a well-attended resort in the summer. There is also a rather shabby shanty town of flimsy cabins tucked away on the western hillside, but along the lake are some more substantial houses and the premises of the yacht club - a place of great character.

It was whilst walking by the lake that Lockwood Kipling proposed marriage to Alice Macdonald, and when their son was born in India some time later they named him Rudyard after the place where they had become engaged.

Rudyard Hall is a good 17th Century stone house of two storeys to a 'T'-plan. It also has good gate piers and a barn with mullioned windows. Cliffe Park Hall lies above the west bank of the lake, a Gothic, ashlar house of about 1830 with turrets and battlements. It has a coach porch to the south side and, facing the lake, a symmetrical front with a bow.

Cliffe Park Hall was built in 1811 as a private house but over the years has also been the club house of the Rudyard Golf Club and a Youth Hostel.

Spite Hall, north of Rudyard and to the west of the lake near Horton Lodge, is a large, barn-like cottage built, it is said, to deliberately spoil the view of the lake for the owners of Rudyard Villa, which is only a few yards away.

Who the parties were, or what the disagreement was over, is unknown but the cottage builder even went to the lengths of installing ugly gargoyles with their tongues sticking out on the side facing Rudyard Villa. These have now been removed but some are still in the garden.

RUGELEY *7.5m ESE of Stafford*

The name means 'red pastures'. Rugeley was one of the many substantial manors owned by the Anglo-Saxon thane, Earl Algar, which were usurped by King William after the Norman Conquest. Rugeley Hay was one of the eight Hays, or separate divisions, of the Royal Forest of Cannock.

Rugeley is a small town, not a village, with a sizeable shopping centre which is now mostly pedestrianised. Without being busy it is quite a lively place and not altogether unpleasant. There are no buildings of special merit but there is a Victorian Gothic Town Hall and a Market Hall in Market Square, both of 1878. On the edge of the town, on the road to Lichfield, are a couple of black and white cottages.

All that is left of the old medieval church of St Augustine is the tower, chancel and north chapel, joined by the four-bay north arcade of the ruined nave. The chancel is still in use and inside there is a monument to Thomas Lauder, died 1670, in his winding sheet, but looking as though he is in a hammock. The new church of St Augustine is of 1822 by H J Underwood. It is large, with galleries, and has glass by Kempe in the east chancel window and the north chapel window. In Heron Street is the Catholic Church of St Joseph and St Ethelfleda, of 1849, with a bizarre steeple; and St Anthony's convent (RC) which was originally a brick house called Heron Court, of 1851, in a pretty Elizabethan style.

The dominant buildings in Rugeley, though, are the two enormous power stations: Rugeley 'A' and Rugeley 'B' (and until a few years ago the adjacent Lea Hall Colliery), which lie to the north-east of the town between the Trent and Mersey Canal and the River Trent. The canal was constructed in 1777 and is 12 feet wide and three feet deep. It was designed to take boats, 70- feet-long, carrying loads of 20 tons with a draft of two feet six inches.

The town has had a varied industrial history. From the Middle Ages to 1963 there was a leather tanning industry here. In the 14th Century there was a fulling mill and in 1418 John Glasman of Rugeley sold white glass to York Minster. (See Etching Hill later in this article.) In the 17th Century William, Thomas and Walter Chetwynd of Rugeley were renowned iron-masters with furnaces and forges on Cannock Chase and other places. In the 19th Century there was a plaster works and in the 20th Century shoes were made here (Lotus 1953), not to mention coal mining and brick making for which the local heavy clay is ideal. Today, there is a modern industrial and trading estate on the road to Colton. As to transport, the town has a main line railway, a canal, a river and an old coaching road.

Hagley, now a southern suburb of Rugeley, was formerly a separate manor. The name means 'the clearing where haws are found'. The site of the early manor houses was 300 yards east of the present Hagley Hall, which was built in 1620 for Sir Richard Weston. This was remodelled and extended in the 18th Century for Assheton Curzon, who also improved the grounds. There is an ornamental stone and wrought iron bridge, and in a cliff below the Hall are man-hewn caves and caverns. In one of these is an altar niche where once stood a lead statue of a river god called The River God of Cannock Chase. In the caretaker's garden is a circular, domed, brick ice-house. By 1971 the Hall was occupied as the Rugeley Arts Centre.

The **Pear Tree Estate,** on the south-west fringe of Rugeley, was built in the 1950s to house miners at the Lea Hall Colliery. The church of The Good Shepherd was built in the early 1960s.

Slitting Mill, 0.75m SW of Rugeley, is a most pleasant little village carved out of a wooded corner of Cannock Chase. Here are some attractive modern villas, properly spaced apart, and the 19th Century mission church of St John the Baptist, which is attached to a later private house. Originally, the settlement was called Stonehouse, after the large stone house in the village called Stonehouse (1584). This was an old home of the Weston family.

A large, brick water pumping station (SK 029171) is tucked out of sight down a lane by the pub. This waterworks stands on the site of the old iron slitting mill, established here 1625 by Thomas Chetwynd. A slitting mill cut iron bars into thin rods from which nails were made. The now dry mill-pond and pond bay still exist to the rear of the waterworks and alongside the stream, the Rising Brook. There are also some overgrown brick culverts, brick walling and stone slabs by the ford across the stream at SK 029171

Half a mile west of Slitting Mill, in **Birches Valley**, are the huts of the Cannock Chase Forest Centre and Deer Museum. All kinds of tourist and commercial information about the area can be obtained here. Nearby is a reconstructed Deer leap, an arrangement that allows deer to jump into an enclosure but stops them from jumping put again. These were very common in medieval times. The best way to describe a deer leap is to imagine a fence separating two fields. At the point where the leap is to be constructed the fence is lowered by about two feet and a mound of earth is raised against it so that the deer can walk up to the level of the top of the fence. On the other side of' the fence is a shallow pit about two feet deep. The deer can jump (or leap) into or over the pit and so into the adjoining field. However, they cannot jump back over the other way because the height of the fence, from the bottom of the pit to the top of the fence, is too great (at least six feet).

Rugeley's most infamous son is William Palmer, the Rugeley Poisoner. He was born here in 1824 and educated at the grammar school. He became a doctor of medicine and lived in a house opposite the Talbot Arms. His practice did not earn him enough to live on and he took to gambling and forgery. In 1854 his wife died suddenly and he collected £13,000 from his insurance company, an enormous sum in those days. Within a year his brother also died, but the insurance company was suspicious and refused to pay. Palmer then poisoned a bookmaker to whom he was in debt. He administered the poison at Shrewsbury Races. The bookmaker fell ill and Palmer brought him back to Rugeley. He got him lodgings at the Talbot Arms so that he could look after him. That night the bookmaker died. A coroner's court accused him of murder and he was duly tried. It was suspected that he had poisoned many other people but he was only charged with the murder of the three people mentioned above. The case was of national and international interest. Although he was found guilty the prosecution never established which poison had been used. Palmer was hanged in public outside Stafford Gaol.

On the north-western outskirts of Rugeley is **Etchinghill**, a place known to prehistoric men who built a large burial mound here. Here too there were regular horse race meetings from 1824 to 1839 and from 1848 to 1860. Now, alas, it is smothered in countless rows of modern, and definitely not upmarket houses.

In the early Autumn of 1991 a man out for a stroll on Cannock Chase found pieces of bead-like glass near the Wolseley sand and gravel quarry, Etching Hill, Rugeley. Archaeologists performed a magnetic gravity survey and discovered the remains of an ancient glass manufactory. The site lies on high ground, beside a small stream, on a slope near the head of a wooded valley. The remains lie within a 40-yard-diameter circle. They include: the foundations of a brick and stone, six-siege kiln building, roughly 13 feet by 10 feet, which encompasses a vitrified grey-green mass; the probable foundations of a second, older kiln near the stream; Cistercian domestic pottery; several wheelbarrow loads of broken fire-clay crucibles; mounds of black earth and half-broken pebbles; and numerous small pieces of green, blue, red and clear glass.

It is likely that this is the glassworks known to have existed in the Rugeley area during the 15th Century. In 1418-19 John Glasman of Rugeley supplied white glass to York Minster and in 1452 the 'glashoushay' at Wolseley is mentioned in contemporary documents. The better preserved of the two kiln sites is of about 1485. There were almost certainly other kilns in the area, and they are either yet to be discovered or already destroyed by quarrying. (The land is owned by Sir Charles Wolseley and the sand and gravel extraction is in the hands of Western Aggregates Ltd.)

The exact location of the glasshouse site is SK 00801896. It lies about 150 yards east of the well-made-up forestry track called South of Sow Street. At the time of our visit in 1988 it was easily approached along a subsidiary track, to which it stands adjacent. However, there are plans afoot to extend the workings northwards, beyond the present high perimeter bank, regardless of the fact that these woods (Little Birches) are a Forestry Conservation Area.

Beware of venturing too close to the quarry sides. They are very steep and crumbly. On the January day that we visited there was mist and a steady drizzle which loosened pebbles on the sheer faces. As they fell they chattered, an eerie sound like people talking in the distance. We also saw a sizeable herd of deer which took flight at the sight of my canine companion. Postscript: sixteen of the windows at York Minster are made from Rugeley glass and the Minster's expert, Peter Gibbons, considers them to be the finest, not only in Europe, but in the world. High praise indeed.

There are now three known sites within the diocese of Lichfield: at Bagot's Wood, Abbot's Bromley, where glass was almost certainly made during the 13th Century and where there is a complex of several kilns; at Bishop's Wood, Broughton near Eccleshall, where the glass furnace of 1580 has been restored and, of course, near Etching Hill, Rugeley.

All these works were in relatively remote areas because they required abundant supplies of timber to fuel the furnaces, fern to burn to make potash; fire clay from which to fashion the crucibles, water, and white sand, the basic raw material of glass. These rural glassworks closed in 1615 when a law was passed forbidding the use of timber as a furnace fuel. The glassmakers duly moved to the coalfields.

RUSHALL *1.5m* NE *of Walsall*

The name Rushall means 'rush-nook', that is, 'the isolated farm by the rushes'. In the Domesday Book Rushall is entered as an established manor, whereas Walsall is not even mentioned; but times change and today Rushall is a suburb of Walsall. The present Rushall Village, 0.75m N of 'Old' Rushall (the Hall and church), developed into its present suburban sprawl after the Second World War. The residential areas are fringed with open land along the banks of the Rushall Canal.

The church of St Michael is by James Cranston and was built in 1856. It has a nave, chancel, transepts, and a tower. In 1867 it was lengthened and the spire was added. The font is 13th Century and the wall paintings in the transepts are by Reginald Frampton, of 1905.

Just to the south-east of the church are the ruins of the 15th Century Rushall Hall, with its high curtain wall in which there are signs of fireplaces. The Hall site has been occupied since Anglo-Saxon times. Coins of that period have been found in the mound by the Hall. The first Hall was built in the 12th Century and parts of this sandstone building are to be found in the present gateway with its segmental arches. There have been a succession of Halls on the site: many could be called castles. Families resident here include Rushall, Bowles, Grubbere (or Ive), Harpur (15th Century, who built the gatehouse) and Leigh.

The Hall was held for Parliament by Colonel Leigh at the beginning of the Civil War. In 1643 it was taken by Colonel Lane of Bentley for the Royalists, but was recaptured by Parliament the next year and was dismantled at the end of the war. The stone house that stands near the ruins was built in the 19th Century.

Just to the north of Rushall is **Shelfield**. The name is from the Anglo-Saxon 'scylf-hyll', meaning 'the hill with a flat top'. There was a settlement here by at least 1276 but today it is a place of 20th Century houses and the church of St Mark (1965), bounded by the broad, marshy pastures of the Ford Brook flood plain to the west and a tributary stream to the east. There is a dour purple and red brick mill, hidden behind the hedges of the mill house, on high ground above the river plain. **High Heath** is the name given to the modern housing estates that lie north of Mill Lane Road.

Daw End is the southern suburb of Rushall, but is 0.75m NNW of Rushall church. The name Daw is probably from the Old English 'dad' or 'denu', both of which mean 'valley'. Indeed, Daw End is more or less at the end of a shallow valley, the broad green lowland followed by the Daw End Branch of the Rushall Canal which opened in 1802. There are houses, the Royal Oak Inn and the Red House Industrial Estate, which stretches from Bosty Lane to Dumble Derry Lane in Aldridge. In Park Lane, off Daw End Lane, are the Park Lime Pits, a disused limestone quarry with woodland, grassland and pools. Next to the car park is a small visitor's centre. The Wenlockian limestone quarried here, or at nearby Linley, was used for the foundations of the bath house at Letocetum just to the east.

At Calderfields Farm, 1m ESE of Rushall, is a circular moat which once encompassed Caldewelle Hall, built in about 1300 by Sir Hugh de Boweles for his son, Norman.

RUSHTON SPENCER *5.5m NW of Leek*

In Domesday Book the manor is referred to simply as Rushton. It belonged to the King and at that time was 'waste'.

Today, the village lies along the A52, Leek to Macclesfleld road, about 1m N of the northern end of Rudyard Reservoir. The village is ordinary enough but overlooking it on the bluff to the west, and visible from the main road, is the 'Chapel in the Wilderness'.

The church of St Lawrence, to give it its more prosaic name, can be approached either from the village, by way of a lane that crosses the route of the now-dismantled railway (past the old railway station, now a house) and up the hill of Rushton Bank, or from **Ryecroft Gate** (0.75m S of Rushton) by turning right at the pub on the top of the hill. The church is embowered in firs and yews at the end of a track that leads across a field, and has to be looked out for. The exterior is largely of stone and has a date of 1690 above the east window and one of 1713 above the south doorway. Within the stone walls and the mullioned windows, and below the weather-boarded bell-turret, is a much older timber-framed church, possibly of the 14th Century. It has low beams, oak piers and trusses, one of which carries the gallery. St Lawrence is a very rare church. The hatchments in the church are of the Trafford and Brocklehurst families who lived at Swythamley Hall, 3m NE of Rushton Spencer. It is highly probable that the original village stood close to the church and moved down into the valley below when the road became important as a trade route.

It was along this road that the body of Thomas Meaykin was brought by his family from Stone. Thomas was a groom who had dallied with his master's daughter. His master, an apothecary, was horrified. Shortly after, young Meaykin died suddenly and was hastily buried, but his favourite pony kept returning to his grave and pawing at the ground. The body was exhumed and was found to have turned over on to its face. Had the groom been poisoned and then buried alive, asked the locals? After his family had brought his remains back to Rushton they were re-buried at St Lawrence's. Meaykin's grave is the only one facing east.

The Staffordshire-Cheshire border is marked by the Dane River, which is crossed by the **Hug Bridge**, 0 75m NE of Rushton Spencer on the A523. In 1620 this bridge was destroyed in a flood. Responsibility for maintaining it was divided between Cheshire and Staffordshire. The Cheshire half was rebuilt in stone, but for some time the Staffordshire side consisted of 'long, tottering and loose poles'. Today there is the works of a water extraction plant beside the bridge.

Just south of the bridge there is a right of way leading west. This follows the gently curving terrace of the flood plain of the River Dane, and then heads up hill to the earth embankment of the feeder canal engineered by James Brindley. This draws water from the Dane near Bearda, a mile or more to the east, and carries it to Lake Rudyard, constructed at the end of the 18th century as a reservoir for the Caldon Canal. This steeply banked little channel still holds water – or should I say a slimy, foetid, insect-infested liquid. Anyway, Bruno, my dog, thought it rather splendid stuff and bathed in it, several times. Not being a selfish beast he shared it with me by rubbing himself against my trousers, several times. Nevertheless, this is a charming area with long views into Cheshire, tall grasses and varied wildlife.

Rushtonhall, 0.5m SW of St Lawrence's at Rushton Spencer, was formerly called Rushton James. The original manor probably stood on the site now occupied by Rushton Hall Farm (sic). From the end of the 15th Century until 1752 it was owned by the Rode family. The Rushton Hall we see today is 17th Century with 19th Century additions. The James of the name could be either from James de Audley of Heighley Castle, an early holder of the manor, or from the Fitz James family.

The Rushton Spencer ice factory was 0.5m NW of the village at SJ 931630. The water came from a spring and it was mechanically frozen. The station, on the NSR Valley line at Rushton Spencer, opened in 1849 and closed to passenger traffic in 1960.

S

SALT *3.5m NNE of Stafford*
Salt brine, from which salt is obtained by evaporation, has been obtained from natural springs and by pumping in Stafford, at Rickerscote and the Common), and at Shirleywich, near Weston on Trent, 1.75m SE of the village of Salt. However, there are no historical records or signs on the ground that salt was produced at, or close to, Salt itself. The name is at least as old as Domesday Book where it is called Selte, so one must presume that it had some ancient connection with the trade, if not as a producer then as a market place.

The village is pleasantly situated on a minor road in the Trent valley opposite Sandon park. Modern houses now line the road on both sides of the old centre which lies around the Holly Bush pub. The church of St James is on the eastern fringe of the settlement. It was built by Thomas Trubshaw in 1840-2 and paid for by Lord Talbot. The tall bellcote, the lofty nave, the high vaulted sanctuary, the large rose window and irregular nave windows delight some but are disparaged by others.

Little known, even to locals, are the ruined cave houses on **Salt Heath**, 0.66m S of the village, on a wooded hillside (SJ 956272). The public footpath from the village starts alongside a house called The Hollies. The path is not defined on the ground but if one heads leftwards, towards a gap between two woods, the caves will be seen near the top of the bluff to the right. They are well camouflaged by undergrowth and have to be looked for. The caves were extended at the front by the addition of orthodox house fronts built of stone blocks. There is a path, like a small terrace, in front of them. The caves, fireplaces and stone blocks are now in ruins, but were lived in until the early part of the 20th Century by people who followed the tinkers' trade. The area is called **Tinkerborough**.

A few yards NE, on the side of the hill facing the village, is another much older looking cave, made in the apparently softer rocks below a striking unconformity between the sandstone strata. One suspects that man may have lived in this area since prehistoric times, but as far as we know it has not been expertly investigated. Salt was very highly prized in ancient times, and the Romans even paid their soldiers' wages partly in salt - hence 'salary'. It is not unlikely that ancient man would choose to live near the source of a mineral so useful in many ways and, indeed, necessary for life itself.

SANDON *4m NNE of Stafford*
The village lies along the A51, Rugeley to Stone road, in the Trent valley. The centre of the settlement is at the junction with the road to Stafford, and was rebuilt about 1905 in Arts and Crafts black-and-white by Sir E Guy Dawber at the expense of Lord Harrowby. The pub, the Dog and Doublet, the village hall and a few cottages were all made to match. They are somewhat artificial but not unpleasing. A little further northwards there are some good brick houses, a Post Office and an old chapel now used as a furniture workshop. The Sandon we see today is a relatively new creation.

The manor that Earl Algar owned in 1066, and which passed to the King after the Conquest, lay 0.33m ENE of the new centre, between the church and the moat that marks the site of the medieval and Tudor manor houses. It was the fashion in the 16th and 17th Centuries to empark the land around the Hall or Manor House. Some landowners built themselves a new Hall away from the village and others chose to keep their old houses and remove the village. At Sandon the lord chose the latter and the old village of Great Sandon was obliterated, though the house platforms and holloways remain by the church. The tenants moved down to Little Sandon, which had grown up along the main road, so the Sandon of today should really be called Little Sandon.

The church and the moat of the old Hall are in Sandon Park whose woods line the main road. It is a large and beautiful estate, very little of which can be seen by the public, although the road from Sandon to Milwich passes through similar undulating and slightly mysterious country. The estate used to belong to the Erdeswick family, one of whom was Samson Erdeswick (died 1603), a local historian of some repute. His son sold the manor to George Digby, his half brother, whose daughter and heiress married Lord Gerard of Gerard's Bromley (near Ashley). His grand-daughter married the 4th Duke of Hamilton in 1698.

The old manor house in which the lords had lived until then is that depicted in Dr Plot's 'Natural History of Staffordshire' (1686). However, the 9th Duke of Hamilton, Lord Archibald, demolished the old manor and built a new classical house, designed by Joseph Pickford, half-a-mile south, near the main road. The 9th Duke sold this house and the estate to the 1st Earl of Harrowby in 1777. In 1848 the house burned down and the 2nd Earl commissioned William Burn to build another.

The new, handsome, stone-built Jacobean mansion with gables and turrets was completed by 1852. The entrance side has nine bays, two storeys and a coach porch. Attached to the house is a fine Victorian Conservatory of 1864. Today, the house is still a private home but is also let out for weddings and the like. In the grounds are an Ice House by the drive; the Italianate belvedere Tower Top from the dismantled Trentham Hall; the Perceval Shrine in memory of the murdered Prime Minister, Spencer Perceval (died 1812); the Pitt column, at the most southern tip of the Park, near the road; a Doric pillar of 1806; and the Home Farm of 1777-80 in classical style, of ashlar with low roofs by Samuel Wyatt.

By the railway is the Sandon Estate Station, a delightful neo-Jacobean building of 1849, which contained private apartments for the Duke and a coach-porch for his carriage. The station can be seen quite clearly from the road to Stafford, near to the village centre. It had fallen into shameful disrepair but, fortunately, the Harrowby estate decided to sell it and the new owners have renovated the old building in a most excellent way. Just south-west of the station and the railway line is the Trent and Mersey Canal which follows a parallel course to the River Trent.

The church of All Saints now stands alone save for one little cottage at the back of the churchyard. There are lovely views across the Park from here. The oldest part of the church is the 13th Century south aisle, which was in fact the original church. To this was added the tower; then a north aisle; then, in about 1300, a new chancel; then a new nave was built in place of the north aisle; and lastly, a new short north aisle was added in the 14th Century.

The furniture and furnishings are very fine - bleached oak pews, pulpit and reredos, all of the 17th Century. There is a fragment of early 14th Century glass in the west window, heraldic glass of the 17th Century in the east window and glass by Wailes in the west window of 1845. The monuments include memorials to the Erdeswickes, George Digby and the Harrowbys. The north aisle became the Harrowby Chapel in 1851. The epitaph to the 5th Earl reads: 'He built the central layout of Sandon Village and many farms, smallholdings and cottages, and planted some 100,000 trees. He loved every sod of soil on the Estate.' The present Earl, the 7th, is a banker. The family name is Coutts Ryder, of the same line that established Coutts & Company, bankers to the Queen.

SAREDON *2m SW of Cannock*
There are two settlements: Great Saredon and, 0.75m SW, Little Saredon. Great Saredon lay in Cannock Chase in early medieval times. Great Saredon Hall is a brick house, some of which dates from about 1700; a brick outbuilding with stone dressings is of about 1600. Great Saredon Low, to the east of the settlement, is probably of Roman origin. It is now nearly ploughed out. Saredon Hill is 500 feet above sea level. The 'don' suffix means 'hill'. The prefix 'Sare' is open to many interpretations.

SAVERLEY GREEN *4m NE of Stone*
The settlement takes its name from the nearby Sale Brook and was originally called Saley Green. However, it also lies on the banks of the River Blithe. In the 19th Century Saverley Green was well known as a venue for cock fights. The village retains its green and also a 1.5-acre remnant of its common land. The local hostelry is The Greyhound Inn which has elaborate November Fifth celebrations. Saverley Green is joined to Cresswell by a bridge over the River

Blithe.

Cresswell has a roman Catholic church with early parish registers. The suffix 'well' is from 'wall', thought to be a reference to the Limes Britannicus, the earth wall and ditch built by the Romans from Doncaster to Gloucester.

SEDGLEY *3m S of Wolverhampton*

In early medieval times Sedgley was a large parish and a large manor which had, prior to the Conquest, belonged to Earl Algar. The manor comprised nine villages, namely: Sedgley, Cotwall End, Gospel End, Woodsetton (which included Dudley Castle and Priory), Coseley, Ettingshall, Brierley, Upper Gornal and Lower Gornal.

Sedgley itself lies at the northern end of the high watershed ridge that runs from southern Wolverhampton to Dudley, and which divides the Black Country. From Beacon Hill there are wide views over Shropshire and Wales to the west and over the Black Country and Cannock Chase to the east. On top of the hill is a late 19th Century stone tower, built by Lord Wrottesley as an astrological observatory.

The town centre of Sedgley is a thriving place, although its northern fringes degenerate as Wolverhampton is approached, and it has its share of modern housing estates. The actual centre is the Bull Ring, a reminder that blood sports were widely practiced in the area during the 18th and 19th Centuries. Here is the Red Lion, an old coaching inn, and the even older Court House. The manor court, established in Norman times, was held here until the end of the 19th Century. A plaque on the inn wall explains the origin of the expression 'give him a fourpenny one'. This referred to the cost, and therefore the size, of the stick used to thrash miscreants by way of punishment.

The medieval church of All Saints in Vicarage Street was rebuilt by Thomas Lee in 1826-9 at the expense of the 1st Earl of Dudley. It is an impressive Gothic building with a tall, recessed pinnacled spire, high aisles, and long, two-light windows. The ashlar Roman Catholic church of St Chad and All Saints in Catholic Lane is of 1823, an early date for such a grand church because Catholics were only allowed to worship in public from 1829. The presence of the church is explained by the fact that there used to be a Roman Catholic college, 1.5m N of Sedgley town centre, at what is now the Park Hall Hotel (technically now in Wolverhampton).

Park Hall is approached along the Ednam Road, off the A4039. It is probably of the early 18th Century and is of brick with five bays, three storeys, a centrepiece of various columns and a carved frieze in Jacobean style. On both side are long two-storey wings. The gardens are largely given over to a tarmac car park. Park Hall was an old home of the Dudley family.

In Ettingshall Lane, which used to be called Hell Lane, there lived a witch who could turn herself into a white rabbit which regularly snooped about the gardens and even the houses of her neighbours. (See Hell Lane.)

About a mile west of Sedgley town centre, down Bush Bank, at Gospel End is the site of **Baggeridge** Colliery, the last large pit to close in the Black Country. The area has been landscaped and in 1983 the newly formed Country Park, complete with a visitor centre and signed trails, was opened by Princess Anne. Close by, sign posted by its tall chimney, is Baggeridge Brickworks which is still a going concern. Adjacent to the sheds, ovens, and large multi-coloured spoil heaps of the brickworks is Woodfield Equestrian Centre. The fields for miles around are well stocked with horses of every size, shape and colour. Baggeridge appeared as Badgering in Ellen Thorneycroft Fowler's novel 'The Farindons', published in 1901.

Gospel End is a pleasant little place of mainly modern, middle-class houses. There is a pub, The Summerhouse, and the yellow stone Anglican chapel of St Barnabas. This is now a dwelling. Between Gospel End and Wombourne is a mile or more of open country.

Cotwall End lies 1m SSE of Sedgley town centre. Here, on the gentle slopes of a valley and surrounded by suburbia, is the Cotwall End Nature Centre, a site of Special Scientific Interest. There is a variety of plant and animal life, some in natural habitats, others in aviaries and freshwater pools. There are large numbers of birds, sheep, goats, rabbits, foxes and badgers and also a craft centre with resident artists. It is a charmingly informal place with large lawned areas, a cafe, car park and friendly staff. Admission is free.

Hurst Hill, a limestone hill of 705 feet, about 0.5m ENE of Sedgley, is now a residential suburb. John Cornfield (c 1820-1890), the Coseley Poet, was a brick maker and later a pawnbroker in the Hurst Hill area. He was found drowned on his Coseley estate.

SEIGHFORD *2.5m NW of Stafford*

The old name of the village was Chesterford - Cesteforde in Domesday Book - which implies that there is an undiscovered Roman settlement hereabouts. The village consists of red brick cottages, farms, the half-timbered Church Farm, a pub and the village green, which lies between the school and the church. The 'ford' of the village's name is where the Gamesley Brook is crossed by the lane that leads off the village green, opposite the school.

St Chad's church has a 17th Century brick tower with Gothic details, buttresses and stone pinnacles of 1748, and a brick south wall. The north wall and chancel are medieval stone. Inside, the north arcade and chancel arch are Norman, probably of the late 12th Century. The south chancel window has 15th Century figures and fragments. The monuments include alabaster effigies of William Bowyer, died 1595, and wife, and an obelisk commemorating Francis Eld of 1777. The pulpit and communion rail are Jacobean and the Squire's pew is of 1748. It is a church which has great atmosphere.

Seighford Hall lies 0.25m NW of the village green. It is a large, timber-framed house with a late 16th Century core and considerable late Victorian extensions. The Hall was the home of the Eld family. In recent years it was a hotel, then a home for old people and is now in the process of being restored

To the left of the house are the sizeable outbuildings. The brick, church-like structure adjacent to the Gamekeeper's Cottage is said to be of the 14th Century and to have come from Ranton Abbey. The timber-framed stables have recently been renovated and converted into dwellings. Just to the north-east of the Hall (on the road to Great Bridgford) is Cooksland Hall Farm, and at the end of the track is a large timber-framed barn.

Seighford Aerodrome lies 0.5m W of the village. It is now very little used but the runways are still intact and relatively clear of undergrowth. A light aeroplane is stored in a hangar hidden by a wood. The airfield opened in 1942. Wellington bombers flew from here until 1945 and it was a base for 'D-Day' gliders. The RAF left in 1946, and from 1956 the airfield was used by civilians. It officially closed in 1966.

Close to the southern tip of the aerodrome is **Coton Clanford** Hall Farm, a good timber-framed house with a three-storey brick porch. (Coton Clanford is a hamlet 0.75m S of the Hall.) As one might suspect by the presence of the wartime aerodrome the land here is relatively flat The scattered farms and cottages are joined by a mass of narrow, un-signposted winding lanes, many of which form rough circles, as not a few strangers have found to their fury.

SEISDON *1m NW of Trysull*

Tucked up against the Shropshire border Seisdon was something of a forgotten place. However, it is now on the route of the Staffordshire Way long-distance footpath and is therefore becoming better known. The name is from the Old English 'Scaxcsdun', 'the hill of the Saxons', probably the 300-foot hill just to the west of the settlement. Seisdon was one of the five Anglo-Saxon Hundreds of the County of Staffordshire. The other four were Cuttlesdon and Totmonslow in the north, and Afflow and Pirehill in the south. The Hundred was an administrative unit, and amongst the duties of its officers were the collection of taxes and enforcement of the law. Although now defunct, some Hundreds were involved in local government into the early years of the 19th Century.

Today, Seisdon is a substantial, spread-about village in the valley of the Smestow Brook. Most of the houses surround an extremely large village green. Only the noisy lorries from the extensive Tarmac sand and gravel quarries on the hill disturb the quiet of this otherwise thriving but peaceful place. By the willow-lined brook is an old brick mill and mill house. They bear a plaque 'RW 1749', but there was doubtless a mill here long before that. There are several substantial red brick farms and three 'big houses': the modest but attractive red brick Old Manor House, dated 'HE1684', which has two gables, string courses and ball finials; the substantial Seisdon Hall, small red bricks with stone dressings, shaped gables, tall chimneys and reputed to be Elizabethan with a half-timbered core, presently occupied by the Foster family and their pack of varied and vociferous dogs; and Seisdon House, five bays, low red brick Georgian with a columned porch.

Between the grander houses are an old sandstone cottage, some black-and-white buildings, the old, white-painted Smithy (dated 1787), some pleasant modern houses, a Post Office/general store and the Seven Stars. The modern pub stands on the sight of an ancient hostelry.

Of ancient monuments the Victoria County History records: "On Seisdon Common, near Abbot's or Apwood Castle (0.75m SW of Seisdon), is a small square entrenchment with a single ditch, situated on a round promontory; near the common (1.33m S of Seisdon) is a large triangular stone called War Stone, which Mr Coote suggests is a 'trifinnial boundary stone'; 1.25m W of Seisdon at Moat Rough is a dry, rectangular moat, 177 feet by 143 feet."

Seisdon is on the southern boundary of the ice sheet of the last Ice Age, and there are heavy deposits of clay which contain granite and other igneous boulder-stones commonly used for walling in the area.

SHARESHILL *4.5m NNE of Wolverhampton*

An old, pre-Norman settlement. The present village lies just beyond the suburbs of Wolverhampton but has been ensnared by motorways, with the M6 one mile to the east (at junction 11) and the M54 just over one mile south (at junction 1). A few of the older houses have survived but, as always, new housing has done little to enhance the townscape.

The church of St Luke has a stone tower, the lower part of which is 15th Century and the upper of about 1562 with a frieze of saltire crosses below the crenellations. The rest is Georgian with stone dressings of about 1742. The windows have round heads and pilasters; the porch has Tuscan columns and the apse has a Venetian window. The furnishings are of the period - box pews, pulpit and altar rails. The alabaster figures are of Sir Humphrey Swynnerton, died 1562, and wife. William Havergal (died 1870), a respected composer of hymns and church music, was a vicar here. Frances Ridley Havergal, also a writer of hymns, was his daughter.

Little Saredon lies 0.25m NE of Shareshill. It is a small village with a windmill of about 1800, converted to a cottage in 1943; and an old Manor, the central timber-framed portion of which is probably 16th Century.

One mile SE of Shareshill is Hilton Hall . (See Hilton.)

SHEEN *2.5m SSE of Longnor, which is 6m SSE of Buxton*

The name Sheen is probably from the Anglo-Saxon 'scine' meaning 'scenic, but especially beautiful'. Sheen is a remote village in the North Staffordshire Moorlands between the upper reaches of the River Dove to the east and the River Manifold to the west. The farms and cottages straggle along the road. There is a school, a Post Office and a church.

St Luke's was rebuilt in the 19th Century. The work was started by C W Burleigh but finished by William Butterfield who was appointed by Alexander Beresford Hope, the squire of Beresford Hall. (Beresford Hall was previously the home of Joseph Cotton of 'Compleat Angler' fame. It lay about 2m to the SSE but has been demolished - see Dovedale.) Beresford Hope was a wealthy Anglo-Catholic and a friend of the founders of the Camden Society to one of whom, namely Benjamin Webb, he gave the living of Sheen parish. All the stained glass in the church is of 1854 by O'Connor. The monuments include: a defaced effigy in the churchyard; a memorial to the Crichton family of about 1855, also in the churchyard; and tablets to Beresford Hope, died 1887, and Lady Mildred Beresford Hope, died 1881.

The school is by Burleigh and the most excellent and interesting Parsonage is by Butterfield of 1852. It has varied roof lines, broad chimney stacks, a polygonal stair turret and pointed arch windows.

Broadmeadow Hall, 1m NW of Sheen, was the manor house of Sheen. There was a house here from the late 16th Century and it was the seat of the Sleigh family until 1709. The present house is 17th Century and was restored in the 1990s after having lain empty for some years.

About 1m SSW of Sheen is **Hulme End**. Here is the Light Railway Hotel, a reminder that the narrow gauge (2 feet 6 inch) Manifold Valley Light Railway operated between Hulme End and Waterhouses (where it connected with the normal gauge railway) between the years 1904 and 1934. When the line was dismantled the trackway was metalled and is now a footpath.

To the WSW of Sheen, by 0.75m, is **Brund**. Here is Brund Mill (SK 099613), a three-storey watermill which, though partly ruined, is of great interest because of the machinery and engineering technique used here for grinding. Brund Mill Bridge is a packhorse bridge on the salt road from Northwich to Chesterfield. In the hills to the east of Brund are two ancient burial mounds: Brund Low and Rye Low.

SHENSTONE *4m E of Brownhills and 3m S of Lichfield*

The village lies 1m S, off the busy junction of the A5, the A5127 and the A5148. It sits on a hill with two church towers, making it easily identified. Shenstone has a history as old as history can be, for here was found an early stone hand axe made some 30,000 years BC, before the last Ice Age. The Romans were busy hereabouts. Watling Street passes 0.33m NE, Ryknild Street 0.25m W and the Roman fort-settlement of Wall (Letocetum) is only 1.5m NW. In the vicinity of Shenstone Hall Farm there are crop marks indicating Iron-Age/Roman farming activities. The name Shenstone is from the Anglo-Saxon and means 'shining (or beautiful) stone'.

There can be little doubt that the Anglo-Saxons had a settlement at Shenstone from soon after the Roman departure. In 1066 the manor was held by Godwin who lost it to the great marcher lord Roger de Montgomery after the Conquest. In 1086 it was a settlement of some considerable size for its day with a population of at least 26 families. In Shenstone Park is an isolated rectangular moat, presumably the site of an early timber-framed manor house.

Shenstone Hall is 0.5m NE of the village, surrounded by high walls. The facade and forecourt facing the road is Jacobean, with mullioned windows and three gables made Gothic at the end of the 18th Century. The garden facade is even more strongly Gothicized with an ornate porch and decorated gables - altogether an attractive house. Shenstone Court lay 0.5m south-east of the village but was pulled down before the Second World War. The church of St John is surprisingly impressive though somewhat stern. It was built in 1852 by John Gibson - nave, aisles, tower, outer south chapel and large rose window. North-west of the new church stands the tower and some walling with an Early English doorway of the old medieval church. Shenstone has such excellent road communications that it is in danger of being spoiled by developers.

Footherley, 1m WSW of Shenstone, is a hamlet which straggles along a minor road, part of which follows the track of Ryknild Street. A Roman coin, an aureus of Claudius, was found south of the settlement at Forge Mill (SK 090018) in 1924. In Elizabethan times Footherley Hall was the home of Francis Floyer. Today it is a nursing home for the elderly.

SHIRLEYWICH 0.75m SE of Weston on Trent, which is 4m NE of Stafford

The area was originally called Brinepits, but at the end of the 17th Century Robert Shirley (Lord Ferrers) developed the salt workings here commercially and within a few years the name had changed to Shirleywich. The Earl dug new pits until he found a brine stream. The new brine pit was 27 feet deep and six feet square. The brine was evaporated in three iron pans, 8 feet by 5 feet, and it took one ton of coal and 16 hours to produce 14 bushels of salt. This was twice as long and twice as costly as anywhere else, but the quality was good and the product commanded a higher price. In about 1700 a new, stronger brine stream was tapped and a new works was built. Production rose to about 800 tons a year. Demand then dropped and the works were leased to a local farmer, Preston Moore. In 1777 the Trent and Mersey Canal came within a few hundred yards of the works. During the Napoleonic Wars trade increased. There were now eight pans and production had risen to 4,000 tons of salt a year. About 20 families, totalling about 100 people, lived in Shirleywich and all were employed at the works. By the 1830s production was 12,500 tons a year, but by 1870 it was falling because the supply of brine was getting weaker. By the 1890s the works only operated intermittently and by 1901 they were closed.

As the Shirleywich works closed so a new company began to expand at Stafford. (See Stafford.) Today there is very little to see at Shirleywich. The brine pits were behind the three pairs of semi-detached houses, opposite the

Shirleywich Service Station. Next to them, on the right, is an area of disturbed ground. There was a row of 13 cottages here. The people who lived in these houses grew to be very old and the local people think that it was the salt in the air that kept them fit and healthy.

SHORT HEATH *1m SW Bloxwich*

In the 19th Century it was a small mining settlement. Today, it is a pleasant residential area. It has a small, village-like shopping centre spoiled only by the Spar food store with its hideous red windows - a real blot on the landscape. There is a pub, The Woolpack, and a neat estate of white-painted Council houses which are graced with little gables (like windowless dormers). The Commissioners' church of Holy Trinity (1854) is built of smoke-blackened, red sandstone and stands embowered in mature trees.

Nearby is Pimbury Road, which encircles a raised grey mound. This is the spoil of an old coal mine, and is also adorned with tall, mature trees. Indeed, it is trees that are the feature of Short Heath. The area was once a part of the great Royal Hunting Forest of Cannock Chase. From the 17th Century the trees were cut down for use as fuel in iron forges. The old woodlands, now grassland, were then stocked with sheep which ate any new young tree growth. It remained as moorland until the earth was ripped apart for coal. When the pits closed it was left an industrial wasteland.

The oaks, alders, elders, buckthorn and birches we see today in the 80 acre **Rough Wood** at Short Heath have all naturally regenerated. A handful of the oaks are over 200 years old, although most of the wood has a very gnarled, ancient feel to it. From the 1950s the area was made safe and is now open to the public. The small pits and mounds which can still be seen were made by local people digging for coal for domestic use. Rough wood can be entered from Myrtle Close, off Woodside Way, where there is a notice board with useful maps and information on the whole Nature Reserve. In total, the Nature Reserve encompasses 360 acres and stretches from the Bentley Coal Wharf Bridge in the south to the Sneyd Canal Reservoir in the north.

The canal that forms the southern boundary is James Brindley's Wyrley and Essington (1792-1795), which follows the 400-foot contour. (By keeping to a constant height above sea level the early canal builders minimized the number of expensive locks, cuttings, tunnels, and embankments needed. The price paid, however, was often a circuitous route.) In 1905 subsidence caused the canal to sink at Short Heath. The coal mine below was flooded and three miners were drowned.

Lane Head lies around the canal bridge, just south of the parish church. There are a few shops, the Bridge Tavern, a red brick Board School of 1880 and a Methodist Church. The area still retains some traditional character.

SILVERDALE *1m W of Newcastle-under-Lyme*

Silverdale lies in a valley and, seen from the high road to Keele, the roofs of the houses and factories often gleam in the sun. It was a mining village but the large British Coal Kent's Lane Colliery (lately called Silverdale Colliery) closed in the 1990s. The considerable estate of the colliery is now (in 2004) being developed as a business park. The houses in the Victorian terraces are wonky in the extreme, but no one complains. After all, the inhabitants earned their living digging out the ground below that caused the settlement above.

It is a mature, work-a-day place centered on the church. Saint Luke's is a

33. Aldridge, near Walsall: the BP oil and lubricant plant. The older industries were coal and lime-stone mining and brick and tile manufacture. Today light industry prevails. (1991, slide 7741)

34. Kings Bromley: Manor Thatch, a chocolate-box cottage used on the back cover of my 1989 topographical guide to *Staffordshire and the Black Country*. (1987, slide 882)

35. Silverdale Colliery, near Newcastle-u-Lyme, and George Jones. At the time of the photograph it was a working mine but has since closed, the last deep pit in N Staffordshire. (1992, pkt 124 neg 23)

36. A gypsy family camped near Tutbury: the young lad in the canary-yellow sweater snatched £300 from my wallet and ran off as I gave his father my business card. (1998, pkt 283)

37. Hanley: the Etruria Marina is built beside the Trent and Mersey Canal. Pictured are narrowboat-dwellers Jack Hancock and his football playing Jack Russell dog, Shammy (1992, MD2).

38. Stafford: a 'totter' plies his trade in Burton Manor. Those operating with traditional horse-drawn carts are now few and far between. (1987, slide 118)

39. Blithfield Reservoir: a summer sunset. The lake was made in 1953 by damming the River Blithe. It is two miles long and there is a yachting club and a bird sanctuary. (c.1987, from a print)

40. Wetton Mill lies 1m NE of Wetton in the Manifold Valley. On Summer weekends it resembles a resort. In Winter the river disappears underground and re-emerges at Ilam. (1987 slide 777)

41. On Biddulph Moor, looking north. Amongst the scattered homesteads are those of the descendants of Saracen slaves brought here by a medieval crusading lord, it is believed. (1987, slide 536)

42. Lake Rudyard, North Staffs: Rudyard Kipling's parents courted here. A small natural lake was greatly enlarged to be a feeder reservoir for the Caldon Canal in 1797. (1997, pkt 45)

43. Jon Raven, of Wolverhampton: researcher of West Midlands folk music and singer-songwriter with numerous recordings, publications and TV and radio broadcasts to his credit. (2004, digital)

44. Black Dog Molly: a lively mixed team of morris dancers from Stoke-on-Trent, photographed at the First Market Drayton Folk Festival, organised by the author. (2000, pkt 291 neg 17)

45. Tipton Green: a Youth Afloat narrowboat near the Factory Canal Junction. Tipton has been called the 'Venice of the Midlands' because it has so many miles of canals. (1991, slide 7692)

46. Tipton: Ocker Hill electrical power station over the ruins of its predecessor. My father was the Borough Electrical Engineer in several towns, including Wolverhampton. (1991, slide 5028)

47. Biddulph Grange: the Chinese Garden. The house was built for James Bateman, 1814-97, but is now divided into apartments. The gardens have been restored by the National Trust. (1987, slide 494)

48. Madeley Old Hall, Staffordshire, is a former farmhouse of 1647. The parish church has stained glass windows by William Morris and Sir Edward Burne -Jones. (2003, digital)

49. Acton Trussell, near Stafford: a wedding at the Moat House. Dull days are the best for wedding photography because the brightness range is reduced. (1989, slide 6407)

50. Worfield, near Bridgnorth, is a delightful village that nestles between the River Worfe and a sandstone cliff. The church is of the 13th and 14th centuries. (1987, slide 1432)

51. Barlaston Hall was built about 1756. It was affected by mining subsidence and fell into disrepair. Wedgewood's bought it and wanted to demolish it, but it was saved and restored. (1987, slide 1075)

52. Black Ladies, Brewood, is a splendid house built on the site of a Norman Benedictine monastery founded about 1140. Some parts of the abbey are incorporated into the house. (1987, slide 1481)

53. Cheadle is a pleasant market town in the North Staffordshire Moorlands. The Gothic-style church of St Giles is by Pugin. It is richly decorated and nationally known. (1987, slide 449)

54. Coseley: The Delves, at Junction 8 of the M6, near its confluence with the M5 and the culverted River Teme - a good place for a picnic, don't you think? The dog is Pirate. (1991, slide 7244)

55. Norbury Junction, near Newport, is no longer a junction. The Newport Canal is derelict but it has a British Waterways maintenance yard and a holiday hire company. (1987, slide 602)

56. Beech Caves, Beech, were made by quarrying limestone for building Trentham Hall. Later they were used for storing ammunition. The escarpment has beautiful bluebell woods. (2004, digital)

57. Willey Moor Lock, Bradeley Green, north of Whitchurch, off the A49, stands on the Llangollen branch of the Shropshire Union Canal. The dog is my good friend Bruno. (1992, pkt 163 neg 30)

58. Hamstall Ridware: the church of St Michael with its 14th Century tower and chancel seen over the lush meadows of the River Blythe. The Hall ruins stand close to the church. (1987, slide 656)

59. Newcastle-under-Lyme, Morris Dancers, but not as traditional teams would know it. These young girls were parading at an area meet. The 'sport' is very popular in Lancashire. (1999, slide 8826)

60. Broughton church, near Eccleshall: a pre-Raphaelite stained glass window . The church is also well known for its high-backed wooden pews, which creak a lot during services. (1987, slide 1565)

61. Netherton: Lodge Farm Reservoir is the twinkle in the eye of this Black Country town. Netherton is known for Real Ale, Jews Harps and nailmaking. The church is St Andrews. (1991, slide 7547).

62. Staffordshire Police Headquarters: the Band of the Mercian Volunteers plays at the Gala Day in the grounds of Baswich House, Weeping Cross, Stafford. (1987, slide 129)

63. Stone: canoeist on the rapids of the River Trent, an important practice area for followers of this sport. Camera movement gave the effect, not computer manipulation. (1987, slide 1688)

64. Tutbury: the Dog and Partridge in the main street, down which bulls were run in the days when John of Gaunt held court here at his castle, which is open to the public. (1987, slide 284)

gaunt, yellow sandstone building strapped together with iron rods and plates. Behind it once stood the grey-green sheds, gantries, conveyers and engine house of the now demolished colliery. Beside it is a surprisingly large, modern and cheerful-looking old people's home called Brighton House, and opposite is the Victorian Conservative Association building.

Silverdale House is a 19th Century stone villa which has latterly been converted into the Parkside Working Men's Club. It was the home of the Cadman family. James Cope Cadman was the General Manager of the Butterley Company iron and coal works at Silverdale. His son, John Cadman (1877-1941), became Professor of Mining and Petroleum at Birmingham University and pioneered the exploration of the Persian Gulf oilfields. He was Chairman of the Anglo-Iranian Oil Company and was made 1st Baron Cadman of Silverdale.

'Red Fanny', Fanny Deakin (nee Davenport), a locally well-known Communist Party member and social activist, was born at Spout Head Farm, Abbey Street in 1883. She married a miner, led strikes and hunger marches and visited Russia twice on funds supplied by the people of Silverdale. She campaigned for the maternity hospital (1947) in Newcastle-under-Lyme, which bears her name. She died in 1968.

At **Black Bank**, 0.5m N of Silverdale, is a 162 square-foot, underground nuclear bunker. It was built by the council in the 1950s during the Cold War but was sold to a private buyer in 1973. There is also a Primitive Methodist Chapel of 1861 and a disused coalmine

The Silverdale area is rich in industrial archaeological sites. The following is a drive that encompasses some of these. We start at Scot Hay Road at the old Silverdale Ironworks furnace pool. This still holds water and is used for fishing. The furnaces stood just west of the pool and some of the connecting pipes can be seen. The slag heaps have been quarried for road metal since the works closed in 1902.

North-west of the pool is **Little Sheriff**, a small working drift coal mine in private ownership. On the other side of the road there was another furnace pool, now filled in, and more slag heaps. Proceed westwards along Scot Hay Road to the junction with **Crackley** Lane at Crackley Gates (SJ 804471). The gates are gone but the gatehouse still stands. Behind the red brick tollhouse is a commercial vehicle yard. It stands on the site of the Crackley Colliery.

Turn south (left) at the junction and go down the unmade lane, passing broiler chicken sheds. On the hillside are old spoil mounds, colliery engine pools (now waterless) and embankments of old tramways. The trees above them are part of the most attractive **Haying Wood** in which there are many 'gin pits'. Gin pits are so called because coal was hauled up the vertical shaft by a horse walking in a circle and turning a barrel windlass, or gin. Until recently there were still some brick remains of the Haying Pit colliery engine house, which powered the tramways that linked the mine to the ironworks below.

A side track to the right of the main lane leads past a ruined farmhouse, inhabited by hens and ducks, to the small, working **Bank Top** drift mine. The main lane continues on to a T-junction where, hidden in a hen farm, are the remains of the **Hollywood Mine**.

Turn left at the junction and pass between the abutments of the bridge that once carried the tramway from Hollywood to the Hayling engine house. Continue through the wood and its 'gin pits' to the junction of Pepper Street, where there is a garage. Behind the garage are the remains of a brickworks, latterly used as a waste disposal site and fishing pool. Turn left into Pepper

Street (B5044) at SJ 807463 and continue back to High Street in Silverdale.

The railway track that runs parallel to Pepper Street is the Market Drayton branch line, last only used to take coal from Silverdale and Holditch to the West Coast main line at Madeley. Across the High Street, near a footbridge over the railway, is the former Silverdale Station, tiny and complete but about to be demolished, we understand.

Turn left into High Street. On the right-hand side of the road is the track of the railway that connected the colliery to the ironworks. On the left-hand side is Parkside Social Club, in what was Silverdale House, the residence of one of the early ironmasters, as already mentioned.

SHUGBOROUGH *5m ESE of Stafford*

Shugborough is an estate, not a village. There was a village here once but it was removed by the Anson family, between about 1750 and 1825, to improve the view from the Hall. Some of the dispossessed tenants were re-housed at Great Haywood near the Essex Bridge. The estate covers some 900 acres of Cannock Chase and the greater part lies on a promontory of low land, south of the confluence of the River Sow and the River Trent. It can be approached on foot from Great Haywood but the main entrance is off the A513, Stafford to Rugeley road, at Milford Common.

The square entrance lodges have pyramid roofs and pairs of columns. They were designed by the architect, Samuel Wyatt, who worked at Shugborough between 1790 and 1806. The drive passes through woods of tall trees. To the left is a marshy area with pools and dense undergrowth. The road leaves the woodland and enters the agricultural Park. The main-line railway emerges from a tunnel here and it is a surprise to find such an intrusion.

A little further along, the Home Farm is passed on the right. Here are found: the Dairy where butter is made using 19th Century equipment; the Farmhouse Kitchen, restored and furnished as it was in 1805; the Scullery, with both washing facilities and a bread making oven; Noah's Park, with Jacob sheep and poultry for young children to see at close quarters; shire horses; northern shorthorn cattle; longhorn cattle; white park cattle, an ancient 'Roman' breed; Tamworth pigs; Gloucestershire Old Spot pigs; bearded Bagot goats; and various breeds of sheep. The mill has been restored and grinds corn grown on the estate. The farm buildings were constructed in about 1805.

The entrance drive ends at the County Museum, which is housed in the out-buildings of the Hall. These are arranged around a courtyard. There are recon-structions of domestic rooms, craft workshops, a school room and retail shops etc, together with a collection of coaches, the restored Estate Brewery and much more. The buildings have been painted in pale grey to match the painted brick Mansion.

It is a surprise to find that the eight giant columns which front the impressive portico of the Hall are a sham, being made of wood dressed in slate and painted. The history of the house is this: the centre is of 1693; the wings are of 1748, though originally only of one storey and heightened after 1768 by James Stuart; the columned portico was added by Wyatt in 1794, and at the same time the high centre block was lowered by removing the balustrade and placing it over the wings; the Saloon with convex front, a Drawing Room and other rooms at the rear were added in 1803-6. The rooms presently open to the public exhibit splendid plasterwork and decorative mouldings on ceilings, covings, arches, friezes, columns and chimney pieces and are beautifully furnished with a collection of paintings, 18th Century ceramics, silver and French furniture.

The house was bought by the Anson family in 1624. The man who made their name and their fortune was George Anson, died 1762. He was in turn Admiral, Commander-in-Chief and First Lord of the Admiralty. He died childless and his fortune passed to his elder brother, Thomas (1695-1773), and it was he who employed James Stuart to work on the house and the monuments in the grounds. When Thomas died he was succeeded by his sister's son, George, who changed his name to Anson. George's son was created Viscount Anson in 1806 and he employed Samuel Wyatt as architect at Shugborough after the death of James Stuart in 1788. The 2nd Viscount was created Earl of Lichfield in 1831.

When the 4th Earl died in 1960 Shugborough passed to the National Trust and is now administered by them in conjunction with Staffordshire County Council. The present Earl of Lichfield is Patrick, the professional photographer and blood sports enthusiast. He has a private apartment in the south wing and stays there quite regularly. The Mansion, though handsome enough, is, by stately home standards, not especially noteworthy.

It is for the Park Ornaments that Shugborough is famous. These are a collection of mostly Classically inspired buildings scattered around the grounds at strategic points, and whose purpose was simply to delight the eye. They include: the Lantern of Diogenes, 1764-71, a copy of the Choragic Monument by Lysikrates, probably by James (Athenian) Stuart; the Arch of Hadrian, a copy of the Roman original with busts of Admiral Lord Anson and his wife, to commemorate the Admiral's circumnavigation of the world in 1740-4, again by Stuart between 1764-71; the Tower of the Winds, yet another copy of a Classical original, made about 1765 and positioned near the site of the old village before it was demolished; the Doric Temple, with its six column front and a rear blank wall - a rather miserable affair but nevertheless of historical interest because it is the second earliest such work of the Greek revival in the world; the Chinese House of 1747, delightfully positioned in a wooded corner near the Mansion and set behind the iron Chinese Bridge of 1813; the Ruin at the back of the house, an absurd concoction, originally much larger and even more absurd; the Monument to a Cat, a pet of either Thomas Anson or the Admiral, commemorated by an urn on a base to a height of about 20 feet; and the Shepherd's Monument, a highly acclaimed piece.

Of functional purpose are: the Railway Bridge, 0.75m E of the tunnels; a rusticated arch with Ionic columns and good retaining walls; the Trent Lodge, an Italian-style house near the Essex Bridge; the Lichfield Drive Lodges, moved here in 1845, which lie hidden amongst trees on the road to Rugeley and are now used as dwellings as the drive is disused; the eastern Railway Tunnel Entrance (SJ 981216), looking like a castle gatehouse with turrets and battlements by Livock, 1847; the western Railway Tunnel Entrance (SJ 988215), looking somewhat Egyptian; and the Lichfield Drive Bridge (SJ 997211), in Classical style to match the nearby monuments.

During the summer various exhibitions, sporting events and fairs are held in the grounds and the Staffordshire County Police Dog Training School let their Alsatians practice attacking human beings on fields here. Salon musical concerts are occasionally held in the Mansion house. The Staffordshire Way long-distance foot path cuts through the Park, entering at the south-west near the farm and exiting at the Essex Bridge.

SLINDON *2m N of Eccleshall, which is 7m NW of Stafford*
A sparse little hamlet on the road from Eccleshall to Newcastle. It consists of a few houses, a roadside fountain, a farm shop and the charming little church of St Chad. The church is of 1894 by Basil Champneys and was commissioned by J C Salt, a Stafford banker. The overall style is Gothic with a central tower, nave, chancel and short transepts. The stained glass windows are by Kempe, of about 1900. It is a building which is well thought of.

One mile north-east is **Millmeece** (water) Pumping Station, still standing and in good order though not in service. Millmeece was built in 1914 and was designed by William Campbell of Hanley. It closed in 1979 but at regular intervals the two large, horizontal tandem steam engines are fired for the benefit of enthusiasts. Both the engine house and boiler house have semi-circular headed windows, the hipped roofs have hand-made tiles and the chimney stack is 125 feet high. The hamlet of Millmeece, 0.5m NE of Slindon, is on the Meece Brook. There was a mill here by 1298, hence its name.

Aspley, 1m NW of Slindon, is little more than two farms but the manor is in Domesday Book as Haspeleia, 'the clearing in the aspen wood', or 'the aspen wood'. An aspen is a type of poplar tree with especially tremulous leaves.

SMALLTHORNE *1.25m NE of Burslem on the B5051*
The main road (B5051) cuts across the valley. On the slopes is industrial suburbia but in the valley bottom is a small nature reserve. The stream regularly floods and recently caused a good deal of damage to the newly restored Ford Green Hall - a good, 16th Century, half-timbered, yeoman farmer's house with a two-bay, 18th Century extension to the east side. The Hall is now a museum which is occasionally open to the public when it is not booked by school parties, which is most of the time. A quarter-of-a-mile south is a disused coalmine, and 1.75m N was the Chatterley-Whitfield Mining Museum, now closed.

SMETHWICK *3m SSE of West Bromwich*
Here we are mostly concerned with West Smethwick. The larger part of the settlement lies to the south-east and traditionally belongs to Birmingham. The name Smethwick is Anglo-Saxon and means 'the dwelling of the smith'. The Domesday manor of Smedwich developed as an industrial area late, well into the 19th Century. This is demonstrated by the population figures:1801-1,100; 1901-54,000; 1930-84,00.

Today Smethwick is a part of the Metropolitan Borough of Sandwell. If approaching the settlement from the north one travels down the new Telford Way. This crosses first the old, meandering canal built by Brindley, and then the later, straight and deeply entrenched canal constructed by Telford. It is quite a dramatic sight. Within a stone's throw of the embankment that carries the new road are the old, disused bridges: the brick Summit Bridge of 1790 by John Smeaton (for Brindley) and the very smart cast-iron Galton Bridge of 1829 (by Telford).

The Wolverhampton-Birmingham main line electrified railway (the old Stour Valley Railway) runs parallel to the Telford canal and is now joined by the fast new road. This unholy triumvirate lies adjacent to Smethwick High Street. Indeed, the whole of the northern side of the High Street was demolished to make way for the road. Only one building was spared, the stucco-clad Toll House. This has round-headed windows and chamfered corners and is now a People's Shop, where the inhabitants of Smethwick can facilitate themselves of a self portrait studio, a sound studio, a video box and a photocopier.

As we entered the High Street we noticed that the shop signs tell it all: Ludiana Fashions, Pakeeza Foodstores, Sudara Fashions, Malhi's Boutique, Lal's Superstores, and Ratti and Sons. The latter reminds us of the charming A S Mathara and Daughters (well, why not?), just down the road at Langley Green. Indeed, the odd man out in Smethwick High Street is Yeume Ping, a chinese restaurateur. Many of the shops have been gaily painted and even on a Sunday trade is brisk - a jolly place. Needless to say the two cinemas, the Empire and the Prince's, are now both closed.

Beyond the Blue Gates pub the High Street rises gently to the well-attended temple of the Guru Nanak Gurdwara. Slightly higher still stands the far less-well-attended and smoke-blackened church of the Holy Trinity. Continuing east, past a small estate of flat-roofed houses, the shops are predominantly Western once again and the area becomes half well-heeled. Here is the rather grand Council House, constructed of red brick and stone and complete with a clock tower. It stands a little aloof beside Victoria Park.

A little to the west is West Park. This was given to the community by the Chance family in 1896 and has a statue of James Chance. The Chance Brothers set up in business in 1814. They were the first in England to manufacture sheet glass and supplied some 114 million square feet of glass for the construction of the Crystal Palace of the Great Exhibition in 1851. They also made optical glass as well as crown glass at their works in Spon Lane. In 1953 the company was taken over by the Pilkington group.

Finally, mention should be made of the new concrete village that is home to a thousand hapless souls. It lies astride the main road to Oldbury. These green-and-brown-painted, barrack-like blocks are guarded by two tall towers, a landmark for miles around.

As mentioned at the outset of this article most of Smethwick lies outside the Black Country. However, as the whole area is now administered as a part of Sandwell a few words on the rest of Smethwick would not be out of place. For the most part it is an established suburban desert, a place to get well and truly lost in. Take a course on navigation at the SAS school in Hereford before venturing forth into this neck of the woods.

In fact, there are woods and green spaces in abundance. **Causeway Green** and **Bristnall Fields** are graced with Barnford Hill Park and Brandhall Golf Course; at **Warley Woods** there are indeed a few trees, another golf course and greens on which to run the dog; and just east of Dog Kennel Lane are the playing fields of **Londonderry**. In addition, there are eight sports grounds and a large, open cemetery, and **Beech Lanes** and **Bearwood** have the benefit of **Lightwoods Park**.

Lightwoods House and Park, 1m S of Smethwick, were bought for the public by A M Chance in 1902, and by 1989 a studio was established there which produced stained glass that has a worldwide reputation. The House itself is late 18th Century and was built by the Grundy family. The Park has a Shakespeare Garden that contains flowers, herbs and other plants mentioned by Shakespeare in his plays.

Cape Hill, an ESE area of Smethwick, gets its name from an inn, the Cape of Good Hope, which stood on Grove Lane from at least 1814. It was rebuilt in 1925. In the 19th Century there were two windmills on Cape Hill. The annual fair of Smethwick was called the Cape Fair.

The Steward (Stewart) Aqueduct, to the west of Spon Lane, was built by

Thomas Telford in 1828 to carry the Birmingham Canal Old Main Line over his New Main Line. The aqueduct is crossed by the M6.

North of the canals is the largely industrial area of **Sandwell Village**. To the east of Halford's Lane is a small residential area and to the east of that is **Soho**, named after the famous Soho Foundry. This was opened in 1796 by James Watt (1736-1819) and Matthew Boulton (1728-1809) to manufacture parts for Watt's improved Newcomen-type steam engine (patented in 1769). All engines made before 1796 were manufactured by other companies under licence, Watt only supplying drawings and valves. The cylinders were bored by John Wilkinson at his Bersham, Denbighshire works. Wilkinson was the first to use a steam engine - a Boulton and Watt in 1776 - to blow air into a blast furnace. This was a major technological development because, henceforth, iron-making was freed from a dependence on waterwheel power. From now on iron could be smelted on the coal fields, close to the source of fuel, and the Black Country could blossom. (Note: the essence of Watt's invention was the addition of a steam jacket around the piston cylinder and the installation of a second cylinder in which the steam condensed back to water. These modifications greatly increased the efficiency of the steam engine. In 1782 Boulton and Watt brought out their 'engine without a beam', the first rotative engine. More compact and more efficient still, it was soon being used the length and breadth of the land. The age of steam had really arrived.)

Manufacturing still proliferates in Soho, and even the local recreation ground is called the Black Patch. The Soho Foundry itself is now occupied by Avery. Boulton and Watt actually assembled their engines at a Manufactory, something less than a mile to the east on the Handsworth-Winson Green border, but of this nothing remains.

The actress Julie Walters was born at Smethwick in 1950 and Chris Collins (aka Frank Skinner), the comedian, is also from the town.

STAFFORD

Stafford is the county town of Staffordshire and is situated approximately in the centre of the shire. It is on a main-line, Inter-City railway route and the M6 by-passes the town to the west. The first settlement was on a mound of gravel surrounded by the River Sow to the east and south, and by marshes to the north and west. This is a typical Anglo-Saxon defensive position. The name Stafford means 'the landing place by the ford' and by the late 9th Century it was established as the county town. In 913 the settlement was rebuilt and fortified by Queen Ethelfleda of Mercia.

Three years after the Norman Conquest there was a rebellion against the Normans, and King William himself came to Stafford. He fought and beat the rebels but the next year (1070) more trouble broke out. The King's wrath was extreme and he devastated the area, burning houses and destroying crops. To maintain order he built a castle, probably at Broad Eye near where the present windmill stands. By 1086 the castle, almost certainly a timber structure, had fallen into disuse and disrepair.

King William's standard bearer, Roger de Toni, was given large estates in the Midlands generally and in West Staffordshire in particular. He took a new name to reflect his new territory and the Stafford family became the leading line in the county. In 1086 Robert de Stafford, the younger son of Roger de Toni, was the largest landowner in the shire after the King, and it was probably Robert who built the motte and bailey castle on a hill to the west of Stafford.

Below the castle lay a village, possibly the Monetville mentioned in Domesday Book. The village had been deserted by about 1450 but the church survived and St Mary's Castle Church still stands.

In 1299 Edmund de Stafford was summoned to Parliament as a baron. His son, Ralph, was created Earl of Stafford in 1351 for his military and diplomatic services during the Hundred Year's War. By marriage and inheritance he acquired the estates of the Audley family and by inheritance the Corbet estates in Shropshire. By 1438 the family was one of the wealthiest in England and in 1444 Humphrey, the 6th Earl, was made Duke of Buckingham. His grandson, the 2nd Duke, rebelled against Richard III and was executed. The 2nd Duke's son, Edward, the 3rd Duke, was also executed (by Henry VIII), after having been found guilty of a false charge of treason.

The titles were forfeit, but though restored in 1547 the family fell into decline and in 1762 the earldom became extinct. In 1824 Sir George Jerningham, who was descended through the female line, acquired the barony but his family also died out.

In 1913 the title passed to Francis Edward Fitzherbert of Swynnerton, who became the 12th Baron of Stafford. The present Baron lives at Swynnerton, a village 10m N of Stafford.

Stafford Castle was started in the late 11th Century with a motte and two baileys. In about 1200 a stone keep was constructed and about 1350 the whole castle was rebuilt in stone by Ralph. the 1st Earl of Stafford. After a siege in 1643, when the castle held out for the Royalist cause, it was captured and demolished.

In the early 19th Century Sir George Jerningham built a Gothic house designed as a castle, and though it was never completed it was inhabited for a time. However, it literally started to fall down and was abandoned in 1949. Lord Stafford then sold it to the local council who, after a youth was killed playing in the building, had the ruins largely dismantled. In the 1980s major excavation of the site were carried out by unemployed people supervised by qualified archeologists. The trees around the castle were cleared and the moat baileys and medieval village were all exposed. The site is now a tourist attraction, and a medieval herb garden has been established as an additional feature.

Stafford, as well as being the administrative and judicial centre of the county, was a market town of great importance The present Market Square, though substantial, was originally much more extensive. The pig market, for example, was where the old Borough Hall (now the Gatehouse Theatre) stands. The cattle market was held just north of the Market Square, until it was moved to the south of the town behind the Sun Inn.

Stafford participated in the wool trade of the Middle Ages and in the 18th Century became known nationally as a centre of shoe manufacture. At first this was a cottage industry, the leather pieces being stamped out and then sewn into finished shoes by workers in their own homes. The factories came comparatively late. Many of them still stand, clustered in the north-east of the town in the Wogan Street, Sandon Road and Marston Road area.

The leading shoe master was William Horton (1750-1832), who lived for a time at Chetwynd House, now the Post Office. His factory, the first in Stafford, was behind Chetwynd House, in Mill Street. In 1818 there were 20 shoe and boot manufacturers in the town. Only Lotus survived into recent times and even they have now gone.

It was Lotus who, in the 1960s, were largely responsible for the demise of the other product for which the area was famous, namely salt. In 1877 brine deposits were discovered in the north of the town at Stafford Common, during boring operations connected with the town's waterworks. In 1893 local businessmen formed the Stafford Salt and Alkali Company and began to produce salt at Stafford Common by evaporating the water from the brine in large iron pans.

In 1894 they opened another works at Baswich so that the salt could be transported easily and cheaply by the canal that passed close by. This was on the site of the present 'Saltings' mobile home park. Just south of the park are the remains of the pipes and the pumping station, close by the canal and the railway.

The brine was pumped from Stafford Common to the Baswich works through a pipe that passed under the town, and which had been laid originally to feed the Royal Brine Baths in Bridge Street. Two other works by rival companies opened on the Common in 1900, one of which was taken over by ICI who manufactured salt in Stafford until 1958. British Soda took over the Stafford Salt and Alkali Company.

In the 1950s settlement fractures began to appear in buildings at the northern end of the town. The shoe manufacturing company, Lotus, had an affected building and took British Soda to court to obtain damages. After a long battle they won compensation for themselves and a small fund of £38,000 was set up to reimburse those private people whose houses had been affected. The salt company was wound up. The average compensation per house was a paltry £80.

Salt production ceased on Stafford Common in 1963 and at Baswich in 1968. Altogether, nearly seven million tons of salt had been extracted between 1893 and 1968. This represents a cube 500 feet square.

The town does not have any great depth of manufacturing business. Bricks were made here from local heavy clays on the southern outskirts, near Wildwood and Brocton, but today Universal Grinding Wheel, GEC, and Dorman Diesels are the only major, basic wealth producers in the area. Stafford is not an especially picturesque place and of recent years it has been savagely treated by the local council, who have raised huge new public buildings which are all out of proportion to those that previously existed. From afar the town announces itself, not by its church towers or the old windmill, but by three high-rise blocks of flats, two at Highfields and one at Pennycrofts. Within the old town centre there is an ugly telecommunications' tower and a new Civic Offices' block with acres of dark glass.

Adjoining the Civic Offices is a food store. This stands on the site formerly occupied by the Royal Brine Baths of 1892, a multi-gabled building of character. On the river alongside it rowing boats could be hired.

The town centre is very compact and still lies within the area that was enclosed by the old medieval Town Walls. Stafford was the only town in the county to have walls, but they were not very substantial, being only some 14 inches thick. They could never have withstood a siege. Two small sections have been preserved, one at the south end of Eastgate Street and one at the north end of Lichield Road. The main shopping area is Greengate Street. This is dominated by the national chain stores, banks and building societies. There are very few individual, privately-owned shops. This street was pedestrianised in the 1980s.

However, there are some good buildings and quaint corners in the county town, and a few surprises too. In the centre of Stafford, just off the Market Square, is St Mary's church. Alongside the church, in the green that adjoins it, are the restored sandstone foundations of an Anglo-Saxon chapel, of about 1000

AD. It consisted of a nave, 20 feet wide and 35 feet long, and a chancel, 15 feet wide and 16 feet long. The walls are two foot thick. The end wall of the chancel is missing. This is the church of St Bertelin, who had a hermitage here and was possibly the founder of the town. This church existed until 1800 when it was pulled down, an inexcusable act of vandalism. When the site was excavated in 1954 signs of a much earlier wooden chapel were found five feet below the present ground level. Amongst these were the remains of a short, squat, oaken preaching cross. A replica of this is displayed on the site. The cross and the wooden chapel are believed to be of about 700 AD.

The church of St Mary was a Royal Free Chapel, which owed allegiance to the King, not the church. At the time of Domesday Book it had 13 priests. It later became a Collegiate church, still a Royal church, and had a college of canons. They were disbanded in 1546. The church of St Mary is large and impressive. Unfortunately, it was seriously over-restored by George Gilbert Scott in 1841-4, which explains why the medieval church no longer looks medieval. The older parts that remain include; the east end, the south transept, the choir aisle and the west front portal, which are Early English and Decorated; and the north transept, the upper parts of the well-known octagonal central crossing tower, and the nave clerestory, which are Perpendicular. The nave and aisles are divided by 13th Century arcades of five bays. The interior is extremely spacious with a Norman font, an organ case of 1790, and stained glass by Gerante in the west window and by Kempe in the east window of the north transept. The monuments include memorials to: Humphrey Hodgetts, died 1730; Barbara Clifford, died 1786; and effigies of Sir Edward Aston of Tixall, died 1568, and his wife. There is also a bust of Izaac Walton of 'The Compleat Angler' fame who was born at Stafford in 1593.

Adjacent to the church is the school of St Mary, built of stone around three sides of a quadrangle, by Gilbert Scott in 1856, and now given over to trade. St Mary's Grove, on the other side of the church, has some good Georgian houses which have been beautifully restored as part of a town redevelopment scheme.

In Market Square is the handsome, ashlar-faced Shire Hall, designed by John Harvey and built in 1795-9. For many years it housed the Crown Court, but is now an art gallery. The court has moved to new, purpose-built premises. To the right of the Shire Hall is the Judge's House, of about 1800, also ashlar-faced. Opposite is The Chains pub, a place that is not unknown to some of the judges' regular customers. Around the corner are the County Buildings in Martin Street, by H T Hare, of 1893-5. These are of brick with stone dressings and add considerably to a street of great character. The main staircase is a grand affair that leads up to some good panelled rooms, one of which has, horror of horrors, been smothered from head to toe in white paint. It is called the White Room.

Martin Street joins Eastgate Street which, despite the new, ungainly Magistrates' Court and Police Station, is one of the pleasanter streets in the town. Here is the Borough Hall, of 1875-7 by Henry Ward, a slightly whimsical structure in 14th Century French Gothic, which now houses an entertainment complex based around the Gatehouse Theatre. A modern glass bay window has been installed above the main entrance.

On the corner of Eastgate Street and Martin Street is the most handsome Eastgate House, which was built in 1683 by General John Dolphin. In the 18th Century it was given a new facade, the one we see today, and in 1839 it was occupied by T B Elley, one of the town's leading shoemakers. The County Council bought the house in 1891 and it became the residence of the Chief

Constable (see the letterbox on the wall). It is now used as offices by the Registrar of Births and Deaths, and has been the backdrop for thousands of wedding photographs. The Registrar also occupies the handsome red brick and stone, Tudor-style building next door.

Close by, on the opposite side of the road, is the William Salt Library, which occupies an attractive house of about 1730-5. Here are kept the county historical archives, a treasure house of old books, papers, maps and records of all kinds. William Salt was a banker of the firm of Stevenson, Salt & Co, whose ashlar-faced premises, of about 1795, are now occupied by Lloyds Bank in Market Square. Next to the bank is the Old William Salt Library, which was previously the Old Bank House, and now houses the Staffordshire Railway Building Society.

In Greengate Street is the High House, a large timber-framed town house of 1595 (not 1555 as was previously thought), constructed of oak from Doxey Wood. It has four gables and overhangs on brackets and is, indeed, a high house. In the 1980s some one million pounds was spent on restoring the building and yet it still has a large, incongruous, plate-glass window on the ground floor. Local planners really are a law unto themselves.

In 1642, during the Civil War, Prince Rupert stayed for three days at the High House as a guest of Captain Richard Sneyd. The prince is reputed to have fired at the weathercock on the tower of St Mary's church, either for target practice or to demonstrate the merits of a newly-introduced, rifled pistol from the Continent.

The house to the left of the High House is of a similar style and age but has been covered in stucco. Left of this, and also stuccoed, is the Swan Hotel which has some early interior features including a section of Jacobean staircase with unusual balusters and a vaulted stone cellar. It is now in the control of a national chain of pub-restaurants, which may not have pleased George Borrow who found the place full of individuality and character; but would not have surprised Charles Dickens who found it 'the extinct town inn, the Dodo'. In fact, Dickens did not like Stafford in general and was most scathing. The Swan Hotel was a coaching inn but only for the local trade between Wolverhampton and the Potteries. The great national coaching road passed through Sandon and Haywood to the west of Stafford.

Opposite the Swan Hotel is the little church of St Chad, an architectural jewel. This was the town church built by the Lichfield Diocese, for we must remember that St Mary's belonged to the King. St Chad's is a Norman church with a Perpendicular crossing. It was called 'ruinous' as early as 1650 and there were shops between it and the street. In 1854 Henry Ward of Stafford began the restoration, which was completed in 1873 by Sir George Scott, who entirely rebuilt the front and donated the statue of St Chad. The Norman work is: four-bay nave with sturdy round piers and one-step arches; clerestory; crossing arches with two demi-shafts; and the blank arcading in the chancel. The octagonal tower is by Sir Charles Nicolson, the aisle walls are of 1874-5 and 1880, and the north transept is of 1886. Many of the carved Norman designs have an Eastern flavour, a feature that is explained by the tradition that the workmen were Saracens, who were captured in the Holy Land by medieval knights of the Biddulph family (See Biddulph).

Also in Greengate Street is Chetwynd House, a Queen-Anne-style house of 1740, of brick and stone with giant pilasters and moulded window surrounds. The paved forecourt is enclosed by good wrought iron gates and railings. This was the home of R S Sheridan, the playwright and MP for Stafford between

1780 and 1806. It is now the Head Post Office.

Church Lane, which runs between Mill Street and St Mary's church, is a delightful little thoroughfare and would be an attraction in any town, with its Georgian brick and stuccoed shops and houses, and the quaint black-and-white Sheriff's Office.

In Earl Street are the handsome Almshouses, of about 1660, founded by Sir Martin Noel. There are six stone houses on either side of the Chapel which has a large ogee-shaped gable. Around the corner in Water Street is the Old Malthouse, which has been converted into an attractive terrace of shops. Opposite are some good modern flats in red brick with stone dressings.

At the bottom of Water Street are the two waterwheels of the old Town Mill which was working until 1957. There has been a mill on the River Sow, at or near this site, since at least 1086. At Broad Eye is the windmill, built in 1796 with stones from the old Elizabethan Shire Hall which was demolished to make way for the building we see today.

Around the town centre are some buildings that should be mentioned: the Masonic Lodge, an abandoned Methodist chapel of 1848 in Gaol Road: St Georges Hospital, the old lunatic asylum, a vast place, begun in 1814-18, with a frontage of 31 bays and numerous additional blocks; the General Hospital in Foregate Street, of 1766-7, of which the long front of 1892-7 is by Aston Webb but which has much diminished during recent development; the Lock-up, rebuilt adjacent to a part of the old town wall, on the island at the end of the Lichfield Road; Forebridge Villa, in Lichfield Road, which is now incorporated into St Joseph's Convent; The Shawms, a house at Radford Rise by T Sandy, in the style of Voysey, now converted to flats; the Borough Library, of 1914, at the junction of the Lichfield and Newport roads; St Paul's, Lichfield Road, by Henry Ward, of 1884, with a steeple of 1887 by Robert Griffiths; the Friends' Meeting house in Foregate Street, a tiny, hemmed-in brick building of 1730 with a good collection of original fitments, including the gallery, the elders' gallery, the staircase, the overseer's bench and the panelling; Burton Hall in Burton Manor Road (at the south end of the town), a Gothic, gabled, red brick mansion with blue-and-yellow brick ornament and pointed trefoiled window lights, built in 1855 by E W Pugin and now too close for comfort to the roar of the M6; Rowley Hall (south-west of the town centre), of about 1817, by William Keen, an unimpressive ashlar building decorated with a colonnade and a bow of three bays with six detached Ionic columns, set in a small park, which was abused as a kind of reform school and is now a home for old people; the impressive row of ornate Victorian terraced houses in Lawn Road, a part of the Rowley Park housing development of the 1850s, which was built on land severed from the estate of Rowley Hall; the Regimental Museum of the 16th the Queen's Lancers and the 5th Royal Irish Lancers, housed in Kitchener House, Lammascote Road, an horrendous modern building but with a good small museum; and, finally, the Gaol in Gaol Road, of 1793, with extensions of 1852, which is one of our overcrowded Victorian prisons. The last public execution was in 1866, and the last execution in the prison was in 1914.

It is not unusual to find companies of funeral directors located close to prisons. The reason, of course, is that they were a regular and reliable source of corpses. In former times public hangings were not uncommon and the scaffold was usually erected in front of the prison. In Stafford the undertaking firm of Emery's is situated opposite the main gate of the jail and the establishment of John Rose is within 100 yards of the prison.

The Staffordshire General Infirmary in Foregate Street was founded by Mr Eld of Seighford Hall in 1766. It closed in 1997, became derelict and has recently been partly demolished and partly redeveloped. In 1919 a portrait of Mr Eld was found at the hospital and the artist was none other than Thomas Gainsborough. In 1912 it was purchased by the Museum of Fine Arts, Boston, USA.

The town is surrounded by housing estates: Parkfields to the north, Western Downs to the west, Wildwood to the south and Kingston Hill to the east.

Close to the windmill at Broad Eye is **Castletown**, a cluster of narrow streets and mean terraced houses, which developed from about 1837 when the Grand Junction Railway was opened. There was a maintenance depot at Castletown and the new 'village' housed the workers. The middle management lived in Brunswick Terrace, off the Newport Road. In 1876 Bagnall's manufactured locomotives and allied products at their Castle Town Works.

In Newport Road, at the town end, is the King Edward VII Grammar School (now called Chetwynd Middle School), a handsome, Gothic, brick building of 1862. The chapel was added in 1928. Further out, at the junction of West Way, is the flat-roofed Edgar Wood Modernist house called 'Upmeads' of 1908, which is interesting to architects but somewhat mundane to the layman and is now completely spoiled by the planting of houses in its once extensive gardens. It is said to be the first flat-roofed house in England. On the hill of Castlechurch is the church of St Mary, with a Perpendicular west tower and the rest by Scott and Moffatt, of 1844, with a north aisle of 1898 by John Oldrid Scott. At the church is a stone slab, with abstract designs, that is a puzzle. Its purpose and age are unknown, except that it is probably at least Norman if not much older. An avenue of yew trees leads to the church.

Of the many other churches and chapels in Stafford and its suburbs one other deserves mention, namely Holy Trinity in Baswich Lane, **Baswich**. The lower part of the tower is medieval, the upper of the 18th Century. The red brick nave and chancel are of 1740 and the transepts are of recent origin and not altogether sympathetic. Amongst the furnishings and fittings are the 18th Century west gallery and pulpit. There is a monument to Brian Fowler and wife, of 1587.

Baswich itself is a large, good-quality suburban residential area but does have the HQ of Staffordshire Police at Baswich House. This stands at the junction of the Stafford to Lichfield road and the Stafford to Cannock road. It was formerly an inn but was either converted or rebuilt as a house in about 1814 by John Stevenson Salt, a London banker. His third son, William Salt, was an antiquarian and his collection of Staffordshire documents formed the nucleus of the William Salt Library in Stafford. From 1904 to 1952 it was a boys' preparatory school, and was used by the police as a motor training centre. In the 1960s the Staffordshire Police Headquarters was housed in new premises in the grounds of the house.

Weeping Cross, Baswich, was a former separate hamlet on high ground, above the confluence of the River Sow and the River Penk, but is now a suburb of the county town. It is presumed that there was once a 'penitence cross' here, a cross where, in pre-Reformation times, those who breached Canon Law knelt and did penance. Such crosses had hollows in the base steps to support the offenders' knees.

Stafford Port, also called Radford Port, was the Stafford wharf on the Staffordshire and Worcestershire Canal (1772). This is a contour canal, which follows river valleys hereabouts, and ran from Stourport to Great Haywood. The canal buildings stood opposite the Trumpet Inn on Radford Bank until demolished in the 1960s. The canal is still very much open.

There were three monasteries, or at least settlements of monks, in Stafford. Outside the north walls of the town, in the area of Foregate, a community of Grey Friars (Franciscans) was established in 1297, and outside the south walls of the town, in the area of Forebridge, a community of Black Friars (Augustinians) was established in 1344. At Baswich an even earlier Augustinian Priory was established in 1179. There are substantial remains of their Priory of St Thomas (SJ 951230) on the banks of the River Sow. The ruined walls and windows have been built up with bricks to make farm buildings. The name Baswich is Anglo-Saxon and means 'Beorcal's dwelling'.

Moss Pit, 1.5m S of Stafford, was a small separate hamlet by the mid-19th Century. From the mid-20th Century it expanded greatly and is now a suburb of Stafford. The name describes the original land condition, a 'damp depression', and the author remembers his surprise to see several four-bedroom, detached houses being built on a site which had long been a marshy pool. Problems in the offing, methinks.

It is not widely appreciated that today Stafford is a garrison town. Touching the north-eastern fringes is the mammoth RAF Stafford Supply Depot covering hundreds of acres. The warehouses, offices and staff accommodation stretch along the five miles of public roads that encircle the village of Hopton and Beacon Hill. It is a very sensitive establishment indeed and air force personnel are ordered not to appear in the town in uniform. There are regular mock attacks to test the defences.

Visitors to Stafford will be surprised to find that the inner eastern ring road is, for several hundred yards, raised above a marsh. These swamps are quite extensive and originally formed a part of the Anglo-Saxon defences of the town. After a period of wet weather one can see just how formidable they were. There can be few towns of any size in the whole of Europe that have what is virtually a primeval swamp within a hundred yards of their Civic Centre. The **Doxey Marshes,** north-east of the town centre, are a protected area with 130 species of plant and bird life. Some 360 acres are an SSSI in the care of the Staffordshire Wildlife Trust.

Coton Hill, on the north side of Weston Road, Stafford, is the site of the big new Stafford District General Hospital, which was opened in 1984. A year later there was an outbreak of Legionnaires' Disease. The author remembers it well. He had attended a diabetes' clinic there and within hours had the most intense, flu-like symptoms which put him in bed for a week. The bright side of that cloud was that he stopped smoking during that illness and never smoked again. The Mid Staffordshire Post Graduate Medical Centre is housed in the private lunatic asylum, of 1854, close to the hospital.

Rickerscote, 1m S of Stafford centre, was a separate settlement but is now a suburb of Stafford. The name means 'Richard's cottage'. The settlement developed around a salt spa in the 19th Century. The waters were said to help sufferers from jaundice, scrofula and complaints of the liver. The church of St Peter was consecrated in 1957 and the parish was created in 1962. In 1996 there was a railway accident at Rickerscote when a Royal Mail train collided with a goods' train. One man was killed and 19 were injured.

Burton Hall, 1.5m SSW of Stafford, was a moated manor house in the 13th Century. However, it was pulled down and replaced by a new hall, designed by E W Pugin, in 1855. It has blue-and-yellow brick decorations and is now the newly-created Stafford Grammar School (1982). The Hall gave its name to the modern Stafford suburb of Burton Manor.

STANDON *5m N of Eccleshall, which is 6m NW of Stafford*
In 1066 Siward held Standon. In 1086 it was owned by Robert of Stafford and held from him by Bryant. There was a village of some size with at least 18 households and a mill.

Today, the village straggles up the hill from Cotes Heath and the ugly gantries of the electrified main line railway. There are a few cottages and a mill on the banks of Millmeece Brook, a handful of houses and the modern, yellow brick All Saints CE (C) First School which stands at the crossroads, near the church.

All Saints has a 14th Century tower that was built into part of an existing Norman church, to which belong the present nave and north aisle. The north doorway of the old church is still in its original position The whole building was restored and partly rebuilt by Gilbert White in 1846. Of the windows only those in the clerestory are original. There are memorials to Francis Ross, died 1500 (in the vestry), and to Nicholas Hyde, died 1526.

Standon Hall lies in attractive country, 0.75m WNW of the church. It was built in 1910 and the architect was J Francis Doyle of Liverpool. The 'L'-shaped mansion is of red sandstone, in Elizabethan style, with mullioned and transomed windows. The Hall was used as a National Health hospital for some time, but is now a private residential and nursing home in lovely wooded grounds. At the entrance to the drive the sandstone lodge still stands, but the two long, separate, modern annexes do not add much to the genteel ambience of the rather splendid Hall. It is very quiet here and the country around is most pleasant.

Standon Old Hall, 1m WNW of Standon, is a timber-framed house, half being of the 16th Century and half of the 17th Century. The sandstone cellars quite possibly belong to the earlier Norman house. Two ancient customs were practiced at the Old Hall, which was the former Manor House of Standon: in one, a dead calf was hung on a wall as a warning to pregnant cows not to abort their young prematurely; and in the other, the household gathered around burning bundles of straw to ward off witches and evil spirits from causing mildew to the wheat and killing young lambs.

In Weston Lane, **Bowers Bent**, 0.5m N of Standon, is the Standon Bowers Farm School and Outdoor Activities Centre, which provides children from Staffordshire towns with short 'country learning' holidays of a week or two's duration. It is run by Staffordshire County Council, and when we visited the young children were tearing around the place having a wonderful time. The history of this institution is very interesting, involving what has been described as white slavery and the murder of the headmaster. Standon Bowers, as it is referred to by staff, started life in 1885 with the building of the Home block and an adjacent Farm. A plaque on the Home reads: "Church of England Industrial Home for Waifs and Strays. Erected at the cost of Maria E Anderton for the Glory of God and the benefit of his poor children."

A piece in the Staffordshire Advertiser of 1885 reads: "The Home is for boys of 12 – 14 years of age, brought up in our large cities and learnt all manner of evil who might be trained in useful outdoor pursuits and then sent abroad to the colonies where, in a few years, it was hoped that they would be able by considerable industry to become landowners instead of street arabs."

There was a concern about over population in England at the time and it was cheaper to export these 'waifs and strays' than to maintain them here. It cost £2 for their passage to Canada and three shillings and six pence a week to provide for them at the Home.

Between 1869 and 1919 some 73,000 children sailed, unaccompanied, to Canada. (In 2003 there were several television and radio programmes about how these children were exploited as unpaid labour and refused all knowledge of their parents. They were literally treated as slaves, especially in Australia.)

At the Home they were trained in farming, carpentry, tailoring, shoemaking and gardening. Some – the lucky ones – became bandsmen for the British Army.

In 1935 Standon Bowers became an Approved School for 'naughty boys', and in 1947 one of the inmates shot dead the headmaster, Mr Fieldhouse. In the same year the school closed. It then re-opened as a Special School and closed in 1971. The buildings and land failed to sell at auction and in 1973 it opened as the Outdoor Education Centre we see today. Some 3,000 children a year pass through the Centre which has courses on academic subjects and environmental studies, together with outdoor pursuits such as canoeing, caving, climbing, camping, orienteering, archery and expedition work. "Courtesy, politeness and good manners are encouraged at all times."

Standon Bowers still gets visits from 'old boys' and their descendants from Canada. The original buildings still stand, although they have accumulated extensions at various times. The headmaster's offices are oak-panelled, and in the centre of the playground is a circular stand of 10 pine trees.

There are four other similar outdoor activity centres run by the Staffordshire County Council at Shugborough, Coven, Chasewater and Stanley Head.

STANFIELD *0.75m N of Burslem*
Stanfield is now a residential suburb of Burslem. If it has a centre at all it is around the Haywood High School and the Haywood Hospital on High Lane (B5049). The present church of St Werburgh was only built in 1953. Stanfield has a famous son and a famous daughter. The son is Daniel Blakeyfield VC, born here in 1922. He served in the Staffordshire Regiment and was awarded his Victoria Cross posthumously for manning an anti-tank gun during the battle of Arnhem in 1944. His bronze statue was erected at Festival Heights, Hanley, in 1966. In Christ Church, Cobridge, there is a collection of photographs relating to him.

The famous daughter is Susie Cooper, the ceramics designer (1903-1995). She was born at Stanfield but her parents later moved to Milton. She worked for the firm of A E Gray and Company, Hanley, from 1922 but founded her own company at the Crown Works, Burslem in 1929. In 1966 her company, Susie Cooper Ltd., was taken over by Wedgwood. Her work is now very much collected.

STANTON *3.5m W of Ashbourne*
Stanton is a small, isolated village of stone farms and cottages on the Weaver Hills. It is known for the prehistoric circular burial mounds that lie to the west of the village: Skrip Low, 0.25m N, and Over Low, 0.33m W, both of which are about 90 feet in diameter. Near Thorswood House Farm, 1m NW of Stanton, at SK 121467, a gold torc of Middle Bronze Age (1350-1000BC) was found. It went to the British Museum. In 1955, just south of the farm, a simple gold strip bracelet of Irish gold was found and went to Stoke-on-Trent City. There were at

least eight burial mounds in the vicinity of the house, some of which have disappeared.

Gilbert Sheldon (1598-1677), Archbishop of Canterbury, was born at Stanton and buried at Croyden. His father was Lord Shrewsbury's steward and the cottage in which Gilbert Sheldon was born still stands in the middle of the village. Although his parents were poor, he accumulated great wealth and became Chancellor of Oxford University. He paid for the theatre, built in Oxford by Sir Christopher Wren, which was named the Sheldonian (1669) after him.

The church of St Mary at Stanton is of 1846, by W Evans of Manchester. It has lancet windows and a bellcote and is an unassuming and pleasant little building of nave and chancel only, but beautifully positioned with wide views over the surrounding countryside.

Smithy Moor Farm, 0.5m SE of Stanton, has a slightly raised circular mound that marks the site of a 17th Century iron furnace. The mound is only visible after a period of dry weather.

STATFOLD *3.5m NE of Tamworth*

Statfold Hall lies close to the Warwickshire border on the edge of its small Park, which is adjacent to the A453, Tamworth to Ashby de la Zouche road. The Hall and its stables lie close to the medieval chapel, which was once the parish church, and to the north are the earthen platforms of medieval houses. In front of the Hall are pasture fields with the characteristic ridge and furrow marks of old, ploughed arable land.

There was a village at Statfold, but in the late Middle Ages it was deserted. The change from arable to pasture was a major cause of rural depopulation. An acre of pasture grazed by cows and sheep requires much less labour than an acre of corn or any other crop which entails ploughing, sowing, fertilizing, weeding, cropping and storing, all of which are labour-intensive activities.

The Hall has an Elizabethan core, and is dated at about 1571 from a now-demolished dovecote. The narrow polygonal tower at the back of the house is of 1671; the east and west bay windows were inserted in 1777; the north and south wings were added in 1817-19; and the north wing was demolished in 1937. The overall appearance of the house is Georgian. It was the home of the Pipe-Wolferstan family who first arrived at Statfold in 1465.

The Chapel is at the back of the house. It has a plain, Norman, west doorway, a Decorated south doorway, two small 13th Century windows in the nave, a 14th Century window in the chancel, a window of about 1600 in the east chancel and a window of 1906 in the nave. Amongst the memorials are effigies of two ladies holding their hearts in their hands, of the late 14th Century, and a large tablet to Francis and Frances Wolferstan, of 1676. In the south window is a stained glass medieval bishop.

Syerscote, 1m WNW of Statfold, is a tiny scattered hamlet, the nucleus of which is Syerscote Manor. The name is from the Anglo-Saxon and means 'Siric's cottages'. Siric is a personal name but also means 'victorious'. In the 1330s there were at least 10 dwellings here. Aerial photographs show the outlines of the house platforms, paths, and ridge-and-furrow strip system field patterns of the deserted village, which had been abandoned by the mid-16th Century. The Syerscote estate was a prebend of Tamworth Collegiate Church. A prebend is something that produces an income, a stipend. In the late 1840s the Manor was home to Mary Elizabeth Smith, who sued the 9th Earl Ferrers of Chartley for breach of promise. In 1846 she published a Statement of Facts about the case.

STEWPONEY *2m NW of Stourbridge*

Stewponey is a small residential area on the busy A449, at its junction with the A458, the Bridgnorth-Stourbridge road. A little to the north, at Stourton Junction, the Stourbridge Canal (1776) joins the Staffordshire and Worcestershire Canal (1772), and a little to the west is the River Stour.

The name Stewponey is said to be derived from Estepona. The story is that a soldier returned from the Peninsula War with a Spanish bride and named his farm (inn) after her home town. The Reverend Sabine Gould wrote a novel called "Bladys of the Stewponey". (See Oldbury.)

The large crossroads' pub, the Foley Arms, is named after the Foley family who were ironmasters in this area. They lived at **Prestwood,** lm N of Stewponey, in a 16th Century house made Gothic in the early 19th Century, but which was burned down and demolished in the 1920s. The gardens were landscaped by Humphrey Repton. A hospital was built on the site and all that now remains of the old house are the stone edgings of the flower beds. By 1996 the hospital had become a nursing home.

Yew Tree Farm, near Prestwood, Stourton, at SO 870865, was the scene of a murder which made national headlines over a protracted period and was the subject of several TV documentaries. Karl Bridgewater, a 13-year-old newspaper delivery boy witnessed a burglary at the farmhouse on 20th September 1978 and was murdered. Three men were convicted of the crime but were later found to be innocent. Two were released from prison, but the third one had already died whilst in custody. After the murder the house became derelict but it has been sold to renovators and renamed The Beeches.

Across the river, opposite Stewponey, is **Stourton Castle,** which is in origin a 14th Century brick house and former royal hunting lodge. It was rebuilt in the early 19th Century by Sir Robert Smirke, in Gothic style with battlemented walls and a gateway. It was the home of the late Mr Fred Phillips, the world's leading authority on, and breeder of, Staffordshire Bull-terriers. He had a museum-cum-library in an outbuilding, where the author photographed him for his 'Midlands Digest' series of magazine-style books.

Stourton Hall, 0.25m W of Stourton, was built in about 1850 and later extended. It was the home of the poet Mrs Downing in the 1920s, and well known for its glasshouses and crops of tomatoes.

Lawneswood House, 1.25m N of Stewponey, is an attractive Italianate building, of about 1845, with a tower and stuccoed walls.

Gibbet Wood, 0.5m S of Stewponey, is so named after the gibbeting here of William Howe in 1813. Howe was a notorious footpad but in 1812 he shot dead a man called Robins during a highway robbery. Howe was tried and hanged at Stafford. However, the dead man's relatives and the Stourbridge magistrates collected the body and placed it in a gibbet (an iron cage) at the site of the murder. It remained there for 12 months until the flesh had rotted off, and many thousands of people came to view it. This true story has gone into the realms of folklore and there are now numerous versions and fanciful elaborations.

STOKE ON TRENT *an introductory note to the Potteries*

Stoke on Trent is both the name of an individual town and the collective name for the six towns that comprise the Potteries - Tunstall, Burslem, Hanley, Fenton, Longton and, of course, Stoke on Trent (or Stoke upon Trent as the individual town is sometimes called).

The six towns were federated by the Potteries' Federation Bill of 1910, which gave the federation the status of a county borough. In 1922 Abbey Hulton, Meir and other satellite developments were added to the borough, and in 1925 it became a City. In 1974, with local government reorganization, the federation lost its county borough status and became a mere district council under the county council at Stafford.

Although the towns have grown outwards towards each other, and now form one more or less continuous built-up area, they all still have quite separate identities. Their one common link is a tradition of pottery making.

There have been finds of ancient pottery in the area dating back to Neolithic times (in the Manifold valley), and 1st Century Roman pottery has been discovered in Trent Vale, south of Stoke on Trent. In the Middle Ages names such as 'le Potter' (1280 at Audley) and 'le Throwere (1327 at Biddulph) began to occur. By the middle of the 17th Century Burslem had developed as a centre of pottery making, and from then on the trade became established and spread southwards to the nearby villages now called The Potteries.

The industry developed here for two reasons: the close proximity of ample supplies of coal, clay and water and the availability of the men to organize and develop the trade, both technically and commercially - Wedgwood, Adams, Whieldon, Astbury, Elers, Bentley, Twyford, Davenport, Spode, Littler, Minton and others.

The major development in the pottery industry - the event that took it out of its small craft roots - was the opening of the Wedgwood factory at Etruria in 1769. The Dutchman Elers had shown the way 70 years earlier in Newcastle-under-Lyme, but now there was a large factory dedicated to producing quality ware using refined techniques.

A major cohesive force in the Potteries was the North Staffordshire Railway (NSR), which was affectionately known as 'The Knotty' after its emblem, a Staffordshire Knot. It was formed in 1845 with eight lines and had three gauges: standard; two feet six inches on the Leek and Manifold Valley line; and three feet six inches on the Caldon limestone quarries' line. Between 1873-5 a Loop Line was constructed which left the main line at Etruria and rejoined it at Kidsgrove. Parts of the NSR tracks can still be discerned in greenways, gaps in the building line and bridge tunnels. It was a progressive and successful company, with connections to the LNWR and the Midland Railway, but after Grouping the LMS began branch closures and British Rail continued this process under Dr Beeching in the 1960s. Stoke (the town) was the hub of the NSR and its station, of course, still very much stands.

The Pottery towns lie in a line from north to south - the line of an outcrop of long-flame coal. (The long-flame with which the local coal burned had the great merit of heating large surfaces evenly.) Today, they are linked by the main-line railway, the Trent and Mersey Canal and most recently by the A500 dual carriageway.

The A500, also called Queensway and the 'D' Road, was begun in 1973. It runs from Junction 15 on the M6 to Junction 16 and links the towns of Tunstall, Burslem, Hanley and Stoke. About 30 years later the A50 (T) was constructed. This links the A500 at Stoke (Sideway) to Fenton, Longton, Meir and Blythe Bridge. The A50 (T) is a major work of civil engineering with numerous cuttings, bridges and a tunnel.

In this book the articles on the six towns appear under their own names

STOKE ON TRENT *1.75m ESE of Newcastle-under-Lyme*

In 1910 the pottery towns were federated and instead of being named after Hanley, which was easily the largest of the six towns, Stoke gained the honour. Strangers are always surprised to find that the town of Stoke is apparently quite small. In fact, it is larger than it looks but is very spread about and broken up. First the canal, then the railway and more recently the A500 (Queensway) have effectively divided the town into two parts. East of the road are the Station and the Polytechnic and west of the road is the old centre where most of the shops, the church, the Town Hall and the Spode factory are to be found.

Up until about 1700 Stoke appears to have consisted of the church of St Peter and Vincula and three houses: those of the Rector, his Curate and the Parish Clerk. The land about was flat and muddy. On the hill nearby was the medieval village of Penkhull (a Celtic name). Stoke, or Stoc, is old English for 'a place', but usually means a holy place. The church was old, an Anglo-Saxon foundation, and when the present church was being constructed in 1829, to replace the previous Norman church, pieces of an Anglo-Saxon preaching cross were uncovered. The font is also Anglo-Saxon. In the churchyard are two arches, two piers and some other pieces of stone. These are reconstructions, by Charles Lynam in 1888, of medieval church remains discovered in the mill race of Boothen Mill when the mill was demolished in 1881. (Old churches were often quarried and the stone reused for other buildings).

The present church is a Commissioners' type, designed by Trubshaw and Johnson, with tower, nave and chancel, Perpendicular windows, a five-light east window, and battlements. Josiah Wedgwood's grave is by the reconstructed arches. A few years ago he was joined here by Sir Stanley Matthews.

The Hide Market was built in 1835 as a covered market, although it was subsequently used as a fire station and the cellar as a jail.

The New Town Hall at Stoke is one of the grandest buildings in the Potteries. Work began on it in 1834 but the wings were not completed until about 1842 (north) and 1850 (south). It has a 19-bay ashlar front with a giant upper portico of Ionic columns in an overall classical design. The centre was originally designed as a market and this duly moved there in 1845. However, in 1888 it was moved out and the accommodation converted to house the mayor's parlour and offices. In 1911 the Kings Hall was added to the rear of the Town Hall. The Spode China works are in the main street of the town, opposite the old Town Hall.

Josiah Spode came to his Stoke works after his training at Thomas Whieldon's factory in Fenton. He came as Master Potter and Works Manager but by 1776 was the owner. Much of the old factory still remains amongst the present buildings. Josiah I died in 1794 and his son Josiah II took over. About 1800 he perfected his bone china. Calcined bone was mixed with clay and glassy material and the result was an excellent imitation of true porcelain. Josiah II made a fortune and expanded the factory by buying up adjoining property. Many of the houses he bought were incorporated into the works with very little alteration, a remarkable conglomeration covering 14 acres, some of which still stands. In 1842 there were 19 ovens, 272 working rooms, 19 slip kilns, 42 warehouses and 33 offices.

The third Josiah had an accident in the factory and lost an arm. He spent most of his time at The Mount, a large brick house with two large domes, which stands in wooded gardens on the hill at Penkhull. The house was built in 1803 by Josiah II and has seven bays, two storeys and an ashlar central bow with columns. It was used as the Blind and Deaf School and extensions were added to provide further accommodation, but in the late 1990s it was sold and is being 'developed'. When Josiah III inherited the business he left the management of it to William Copeland. After the death of Josiah III his widow and Josiah IV left the area. (See Armitage.) William Copeland took control of the business and it has remained in the hands of that family to the present day.

The other pottery firm based in Stoke was Minton's. Thomas Minton was the equal of Josiah Spode and Josiah Wedgwood. He had been apprenticed at the Caughley works in Shropshire, a factory renowned for the excellence of its wares which are highly sought after by modern collectors. His reputation for quality was such that he attracted the very best craftsmen, many coming from the workshops of his competitors - from Spode and from works in Derby and Worcester. 'Nearly as good as a Minton' became a phrase of high praise. The Minton factory of 1950-2 was demolished in recent times and the site is now occupied by a gleaming silver Sainsbury's food store. The Minton brand name is now owned by Royal Doulton.

Opposite Safeway is the seven-bay Gothic School of Science and Art, of 1858-60, by James Murray. Next door is the Library of 1878 by Charles Lynam, a building of some character with wide eaves, large round windows and mosaic and tile panels.

Perhaps the most important event in the development of Stoke was the coming of the railway. The North Staffordshire Railway Company built the handsome station in 1848. A year later an equally handsome Hotel and Regional Offices were built with black diapers in a Jacobean style with mullioned and transomed windows. The area between the station and the hotel is called Winton Square and here is the statue of Josiah Wedgwood by Edward Davies, 1863. There are a few trees and the whole area is most pleasing. Stoke had become the railway centre of the Potteries and this, perhaps more than anything else, established her name nationally.

In this respect, and of no little consequence, was the publicity the town achieved through its Football Club. Stoke City FC was formed in 1863 and is the second-oldest club in the country. The club has produced more than 30 international players. Perhaps we can now explain why the federation of pottery towns was called Stoke. That was the name the nation knew because of a railway station and a football club. In recent times the club has moved from the old Boothen Road pitch to the brand new Britannia Stadium on high ground near the rubbish dump at Sideway (pronounced 'sidaway')

Some churches and their dates: St John, Newcastle Road, Trent Vale, 1909 by A R Piercy who incorporated the nave of the previous church as the south aisle; All Saints, London Road, Boothen, 1888 by Lynam and Rickman; Our Lady of the Angels (Roman Catholic), Hartshill Road, 1857, by Charles Hansom, a striking building of yellow and red brick, Gothic with presbytery and convent attached: St Thomas, Penkhull, by Scott and Moffatt, Middle Pointed and paid for by the Rev Thomas Webb Minton; Holy Trinity, Hartshill Road, 1842, by Gilbert Scott, in Middle Pointed and paid for by Herbert Minton, who also paid for the school, the parsonage and the Gothic brick houses near the church. In Aquinas Street there is a Quaker burial ground used until 1951.

To conclude, mention should he made of The Villas, a charming cul-de-sac off the London Road, with Italianate houses, of about 1840, which have short towers, pantile roofs and stuccoed, colour-washed walls; and Whieldon's Grove, the great Thomas Whieldon's 18th Century house of two storeys, five bays with a later wing, Ionic columns and a pediment, located east of Stoke, off City Road, and technically in Fenton.

Boothen is a suburb of Stoke, 1m S of the town centre. On the east side of London Road at Boothen is a 12-foot-high obelisk raised by public subscription to the memory of Timothy Trow, a 21-year-old tram conductor. He could not swim but plunged into the Newcastle-under-Lyme Canal in an attempt to save a four-year-old girl. Two other men then arrived and pulled out both Trow and the girl; the girl lived but Trow died. This sad little event touched local people greatly. The old Stoke City football ground, The Victoria ground, was at Boothen. As we write the area is a cleared wasteland awaiting redevelopment. It was at the old racecourse, Boothen, that Buffalo Bill Cody performed his Wild West Show in 1904. (For more on Penkhull see the article on page 244.)

STONE *7m N of Stafford*

Here Iron Age man built a fort, here an Anglo-Saxon king slew his children, and through here passed one of the country's greatest coaching roads. Stone is a very old town and we have yet to unravel much of its early history.

The Iron Age fort is on high ground at Bury Bank, overlooking the river Trent. It has a much-eroded, single bank and ditch with an inturned north-west entrance, and covers three acres on top of the heavily-wooded hill at the junction of the A34 and the A51 at Darlaston, 1.3m NW of Stone. It will have been passed by millions of travellers because this was the point where the medieval road from London (now the A51) forked left to Nantwich, Chester and Ireland, and right to Newcastle-under-Lyme, Carlisle and Scotland. (Chester was a port before it silted up in the 18th Century, the actual docks being on the site of the present racecourse.) **Darlaston** itself never developed much beyond its present size - a handful of cottages, some new houses, a garage and a pub called 'Yesterdays' - but Stone, being the nearest town of any size to this important junction, thrived on the coaching trade, especially in the 18th Century when the roads were improved by turnpiking and the traffic greatly increased.

Industries of some importance in Stone in the 18th and 19th Centuries were leather tanning and shoe making. The tanneries were mostly alongside the south Bank in Stafford Street, but were pulled down when the stream was culverted and the area turned into a road and a car park. The shoe factories were numerous. Behind the shops in the High Street are several small factories. There are also larger works in Lichfield Road, behind the old cinema in High Street and around the modern Lotus factory.

Today Stone is a flourishing small market town with a busy centre, a small market square and an essentially Georgian look. At the north end of the High Street is Granville Square. Here is the handsome Post Office and an attractive thatched pub called the Crown and Anchor. Half-way down the hill is the Crown Hotel, which is a lot bigger then the facade would suggest. It was built by Henry Holland in 1778, presumably replacing an earlier inn. It has two brick bays and a central porch of Ionic columns. This was the most important coaching house in Stone. It still retains an atmosphere of days gone by and customers have armchairs and spacious surroundings in which to eat and drink at very modest prices.

Back up the hill a bit is the very Georgian facade of Joules' Brewery Offices, with two ground-floor bow windows and a porch with Tuscan columns. At the back was the old brewery, which operated until 1974 but is now demolished. It was established here in the early 18th Century and became Joules & Son in

1785.

There was another brewery on the north-west outskirts of the town at Stonefields, off Mount Road, near the station. This belonged to Bents and most of the buildings still stand. It has a large tower block and chimney, which are a major landmark in the town. The works are now a trading estate. Adjacent to it are the mysterious Mottley Terrace earthworks, about which more is said later.

At the bottom of the hill the High Street crosses the Scotch Brook, though sharp eyes are needed to see it, except when it causes the road to collapse, as happens not infrequently. The stream is fast flowing - it had to be to power the 10 flint mills of the Moddershall valley, 0.5m NE, and at times of heavy rain it sometimes bursts the culvert that carries it to the River Trent.

Stone Workhouse (1792), in Crown Street, became Trent House when it ceased to be the workhouse and then became the Trent Hospital.

The River Trent passes within 400 yards of the town, and Stone is known throughout the country as a 'white water' site. Canoeists travel here from as far as Lincolnshire to practice in the swirling waters of the river, especially in the area adjacent to the big new bridge. This carries the A520, Leek road, to its junction with the A34 at the suburb of **Walton**, a residential area with a garage and some retail shops and a new industrial park tucked away at the back.

The Trent and Mersey Canal almost touches the High Street, and on its banks at the southern end of the town are two red brick, canal warehouses. Having lain derelict for many years, they have now been renovated and converted into flats. They are listed buildings so the facades will remain largely unaltered.

The oldest religious site in Stone is that at The Priory in Lichfield Street. This is a three-bay detached house set back off the road, near the church, and is currently used as offices. In the cellar is a rib-vaulted undercroft of at least four bays, and in the right-hand garden are some stone fragments which include part of a large pier of four-leaf section, probably of the 14th Century. It was the Priory that developed the town and which probably laid out the burgage plots, which can still be traced in the boundaries and alleys of today. It was the Priory which obtained Borough status and the Tuesday market for the town in 1251. This medieval monastery was almost certainly on the same site of an even earlier 7th Century Priory, established by Queen Ermenilda in memory of her two sons. They had been murdered by their father, King Wulphere of Mercia, in a fit of rage because they would not renounce the Christian religion. The Anglian name for the fort on Bury Bank was Wulpherecester, which suggests that King Wulphere re-occupied the old Celtic site and possibly had his palace there.

The present parish church of St Michael was built in 1753-8 by William Robinson, partly on the site of the old Priory church. St Michael's is noted for being a very early example of the Gothic revival. It is plain and simple inside. The galleries and pews have survived but the chancel was spoiled in 1887 when it was restored in Perpendicular style. Inside, the church are two effigies of unknown persons, circa 13th Century and almost certainly from the old Priory, whilst in the churchyard are the effigies of two members of the Crompton family, died 1606. There is a tablet at the west end of the nave to Admiral John Jervis, Earl St Vincent, died 1823, with a bust by Chantrey. In the churchyard there is also the Jervis Mausoleum, a small Palladian building with pediments designed by Robinson. Here lie the Admiral and many members of his family.

Jervis's most famous victory was at the battle of Cape St Vincent (St Valentine's Day 1797), when he and Nelson routed the Spanish fleet and prevented it from joining with the French in attacking England. The Admiral was born at Meaford Hall, 1.25m NE of Stone. (See Meaford.)

Just to the north of Stone town centre, in Margaret Street, is the large Roman Catholic church of the Immaculate Conception and St Dominic. It is built of brick in 13th Century style. Attached to the church is a Dominican Convent. The symmetrical front is of brick, with gables, and the building incorporates work by Hanson in 1853 and Blount in 1863. There is a chapel of St Anne in the garden by A W N Pugin, a simple little place.

In 1848 the main-line railway came to Stone and the original neo-Jacobean station still stands. It is of brick, with shaped gables and was designed by H A Hunt.

Darlaston, 1m W of Stone, was Deorlavestan in 956. The name is Anglo-Saxon and means 'Deorlaf's settlement'. At the time of Domesday it belonged to Burton Abbey. There is confusion as to what is Darlaston and what is Meaford, but the houses at the foot of Bury Bank are historically in Darlaston, as is the bridge over the River Trent. Darlaston Hall stood to the west of the River Trent between Filleybrooks and Darlaston. Richard Barnfield, the Elizabethan poet, spent his adult life at the Old Hall and died here in 1627. Two of his poems were ascribed to Shakespeare and became very well known. One begins: 'If music and sweet poetry agree'; and the other, 'As it fell upon a day, In the merry month of May, Sitting in a pleasant shade which a grove of myrtles made'. This Hall and its successor were both demolished and a large bungalow built on the site in 1910. Peter de Wint (died 1849), the respected landscape painter, whose work hangs in the National Gallery, was born in Stone.

Archeological sites in the Stone area include: Saxon Lowe, a burial mound on Tittensor Chase, 0.5m NW of Bury Bank fort; a square entrenchment, one mile from Stone at Hollywood, in a wood known as Campfield, believed to be Roman; in the meadows near Hilderstone Brook another earthwork with a double ditch (or fosse), the outer one forming a rectangle, 200 yards long, in which a Roman coin was found; a moated site at Hartwell Farm, Hartwell, 2.5m NNE of Stone, off the Barlaston to Meir Heath Road at SJ 917390; a moated site at Priory Farm, near the road between Eccleshall and Stone and near the junction with the Stafford road; and a moated site at Aston Hall, Aston by Stone at SJ 914316.

Finally, a mystery. About 0.25m NNE of Stone station, on Stonefield Common, are the Mottley Pits Terraces. The Terraces are variously straight and curved, and cover a large area. At the top of the hill is an area, about 100 yards by 50 yards, which is covered in mounds with gulleys in between. Who made these terraces no-one knows. They could he prehistoric, they could be Roman or they could he the remains of Civil War defences. Just south-east of the mounds is a spring surrounded by a hedge. A line of ancient trees with gnarled and twisted roots and trunks leads from this spring to the road.

Rough Close, 3.5m NNE of Stone, is a small hamlet which lies just beyond the clutches of the suburban housing of Meir Heath and adjoins Barlaston Common. It is hilly country and the land in places is indeed rough in appearance. It is basically a road junction settlement where the Longton-Stone road meets the Leek-Stone road. The mission church of St Matthew was built in the 1890s but suffered subsidence from coal mining and was rebuilt in 1961. On the north side of the common is the Church of England Primary School. Rough Close is not a place of any great antiquity. In the late-17th Century there was only a single farm here.

STONNALL *1.5m SE of Brownhills*

Stonnall is a small nucleated village with a 'tail' that straggles down the A452, Brownhills to Sutton Coldfield road. The church of St Peter was built in 1822. It has a nave and battlemented tower in Gothic brick, and a Gothic stone chancel of 1843 by Joseph Potter.

One mile SW of Stonnnall, on the other side of the A452, on a wooded hill just to the east of **Holly Bank** (a suburb of Walsall Wood), are the remains of a fort (SJ 062033) called Castle Old Fort, which is believed to be Roman. Spear heads and other implements of uncertain age have been found on the site. The north part of it has been built on and the enclosure used as a garden.

At the junction of the A452 and the A461 are large sand and gravel pits. The A452 was part of the 'Old Chester Road' coach route from London. It joined the A5 (Watling Street) for a few miles before turning north to Newport and Whitchurch, and on to Chester. The Welsh Harp at Stonnall was a well-known coaching inn

Owlett Hall, 1.25m NE of Stonnal, is of about 1700. In 1956 a prehistoric axe was found here which went to Birmingham museum. The Hall was the childhood home of Rosalind Prince, the writer of Staffordshire ghost stories.

STOURBRIDGE *2m SW of Dudley*

Almost the whole of the Black Country used to lie within the boundaries of the County of Stafford. The major exception was the Stourbridge area, which belonged to Worcestershire. However, in recent years boundaries have been moved and today Stourbridge is a part of the Dudley Metropolitan Borough. This is, in turn, a part of the new County of the West Midlands, which now encompasses the whole of the Black Country. United at last. In fact this is history come full circle because at the time of Domesday Book the place later to be called Sturesbrige ('the bridge over the River Stour') lay in the manor of Swinford.

Now called **Old Swinford** this ancient Anglo-Saxon settlement belonged to the Norman lord, William Fitz Ansculf, who controlled his extensive estates from his castle at Dudley. Very little is known of the early settlement at Stourbridge but in 1482 the holders of the manor (the Dean and Chapter of Windsor) were granted the right to hold a weekly market and two annual fairs. The wool industry flourished in the countryside around, and the Gig Mill pub on the corner of South Road and Broadway reminds one of this. (A gig was a machine that raised the nap of a piece of cloth). There was also some early exploitation of the local limestone, coal and fireclay, and in the first half of the 17th Century the Foley family of ironmasters from Swinford rose to be of more than local importance. (The notable Old Swinford Hospital was founded in 1667 by Thomas Foley). Nails, edge tools, heavy engineering and brick manufacture were the industries on which Stourbridge thrived.

In 1779 the Stourbridge Canal came to the heavily industrialized area north of Stourbridge, but the town itself had to wait until 1849 for the extension spur that linked it to the waterway that bore its name. New roads and a new bridge were followed by the coming of the railway in 1852.

But what of the glass industry for which Stourbridge is today world famous? Stourbridge was one of the very first centres of glass production. However, the glass industry was, and still is, centred not so much on Stourbridge itself but a little to the north in Wordsley, Amblecote and Brierley Hill, and especially along the banks of the Stourbridge Canal. Glassmaking was introduced to the area in the early 17th Century by refugee Protestants from Lorraine, but was of little importance until the 19th Century when the industry grew rapidly. Advanced techniques of decoration - etching, cutting and new colours - were developed in the factories of pioneers such as the Richardsons, Stevens and Williams, and Thomas Webb.

Ruby glass was a particular local specialty. This colour was created by the addition of powdered gold to the molten glass. Very often this glass was used as a thin second coat to a clear glass object, giving an attractive pale-pink finish. Most of the manufacturing processes were carried out within a tall, cone-shaped building built of brick. Alas, all but one of these have been demolished; only the Red House cone at nearby Wordsley still stands. (See Wordsley.)

Perhaps the area's greatest craftsman in glass was Frederick Carder. He was born in Brockmoor (see Brierley Hill) in 1863. Carder was both a scientist and a creative artist but early on he emigrated to America where he built the famous Steuben works, later taken over by Corning. He was doing a full day's work well into his nineties.

Another emigrant to America was Harry Northwood, who set up a factory in West Virginia where he produced what many consider to be the finest Carnival Ware ever made. Carnival Ware was made by sprinkling metallic salts on to the pressed molten glass. This produced an iridescent effect. Done less than skillfully this can be very garish, and cheaply produced goods were popular as prizes at show-grounds and funfairs - hence 'Carnival' Ware. Northwood's glass is highly collectable; it is marked with a letter 'N' within a circle.

Today the centre of Stourbridge is an island encircled by a race-track of a ring road that has more than its fair share of critics. It is a mature place with an air of affluence. There are two shopping malls - the Crown Centre and the Ryemarket - but these are of modest proportions and have not denuded the traditional shopping areas. High Street still flourishes and there are numbers of small, individual shops that are so important to the character of a town. The oldest building is the Talbot Hotel. It was built in the early 17th Century but the street facade was renewed in brick during the 18th Century. The sign shows a white dog, although we always understood the Talbot to be a dog of French origin that was white, yes, but with large black spots.

The early Georgian parish church of St Thomas dates from 1728-36. It is of brick with stone dressings and hides away in Market Street, now a cul-de-sac. The substantial red brick Town Hall, complete with tower, is of 1887 to a design by Thomas Robinson. The most interesting street, architecturally speaking, is High Street. Unfortunately, this has been given the kiss of death by being cut off from the town centre. It runs downhill, northwards to the river and the canal. At the top is the Mitre Hotel, known for its folk club, and at the bottom are two handsome houses. One of these, Stourhurst, is built of brick with stone dressings and has unusual, canted-bay, Venetian windows. On the same side of the street, higher up the hill, is probably the most eye-catching building in Stourbridge, namely the yellow brick, Gothic-Tudor King Edward Grammar School. This was built in 1862 to a design by Thomas Smith. It has a castellated tower complete with side turret. The right-hand side was demolished and rebuilt in 1931 by Webb and Gray; in no way did they improve on the original.

Alongside the Canal Basin is the 18th Century Bonded Warehouse. Next to the warehouse are the old Canal Company Offices and the Mooring Tavern. Nearby, is the site of the Stourbridge Ironworks where the Stourbridge Lion was built in 1829. This locomotive had the distinction of being the first to run on commercial rails in America.

Stourbridge has two public parks, both the gift of Ernest Stevens, a millionaire holloware manufacturer. In 1929 he gave the Studley Court Estate to Stourbridge. The big house became the Council House and the surrounding land became the Mary Stevens Park, a memorial to his wife. In 1930 he gave the Wollescote Hall estate to Lye and Wollescote Urban District Council. This became the Stevens Park.

South of the town centre lie Old Swinford and **Pedmore**, two ancient manors, and **Norton**: all are now suburban residential areas. Likewise, **Wollaston** to the north-west, where there is a good local shopping centre and Gibbet Lane, so called because one Bobby Howe was hanged here for murdering a farmer. Wollaston lies on the road to Stourton. At the junction of this lane and the busy A449(T) stands the Stewponey and Foley Arms. (See Stewponey.) The famed hostelry looks across the green water meadows of the River Stour to the almost romantic remains of Stourton Castle. The castle was the home of Fred Phillips, the leading living breeder of Staffordshire Bull-terriers. Further west again the road passes through the charming woods of The Million to the unspoilt village of Enville. Many a Black country man has retreated here on a summers weekend.

Whittington lies 2m W of Stourbridge on the A449. The hamlet is widely known for its hostelry, the Whittington Inn. This attractive half-timbered building was originally the Manor House. However, in 1788, Lord Stamford, wishing to distance himself from his tenants, built a new Hall to the south. This still exists and is now used as a farmhouse. The association of Dick Whittington with the Inn is by no means proven and owes more to commercial opportunism than historical fact. Certainly the building we see today cannot be of 1310, as claimed, and is more likely to be Elizabethan.

Man's earliest marks on the countryside around Stourbridge are the Iron Age earthworks of **Wychbury Ring** on Wychbury Hill, just south of the town; and to the west, the track of the old Roman road that ran from the Roman military camp at Greensforge to West Hagley and beyond. (Note: Lye, Amblecote, Wordsley and Brierley Hill all have associations with Stourbridge but have their own articles).

STOWE BY CHARTLEY *6m NE of Stafford*
The village of Stowe lies 0.66m S of Chartley Castle, on the other side of the A518, Stafford to Uttoxeter road. It is an old village, but is not mentioned in Domesday Book. There is a pub, the Cock Inn, a very good black-and-white thatched cottage called Old Thatch, some old red brick houses and, mercifully, very little new building.

The church of St John is quaint. It is essentially Norman: chancel south window, chancel south buttress and both nave doorways, with their scalloped capitals and zig-zag decoration in the arches. The tower is probably Decorated and the north aisle is by Habersham and Pite of 1895. There is a monument to Walter Deveraux (died 1537), grandfather of the famous Robert, 2nd Earl of Essex and favourite of Queen Elizabeth I. There are also monuments by Sir Edwin Lutyens to General Sir Walter Norris Congreve (died 1927), who was Governor General of Malta, and his son, William, VC, DSO, MC, killed in 1916 aged 25.

Just to the west of Stowe is the track of the overgrown disused railway line that joined the main line just south of Bramshall, near Uttoxeter.

To the east of Stowe is the site of the old gypsum mines. Memory of these mines had all but vanished in the area and we had difficulty in locating the site. Softer, lower-grade gypsum is used for making plaster, but when it occurs as large, stone-like blocks suitable for carving it is called alabaster and is used for making ornaments and church effigies. There are only two places in the county where alabaster is found: in the valley of the River Dove near Hanbury, and at Chartley.

The Chartley mines were worked from the 1860s to the 1880s when production ceased. In 1948 exploratory borings were made and in 1958 production was started again, but only for six months when excessive salt in the gypsum and problems with flooding made the workings uneconomic. The mine buildings have been leveled and the shaft capped in concrete. There is no visible evidence left to show that mines were ever there. The site is at Norman's Wood Farm (SK 013272). The farm is 0.5m E of Stowe. Take the Drointon lane out of the village, fork left when the road divides and the farm is on the left with white entrance fences and gates and lamp-posts. The mine was in the field to the right of, and adjoining, the entrance drive. The small bush near the middle of the field marks the site of the shaft.

The alabaster that was mined here was taken to be processed at Weston, 1.5m W of Stowe. Here was a factory. The building is still there. It faces the large village green and stands near the village hall at the entrance to the Laing construction equipment depot. The same building has also operated as a dairy.

STOW HEATH *1m WNW of Bilston*

Stow Heath was once a large manor in its own right. It is conjectured that the manor house was the timber-framed building at Bilston now called the Greyhound Inn. Stow is an Anglo-Saxon word that can mean many things but when used as a first element usually has a religious significance. Thus, Stow Heath probably means 'the church on the heath'.

The heath was long ago ripped up by coal miners. Mounds of their spoil can still be seen in the rather drab and otherwise very flat East Park (east of Wolverhampton). This park was laid out in 1896 by T H Mawson. His partner, Dan Gibson, designed the entrance lodge. A few terraced houses survive near the main Wolverhampton-Bilston road but Stow Heath is dominated by a big new industrial estate that runs the length of Hickman Avenue and incorporates the old Chillington Tool Works.

In a charter of 994, made by Lady Wulfrun, **Monmore** was referred to as Wetmere. In former times there was a windmill and a sulphur holy well here. The church of All Saints in Steelhouse Lane was built in 1877-79. Rising above these big industrial sheds is the grey-painted tower of **Monmore Green** greyhound racing stadium, looking very smart indeed these days. It was here as a very small boy that the author picked the winners of five successive races by simply 'liking the look' of the dogs. This so upset his father's faith in canine form that for the rest of his life he wagered only on horses. The name Monmore is Anglo-Saxon and means either 'Manna's lake' or 'the men's lake.' Most of Monmore Green lies south of the Wolverhampton Road, a place of old iron works, Victorian terraced houses and ubiquitous new developments. To the west of Stow Heath Lane are estates of small, modern houses and bungalows. The Lane leads to **Stow Lawn**, where indeed there is a large, undulating open green graced with daffodils in the Spring. South of this is the residential area called **Green Lanes** which adjoins the extensive Bilston Cemetery.

STRAMSHALL *2m NNW of Uttoxeter town centre*

A rather drab dormitory village for Uttoxeter. Alric, a freeman, held the manor both before and after the Norman Conquest, a most uncommon feat. The church of St Michael has a nave and chancel, a steep roof, lancet windows and a turret, all of 1852 to a design by Thomas Fradgley of Uttoxeter.

West of Hill House are the Hill House Terraces, rectangular earthworks some 420 feet long. North-east of St Michael's is another prehistoric earthwork, 120 feet by 90 feet. In a field near the village five trenches were dug and fragments of pottery, probably Romano-British, were found at each place.

A mile to the north-east of Stramshall, on the Uttoxeter to Rocester road, is the hamlet of **Crakemarsh**. The name means 'the marsh frequented by water-crakes' and the manor appeared in Domesday Book as Crechemers. The marshes were common land but were enclosed in the reign of Edward IV. When the author first visited the area in 1988 he wrote: 'Hidden in the wooded grounds of its small park are the fire-charred ruins of the once elegant Crakemarsh Hall. Inside this stuccoed Georgian mansion was once a beautiful 17th Century staircase. The coach-house has been converted to dwellings. The gardens are all of a tangle and an air of desolation pervades the place.'

Since then it has been pulled down (1998) and redeveloped. The Hall was built on the site of a grange of Croxden Abbey and there is Norman work in the cellars. It was formerly the home of the Cotton and Cavendish families but in the 1970s it was bought by J C Bamford who lived there for a while. It seems that the JCB company had its beginnings here in about 1947 when it occupied the coach house and stables (presumably renting them) as workshops before moving to larger premises at nearby Rocester. Today, of course, they have a splendid new factory in landscaped grounds alongside the B5030.

STREETLY *4m W of Walsall*

The name means 'the open land by the Roman road'. Ryknild Street runs through the settlement. Streetly is not in the Black Country but is included here because, since 1974, it has been administered from Walsall. It is not a town; it is a substantial residential area with pubs, schools, churches and several small clusters of shops. It has the great good fortune of adjoining the oak woods, moors and pools of Sutton Park, a carefully preserved wilderness area of considerable size. Note the traditional paling fence that surrounds it.

At **Hardwick** there are leafy lanes lined with very upmarket houses, such as those in Streetly Wood, a gated road noted for its rhododendrons. The red brick parish church of All Saints is long and low and rather plain, as though subdued by the opulence of nearby houses.

To the north the old Roman Road passes through Little Aston Park. Here are some very expensive houses indeed. These mansions have security systems to protect their security systems. Watch out for the 'sleeping policemen'; they mean business, as the numerous grooves in the road testify. Roman Road runs from the irregular brick Methodist church in Thornhill Road to the ashlar, sandstone church of St Peter, one mile further north. St Peter's lies embowered in trees and was built in 1874 by G E Street. It has a broach spire with groups of slender, stepped, pointed, arched windows, and was paid for by the Honourable Edward Swynfen Parker Jervis of **Little Aston Hall**.

The Hall stands close by the church. It is a handsome Italianate building, designed by Edward J Payne of Birmingham, and built in 1857-9. It possibly incorporates parts of an older 18th Century house by James Wyatt. Payne's house is symmetrical with a seven-bay, 2.5-storey centre with three three-bay wings of two storeys on both sides. It has been converted into apartments but is immaculately kept. There is a large lake behind the house and, surprise, surprise, here is a cluster of tall, three-storey blocks of brick built flats. They are undoubtedly expensive, but they are certainly not handsome. Elsewhere in the lovely grounds there are more modern mansions and a bland red brick BUPA hospital.

But return to the church of St Peter. Opposite the church is the entrance to Forge Lane. In this country place the name might conjure up pictures of the village smithy. Far from it. The lane leads to Forge Farm and the undisturbed slag heaps and reservoir pool of John Wood's mid 18th century iron forge. Here water-powered hammers were used to beat out the impurities in brittle pig iron to make it more malleable. Wood also had a much larger works in Wednesbury where malleable iron was made using coal (not charcoal).

STRETTON *3.5m SW of Penkridge*

The village lies 0.5m N of the A5 (Watling Street), about 2m WNW of Gailey Island. The Roman road to Whitchurch passes through the settlement. In the general area of its junction with Watling street were the several Roman forts and civilian settlement collectively called Pennocrucium (after Penkridge). There is very little to see on the ground and, indeed, the ancient ploughed out earthworks were only discovered from the study of aerial photographs.

The River Penk (a Celtic name) crosses Watling Street here and powered the waterwheel of Stretton Mill. In the village of Stretton is the attractive church of St John. It has a Norman chancel and a priest's doorway, but the nave and transepts were rebuilt in 1860. Adjacent to the church is Stretton Hall, a charming, early 18th Century country house set in a pleasant park with a lake. It originally had only two storeys but a third was added about 1860. The house is built of brick and has even quoins, a central pediment and cupola, long sash windows with moulded surrounds, a Victorian porte-cochère, and inside a fine staircase.

The Congreve family had acquired Stretton by marriage in the 14th Century and built a house here shortly afterwards. The present mansion was built by John Congreve. It was sold to the Conollys in the mid-18th Century. In 1758 Thomas Conolly married Lady Louisa Lennox. She and her sisters are the main players in Stella Tillyard's book 'Aristocrats', which became a TV series of the same name in 1999.

From the Conollys it passed to the Moncktons of Somerford who are the present occupiers. The Staffordshire Moncktons are descended from the 5th son of the 1st Viscount Galway, who married the daughter and heiress of Lord Pigot of Patshull. Several members of the family have been Members of Parliament.

One mile south-west of Stretton the Shropshire Union Canal crosses the A5 via the black-and-white aqueduct constructed by Thomas Telford in 1832.

SUGNALL *2m NW of Eccleshall*

The name is from the Anglo-Saxon and means 'Sucga's hill'. Sucga was both a personal name and that of a bird, and earlier forms of the suffix are 'hulle', from 'hyll'. Sugnall Hall stands just north of the Croxton-Eccleshall road. It is a 2.5-storey, four-bay red brick house spoiled by the replacement windows; such houses lose their character when shorn of their small, glittering Georgian panes. Nevertheless, it is a friendly enough looking place. The house cannot be seen from the road being shielded by trees and approached down a gravel drive.

The Old Hall has disappeared but may have been replaced by Sugnall Home Farm, just south of the road, some outbuildings of which are now rented out to trade.

In 1807 a driverless stagecoach arrived at an inn in nearby Eccleshall. The horses stopped by themselves, out of habit. The driver had fallen off and was later found dead beside the road at Sugnall.

Copmere, a most lovely natural lake lies 1m S of the Hall and is part of the estate. My dogs have spent many happy hours there. (See the Copmere article.)

Pershall, 1.5m SE of Sugnall, on the road to Eccleshall, is a small farming hamlet, most of which lies south of the main road. The Blest family have held land at Pershall from 1298 to the present day. In 1622 John Blest held his land from the Bishop of Lichfield by supplying the Bishop with two pairs of gloves, and two pence yearly, and providing two beaters to the Bishop's hunt for three days three times a year.

Pershall Pool, on the lane to Copmere, appears to be privately owned and there is no public access.

SWINDON *2m SW of Wombourne*

The name Swindon means 'pig hill'. It is a pleasant little village in a delightful setting on the banks of the Smestow Brook, which is here shadowed by the Staffordshire and Worcestershire Canal (1772). There is a row of shops, a Post Office, the Ebenezer Chapel (1820), The Old Bush, The Greyhound, The Green Man, a water well guarded by two white goats and a rabbit, a few too many modern houses and the small, red sandstone church of St John.

It is strange to think that such a charming country place was once a hive of industry. There was an iron forge here from at least 1668 when the ironmaster, Thomas Foley (died 1677), took the lease on it. There was an iron furnace here even earlier, in the 1620s, which was said by Dud Dudley to be smelting iron ore by burning coal (rather than by burning the usual charcoal) more than 100 years before Abraham Darby 'rediscovered' the techniques at Coalbrookdale. By the brook there is a new road called Swin Forge Way.

The old craft of working tempered iron into edge-tools such as scythes, reaping hooks, axes, etc, was called 'whitesmithing'. There were several whitesmiths in the region during the mid-17th Century, and in Swindon there was a blade-mill that ground a sharp edge on the tools they produced. There was also a blade-mill at nearby Himley.

An unusual feature in Swindon today is to be found in the back garden of No 6, Reynolds Close, a modest detached estate house. This dwelling backs on to the canal and the owners have dug out their own private little concrete lined dock in which to moor a boat.

The hamlet of **Smestow** is 4m NNW of Swindon. It lies along the east side of the lane close to the Smestow Brook just a handful of old cottages with a few modern houses and a chapel. The sheds that can be seen behind the trees are on the Wombourne Enterprise Park. The name Smestow is a contraction of the medieval Smethestall. Both the first and the second element mean the same thing, 'smooth, or stagnant'. This could refer to either a deep, slow moving section of the river, or to a pool on its course. In 1912 a bore hole was drilled by Germans to extract water, to lower the level of the water in the Earl of Dudley's coal mines at Baggeridge and Himley. It is 886 metres deep and is said to be the deepest well in Britain. This created a rivulet called locally Hun River.

Ashwood, 1.5m S of Swindon, is a scattered hamlet which was given to the Wolverhampton monastery in 994. It was later laid waste when Kinver Forest was created. The wharfage on the nearby Staffordshire and Worcestershire Canal is called Ashwood Basin. In 1776 the 1,400 acres of Ashwood Hay and Wall Heath were enclosed by an Act of Parliament.

SWINSCOE *3m WNW of Ashbourne*

Swinscoe is a small village of cottages and farms with a main-road motel and a pub, the Dog and Partridge. The name means 'the swine's wood'. Swinscoe Green is the centre of the settlement and lies just south of the A52, the Ashbourne to Leek road. In 1745 three marauding Jacobites were shot dead by the Smith family and buried in the 'Flats' behind the lime-kilns. A spectral black dog haunts these graves protecting its master.

A Neolithic or Bronze Age axe-hammer was found at Commonend Farm, 0.5m NW of Swinscoe, and there are at least three burial mounds in the vicinity of the village.

SWYNNERTON *9m NNW of Stafford and 5m NNE of Eccleshall*

In 1086 Swynnerton was part of the vast estates of Robert de Toni, standard bearer to King William during the Conquest. The lord of the manor was the Anglo-Saxon, Wulfgeat, who had also held it before 1066 and was one of the few to keep his position under the new Norman aristocracy.

Swynnerton is a handsome village that lies on a gentle hill amongst pleasant pastoral country. There is a pub, a rustic garage, a thatched cottage amongst several old red brick houses, and on the fringe of the village is a beautiful water tower. This has tall arches in yellow and red brick and was built in the 1890s.

There once lived in the village an eccentric odd-job man who, until his death in 1987, lived in a tiny hut, without water and electricity, in the grounds of the Fitzherbert Arms, the village inn.

The parish church of St Mary has two Norman doorways in the base of the tower; the upper part is of the 16th Century. The nave, chancel and nave arcades are 14th Century Early English, and there are Perpendicular traceried windows. The south chapel was the original church. In the south-east chapel is a seven-foot-high statue of Jesus, dated between 1260 and 1280. He is seated and pointing to the wound in his side. This sculpture was certainly never meant for a humble country church and probably came from Lichfield Cathedral. It was found buried under the floor of the chapel and had probably been interred at the time of the Reformation. The stained glass of the east window was made by Powell to a design by J D Sedding.

Under a canopy in the south wall of the chancel is the effigy of a cross-legged knight of the mid-13th Century, probably Sir John Swynnerton who died about 1254. In 1856 the tomb was opened and a body covered in lead an inch thick was found. When this was removed a young man of ruddy complexion, with auburn hair and beard and with two front teeth missing was revealed. The body and the effigy agreed in measurement and other details, but on exposure to air the body quickly turned to dust.

East of the church is the former Vicarage now called Queenswood, a house of five bays and two storeys, of 1760, by Charles Cope Trubshaw.

Swynnerton Hall stands within the village but turns its austere back towards the humbler abodes of the common folk. The park, which is now a conservation area, lies to the front of the south-facing Hall and is cut through by public roads.

Amongst the green pastures is the ground of the village cricket club. The Hall itself was built by Francis Smith of Warwick, for Thomas Fitzherbet, in 1725-9. It is a classical ashlar house of three storeys, with a substantial cornice below the top storey. The three-bay centre has giant Roman columns, the quoins are of equal length and the windows have moulded surrounds. In 1812 there were additions and alterations by James Trubshaw but some of these have recently been demolished. From the front of the house there are splendid views over Staffordshire to the south and Shropshire to the west.

The estate passed by marriage from the Swynnerton family to William Fitzherbert in 1562. In the 18th Century the widow of Thomas Fitzherbert married George IV and played an important part in public life. The house is still home to the Fitzherberts and they still farm the estate of some 8,000 acres.

Although the line of the original Lord Stafford died out several centuries ago, the present squire of Swynnerton still carries the title. He is well known for his obsession with blood sports, especially the shooting of game birds. His estate is littered with traps designed to kill small animals that might interfere with the birds he breeds. We found a young male blackbird crushed in one of these traps close to the Hall. Both Lord Stafford's wife and his gamekeeper, Mr Green, were quite scornful of my concern. The police were called and I was threatened with prosecution for trespass because I had strayed one yard off the public footpath to try and rescue the blackbird.

The Roman Catholic church of Our Lady of the Assumption stands close to the Hall and was built for the Roman Catholic Fitzherberts in 1869 by Gilbert Blount. It is a little austere without, but within it is richly decorated. The overall style is Gothic Middle Pointed. Due to the influence of the Fitzherberts a good half of the church-going population of Swynnerton is Roman Catholic.

West of the church and tastefully hidden from sight is an estate of modern houses. Two miles south of the village, on the road to Eccleshall, is the entrance to the huge Swynnerton Camp where training is given on new weapons and equipment. A few years ago the area was coated with a radioactive dust during an exercise to simulate a nuclear attack. It is here that convoys carrying atomic warheads, en route from Scotland to the south for servicing, are parked overnight. Close by was the Weapons Testing Centre at Coldmeece, now closed.

At the beginning of the Second World War the Royal Ordnance Factory at Woolwich was moved to Swynnerton where a large munitions' factory was built. There were up to 23,000 workers here and several halls of residence were built nearby to accommodate them: Howard Hall, Frobisher Hall, Raleigh Hall, Drake Hall, Beatty Hall, Duncan Hall and flats and houses at Stone and Walton. The factory closed in 1959.

There are several marl pits in the Swynnenton area. Marl is a clay rich soil which is mixed with poor, light soils to bind the particles together.

SWYTHAMLEY *3m NE of Rushton Spencer, which is 5m NW of Leek*
Swythamley lies in the North Staffordshire Moorlands amongst some of the finest countryside in England. There is no village in the accepted sense, just a scatter of farms and cottages. The Hall is not large and the church (of 1903) has been abandoned; yet there is magic in the air, for this is the setting of the great medieval epic poem 'Sir Gawain and the Green Knight'.

In the Middle Ages Swythamley belonged to the Earls of Chester and in 1180 the 5th Earl died at his hunting lodge here. (Swythamley lay between the Forests of Leek and Macclesfield.) In 1214 the Cistercian Abbey of Dieulacres was established at what is now called Abbey Green, 1m N of Leek. This monastery had been founded at Poulton, on the River Dee near Chester, in 1146, and probably moved to Leek at the request of the Earl of Chester. The Earl endowed the Abbey with lands which included Swythamley. In 1540, at the time of the Dissolution of the Monasteries, Henry VIII granted Swythamley to the Trafford family.

Their manor house was burned down in 1813. In the mid-19th Century the estate was purchased by Philip Lancaster Brocklehurst and he rebuilt the house. However, the centre block of the present Hall seems to be from the old, original manor. It is made of sandstone, whereas the wings to either side and the porch to the front are of brick. The house is irregular, of two storeys and has dormer windows. It is not altogether a friendly building, an opinion shared by the organisers of the Transcendental Meditation group who occupied it for several years before leaving in 1987. There are various outbuildings and two lodges with good iron gates. The abandoned rock-faced church lies near to the east lodge.

Although the house is nothing special the setting is magnificent. To the front of the Hall is a delightful small Park in which sheep graze and to the rear are the jagged rocks of the Roaches. Close by are wild moors and deep wooded valleys, an archetypal romantic landscape. The dramatic rock called the Hanging Stone (SJ 974654), lies 0.5m N of Swythamley Hall. It juts out unmistakably from Back Forest Hill. There are many legends connected with this rock: that it was used for public hangings (doubtful); that in prehistoric times it was used to make sacrifices to the goddess Dana (possible). Two plaques are affixed to the stone, one commemorating Lt Col Courtney Brocklehurst (1888-1942) of Swythamley Hall, and the other to a dog. This reads: "Beneath this rock August 1, 1874, was buried Burke,

A noble mastiff, black and tan,
Faithful as woman, braver than man:
A gun and a ramble his heart's desire,
With the friend of his life, the Swythamley Squire."

It has been suggested that the Hanging Stone was positioned by the hand of man, but we are convinced that it is a natural formation; there are similar features in the area.

It is very likely that the author of '**Sir Gawain and the Green Knight**' either lived at Swythamley Hall or very close by. Briefly, the tale tells of Sir Gawain's quest for the Green Knight, an elfin knight whom Sir Gawain had beheaded but not killed. Gawain journeyed from South Wales to the Wirral and from there he followed the old 'Earlsway' route used by the Earls of Chester to visit their lands in Staffordshire and Derbyshire. He reached the Meerbrook marshes and turned north into the valley between the Roaches and Gun Hill to Swythamley. Here he found a beautiful white castle with towers and turrets and here he sojourned as a guest of the owner, Sir Bertilak. Whilst Sir Bertilak was out hunting deer, boar and fox, Sir Gawain was seduced by his host's wife. To say more would spoil the story.

The descriptions of the scenery in the poem are very fine indeed, and so many tally with natural features around Swythamley that there can be little doubt that the poem was set here. The cliffs called 'the rocheres' are the Roaches; 'the flosche', meaning a 'marshy place' is Flash; 'a knot', a rare word meaning 'a rocky formation', is Knotbury (a plateau just beyond Flash with semi-circular layout of tracks and houses around the common, which is quite possibly an ancient settlement site); the place where the boar is trapped in a hole in a water course near a rock is probably Pincher's Hole in the valley of the River Dane, just south of Knar Farm, where there is a hollow between the river banks; 'valley to wild valley' is Blackbrook to Dane; the 'rughe, knokled knarres with korned stones' are the Castle Cliff Rocks near Lud's Church; and lastly, the mysterious 'Green Chapel', the forbidding cleft in the rock where the story reaches its conclusion, just has to be Lud's Church itself which lies in the woods of the Back Forest, lm NE of Swythamley Hall. (see below.)

'Sir Gawain and the Green Knight' was written by an anonymous author in about the year 1400. He used a dialect peculiar to the north-west Midlands. The ballad is considered to be 'the finest alliterative poem of the age outside Chaucer's works', though comparison with Chaucer's writings is impossible because of stylistic and language differences.

The mystery of the poem is the location of the castle. There is no sign of a castle at Swythamley, or of any other building that even remotely fits the description. It is likely that this was simply a poetic invention, though who is to say what excavation on the site of the Hall may reveal. There might have been clues in the estate papers but when the Brocklehurst family sold Swythamley they burned most of the old papers relating to the house, much to the chagrin of the County Archivist.

There are two translations of 'Sir Gawain and the Green Knight' currently available. One is by Brian Stone, published by Penguin Books, and the other is by R R Tolkien, published by Unwin Paperbacks.

Lud's Church is most easily approached from Gradbach in the Dane valley. A footpath leads westwards through lovely country along the banks of the river. Lud's Church is not well signposted and the actual entrance could be easily be missed. The cleft in the rock is initially narrow but widens and deepens as one progresses. It is quite eerie. The moss-covered rocks drip with water and trees and ferns overhang from above - hence the 'Green' Chapel. The sun never shines here. Altogether, Lud's church is about 100 yards long, 30 to 40 feet deep and 6 to l0 feet wide. The cleft was caused by the Millstone Grit rocks slipping along a bedding plane which caused fractures, which were later eroded. It is a place that one should visit, though the climb is steep and rough in places.

Lud's Church is said to have been used for secret services by the Lollard religious sect, who were followers of John Wycliffe (1330-84). On one occasion their singing betrayed their presence to soldiers who were searching for them. In the struggle that ensued a beautiful 18-year-old girl called Alice was killed and was buried beneath an oak tree at the entrance to the cleft. She was the daughter of Walter de Lud-Auk after whom the 'church' is named. The Lollards were early Nonconformists who despised the wealth and arrogance of the established Roman Catholic church.

Another local name for Lud's Church is Trafford's Leap, after one of the squires of Swythamley Hall, whose horse leapt over the chasm whilst they were out hunting.

The Swythamley Estate is famous for its wild wallabies. In 1938 the brother of Sir Philip Brocklehurst introduced imported wallabies into his enclosed private zoo at Roach House at the southern end of the Roaches. Some of these animals escaped and bred in the wild. Their descendants were still living in the rocks and woods hereabouts until about 1990 but sightings are no longer reported and it is likely that they have died out. One of them can be seen at the

Potteries Museum in Hanley.

Old Hag Farm, 1m SSE of Swythamley, is said to have been named after the Witch of Frith, and is thought to be on the Limes Britannicus, the Roman defensive earthwork that ran from Doncaster to Gloucester and was a predecessor of Hadrian's Wall.

Turner's Pool was Thurnehurst-pole in 1541 and lies 0.5m SE of Swythamley. It may have been made by the monks of Dieulacres Abbey as a fish pond. The farmhouse nearby was once Swythamley school, which closed in about 1870.

Gun Hill, 1.75m S of Swythamley, rises to 1,200 feet (or a little more), and there is an earthwork running down the side of the hill. It has been suggested that there was a battle between the Romans and the British on Gun Hill in about 22 BC. In medieval times the hill was forest-clad. The Trussway, an ancient trackway, has been traced from Cleulow Cross in Cheshire, over Gun Hill, to Fould, to Leek, Leekbrook and Cheddleton to Basford Green.

T

TALKE O'TH'HILL *1m SW of Kidsgrove*

Talke is a large, former-mining village which lies along the old London-Carlisle road, turnpiked here in 1741 but now bypassed to the east by the improved A34. There has been a lot of recent residential development in the southern suburb of Talke Pits, and the High Street has been turned into an obstacle course by the construction of many annoying chicanes, which periodically and unexpectedly reduce the road to a single track. The old village lies on high ground to the north. Indeed, the name Talke is from the Celtic for 'high hill'.

The parish church of St Martin was built in 1794 of dull red brick and has a Victorian bellcote, a stone-built north transept, a modern parish room adjoining, and a large wooded churchyard.

The market cross in High Street was first erected in 1253 and restored in 1887, and marks the site of the market place. There are a number of inns along High Street. The Plume of Feathers was a noted wagoners' stopping place. In 1781 a wagon carrying gunpowder exploded in the village killing the horses and the coachman and injuring the occupants of a cottage. George III commanded collections to be made throughout England to aid the bereaved and injured.

Today Talke is becoming best known for the new, large and rather smart, shopping centre called Talke Freeport on the Jamage Industrial estate, Talke Pits, which adjoins Talke to the south.

On the A34, east of Talke village, is Harecastle Farm, a Jacobean stone house with a recessed centre. The upper windows are regular but on the ground floor the door is left of centre and the middle window right of centre. This is because the hall is not centrally placed. The house has recently been developed as an inn-cum-restaurant. The Harecastle tunnels run below the hill, 0.75m E of the house. (See Kidsgrove.) Further north, on the A34, are the two lodges of Clough Hall, the now-demolished 19th Century home of the Kynnersley family.

Talke's most famous son is Reginald Mitchell, the designer of the Spitfire aircraft so much admired both by the enthusiast and the general public alike. He was born at 115 Congleton Road, Butt Lane, Talke in 1895. In 1995 a statue of him was erected in front of the Potteries' Museum in Hanley. Butt Lane is a northern residential suburb of Talke.

Dunkirk, 1m SW of Talke, is a hamlet which consists of a cluster of terraced cottages in a charming, watery dell.

Parrott's Drumble, just to the west of Talke Pits, is a wooded valley leased by the Staffordshire Nature Conservation Trust from the Coal Board. Parrott is (was) the name of a local family.

TAMHORN *1.25m NNE of Hopwas, which is just W of Tamworth*
The name is from the Anglo-Saxon and means 'the horn-shaped piece of land near the River Tame'. On the west side of the Birmingham and Fazeley canal, near Tamhorn House Bridge, is the site of an early medieval village (SK 180070), which was deserted between 1334 and 1529. Today, there is no actual settlement and the area is in the 'danger zone' of Whittington Barracks. Tamhorn Park Farm was the former manor house of Tamhorn and the Tamhorn family. The present house was built in the early 18th Century.

TAMWORTH *24m SE of Stafford*
The name is from the River Tame which is joined here by the River Anker. Tamworth Castle stands guard at their confluence. For over a thousand years it stood alone, but now has the incongruous company of six blocks of council flats 15 storeys high. Below the castle are attractive public gardens leading down to the wooded banks of the river. Beyond the river, on the wide reaches of its flood plain, are the Castle Pleasure Grounds, and west of the now-pedestrianised Lady Bridge is Lady Meadow.

Tamworth itself lies on higher ground beyond the castle. It is a busy market town of some 50,000 people with a good range of shops and two modern shopping precincts. In 1965 it was designated an Expanding Town to absorb the overspill population from Birmingham. This explains the acres of modern housing that now surround the ancient settlement. Tamworth has come down in the world not a little since it was the capital of the Kingdom of Mercia. Indeed, it was virtually the capital town of the country during the reign of King Offa, from 757 to 796, for he was overlord of England, the acknowledged King amongst Kings. He was a figure of international repute who dealt on equal terms with the great Charlemagne. Offa had his royal palace at Tamworth, probably in the area now occupied by Market Street. The town continued to be the royal seat until it was burnt to the ground by the Danes in 874 and Mercia ceased to be an independent kingdom.

In 913 Tamworth was fortified by Ethelfleda, daughter of King Alfred. Ethelfleda died in 918 and when her nephew, Athelstan, became King of England in 924 he again established a royal residence at Tamworth. His sister, Editha, married Sitgtryg, the Danish King of Northumbria. However, the marriage failed and Editha established a convent at Tamworth and gave the rest of her life to God and good works.

In 943 the town was again attacked and burned by the marauding Danes. It was never to be the seat of a royal residence again. The Anglo-Saxon fortifications were of earth and timber and, except for the castle mound, there is nothing above ground to be seen of these, though excavations in the town centre have recently produced some archaeological finds.

In 1971 a two-storey, Anglo-Saxon watermill was discovered in Bolebridge

Street, which had probably been powered by a horizontal overshot wheel. It would have stood at the south-east corner of the Anglo-Saxon defences by the River Anker and is one of only two Anglo-Saxon watermills found in Britain.

A hoard of 300 William I and II coins were found when the Marmion Steeet schools were built in 1877. Thirty-three were from the Tamworth mint.

After the Norman Conquest the castle and the manor became the property of Robert le Despencer and then of his nephew, Roger le Marmion. They then passed by marriage to the de Frevilles in 1291, the Ferrers in 1423, the Shirleys in 1688, the Comptons in 1715, and finally in 1751 to the Townshends. In 1879 Tamworth Corporation bought the castle.

The castle they bought was the work of the Normans. The circular shell keep was built by the Marmions; the lower part of the herringbone walling is 11th Century and the main battlemented shell keep is 12th Century. Incorporated into the keep is a tower. Within this ancient framework are buildings of a later date, principally the Hall which has survived in its Jacobean dress of the time the Ferrers held the castle. The exterior front was faced with ashlar and the Jacobean mullioned and transomed windows were Gothicized by the Marquess Townshend in 1786. The gabled Warder's House adjacent to the tower is original Jacobean. There is a beautiful wooden chimney-piece here, and two more in upper rooms south of the Hall. All the main rooms - the State Drawing Room, the Oak Room, the Haunted Room, the Long Gallery etc. - are well furnished and the castle houses the local authority Museum. The exhibits include displays of Anglo-Saxon and Norman coins from the Tamworth Mint and information on the unique Anglo-Saxon watermill.

The castle has been lived in continuously from Norman times to the present day, although in 1790-2 the Banqueting Hall was used to house a forge in association with a cotton factory in Lady Meadow owned by Robert Peel's third son. One of Mr Peel's other sons was Sir Robert Peel, MP (1788-1850), who represented Tamworth and who became Home Secretary and later Prime Minister. His famous Tamworth Manifesto of 1834, which expounded his ideas on free trade, was delivered from the steps of the Town Hall, in front of which his statue now stands. In 1846 he repealed the Corn laws, an action which split the Conservative party and forced him to resign.

The Town Hall in Market Street is one of Tamworth's few buildings of note. It was built in 1701 and paid for by Thomas Guy, of Guy's Hospital fame, who was an MP for Tamworth between 1695 and 1707. It is a building of some character with broad, open, stone arches supporting a two-bay brick front with arched windows, a pediment and five-bay sides with a cupola on top. Thomas Guy, who made a fortune out of the South Sea Bubble Scandal, also paid for the charming Almshouses in Gungate (a Danish name), which were completely rebuilt in 1913. In Market Street there are a few Georgian houses but also some untoward modern development.

As for sporting facilities the town is well served. There is an indoor and an outdoor swimming pool, a challenging municipal golf course, fishing and sail-boarding on Borrowpit Lake, a championship-standard BMX track, four sports centres and an athletics' stadium

Buildings deserving mention include: the facade of G Griffith and Son Jewellers, in George Street; the Job Centre in Church Street, a splendid 18th Century, Georgian, stuccoed house of three storeys and five bays with giant angle pilasters and a pedimented doorway; Rutherfords, solicitors' offices in Holloway, neo-Gothic of 1845, built to house Sir Robert Peel's Savings Bank;

the Assembly Rooms in Corporation Street of 1889, a somewhat ungainly edifice with a five-bay front, columned porch with mock parapet, arched widows, three rectangular attic windows and a top-heavy segmental (semi-circular) pediment, all in brick with stone dressings; Bole House in Amington Road, to the south-east of the centre, a tall, handsome, early Georgian house of three bays with giant pilasters and segmental pediment over the door; Spital Chapel (see over page) in Wiggington Road is the small, much amended Norman chapel of the long-gone 13th Century hospital built by the Marmion family; and the Moat House (1572 in Lichfield Street, set back on the south side, is now a public house but was formerly the town house of the Comberford family who entertained Prince Charles, later to become King Charles I, here in 1619. It has five stepped gables. The windows are mostly 18th Century. In the garden by the river is an unusual 18th Century gazebo with pyramid roof and a wind dial painted on the ceiling. Finally, the Manor House, also in Lichfield Street, has a late 18th Century facade hiding a 16th Century core and is believed to have been the childhood home of Thomas Guy.

The only church of interest is St Editha. It lies in a small churchyard by a shopping precinct and is a large building, some 190 feet long. Outside, the church has been so restored (successively by Scott, Ferney and Butterfield) that suggestions as to dates are virtually impossible from external evidence. There was a church on this site at Tamworth as early as the 8th Century, and in 963 King Edgar founded a Collegiate church with a Dean and six Canons, which was largely rebuilt by the Normans. Most of this church was burnt down in 1345. What we see today is a much modified version of the rebuilding. Inside, the following are Decorated: arcades in the nave; blocked south transept window; south aisle windows; north doorway; north chancel wall with tomb recesses; and west and north arches in the north transept. The west tower is Perpendicular with a door by Champneys. In the south-west turret of the tower is a remarkable and very rare double spiral staircase. The clerestory windows and the roofs are Perpendicular. Possibly the feature of most interest to students of church architecture is the large, apparently Norman, south and north crossing arches which originally supported a central crossing tower. (The east and west arches were removed when this tower was dismantled after the fire of 1345.). Are these arches Norman or Anglo-Saxon? The hint that they might be Anglo-Saxon is that the external angles of the old tower project into the nave and chancel aisles. Norman crossing towers left the aisles uninterrupted. Despite this, expert opinion is that the arches are in fact Norman. Of the stained glass there is work by William Morris, Ford Maddox Brown, Burne-Jones, and Holiday and Powell.

Amongst the monuments are memorials to: Sir Baldwin Freville, died 1400 and wife; Baldwin de Witney, died 1369, an ecclesiastic who rebuilt the church in 1345; Sir John Ferrers, died 1680, and his son Humphrey, died 1678. This last monument was commissioned from Grinling Gibbons but was probably actually carved by Arnold Quellin. It is a splendid baroque piece with cherubs, garlands, two figures, a sarcophagus and an urn.

The Railway Viaduct (SK 213037), over the River Anker at Kettlebrook, was highly praised as an adornment to the landscape when it was built in 1851 to carry the Birmingham and Derby Railway, and was the most expensive engineering work on that line. The track is carried over 19 arches at a height of 23 feet.

Perry Crofts, 0.75m NNE of Tamworth, was a medieval manor held from the king on duty of supplying coal and bed litter should the king be staying at Tamworth. Today it is a residential suburb of Tamworth.

Spittal House, 1m N of Tamworth on the Wigginton Road, is today a two-cell mission church dedicated to St Peter. However, it has ancient, if confusing and uncertain, origins. It is probably Norman but has been restored and rebuilt several times and is believed to be the medieval Hospital of St James, or a chapel attached to the hospital, or it became a chapel after being a hospital.

Bassett's Pole, 4m SW of Tamworth, takes its name from a tall pole erected in 1201 by Lord Bassett of Drayton Bassett as a boundary marker. It no longer exists but its position is marked by a concrete finger post facing the Bassett's pole Inn car park.

Brief mention should made of the old broadside ballad, registered at the Stationers Company in 1564, that outlines the meeting of 'Edward IV and The Tanner of Tamworth' which begins:

In summertime, when leaves grow greene,
And blosomms bedecke the tree,
King Edward wolde a hunting ryde,
Some pastime for to see.

TATENHILL *3.5m W of Burton upon Trent*

Tatenhill is a small, linear village with a recent development of large modern houses which lies in the hills of Needwood Forest that fringe the Trent plain to the west of the busy A38.

Tatenhill was an established village by 941 when it is mentioned in a grant of land made by King Edmund. In the same charter Barton (under Needwood) is also mentioned. Barton means 'outlying grange', in this case of Tatenhill.

The settlers in the Trent valley were Angles (not Saxons). After the Norman Conquest the Forest of Needwood became a valued resource. In the 1330s Philip de Somerville actually held the manor of Tatenhill and Draycott by hunting venison for the Earl of Lancaster.

The large church of St Michael has Early English walls, south doorway and priest's doorway, a Perpendicular tower and windows, and was restored by G F Bodley in 1890. The reredos, stalls, pulpit and black-and-white marble floor are also by Bodley. There is a monument to the wife and two daughters of Sir Henry Griffiths. Mr Griffith died in 1641. To the left of the church stands the very fine, early Georgian Rectory. It is a two-storey brick house with five bays, dormer windows and a doorway with fluted Doric pilasters. Together, the church and the Rectory make a most attractive group.

To the east, just over the stream, is Battlestead Hill. Which battle does this commemorate? - perhaps a skirmish between the British and the invading Angles, or the Angles and the marauding Danes. At the hamlet of **Callingwood**, 1.5m NW of Tattenhill, a hoard of 32 Roman gold coins was found at SK 195235 in 1793. They dated from 20 BC to 96 AD.

Rough Hay, 1m N of Tatenhill, was a tiny hamlet, now made large by recent housing development. The area was a former woodland and waste on the fringe of Needwood Forest, which belonged to Burton Abbey before the Dissolution.

Anslow, 2m N of Tatenhill, is a hamlet on the Needwood plateau. In the 10th Century the name was Eansythledge, meaning 'Eanswyth's clearing in the woodland'. In medieval times it belonged to Burton Abbey, but in the 1540s it passed to Sir William Paget of Beaudesert.

TEAN *2.5m S of Cheadle*
There are two settlements here - Upper Tean and Lower Tean. Both lie on the A522, Uttoxeter to Cheadle road and both are adjacent to the River Tean on the edge of the North Staffordshire Moorlands.

Lower Tean is a very pleasant village indeed, with mature houses well spaced apart and set in open country. The contrast with the grim terraces of Upper Tean is dramatic. Heath House lies 0.5m NE of Lower Tean, at SK 027392 in a small agricultural park, and the house is embowered in mature specimen trees and evergreen bushes on high ground. Both the site and the house are verging on the magnificent. However, the main road lodges are drab, uninspired, pyramid-roofed buildings, although there is another on a side lane, which is very handsome with gables and tall chimneys in decorated grey stone.

Heath House is an impressive mock-Tudor mansion, built of stone in 1836 for John Burton Phillips by Thomas Johnson of Lichfield. The windows are slim, the gables steep and irregular, the front (complete with portecochère) and the bay-windowed garden side are symmetrical, and there is a tower. Inside, it is quite medieval, though rather dark, with a fine staircase and some good ribbed ceilings. There is a handsome orangery of five bays by Thomas Trubshaw (1831) and 0.5m. NE is a classical temple with a stone dome and eight unfluted Ionic columns, which were formerly incorporated into the verandah of the old hall, now demolished. The House is still owned and occupied by the Philips family though it is sometimes rented out to film companies. We know of at least two television productions filmed here: 'The Hound of the Baskervilles', in which it became Baskerville Hall (whilst the Roaches, near Leek, stood in for Dartmoor), and Agatha Christie's 'They do it with Mirrors'.

The Philips family made their fortunes from the large mills they built at **Upper Tean** and Cheadle. It is believed that in 1747 John and Nathaniel Philips brought to England a Dutchman called Sanfort, to teach local carpenters how to make looms for the manufacture of woven linen tapes. The earliest machines were installed at Tean Hall, the black-and-white house adjacent to the present mill. By the 1790s the business was well established, both at the Tean and Cheadle factories and as a cottage industry. (Loom sheds were built on to some of the weavers' own houses and they had the looms on loan from the Philips family.)

By 1817 there were 300 looms at the Tean factory and 200 at the Cheadle factory, with the total number of employees exceeding 5,000. Brown yarn was imported from Russia, Germany and Ireland and bleached at a works on the banks of the Tean near Tenford. In about 1824 all the looms were brought from the smaller factories at Kingsley, Draycott in Clay and Lower Tean and placed in factories at Upper Tean and Cheadle.

The Tean mill still exists and dominates the main street of the town. The earlier parts are three storeys high and 11 bays wide, with a central pediment and a cupola with a bell. In 1823 a large extension of four storeys and 27 bays was built at right angles to the existing block. At the same time steam power was introduced. Another block was built in 1885 with a road frontage of four storeys, eight bays and bay pediments. On the left of the factory block is a timber-framed house which was occupied by the Factory Manager. From 1959 the mill was called Tean Hall Mills Ltd. Today, the big red brick part of the mill is derelict with broken windows and looks very ugly. Nearby the terraced houses are very close to the road and add to the dismal scene.

Scattered around Upper Tean are several rows of weavers' cottages. Some have very unusual, octagonal lavatory blocks - behind Nos I and 3 New Road and Nos 4, 6, 8, 10, and 12 Old Road. The best of the remaining weavers' cottages built by the Philips' Company are Nos 1- 8 Holborn Row. The Company also had a works at The Croft, Upper Tean, where, from about 1750, they carried out bleaching and dyeing operations. This became a welding works in 1971.

There are three churches in Tean - the Anglican Christ Church of 1843, the Providence Chapel of 1822 and the Wesleyan Chapel of 1843.

TETTENHALL *2m NE of Wolverhampton*

It is the prime residential area of the Wolverhampton conurbation. There are some streets of meaner houses in Tettenhall, and even some council flats, but these are placed so as not to detract from the upper-middle-class ambience of the area, and its claim to be the leafiest of Wolverhampton's leafy suburbs.

Tettenhall is an ancient Anglo-Saxon Manor perched high on a rocky ridge, 2m NE of Wolverhampton town centre. In AD 910 the invading Danish army was defeated at the Battle of Tettenhall by Edward the Elder, son of Alfred the Great. The Danes had rampaged over the whole of Mercia, as far as the River Avon and then along the western bank of the River Severn to Bridgnorth, where they turned east to the Midlands. They were caught at Tettenhall and were annihilated by the Anglo-Saxon army. Three Northumbrian Kings amongst their number died that day. (Tettenhall is given as the site of the battle in the Anglo-Saxon Chronicle, but an account by Athelweard says the battle took place at Wednesfield on 5th August 910.) See the poem on page 380.

Under the Normans Tettenhall was a Royal manor, though only four villagers and three smallholders were recorded as living there in 1086. It was long a separate village and even now is not really joined to Wolverhampton because of the nature of the terrain - the cliff edge with the canal at the bottom. Indeed the road up the hill was notoriously steep, crooked and narrow until widened and improved by Thomas Telford in 1816. This road, the A41, was of some importance, being part of the 'Parliamentary' mail-coach route from London to Holyhead.

The village of Tettenhall is split into two parts. Half-way up the hill is **Lower Green**. Here is a sloping green with some attractive old houses and the church of St Michael. This was an important medieval church, a Collegiate church under Royal control. Sadly, in 1950, it was almost totally destroyed by fire. Only the Perpendicular tower and the much later porch, by A E Stuart of 1883, were salvaged. The rest was rebuilt by Bernard Miller. He made no concessions to the past and based his design on unusual cross-gables with circular and oval traceried lights. Some like it; some hate it.

At the top of the hill is the large **Upper Green**, studded with mature trees and cut through by roads. Shops face the lawns on two sides and only parked cars mar a most picturesque area. On the other side of the main road there is a paddling pool, and beyond that a huge open area on part of which is the cricket ground - a ground of sufficient standing for it to accommodate Minor County matches. A few old houses have survived: The Old Farmhouse, of 1520, with stone mullions, in Stockwell Road, for example, and the black-and-white cottage opposite the Roman Catholic church. The longest established residential areas are along the rock edge, where handsome houses lie in large gardens, though the gardens get smaller every time a house is sold. The temptation to make an extra £100,000 or so by splitting off a building plot is irresistible to most vendors.

Tettenhall College is a fee paying school in Wood Road. The dour Gothic College buildings are of 1865, by G Bidlake, but the school has expanded to include the adjoining large, stuccoed and equally-dour, late Georgian house called Tettenhall Towers, which gained it polygonal towers as an afterthought in 1866.

In the past sandstone, sand and alabaster have been mined in Tettenhall. The largest stone quarry was at the junction of Henwood Road and the Wergs-Tettenhall Road, but the location of the medieval alabaster mines are unknown. In 1991 Mrs Budge of Limes Road Tettenhall found a piece of alabaster in her garden, which might indicate that the mines were in this area. Alabaster is a soft, soapy rock once much used for carving effigies of the noble dead. It is formed by water rotting gypsum (anhydrite CaSO4, formed by evaporation of sea water) and all the known beds in Britain are now virtually worked out.

Water pumped up from boreholes is a natural resource that is still utilized at Tettenhall, though in very recent times the reservoirs were sold off for housing. A special pipeline runs from the Tettenhall waterworks to Banks's Brewery in Chapel Ash.

There is a tale told in Tettenhall concerning an old gypsy woman who, on a Sunday, was knitting in the shade of a willow tree in the churchyard. The vicar scolded her for working on the Lord's day and she cursed him in reply. Shortly after, she was struck by lightning and buried in the churchyard. It is said that her gravestone, which is carved with a head and shoulders portrait, moves towards the willow tree at the rate of one inch every year. Rachel Heyhoe-Flint, the champion, and leading exponent, of women's cricket lives in Tettenhall.

Adjoining Tettenhall to the south-west is **Tettenhall Wood**. The area was originally called Kingsley Wood and was a remnant of the large medieval Kinver Forest. Here, in Mount Road, is the Mount Hotel, built for Charles Benjamin Mander as a private house in 1870. It is constructed of brick with stone dressings and was enlarged in 1891 and 1908. The mansion is chiefly noted for it sumptuous ballroom, the work of Edward Ould, who also built Wightwick Manor for Theodore Mander. In Mill Lane is a short, red brick tower windmill with an octagonal-pyramid roof. It was built in 1818 and was probably at least one storey taller. The church of Christ was built in 1866.

Today, Tettenhall is probably best known to the outside world for the Tettenhall Horse Sanctuary. This is funded entirely by charity and is the life's work of the admirable Billy Wilson. It is situated in Jenny Walker Lane, 2m W of Tettenhall and best approached off the Bridgnorth Road, the A454.

Stockwell End adjoins Tettenhall to the east, on the other side of the Newport Road. It, too, is a good class residential area and includes the paddling pool and the greater part of the Upper Green and the cricket pitches. There was once a large mansion here called Danescourt, but this has been demolished and now there is a special school with residential facilities in its place.

Newbridge, 0.25m SE of Tettenhall, is a mature residential area with a small shopping centre, a large pub, an old tennis club and a new bridge. The bridge crosses the Staffordshire and Worcestershire Canal (1772) and the Smestow Brook. There are pleasant tow path walks and large playing fields. As to the bridge, it should really be called the New, New Bridge, but let the plaque riveted to its guard wall explain: "When the Union with Ireland Act was passed in 1800 the mail coach route from London to Holyhead became very important. Thomas Telford (1757-1834) was appointed to improve the London-Holyhead road. The earlier road crossed the canal on the old bridge which you can see from here. For the improved road a new bridge was built in the 1820s. It was replaced by a wider bridge in 1939." The old canal bridge is still there, west of the new one, as is the old bridge over the Smestow Brook.

The Wergs, which adjoins Tettenhall to the north-west, is a good-class residential area. The attractive, but modest, mid-19th Century Italianate Hall is now the headquarters of Tarmac Building Materials Ltd. The name Wergs is a corruption of the medieval Withegis, which in turn is from the Anglo-Saxon 'wipigas', meaning 'the willow trees'. There is a stream and a man-made lake by the Hall. On the Wergs Road is The Crown pub and the showrooms of a car dealer and further up, in the direction of Tettenhall, are the offices of The Ministry of Agriculture and Fisheries, built in 1980. They stand on the site of a house called Woodthorne, which was demolished in 1978. This was the home of novelist Ellen Thorneycroft Fowler who wrote at least six of her novels here, many of which are set in the Black Country.

The Dovecotes is a modern housing estate, 1.5m N of Tettenhall, which was built on the site of the former Wolverhampton Airport at Pendeford. The Dovecote, which still stands, belonged to Barnhurst Hall, a substantial Elizabethan moated manor house, now demolished.

Aldersley stadium, opened by actor Jack Hawkins in 1956, has been redeveloped and is now a Leisure Village. (Hawkins was making the film 'The Man in the Sky' at Pendeford Aerodrome at the time.) The author, prior to becoming the Midlands' Decathlon Champion in 1956, used to train at the Aldersley Stadium.

THORNCLIFFE *1m SE of Blackshaw Moor, which is 2.5m NE of Leek*
A moorland hamlet which stands around a deep gully. It is a stone-built place of cottages and farms with an abandoned church. The dramatic road that follows the Morridge lies above, and below lies Tittesworth Reservoir. A land so full of greys and greens that the red telephone box seems almost garish.

THORPE CONSTANTINE *5m NE of Tamworth*
All that remains of the medieval village of Thorpe is the big house and the church, but this is a beautiful place with spacious grassed areas, tall trees and an air of graciousness. The view from the road to the church is especially fine.

The village was probably deserted in the late Middle Ages when half of the pre-Conquest villages in the valley of the River Mease suffered a similar fate. The reasons are thought to be connected with problems of flooding, caused by a period of increased rainfall and the change from arable to pastoral farming which is less labour intensive. The site of the deserted village is at SK 260089.

However, today there are several estate cottages and the village may be said to have been rejuvenated. The name Thorpe is one of a very few in Staffordshire that is of Danish origin. (Croxton, Croxall, and Thorpe, near the entrance to Dovedale, are the others.) In the 13th century the Constantine family were Lords of the Manor here. They were Earls of Breteville in Normandy.

The Thorpe estate lies on a low rise within yards of the border with Warwickshire. It has been the home of the Inge family since 1651, and the five-bay centre of the Hall is of this date. The Hall originally had three gables, but these were removed when it was remodeled in the 18th Century and made Georgian. The wings were added in 1800 (north) and 1812 (south) by Thomas Gardner of Derby. Inside, there is a handsome staircase with an iron ballustrade, a good plaster ceiling in the drawing room, and oak panelling with heraldic emblems which came from Drakelowe Hall, home of the Gresley family, when it was demolished in 1934.

The charming church of St Constantine has a medieval tower and recessed spire, but the nave and lower chancel were rebuilt by J Oldrid Scott in 1883. The Glebe House is a striking building in blue brick with gables and many tall chimneys. It was built by one of the Inge family for their parson son.

THREAPWOOD *1.5m E of Cheadle*

Threapwood is a hamlet on the 5032, the Cheadle to Alton road. The name means 'disputed woodland', referring to a boundary dispute. At the crossroads there is a large rambling pub called The Highwayman, once the haunt of local biker clubs but closed and put up for sale in 2004. There are a mission church and a few cottages. Most of these lie on the lane that leads north from the pub. This lane leads through the woods at Threapwood to **Old Furnace**, a handful of cottages at the junction of Greendale Lane and Stoney Dale (lane). There is a small stream here and a footpath leading to the beautiful Dimmingsdale (a corruption of Dead Man's Dale, after a Civil War skirmish).

Iron ore was smelted here from the 13th Century. In 1593 the first water-driven blast furnace in North Staffordshire was built on the site by Sir Francis Willoughby and Lawrence Loggin. The furnace at Old Furnace and the forge at nearby Oakamoor (which closed in 1608) were collectively referred to as the Okymoor Works.

We will leave Old Furnace and head north-east along Stoney Dale, a narrow lane that leads through beautiful woods and lovely countryside to the valley of the River Churnet. At the 'T' junction you can turn left to Oakamoor, or right into Red Road, and follow the river to the **Ramblers' Rest**. This is at an idyllic spot where Dimmingsdale joins the Churnet Valley. The café was originally a hunting lodge and on some maps is called The Lodge. There is a Forestry Commission car park here. This is truly lovely walking country, a place where nature is at its most majestic.

The lane continues on to Alton. However, a footpath leads from the Ramblers' Rest to Smelting Mill. Some remains of the 18th Century lead smelting mill, which processed ore mined at Ecton (see Ecton), can still be seen. A little further on one passes the Smelting Mill Cottages, and can enjoy the woods and rocks of Ousal Dale, before arriving at the Little Ranger Youth Hostel on the Staffordshire Way Footpath. The traveller can then return to the Ramblers' Retreat down Dimmingsdale. The Threapwood-Churnet Valley area really is superbly romantic country.

THROWLEY *2.5m NW Ilam*

Throwley is first mentioned in documents in 1208. The name apparently means 'clearing with a conduit'. (A conduit is a pipe which carries water, probably for drainage purposes.) Throwley is an area rather than a village. It constitutes the tongue of land that lies between the River Hamps and the River Manifold, immediately below their confluence. It is like a huge bowl, with Throwley Hall situated in the centre and ringed by high moorland hills.

Primitive man was attracted here and has left considerable remains. Throwley Hall can be reached from the lane that runs between Ilam and Calton. The early 16th Century house stands as a spectacular ruin. It is stone built and has uncusped four centre heads to the lights. A large bay window has collapsed. Very little is known about the Hall. It was the home of the Meverells in the late

Middle Ages but when Robert Meverell died in 1626 his daughter and heiress married the 4th Lord Cromwell (who was distantly related to Oliver Cromwell). The ground about the house is much disturbed and there is a pond near the road. The site is almost certainly very ancient and is likely to have been occupied in prehistoric times.

Next to the Hall is a farmhouse. The outbuildings of the farm include several very substantial, stone-built barns with mullioned windows. One has two floors of seven bays and is called The Barracks.

The hills around are littered with prehistoric tombs. Some are marked on the Ordnance Survey map and some are not. Even more have doubtless been destroyed by farmers and treasure seekers. A hoard of Anglo-Saxon gold coins and brooches was found in **Beeston Tor Cave** (SK 108541) in the Manifold Valley, 1m N of Throwley Hall. The site is best approached from the road that runs just to the north of the caves or from the path that starts at Weag's Bridge. Throwley and the area around was intensively investigated in the middle of the 19th Century by S Carrington of Wetton, a local schoolmaster. He showed that there had been a large population here during the Neolithic, Beaker and Food Vessel periods than there is today. Recent excavations have been made at the Cheshire Wood Cave (SK 114536) and Falcon Low (SK 104532) by Keele University Extra Mural Archaeology classes. In Falcon Low, on Old Park Hill, they found a sepulchral cave, probably of Neolithic age. Six people had been buried there - two adult and four children. There were also the remains of dog, hare, wildcat, marten, pig, sheep and water vole. The cave had been blocked with boulders and covered with earth.

At the top of the hill to the south-west is Throwley Cottage. Note the tall trees. They were planted primarily as a windbreak but also function as a landmark. When the hills are covered in snow and visibility is bad, even people born and bred on the moors can become disorientated and in need of help to find their way home. There is also a small disused quarry. Much of the material for the dry-stone walls came from such local quarries; it was not all just picked off the land when clearing fields.

It is strange to think that these bleak, green hills were once forested. Prehistoric man cut down much of the woodland. Once the land was grassed over grazing animals ate the seedlings of any new natural tree growth that attempted to establish itself. Experiments in Scotland have shown that if hillsides are protected from sheep, woodland can regenerate without any assistance from man. Of course, if existing woodland is not close by, the process can be very slow because it takes time for sufficient seeds to be brought in by natural processes such as the wind and droppings from birds, etc.

TIPTON *5m SSE of Wolverhampton*

The Norman scribes who compiled Domesday Book often made mistakes in writing down the names of the towns, villages and manors they visited. They were, after all, French speakers writing down colloquial Anglo-Saxon. Whether or not their notation of a place we now call Tipton is correct we will never know. They called it Tibbintone, a delightful name if ever there was one and certainly an improvement on Tipton. The original name was in fact probably Tipstone. A 'tip' was a stave or spear, and Tipstone might well have referred to a spear shaped stone - a megalith of prehistoric origin - that once stood here.

Tipton is the archetypal Black Country town, a place of character with some unusual claims to fame. For example, before some of the canals were filled in it is reputed to have had more miles of waterway than Venice, and is indeed often called the 'Venice of the Midlands'. At one time, almost unbelievably, the town had seven passenger railway stations and six goods' depots belonging to different 19th Century companies. Yet another surprising fact is that the Parish Registers here date from December, 1513, the earliest in the whole country. (This has been challenged. G P Mander suggests that '1513-19' can be interpreted as 1573-9, the handwriting being ambiguous).

Until about 1700 Tipton was a small village surrounded by fields. The only event of note to have occurred in the area was the Battle of Tipton Green in 1644. This was an indecisive engagement between the troops of Lord Denbigh, who were intent on taking Dudley Castle, and the Royalists. By the early 18th Century the small medieval coal, iron and limestone workings were rapidly expanding.

In 1712 Thomas Newcomen (1663-1729) installed the first of his revolutionary steam cylinder and piston beam engines at Lord Dudley's **Coneygree** Colliery at Burntwood, on the Tipton-Dudley border. It was used for pumping water out of the mine and was so efficient that its use spread rapidly. A replica of this first engine has been built at the Black Country Museum in Dudley. (There is more about Coneygree later in this article, under Burntwood.)

Mining continued through the 18th and 19th Centuries, and coal was being extracted until about 1920 when excessive flooding, amongst other reasons, forced the last of the pits to close. The extent of the old workings was illustrated by a report on the area in 1984, which said that 25 acres would have to be abandoned because the ground was too unsafe for new building, or even for use as recreational parkland. There is a honeycomb of old limestone caverns beneath the surface, and 37 uncapped mine shafts have been discovered.

The iron trade flourished in Tipton, and Barrows and Hall at **Bloomfield** (presumably the site of an early 'bloomery' iron works) were the largest producers of iron in the Black Country until the firm closed in 1906. Another famous works was the Horsley Iron Company who, in 1821, made the world's first iron steamship, the Aaron Manby. The old Horsley works still exist as a part of a larger company.

The centre of Tipton is Owen Street, which was once a lively, thronging place between the canal at Factory Road and the level crossing. However, in the 1980s it was redeveloped. The south side was demolished and replaced by a small shopping centre and some town houses. The street now has no character whatsoever.

On the corner of Factory Road is the Fountain Inn, for long associated with the Tipton Slasher, a pugilist of great repute. His real name was William Perry, and from 1850 to 1857 he was the champion prize fighter of England. The 'Slasher' was a canal boatman who became a publican in West Bromwich on winning the title, and is buried in the churchyard of St John's, Kate's Hill, Dudley. He was born in 1819 and died in 1880.

The railway station of **Dudley Port** is actually in Tipton. It got its name in the days before the Dudley Canal Tunnel was cut under the limestone ridge that bisects the Black Country. Here, goods for Dudley, or for the canal system on the other side of the ridge, were unloaded from boats on the Birmingham Canal (1772), and carried by packhorse up the hill. So, although actually in Tipton, this was the port for Dudley. Later, when the railway came through, it became the station that served Dudley, and a branch line to the town - the Dudley Dodger - was built. The canal crosses the main road on the Ryland Aqueduct. Like the adjacent railway bridge it is painted blue and cream.

Just south of the station is the old Vono Works, now an industrial estate, and the magnificently grim Duport Harper Foundries, massive red brick and real, old Black Country.

The Tipton Harriers are a well known athletics' club. Their most famous member is Jack Holden, born in 1907. In 1950 he won the AAA Championship, the Commonwealth Games and the European Games' marathons. The Jack Holden Gardens in Queen's Road are named after him.

Tipton has two parks. Jubilee Park, Toll End, opened in 1935, but for centuries before had been a place for huge ceremonial bonfires to mark occasions such as coronations and success in major battles, such as Waterloo. Victoria Park (1901), off Park Lane, has a lake and is overlooked by one of the few buildings of note in the town.

This is the Library of 1906 by George H Wenyon, built in brick and yellow terracotta, with a tower and a variety of ornamental motifs. It stands in Victoria Road and really is quite impressive.

Of the churches, the first ranked is the parish church of St Martin in Lower Church Lane, 0.25m from the town centre. It was rebuilt of plain Georgian brick and stucco in 1795-7, by J Keyte, and the chancel was extended in 1876. The whole was restored in 1963. Other churches are: St Paul's, of 1838, in the main street (Owen Street), of brick with buttressed nave and tall lancet windows; St Matthew's, 1876, of brick, by J M Gibbons; and Sacred Heart, 1940, a Roman Catholic church by Sandy and Norris.

Half-a-mile to the east of Owen Street is **Great Bridge.** This is a settlement in its own right but has for long been considered a part of its more famous neighbour. Certainly, it is the main shopping centre of the area, and a flourishing one at that. As to the name, there are many bridges, both over canals and the murky River Tame, but none that can be called 'great'. In fact, the name is probably a corruption of Greet Bridge, Greet being the medieval name of the River Tame.

At the eastern end of the main shopping street is the recently restored Wellington Works, partly occupied by Continental Tubes. Opposite the main gates is a canal bridge. From here there is a fine view of the seven **Ryder's Green** Locks, which climb the hill between New Town and Swan Village to the **Greet's Green** canal basins. Industrial buildings line the canal banks all the way along. Just up the road (the A4035) is a tiny, red brick Methodist church, fighting off the factories that seem to be threatening to squeeze it out of existence. Between the Wellington Works and the Great Bridge Tavern stand the shops and the indoor and outdoor markets. Here, too, are some modern houses and residential blocks.

From the Tavern the road to Bilston crosses the Walsall Canal (1809), now reduced to a concrete gutter, continues through **Toll End**, 1.5m ENE of Tipton, and past the ungainly seven-storey MEB office building (where the author's father spent the last years of his working life). In 1460 a John de Tolle resided here, hence the name.

The road continues up to **Ocker Hill**, 1m NE of Tipton. Ocker is probably from the Anglo-Saxon personal name 'Occa'. When we visited in 1992 Bayley Lane led past a small park and fishing pool to a wilderness area of abandoned canals, a murky tree-fringed pool, great piles of smashed reinforced concrete and derelict land. This was the site of the old coal-fired electricity power station, demolished in 1985, and the concrete blocks were the remains of the water-cooling towers. The new, oil-fired station with its two, tall, thin towers stood 0.25m E of the canal. It was a desolate, watery place, abandoned and forlorn. Today, the Black Country New Road of 1995 passes through this woebegone area between the new power station and the site of the old. The parish church of Ocker Hill is St Mark's, built in 1849.

Prince's End lies 0.25m. N of Tipton station. Here there is a large, modern shopping centre. The settlement stands on high ground and, to make its mark on the skyline even further, has many blocks of flats. They come in all shapes and sizes. Perhaps the most eye-catching are those in Churchfield Avenue. They stand continental-fortress-like, their bricks painted cream, their windows set in steel frames with leaded lattices, and fronted by bowed iron verandahs.

Just down the road is **Summerhill** and the parish church of St John, its short stone tower overpowered by the high-rise flats. The nave is of blue and red brick and the lancet windows have cast-iron diamond lights. One would not be surprised to see it in a rural Shropshire village. On the main road there is no scarcity of pubs - The Lagoon, the George and Dragon, the lopsided Tilted Barrel, and The Royal. There is also an Asda superstore.

Adjoining Prince's End to the east is **Wednesbury Oak**. It has the air of a country place. At the junction of Wednesbury Oak Road and Gospel Oak Road (the road to Tipton) is the Gospel Oak pub.

Opposite the pub is the large, modern **Willingsworth** School, which has many wide green acres of playing fields. This is not virgin country, however - far from it. Into the late 1970s this was derelict land: spoil heaps, slag heaps, old railway tracks, ruined factories and scrub woodland. The area has lost its ancient oak trees but gained the Tipton Sports Centre, home to the famous Tipton Harriers Athletics' Club. They still turn out athletes of international standard. East of the crossroads are several pleasant, modern housing estates and west of these is the Rocket Pool. (See Lower Bradley in the Bilston article.)

Bloomfield lies 0.5m SW of Prince's End, along the main road, the A4037. Starting at the King's Head one passes a rope works, varied small industrial units, the eye-catching globe of the Angle Ring Company, the dour sheds of the British Rolling Mills works, semi-detached houses and the Star Inn; before passing under the railway bridge at Brook Street and over the canal (much used these days by Youth Afloat) to arrive at **Tipton Green**.

Here, there is a touch of elegance: managers' and owners' houses and the church of St Matthew. A little to the east, at the southern end of Owen Street, are the Coronation Gardens of 1937, which adjoin the canal at a narrow-boat turning point.

Horseley Heath is lm E of Tipton station. With the wide green spaces that line Alexandra Road it is one of the few Black Country places that does not belie its name. Nevertheless, there is grimy industry a-plenty ('steel pipe fabrications at short notice'), gas holders, ubiquitous modern housing, a large High School, an even larger cemetery and the Rising Sun with leaded glass and canted bays.

Horseley Heath was the birthplace of Ben Boucher (1769-1851), the Dudley poet. He was a miner who turned to making a living by writing and selling his poems at a penny each in the streets of Dudley. There is a well known sketch of him. He died in Dudley workhouse.

Burnt Tree, lm S of Tipton station, is known to many as a traffic island on the Birmingham New Road and a van hire business. There is a pub-restaurant, a service station, an office block and some semis. But Burnt Tree is also an area which lies between the traffic island and the Birmingham Canal (1772). This is

Coneygree Iron Foundry country, or rather it was. The old works has been demolished, the land cleared and already mock-Elizabethan detached houses are appearing. Just to the west of the ironworks site, cut through by the railway where it crosses the canal, is Lady Meadow (SJ 958916). Recent research suggests that it was here, at Lord Dudley's Coneygree Colliery in 1712, that the first Newcomen steam engine was set to work pumping water out of the mines. This was a landmark in industrial history; the age of steam had really arrived. Indeed, with records of iron ore being mined here as early as 1291, Coneygree is one of the oldest documented industrial sites in the Black Country.

To the west of Burnt Tree is **Tividale**. It lies between Dudley Road West and the Birmingham New Road. Here there is a large, yellow brick Comprehensive School, an industrial estate alongside the canal, a sports ground, semis, a Lada dealer, the Wagon and Horses, and an estate of rendered council houses. On 29th May 1991 a man was sentenced to four years in prison at Wolverhampton Crown Court because he had been caught growing over one million pounds worth of cannabis plants in the garden of his house at Tividale. At Tividale! South of the New Road is **Tividale Hall**. We could not find a Hall, just more semis climbing Darby's Hill to the old hard rock quarry. (See Dudley.)

TITTENSOR *10.5m N of Stafford*
Tittensor lies on a hill, 3.5m NNW of Stone, on the A34. It has a pub (The Winghouse), a shop, a Post Office, a part-timber-framed cottage, a church, a school, an estate of new houses, a Manor House and the sheds of Basset's Transport.

In 1066 the manor was held by Wulfgeat and Godric but after the Norman Conquest it passed to Robert de Toeni (or Toni), King William's standard bearer. There were at least 12 families and a mill in 1086. The site of the old manor house is behind the church. It was demolished in 1963 to make way for new houses.

The new Manor House is said to have been built by the Dukes of Sutherland. It lies alongside the busy dual carriageway of the A34, behind a wall. The house is built of brick, to an irregular pattern, in a vague Tudor style and has many tall chimneys. It stands on the site of a much older house, and leading from the cellars are at least two tunnels that pass under the road towards the church. They are still intact but the entrances have been bricked up. The attractive grounds border the River Trent and there was a pool that has been filled in because it was a danger to the old people who now live there in the care of the council. Adjacent to the Manor House is the now-abandoned School.

This is built in an identical style to the church, which stands on the opposite side of the road. St Luke's was built in 1881 by Roberts of Trentham and presumably replaced an earlier church. It has been laughed at by some authorities on church architecture but most laymen would find nothing amiss. The mixture of brick and stone in a random pattern is most unusual but not displeasing. The upper part of the tower is timber-framed and there is a timber-framed gable to the west side. Inside, there are some carved wood panels which were taken from the old manor house when it was pulled down. The newly-built parish hall is joined to the church in its upper parts, but at ground level there is a path between them.

Tittensor Chase, 0.75m S of Tittensor, is a mock Tudor mansion built in 1856 in high, wooded, rolling country on the Tittensor Chase estate. In the 1990s it was owned by the Chairman of Severn-Trent Water and his wife, Pru, who left him and went to live in Ludlow with Sir Julian Critchley MP, who died shortly after of cancer. The attractive thatched lodge, on the busy A34, is now detached from the estate and is called Wrens Nest Cottage. The large bronze statue (1834) of the First Duke of Sutherland (1758-1833), which overlooks Trentham Park, stands on Tittensor Hill, 0.5m NNW of Tittensor. The sculptor was the illustrious Sir Francis Chantrey.

Groundslow, 0.5m SW of Tittensor is a small hamlet known for its former hospital. It takes its name from the two prehistoric burial mounds, both called Ground's Lowe. One lies on a hill opposite Groundslow Lodge, marked by four trees at SJ 867373; the other is 0.25m SE of Groundslow. There seems to be some confusion about the name of the house which, in the 1920s, became a tuberculosis hospital annexe to the Staffordshire General Infirmary (in Stafford). It could be Groundslow Villa or Groundslow House, but on the site plan of the builders (Wimpey), who are currently developing the site for houses, it is called Groundslow Manor House. This still stands and is a large, irregular house of brick with over a dozen chimneys, three forward-facing gables and a date plaque of 1832. Hard by the house, to the north, is Groundslow Farm, which is also being developed for housing. The gardens are heavily wooded but have been very much diminished, first by the low-quality hospital additions, now demolished, and now by the housing estate. Of the 'new' hospital buildings only one remains: a 15-bay, two-storey structure in pale-pink brick with iron window frames, which is close to Groundslow Lodge. The hospital changed from caring for TB patients to a maternity home, and closed in 1982. It then became two old people's homes and, as already mentioned, is being developed for private housing. The hospital chapel has been demolished by the developers

We think it likely that the 1832 house we have described is that built by the Duke of Sutherland and later occupied by the Earl of Huntingdon and members of the Copeland (Spode pottery) family. One source says that Groundslow 'House' was built in 1832 by the Duke; another says that Groundslow 'Villa' was the house developed as the hospital. We could only find one old house, and the developers had plans going back to 1900 which only showed one house and the farm. I do not suppose that anyone really cares, but these incongruities can be very annoying to tidy minds.

At Groundslow Grange aerial photography has located crop marks, indicating a former prehistoric, oval enclosure probably used as a cattle pound.

Strongford, 0.5m N of Tittensor, is a hamlet just off the A34 on marshy ground. The A34 was the important London to Carlisle road, and where this crossed the River Trent there was a bridge which had an unhappy history. It was destroyed by flood in 1605, fell down in 1790, was rebuilt and fell down again in 1792, and rebuilt and damaged by 'hearty rains' in 1796. You can see the marshy ground from the road today.

TIXALL *3m E of Stafford*

Tixall is a most charming village set amidst pleasant country. It lies on the gentle northern slope above the flood plain of the River Sow, which is paralleled here by the Staffordshire and Worcestershire Canal. (One mile to the east the Sow joins the Trent, and the Staffordshire and Worcestershire joins the Trent and Mersey at Great Haywood.) The village consists of little more than the church of St John by Wyatt and Brandon, of 1849, a lane lined with varied old houses, an obelisk milestone of 1776 on the tiny village green, a disused school, an 18th Century Rotunda, at the end of an avenue of young lime trees, and some good hedges.

A track leads away from the village, behind a small copse, to the handsome crescent-shaped, early 19th Century stable block of Tixall Hall. This was designed by John Ireland and is a single-storey range with higher pavilions at each end and one in the middle, with a three-bay, Tudor-Gothic porch. These have been well converted into mews dwellings.

The Hall was demolished in 1926, but like the stables the Gatehouse has survived. The general concensus of opinion is that Tixall Gatehouse is the best late 16th Century gatehouse in the whole of England. It was built for Sir Walter Aston about 1575. It has three bays, three storeys, a central archway, four polygonal turrets with ogee caps, four-light transomed windows framed by pairs of columns (from the ground up, Doric, Ionic, and Corinthian), and a top-most parapet. Like the stables it has also been converted into a dwelling (1977). There were some deer-lodge shelters but they were dismantled by the farmer who owned the property and now lie as jumbled heaps of stone. Along the road from Tixall to Ingestre are some large, forbidding, red brick farm buildings. Opposite these is the delightful Bottle Lodge, a tiny octagonal building with an ogee-shaped roof, the whole resembling a bottle. This looks as though it is also of 1575 and may have been used later as a toll house.

The original Tixall Hall was a half-timbered mansion built by Sir Walter Aston in 1580, ten years after the Gatehouse had been constructed. Mary Queen of Scots was held in the Gatehouse for two weeks in 1586. In 1720 the 6th, and last, Lord Aston died and the Hall passed by marriage to the Clifford family. The Hall burned down and a new house on a new site, to the side of the great Gatehouse, was built in 1780. The Cliffords sold Tixall to Earl Talbot of nearby Ingestre in 1840. The Catholic chapel at Tixall was dismantled and rebuilt at Great Haywood. (The Astons and Cliffords had been Roman Catholics, but the Earl Talbot was not.)

In the 19th Century the stone quarried at Tixall was highly thought of for its texture and colour, and for the fact that it was soft and easily worked when first cut but hardened over time. It was used in the building of Tixall Hall, the Shire Hall in Stafford, Radford Bridge and in public buildings in Worcester and Birmingham.

Tixall Heath, 1m WNW of Tixall, is former common land. In 1492 Sir William Chetwynd of Ingestre Hall was murdered on Tixall Heath, just east of King's Low at SJ 951234. He had received an appointment from Henry VII, which made Sir Henry Stanley of Pipe, Lichfield jealous. Stanley and a band of 20 of his men waylaid Chetwynd and killed him.

Tixall Wide, or Broad Water, is a widening of the Trent and Mersey Canal to give it the impression of being a lake when viewed from Tixall Hall. Josiah Wedgwood did the same at Etruria.

In **Blackheath Covert**, woods about 1m NW of Tixall, there is a flat-roofed utility building that was used as a secret factory for testing aeroplane engines during the Second World War. It has attracted satellite buildings since the war. Also in the woods is King's Low, a burial mound at SJ 955237. Queen's Low is 0.5m ENE of King's Low.

TOTMONSLOW *0.75m W of Upper Tean and 2m S of Cheadle*
Totmonslow was the north-east hundred of Staffordshire, established in Anglo-Saxon times and named after a burial mound at which it is presumed the court met. There were five hundreds altogether: Pirehill, Totmonslow, Offlow,

Cuttlestone and Seisdon. As an administrative unit the hundreds lasted from the 10th Century, when the county was first defined, until the 19th Century, although by then it only had residual powers.

TRENTHAM *3m SSE* of *Newcastle-under-Lyme*

Trentham was one of the royal manors of William the Conqueror. It lies astride the A34, the old coaching road from London to Newcastle-under-Lyme, Carlisle and Scotland. On the east side of the road is the largely modern village. On the west, along the banks of the River Trent, is Trentham Park (or Gardens as it is sometimes called). Today, this is an expanding pleasure garden and entertainment centre.

The great and famous palace of the Dukes of Sutherland is gone but some of the service buildings have survived. The setting itself would be difficult to better, with grand vistas over the huge lake to the wooded hills beyond, but the outbuildings are on the whole most unimpressive and often shoddy. The Palace stood on the site of an Augustinian priory, founded about 1150 and dissolved in the 1530s. The priory had in turn replaced the nunnery of St Werburga (died 699).

In 1540 James Leveson bought the estate. In the 17th Century the Leveson heiress married Sir Thomas Gower who changed his name to Sir Thomas Leveson-Gower (pronounced Lewson-Gore). This family acquired a barony and an earldom and became Marquesses of Stafford. The 2nd Marquess married the Countess of Sutherland and for the rest of his life used and enjoyed her immense wealth. He was made the Duke of Sutherland but only at the very end of his life. He was only a Duke for eight months! It was the 1st Duke who drained marshes in Shropshire and Staffordshire. He also built roads and bridges in his wife's huge Scottish estates, and was responsible for the terrible sufferings of the crofters he dispossessed during his Highland Clearances.

It was his son, the 2nd Duke, who commissioned Sir Charles Barry (the architect of the Houses of Parliament) to enlarge and remodel the house at Trentham which had been built by Francis Smith, 'Capability' Brown and Henry Holland. Between 1833 and 1842 Barry created the grand, irregular Italian-style palace that was to provide inspiration to Prince Albert when he designed Osborne on the Isle of Wight, and which in turn inspired the design of other great houses in Britain and Germany.

The imposing semi-circular entrance with its ornate porte-cochère still stands; likewise, the stable yard and the clock house. The lake (1759) had been created by Capability Brown but the gardens of the parterre, between the house and the lake, were laid out by W A Nesfield. Beyond the southern end of the lake, 1.25m away, on Beechcliff Hill, is a plain column on which is a huge bronze of the Duke sculpted by Chantrey.

In 1907 the great house was abandoned because sewage in the River Trent caused such an awful smell. It was offered as a gift with 200 acres to both the Staffordshire County Borough and the Borough of Stoke on Trent, but both refused. In 1907 demolition began and was completed in 1912. (The top of the impressive palace tower is now in the grounds of Sandon Park, Stafford.)

Behind the great empty space where the house once stood is the church of St Mary and All Saints. It was built in 1844 by Barry but he never intended the south side to be seen, not envisaging the demise of his great house. This side is, in fact, what most people see and it forms the backdrop to innumerable wedding photographs. Poor Barry would be horrified. The church incorporates much of the stone work and fittings from the previous priory church. The four-bay arcades are part Norman (the round shafts), and part reproduction (the capitals). The Screen is partly Jacobean and partly a copy, and the west gallery is 18th Century Georgian. Amongst the monuments are memorials to: an unknown Knight of about 1215 in effigy; Sir Richard and Lady Leveson-Gower, died 1559 and 1591; the 1st Duke of Sutherland, died 1838, in statue by Chantry; and Florence Chaplin, died 1881.

Opposite the old main gates, which are north of the new main gates, is the Mausoleum, of 1808, by Charles Heathcote Tatham. This is the only Grade One Listed building in the Potteries. It is grim, dour, forbidding, large and heavy. It has only one door and one window. Although close to the road it is fringed with trees to three sides, which partly obscures it from the highway. It was, of course, quite deliberately placed here to remind passers-by of the family that built it. Inside, the plan is that of a Greek Cross with tunnel vaulted arms.

What would the old Duke have thought about his Park today? It is now a venue for dances and concerts by popular big bands, there is boating on the lake and a Garden Centre; fairs and festivals are held here and there are plans for major development. There is little doubt that the Duke would have approved, as he regularly opened the Park to the public, even when he was in occupation.

Trentham was the model for the house called Bentham in Benjamin Disraeli's novel 'Lothaire'.

The site of **Hem Heath** colliery lies 1.5m E of Trentham Gardens, alongside the main-line railway, on the road to Longton. This pit was sunk in 1929 and closed in the late 1990s. The colliery site, and a large area of derelict land and marsh to the north, is now being developed for housing. On the opposite side of the road is Hem Heath Wood. This was planted some 120 years ago and contains about 34 species of trees and shrubs. There is a printed trail guide.

TRYSULL *1.5m NW of Wombourne, which is 5m SW of Wolverhampton*
The name Trysull is derived from 'Tresel', the Anglo-Saxon name for the Smestow Brook. The first element, 'tres', is a Welsh word meaning 'to work, to labour, to toil'. The name Trysull is pronounced Tree-sul. The manor was owned by the Anglo-Saxon freeman Thorgot before the Norman Conquest, when it passed to William, son of Ansculf. He leased it to Baldwin who had five slaves, or serfs, and a mill.

The Smestow Brook flows through the north of the village and until 1940 it powered the Trysull Mill. The mill stands complete with iron waterwheel, 17 feet 6 inches by 6 feet 2 inches, all the gearing and three pairs of grinding stones. It is dated at 1854 and belonged to Lord Wrottesley. The Staffordshire and Worcestershire Canal passes by, 0.5m to the east at **Awbridge,** where there are some handsome locks.

Houses in Trysull that are worthy of note include: the Redhouse, west of the church, Georgian brick with Venetian windows; The Croft of 1808, a tall house built by 'Gentleman Perry'; the Manor House of 1633, half-timbered and with an inscription on the porch which reads stranger, should this catch your eye do a favour, passing by Bless this House...' Dr. Johnson's aunt lived in the house and the great man stayed here on at least one occasion.

The church has a reset Norman arch outside the north aisle, a decorated tower and most of the rest is early 14th Century. The Jacobean pulpit is made from pieces of an original three-decker and the roof has some excellent woodwork. Amongst the ornaments is a small bust of a bishop under a pointed arch, of the

13th Century. In the east window are two very fine, 14th Century, stained glass figures. There is an inscription in the church that tells of the foundation made by John Rudge, in 1725, to pay one pound a year to the Sleep Rouser, whose job it was to awaken members of the congregation who fell asleep during the service, and to clear the church of dogs who became a nuisance. In those days it was not uncommon for dogs to be taken into churches.

The boundary with Shropshire runs along the wooded ridge called Abbot's Castle Hill, about a mile from the village. The names Gibbet Bank and Gibbet Plantation suggest the obvious.

Trescott is a hamlet 1.75m NNE of Trysull It was held by Combe Abbey, Warwickshire, from the later 12th Century, and then passed to the Wollastons and the Bagots. The present brick house, called The Grange, is of 1682 or a little earlier. In the grounds there is a dovecote.

TUNSTALL *3.5m NNE of Newcastle-under-Lyme*
This is what I wrote in 'Staffordshire and the Black Country' in 1988.

"A good place to start a journey through the Potteries is at the junction of the A500 and the A34, north of Newcastle. There is a road to Tunstall from here, called Peacock Hay Road, and as it descends into the Chatterley Valley there are good views of spoil heaps, slag heaps, stagnant pools interspersed with infill rubble, battered iron railings and illegally dumped household refuse. Nature is doing her best and grass grows bravely in an attempt to heal the old industrial wounds. Strangely, there are still farms here though the farmhouses have suffered from settlement and lie at odd angles. The road crosses the railway and passes by Bathpool Park at Ravenscliffe, an area of derelict land that has been landscaped by the local council. Further along Chatterley Road, on the bank above the road, stands a well-stocked cemetery. At the handsome, blue-brick pub called The Cottage the road swings right and the tall, red brick Old Court Pottery announces that here the Potteries begin. Opposite the pottery, along America Street, are acres of derelict lands made so by the demolition of several streets of terraced houses. The road runs on to a roundabout. This is Tunstall."

Things have been tidied up since then and the America Street area has been redeveloped. There is also a small 'traveller' camp site inhabited mostly by Irish itinerants. (There is a large gypsy camp at Ravenscliffe.)

The main street at Tunstall runs down hill and here is to be found the nine-bay Town Hall of 1883, designed by A R Wood. At the back of the Town Hall is the Market designed by G T Robinson and built in 1857. Opposite the Town Hall is the old market place, now called Tower Square after the Clock Tower of yellow tile placed there in 1893. It is most pleasant and very quiet here compared with the hustle and bustle of the thriving High Street.

Tunstall is something of a centre for the nearby moorland country, and despite all the industry around has very much the feel of a rural market town. In fact, the settlement has a long industrial history. Millstone Grit and iron ore was mined in the 13th Century. Bricks and tiles have been made here since at least the mid-17th Century, including 'Staffordshire Blue' engineering bricks. It was not uncommon for a potter to own his own coal pits. John Beeze, who owned the Greenfield potworks in about 1800, worked many coal pits as did William Adams when he took over the works in 1834.

In 1887 the earthenware manufacturers formed the Staffordshire Potteries Manufacturers' Association which had its headquarters in Picadilly, Tunstall.

The most striking piece of architecture in the town is the Roman Catholic

Church of the Sacred Heart in Queen's Avenue. It was built in 1925-30 by J S Brocklesby and finished by Father P J Ryan. There are two towers - a square west tower and a smaller round tower with a conical roof. It also has three copper-covered domes which are a landmark for many miles around. The overall style of the church is Romanesque.

The architect A R Wood designed the red brick Queen Victoria Jubilee Building in The Boulevard, of 1889 and 1898, and also the transepts and chancel (1885) of Christ's Church, a Commissioners' church, of 1830, by F Bedford. North-east of the town centre is Westcliffe Institution in Ternhurst Road. This was the old Workhouse, of 1838, but has been much added to. The old core includes the yellow brick Tudor Gothic range.

Nearby, in Furlong Road, are the premises occupied by the old Greenfield Pottery. It has two storeys and a pediment and stands at right angles to the street. From the centre of the town the High Street, as the A527, leads southwards towards Longport. H R Johnson's huge tile factory (they make Crystal tiles here) is passed on the right. Johnson's were founded in 1900. By 1965 they had four works in the area, and in 1969 they merged with the Richards-Campbells company and became the largest manufacturer of tiles in Britain.

At the back of the factory, off Ladywell Road, are enormous numbers of two-storey blocks of flats with white plastic cladding on the upper parts. Seen from a distance, say from the A500, they present a remarkable sight. It is almost as though a piece of an Italian seaside town has been transplanted.

Victoria Park, off Victoria Park Road, is now called Tunstall Park. It lies just to the east of the town centre and was opened in 1908. Local gypsy wedding parties come here to have their photographs taken. The entrance gates are dedicated to Thomas Peake, a tile maker of Tunstall. Some of the famous Bridestones' burial chamber were brought here (shamefully).

The main road passes on through inter-war houses to the Steetley Brick Works. A right-hand turn leads down a track and over the yellow-stained waters of the Trent and Mersey Canal to **Westport Lake Park**.

The two large lakes were formed by mining subsidence about 1880. By 1971 they had been landscaped and there are now ducks, swans and fishermen, all surrounded by factories to one side and the railway to the other. From here one can see into the rear of the former Arthur Wood's Teapot factory, with its tall brick chimney encircled by iron bands but still leaning at a wildly improbable angle. Back on the main road, just past the teapot factory, is a traffic island. This is Longport. (See Burslem.)

Greenbank, 0.75m E of Tunstall, was a small, separate settlement, but is now engulfed by suburban sprawl. The place name is only preserved in Greenbank Road, which now has its footnote in history because the popular singer Robbie Williams (born 1974) had his childhood home here. Before emerging as a solo artist he was a member of the group Take That. A large part of his success is due to his 'roguish charm'. Clarice Cliff, the Art Deco pottery designer, was born in Meir Street, Tunstall, in 1899.

Goldenhill, 1m NNW of Tunstall on the road to Kidsgrove, is now a residential suburb on high ground on the northern fringe of the Potteries. The name might well be derived from the local tradition that a hoard of gold was hidden here during the Civil War. This might relate to the leather purse found in 1832 in the thatched roof of a cottage in Goldenhill. This contained silver coins of the reign of Elizabeth I and gold coins of Charles II and James II.

The rather dour, blue brick parish church of St John the Evangelist was built in 1841. In the garden of the Rectory was found a Romano-British bronze figurine of Hercule. This is now in the Potteries' Museum at Hanley. Adjacent to the church is the old Victorian school, now looking very glum with boarded up windows and a banner proclaiming that it is now used by a Combat Arts Academy. On the opposite side of the road is a modern Community Hall. To the north-west of the settlement is Goldenhill Golf Course.

There is a small community of Irish 'travellers' now housed in the council estates of Goldenhill. The author has video filmed many of their weddings in the yellow brick Roman Catholic church of St Joseph. These affairs have certain characteristics.

The young men tend to be somewhat surly and not a little bored. They live their lives according to the laws of Mr Machismo and on more than one occasion the groom has taken his vows with swollen cheeks and a black eye. The young girls dress somewhat provocatively, their ample bosoms heaving like a swelling sea against the restrictions of white satin cliffs. The older women are attired in the fashion of country ladies with field-wide hats and eyes that miss nothing. The children do pretty much anything they like pretty much all of the time, much to the annoyance of the officiating priest who has to contend with high speed, miniature gypsies zipping around his church in full voice.

Everything is larger than life: bouquets are bigger, button holes become hanging gardens and one bride had a dress with a 15-foot-long train. Many would think this over the top, but it makes brilliant video.

At the wedding reception it is sometimes the custom for the bride to dance, not only with her new husband but with every male relative in turn, ending with the females dancing in a ring around her. This can take up to two hours without rest and is truly an ordeal, not only for the bride but for the poor video man. Another little custom is that if the bride's father has died before her wedding the car number plates are changed to his initials. The car is always, of course, an American stretch limousine, usually a matching pair.

I am not likely to forget one evening wedding reception at Chorlton-cum-Hardy when I was surrounded by five Charles Bronson lookalikes and informed that I would be staying on beyond my pre-arranged departure time: "Won't you now Michael?" said one; "To be sure he will", said another, his profusely sweating nose touching mine.

Pitts Hill, 0.75m NNE of Tunstall, lies along the road from Tunstall to Biddulph, which here climbs a long, fairly-steep hill lined with affordable Victorian terraced houses, a few shops and a Spiritualist church.

Clanway, an area at Pitts Hill, north of Hoskins Road, is known for its sports stadium. Clanway Hall was once home to John Henry Clive (1781-1853), a nephew of Clive of India. Henry Clive was a pottery manufacturer but he also invented a system of shorthand, part of which was adopted by Pitman. The Hall became a farmhouse and was still standing next to Clanway Brickworks in 1958.

Great Chell, 1m NNE of Tunstall, stands at the top of Pitts Hill. It is dominated by the large church of St Michael and All Angels, built in 1894. There was a village here by the late 18th Century.

TUTBURY *8m ESE of Uttoxeter*

It would seem very likely that Tutbury was the site of an Anglo-Saxon fort, if not an even earlier Iron-Age settlement. The hill on which the present castle stands has a commanding view over the wide and well-watered plain below. The River Dove flows by within 0.25m of the castle, which stands guard over an ancient crossing place.

The Domesday Book entry on Tutbury (Totoberie as it was called) reads: 'Henry Ferrers has Tutbury Castle. In the Borough around the castle are 42 men who live only by their trading; in the market, they pay £4.10s.' In 1205 the castle and the borough passed to the Duke of Lancaster, John of Gaunt, who was the fourth son of King Edward III. It belongs to the Duchy of Lancaster to this day. During the Civil War the castle was besieged and captured by the Parliamentarians, in 1646, and much of it was demolished. The entrance is through the north-east gatehouse. This leads to the great lawn of the Tilting Ground (or bailey). On the south side are the King's Lodgings of 1631-5 which were built as a Hunting Lodge. James I and Charles I both hunted in Needwood Forest. Adjoining, is the South Tower of 1442-50, which actually consists of two towers, side by side, with a staircase between them.

This leads to the Tilting Ground. Along the east wall is John of Gaunt's Tower. To the west of the King's Lodgings, on the site of the original keep, is the round Julius Tower, or Folly Tower, built in the 1760s by Lord Vernon. Near the centre of the Tilting Ground lawns are the foundations of the free-standing Norman Chapel. Today, the castle is by no means spectacular but it is well tended and a pleasant place to be. The views are wide and the skies here seem large.

On the right of the drive that leads to the castle is the church of St Mary, which was the church of the Priory, established by Henry de Ferrers in the 1080s and attended by monks from Pierre-sur-Dives in Normandy. The monastery is gone and the church is not complete. It originally had an apse, a large choir, transepts and a crossing tower. A new chancel and apse were added by Street in 1866. The outstanding feature of the church is the great, and much photographed, west front doorway, which has seven orders of receding decoration most elaborately carved. The outside order is alabaster, this being the first use of that material in England. The nave has large Norman columns and the present clerestory was the original Norman triforium, into which Perpendicular windows have been inserted. The south aisle door is Norman and on the lintel is depicted a boar hunt. The north aisle is of 1822 by Joseph Bennett.

In medieval times Tutbury was famous for its **Minstrels' Court**. John of Gaunt spent quite a lot of time at Tutbury, which was the administrative centre of the Honour of Tutbury and included within its boundaries the present counties of Stafford, Derby, Warwick, Nottingham and Lancaster. The Duke encouraged minstrels to attend his court and granted them a charter. Authority over the minstrels was in the hands of the King of the Minstrels, who was elected annually, and disputes amongst them were settled at the Minstrels' Court. The Court ensured, amongst other things, that the minstrels served a seven-year apprenticeship before playing for gain. The court was held on the Feast of the Assumption of the Virgin Mary and every musician in the Honour had to attend. This organization and assemblage was unique in England. After the election of a new King of the Minstrels there was a banquet, and after the banquet all the musicians assembled for the bull-running.

A bull was shorn of his horns, had his ears cut off, his tail cut to a stump, his body smeared with soap and, finally, his nostrils blown full of pepper. The populace of the town was commanded to 'attend to their safety' and not to come anywhere near the enraged bull. The animal was released and the musicians had to try and take a piece of the bull's hair or hide. He who did so won the bull, which was then brought to the High Street, baited with dogs and killed. This bull-running was practised from about 1377 to 1778, when the custom was abolished because one of the participants was killed.

Tutbury is also famous for its **Great Lost Treasure**. In 1320 Thomas, the 2nd Earl of Lancaster, along with other English Lords, allied himself to Robert the Bruce, King of Scotland, and received a large quantity of silver coin to finance his fight with Edward II, King of England. At the battle of Burton Bridge Lancaster was defeated and fled to his castle at Tutbury where he ordered his treasurer, Leicester, to convey his treasure chest of English, Flemish and Scottish coin to Pontefract with all possible speed. However, as the train was crossing the River Dove, at the foot of the castle, the chest fell into the raging flood waters. The King was only half an hour behind him so Leicester had no time to recover the treasure, being more intent on saving his life. The treasure then appears to have been forgotten. At least it was not recovered by Leicester or anyone else in his retinue.

Then, on the first of June 1831 the workmen of a Mr Webb were removing a quantity of gravel from the bed of the River Dove, on the south side of the bridge, in order to accelerate the flow of water to the mill. "While thus employed the workmen found small pieces of metal, which on examination they perceived to be silver coins. Upon this discovery a general scramble commenced and large numbers of people soon flocked to the place. Almost numberless coins in close rows came forth together with many beautiful encrustations of horse shoes, sword handles, with other war-like remains." The Chancellor of the Duchy ordered the place to be cleared and soldiers patrolled the river banks. A search was made by Duchy officials and 1,500 more coins were found. The workings were then back-filled with gravel. In 1838 further official diggings were made and a large number of coins were again recovered. It has been estimated that the total number of coins found exceeded 100,000. This has to be a guess, of course, because so many were taken in the first, unauthorized scramble. Some of these coins are on display in the museum at Hanley. It should be noted that the old bridge over the Dove was further upstream from the present bridge.

The town of Tutbury is a pleasant enough place. The wide High Street lies on the slope of a hill and has some handsome and varied buildings. The Dog and Partridge is a timber-framed public house of great character, and opposite is a house with a charming little doorway in Venetian style. The Croft House is Georgian with three bays and a pedimented doorway. There are several other good Georgian houses, both here and in Castle Street.

Tutbury has two craft manufacturers of ornamental glass and crystal ware. Both are situated near the centre and both have factory shops.

Tutbury alabaster is world famous but in fact the mines were all nearer to Hanbury, 2.5m WSW of Tutbury. The last of these, which is still producing gypsum, is the huge mine at Fauld, 1.5m W of Tutbury. (Alabaster is a special kind of gypsum suitable for carving. It is now in very short supply and is only used for small craft ware. (See Hanbury.)

Tutbury Woodhouse, now Woodhouse Farm, stands 0.25m W of Tutbury on the road to Fauld. In medieval times the manor was held on duty of making and repairing wooden vessels used at Tutbury Castle.

U

UPPER HULME *2.25m NNE of Leek*

The access road to Upper Hulme leaves the A53, Leek to Buxton road, and drops into a little valley, where the tiny village lies crammed between the hills, a waterfall and a factory. A factory is not exactly what one expects but this is just the kind of place in which the early mills were sited. Manufacturing began in the country and only later became centralized in towns. In fact, the mill at Upper Hulme was once world renowned as Tatton's, the yarn dyers, who were especially famous for their black dyes. It is still a dyeing works though part of the premises are now occupied by an engineering company and a furniture manufacturer. The original stone mill-house still stands and is some 300 years old. It was a rope works before the dyeing trade came. The dyers found the water from the stream especially good.

The road continues on around Hen Cloud, the outlying hill of the Roaches, and passes above Windy Gates (SK 004618). This house is dated at 1634 and is superbly positioned with long views over Tittesworth reservoir. It has two gables and transomed windows, and the porch has a stepped lintel.

On the other side of the road from Windy Gates, in the rocks of the southern tip of the Roaches, is Rock Hall (SK 006622), which has no water and no electricity, and which was made a Listed Building in 1987. This remarkable and extremely picturesque cottage includes a room which is actually a cave. Doug Moller and his wife Ann bought Rock Hall in 1978, but the building was condemned and they left in 1989. It is now a British Mountaineering Council Climbers' hut. Doug Moller, 'the Lord of the Roaches', once gave the author a photograph of a wallaby he had taken on the Roaches. Rock Hall was built by the squire of Swythamley Hall for his game-keeper. Queen Mary visited the house as a child. It is said that there were caves here, which were destroyed, and the stone taken to build cottages.

The flat stone to the right of Rock Hall, called The Bawd Stone, weighs about 20 tons and is balanced on short pillars. The name Bawd could be from 'Baal', the Celtic sun god, and it is surmised that this stone could have been an altar and a place of sacrifice. A few yards from the stone is a mound, about 40 yards in diameter, encircled by two concentric oval stone circles.

The road runs parallel to the Roaches and continues past the disused quarries and the Five Clouds to Roach End. Roach means 'rock' and these rocks are millstone grit, a hard, coarse sandstone which was used for grinding wheels before synthetic carborundum was developed. To the left are magnificent views over the green meadows of Gun Hill, and to the right are jagged rocks with ruined stone cottages standing forlorn in rough hill pasture.

At **Roach End** there are farm gates to be opened and closed before proceeding. The road circles around the Roaches and there are more incredible views over the great bowl of Goldsitch Moss. Ultimately, one returns to the Leek-Buxton road - a journey not to be missed. This is not a place that only looks right in the summer sun. It looks good in any season, but in different ways at different times.

The Roaches used to belong to the estate of Swythamley Hall. In 1938 the squire of Swythamley was Sir Philip Brocklehurst. His brother lived at Roache House (SK 011605), which is at the southern end of Hen Cloud (at the southern end of the Roaches), where he had a private zoo. In 1938 wallabies were introduced here, but shortly after Sir Philip's brother left to fight in the First World War. Whilst he was away the fences became broken and the animals escaped. All of them were recaptured, apart from some of the wallabies. Sir Philip's brother was killed in Burma, but the wallabies managed to survive and breed on the Roaches until the late 1990s when sightings ceased. One of their regular haunts was the atmospheric Doxey Pool on the summit of the Roaches. It has never been known to run dry.

Roche Grange (SJ 992633) is a tiny settlement on the west end of The Roaches, 2m NW of Upper Hulme. By 1246 there was a grange of Dieulacres Abbey here which, by 1900, was the seat of the Hulme family.

UTTOXETER *13m NE of Stafford*

The name Uttoxeter (or Uttcheter, as the locals pronounce it) is from the Anglo-Saxon and means 'Wittuc's homestead in the heather'. The 'xeter' is not a corruption of 'cester', meaning a Roman fort. Early British man has left numerous artifacts in the area and it is likely that Uttoxeter was a pre-Roman settlement.

However, in the fields to the south of the town is a large, quadrangular earthwork, believed to be the remains of a Roman defensive position. The north entrenchment is the best preserved and lies in a field called Sandfort. The south and west sides are also discernable. Pottery has been found on the site and nearby an amphora was located. Many finds were made in Bradley Street which was probably the site of a Romano-British pottery. Finds include a quantity of grey clay, an unfinished pot, a bronze disc, the handle of a bronze key, a quern, a coin, pieces of iron, pottery, boars' tusks and part of a glass fibula enamelled in red, etc. Small potsherds and coins have been found all over the town. Near the church was an old well surrounded by a pavement, a foot below ground level, that was believed to be Roman. It was lined with sandstone for its full length and pottery was found in a bank nearby. Very little Roman Samian ware has been found and much of the pottery found is Romano-British. In fact, it is unlikely that Uttoxeter was ever a Roman town as such, and some doubt has been cast on the age and origin of the artifacts said to have been found in the area. No new finds have been made for many years.

Little is known about the area in the Dark Ages, but in 1066 Uttoxeter was held by the great Earl Algar. After the Norman Conquest King William took the manor for himself and at the time of Domesday Book there were at least 37 families living here, a considerable settlement for the time. The Norman scribes called Uttoxeter Wotocheshede. The village officially became a town about 1140, when the Earl of Derby sponsored a borough and the right to hold a market was obtained. To induce new tenants to take residence the burgesses were offered the right of grazing and other rights in Needwood Forest. The new town was a great success and both the landlord and tenants prospered.

By the 15th Century Uttoxeter, and the lower Dove valley in which it is situated, was an area renowned for its dairy products. Leland, who passed through in 1540 said, 'there be wonderful pastures upon the Dove'. The potters of Burslem were kept busy making butter pots for the traders and farmers at Uttoxeter market. Indeed, they had to be constrained from making pots too shallow - done no doubt at the request of the farmers - because customers were getting short measure.

In 1596 and again in 1672 there were major fires which destroyed almost all the old timber-framed, medieval houses. Elizabeth I visited Uttoxeter in 1575 during her tour of the country, and in 1645 Charles I and Prince Rupert stayed at the Manor House.

Despite its prominence as a market Uttoxeter was the last North Staffordshire town to be linked (in 1763) to the new, improved, turnpike-road system. Today it has the benefit of the new A50(T) dual carriageway which swoops by on its way from Stoke to Derby. This improved road is carried over both the River Tean and the River Dove at their confluence on a new bridge, 1m NE of Uttoxeter. The handsome 14th Century, stone-built Dove Bridge was rebuilt in 1691 and widened in 1915. In 1987 a hoard of coins from the reigns of Edward I and Edward II was found nearby This old stone bridge is now not used but it can be seen from the new, and a splendid sight it is.

The Uttoxeter branch of the Caldon Canal ran from Froghall to Uttoxeter and was completed in 1811 but it has long been abandoned and the warehouses converted to other uses - as a corset factory in Uttoxeter and a railway warehouse in Rocester. Indeed, the track of the railway from Uttoxeter to Maccclesfield used the drained canal bed.

The town centre consists of two adjoining, irregular squares collectively called the Market Square. In the larger square is the small, domed and pedimented classical structure that was built in 1854 as the Weighing House. It is now used as a newsagent's kiosk. It was in Market Place (about 1780) that Dr Johnson, as an old man, stood bald-headed in the rain and did penance for having disobeyed his father 60 years earlier. Johnson's father was a seller of second-hand books and had a stall at Uttoxeter market. (Dr Johnson himself suffered from Tourette's Syndrome which manifests itself as facial and bodily tics, convulsive movements, whistles and noises, gesticulations and compulsive actions like touching posts and measuring one's footsteps.)

There are attractive and interesting buildings around the Market Street corner of the square. The Talbot Inn is part black and white; the shop of T G Sargeant is timber-framed, of about 1600, restored in 1980; and opposite is an ironmonger's shop in Gothic stone with a gable, an arched window with carvings and a turret. The building, of which this front is a part, housed the old Bamford (JCB) offices. The firm is now at Rocester but its original factory was in Uttoxeter, on the road to Stafford. The premises still stand.

The main shopping street in Uttoxeter is High Street, a busy place at most times but thronging on market days, despite the great lorries that still vibrate their way along the narrow road. Here is the Classical Town Hall of 1854 by Thomas Fradgley, now standing forlorn with shuttered windows and flaking paint. A passage leads to the Cattle Market that stands behind the Town Hall. Also in the High Street is the three-storeyed Uttoxeter House, still handsome despite the later work of unsympathetic hands. Here, too, is the Old Bank House of 1798, with five bays and an engaged Tuscan columned porch. There is a small shopping precinct off the High Street, a rather miserable affair done on the cheap and completely out of character with the rest of the town. The brick Methodist church is of 1812, in Classical style with arched windows and a pediment.

Other buildings worthy of mention include the following: starting in Church Street there are the County Court Offices, with a Gothic pointed arch doorway; the Manor House of five bays and 2.5 storeys with a three-bay pediment, three tall urns and a handsome Tuscan columned doorway - possibly the best house in

Uttoxeter; the Jervis House with two canted bay windows; and the Headmaster's House of Alleyne's Grammar School (about 1858).

In Carter Street is the white-painted White Hart, which has Tudor panelling in the dining room taken from Beaudesert Hall when it was demolished. Opposite the White Hart is a group of three timber-framed cottages. In Balance Street are some good Georgian brick houses and the R C church of St Mary.

The parish church of St Mary faces straight on to the pavement at a busy corner. The tower is early 14th Century and has a recessed spire. Most of the rest was rebuilt by Trubshaw and Johnson in 1828 with alterations to the chancel in 1877. It is a light, airy church with galleries and contains the 16th Century tomb of Thomas Kinnersley of Loxley.

Market towns are often venues for horse racing and Uttoxeter is no exception. Regular meetings have been held here since the late 18th Century. The Racecourse is situated alongside the railway line to the south-east of the town, on the back road to Marchington. There has been horse racing in the Uttoxeter area since 1720. The present, purpose-built course at Town Meadow was opened in 1907. In 1988 the businessman Sir Stan Clarke (d 2004) became a major shareholder and a new grandstand was opened in 1994. On the slopes of the wooded hills overlooking the course are some attractive old houses.

Bartley Gorman (1944-2002), bareknuckle fighter and 'King of the Gypsies', lived in a caravan near Uttoxeter and was buried at Rocester.

Loxley Hall lies on the hill above the hamlet of Lower Loxley, 2m WSW of Uttoxeter, along the A518 to Stafford. Legend has it that this is the Loxley mentioned in the old Robin Hood Ballads. The Hall is a large 11-bay house, with an ashlar facade of about 1795, and a four-columned porch. Much of the house was rebuilt in 1817. Parts of the previous house remain, notably the old panelled hall which has been brought into the house by the extension of the front. The panels are of about 1650 and the small inset pictures are Catholic. In the frieze over the large mantelpiece are heraldic shields, dated at 1607. The Hall is located on a good site and it is likely that there has been a house here since Anglo-Saxon times, although in 1066 the land was said to be waste and in 1086 was still in that condition. Robin Hood's Chapel, 0.5m SSE of Loxley Hall, is made of ornamental stone from the old hall and features the arms of the Sneyd-Kinnersley family. Robin Hood is said to have courted Maid Marion in the woods hereabouts.

Blounts Green is now a south-west suburb of Uttoxeter, which lies along the Stafford-Uttoxeter road. The name is from the Blount family who lived at Blount Hall. In 1638 Sir Harry Blount succeeded to the estate. He was a well-known traveller and author of 'A Voyage to the Levant with Observations concerning the Modern Condition of the Turks'. The Hall is no more; Blount's Hall Farm probably stands on the site. In the village there is a rectangular pound with 12 sandstone posts. Popinjay Farm (SK 075323), Blounts Green, may once have been an inn. A popinjay was a parrot-like bird used in medieval times as a target by archers. Highfields Hall, 0.5m S of Blounts Green, was once the home of Judge Alfred Ruegg KC (died 1941), who was also a novelist, and Captain Ridout, who had terminal cancer and took his own life by falling on his sword. The Hall was demolished in about 1986 and replaced with a purpose-built nursing home.

Upper Nobut, 2m WNW of Uttoxeter, and nearby **Lower Nobut**, are hamlets whose name is perhaps from the Irish celtic 'noeb' meaning 'holy', hence 'holy grove'. Alternatively, it may have originally been 'north butt', meaning 'north archery practise ground'.

Thorn Tree House, 2m S of Uttoxeter, is a farm, just north of which are the remains of two side-by-side, rectangular moats (SK 086303).

Toot Hill at **Woodgate**, 1m SE of Uttoxeter, is a hill with a listed burial mound which was excavated in 1860. Celtic and Roman pottery was found with two cremations. Toot is not an uncommon name for small hills and Norman mottes. There are many explanations but the one we like best is 'observation post'.

WALL *2.25m SSW of Lichfield*

Wall lies along Watling Street. The A5 makes a slight detour south of the Roman road here. The village is presumed to have taken its name from the upstanding remains of the old Roman fort and settlement of Letocetum. Most of the modern village lies on the hill above the Roman site. It is a dignified settlement of mostly large, red brick houses and farms. Near the church is a substantial Classical mansion with stuccoed walls.

The small church is of 1843 by Scott and Moffatt. It has a nave, a short chancel and a small steeple.

The site must surely be old and indeed there is good reason to believe that here, or hereabouts, was a pagan temple – a Celtic church of the Cornovii. A number of carved stones with human horned heads have been found built into the walls of the Roman settlement just below the church. It is believed that the name Cornovii means 'worshippers of the horned one'. (The Cornovii were the Celtic tribe that occupied most of Staffordshire, Shropshire, Cheshire and Herefordshire at the time of the Roman invasion.) It is thought that the Romans destroyed the shrine but reused the stones, which they turned upside down, as a small gesture to the Celtic gods should they in fact exist. The bones of Celtic oxen with down-turned horns have also been found in the area, and they may be the remains of animals ritually slaughtered and then eaten.

The name Letocetum is a Latinised version of the Celtic word meaning 'the grey wood'. The Romans first had a large but simple marching camp here. Later, they built a succession of 1st Century wood and earthen forts. The last of these forts was abandoned about 80 AD because the area had been pacified. In the 3rd Century new defences were constructed to make a strong point on the road. Parts of this were built in stone and stand astride Watling Street.

The Civil Settlement has been partly excavated and can be viewed by the public. Here are the sandstone foundations of a mansio (an inn) and of a bath-house with the usual sequence of rooms of different temperatures. There was also a stable where a change of horses could be obtained.

Pipe Place, 0.75m WNW as the crow flies, is a house with five bays, two storeys, cross-shaped windows and a hipped roof, dated at about 1764. However, what is of interest here is the palisade of oak trunks found below the present ground level. This was traced for 500 yards and was protected by a 'V'-shaped ditch. It is probably of Roman origin, a protective barricade that probably once stood 12 feet high and connected with Wall. It is not quite straight and follows the contours of the hill, which suggests it could also have been an aqueduct. This earthwork was discovered in the late 18th Century, probably during the excavation of the Wyrley and Essington Canal.

Aldershawe House, 0.5m N of Wall, has half-timbered gables above, and brick below, to a design by Samuel Luxton of the 1890s.

WALSALL 6m E of Wolverhampton

The surprise here is the remarkable collection of internationally important paintings and sculptures housed in the New Art Gallery in Gallery Square, which was opened by Queen Elizabeth II in 2000. The Garman Ryan family, who lived locally, donated paintings by Monet, Degas, Blake, Van Gogh, Turner, Matisse, Modigliani, Constable and others; and the Epstein family gave examples of the work of the 20th Century's most illustrious sculptor, Sir Jacob Epstein. Few provincial towns have been so blessed.

As to Walsall itself, well, the town planners have tried but they have failed. The centre of the town is cut through by nightmarishly busy roads and junctions, made worse by a one-way system, which so infuriates drivers that many become homicidal maniacs intent on mowing down anyone who dares even to think of crossing the road.

Although Walsall is not mentioned in Domesday Book there was almost certainly a settlement here before 1086. The name is derived from 'Wealh's halh', 'the valley of the Welsh(man).' 'Wealh', or 'walh', was an Anglo-Saxon term of abuse meaning something like 'bloody foreigner', despite the fact that the Welsh (Celts and Ancient British)) were here first. About 1159 the manor passed to the Ruffuss family.

The town has two charters: one granted by William Ruffuss in, it is thought, the early 13th Century and another of 1309. In 1390 the manor passed to the Earls of Warwick and remained with them until 1488. (This explains the appearances of the Warwickshire bear and ragged staff symbol in the Walsall coat of arms.)

The old town lay on the slope between the church at the top of the hill and the bottom of the valley below. It was a crowded place of mean, dark houses and narrow, cobbled streets. These have been demolished and there are now some new dwellings and open green areas.

The church of St Matthew (formerly the church of All Saints) almost certainly replaced an Anglo-Saxon church. St Matthew's was built in the 13th Century but all that remains from this time are the tower and the crypt, which is something of a feature of this church. It was altered in the 15th Century and in 1819-22 the nave walls were encased in ashlar stone and the windows re-made and given iron tracery by Francis Goodwin. Ewan Christian remodelled the chancel in 1877-80 and the spire was largely rebuilt in 1951. Inside there are three galleries and a good Georgian Gothic ceiling. There is a battered effigy of Sir Roger Hilary, died 1399, in the south aisle. From the rear the church looks most dramatic, standing amongst a cluster of abutments.

Other churches are: St Mary, Roman Catholic, 1825-7 by Joseph Ireland; Vicarage Walk Baptist Church, 1879, Italianate; St Paul by J L Pearson, 1891-3; St Peter, 1841 by Isaac Highway, brick with polygonal buttresses; and St Michael at Caldmore, 1871, by J R Veall, Early English style in red sandstone.

Coal, iron-ore and limestone have been quarried and mined in and around Walsall since the 14th Century. Iron was worked here from at least 1554, and in 1570 men from Walsall were felling trees at Bentley Hay (which was part of

Cannock Chase) to make charcoal. Iron was also exported to several other areas, including the Paget furnaces on Cannock Chase and Middleton in Warwickshire (1592).

The limestone workings are very extensive and there is a honeycomb of uncharted tunnels and caverns below the town, which could one day cause a disaster. In 1824 the Mayor of Walsall was drowned in a flooded, derelict quarry along the Lichfield Road, and another man died trying to rescue him. In 1874 the Arboretum and Lake Company was formed to convert this quarry (which belonged to Lord Hatherton) into a pleasure garden. The company failed and the council took over and made it into a public park. The Arboretum now covers some 80 acres and its annual illuminations are well known. Limestone was quarried in Walsall until the 20th Century.

However, the trades most closely linked to the town are those connected with the supply of 'equine accessories'. In the 16th Century the town was famous for its bits, spurs, stirrups and other such metalwork for the rider, and buckles for the shoe trade. In the first half of the 19th Century the leather making and saddlery trades developed in Walsall. Tannin was available from local oak trees and hides from local cattle and sheep. In the 19th Century the town became a major producer of saddles and whips, known the world over, and the trade continues to this day. Indeed, the local football team is called 'The Saddlers'. There is now a substantial Leather Centre, housed in a large, red brick industrial building recently restored and showing just how handsome such structures can be.

Not far away two roads intersect - Littleton Street and Hatherton Street. These commemorate a local landowner who, amongst other things, was chairman of the company that financed the construction of the Staffordshire and Worcestershire Canal (1772). He was Sir John Littleton who became Lord Hatherton in 1835. Hatherton is just west of Cannock. (Incidentally, General William Booth, 1829-1912, founder of the Salvation Army, and his family once lived at No 5, Hatherton Street.)

Another trade of some local importance from the 1760s onwards was brush making. Every conceivable kind of brush was made, using materials bought in from all over the world: bristles from Siberia, fibres from Mexico, horsehair from the USA and ivory from Africa, etc.

The modern town centre of Walsall has neither rhyme nor reason, being cut into bits and pieces by roads and shopping precincts. The High Street was the medieval main street. It leads down from the church to the area called The Bridge. (There was a bridge here but the stream now runs through an underground culvert.) The Tuesday and Saturday markets are now held in the pedestrianised High Street. Also in the High Street is the Italianate Guildhall of 1876, designed by G B Nichols.

On The Bridge is the statue of Sister Dora - Dorothy Wyndlow Pattison (1832-1878) - a nun of the Christ Church sisterhood, who, through her great concern and tireless efforts as a medical nurse, so won the affection of the people of Walsall that when she died the whole of the town went into mourning. Somewhat disrespectfully, the pigeons find her head a useful perch.

At her back there are modern buildings that stand in the place of the George Hotel. This was Walsall's most famous coaching inn and was demolished in 1933. Near the Bridge is a Victorian shopping arcade that leads into the modern Saddlers Shopping Centre, which in turn leads to the railway station.

In Bradford Street is the 19th Century School of Art, and on the corner of

Caldmore Road is Belsize House, the birthplace of Jerome K Jerome who was born in 1859 and died in 1927. His middle name was Klapka. He actually left Walsall when he was two years old and never lived there again. Nevertheless, Walsall opened a Jerome K Jerome Museum in 1984. However, the public is denied sight of the prize exhibit, his desk, which has apparently been commandeered by the Mayor for his Parlour in the Town Hall.

The Town Hall of 1905 is in Leicester Street. Also in Leicester Street is the old Walsall Literary and Philosophical Society building of 1831, with its impressive Classical Greek Doric portico. It now houses the County Court. Adjoining the Town Hall, but in the tree-lined grandeur of Lichfield Street, is the Council House. It is ashlar, in Baroque style and has a high tower. Here, too, are the Library and the old Art Gallery, fronted by the statue of John Henry Carless who was awarded the Victoria Cross posthumously for his part in the Battle of Heligoland Bight, 1917. The sculptor was R J Emerson of Wolverhampton.

Most of the suburbs of Walsall are best forgotten but there are some isolated buildings of interest. In **Caldmore Green** is the White Hart, a large irregular Jacobean house with shaped gables, two canted bays and mullioned windows. It stands on a corner near the old village green. This is a famous 'haunted house' where a variety of metaphysical incidents have occurred. In 1870 the mummified hand of a small child and a Cromwellian sword were found in the loft. The Hand was thought to be a 'Hand of Glory', a felon's arm cut from his body after he had been hanged and often used in witchcraft. It was, in fact, a medical specimen. The ghost of a girl who committed suicide in the house over 100 years ago has been seen on several occasions, and in the 1950s there were several reports of strange phenomena. In the southern suburbs, between Broadway and Gorway Road, is the West Midland Teachers' Training College of 1964 by Richard Sheppard, Robson and Partners. It is a modern glass and concrete construction. Seen from a distance through a screen of trees it looks half handsome.

Bescot lies 1.25m SSW of Walsall town centre, at junction 9 of the M6. This is not a major junction, as junctions go, but aerial concrete is everywhere. It even totally overshadows the famed Bescot Railway Sidings. There are broad acres of cleared and levelled land on both sides of the Motorway. That encircled by Bescot Crescent has given birth to the smart new Bescot Stadium, now home to Walsall Football Club. Amongst the comprehensive schools and metal works the gloomy river Tame winds its weary way. Never has a river been so mucked about. Half its life is spent in concrete tunnels and wired-stone banks, its course altered and its level lowered by dredging. Help! it cries. But the dark glass of the RAC Rescue Control Centre glares sullenly at the hurrying hot metal on the motorway and turns a deaf ear.

The name Bescot is a contraction of the Domesday Bresmundescote, meaning 'Beortmund's cottage (or shelter for cattle or sheep)'. The Hilarys, lords of Bescot Manor, were given permission to crenellate the moated Bescot Manor House in 1345. In 1731 it was demolished and replaced by Bescot Hall, which in turn was demolished in 1929. These two, once-proud edifices stood in what is now Pleck Park, between the Pleck Park entrance from Bescot Drive and the M6 at S0 997968. Doctor John Fletcher, a lecturer at Aston University, Birmingham, and an authority on Black Country culture, lived at Bescot.

Horden,1.5m N of Walsall centre, was anciently an enclosure in Cannock Forest and was recorded as a settlement in the 13th Century, with its nucleus at the crossing of Horden Road and Well Lane. Cromwell Cottage is probably the oldest building still standing in Horden. In about 1800 it was a shop and was later converted to a Roman Catholic chapel. Horden became a ward of Walsall in 1931. Today it has some forbidding council estates.

Palfrey, a suburb 1m SW of Walsall centre, was formerly an independent settlement. The name could be from the Middle English 'palfrey', meaning 'a riding horse', especially for a lady; or from the Old English 'pall', meaning 'still or firm'; or from 'palfrey', meaning 'a fire', which is the explanation most favoured. Palfrey is an ecclesiastical parish, created in 1902, and the church was built in 1893. Palfrey Park was opened in 1886 and extended in about 1935. At Palfrey Green there is a green no more. There was iron working at or near here in medieval times.

At **Birchills**, 0.5m W of Walsall town centre, there are Victorian terraced houses (an increasingly rare commodity these days), many Asian faces, a small shopping centre, the Four Ways Inn, blocks of yellow brick flats, the Rose and Crown, and a Liberal Club with green area beside. All are set on a low hill climbed by the Walsall Locks of the Wyrley and Essington Canal, which heave the leaden water up to a desultory 'Local Canal Museum', a collection of old waterways' buildings. St Andrew's church is of brick with clerestory windows and was built in 1884-7 to a design by J E K Cutts. In the 19th Century there were large collieries and steelworks here. There was a boiler explosion at the Birchills Hall Ironworks in 1880 when 25 men were killed. The prefix of the name Birchills is from the Anglo-Saxon 'bryce' and means 'newly cultivated land', not 'birch tree'.

Little London lies 0.25m S of Walsall centre. On high ground, amongst the houses, is a creeper-clad tower windmill, of brick, five storeys high and topped by a castellated parapet. It was probably built in the early 1800s and ceased working in the 1860s. In the 1920s the Skidmore family rebuilt the tower-top and converted it to an observatory. The windmill is situated between Sandwell Street and Highgate Road at Ordnance Survey reference SP 016976.

Pleck is 1m SW of Walsall town centre. Starting at Old Pleck Road and progressing northwards the traveller passes high rise flats, the Bradford Arms, the Hymac Works, houses old and new, Walker Brothers Galvanising, The Forge pub, Gill Russell (tubes, fittings, valves and flanges), a sub Post Office and finally the sprawling Manor Hospital.

The nucleus of the hospital is the Old Workhouse, built in 1842. Maps still show the U-shaped medieval moat of the old Manor House lying beside the Belle Vue pub in Moat Street. Alas, it was filled in (about 1987) and is now yet another hospital car park. It is sad to see the red brick and imitation slated blocks of nurses' flats occupying the site (now called Cavall Close) of the scrap dealers Steptoe and Son. Their name was emblazoned here in large, faded letters long before the television series was broadcast. It is hard to believe that their name was not "lifted' by the author of the original play.

The Chuckery, 0.5m ESE of Walsall centre, is a largely residential area. It is bounded by the Broadway, which itself has some substantial Victorian and 20th Century houses. The name Chuckery stems from the word church. A medieval title deed refers to 'church grove field'. The church to which the land belonged was, of course, St Matthew's. The church of St Luke was built in 1879, and rebuilt twice in 1879 and 1934.

The Chuckery covers a hill and contains a wide variety of domestic dwellings, from the desirable detached in leafy Prince's Avenue to the recently refurbished terraces in Tantarra Street. There is the odd corner shop, a Peugeot car dealer, the handsome Spring Cottage pub (which has stained glass windows and shaped gables), an art college in an old school in Tong Street, some tower blocks, and in the middle of all this is a huge iron works, the iron casting foundry of Chamberlain and Hill. In the 1980s the entire side of Beacon Street was demolished and replaced with a tall, yellow brick wall in an attempt to contain the roaring hum and fumes from Chamberlain's. Still, this is the Black Country. By way of contrast the mighty Crabtree Electrical Industries works, also in Beacon Street, hides (to the point of disappearing) behind a high hedge and an even taller wall of trees. Opposite the Crabtree works, on the other side of Broadway, is a large parkland with a nine-hole golf course, a miniature steam train and the Grange Playhouse. To the south this is bounded by Sutton Road, another wide, leafy avenue.

Daisy Bank is a 20th Century residential area adjoining the Sutton road and backing on to open country. Services include The Longhorn pub, a red-windowed Spar shop and the modern, yellow brick church of St Martin. This has a wood shingle roof, most unusual. The **Hay Head** Wood Nature Reserve is 0.5m N of Daisy Bank, down Longwood Lane. This 13-acre site was once occupied by the Hay Head Lime Works.

The Delves lies 1.5m S of Walsall. Between Walsall and West Bromwich the A4031 runs through a suburban no-man's-land. At The Delves there are a shopping precinct, a big red pub and playing fields. The name could be derived from either the old English 'delf', meaning 'a mine', or from 'dell', 'a hollow'. Adjoining it to the south-east is **Yew Tree**, a place also largely given over to housing. The council estate was completed in about 1966 and the mission church, The Annunciation of Our Lady, opened in 1958.

The M6-M5 interchange (at junction 8 on the M6) lies 0.5m S of The Delves. Here the River Tame, in all its murky glory, is channelled through concrete gutters. My dog, 'Pirate', accidentally slid down a steep concrete slope and into the water. For two minutes or more he tried to scramble out in several different places before finally thrashing downstream to a natural earth and grass bank. What fate might await a child in this well frequented place?

Coalpool lies 1m NNE of Walsall town centre. Today it is an open, airy residential place of brick and render houses. To the south is the large, well-wooded and well-tended **Ryecroft** Cemetery. It is set on a hill and looks more like a park. To the north is **Goscote**. The name means either 'the cottage in the gorse field', or, 'the hut for geese'. There are large commons grazed by horses of all kinds and colours, a canal, a hospital and an adult training centre. At **Heath End** are the old Elkington Copper Refinery works.

Addendum: **Making the Limestone Mines Safe.** In the early summer of 1991 we spoke to the engineers who were infilling the subterranean limestone caverns in the Mellish Road area. There are three old mines here: the Arboretum Mine, which adjoins the Arboretum to the west; the Moss Close Mine, centred on the roundabout where Lichfield Road meets Mellish Road; and the large James Adams Mine which lies north-west of the roundabout and extends to Eastbourne Street. The Adams mine has collapsed because the support pillars were either weakened or even removed, as last-fling easy pickings, shortly before the workings were abandoned. Signs of ground settlement are evident in many buildings. The offset spire of the Wesleyan Methodist Church (1910) is in the process of parting company from the main body of the building, and recently a hole appeared in the main road when an uncharted shaft cap collapsed. Indeed, mining engineers estimate that there are between 10,000 and 20,000 unmapped shafts in the Walsall area. Only 10 have been located and properly capped! The mine caverns are now flooded. To make them safe, first the water is pumped out and then a Rock Paste is pumped in to completely fill the void. This paste consists of 'pulverised fuel ash' (the powder that is left after coal has been burned in a power station) mixed with lime and water and bulked out with graded colliery spoil. These ingredients are mixed at a central yard located at the corner of Lichfield Road and Westbourne Road. The liquid is pumped out of the mixer, and feeder pipes direct the Rock Paste to 16 inch boreholes drilled from the surface into the caverns 30-150 feet below. The paste slowly hardens and becomes rock-like. The 'average' mine requires some 200,000 tons. The contractors on this site are Douglas and the consulting engineers are Ove Arup and Partners. The men we spoke to had recently filled in old limestone workings at other parts of Walsall (Littleton Street and Wolverhampton Street), Dudley, Lilleshall and Ironbridge (Lincoln Hill). The work is paid for by grants from Central Government.

WALSALL WOOD *4m NE of Walsall*

Presumably Walsall Wood was a medieval daughter settlement of Walsall in the woodland of Cannock Chase. It developed late, as a coalmining and brick making centre, but by 1850 the Springfield Brick Works were producing over a million bricks a year. The Walsall Wood Colliery was sunk in the late 19th Century, very late by Black Country standards.

At the centre of the village is the parish church of St John. The early parts, including the tower, are by Isaac Highway of 1837; and the later parts, including the south aisle and the chancel, are of 1895 by M E Lavender. Some work was also done in 1886. Inside are ornate cast-iron arcades.

Opposite the church is a row of small, traditional shops. (The superstore and newer shops have been banished to Aldridge-Walsall crossroads.) The old railway line has been landscaped and lawned and there is a certain airiness here. Industrial activity is now minimal; suburban housing rules hereabouts. Amongst the social facilities are the bright and breezy Bar-Restaurant, the Oak Park Sports & Leisure Centre, a dancing school, a snooker-club and the Megan de Boisson complex of old people's dwellings.

The area called **Vigo** (a Spanish port) is named after the Vigo Brickworks. This is no more, but the huge pit from which the clay was taken remains. Beside it is a half-hearted Recreation Ground, a run-down Progressive Club and a few Victorian terraced cottages that have escaped the onslaught of 20th Century developers. On the main road, the A461, is the quite startlingly-large Baron's Court Hotel, a truly gigantic edifice for such a small place.

Shire Oak is a northern residential area. However, there is no sign of the old tree now and, worse still, we are now treading on the toes of Brownhills, cursed by the presence of Leigh Environmental in Lindon Road which bounds Shire Oak to the west. Leigh Environmental dispose of noxious waste substances in big holes in the ground and have been a cause of great concern to local people for many years.

The eastern suburbs of Walsall Wood are called **Holly Bank**, after the lane that leads steeply downhill to the busy A452 trunk road. Here are the evocative earth walls and ditches of a prehistoric fort, now embowered in mature trees. A handful of old cottages decorate the descent, so nice compared to comfortable but 'oh-so-dull' abodes that are home to most of us these days.

Clayhangar lies 1m N of Walsall Wood. This is an isolated little settlement with a few old cottages and rather more modern houses. No 2 Bridge Street is a delightful old, brick and stucco cottage. All around is rough, drained pasture and derelict industrial land. The name Clayhangar is Anglo-Saxon and means 'a slope on clayey soil', though to us the land looked rather flat.

WALTON-ON-THE-HILL *2.5m SE of Stafford*

The Anglo-Saxons referred to the Celts as 'Wahls', which was a term of abuse. This name was later adapted to 'Wales', the land of the Celts. The Welsh call their land Cymru. Settlements, either lived in by Celts or associated with them, were often called Walh-ton or Walton.

In 1066 Walton-on-the-Hill was part of the manor of Baswich and belonged to the Bishop of Chester. He had taken over the estates that formerly belonged to the Anglo-Saxon diocese of Lichfield. Today, Walton is joined to Stafford by an unbroken line of suburban houses. The centre of the village is called The Village and is most attractive. It has a variety of red brick houses and the occasional timber-framed cottage, set amongst mature gardens along narrow lanes. Around the old part are the inevitable soulless estates, and within the village itself large, modern houses are crammed into any odd spot the planners will allow. There are a school and a garage on the main road. The small church of St Thomas is set in the old part of the village and is quite delightful. It was built by Thomas Trubshaw in 1842 in a simple Gothic style of red brick with lancet windows and has a striking tower and spire. Inside, there are memorials to the Levett family of Milford Hall.

Milford Hall lies on the main Stafford to Rugeley road. It is a late 18th Century stuccoed house of three storeys. It was built on the Mill House estate and utilizes the mill stream to supply a small lake which has a boathouse and a bathhouse. In the gateway to the garden are stones from the gatehouse to St Thomas's Priory, Baswich.

Just down the hill is the village of Milford which has a shop, a pub, a classic English village cricket ground and the Common. In the summer Milford Common is akin to a seaside holiday town. Cars park in rows, dogs frolic and children eat ice cream. The actual Common is not very large but it adjoins the wide acres of Cannock Chase, and opposite are the main gates to Shugborough Park and Hall. A little way down the road, on the left, in the direction of Walton, is the house where the retired Governor of Gibraltar, Air Marshal Sir Peter Terry, was shot by the IRA in revenge for the SAS assassination of IRA bombers in Gibraltar.

The Hole, 0.5m S of Milford, on the north-west side of Broc Hill, is a hollow with pitted ground. Squatters made shelters here and in the rock face. The last rock cottage was demolished after the Second World War.

WARSLOW *7m N of Leek*

The village lies high in the wild Peak District moorlands with splendid views all round. It belonged to the manor of Alstonfield and is called Wereslei in Domesday Book. In 1086 there were 4 villagers, 2 smallholders with 1 plough and 8 acres of meadow and woodland, 1.5m long by 0.75m wide.

The village is stone-built and attractive, but is rather spoilt by a terrace of rendered houses and a ghastly modern school. There is a well-used pub, an abandoned chapel of 1848 and iron stocks at the point where the lane to Ivy House Farm leaves the main road, close to the school. The stone-built Memorial Hall has that boon to the traveller, clean public toilets that are actually open.

The church of St Lawrence was built in 1820 and the chancel was added in 1908 by Charles Lynam. Inside, there is a two-decker pulpit, box pews and a large pew for the squire and his family. There are stained glass windows by Morris & Co (between 1909 and 1923), and in the sanctuary there is much Art Nouveaux decoration. The churchyard is graced by some splendid beech trees.

Warslow Hall lies on a wooded slope, 0.5m NNE of the village, on the road to Longnor. It is stone-built and has a porch with two pillars and a pediment. Adjoining the Hall is a courtyard, enclosed by ranges of handsome stone barns and stables with slit windows.

The Hall was built by Sir George Crewe (of the Harpur-Crewe family of Calke Abbey in Derbyshire). It was used as a summer residence and later as a shooting lodge. The grounds were landscaped in the 1830s and features include a grotto and a series of cascades and pools in the woods of the steep-sided valley to the south of the Hall.

About 1548 the Lord of Warslow agreed to enclose some of the waste land on his manor, not for pasture and not to deprive his tenants, as was usual; far from it, he made the land good 'for the better maintenance of tillage and corn which they then greatly wanted'. Good for you, Sir.

Swainsley, 0.75m SE of Warslow, is a small hamlet which lies in a loop of the River Manifold. The name probably means 'clearing where pigs are kept'. Swainsley Hall was built in 1864 with later extensions. Sir Thomas Wardle occupied the Hall in the late 19th Century. He was a friend of several pre-Raphaelites and William Morris and Burne-Jones were guests here. The Dovecote was built to a French design in about 1920 to house 200 birds.

Wigginstall, 1.25m N of Warslow, is a cluster of grey stone buildings which constitute two farms, situated close together in a secluded valley. One barn is dated at 1780 but the settlement must be much older than this; stone is so difficult to date. Access is along an unsigned limestone chatter track off the B5053, Ipstones to Longnor road. The farmers here keep dairy and beef cattle and some sheep. The name is from the Anglo-Saxon 'Wicga's-stall', where 'Wicga' is a personal name and 'stall' can mean 'place, stable or stall'.

Upper Elkstone, 2m WNW of Warslow, is a village on a hill in the Moorlands. There are three listed burial mounds on the hill. In medieval times the manor belonged to Trentham Priory. Copper was being mined here by 1750 and in the 1780s the old church was replaced by a new one dedicated to St John the Baptist. The village had a pub, the Cock Inn, but when it closed in 1976 so did the annual wake, which tells you something about the nature of wakes.

Lower Elkstone, 0.75m NW of Upper Elkstone, is smaller and younger than Upper Elkstone and was a separate manor by the late 13th Century.

Hulme End, a hamlet 1m ENE of Warslow, was the northern terminus of the Manifold Valley Light Railway, which opened in 1904 and closed in 1934. The engine shed and booking office still stand. There are several burial mounds in the area about Hulme End. One, at the junction of the Sheen and Harrington roads, is thought to be the grave of John Bonsall, who died in about 1770 and wished to be buried on his own land. In Old Danish 'hulm' means 'piece of land by a stream'.

WATERFALL *1m N of Waterhouses, which is 7m NW of Ashbourne*
It lies in the hills of the Staffordshire Moorlands, a small stone-built village with a pub, a church and the old stocks on display at the crossroads. A Roman crucible was found at Earls Cement Works in 1961. Waterfall is believed to have

existed at the time of the Domesday book but was omitted. In the early 12th Century the manor was acquired by Burton Abbey.

The church of St James and St Bartholomew is of 1792 but incorporates parts of the previous Norman church, namely the restored chancel arch with its zig-zag and saltire cross ornament, and the arch top of the south doorway. The font is 17th Century and the screen Jacobean. There is an inscription on the altar:

The river of God is full of water.
Let the floods clap their hands,
and let the hills be joyful before the Lord.

Lamber Low and its burial mound lie 0.33m SE of Waterfall, and the River Hamps flows by 0.33m mile E; at least it does in the winter for in the summer it usually runs dry, the waters sinking through the limestone and running underground. It is from this falling of the water underground that the village takes its name, not from a waterfall as is normally surmised.

WEDNESBURY *4.5m ESE of Wolverhampton*
The name is pronounced Wensbury, or Wedgebury in the local dialect. It is a very old settlement and is dedicated to the Anglo-Saxon god Woden. The church stands high on a hill, inside the worn banks of a Celtic Iron-Age fort. As befits a former country village, Wednesbury had a full compliment of traditional 'hardware' - pinfold, market cross, gallows, whipping post and ducking stool – now all gone .

Alas, today the town is dying. There are many empty, boarded-up shops and on top of that the roads and road junctions cut the place to bits. The main road is in fact a section of the Holyhead Road, the famous 'Parliament' coaching route laid out by Thomas Telford in the 1820s. The Wednesbury Branch of the Birmingham Canal was constructed by James Brindley in 1769, but subsequent alterations and name changes to the canal system of the Black Country are extremely complex and confusing.

The town has a long industrial history. There was an iron working forge here in the reign of Elizabeth I (see Wood Green in this article) and John Wood, a contemporary of John Wilkinson, had an early iron furnace in Wednesbury, which was important because it produced malleable iron using coal (instead of charcoal). Coal was mined through the ages, though it was prone to instantaneous combustion - the ground smoking and fuming - a fearful sight. Limestone was worked and has left perilous subterranean caverns, many of which are uncharted and liable to collapse at any time.

But, above all, Wednesbury is known for tubes and is sometimes called Tube Town. In the 18th Century the most important industry in Wednesbury was the manufacture of gun barrels and gun locks. After 1815 the demand for guns slumped but a new market developed for tubes, especially for the new gas mains. In 1825 Cornelius Whitehouse, an edge tool worker at the Wednesbury Forge of the ironmaster Edward Elwell, invented a method of forging hollow tubes. This process was developed by James Russell, who bought the patent and became the largest manufacturer of tubes in the whole country. After 1845, when his patent ran out, rival firms were set up and the town became an even larger centre of tube production.

Shafts for vehicles and engines were also a specialty of the area. The leading company in this field, Patent Shaft, closed in 1980, but the town is still a centre of the iron trade. It is nice to see some small firms, comprising only two or three men, surviving in old buildings. One such is the drop forge works, tucked down an alley between the houses numbered 98 and 100, in Walsall Road, King's Hill.

Wednesbury is known in the region for the Riots of 1743, caused by the preaching of John Wesley who was manhandled by angry mobs. In time, however, Wednesbury and the Black Country in general became centres of Methodism and Nonconformity.

The parish church of St Bartholomew, on its high hill, is a landmark for many miles around. It was largely rebuilt in Victorian times; nave and north transept of about 1827, and the south transept and east end by Basil Champneys in 1890. However, there are still some medieval parts, such as the 14th Century tower arch and the re-set chamfered arch in the north aisle, which is probably of about 1200. There are 16 stained glass windows (1889-1910) by C E Kempe and a painting by Jean Jouvenet of 1698. Amongst the monuments are memorials to: Richard Parkes, died 1618, and wife in alabaster effigy; Thomas Parkes, died 1602; and Samuel Allison, died 1817. The most remarkable piece of furniture in the church is the lectern. This incorporates a carved, wooden fighting cock and is dated at about 1400.

There is also a famous, and very long, 19th Century broadside ballad called 'The Wedgebury Cocking' which tells of the tough, rough and not-for-your-maiden-aunt tale of a typical match.

There have been at least three, and possibly five, windmills on Church Hill. Locally, the hill was known as Bull Hole because it was a place where bulls were baited.

Adjacent to St Bartholomew's is the Roman Catholic church of St Mary. It has a tall, thin, copper-clad spire designed to compete with the tower of its Anglican neighbour. St Mary's was built of red brick, with some black brick decoration, by Gilbert Blount in 1874.

Other buildings that should have some mention include: the Town Hall, of 1872, with a facade of 1913; the Art Gallery, 1891, by Wood and Kendrick; the Market Place Clock, 1911, by G W D Joynson; the attractive Library, 1908, by Crouch, Butler and Savage; the Memorial Gardens, 1926, by Bateman of Birmingham; St James, 1848, by W Horton, a Commissioners' church with a chancel of 1857 and an apse of 1865; St John, 1846, by Dawkes and Hamilton and the gaunt sandstone rectory in Lower High Street. This has lost its church, demolished some years ago, and is now the chapel of a Masonic Lodge, which explains the shuttered windows.

An ancient, pre-Christian, 'magical transference' cure was practised in Wednesbury by colliers and forge-men until the early part of the 20th Century. A child suffering from croup would be treated by holding a pigeon against its throat. The bird was allowed to die of starvation. As the life passed from it so the disease would transfer to the poor creature, it was believed.

Mesty Croft lies 0.25m SW of Wednesbury parish church. Between the high ground of Brunswick Park and the Tame Valley Canal is a residential area of mostly modern houses. The parish church of St Luke is small and also very modern, likewise the Village Inn. The big, red brick building with a tall chimney is the old Water Pumping Station. It now houses several small, light industrial units. Just down the road is St Paul's Church Hall, red brick with stone dressings, opened in 1906 with the blessing of the Roman Catholic Viscountess Ingestre (near Stafford).

Down by the River Tame, alongside Woden Road South, there are wide, open, green spaces. This was once derelict industrial land and even now the river runs well below ground level, a level raised by shaley spoil heap waste. Some of the old pools remain but "Danger Deep Mud" reads the sign. The water of the Tame is an utter disgrace. Near Wodensborough High School the thick green liquid is joined by a busy little stream of chocolate hue. What a brew they make as they mingle. Ironically the name Tame is Celtic and probably means 'dark river'. The Welsh 'taf' and 'tam' have the same meaning and in Sanskrit (the ancient northern Indian mother of most European languages) 'tamas' means 'darkness'. By way of contrast, the pool near the dismal modern block that houses the College of Commerce and Technology is quite delightful, with ducks and swans and reeds and willows.

The largely residential area of **Wood Green** lies 1m NE of Wednesbury centre. The red sandstone church of St Paul, with its fiercely pitched roof, was built in 1874 by the ironmaster family of Elwell. The Elwells owned the Wednesbury Forge, first recorded in 1597 during the reign of Elizabeth I. Remarkably, it is still there. At least its descendant is - the Bescot Drop Forgings works (SJ 002963). These can be approached down St Paul's Road, off Woden Road East. The old forge used water from the mill race to drive a waterwheel. This worked the bellows that blew air into the furnace and lifted the great hammers that beat out impurities from the brittle pig iron blocks that had been smelted elsewhere. The reservoir pool still survives, empty now and grassed over. But as proof that it still had water when the railway came, the tracks crossed the pool on a brick viaduct, rather than a much-less-costly earthen embankment. Opposite Bescot Drop Forgings is the even bigger Spear and Jackson tool works. A public footpath leads from here to Bescot Station, crossing first the railway and then the River Tame by two tall bridges, from which there are long industrial views. Opposite the Queen's Head pub, in Brunswick Park Road, is another industrial monument - a wall built of blocks of furnace slag. The Sandwell College in Wood Green Road is a memorial to 20th Century architectural bad taste. There are still trees about in Wood Green and even a cricket ground.

The Woods adjoins Wood Green. It is a rather dreary, 20th Century residential area with schools, a Methodist church, the Windmill pub and a block of shops. The drainage ditch that runs parallel to Coronation Street is the blighted River Tame.

Friar Park, 1m E of Wednesbury centre, is very much a place of council houses. There are a few shops, an industrial estate, the Coronation pub, a service station and the church of St Francis of Assissi in yellow ashlar with a pantile roof. This stands at the head of Carrington Road, which can only be described as a 'boulevard' - an unusually wide avenue with a double row of trees on both sides.

To the south, over the deeply entrenched Tame Valley Canal (1844), is **Hall Green**. A couple of shops and the Golden Lion do nothing to prepare one for the treasure that lies in Hall Green Road (west). This is the ancient Manor House, not of Wednesbury, but of West Bromwich. For something on this jewel of the Black Country, see the article on West Bromwich. The estates hereabouts are pleasanter places - tree-lined avenues on higher ground.

At **King's Hill,** 0.66m NW of Wednesbury town centre, is a small park on a high knob (like a spoil heap) next to the red brick church of St Andrew. To one side are new houses, to the other bleak sheds that house metal industries. Opposite, is the Scott Arms and to the south are Woodstone Rolling Mills (derelict land), and the Wednesbury Trading Estate.

WEDNESFIELD *2m NE of Wolverhampton*

'At Wedgefield at one village wake the cockers all did meet', so begins a 19th Century street ballad, and makes the point that Wensfield (as it is pronounced, or Wedgefield in dialect) was still a village well into the industrial period. Wolverhampton spread out and swallowed it up, a process not hindered by the fact that the link canal, joining the Staffordshire and Worcestershire Canal (at Wolverhampton), and the Essington and Wyrley Canal (at Bloxwich) passed through Wednesfield. However, Wednesfield had long been associated with Wolverhampton, having been given to the monastery at Wolverhampton by Lady Wulfrun in 994. The Anglo-Saxon Chronical records that Edward of Wessex defeated the marauding Danes at Tettenhall in 910, but many historians are of the opinion that the battle was actually fought at Wednesfield. In Domesday Book it is called Wodensfelde. The Anglo-Saxon word 'felde' implies a naturally-occurring open plain, not a man-made cleared field. Wednesfield lay on the road that connected the Roman forts at Pennocrucium and Metchley.

Locally, it is held that there was an Anglo-Saxon shrine to Woden (their God of War) at Wednesfield and that this took the form of a large stone altar used for human sacrifice. (In 1909 it is recorded that an unusually large number of basalt boulders were evident in Wednesfield, brought here by glaciation.)

Despite its ancient roots the village does not seem to have had a church of its own until 1875 when St Thomas's was built as a 'chapel of ease' for St Peter's in Wolverhampton, which was the parish church for Wednesfield. St Thomas's was burnt in 1902, and repaired and partly rebuilt in 1903. It is constructed of brick and has a pedimented doorway.

In Church Street is a row of seven old shops, quite charming when compared to the rest of the mostly modern, flat-roofed things which now dominate the High Street.

There is a variety of metal works and light engineering industries in the area, but perhaps the product for which Wednesfield was best known was not one to be proud of - namely animal traps, especially those used to capture large animals. One of the old trap works has been dismantled and rebuilt at the Black Country Museum.

A massive house building programme increased the town's population from some 17,000 in 1951 to 28,000 in 1958. The huge **New Cross Hospital** lies 0.5m along the road to Wolverhampton. It started life as the new Wolverhampton Union Workhouse of 1901, designed by Arthur Marshall, and had become a hospital by the 1930s. Opposite the hospital is an old house with very ornate garden wall railings. Behind this, the now-abandoned Bentley Canal comes to rest, the locks falling to bits. So sad.

The main industrial area lies south of Wednesfield town centre, along Neachell's Lane. Here, old iron foundries mingle with brash new sheds of many colours. On the 50-acre site of a seamless tube works, which closed down in 1995, Corus built Steelpark, a steel distribution centre in 1999. At **Neachell** itself is Strawberry Lane, an industrial estate now. The name Neachell means nothing more exciting than 'land added to an estate'.

East of Wednesfield town centre is **March End**; March is probably from the Anglo-Saxon 'mearc' meaning 'boundary'. Today, it is a residential area with two large comprehensive schools. To the north is **Wood End,** another residential area. In Amos Lane, once stood the attractive Cottage Homes. These were built for pauper children by the Board of Guardians, in 1889-90, to a design by George H Stanger. Their place is filled by yet more modern 'homes', which overlook the substantial playing fields behind.

Ashmore Park is an overflow residential housing estate for Wolverhampton, developed from 1951. A shopping precinct was built on the site of the old medieval Ashmore Hall, though the moat which surrounded it was preserved and can still be seen.

WEEFORD *4.5m W of Tamworth*

Weeford is a tiny hamlet that lies in the charming valley of the Black Brook, a mile or so upstream from Hints. Just to the north is the busy A5, and just to the south are large gravel pits.

Thickbroome Hall, on the road to Shenstone, is a modest country house which, from at least 1562, was the home of the illustrious Wyatt family. John Wyatt I (1675-1742) spawned a dynasty of architects, inventors and builders, sculptors, painters and carvers. The most famous was James Wyatt (1746-1813). His father Benjamin was a well-known local builder. James worked on several cathedrals and designed many country houses and stately mansions including Hagley Hall, Little Aston Hall, Beaudesert, the London Pantheon and Fonthill Abbey. He was actually born at the modest, early Georgian, red brick, five-bay Black Brook Farmhouse, 0.5m SW of Weeford.

The cruciform church of St Mary at Weeford is of 1802, in a Gothic style, with a later bell-turret and chancel. In the south transept window is 16th Century stained glass brought here in 1803 (during the French Revolution) from the chapel of the Duke of Orleans near Paris. There are monuments to the Manleys of Manley Hall and the Swinfens of Swinfen Hall.

Manley Park lies 1.5m S of Weeford, but the neo-Elizabethan Hall with its towers and pinnacles is no more. Swinfen Hall, 1.5m NNW of Weeford, was built in 1775 by Benjamin Wyatt, father of James. It is now part of a Youth Custody Centre. The seven-bay house is of brick with stone dressings to the front, 2.5 storeys high with a top balustrade, giant angle pilasters and a pedimented doorway. Inside, are good ceilings, a good staircase and Art Nouveau bathrooms which are listed.

The Bishop's Stones at Weeford were said to have been piled by the roadside to mark the places where the bodies of a Bishop of Lichfield and his entourage were found after they had been murdered by robbers.

WERRINGTON *3.5m E of Hanley*

A main-road village, dominated by modern housing, that lies on high ground along the A52, the road from Hanley to Ashbourne. Next to the fish and chip shop is an old windmill, of about 1730, now used in connection with the ugly telecommunications' mast which stands beside it, next to the handsome Windmill pub. On the opposite side of the road is a government penal institution, currently used as a Youth Custody Centre. In 1936 flint knives and scrapers of the late Bronze Age - Iron Age were dug up in the grounds of the Centre.

Cellarhead lies 0.5m E of Werrington. This is an ancient north-south, east-west crossroads around which has developed a small settlement. There was a bull-ring here to which bulls were tethered whilst they were baited by dogs. The ring and the stone to which it is anchored are now on display at the County Museum, Shugborough Hall, near Stafford. One of the crossroads' pubs at Cellarhead is a venue for car boot sales. In 1838 Gervase Forester of Cellarhead was made bankrupt when his business as a maltster failed. He then turned his hand to writing street ballads.

Ash Hall, in **Ash Bank** is a Tudor 'baronial-style' house built for Job Meigh, a pottery manufacturer, shortly after the Elizabethan mansion that previously occupied the site was demolished in 1841. In the 20th Century it became a hotel, then a country club and in 1992 a nursing home. It has two ghosts: a lady in white in the grounds, and a Mr G Wood, a former resident in the house. Werrington expanded greatly after the sale of the Ash Hall estate in about 1925.

The Fireman's Rest, a house on the Leek road, 1m E of Werrington, was a venue for cock fighting.

Washerwall, 0.5m W of Werrington, is a very large residential area adjacent to Werrington and lying north of the A52. It takes its name from the Wash Well, at SJ 934478, on an old saltway over Wetley Moor. The stream rising from it flows to Bucknall. In Washerwall Lane, opposite the well and behind a shop, is a badly worn and broken cross shaft. There were two quarries at Washerwall, one for sand and one for stone. On the main road is the plain, rock-faced church of St Philip. Just where Werrington and Washerwall divide is very debatable.

WEST BROMWICH *7.5m SE of Wolverhampton*

The best thing in West Bromwich is really in Wednesbury. The discovery and restoration of the superb Old Manor House of West Bromwich in Hall Green Road, two miles from the High Street, is really rather marvellous. A tumble-down jumble of old brick and stucco buildings was on the verge of being demolished, when it was found that behind the more recent brickwork was a long-forgotten, timber-framed manor house of the 14th and 16th Centuries. The complex consisted of an Elizabethan Gatehouse, a Great Hall, a north Solar Wing, a Chapel and a Kitchen Block around a small courtyard. The restoration was done on behalf of the council by James A Roberts of Birmingham and he did a superb job. The Manor House is currently leased to a brewery as a restaurant and licensed premises.

Early holders of the property were the Deveraux and the Marnham families. The manor passed by marriage to the Stanley family and was later bought by Sir Richard Shilton, who was the Solicitor General to Charles I. It then passed to Sir Samuel Clark, whose family became Clark-Jervoise with property in Hampshire and it was they who abandoned the Old Manor.

The Oak House in Oak Road, **Lambert's End,** is another unexpected timber-framed house which, like the Old Manor, now stands marooned in a sea of houses. It is an impressive building of the 16th Century with stepped, upright studding. The earliest parts of the house are the central hall and the side wings. The earliest known occupants were the Turton family, who came from Lancashire in the mid-16th Century and who became some of the earliest nailmasters. The Turtons left in 1768 and in 1894 the house was bought by Alderman Ruben Farley, five times Mayor of West Bromwich, who had it completely restored and gave it to the town in 1898. It is now a museum and has some good furniture.

Unfortunately, the Manor House and the Oak House are not representative of West Bromwich. The town is spread-about and has very little character. It does have a centre of sorts, the long, partly-pedestrianised High Street, but this is too long for comfort. Here is the Old Library of 1907 by Stephen Holliday, built in brick and stone with fluted columns and pediments, and paid for by Andrew Carnegie. Next door is the Town Hall of 1875, by Alexander Hunman, in brick to a Gothic style. The only other building of note in High Street is Christ Church, of 1821 by Francis Goodwin. It is in Perpendicular style with iron window tracery and three galleries. On the roundabout at the south end of the High Street is an arched stone gateway, which came from the now-demolished Sandwell Hall, a reminder that West Bromwich is the centre of the new Metropolitan Borough of Sandwell.

Sandwell Park, on the estate of Sandwell Hall, covers a large area to the east of the town. There are nature trails, woodland and pools, totally surrounded by suburbia and sliced through by the M5. Here, too, is the Sandwell Valley Farm where you will find Longhorn cattle and Shropshire sheep, not to mention many men with many dogs, most of which seem to be Staffordshire Bull-terriers. The site of the Benedictine Priory and the Holy Well are close to the farm. South of them is Sandwell Golf Course.

Excavations have revealed the foundations of both the Benedictine Priory and its church, and the drinking fountain fed by a natural spring, the 'sanctus fons' or holy well which became San(d)well. Sandwell Hall was rebuilt in the early 18th Century, on the site of the ruined Priory, by the Legge family who were to become the Earls of Dartmouth. They exploited the natural resources of the area, principally coal. When the industrial region encroached upon their private domain they abandoned Sandwell Hall and went to Patshull near Wolver-hampton. Sandwell Hall was demolished in 1928.

Signs of early man at Sandwell include flints, a Roman coin and three burnt pebble mounds.

Although the first known blast furnace in the Black Country was at West Bromwich (1590) the area did not develop much until the early 19th Century. Coal and ironstone were discovered in the open heath to the south of the old village centre and the area became a 'boom town'. This explains why today the modern centre is so far away from the parish church and the Old Manor House. Between 1801 and 1901 the population increased from 5,700 to 65,000. In 1825 there were three collieries; in 1865 there were 65. Many things were made here but especially irons, stoves, bedsteads, grates and coffee mills.

The church of All Saints lies 1.5m NE of the town centre. It has a tower of the 14th and 15th Centuries but the rest was rebuilt in 1872 by Somers Clarke. Inside, there are alabaster effigies believed to be of Anne Whorwood, died 1599, and Field Whorwood, died 1658, both members of the family who lived at the old Sandwell Hall, before it was rebuilt by the Earls of Dartmouth. There is also a wooden chest, all of one piece, carved out of a solid block.

Local personalities include William Salter, a late 18th Century businessman, who made several things but especially springs. His firm continued and by 1960 was making over 500,000 different kinds of springs! Jess Pennington played for West Bromwich F C and England (25 times) in the early 20th Century and is still remembered as a great player. Madeleine Carroll, the film actress, was born in West Bromwich in 1906. She starred in several classic films, including 'The Thirty Nine Steps' of 1935 and 'The Prisoner of Zenda' in 1937. In 1837 James Fellows started the most famous of the canal transport companies, namely Fellows, Marton and Clayton, which at one time had 200 narrow boats. They were known at Joshers after Joshua Fellows. The firm closed in 1948.

At a crossroads in **Carter's Green**, West Bromwich, a suicide called Edward Lane was buried with a stake through his heart. His bones were removed in 1835 when the road was altered. The church of St Andrew, Carter's Green, was rebuilt in 1940.

Hill Top is 1.5m NNW of the High Street at West Bromwich. The parish church of St James was consecrated in 1844. William Henley, the English Paganini, was born at Hill Top in 1884, and by way of contrast Ken Downing of the heavy metal band, Judas Priest, also hails from Hill Top

Lyndon, 0.75m N of West Bromwich High Street, was the original centre of population in the area before 1800. Here were the Market House, the Lock up, the Stocks and a Windmill (SP 008925). Lyndon village clustered around the junction of the present Hargate Lane and Lyndon Street. Lyndon ward has three parts: Hateley Heath, Friar Park and Charlemont.

At **Grove Vale,** 2m NE of the West Bromwich High Street, is Bishop Asbury's Cottage. Asbury spent his childhood here, became a Methodist preacher and went to America to spread the gospel according to John Wesley. He travelled extensively in the new continent and fought for many social improvements. He became the first Methodist Bishop, much to the despair of his old teacher, Wesley, who decried such pomp. Nevertheless, Asbury is highly regarded in America and is considered to be one of the 'founders of the nation'.

In the mid-19th Century a man called Hudson invented dry soap powder. For many years he had a small works at West Bromwich before opening a large factory in Liverpool. This was taken over by Lever Brothers of Port Sunlight in 1908.

To the north and the south of West Bromwich are long, straight stretches of canals with deep embankments which can be quite dramatic. The best known is the New Main Line (1829), to the south of the town, on the border with Smethwick. At one point (SK 002898) the M5 crosses the main-line railway and the canal, which here are within yards of each other.

Guns Village lies at the east end of West Bromwich High Street. There are new houses, an old railway line, a service station, terraced houses, the Black Cock pub, a YMCA, and Vubrake Technologies. **Swan Village** is 0.5m NW on the A4035. It is an industrial place with metal works, such as the Speedway Foundry, and gasometers in Swan Lane. At the top of Swan Lane is **Black Lake,** where the Express & Star newspaper has offices and a printing works in lack-lustre modern buildings. These stand near a deeply entrenched canal, now disused. The road leads uphill, past chemical factories, houses ancient and modern, and the New Talbot (in brick and stone mock-Tudor) to Hill Top. (See Hill Top.)

At **Mayers Green,** 0.5m E of West Bromwich High Street, is Dagger Lane. Here is Hill House, an early 16th Century, timber-framed building with later additions. **Stone Cross** lies 2.5m N of West Bromwich High Street, on the road to Walsall. Here there is a colourful shopping centre around a large traffic island on which stand, in splendid isolation, the Stone Cross pub and the Top Rank Bingo Hall. The place takes its name from a sandstone wayside cross that stood near the pub until the 1890s. The church of The Ascension in Walsall Road was built in 1938.

Charlemont adjoins Stone Cross to the south. It is a residential area with a large and well known cemetery. The florist opposite the main gates does a roaring trade on Sundays. As to the name, 'Charl' in English place names usually means 'free peasant', from the Anglo-Saxon 'ceorl'. Thus Charlemont might mean 'the hill of the free peasant.'

There can be very bad traffic jams in Charlemont. One way to avoid them is to head east, through **Wigmore**, 3m NE of West Bromwich centre to the Newton Road. The suffix 'wig' in Wigmore is probably from the Anglo-Saxon and probably means 'Wigca's moor'. However, the first element of the name, 'wig', is also used to mean 'a battle', hence Wigmore could mean 'a moor where a battle took place'. On the high ground at Wigmore is the imposing school built in 1869 by the Walsall and West Bromwich School District Board. In fact, it has the appearance and trappings - gatehouse and coach block - of a stately home. The 2.5 storey entrance porch with shaped gable, is surmounted behind by an ogee capped tower and flanked by canted bays. Most of the building is red brick with stone dressings. Today it is home to the Sandwell Municipal Borough Technical Services Department. This includes Planning, though you would never believe it were you to judge by the ugly satellite buildings they have erected around the old school to provide more office space. I challenged one of the senior staff members. His reply was: "We don't care what it looks like. All we want is the cheapest building that will do the job." Little wonder that parts of Sandwell leave much to be desired.

At the bottom of the hill is an old farm, now a riding centre. There is an air of unreality here. Young girls lead horses between high rise flats and through the roaring gloom of the shadows cast by the looming concrete roads that curl all around the M5 at its junction with the M6.

WESTON ON TRENT *5m NE of Stafford*

Weston lies in the valley of the River Trent, which here is paralleled by the Trent and Mersey Canal (1777). The village stands at the crossing of the A518, Stafford to Uttoxeter road, and the famous coaching road now called the A51 from Rugeley to Stone. It is an attractive place with an enormous village green and retains a deal of character despite the new houses.

Facing the green is The Woolpack and almost opposite the pub is an old factory with a chimney. This has been various things including a dairy and an alabaster works. Alabaster was formerly mined at Norman's Wood near Stowe by Chartley and brought down to Weston to be processed. Behind the factory is the Laing Construction equipment depot. The firm came here in 1963-4 when the M6 was being constructed and has been here ever since. The yard occupies the site of the old Salt Works, established alongside the canal by Earl Talbot in 1820. Parts of the impressive brick building designed by James Trubshaw survived until 1963. There were eight large pans in which the brine was heated and the water removed by evaporation. (See Shirleywich.) By the short canal spur that served the works is a cluster of cottages, which probably had a connection with the industry.

The parish church of St Andrew is well known for its sturdy and handsome 13th Century, Early English tower with lancet windows. Above the tower arch, the arcades and the chancel arch are also 13th Century. However, much of the church was rebuilt by Gilbert Scott in 1860 (north aisle) and Butterfield in 1872 (south aisle and clerestory). The chancel windows are of about 1400 but are not in their original positions. The east window glass is by Gibbs. The church has two bells of about 1400, some of the oldest in Staffordshire.

Opposite the church, screened by trees, is a handsome Jacobean-style house called Abbeylands, built in 1858 by Gilbert Scott. Here lives Lord Harmer Nicholls, father of Sue Nicholls, the actress, who has appeared in the television soap operas Crossroads and Coronation Street. The house is said to be haunted. Also opposite the church is a most attractive stuccoed dwelling, and to the right-hand side of the church, almost totally hidden by trees, is a splendid and substantial thatched cottage.

The most impressive building in Weston is Weston Hall. Indeed, it is one of the most impressive houses in the county. The Hall stands 0.5m W of the village, on the lower slopes of Weston Bank, on the A518. Gaunt and strong-looking, it is a stone Jacobean house with four gables, three storeys plus attic, and mostly transomed windows. The porch was added in Victorian times. At the turn of the century it was sold to pay gambling debts and for a time, from about 1912, it was a county lunatic asylum. During the Second World War it was requisitioned and occupied by Land Girls. Subsequently, it has been in multiple occupation and is now a restaurant and a venue for wedding receptions. The owner is Paul Reynolds who lives in the cottage adjacent to the Hall. It is a pity that he has seen fit to plant the tall, straight line of fast growing coniferous trees that now partly obscure the Hall from public view.

The small brick shed in the valley below is the old pump house which supplied water to the Ingestre Estate. Close to it is an area of landslip where springs issue forth. The River Trent has been lowered hereabouts by dredging, as a flood control measure.

WESTON UNDER LIZARD *7m E of Telford (Oakengates)*

Two miles to the south-west of the village, over the border in Shropshire, is the wooded Lizard Hill under which the settlement lies. Lizard itself is said to be either a corruption of the name of a local Norman lord of the manor or of Lazar, meaning a leper, of which there is reputed to have been a colony hereabouts. Weston is very much an estate village and had it lain on a more peaceful road than the busy A5, it would be considered most attractive. The cottages are of several styles, all handsome, though it was sad to see the proud vicarage in its wooded gardens being sold for 'development'.

The Hall and the church are hidden from the road by a high wall and a screen of trees. Weston Hall is very much open to the public and the main entrance is to the west of the village at a minor, and very dangerous, crossroads. Opposite the entrance gates is the estate plant nursery and sawmill. In the Middle Ages the Weston estate passed from the Weston family to the Myttons and then by marriage to the Wilbrahams, and again by marriage to the Newports (Earls of Bradford). Finally, in 1762, it passed to the Bridgemans (Earls of Bradford of the second creation). The present, 6th, Earl of Bradford is no longer the owner of Weston Hall and its immediate estate. He was forced to sell it some years ago and now lives in a nearby farmhouse. The company that now runs Weston Hall holds a variety of events in the grounds, from game fairs to steam engine rallies and pop concerts. The Virgin concerts are mammoth affairs with huge security fences and battalions of sour–faced guards, who herd their customers around as though they were cattle. Like cattle they defecate everywhere, including Lord Bradford's drive and garden. He is not a happy bunny.

The present classical house was built in 1671 to a design by Lady Wilbraham, wife of Sir Thomas Wilbraham. The south front has a central stone bay, and to the left and right segmental gables. Above the east front is a pediment and a Victorian porch (1865). There is a balustrade around the whole of the top of the house and some good chimneys. The low east wing was added in Victorian times and joins on to the 11-bay, 17th Century Stable Block which has a central pediment, weather vane and cartouch of arms. Beyond the stables are the handsome 18th Century Farm buildings. Alongside these there is now a small menagerie - ducks, donkeys and exotic birds etc. - and also a pottery and a shop. In the Orangery of 1865 is a cafe.

The church of St Andrew (1701) has an entrance to the north, from the main road, but is attached to the Hall. Like the Hall it was designed by Lady Wilbraham. Part of the previous church was incorporated: namely the tower, in which there are some Norman stones; and the east wall, which has a 14th Century window. In 1877 Ewan Christian added a family chapel in Norman style. In the east window are reset parts of the original 14th Century glass in a work by Hardman, of 1876. There are monuments to various members of the Bradford families including, of course, Lady Wilbraham, died 1705.

The Park was landscaped by 'Capability' Brown. The woods contain many specimen trees, such as the magnificent plane tree by the house, and in the meadows are deer and rare breeds of sheep. In the grounds are several ornaments. The Temple of Diana is a domed orangery standing above the deer wall. This, and the Roman Bridge with its 'sentry boxes', are by Thomas Paine, of about 1760. Beyond the bridge is the Swiss Cottage with its wooden trellis verandah. There is also an Obelisk, a Mausoleum of 1870, Boat-houses and various urns and vases. To the south, on Tong Knoll, is The Tower, a Victorian folly with a polygonal turret. Some of the Park ornaments are now houses.

To these attractions of old, the new owners have added: an Adventure Playground in Temple Wood and beyond that a Miniature Railway; an Aquarium in the old boiler room beneath the Orangery; a Butterfly Farm beside the Church Pool; and the Museum of Country Bygones. There are walks in the woods, the charming Temple Pool, and the freshwater tanks in which fish from the lake were kept for some weeks to improve their taste before being killed and eaten. (These are by the Toddlers' Playground.)

Inside the Hall nothing is left of the 17th Century. The finest rooms are the Tapestry Room, with Gobelin tapestries (1766), and the Dining room made in the mid-19th Century. There is a marble staircase and an important collection of paintings, including works by Holbein, Reynolds, Gainsborough, Hoppner and many others. In the former dining room, now the Library, there is a collection of rare books.

One mile north of Weston Park is Blymhill, which is very much a Bradford estate village. (See Blymhill)

WETLEY ROCKS *6m S of Leek*

It lies on the A520, Leek to Stone road, 1.25m NNE of its junction with the A52 at Cellarhead. The Rocks are an outcrop of Millstone Grit, which has been quarried since the early 19th Century. The red-and-white stone was originally used only for kerbstones and steps, but in 1833 St John's at Wetley Rocks was rebuilt of local stone, and by 1850 Wetley stone was in great demand as a building material for churches and chapels. The stone was being worked until at least 1890.

St John's has a nave, tower and aisles of 1833, paid for by the Sneyd family of Ashcombe park, and a chancel of 1901 by J Beardmore. Wetley Abbey lies 0.75m SW of the village, down a track off the main road (A520). It was probably an old house, enlarged greatly in 1836. It has a cruciform shape and Gothic features with a pediment and an ornamental motif of the cross and mitre - a somewhat strange house. The Victorian painter George Mason Mills lived here. It is now a Nursing Home. A custom which is still practised at Wetley Rocks is the Palm Sunday procession of three wooden crosses being carried through the village streets and up to a high point on the rocks.

Rownall, 0.75m WNW of Wetley Rocks, was Roughenhall in the 13th

Century, which means 'rough land'. There was a possible deserted medieval village to the north of Rownall Hall. The Hall was home to the Arblasters in the early 17th Century and to Smith Child, MP for North Staffordshire, in the mid-19th Century. Rownall had a witch in the early 19th Century. She was a herbalist whose cottage was burnt down in about 1820 by a gang of her neighbours, led by their landlord Captain Powys.

Westwood Manor, 1m NNW of Wetley Rocks, is a neo-Elizabethan house of 1870 built by the potter, William Meakin. After several owners it was given to the Stoke-on-Trent Education Authority, who use it as a Special School. The previous house on the site, Westwood Hall, was a square, grey-stone building.

Wetley Moor is 2.25m WSW of Wetley Rocks and is a high, barren, former common which was originally much larger and reached almost to Wetley Rocks. There have been squatters on the moor since about 1800 and they had a lawless reputation. More squatters built humble cottages after the Second World War. During the General Strike of 1926 coal miners made small bell pits, which now look like shell craters.

WETTON *8.5m NNW of Ashbourne and 1.25m W of Alstonfield*
This is the heartland of the Staffordshire Moorlands - hills and dales with pastures divided by dry-stone walls. Even in summer the village looks cold. In this high place prehistoric man lived and died. His burial mounds are still numerous here, though many have been ploughed out. In the 19th Century most of the larger tumulii were opened and their contents removed by Samuel Carrington of Wetton and Thomas Bateman of Hartington. The pottery, bones, coins and other grave goods that they found are now mostly in Sheffield museum.

There are caves too. The best known, of course, is **Thor's Cave** which lies 0.5m SW of Wetton, approached by a track. The cave overlooks the Manifold Valley and the views are dramatic. It is, however, quite dangerous. The rocks at the entrance to the cave are very worn and shiny, making them quite slippery. Anyone falling from here would be unlikely to survive. The approach track is safe enough though and the views from the bluff are excellent. Many prehistoric and Romano-British finds were made in the floor of the cave when it was excavated.

Elderbush Cave is situated at SK 098549, on the 900-foot contour just south of Thor's Cave. When it was excavated finds from the Old Stone Age, New Stone Age, Bronze Age and Romano-British period were found. When the cave was first rediscovered in 1935 the entrance was obscured by an elder bush, hence its name.

Between 1848 and 1852 the fields known as the **'Borough Hole'**, near Wetton, were archaeologically examined and the remains of many dwellings found. These were probably the homes of workmen in the Roman lead mines. There were numerous finds of pottery, iron utensils, coins (from AD 253-337), glass, a bronze ring, skeletons and enamelled jewellery. The site has long been used by local people as a source of building stone.

At **Long Low Cairns** (SK 122539), 1.25m SE of Wetton, at the end of a track that leads directly to them, are two round mounds linked by a stone bank. This is unique. The larger mound is 8 feet high and 75 feet in diameter, and inside was a closed stone grave chamber containing 13 bodies and three leaf-shaped, flint arrowheads. These were probably Late Neolithic people who lived about 2,000 BC.

The village of Wetton is small, nucleated and built of stone. There is a pub and a church. St Margaret's has a strongly-built medieval tower, but most of the rest was rebuilt in 1820 to a Gothic style with pointed windows. The large corner stones are a feature of the structure. Samuel Carrington, the excavator of pre-historic graves, lies buried here. One wonders how he would feel if someone dug him up and removed his bones to a store room in Sheffield Museum.

Redhurst Gorge in the Manifold Valley runs around the foot of Wetton Hill. It might have derived its name from 'red deer hurst' and is said to be haunted by Hob i' th' Hurst. Old Hannah's Cave, named after a witch who once lived there, is in the Redhurst Gorge. Unexplained explosion sounds were heard emanating from the cave in 1855, 1869 and 1896. (For Wetton Mill see pages 72 and 181.)

WHEATON ASTON *8.5m SW of Stafford*

The village lies 1.5m N of the A5. In the centre are some attractive old houses. One large black-and-white house is especially good but has been spoilt by having lost its garden to development. All around modern estates proliferate. This is no longer a country village.

The church of St Mary is of 1857, with a chancel of 1893 and stained glass by Kempe in the east window. There is also a Primitive Methodist Chapel of 1856 in Georgian style with a round-headed window. The north-west edge of the village is touched by the Shropshire Union Canal, and where landway and waterway meet is the Hartley Arms. The country around is flat and was presumably an area where wheat was grown. Aston, of course, means 'east town'. Wheaton Aston Old Hall lies alongside the A5. The New Hall stands close by but is set back from the road. Wheaton Aston now has an annual Folk Festival which is increasing in popularity. The site of Pennocruciam lies 3m SE.

Marston, 1m NW of Wheaton Aston, is a small hamlet on low ground which, in 1652, was recorded as Marston under le Seard. At one time there was well dressing at Marston. The site of the medieval village, now deserted, can be seen on aerial photographs at SJ 624275. Marston has historically been connected administratively with Whitgreave.

Shushions Manor, 1m WNW of Wheaton Aston, was called Sceotestan in Domesday Book. The name probably means 'Sceto's stone', Sc(e)to being an Anglo-Saxon personal name thought to indicate someone who was a good archer. The present manor house only dates from the early 19th Century, but to the east of the house there is a deep, curved moat and other earthworks, probably the site of a deserted medieval village. In 1780 a skeleton in a full set of Civil War period armour was found in a watercourse near, or at, Shushions - the end of a story with no known beginning.

Motty Meadows, 1.5m WNW of Wheaton Aston, is an ancient water meadow with 240 species of wild flowers and grasses. It is the most northerly location of the lily Snake's Head fritillary in the British Isles. and in 1982 was created a National Nature Reserve. Signs of a shallow water channel remain.

WHISTON *3m NE of Cheadle*

Whiston is a substantial stone-built village on the A52, in the hills lm E of Froghall. The church of St Mildred is of 1910 by J M Becket and is pleasant enough. Whiston Hall (or Manor Farm as some call it) dominates the village. It lies on the top of the hill, large and built of ashlar stone and very blackened. It is now the club-house of the local golf course.

Behind the Hall is the Whiston Incline. The Incline is made of earth and supported a plateway which carried trucks of limestone that came from Cauldon Lowe quarries and went on down to the Caldon Canal at Froghall. Between Cauldon Lowe and Froghall is a distance of four miles and the vertical drop is 649 feet.

Copper from the great Ecton mine, 10m NE, was smelted at Whiston from 1770 to 1890. Almost the only sign of this industry today is slag, some of which has been used as a building material. In the 1680s stone, for use as hearths in iron furnaces was quarried on Whiston Moor. Coal outcrops in the Whiston area.

Whiston Eaves lies 0.5m SE of Whiston along the road to Oakamoor. There is little here but a few cottages and the ashlar gatehouse-stable block of Whiston Eaves Hall. The Hall was pulled down and the stone taken away and reused to build houses for the senior management of British Industrial Sand, a local farmer told us. One of these houses is at Hollington. BIS have huge quarries here from which they extract sand. This is processed in what is said to be the most advanced purification plant in Europe. Flint glass sand is supplied for the manufacture of a variety of commodities - glazes, pottery paint, asbestos sheets, abrasive cleaners and even milk bottles. The quarries are connected to the main line railway by the old North Staffordshire Railway line. This follows the Churnet Valley northwards, through Consall Forge and Cheddleton. Most of the sand is taken to the Pilkington works in St Helens, Lancashire.

In 1866 a poacher, William Collier, was found guilty, on circumstantial evidence, of shooting dead the son of the local squire who lived at Whiston Farm. Collier was hanged outside Stafford prison, the last man to be executed there.

Near Whiston Eaves, on the road to Oakamoor, is a quaint little smallholding. The house is built against a rock outcrop, a place of great character.

Preston Vale, 0.5m ENE of Whiston, is a 17th Century farmhouse. The name means 'the priest's house' and there was a chapel in a nearby field. The tall chimney at the end of the farm buildings of Preston Vale House belonged to a former steam mill here.

WHITGREAVE *3.5m NNW of Stafford*
The name means 'white grove'. It lies between the A34 and the M6, a little rural village spoilt by the roar of the motorway. The church of St John is of 1844, in brick with a bellcote and pointed windows. There was a custom here whereby a young girl would pin an ash tree leaf above her front door. The first man to enter would have the name of the man she would marry. The Whitgreaves of Burton Manor and Moseley Old Hall took their names from this village.

WHITMORE *4m SW of Newcastle-under-Lyme*
Whitmore lies on the A53, Market Drayton to Newcastle-under-Lyme road. It was on one of the notoriously bad bends on this road at Whitmore that Gordon Banks, the Stoke City and England goalkeeper, had the car accident which resulted in his losing the sight of one eye. This ended the career of a man who is generally accepted as having been the best goalkeeper the world has ever seen.

Whitmore is an unpretentious but most attractive village. The first lord of the manor we know by name was John de Whitmore (died 1208), but what we see today is very much the making of the Mainwearings, who can trace their line and tenure of the estate as far back as 1546, when Alice de Boghay married Edward Mainwearing. (Mainwearing is pronounced 'Mannering'.) In all that time the manor has never been sold and has only passed on by inheritance. The present squire maintains a keen interest in the village. There are trim little estate cottages, the Mainwearing Arms, a craft shop in the premises of the original pub, a bridge across the stream and the charming church.

St Mary and All Saints has a timber-framed bell-turret and a timber-framed gable. Parts of the north and south walls are Norman and inside is an alabaster effigy of Edward Mainwearing, died 1586. The Hall faces the church down an avenue of mature lime trees - a most splendid sight. The old four-storey, timber-framed manor house is encased in brick. The handsome south front that faces the church is of 1676. It has nine bays and two storeys with a top balustrade. The porch is of 1847 and the entrance hall, with its Corinthian columns, is mid-Georgian.

The stable block is as good as the house. It dates from about 1625 and the horse boxes are in beautiful, original condition. A road leads northwards to Keele, past the Stable Block, and on up the hill from where one can look down on the fishing lakes and lodge embowered in trees. The lane continues up and a track forks left to the Moathouse and Woodhouse, both names implying late forest clearance.

The Whitmore Gap is a low point in the Trent-Mersey watershed, which is utilised by the main line railway. At the top of the hill, north-west of the village, the A53 is joined by the A5182 to Trentham. This was a new road made in 1845.

Samuel Stone, the author of the famous hymn 'The Church's One Foundation', was born at Whitmore Rectory in 1839.

Baldwin's Gate, 1m SW of Whitmore, is a small residential village on the Newcastle-under-Lyme to Shrewsbury road, the A53. In recent times some new houses have been built. One of these developments consists of superior modern houses arranged around a lake and is most attractive.

There are two village shops, a sub-Post Office, the Sheet Anchor pub and a service station. The village developed after the arrival of the railway in 1837 but the station is now closed.

The name Baldwin's Gate is recorded in a Madeley Manor document of 1511, long before the turnpiking of the roads. Therefore, it is likely that Mr Baldwin was a gate-keeper at one of the gated entrances to the large Madeley Deer Park, just to the north-west.

Whitmore Heath, lies on high ground, 0.5m W of Whitmore. The common land was enclosed as late as 1841. There are two burial mounds: one at SJ 797404 and one at SJ 798405. Today Whitmore Heath is a well-wooded upmarket residential area.

Shelton-under-Harley, 1m SSE of Whitmore, is a tiny place to the west of Swynnerton Old Park. The author remembers the sad time when he spent six months searching for the three dogs who went missing from his home. He had numerous 'phone calls of possible sightings. One was from a farm at Shelton-under-Harley. They had a stray Border-Collie-cross that matched the description of Lady, one of my dogs. It was not her, but the farmer's wife said that dogs who had got lost in the woods of Swynnerton Old Park often came to them.

John Dimmock, a pottery manufacturer, was born in the hamlet about 1819. He was saved from the depredations of the Chartists because he was considered to be a friend of the working classes.

WHITTINGTON *3m E of Lichfield*

To the north and east the village is bounded by the Coventry Canal, and to the south are the 'danger areas' of army rifle ranges. On **Whittington Heath**, 0.5m south, are the grim bastions of Whittington Barracks, home to nine regiments.

The barracks were built in 1881 under the Cardwell Army Reforms and extended in later years. They were originally constructed to house the North Staffordshire and the South Staffordshire Regiments, which were amalgamated in 1959 to form the Staffordshire Regiment (The Prince of Wales'), but there have been many comings and goings of different units over the years. In 1969 the museum of the Staffordshire Regiment was built and is open to the public. There are many interesting items of memorabilia from old wars and far-away places. In the 19th Century horse races were held on Whittington Heath.

In the village church of St Giles is the rather grand Century pulpit of 1671, which had been removed from Lichfield Cathedral by Gilbert Scott during his restoration of the building in the second half of the 19th Century. The tower of St Giles is medieval, the brick nave and the ashlar bays are of 1761, the chancel is of 1881 by Ewan Christian, and there is some restored 15th Century stained glass. Preserved in the church is the flute of William Bass, who accompanied the singing here from 1800 to 1867. All manner of solo instruments and 'rustic ensembles' of violins, trumpets, oboes and the like were common in country churches in the days before organs became commonplace.

Whittington appears to have had five Halls at various times but only Whittington Hall No 5 still survives. It is mostly of 1891, when the 17th Century brick house was much enlarged for Samuel Lipscomb. On the garden side is the handsome stone porch from the original house. The gate posts are also original and dated at 1673. On the road to Fisherwick, just past the Hall, are two splendid half-timbered houses, Old Timbers and Long Meadow. The infilling is of brick and they stand about a cobbled court facing the road. Both have been extremely well renovated and restored.

Fisherwick Park lies 0.75m NE of Whittington on the wide, flat plain of the River Mease. The medieval village was obliterated when the park of the 16th Century Hall was extended in the 1750s. On behalf of the Marquis of Donegal the hall was rebuilt in 1774 by 'Capability' Brown, who also landscaped the park to form noteworthy gardens. Sad to say, in 1810 the estate was bought by the Howard family of Elford, who demolished the house and ploughed up the park. All that remains are the large gate piers, a lodge house and some outbuildings in Fisherwick Hall Farm. There is a local tradition that the bricks used to construct the wall of the Park were originally intended for the unbuilt centre part of the house Charles Pye partly erected at Clifton Campville.

The Fisherwick area is rich in Prehistoric remains: post holes of a Middle Bronze Age settlement; an Iron Age settlement on a terrace beside the river Tame, north of Brook Leasowe; and a Romano-British stock-raising farm (villa) of the 2nd and 3rd Centuries AD, on the west bank of the Tame. The name Fisherwick means 'the homestead of the fisherman'.

Just to the east of Whittington Barracks, and clearly visible from the A51, is the handsome, cream-washed, 18th Century **Packington Hall**. It is fronted by a line of trees and stands amidst huge arable fields. It is now used as offices by Gills Cables Ltd. The sound of gunfire echoes all around from the army rifle ranges which encircle it to the rear.

Darnford, 1.5m W of Whittington, is a small hamlet whose name means 'the hidden (or secret) ford'.

WIGGINTON *1.25m N of Tamworth*
Wigginton is a small village 0.5m N of the suburbs of Tamworth. It is an Anglo-

Saxon settlement and after the Norman Conquest was kept by the king. It lay within the Royal Forest of Cannock and in 1266 it was noted that the tenants of the manor had rights of 'husbote and heybote' in a wood owned by the manor. By 1340 there was a fulling mill here. The attractive brick church of St Leonard is of 1777, by Joyce of Burton, with a later Gothic chancel of 1862. It has a gallery, round-headed windows and two columns which support the small square turret-tower.

Hanging Hill, to the north of the settlement, suggests it was a gallows' site, and there was a windmill at Wigginton Farm, 1m S of the church, which had been dismantled by 1883. An Anglo-Saxon trackway, thought to be a salt road, ran though Wigginton as evidenced by Salters Lane and other signs.

Wigginton Lodge, 1.25m S of Wigginton, is a brick house with stucco made to look like ashlar stone. Tamworth Rugby Union Football Club use a modern annexe to the house. Their ground is in Wigginton Park which adjoins the Lodge.

Comberford, 1.25m WNW of Wigginton, was a medieval village, now reduced to a hamlet. It stands near the River Tame. The name means 'the valley ford'. There is an unconsecrated mission chapel licensed for services. The present Comberford Hall, 0.5m S of Comberford, dates from the early 19th Century. Today, it has been reduced in status to a block of flats.

WIGHTWICK *2.25m W of Wolverhampton town centre*
Wightwick (pronounced 'Whitick') used to belong to the manor of Tettenhall. Today, they both belong to Wolverhampton and both are upmarket residential areas - the leafiest of leafy suburbs. There are many good houses here, ranging from the large, red brick Wightwick Hall (now a council special school) to little, old cottages.

Wightwick lies on the bluff that overlooks the Staffordshire and Worcestershire Canal and is best approached along the A454, Wolverhampton to Bridgnorth road. The star attraction here is Wightwick Manor. Superficially, it looks old, but is in fact of the late 19th Century. It was built by Edward Quid of Liverpool for Theodore Mander, who paid for it from the profits of his paint and varnish business. (His main factory was right in the heart of Wolverhampton where the Mander Centre now stands.) The Manor is not only a beautiful and interesting house, it is also on a scale that is suitable for living in. The left-hand half of the house (as seen from the garden) was built in 1887 and is part timber-framed and part bright Ruabon brick and hung tiles. On this side is the short tower that contains the entrance. The right-hand side is of 1893 and is almost all timber-framed and highly decorated above the low sandstone foundation plinth. The chimneys on this side are tall and have candy twists. The entrance leads to a long corridor. In the left and older part of the house are the Drawing Room and the Library. In the right-hand part are the Great Parlour of two storeys, the Dining Room and the Billiard Room.

All the rooms are decorated with an impressive collection of the works of the pre-Raphaelites and the William Morris school of design. There are stained glass windows by Kempe; rugs, textiles, wallpapers and tapestries by Morris; and tiles by de Morgan. The furniture, though, is a motley crew and includes a settle by Bodley, a folding chair by Swinburne, a cupboard painted by Treffry Dunn, an Italian Renaissance chimney piece and some new-Jacobean plaster ceilings by L A Shuffrey. The gardens around the house have both formal and natural areas and were designed by Alfred Parsons, with a later terrace by T H Mawson. The

Lodge and the Barn are all that is left of the previous late 16th Century Manor House and were grossly over-restored by Ould. In 1937 Sir Geoffrey and Lady Mander made over the house and gardens to the National Trust.

North-east of Wightwick Manor is the Mount Hotel in Mount Road. This was the home of Charles Benjamin Mander, cousin of Theodore. It was built about 1870 and extended in 1891 and 1908. In Church Road is Christ Church, constructed of rusticated stone in 1866 by Bateman and Corser, with some stained glass by Kempe. On the main road is The Mermaid pub, a favourite meeting place of the well-heeled local youth.

To the south, over the Smestow Brook and the Staffordshire-Worcestershire Canal (1772), is **Castlecroft**. It takes its name from a farm in the valley but most of the houses of this good-class residential area lie on the high ground. There is a United Reform Church (St Columba), a Catholic Church (St Pius X), several schools, a family park, a bird sanctuary and the locally well-known Castlecroft Hotel, which is happily surrounded by a cricket pitch, a football pitch and a sports ground. The Windmill, on Windmill Bank, ceased working in the 1880s. It has a red brick barrel tower and was built by John Chamberlin in 1720. Abounding Wightwick to the north was the old wartime Perton aerodrome on which, in the 1980s, have been built several large, modern housing estates.

WILBRIGHTON *2.75m SW of Gnosall*
At the time of the Domesday Book it was called Wilbrestone. All there is today is the Hall. There may have been a medieval village at SJ 795187, which was probably deserted in the 17th Century, and there was a late 18th Century windmill on Windmill Bank, 0.5m W of Wilbrighton, but by 1958 only a few stones were left.

Wilbrighton Hall hit the headlines in 1992 because Kevin Barry O'Donnell was living there with other students. They were studying agriculture at the nearby Harper Adams College. O'Donnell had been on the raid that blew up the Clive army barracks at Tern Hill in 1989. He was later shot dead in an SAS ambush at Coalisland, County Tyrone.

Wilbrighton Hall is a Tudor mansion situated at the end of a long, straight lane that leads off the A518, Newport to Stafford road, at SJ 795186. It stands on a bluff between a copse of pine trees and a yew-screened garden, to the right, and its extensive farm buildings (dated 1831), to the left. Just to the east is the route of the Roman road which connected Whitchurch to Stretton (near Penkridge), and just to the south is the disused track of the Newport to Stafford railway.

The house is not unhandsome - a red brick pile of three storeys with stone dressings, gables, prominent chimneys and cast-iron latticed windows. The north gable is dated 1865, but part of this and the whole of the south and west walls are Tudor. From the north side there are long views over the watery woods of the Aqualate estate. The south side of the house was probably the original front. It has less spectacular views but faces the sun.

The countryside around is most attractive, with many small woods and small marshes between the pastures and along the shores of the beautiful lake of Aqualate. The police anti-terrorist unit is convinced that there is at least one major arms' and explosives' cache hidden in the area. There have been intensive searches but, as yet, nothing has been found. The secret of its location lies buried with O'Donnell.

WILLENHALL *3m E of Wolverhampton*

At the time of Domesday Book 'Winehale' belonged to the king and was a Royal Manor. By the 19th Century the following rhyme was current:

A tumbledown church,
A tottering steeple,
A drunken parson,
And a wicked people.

There is many a true word spoken in jest. The church did in fact become unsafe and was rebuilt three times; the Reverend Moreton was a 19th Century vicar who drank, gambled and interrupted sermons to attend cock fights; and Willenhall was known nationally as a cruel place where young and old worked long hours for little pay and where the children were 'beaten shamefully with horsewhip, strap, stick, hammer, handle, file or whatever tool is nearest to hand'.

The tool nearest to hand would probably have been one used in the manufacture of locks. Ninety per cent of the locks made in England today are made in Willenhall. It was for long a craft industry because most of the parts of the lock mechanism had to be filed by hand. This was not only skilled work, it was hard work and the men of Willenhall were known for their stoops and humpbacks - 'Umpshire' they called the area in other parts of the Black Country. Not until 1856 was the drop forge used to press parts into shape.

Two of the largest firms today are Josiah Parkes, who were originally iron-merchants and turned to lock making in 1896; and Yale, founded by the American, Linus Yale, who invented the pin tumbler lock and set up in Willenhall in 1929.

There are two lock museums in the town. One is the privately owned National Lock Museum in New Road, which is housed in an old locksmith's shop that has been in continuous use since the 1840s. The other is in Walsall Street, next to the library. In the Market Square there is a large stone sculpture of a lock with inscriptions around the base.

The parish church of St Giles is dedicated to the patron saint of cripples, reputedly because in Spring Lane there was a well whose waters cured the sick, especially those who suffered complaints of the eyes and skin. The present church has a tall tower with pinnacles, and was built by W D Griffin of Wolverhampton in 1867. St Stephen's in Wolverhampton Street is also by W D Griffin, of 1854. St Anne's in Ann (sic) Street is by H Jeavons, of 1856.

In 1849 there was an outbreak of cholera in the town and not enough room in the churchyard to bury the victims. In the residential area of **Little London** a piece of land once owned by Dr Richard Wilkes (died 1760) was used to take the overspill, and 211 (out of 292) corpses were interred there. The burial ground is known as Doctor's Piece and is now a well-wooded Memorial Garden. Just north of Willenhall town centre is a traditional industrial area: small workshops in old Victorian buildings and converted terraced houses. Here, facing an almost abandoned cemetery, is the Yale works.

One mile north is **Ashmore Lake**, where in recent times a large industrial estate has grown up on reclaimed derelict land. There are still undeveloped areas, romantically gorse-clad and wild looking. 'Enhancement Schemes' are in progress all about.

Portobello, 0.5m W of Willenhall centre, on the road to Wolverhampton, is a mixed residential-industrial area. The name comes from the Portobello lock works of Josiah Parkes (Union Locks). It was once the fashion to give factories exotic names, and as these were proudly displayed in large letters on walls and chimneys it was natural for local people to call the area by that name. (Portobello, in Panama, was captured by Admiral Vernon in 1739.) The substantial residential area south of the main road is also now a part of Portobello. One mile east of Willenhall is Bentley, which has its own article.

Tony Portlock and his wife Barbara live in Aston Road, Willenhall. Tony is a popular folk singer and finger-style guitarist, who has been a leading figure on the Midlands' folk scene for many years.

Pool Hayes, 1.25m NNE of Willenhall, is a residential suburb with a large comprehensive school, built from 1965. There was formerly a farm here called Pool Hayes.

WOLVERHAMPTON *16m S of Stafford*

Wolverhampton is an ancient hill town, and the raised mound on which the parish church stands was quite probably of significance to prehistoric man. By the mid-9th Century it was an Anglo-Saxon religious centre, and the 14-foot-high pillar that stands by the entrance of St Peter's church dates from this time. It is covered in badly-worn carvings, one of which appears to be of a dragon, and was almost certainly a Preaching Cross. The first church was probably of timber.

In 985 Lady Wulfruna, the sister of King Edgar, was granted land in Heantun by King Ethelred, and in 994 she endowed this land to the church of St Mary. Shortly after, Heantun (meaning 'High Town') became Wulfruna's Heantun, later corrupted to Wolverhampton. The Minster Church of St Mary served a wide area. The parish system was not yet established and the Christian religion was administered by priests who travelled out from Minster Churches. They preached under trees, often yew trees, at specially erected preaching crosses and even in old pagan temples.

In the reign of Henry III (1216-1271) the church of St Mary was re-dedicated to St Peter. It was now a collegiate church - a Royal Free Chapel - answerable to the King, not to the church. Collegiate churches were powerful, influential and richly endowed with land. St. Peter's is a large church and reflects both its own prosperity and that of the town. (There is more about St. Peter's later in this article.)

Wolverhampton grew rich on the wool trade in the 14th and 15th Centuries. There was a large market place to the south-west of the church and the memory of this is preserved in names such as Blossom's Fold, Mitre Fold, Wadham's Fold, Exchange Street and Cheapside. The word Cheapside is derived from the Old English for 'market'. The market place has been in-filled with buildings since Victorian times, and the process was completed in 1978, when the new, red brick Civic Offices (designed by Clifford Culpin) were erected in the last open space between the Old Town Hall and the church.

Wolverhampton in the 15th Century was a handsome place, full of richly adorned merchants' houses, inns and hostelries. As late as 1868 Elihu Burntt was able to write of Wolverhampton: 'Look at this town ... Few in England wear seemingly more antiquity in general aspect. Here are houses built in Elizabeth's day . . .' One of the houses that Burntt saw was the Old Hall, the moated mansion of the Leveson wool merchants and future Dukes of Sutherland, whose house survived to be used as a late 19th Century japanning works. It stood on the site now occupied by the Central Library. The road at the back of the Library is still called Old Hall Street.

Another old house was the Deanery, reputedly the most beautiful Elizabethan house in the town. It stood on the site of the new Polytechnic and was demolished in 1921. The only building to survive from this period is the small, 16th Century, timber-framed house on the corner of Victoria Street and St John's Street, which was zealously over-restored in 1979-81.

After the decline of the wool trade Wolverhampton continued to prosper through the 16th and 17th Centuries as a market town, and in the 18th Century a variety of industries took root. Architecturally the early 18th Century is represented by two buildings. The unexciting Molyneux Hotel is of about 1740-50, the old home of the Molyneux family and has two fronts. The earlier faces the Ring Road and has five bays and three storeys. The new front is at the back and has two richly decorated Venetian windows. The turret is Victorian and there have been several extensions. A little earlier in date, at 1728, is Giffard House, the town house of the Giffard family of Chillington which stands near the Civic Hall. The Roman Catholic church of St Peter and St Paul was built on to the back of the house in 1828. The stuccoed church was designed by Joseph Ireland and has shallow domes and high, moon-shaped windows. (Note: in the 17th Century Wolverhampton was 'the strongest Catholic centre in England'. In 1688 the Pope appointed Boneventure Giffard Vicar Apostolic of the Midlands.)

Also of the Georgian period is the 18th Century George Street with elegant houses leading to the east end of St John's Church. The church was built in 1758-76, by either William Baker or Roger Eykyn. It is ashlar, is not altogether in proportion and inside has three galleries. The organ is of about 1682 by Renatus Harris and was formerly in the Temple Church, London. It is an instrument of some renown.

One of the most attractive streets in Wolverhampton is King Street, where a row of small Georgian houses form a delightful ensemble.

The continuing prosperity of the town can be judged by the fact that in 1763 no less than seven turnpiked roads met here. Not only was there a Corn Exchange, a weekly market and a horsefair, but the metal trades were becoming established, the canals were arriving and Wolverhampton was entering an age of prosperity matched perhaps, but not exceeded, by any other town in England. That this is not reflected in its public buildings has been noted by more than one observer. The explanation seems to be quite simply that 'they took their money home and spent it there'. Certainly, the workers saw little of the profits. However, drive down Tettenhall Road to Tettenhall, Penn Road to Penn or Compton Road to Compton and you will see the houses built by the wealthier Victorians and Edwardians.

Around the town centre were the courts and passages of the artisans, the slums and squalor that led to outbreaks of cholera in 1832, 1849 and 1872. In 1849 an asylum was established for children made orphans by the plague. This became the now highly-respected Royal Wolverhampton School in Penn Road. The impressive buildings date from 1853 and were designed by Joseph Manning, with wings added in 1863. The Headmaster's House is of 1885 and the chapel, which has stained glass by William Kempe, is of 1895.

The town became a Jack of All Trades and because of this diversity was never hit by the recessions that inevitably affected some individual industries. Of particular importance were iron-working (Bayliss), japanning (Mander), lock making (Chubb), railway rolling stock (GWR), bicycles (Rudge), motor-cars (Sunbeam), motor-cycles (AJS), lorries (Guys) and brewing. Little wonder that between 1801 and 1901 the population of the town rose from 12,500 to 95,000.

In 1848 Wolverhampton became a borough and its first mayor was George Benjamin Thorneycroft, an ironmaster. Two years later the Oxford and Worcestershire Railway arrived, followed by the Shrewsbury to Birmingham and Great Western in 1845.

During the 19th Century the town was virtually rebuilt. As was so often the case the wealth created by industry financed wholesale and largely indiscriminate redevelopment. It was 'farewell and adieu to Old England' and 'all hail the Age of Steam'. The greater part of Wolverhampton today is Victorian (1837-1901) and Edwardian (1901-1910) but there has also been some rebuilding in recent years, especially in the Chapel Ash area, at the end of Darlington Street. Here amorphous concrete giants clad with red bricks stand gazing coldly at the traffic rushing around the new Ring Road. Having done their worst at the west end of town the planners are now exercising their talents at the east end. To the sturdy Classical ashlar of St George's church is now attached a flimsy bit of whimsy under whose roof Mr Sainsbury trades. Of more lasting benefit to the community was the recent mass modernisation of Victorian terraces in areas like Whitmore Reans.

From the humble to the high, a further word on the parish church. The red sandstone church of St Peter is an ancient foundation but the fabric that we see today owes much to the vigorous restoration carried out by Ewan Christian in 1852-65. What is old are the crossing arches which support the crossing tower, the excellent five-light east window and the piscina (wash basin) in the south wall, all of which are of the 13th Century. The north transept, the embattled and pinnacled tower itself, and the windows in the south transept and the nave clerestory are all Perpendicular. The nave is of about 1460. The chancel and apse were rebuilt by Christian and the porch is largely Victorian. The pulpit was donated by the Swynnerton family.

There are monuments to the Levesons in the south (Leveson) chapel, including a bronze of Admiral Sir Richard Leveson, died about 1634, by le Scour. In the north (Lane) chapel are monuments to the Lane family, including the tomb of Thomas and Katharine Lane (1582), and the wall monument of Colonel John Lane, died 1667, who aided King Charles II in his escape after the Battle of Worcester.

There are stained glass windows by Kempe and Powell, and some 16th and 17th Century, Dutch and German stained glass medallions in the chancel. The stalls are 15th Century and came from Lilleshall Abbey. They were given to the church by the Leveson family in 1546 (at the Dissolution of the Monasteries).

In 1479 Edward IV united the Deanery of St Peter's with that of Windsor and this Royal Peculiar lasted until 1846.

The markets, both open and covered, have long been banished to the edge of the town centre (Salop Street-School Street) and are housed in a building by A G E Chapman, who must have been given a very small budget. Opposite the new, red brick Civic Offices are the old Town Hall of 1869, by Ernest Bates, and the unprepossessing Civic Hall of 1938 with its giant Classical portico.

The village green of the original settlement was called High Green and occupied the site now called Queen's Square. The Queen, of course, was Victoria. In Queen's Square is a statue of Prince Albert on horseback (1866) by Thomas Thorneycroft. This was unveiled by Queen Victoria herself and was her first engagement after the death of her consort. She travelled by train and is reputed to have ordered the blinds to be drawn over her railway carriage window so that she would not have to witness the horrors of the Black Country. On arrival at the station in Wolverhampton she walked beneath a triumphal arch of coal, especially erected as a symbol of the wealth of the area.

There is an entry off the square to the Mander Centre, a large, modern shopping precinct designed by James Roberts and built in 1968-70. It contains the largest Woolworth's store in Europe. The precinct is built on the site formerly occupied by the Wolverhampton Grammar School, founded by the wealthy wool merchant, Sir Stephen Jenys, in 1512. The school was rebuilt in 1717 and demolished in 1964. Also on the site was the paint and varnish factory founded by Charles Mander in the late 18th Century. The new factory is now more suitably located in Heath Town.

Lichfield Street leads off Queen's Square and here, separated from the church by pleasant gardens, is the Museum and Art Gallery. This most attractive building was built in 1883-5 to a design by J A Chatwin. It is Italianate with coupled Ionic columns of pink granite supporting the porch, and sculptured panels in the upper part, which is windowless, light being admitted by means of skylights. The Polytechnic (College of Technology) buildings, new and old have a large physical presence in the town centre. The main range was designed by P Woodcock and built in 1926, and there have been several additions since. The most recent faces Wadham's Fold. It is of red brick and glass, has a small garden, and is not unattractive. Back in Lichfield Street, but further down and within view of the entrance to the new Station, is the Grand Theatre, built in 1894 to a design by C J Phipps. It is of brick with a loggia of arcading above the entrance. Inside it is superb. A Victorian Baroque theatre to be proud of.

Nearby is Queen Street, said by some to be the best street in the town. Here are the stuccoed offices of the Army Recruiting Centre, with five bays and two entrances, which was built as the Mechanics' Institute and Athenaeum in 1835. The County Court is of 1813, a late Georgian building with an upper floor of 1829. It has seven bays and two Tuscan porches, and was originally built as a Library and Assembly Room. Here, also, are the modern offices of the Express and Star Newspaper and the former Dispensary of 1826, with seven stuccoed bays and Greek Doric half-columns on the upper storey.

Today, Wolverhampton has a very large shopping centre which has the great advantage of being compact. It attracts people from as far away as North and Central Wales. It is a terminus of the new Metro railway.

Here are some buildings and their dates: St Mary & St John RC, Snowhill, 1855, by Charles Hansom; St Patrick RC, Westbury Street, 1867, by E W Pugin; House of Mercy RC, St John's Square with a Gothic brick range in George Street, both of 1860, by E W Pugin; Methodist Chapel, Darlington Street, 1901 by Arthur Marshall, large with copper domes and turrets; the old station ticket office, 1849, on the corner of Railway Street and Horsley Fields, high Italianate in grey brick with columns and turrets; the Polytechnic Department of Art and design, 1969, an eight-storey glass box and pretty awful, with a grotesque collection of iron on the roof; the library, 1900-2, by E T More, an attractive building of brick and yellow terracotta; the Grammar School, Compton Road, 1875, by Giles and Gough in brick to a handsome Gothic design by Thomas Gates; and off Queen's Square there is an eight-bay Georgian house of 1726.

Waterloo Road could have been a gem but large parts have been demolished and redeveloped, although enough remains of the mid-19th Century villas to show what might have been. The house now occupied by Walker Barnet & Hill was the home of the remarkable Macdonald sisters, all of whom married worthy and well-known Victorian gentlemen.

Wolverhampton has produced several other personalities who have gained national and even international reputations. Amongst these is Samson, an ecclesiastic who owned land in Wolverhampton during the 11th Century. He is listed in Domesday Book with the clergy of the town but was in fact a person of some consequence. He was Chaplain to King William and later became the Bishop of Worcester (1096-1112). He was also probably the editor of Domesday Book. The teams of commissioners, who had visited all parts of the country and returned with the answers to their set questionnaires on land ownership and taxable value, reported to the editor. He corrected and wrote the actual book, though not necessarily the fair copy that has come down to us.

In about 1682 one of the most notorious criminals in British history was born at Boningale, a picturesque village seven miles west of Wolverhampton. He was Jonathan Wild, who became a buckle maker in Birmingham, married, deserted his wife and child and went to London. He got into debt and was put into prison where he made the acquaintance of many thieves, highwaymen and robbers. He lived with a prostitute, and from the Cock Inn at Cripplegate set up an organization that virtually controlled the whole of the criminal underworld in London. The criminals brought their loot to Wild who paid them a small commission. He then offered to return the stolen goods to their rightful owners for a brokerage fee. He was amazingly successful and openly advertised himself as a restorer of property and a taker of thieves. Every now and then, a minor criminal would be sacrificed to avoid the charge that he was in collusion with his underworld colleagues. Wild had warehouses stuffed full of jewellery and other valuables, and even had a ship to transport unclaimed goods to the Continent. Indeed, it was the Captain of his sloop who finally betrayed him, and in 1725 he was hanged at Tyburn Hill. When John Gay wrote the Beggars' Opera (1729) he based the central character, Peachum, on Jonathan Wild.

In the 18th Century there was a Bluecoat School in Wolverhampton and on three occasions a small trader in the town signed the minutes of meetings held by the subscribers to the school. His name was Button Gwinnett and he had been born at the parsonage at Down Hatherley, Gloucestershire in 1732. After his sojourn in Wolverhampton he emigrated to America and in 1776 was elected one of the three representatives of the state of Georgia who drew up the Declaration of Independence. His signature was one of 55 that are now probably the most sought after and valuable in the world. Collectors want the complete set of Independence signatories and there are many that are complete except for the signature of Button Gwinnett. He was not a person of great note and there are less than 40 specimens of his signature extant. The Wolverhampton Bluecoat School signatures were sold many years ago for a lot of money. Today a Gwinnet signature would sell for many thousands of pounds.

In Exchange Street there is a plaque to Dame Maggie Teyte, the operatic singer, who was born in Wolverhampton in 1888, the tenth child of a publican and wine merchant. She became a world famous prima donna but died in poverty at the age of 84. She is said to have disliked the town intensely.

In the highly thought of West Park there is a statue to Sir Charles Pelham Villiers (1803-1897), of the motor-cycle engine firm, who lived to be 94 years of age and was an MP for Wolverhampton for 60 years. The West Park itself covers some 50 acres and was originally a racecourse.

Joseph Stawinoga, (born 1921 or 22), is a Polish man with a huge beard, wild eyes and an unkempt appearance, who has lived rough in Wolverhampton since the 1960s. Since the 1970s the council has allowed him to live in a tent on the central reservation of the dual carriageway opposite St John's church. Apparently, he is thought of as a holy man by the Asian community.

Alfred Noyes (1880-1958), the highly-acclaimed poet, author of the popular poems 'The Highwayman' and 'Song of England', and Professor of Poetry at Princeton, was born in Chapel Ash.

In 1968 Enoch Powell, an erudite classical scholar and the Conservative MP for Wolverhampton South-West, made his 'Rivers of Blood' speech, warning of the dangers of mass immigration. This caused a heated national debate.

The present Racecourse is at **Dunstall Park**, off the Stafford Road. The first race held here was in 1886. It lies in a valley bounded by canals to the north-west and north-east and the recently constructed new grandstand and all-weather course have been given a herd of small new houses for company. To the north-east is the impressive blue brick railway viaduct.

Autherley Junction lies 0.5m N of the racecourse. Here the Staffordshire and Worcestershire Canal joins the Shropshire Union Canal. Canals were essential to the early development of industry in the area. One of the most important was the Birmingham Canal. An unusual service was operated on this waterway by the Express Flyboats. These high-speed, passenger-carrying narrow-boats operated between Wolverhampton and Birmingham from the 1780s to about 1850, when the railways made them redundant. Travel by road was not especially comfortable and the boats offered a smooth ride that was beyond compare. Every whim and fancy was catered for and the craft were drawn by two horses instead of the customary one, enabling them to whizz around at about 9 mph.

The Wolverhampton Wanderers' Football Club (The Wolves), was founded in 1887 and moved to Molyneux in 1889. In 1893 it was one of the original 12 members of the Football League. The team and the club have been extremely successful in the past and have had many international players, of whom Billy Wright, the Captain of England for so many years, must be the most renowned. The club's new ground is an extravaganza of yellow steel frames.

Wolverhampton, or its people, are mentioned in the following folksongs: 'Song of a Strike' (by Wolverhampton tin plate workers in 1950), 'Foxy Southall', 'The Wedgebury Cocking', 'A Balloon Flew o'er Ampton Town', 'The Birmingham and Liverpool Railway (1838)', 'A Warning to Servant Maids', 'Hampton Lullaby' (M Raven), and 'Old Sam' (Peter Dodds). Now, a little on some of the suburbs of Wolverhampton.

Chapel Ash is a secondary shopping centre at the end of Darlington Street, within walking distance of the town centre. However, it is now cut off from the town by the new ring road and a monstrous traffic island which is encircled by high rise office blocks. Tucked away in the side streets is Banks's Brewery, frequently evident by its aroma. The company has its own private pipeline to the waterworks at Tettenhall. St Mark's, on the main road, is a Commissioners' church of 1899, to a design by C W Orford.

Whitmore Reans, 1m NW of Wolverhampton Centre, was formerly a part of a barren area called the Hungry Leas. The name is probably from 'white moor reans'; a rean was a gutter that was dug parallel to ploughed furrows to drain water on marshy ground.

When the area was developed for housing, from about 1880, it was officially called New Hampton, but the old name stuck and New Hampton is now only a road name. In the 20th Century the area became very rundown and in the 1980s it was made an Action Area and millions of pounds were spent renovating the houses - new roofs, bathroom extensions, new concrete floors, re-wiring, damp proof courses etc. Some were demolished to make space for new houses, green areas and a modern shopping precinct. However, there are still serious social problems in the area and on more than one occasion the police have had to barricade the police station to protect themselves from angry mobs. In Coleman Street is the stocky, modern, brick church of St Andrews, built in 1967 to a design by Twentyman, Percy and Partners. It boasts a west window designed by John Piper (made by Patrick Reyntiens), a rare treasure to find in Whitmore Reans.

Park Village, 1m NE of the town centre, is another lowly residential area. There are terraced houses and terraced houses, and those in Park village come bottom of the heap. Many have been cleared but some still stand as a memorial to 'the good old days'. The author lived in one, for a short time in the early 1960s, in Powell Street. Once or twice a week one trotted off with towel and soap to the public baths. Next door lived a retired miner, his last years made a misery by the effects of coal dust on his lungs - coughing and wheezing and hobbling painfully to the outside toilet in the rain.

If one follows Powell Street uphill to its end one arrives at **Heath Town**, 1m WSW of Wednesfield. This was formerly known as Wednesfield Heath but now belongs to Wolverhampton. The Grand Junction Railway came in 1837 but the station closed in 1910. The ashlar parish church of Holy Trinity was built in 1850-52 to a design by E Banks. Nearby are six attractive Almshouses for 12 widows, also built in the mid-19th Century. Heath Town developed quickly from the late 19th Century and industries included iron goods, such as locks, hinges, pumps and safes.

South east of the almshouses is a 20th Century mistake. The tower blocks point the way. At their feet are a rabbit's warren of concrete human hutches. Great, slab-like buildings with upper floor walkways that allow young hooligans to commit acts of vandalism, robbery and burglary and escape with ease. At night old people will not open their doors for anyone. These blocks, and nearby drinking places, are widely known to be the centre of drug dealing in Wolverhampton. Heath Town is a dangerous, ugly place. Ironically, when it was first built in the mid 1960s these new blocks were loudly lauded by architects and planners. Even the venerable Niklaus Pevsner had a good word for them.

Springfield adjoins Heath Town to the west. It lies between Cannock Road and Wednesfield Road. The original spring in a field attracted brewers of beer. The whole of Cambridge Street was lined with the tall brick walls that screened the tall, modern sheds of Mitchells and Butlers Springfield Brewery; it closed down in 1991. The spring has dried up because excessive amounts of water have been pumped out by the water authorities. On the Cannock Road, between the brewery and Johal Dairies, there is access to an attractive canal-side walk: distant chimneys, a forge being dismantled, an abandoned railway, a flight of locks on the canal - as Black Country a scene as ever there was. Facing the Wednesfield Road, opposite Inkerman Street, are the mundane offices of the famous Chubb lock and safe making company. They were once an eyesore; now they blend into the high-rise landscape of Heath Town quite nicely. Behind the offices are the works. In Springfield Road the sports' ground is now a housing estate. For the rest, Springfield is a residential area with Victorian terraces, post war council semis, some recent houses, the Freemason's Arms, the Woden Schools and the red brick Parish Church of Stephen the Martyr, built in 1909 to a design by F T Beck.

Neachells, 1m ENE of Wolverhampton and 0.5m S of Wednesfield, was a settlement in the 13th Century and in 1834 was still an isolated village. By the mid-20th Century it was part of the Black Country conurbation. Neachells Hall and its moat had disappeared by the early 20th Century, but we know that it was a 13th Century, two-storey house. At that time two storeys was exceptional and it was this characteristic which gave the place its name. 'Echelles' in Old French means 'ladders'. A ladder was used to get to the second floor in early two-storey houses. In the 1850s it became a beer house called The Board and later became derelict.

Blakenhall, a SSW suburb of Wolverhampton, became a separate parish in 1861. The parish church is dedicated to St Luke (1860-1). It is a mixed residential area, bounded by Penn Road to the west and Dudley Road to the east. Here is the Royal Wolverhampton School, already mentioned. The Blakenhall Gardens' high-rise flats arose in 1976.

Wolverhampton Wanderers' Football Club was founded in 1876 with young people from this parish. After several moves and amalgamations the club moved to Molyneaux in 1889.

In 1996 Lisa Potts, a teacher at St Luke's Nursery School, was awarded the George Medal for bravery for protecting young children from an attack by a deranged, machete-wielding man.

From an earlier time came the ratcatcher called 'Hairy' Kelly. Kelly kept the rats he caught and supplied them to men who organised rat fights. Rats were put in a pit and bets were placed as to which terrier dog could kill the most in a given time. It was not unusual for the dog to be able to kill 100 rats in 10 minutes. Much to my surprise the local naturalist, Phil Drabble, is in print saying: "I have never been to a rat-pit …. much as I should like to go." Shame on you, Mr Drabble.

Horsley Fields, 0.75m ESE of Wolverhampton centre, was formerly an 'open field' but is now an industrial suburb. The workhouse of 1700 was adapted by Chubb as a lock factory in 1841.

In more recent times the Commercial Road/Walsall Street area has become a red light district. At Horsley Fields Junction the Birmingham Main Line Canal joins the Wyrley and Essington Canal.

Merridale is an old residential area west of Blakenhall, across the Penn Road. Bantock Park is the attraction here - not so much the park, which is little more than a lawn, but Bantock House. Here there is a fine collection of Bilston enamels. The name Bantock probably means 'Banna's religious place', but could mean 'the murderer's tree', a gallows. ('Banna' is 'murderer' in Old English.)

Merryhill adjoins Merridale to the south and is 2.25m SW of Wolverhampton town centre. It is a mixed residential area dominated by blue-grey tower blocks. These stand by the shopping centre and the large mock-Tudor pub. St Joseph's is of red brick; St Michael's Catholic Church is round with an offset tower; and St Philip's is rock-faced, with a tower and turret, and is set amongst yew trees. The name Merryhill could mean either 'pleasant hill', 'the boundary hill', or 'the hill where mares are kept'.

East of Merryhill are three mature residential areas: Penn Fields (see Penn); **Goldthorn Hill**, which in the 19th Century had a tower windmill at S0 907969, now demolished; and **Goldthorn Park**, where is the locally well known Park Hall Hotel. South-west of these is **Colton Hills**, another mature residential area. In the narrow, winding Manor Road are boundary walls made of black and grey iron furnace slag. The name is Anglo-Saxon and could mean the 'hills where colts are reared'. **Castlecroft**, north of Lower Penn, is a suburban residential area that probably took its name from a farm. In Windmill Lane there is a windmill and next to it is the church of The Good shepherd, built in 1954.

Graisley Old Hall, in Claremont Road, Wolverhampton, dates from the 1320s and was encased in brick in Queen Anne's reign. In 1930 it was bought by the Royal Wolverhampton School, which built a junior school in its grounds, and in 1991 became a private house once again. Note: the following areas are associated with Wolverhampton but, as most were at one time separate villages which were later engulfed by suburban development, they have their own articles: Tettenhall, Wightwick, Penn, Bushbury, Claregate, Fordhouses, Compton and Ettingshall.

WOMBOURNE *5m SW of Wolverhampton*

The name means 'the winding stream', and indeed the Wom Brook has many a kink and curl in its course between Penn Common and its confluence with the Smestow Brook. Wombourne was a substantial village in 1086 when it belonged to William, son of Ansculf, and has an early industrial history. About 1600 a corn mill was altered to a hammer-mill (in which brittle pig iron was re-heated and beaten to make it more malleable). In the 19th Century there were some 1,000 nail shops in the parish. The industrial tradition continues with the Wombourne Enterprise Park where, amongst others, are Russell Hobbs and FAG.

Despite all this the settlement has the aspect of a rural village. The shops and service offices lie around a large village green and the whole is not unattractive. However, ranged about the centre are row upon row of suburban houses; Wombourne is now a dormitory town for Wolverhampton.

The church of St Benedict Biscop is the only church with this dedication in England. It has a red medieval tower and a grey spire. Most of the rest was restored and furnished by Street in 1862-7. The stained glass is mostly Kempe and Clayton and Bell, and there is an especially good, little, early 16th Century, Italian sculpted relief of the Good Samaritan, brought here by Sir Samuel Hellier. Amongst the monuments is a tablet by Chantrey to Richard Marsh of Lloyd House.

Ounsdale is an industrial-cum-residential suburb of Wombourne on the Staffordshire and Worcestershire Canal with a large school. Woodford Grange, 0.5m NW of Ounsdale, was a tithe-free estate which belonged to St James' Priory, Dudley until the Dissolution in 1540. From 1576 to 1929 it was held by the Wrottesley family. There might have been a medieval village at SO 856936, which was subsequently deserted.

Lloyd House lies 1.25m NNE of Wombourne, on the A449, and gives its name to Lloyd's Hill. It is a handsome, late 18th Century, grey ashlar building of nine bays with a central bow with two giant Ionic columns which was the original entrance. It is set amongst specimen trees and is not a Saint Anthony's Cheshire Home. This is housed in modern bungalows in woods 300 yards behind the House.

There has been a dwelling at **Wodehouse**, 0.25m NE of Wombourne, since about 1170 when William le Coq settled here. His descendants, the Wodehouse family, left in the early 18th Century and the property passed to the Hellier family. The present owner, Mr John Phillips, bought the house in 1981. Wodehouse stands hidden in woods beyond a dark pool and wide lawns. It is a Jacobean building (with an Elizabethan core) that was well restored by G F

Bodley in the 1870s, and given additional external ornament by C R Ashbee and his Guild of Handicraft in the years 1896-8. The following was their work: the gables, the parapet, the sundial in the porch and the wrought iron weather-vanes. The stables are Georgian brick and have a cupola and a central pediment. Above all, the house has a certain serene and mysterious charm. On the other side of the road are a couple of cottages, a red brick farm and a watermill complex with timber-framed barns. Above the mill-pool is a waterfall, a dam and a lake. Taken as a whole, Wodehouse has the classic configuration of an early medieval settlement and is so far unspoilt.

Blakeley, 'the black clearing', is a southern residential suburb of Wombourne. **Giggetty** is an old lane in which are located the ambulance station, the fire station and a school. It crosses the canal by a bridge and the Worn Brook by a ford. To the west is the pleasant residential area of Ounsdale. However, the view from Mount Pleasant is somewhat marred by the surprisingly large factory of Ferro Metalworks whose tall brick chimney is a major landmark hereabouts. In the valley of the Smestow Brook is the ARC quarry and concrete pipe works.

A little further north is **The Bratch**. Here is a well-known and much photographed canal lock and lock-keeper's office complex on the Staffordshire and Worcestershire Canal, where it is crossed by a bridge that carries the road to Trysull. On the opposite side of the road is a car park, and adjacent to this is the red brick Waterworks built by Bilston Urban District Council in 1895. It is dressed up with little corner turrets to give the impression of a Gothic castle. Between the Bratch and Trysull, lm NW, the valley of the Smestow Brook is most pleasant indeed. The stream winds through lush pastures, its banks lined with mature weeping willows.

Orton lies 1.25m NNW of Wombourne. This is an old Anglo-Saxon settlement, with its own entry in Domesday Book. Seen from the lane to Awbridge it looks very picturesque. Substantial red brick houses and farms line the Wombourne-Penn road, which runs along the foot a long bluff of wooded sandstone slopes and cliffs. Some desirable homes lie in the folds of the hills behind. Orton Grange was the home of the Marsh family, local landowners, by 1700. The core of the house is probably 12th Century with a cross-wing of 1685 and a three-storey, 18th Century block on the site of the original main house range. Orton Hall Farm was built in 1754.

Awbridge, 0.5m WSW of Orton, is a canal-side farm with moorings for narrowboats.

WOODLANE *8.5m N of Lichfield*
Woodlane is a hamlet in Needwood Forest, 1.25m N of Yoxall, on the A515. There is a handful of cottages, a telephone box and the Roman Catholic church of St Francis de Sales. The church is of 1795 and was commissioned by the 15th Earl of Shrewsbury, whose father had lived at nearby Hoar Cross Hall. It is of brick, in a Gothic style, and was enlarged in 1834. Attached to the church is the Presbytery. Henry Bamford (1819-1896), founder of the agricultural implement business that was to become JCB, came from Wood Lane. He move to Uttoxeter in 1845.

WOOTTON LODGE *6m WSW of Ashbourne and 1.5m ENE of Alton Towers*
Wootton Lodge must be the most handsome house in Staffordshire and the equal of any in England. In addition, it is set in the most beautiful Park - a valley of woods, meadows and lakes stocked with deer of several kinds. It is such a

terrible misfortune that the strident music from the enormous funfair at Alton Towers drifts across this perfect idyll.

The Lodge was built for Sir Richard Fleetwood, 1st Baronet, in about 1600. The architect was probably Robert Smythson, died 1614. Sir Richard was a recuscant Catholic and a Royalist, and in 1643, during the Civil War, the Lodge was attacked and badly damaged. The 3rd Baronet sold the house in the Late 17th Century and it was bought by an ironmaster from Stourbridge, John Wheeler. He repaired the exterior and completely remade the interior in about 1700. The balustrade, the steps and the detached side pavillions date from that time. The Wheeler family and their relatives, the Unwins, occupied the Lodge until the Second World War.

Since then it has changed hands once or twice and is now owned and occupied by a member of the Bamford family of the JCB company, who manufacture earth-moving equipment in their new factory at Rocester. Joseph Cyril Bamford, the founder of the company, started with virtually nothing after he was demobilised at the end of the war, and yet has built in his own lifetime a large, profitable and internationally-known company of high repute. Mr Bamford has used his own equipment to good effect at Wootton where the lakes have been greatly extended and new terraces constructed.

The house is tall and symmetrical. It is three storeys high, plus basement, and is five bays wide. On either side of the central projecting porch bay are canted bays, all rising the full height of the building. Around the top is a balustrade. The chimneys are small and neatly aligned. The sides have semi-circular bow windows. The fan-shaped entrance steps lead to the entrance porch, which is decorated with pairs of fluted Ionic columns on which are obelisks. The windows are mullioned and transomed. The detached pavilions to either side of the house at the front are quite acceptable, but modern attached extensions at the back are not good at all. There are several other buildings on the estate - farms, workshops, lodges and the like - and all are fitting and well cared for. Wootton Lodge and its park really are most excellent. The beautiful Park is stocked with deer. The old rhyme 'Wooton under Wever, where God came never', may have applied to the village, lm NE, but to the Lodge he most surely came. The entrance to the estate is not signposted. It lies at the end of a lane, off the road from Upper Ellastone to Wooton. Note: Wever is the old name of the Weaver Hills, and is still used by many local people.

WORDSLEY *2.5m N of Stourbridge*
Wordsley hardly has a separate identity merging, as it does, into Brierley Hill to the east and Amblecote to the south. The village lies along the A491, Stourbndge to Kingswinford road, and it is here that the Redhouse Glass Works of Stuart and Sons Ltd stand (S0 894864). The glass industry came here early because all the necessary raw materials - coal, fireclay, sand and potash - were available locally, and was given an impetus when the Stourbridge Canal (1779) was driven through. (See Brierley Hill.)

There are still many companies making glass at Wordsley but Stuart and Sons are the only manufactory to have kept their glass-cone. This kilnhouse is now the only surviving building of its kind in the Midlands. (There are only four in the whole country - two more in the north of England and one in Scotland.) The cone is 87 feet high, and tapers from 57 feet at the base to 10 feet at the top. The building is now used for storage but it originally had a 12-pot furnace, which was in use until 1939. Around the furnace were; the 'dog hole' for pot storage;

the pot arch, which pre-heated the pots (the pots were made of fireclay); an annealing kiln; a metal room, where the glass mix ready for melting into glass was stored; a 'glory hole', where glass was reheated whilst being worked; a second glory hole and another kiln; and the coal entrance to the kilns which connected to the canal. Almost all these ancillary buildings have been demolished. The works probably date from about 1788 when Richard Bradley, a glassmaker, bought the site. The company is still very much a going concern and there is now a museum, a coffee shop, a workshop which repairs minor damage to glass products, and a factory shop. The complex is open every day including Sundays, as are several other glass factory shops in the area.

For the rest, Wordsley is a place typical of the Black Country - factories, large and small, terraced houses, corner shops and the occasional grand Georgian house. Wordsley Hospital was the former workhouse. The central block with gables and tower is of about 1900.

The parish church is Holy Trinity in High Street. It is a substantial and impressive building, raised by Lewis Vulliamy in 1829-30, with an east chancel window of 1857. The traceried side windows with two lights are of about 1300, and inside there are high arcades, galleries and flat ceilings. The School is also by Vulliamy with stepped end gables and a mid gable.

Buckpool adjoins Wordsley to the south-east. One turns off the High Street into Brierley Hill Road and travels up the hill: past Cookson Precision Castings, semis with big rockery front gardens, Kitson Steel Stockholders, a service station, scrub trees in big grassy spaces, narrow red brick houses climbing Ridge Hill, The Swan and the large modern Pens Meadow School. At the top of the hill is a canal basin and locks on the neglected Stourbridge Canal. The Happy Return signals that we are now in Brockmoor. **Audnam** and **Hawbush** are residential estates south of Buckpool and the Brierley Hill Road.

WYCHNOR *7m NE of Lichfield*

Wychnor Bridges Farmhouse is on the horrendously busy and dangerous A38. It is a seven-bay, 2.5-storey house with a canted, three-bay centre supported by Tuscan columns. Opposite this substantial house is the lane to Wychnor. A bridge carries the lane over the Trent and Mersey Canal, which here runs alongside the main road. Half-a mile down this lane is a turning to the left. This leads to the church of St Leonard, which stands on the edge of a low terrace overlooking the flood plain of the River Trent. It is mostly of about 1300 (Decorated), but the east arch of the tower is of about 1200 and the brick top of about 1600. Next to the church is the Old School House. In the field to the front of the church and the school house is an area of disturbed ground. This is probably part of the site which was excavated in 1973, when remains of an early Anglo-Saxon settlement of some size were found.

The Angles came into the Midlands along the valley of the River Trent. The group that settled at Wychnor were the Hwicce, after which the settlement was named. The medieval village was deserted either because of flooding or, more likely, because of a change from arable to pastoral agriculture. Just south-west of the church, on the island, is the site of a moated farmhouse or manor. Today, all that is left of the village is the church, the old school house and, across the fields, two farms.

Wychnor Hall lies 0.75m W of the church. It stands in a small park with a few cottages and a plants' nursery. The old moated Hall has been replaced by an 18th Century mansion, which has a main range of seven bays, and is three storeys high, with a recessed centre and a Tuscan-columned porch. To the right of the main block is a two-storey range of the same height. It is not a handsome house and the grounds are uncared for. What is worse, the present owner tells with glee how he disposed of the ancient custom of the Wychnor Flytch.

In 1347 the manor was granted to Sir Philip de Somerville, by John of Gaunt, on the condition that a flitch of bacon should always be kept in the Hall to be claimed by any man of the manor who could prove absolute fidelity and happiness in his marriage for a year and a day. The custom fell into disuse but a token flytch made of painted wood was kept in the Hall, right up until about 1980, when it was sold to a private person for a pittance.

The A38 is, of course, Ryknild Street, the old Roman road that was kept in repair throughout the Middle Ages, and was a major highway in the 12th Century. The bridges over the River Trent at Wychnor were therefore of some importance.

(Note: The Hwicce were the 'salt people'. 'Wich' is derived from the name and usually denotes an area where salt is, or was, found - Nantwich, Shirleywich near Stafford, etc. It does not necessarily mean that the Hwicce tribe were the settlers in all those places. It is also now believed that Hwicce may be a Celtic name, adopted by the Angles.)

Cat Holme, an island in the River Trent near Wychnor, had an Anglo-Saxon settlement between 450 and 950. There are also two prehistoric listed sites here: a ceremonial monument and circular enclosure and pit alignment. 'Holme' is Norse for 'island'. Nearby, at Fatholme, a house 1.75m NE of Wychnor, a Neolithic henge was found. It consisted of a number of concentric rings of timber posts.

XYZ

YARNFIELD *2.5m WSW of Stone*
Yarnfield is most easily approached off the A34. The road climbs the hill of Bury Bank and passes the Iron Age fort in the woods to the right. A little further along, and also on the right, about one third of a mile from the road, is the conical hilt of Saxon's Lowe (SJ 875366), a large, 38-foot high burial mound. It is most easily seen in the winter when the trees close to it have no leaves. There is some conjecture as to whether the hill itself is a man-made burial mound or is natural with a burial mound placed upon it.

The road crosses over the M6 and on the outskirts of Yarnfield are modern houses erected on the site of the buildings of Duncan Hall, the old GPO training centre. New houses already envelop the old village, to the extent that it is no longer a country place but more like the suburb of a town. Nevertheless, the long village center still retains some kind of character. There is a half-timbered barn at Ivy Cottage, a pub called the Labour in Vain and St Barnabas (1838), the tiniest of tiny churches, which is simply a red brick box with a slate roof, although quite endearing. There was a windmill and a steam mill on the western edge of the village, at SJ 862335, built by Stephen Plant in the 18th Century.

The village green is very large with an unexpected wild area near the stream. It is still common land. There are several older brick cottages, the attractive

Gorsty Hill Farm and a rendered Village Hall of 1932. Close to the centre of the village is the new college, almost a small town in its own right. The large, multi-storeyed, many-windowed teaching blocks of about 1970 are not at all pleasant. However, the student accommodation is quite reasonable and the new buildings constructed in 1987 are superb. They have low, varied roof lines with pantiles, and red brick walls with smooth brick dressings. The green window hoods and dark glass add just the right amount of colour, and they are positioned so that they can be seen to their best advantage. Today, the centre is known as the British Telecom Training College. There are some 1,000 students and about 500 staff to instruct and administer them.

Cold Norton, 0.75m ESE of Yarnfield, is now little more than one farm, Cold Norton Farm. In the 13th Century it was Coldmorton (cold moor town) and there was a medieval settlement of some size at either Cold Norton Farm, where there is a moated site, or Norton Farm to the south. This village was deserted some time between 1334 and 1539.

YOXALL *7.5m NNE of Lichfield*
The village lies in flattish country on the A515, NE of King's Bromley. It is a substantial settlement and although not picturesque is a pleasant enough place. The River Swarbourne flows parallel with the east side of the main road and is crossed by four bridges. The name Yoxall is thought to mean 'a secluded piece of land small enough to be ploughed by one team of oxen'. In 1778 nearly 40 urns of coarse brown pottery were found in the village and it is probable that they marked the site of a Romano-British burial ground. This suggests that Yoxall is a Celtic settlement in origin. (One of the urns is in Lichfield Museum.)

The church of St Peter was rebuilt by Woodyer in 1865-8 but still retains a south doorway of about 1200, Decorated arcades, and a west tower which looks Perpendicular but is believed to be of the 17th Century. There is stained glass by Wailes and monuments to Humphrey Welles, died 1565, and Admiral Meynell, died 1865. Noteworthy buildings include: The Rookery, 0.25m S, an 18th Century house of three storeys and five bays with a pedimented doorcase; and Yoxall Grange, a timber-framed house infilled with brick and with two gables. Yoxall Lodge (now demolished) stood north-east of the village and was the home of the Rev Thomas Gisborne, a friend of William Wilberforce, who often visited here and spent many weeks discussing his reforms with the Reverend.

At **Bond End**, on the eastern fringe of Yoxall, are the remains of a Malthouse. Well into the 19th Century it was not uncommon for innkeepers and the owners of large estates to brew their own beer in their own breweries. Some also had a malthouse, but a large floor area was required on which to spread the barley, so most bought their malt from specialist malthouses. One such was the malthouse at Bond End. It is especially interesting because the accounts have been preserved. Of the buildings, the brick and tile malthouse and part of the kiln still survive. The main range runs alongside the road and is 83 feet long by 21 feet wide and three storeys high. The top two floors are laid with gypsum plaster, a surface prized by maltsters from at least 1680 to 1870. The kiln formed a cross wing at the west end and was built in 1776. The premises are now used as a builder's store.

Reeves End Cottage, at the north end of the village at SK 141191, was built before 1350 and is said to be the only surviving aisle-hall house in Staffordshire.

Longcroft Farm, 0.75m NNE of Yoxall, is at or near the site of the now-demolished, moated Longcroft Hall. In 1576 it was purchased by Simon Arden and it is believed that Mary Arden, Shakespeare's mother, lived there. In World War Two it was commandeered by the War Office, then became derelict and was demolished, probably in 1952, and the moat filled in.

In the late 18th and early 19th Centuries there was a woven cloth tape-making industry in the area. At **Morrey**, 0.5m. W of Yoxall, there was a large tape-mill. It was built in the 1790s and operated in conjunction with a bleaching works until the mid-19th Century.

In **Woodhouses**, 0.75m E of Yoxall, a small tape factory was established in 1817 in the mansion of Highwall Hall, but after 1818 nothing more is known about it. Also in Woodhouses, Yoxall, is the Roman Catholic chapel dedicated to St Francis de Sales. It was built in 1795 for Charles Talbot, Earl of Shrewsbury, of Hoar Cross Old Hall. It was originally designed to look like an outhouse to the priest's house, to disguise its function, but after the Catholic Emancipation Act of 1829 was altered to look more like a religious building. A priest, paid for by the Earl, lived at the priest's house (presbytery) until 1966.

THE END

Some Poems from *A Second Collection*

This book was printed in 32 page sections. When completed there were five pages to spare. Rather than leave them blank I decided to include a few of the poems from my as yet un-published *A Second Collection*

The Cup that Cheers

She is a wanton woman;
Her eyes they shine so bright.
Come morn you can't abide her;
Come night she's your delight.

With worldly woes around you,
With debtors on your trail,
She'll find the words to help you
To tell a likely tale.

And when your ship is sinking,
When all around you flee,
She'll lead you to a lifeboat
And scorn the raging sea.

She laughs at all misfortune;
She's a shortcut to the Lord;
And when they come with daggers
She'll provide a sword.

She's Errol Flynn with bubbles;
She's every man's delight.
She is a glass of ale, my friend,
And she will see you right.

So, raise your glass and sing with me:
"Away with doubts and fears;
No woman was so richly blessed
As is the Cup that Cheers."

Border Lord

He lived in castles strong with stone,
All dressed in rich attire,
In gold and green and ruby red,
And won my heart's desire.

In sunset mist enshrouded,
In valleys full of blood,
He calls his hirelings homeward,
To dine in that dark wood.

I see him now when rested,
The wine his soul has stirred,
And beg my liege's pardon,
As I betray my word.

I see that hated Frenchman,
His hand upon her breast,
And she her eyes disdaining,
This wild man from the West.

I plunged my dagger ever deep,
Laughed at her wails of woe,
The sigh that sails mountains,
That wolves and Welshmen know.

And now that I am hunted,
And death my only fate,
I'll cry no more for Ceinwen,
And all her fine estate.

Evening Light

There's a cosy nook by a babbling `
  brook,
'Tis there I'll lay me down,
And every day the sun will shine,
And no man wear a frown.

There's ducks and geese and an old
  blind dog,
And a cottage thatched with straw;
A jug of ale and an old wive's tale –
Just who could ask for more?

For Sir Stanley Matthews

The sun no longer shines
As once it brightly shone,
And Hanley's hill in shadow lies
Now that he has gone.

The thousands watched and wondered,
Yet he abhorred the fame;
Reward enough for men like him
Was just to play the game.

Sainsbury Lady

There you were in your trendy leather
  coat,
Black, of course, as were your eyes.
Slightly lowered and flashing
At your tall, dark friend
Who ushered you to the checkout.

Heavens above was I jealous
Of that glorious rapport,
That unspoken love and devotion,
Careless of the world around them.

Overcome I had to walk away
And shed tears of happiness in secret.

Just one backward glance
At the tall handsome man
Who wheeled you away –
You, who had no arms
And had no legs,
But bright and laughing eyes
That told the world
How good it was
Just to be alive.

Credo

Lust and greed pay no heed
To birthright or to station.
They are, indeed, the very creed
Of every state and nation.

In Canada

A bit of zest in life,
That's what matters most.
Who cares if you're a goodikins
Or a kind-hearted crook?
Zing-a-long, sing-a-long
Carefree and cunning,
Laugh and be happy,
No cheerful chappie
Was disliked for long.
The sinner repented
Or angel untouched:
Who would you choose
To pass the hours in a
Snowbound log cabin
In Canada?

Devotion

I have had respect from not a few,
Admiration, too, beyond my due,
Loyalty also in some small measure,
But by far the greatest treasure
Is devotion.
No questions asked,
No fault to see,
Some men give it to their God:
My dog gives it to me.

Grim Reaper

Forget the Grim Reaper,
  his scythe becomes blunt,
His grisly visage
  no more than a front.
For I've been prepared
  by the passing of years,
And when my turn comes
  I'll go without tears.

The Battle of Tettenhall

They crossed the waters raging wild;
They crossed the seas of anger;
Crossed the hills of deep despair,
Down by the lakes of languor.

These night riders have ridden far,
Through rain and flood and thunder;
And now rewards they seek to reap
To add unto their plunder.

Their faces are so grey and grim;
No mercy lingers there within.
They only laugh when they can't win,
But then return the stronger.

Viking swords and boats on fire;
Trampled crops and scornful ire:
Do these horsemen never tire
Of pleasing Odin's anger?

Ravens feast on bronzen blood;
Roads and rivers turn to mud;
Lust is all they know, not love.
Our world they break asunder.

Then the crops they grow again;
The storms become but gentle rain,
And soon the sun it salves our pain,
But for how long, we wonder?

Oh Lord, what is that over there?
Those coal-black wings on higher air,
The swish of oars and drunken song?
This fiercesome night will last too long.

But this time we will stand and fight,
Not hide like thieves in dark of night;
So ring the bells and let them peal;
We'll meet these wolves with English
  steel.

At Tettenhall we made our stand,
And drove the Norsemen from our land
Back to their ships on Severn strand,
Their dead their only plunder.

Friday

Friday is not a good day to 'phone;
For all too often they've gone home -
At least the ones who matter have.
Gone to golf or mistresses,
Or drunk again at Joey's Bar,
Chasing that elusive star,
And putting off the going home
To comfort and to loved ones
That are now too well known.

The Nightingale

A nightingale sang in my garden,
And sweet, so sweet sang she:
"I wonder of my Lord above,
Did I make Him or he make me?

Out-of-Work Assassin

Market Drayton, Shropshire,
The land of Jeeves and cheese.

There he stood, pushing a pram,
At the beck and call, quite in the thrall,
Of a little lady, bright and so contrite.
But he, Oh dearie me!
With grizzled silver beard,
He looked so weird,
Dressed in black
And for a hat
He had on a baseball cap -
In leather.
Sneakers on his feet,
A beer gut and,
To make the set complete,
A pair of midnight shades.
His brooding look made it plain:
"Do not treat me with disdain.
Cross me, mate, you'll get a bashin',"
Said this out-of-work assassin.

Bentley Canal

Dreaming,
Dreaming of the days gone by.
Fading,
Fading fast, I'm dying.
Once my waters sang
And touched the sky.

Now I'm sad and weary,
Now the boats are gone
No one even knows my name.

Sailing,
Sailing on a midnight shroud;
Laughing,
Laughing though I'm crying.
When the foundry boats came
I was proud.

Smiling,
Smiling as the day grows dim;
Lying,
Lying though I'm sighing.
Once I told myself
That I would win.

War Games

Where are you going
  and what are you doing?
Who is that singing
  and what is that song?
Raucous the voices
  and who is that crying?
It is the soldiers
  as they march along.

But they don't die, Sir;
  never ask why, Sir,
Their painted feet
  never burn on the sand.
They're never thirsty;
  their uniforms dirty.
If they fall down
  they rise up again.

They can't be counted,
  can never be routed.
They cannot feel
  the rain or the cold.
They'll suck down the sky
  and the wild birds will cry:
"Who are these devils
  so brave and so bold?"

Says Hero to Nero
  as they galloped onwards:
"What are those black specks
  down there on the plain?"
"They are old masters,
  come, let us ride faster.
When they've done fighting
  we'll kill what remains."

Says Captain to Colonel:
  "What is that inferno,
That scarlet red sky
  on the hills to the West?
The sun it cannot be,
  the trees they are burning,
The river's on fire
  and the birds flee the nest."

Now all is still;
  the world it is barren.
How quiet it is
  by the rocky sea shore.
Slowly the grass grows;
  wanly the moon glows.
There are no angels
  Of death or of war

Knight Forlorn

There's many a mile we've travelled,
My old grey mare and me,
And when she goes, then so go I,
They'll not part her from me.

We've battles lost and battles won,
At times we've not agreed,
But doubter I could never be,
Of such a gallant steed

Little John and the Bandog

All on a day in Folly Wood
There I met bold Robin Hood.
"Sir," said he, "is that your hound
That stands four square and guards
  your ground?"

"It is," said I, "and you should know
That should you raise your good yew bow
He'll have your hand from off your arm,
Should you seek to do us harm."

Bold Robin laughed. "Come close," he said,
"And share with me some wine and bread.
The air is clear, the birds sing well;
I warrant you've a tale to tell."

Soon the moon brought in the night,
And Robin called for our delight
A juggler and a dancing maid,
And a minstrel sweetly played.

One by one his men returned,
Of their adventures soon we learned:
How the Sheriff's men were tricked,
And sent away their wounds to lick.

Then Little John, the worse for drink,
Cried "Tis time I truly think
For some sport, give me your hound,
I'll make that brute concede his ground."

 "Be warned," I said, "you seek a thrill,
 But this black beast will want to kill."
 "Be gone! Be gone!" cried Little John,
  And so the contest was set on.

The hound he taunted with his stave,
"I'll teach this brute to well behave."
But in a trice his stave was broke,
And the beast was at his throat.

"Mercy! Mercy!" croaked Little John,
"I think my life it is undone."
And Robin laughed, cried to his men:
"I'll warrant he'll not try that again."

I called my hound off just in time.
Said Little John: "In jest and rhyme
My first defeat will now be known,
And by a bandog, I do own."

*My dog, Bruno, was a large, aggressive
Rottweiler cross who thought I was God.*

The Pride of Delamere

I lay asleep by the boatyard gate.
With dignity I bore my fate,
But often I would shed a tear,
For friends now gone, I hold so dear.

When days are short and nights are cold
I call to mind tales long untold,
And think of times no more can be,
When I was young and roaming free.

When first I came I did not know
That time could pass so dreadful slow,
But then the months turned into years,
And thoughts of hope turned into fears.

And then one day a young man came,
Towed me away and changed my name.
Says he out loud: "I'll do her proud."
And stripped away my mourning shroud.

And now I am a sight to see
In green and gold proud livery.
On Summer days we cruise in style,
And old men wave to me and smile.

But in my heart I'm carrying coal
To Coventry and Sankey Hole,
And way ahead is Bonny Joe,
The best old horse I ever did know.

Old Churches

The stones of old churches speak plainly
To the earth and the sea and the sky;
So why do most men in their wisdom
Smile smugly as they pass them by?

Glossary of Architectural Terms

APSE A semi-circular or polygonal end to the chancel and/or a chapel of a church. It is usually vaulted.

ARCADE A range of arches supported by either columns or piers and usually of structural importance. (See Blind Arcade.)

ASHLAR Blocks of squared stone, smooth faced, even in size and usually laid in courses like bricks. The blocks can either be structural or merely a facing to a brick built building.

BAILEY An enclosed and protected open space within the walls of a castle.

BARGEBOARDS Boards which hide the join of the roof and the wall on a gable and which are often ornamented.

BATTLEMENT The alternately raised (merlons) and lowered (embrasures) configuration of a parapet, usually associated with the tops of the walls and towers of a castle but also used as a decoration on civilian buildings. An alternative word for battlemented is crenellated.

BAY A bay is a vertical division of a building, either by internal or external features. The most common feature used to define the number of bays is the arrangement of the windows as seen from the outside.

BEAKER PEOPLE Late Neolithic (New Stone Age) people who came to Britain from Europe. They introduced weapons and tools made from metal, and buried their dead in round barrows.

BELFREY It can be either a specially built bell tower or the upper floor of the main church tower where the bells are hung. In the Middle Ages a belfry was a moveable siege tower and later came to mean a watch tower from which the alarm was raised by ringing a bell.

BELLCOTE A simple framework from which bells are hung. It is often an extension of a gable end but can mean anything that literally 'houses a bell'.

BROACH SPIRE When an octagonal tapering spire meets the square tower on which it stands, sloping half-pyramids of wood, brick or stone are positioned at the base of the four oblique faces of the spire to 'square the octagon'.

BLIND ARCADE A series of arches supported by columns or pilasters arranged against a wall, almost always as a decorative, not structural, feature. The Normans were very fond of it.

BROKEN PEDIMENT A pediment in which the horizontal base line has a gap at the centre.

BRONZE AGE Bronze is a mixture of tin and copper. It was the first metal that man was able to work with effectively. In Britain the Bronze Age lasted from about 2000 BC (the end of the Stone Age) to about 600 BC (the beginning of the Iron Age).

CABLE MOULDING A decorative band, usually carved in stone or wood, imitating a twisted rope or cable and much used by the Normans.

CANTED BAY WINDOW A protruding window, the front of which is straight and parallel to the main building, and which is joined to the main building by side walls set at an angle of more than 90 degrees.

CAPITAL The top part of a column or pilaster usually highly decorated. It tapers outwards from the column beneath to provide a platform from which an arch may spring or upon which an entablature may rest.

CARTOUCHE An ornament in the form of a tablet or shield with an ornate frame, often in the form of scrolls made to look like paper, and which usually bears either an inscription or a coat of arms.

CHANCEL The part of the church, usually the east end, where is placed the altar. In a cruciform church it is the whole of the area east of the crossing. The sanctuary is the area immediately around the altar.

CHANTRY CHAPEL A chapel either inside, or attached to, a church or other religious foundation in which prayers were said, and the mass was chanted for the founder or other particular person (often a relative of the founder). The founder usually built the chapel himself and endowed (i.e. left money or land) to the church to pay for the clergy to officiate after his death.

CHEVET A French word meaning the east end of the church.

CASTELLATED Identical in meaning to 'battlemented'.

CLASSICAL A building or style based on Roman or Greek architecture.

CLERESTORY Derived from 'clear-storey'. The upper part of the main walls of a church, above the aisle roofs, which are pierced by windows.

COB Walls constructed of mud or clay mixed with straw and, or, cow dung. The exterior surface of the cob was whitewashed to protect it from rain and, if properly maintained, is a durable material. The houses of the poor in Britain were commonly made of cob, and some still exist in the South-West. However, If neglected and exposed to water they almost literally melt away. Whole villages, once abandoned, could disappear in a matter of years.

CORINTHIAN See Order

CORNICE A projecting ornamental moulding around the top of a building, arch or wall.

CRENELLATION Means battlemented.

CROSSING The area where nave, chancel and transepts meet. In a cruciform church the tower is usually built above the crossing.

CRUCK A curved beam that supports both the walls and the roof of a timber-framed building. It was usually obtained from a tree that had a major branch leaving the trunk at an angle of about 45 degrees. The tree was then cut down and the main branch and the trunk trimmed of side branches. This curved timber was then spilt in two. The two parts were then erected opposite each other to form an arch. Several such arches were constructed and these formed the basic structure of a 'cruck house'. The area between the arches were called bays.

CRUCIFORM In the shape of a cross, usually meaning a Christian cross.

CRYPT A room below floor level and usually at least partly below ground level, most commonly positioned at the east end of a church, underneath the chancel. The crypt normally contained graves and religious relics.

CUPOLA A small dome, usually circular but sometimes polygonal, that either crowns the roof of a building or a tower or caps a turret.

DECORATED (Sometimes called 'Middle Pointed'.) A style of English Gothic current in the period 1300-1350 or thereabouts. As the name suggests ornamentation was rich in this period. (See Gothic.)

DORIC See Order.

DORMER A window placed vertically in the sloping plane of a roof. If it lay in the plane of the roof it would be a skylight.

EARLY ENGLISH Sometimes abbreviated to 'EE' and sometimes called 'Lancet' or 'First Pointed'. Early English is the earliest style of English Gothic and was current between 1200 and 1300. It is characterised by a simplicity of line; by tall, pointed, untraceried, lancet windows; and by slender spires and tall piers. (See Gothic.)

EASTER SEPULCHRE A recess in a wall (usually the north wall) of the chancel in which is a tomb chest. An effigy of Christ is placed here during the Easter ceremonies.

EMBATTLED It means there are battlements. (See Battlement.)

FAN VAULT A vault is an arched interior roof of stone or brick. A fan vault is a late medieval vault where all the ribs from the same springer are of the same length, the same distance from each other and the same curvature.

FLUTING Vertical grooves or channels in the shaft of a column.

FOLIATED As of foliage; the materials are ornamented with carvings of plant foliage, especially leaves.

GABLE The triangular upper part of a wall that rises to the slopes of a pitched roof. The gable at the side of a building is called the End Gable. Gables facing to the front or back of a building are simply called gables.

GALLERY In a church a gallery is an upper floor over an aisle which is open to the nave. There is also sometimes a gallery at the west end to house the organ.

GAZEBO A small pavilion or summerhouse in a garden or park. When placed on the roof of a building it is called a Belvedere.

GEORGIAN Buildings constructed in England during the reigns of the four King Georges, 1714-1830, in a style influenced by Greek and Roman (Classical) ideas, are said to be Georgian. Neatness, formality and symmetry are to the fore. Famous architects associated with the Georgian styles include Robert Adam, John Nash, James 'Athenian' Stuart and James Wyatt. Many of the great English country houses were either built, or were given new facades, in the 18th Century.

GOTHIC Gothic is a style that can only be defined by listing its characteristic features: the ribbed vault, the pointed arch, the flying buttress, the traceried window, the lofty steeple, the panelled stonework, triforium, spacious clerestory windows, etc. When all or many of these elements are present in a building it can be described as Gothic. The word 'Gothic' was not used during the period called Gothic, that is between the later 12th Century and the mid-16th Century. It was first used in the late 16th Century to describe the architecture of the previous centuries. It was a term of abuse. To say the style was Gothic meant that it was barbaric and uncivilised, as were the ancient German tribes called Goths. Gothic architecture had absolutely no connection with the Gothic tribes themselves. The style, though always recognizable as one style, underwent changes over the years. The main historical sub-divisions in England were:

Early English   1200-1300
Decorated   1300-1350
Perpendicular   1350-1550

These dates, of course, overlap and are only a rough guide. It should be remembered that individual elements of the Gothic style can be present in buildings that are not Gothic. It is the coming together of several elements that defines the style. Gothic evolved out of the Norman style and so some later Norman churches might best be described as Transitional.

HAMMERBEAM Horizontal timbers 'projecting' out from opposite sides of the walls supported by brackets. From these, vertical timbers called hammer-posts rise to support the purlins.

HERRINGBONE A design created by laying bricks, stones or tiles in order to make a zig-zag pattern.

HIPPED ROOF A roof which has sloping ends, not vertical ends with gables as is usual.

IONIC See Order.

IRON AGE The Iron Age began when iron working was introduced into Britain by invading Celtic tribes, who arrived on these shores in about 600 BC. The Iron Age lasted until the coming of the Romans, which was effectively AD 43. However, in some remote areas the Iron Age continued until the coming of the Anglo-Saxons in the 6th Century AD.

LINENFOLD Tudor panelling, usually of wood to an interior wall, decorated with a stylized representation of a piece of linen laid in vertical folds. The pattern is contained within one panel and repeated in every other panel.

LOWER PALAEOLITHIC See Palaeolithic.

LANCET A tall, slender, one-light window with a sharply pointed arch, much used in early Gothic, 13th Century architecture. They can be either single or arranged in groups, usually of three, five, or seven.

MANSARD A pitched roof with two slopes, the lower being longer and steeper than the other. Named after Francois Mansart (sic).

MESOLITHIC Means Middle Stone Age, the period of man as hunter and fisher from about 8,000 BC to 3,500 BC.

MEGALITH A large stone or block of stone, often irregular and either rough hewn or left as found. Such stones were erected by prehistoric man as monuments between about 4,000 BC and 1,000 BC.

MIDDLE POINTED Another name for the period of English Gothic, more commonly called Decorated. (See Decorated and also Gothic.)

MISERICORD Sometimes called a Miserere. A bracket attached to the underside of a hinged choir stall seat, which, when the seat is turned upright, provide support for a person in the standing position. They are frequently carved and because they are not seen by the congregation the subjects are sometimes non-religious and on occasion even verge on the profane.

MOTTE Means a mound, usually of earth, on which the main fort of a motte and bailey castle was built.

MULLION A vertical post that divides a window into separate lights. The term is usually reserved for substantial uprights of brick or stone. (See Transom.).

NAVE The western part of a church, often with aisles to the sides which are occupied by the congregation.

NEOLITHIC Means New Stone Age, the period of pre-history in Britain from about 3,500 BC, when settled farming communities were established, to the emergence of the Bronze Age about 1,800 BC.

NORMAN What in England is called Norman is really Romanesque. The Norman architects and builders did not have a style particular to themselves. They built in the manner current on the Continent at that time. Indeed, there are in England examples of 'Norman' work, such as Westminster Abbey, that were constructed before the Conquest. (See Romanesque.)

OBELISK A pillar of square section that tapers to the top and ends with a pyramid. It can be of any size but is usually of stone, large and erected as a monument.

OGEE An arch introduced into Britain about 1300 and very popular during the 14th Century. It has a characteristic double curve, one concave and the other convex, something like a parenthesis sign '}' laid horizontal.

ORDER In Classical architecture an Order is a complete system which comprises a column and its associated base shaft, capital and entablature (a horizontal table or lintel supported by the columns). The number of inventions and permutations is endless but a mere handful achieved popular acceptance in Rome and Greece and are still used. They are Greek Doric, Roman Doric, Tuscan Doric, Ionian and Corinthian. For full descriptions of the orders see a specialist book on architecture. Only one can be described briefly and meaningfully and that is the Tuscan Doric, which very plain in all its parts with an unfluted column. The Ionic usually has a 'rams-horn' capital.

PALAEOLITHIC Means Old Stone Age and lasted from the start of the Middle Stone Age (the Mesolithic), about 8,000 BC. As it is such a long period it is sometimes divided into Lower (the early part) and Upper (the later part).

PALIMPEST When a metal plate, usually of brass, is re-used by engraving on the back, the plate is said to be a palimpest; likewise, a parchment reused after removing the original writing; and a wall painting where one painting overlaps and obscures an earlier work.

PANTILE A tile with an 'S' configuration. When laid such tiles give a roof a corrugated surface.

PEDIMENT A low-pitched gable much used in Classical architecture and essentially of an ornamental nature. Pediments can be found not only at roof level but above windows, doors and porticos.

PERPENDICULAR A style of Early English Gothic current in the period 1350-1550. It is characterised by the vertical lines in the window tracery and the vertical articulation of the panelling in the stonework - hence Perpendicular. (See Gothic.)

PIER A pillar-like support but square (or composite) in section, usually of masonry. The brickwork or stonework between walls and doorways in a building can be described as piers.

PILSASTER A shallow pier or rectangular column projecting only slightly from a wall.

PISCINA A stone basin, complete with drain, in which the Communion or the Mass vessels are washed. It is usually set in or against the wall south of the altar.

PORTE COCHERE A coach porch.

PORTICO A porch with columns and a pediment decorating the main entrance to a building. If it projects forward, as is commonly the case, it is said to be 'prostyle'. If it recedes into the building (with the columns arranged in line with the front wall) it is said to be 'in antis'.

PRESBYTERY Has two meanings. It is part of the church east of the choir where the high altar is placed. It is also the name given to the house of a Roman Catholic priest.

PRIORY A monastery whose head is a Prior or Prioress, as distinct from the Abbot or Abbess of an Abbey.

'QUEEN ANNE STYLE' A house style developed in England by Eden Nesfield (1835-88) and Richard Norman Shaw (183 1-1912), and very much influenced by 17th Century Dutch brick architecture and the William and Mary style (1689-1702). Queen Ann reigned from 1702-1714. Characteristically, it has a hipped roof, a pediment, a cornice, a string course and is constructed with brick with stone quoins.

QUOINS Stones, usually dressed, at the corners of a building. Sometimes they are of equal size; more commonly they alternate long and short.

RECUSANT A person who refuses to submit or comply. Most commonly means a practicing Catholic in the period when that religion was suppressed, that is, between the Reformation and Catholic Emancipation in the early 19th

Century.

REREDOS A wall or screen, usually well decorated, that lies behind the altar in a church.

RIB-VAULT A vault with diagonal ribs projecting along the groins. 'A framework of diagonal, arched ribs carrying the cells which cover the spaces between them'.

ROCK-FACED Masonry cut to regular blocks but deliberately roughened on the exposed surface to look rough-hewn. The aim is to look natural but usually the result is most unnatural.

ROLL MOULDING A decorative moulding of semi-circular and more than semi-circular (but less than circular) cross section.

ROMANESQUE A Continental term for what in England is called Norman, and which covers architecture of the 11th and 12th Centuries. The style is characterised by the round arch, thick walling, small windows, bays clearly marked internally by vertical shafts from floor to ceiling, arcading, tunnel vaults and apses. Ornamentation was vigorous and depicted foliage, birds, animals and monsters, and utilised various bold geometric designs such as zig-zags and chevrons.

ROOD A cross or crucifix.

ROOD SCREEN A screen which separates the chancel from the nave. Above, or fixed to it, is often either a crucifix or a cross.

SADDLE-BACK ROOF This is a normal pitched roof, as on an ordinary house, but placed above a tower.

SALTIRE CROSS A cross with four equal limbs laid diagonally i.e. an 'X'-shaped cross.

SARCOPHAGUS A coffin, usually of stone and ornamented with carvings.

SCREEN A porclose screen separates a chapel from the rest of the church.

SCREENS PASSAGE The passage between the kitchen and other work places, and the screen that protected the privacy of the occupants of the great hall of a medieval house.

SEDILIA Masonry seats for use by priests on the south side of the chancel of a church. There are usually three in number.

SEGMENTAL ARCH An arch with a profile that is part of a circle in which the centre of the circle is below the springing line; that means that it will always be less than a semi-circle.

SOLAR An upstairs living room in a medieval house.

SPANDREL The triangular space between the side of an arch and the horizontal line drawn through its apex and the vertical line drawn from the side of the opening below the arch

SPIRE A tall cone, pyramid or polygon that is placed on top of a tower. It has no structural purpose and its function is primarily to act as a landmark.

STEEPLE A term that means the tower and spire of a church taken together.

STRAPWORK Decoration consisting of interlaced bands similar to leather straps. It can be open (like fretwork), as in a vertical partition or screen, or closed as in plasterwork on ceilings. It was especially popular during the Renaissance.

STRING COURSE A horizontal band projecting from an exterior wall.

STUCCO PLASTER or cement rendering to walls or ceilings. The term is most commonly used to describe external wall rendering which is usually given a smooth finish.

THREE-DECKER PULPIT A tall pulpit with three seats, one above the other: a

TOMB CHEST A stone coffin shaped like a chest, often with an effigy of the deceased placed on top. Sometimes the side walls are elaborately carved. It was commonly used in medieval times.

TRACERY In the Middle Ages it was called form-pieces or forms. It is the intersecting ornamental work in the upper part of a window, a screen, a panel, a blank arch or a vault.

TRANSEPT The transverse area of a cruciform church, which usually projects out from the junction of the nave and the chancel.

TRANSOM A horizontal bar across a window opening which divides the window into separate lights The term is usually only applied to a substantial bar, one commonly made of stone.

TRIFORM A galleried arcade facing on to the nave between the wall arcade and the clerestory.

TURRET A small tower, round or polygonal in shape.

TUSCAN See Order.

UNDERCROFT A vaulted room under a church or other building, sometimes below ground level.

VENETIAN WINDOW A tripartite window. The central part is arched and wider than the square-topped parts to each side. It was developed from the Italian Serliana.

VICTORIAN Architecture and general style associated with the period during which Queen Victoria reigned in Britain, 1837-1901.

WEATHER-BOARDING Hortizonal exterior overlapping boards, usually of a timber-framed building but sometimes used decoratively on a stone or brick structure.

Index

Places in bold capitals have gazetteer articles

D

G

XY

Z

LFQPBT